TOYOTA COROLLA
1970-87 REPAIR MANUAL

CHILTON'S

Covers all U.S. and Canadian models of Toyota Corolla

by Tony Tortorici, A.S.E., S.A.E.

CHILTON *Automotive Books*

PUBLISHED BY **HAYNES NORTH AMERICA,** Inc.

AUTOMOTIVE PARTS & ACCESSORIES ASSOCIATION MEMBER

Manufactured in USA
© 1995 Haynes North America, Inc.
ISBN 0-8019-8586-2
Library of Congress Catalog Card No. 94-071963
7890123456 9876543210

Haynes Publishing Group
Sparkford Nr Yeovil
Somerset BA22 7JJ England

Haynes North America, Inc
861 Lawrence Drive
Newbury Park
California 91320 USA

ABCDE
FGHIJ
KLM

Contents

Contents

SAFETY NOTICE

Proper service and repair procedures are vital to the safe, reliable operation of all motor vehicles, as well as the personal safety of those performing repairs. This manual outlines procedures for servicing and repairing vehicles using safe, effective methods. The procedures contain many NOTES, CAUTIONS and WARNINGS which should be followed, along with standard procedures to eliminate the possibility of personal injury or improper service which could damage the vehicle or compromise its safety.

It is important to note that repair procedures and techniques, tools and parts for servicing motor vehicles, as well as the skill and experience of the individual performing the work vary widely. It is not possible to anticipate all of the conceivable ways or conditions under which vehicles may be serviced, or to provide cautions as to all possible hazards that may result. Standard and accepted safety precautions and equipment should be used when handling toxic or flammable fluids, and safety goggles or other protection should be used during cutting, grinding, chiseling, prying, or any other process that can cause material removal or projectiles.

Some procedures require the use of tools specially designed for a specific purpose. Before substituting another tool or procedure, you must be completely satisfied that neither your personal safety, nor the performance of the vehicle will be endangered.

Although information in this manual is based on industry sources and is complete as possible at the time of publication, the possibility exists that some car manufacturers made later changes which could not be included here. While striving for total accuracy, the authors or publishers cannot assume responsibility for any errors, changes or omissions that may occur in the compilation of this data.

PART NUMBERS

Part numbers listed in this reference are not recommendations by Haynes North America, Inc. for any product brand name. They are references that can be used with interchange manuals and aftermarket supplier catalogs to locate each brand supplier's discrete part number.

SPECIAL TOOLS

Special tools are recommended by the vehicle manufacturer to perform their specific job. Use has been kept to a minimum, but where absolutely necessary, they are referred to in the text by the part number of the tool manufacturer. These tools can be purchased, under the appropriate part number, from your local dealer or regional distributor, or an equivalent tool can be purchased locally from a tool supplier or parts outlet. Before substituting any tool for the one recommended, read the SAFETY NOTICE at the top of this page.

ACKNOWLEDGMENTS

The publisher expresses appreciation to Toyota Motor Corporation for their generous assistance.

1

GENERAL INFORMATION AND MAINTENANCE

HOW TO USE THIS BOOK

Chilton's Repair Manual for the Toyota Corolla is intended to help you learn more about the inner workings of your vehicle while saving you money on its upkeep and operation.

The first two sections will be the most used, since they contain information and procedures for both maintenance and tune-up. Studies have shown that a properly tuned and maintained car can achieve better gas mileage than an out-of-tune car. The other sections deal with the more complex systems of your car. Operating systems from engine through brakes are covered to the extent that the average do-it-yourselfer becomes mechanically involved. This book will not explain such things as rebuilding a differential for the simple reason that the expertise required and the investment in special tools make this task uneconomical. It will, however, give you detailed instructions to help you change your own brake pads and shoes, replace spark plugs, and do many more jobs that will save you money, give you personal satisfaction and help you avoid expensive problems.

A secondary purpose of this book is a reference for owners who want to understand their car and/or their mechanics better. In this case, no tools at all are required.

Before removing any bolts, read through the entire procedure. This will give you the overall view of what tools and supplies will be required. There is nothing more frustrating than having to walk to the bus stop on Monday morning because you were short one bolt on Sunday afternoon. So read ahead and plan ahead. Each operation should be approached logically and all procedures thoroughly understood before attempting any work.

All sections contain adjustments, maintenance, removal and installation procedures, and repair or overhaul procedures. When repair is not considered practical, we tell you how to remove the part and then how to install the new or rebuilt replacement. In this way, you at least save the labor costs. Backyard repair of such components as the alternator is just not practical.

Two basic mechanic's rules should be mentioned here. One, whenever the left side of the car or engine is referred to, it is meant to specify the driver's side of the car. Conversely, the right side of the car means the passenger's side. Secondly, most screws and bolts are removed by turning counterclockwise, and tightened by turning clockwise.

Safety is always the most important rule. Constantly be aware of the dangers involved in working on an automobile and take the proper precautions. See the information in this section regarding Servicing Your Vehicle Safely and the SAFETY NOTICE on the acknowledgment page.

Pay attention to the instructions provided. There are 3 common mistakes in mechanical work:

1. Incorrect order of assembly, disassembly or adjustment. When taking something apart or putting it together, performing steps in the wrong order usually just costs you extra time; however, it CAN break something. Read the entire procedure before beginning disassembly. Perform everything in the order in which the instructions say you should, even if you can't

immediately see a reason for it. When you're taking apart something that is very intricate (for example, a carburetor), you might want to draw a picture of how it looks when assembled at one point in order to make sure you get everything back in its proper position. We will supply exploded views whenever possible. When making adjustments, especially tune-up adjustments, perform them in order; often, one adjustment affects another, and you cannot expect even satisfactory results unless each adjustment is made only when it cannot be changed by any other.

2. Overtorquing (or undertorquing). While it is more common for over-torquing to cause damage, undertorquing may allow a fastener to vibrate loose causing serious damage. Especially when dealing with aluminum parts, pay attention to torque specifications and utilize a torque wrench in assembly. If a torque figure is not available, remember that if you are using the right tool to do the job, you will probably not have to strain yourself to get a fastener tight enough. The pitch of most threads is so slight that the tension you put on the wrench will be multiplied, many times in actual force on what you are tightening. A good example of how critical torque is can be seen in the case of spark plug installation, especially where you are putting the plug into an aluminum cylinder head. Too little torque can fail to crush the gasket, causing leakage of combustion gases and consequent overheating of the plug and engine parts. Too much torque can damage the threads, or distort the plug which changes the spark gap.

There are many commercial products available for ensuring that fasteners won't come loose, even if they are not torqued just right (a very common brand is Loctite®). If you're worried about getting something together tight enough to hold, but loose enough to avoid mechanical damage during assembly, one of these products might offer substantial insurance. Before choosing a threadlocking compound, read the label on the package and make sure the product is compatible with the materials, fluids, etc. involved.

3. Crossthreading. This occurs when a part such as a bolt is screwed into a nut or casting at the wrong angle and forced. Crossthreading is more likely to occur if access is difficult. It helps to clean and lubricate fasteners, and to start threading with the part to be installed going straight in. Then, start the bolt, spark plug, etc. with your fingers. If you encounter resistance, unscrew the part and start over again at a different angle until it can be inserted and turned several times without much effort. Keep in mind that many parts, especially spark plugs, used tapered threads so that gentle turning will automatically bring the part you're threading to the proper angle if you don't force it or resist a change in angle. Don't put a wrench on the part until it's been tightened a couple of turns by hand. If you suddenly encounter resistance, and the part has not seated fully, don't force it. Pull it back out and make sure it's clean and threading properly.

Always take your time and be patient; once you have some experience, working on your car may well become an enjoyable hobby.

TOOLS AND EQUIPMENT

▶ **See Figures 1, 2, 3, 4, 5, 6, 7, 8, 9, 10 and 11**

Naturally, without the proper tools and equipment it is impossible to properly service your vehicle. It would also be impossible to catalog every tool that you would need to perform most operations in this book. Of course, It would be unwise for the amateur to rush out and buy an expensive set of tools on the theory that he may need one or more of them at sometime.

The best approach is to proceed slowly, gathering a good quality set of those tools that are used most frequently. Don't be misled by the low cost of bargain tools. It is far better to spend a little more for better quality. Forged wrenches, 6 or 12-point sockets and fine tooth ratchets are by far preferable to their less expensive counterparts. As any good mechanic can tell you, there are few worse experiences than trying to work on a vehicle with bad tools. Your monetary savings will be far outweighed by frustration and mangled knuckles.

Begin accumulating those tools that are used most frequently; those associated with routine maintenance and tune-up. In addition to the normal assortment of screwdrivers and pliers you should have the following tools for routine maintenance jobs:

• Metric wrenches-sockets and combination open end/box end wrenches in sizes from 3mm-19mm and a spark plug socket $^{13}/_{16}$ in. or $^{5}/_{8}$ in. (depending on plug type).

➡**If possible, buy various length socket drive extensions. One break in this department is that the metric sockets available in the U.S. will fit the ratchet handles and extensions you may already have ($^{1}/_{4}$ inch, $^{3}/_{8}$ inch, and $^{1}/_{2}$ inch drives).**

• Jackstands for support.
• Oil filter wrench.
• Oil filler spout or funnel for pouring oil.
• Grease gun for chassis lubrication.
• Hydrometer for checking the battery (unless equipped with a sealed, maintenance-free battery).
• A container for draining oil.
• Many rags for wiping up the inevitable mess.

In addition to the above items there are several others that are not absolutely necessary, but handy to have around. These include oil dry, a transmission funnel and the usual supply of lubricants, antifreeze and fluids, although these can be purchased as needed. This is a basic list for routine maintenance, but only your personal needs and desire can accurately determine your list of tools.

A more advanced set of tools, suitable for tune-up work, can be drawn up easily. While the tools are slightly more sophisticated, they need not be outrageously expensive. There are several inexpensive tach/dwell meters on the market that are every bit as good for the average mechanic as a professional model. Just be sure that it goes to a least 1,200-1,500 rpm on the tach scale and that it works on both 4 and 6 cylinder engines. (A special tach is needed for diesel engines). The

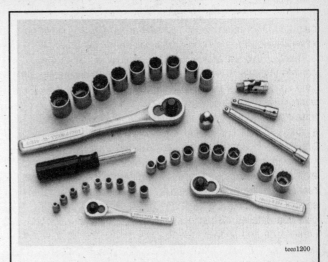

Fig. 1 Most procedures will require an assortment of ratchets, sockets and extensions

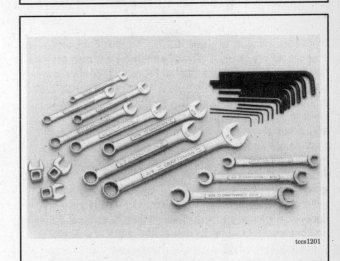

Fig. 2 In addition to ratchets, a good set of wrenches and hex keys will be necessary

key to these purchases is to make them with an eye towards adaptability and wide range. A basic list of tune-up tools could include:

• Tach/dwell meter.
• Spark plug wrench and gapping tool.
• Feeler gauges for valve and point adjustment;

A tachometer/dwell meter will ensure accurate tune-up work on cars without electronic ignition. The choice of a timing light should be made carefully. A light which works on the DC current supplied by the car battery is the best choice; it should have a xenon tube for brightness. Since most later models have an electronic ignition system, the timing light should have an inductive pickup which clamps around the No. 1 spark plug cable.

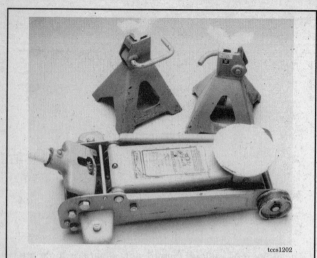

Fig. 3 A hydraulic floor jack and a set of jackstands are essential for lifting and supporting the vehicle

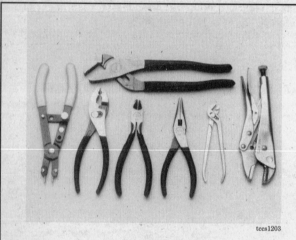

Fig. 4 An assortment of pliers, grippers and cutters will be handy, especially for old rusted parts and stripped bolt heads

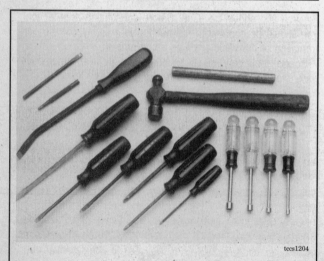

Fig. 5 Various drivers, chisels and prybars are great tools to have around

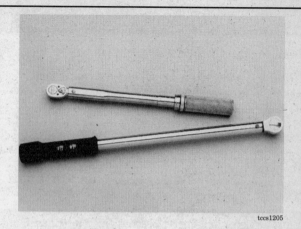

Fig. 6 Many repairs will require the use of a torque wrench to assure the components are properly fastened — DON'T attempt a procedure without one if it specifies a fastener's torque

Fig. 7 Battery maintenance may be accomplished with household items and with special tools like this post cleaner

In addition to these basic tools, there are several other tools and gauges you may find useful. These include:

• Compression gauge. The screw-in type is slower to use, but eliminates the possibility of a faulty reading due to escaping pressure.

• Manifold vacuum gauge.

• 12V test light.

• A combination volt/ohmmeter

• Induction meter. This is used for determining whether or not there is current in a wire. These are handy for use if a wire is broken somewhere in a wiring harness.

As a final note, you will probably find a torque wrench necessary for all but the most basic work. The beam type models are perfectly adequate, although the newer click types (breakaway) are more precise. The click type torque wrenches tend to be more expensive and should be periodically checked and recalibrated. You will have to decide for yourself which better fits your purpose.

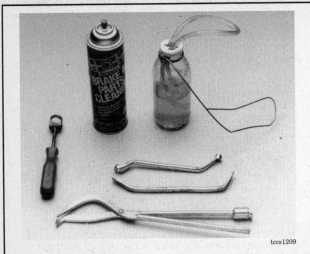

Fig. 8 Although not always necessary, using specialized brake tools will save time

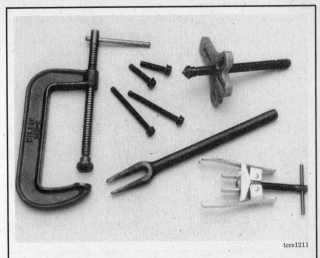

Fig. 10 Various pullers, clamps and separator tools are needed for the larger, more complicated repairs

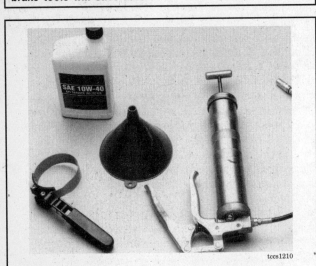

Fig. 9 A few inexpensive lubrication tools will make maintenance easier

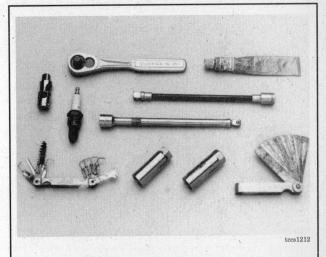

Fig. 11 A variety of tools and gauges should be used for spark plug gapping and installation

Special Tools

Normally, the use of special factory tools is avoided for repair procedures, since these are not readily available for the do-it-yourself mechanic. When it is possible to perform the job with more commonly available tools, it will be pointed out, but occasionally, a special tool was designed to perform a specific function and should be used. Before substituting another tool, you should be convinced that neither your safety nor the performance of the vehicle will be compromised.

Special tools can usually be purchased from an automotive parts store or from your local dealer.

SERVICING YOUR CAR SAFELY

▶ **See Figures 12, 13 and 14**

It is virtually impossible to anticipate all of the hazards involved with automotive maintenance and service, but care and common sense will prevent most accidents.

The rules of safety for mechanics range from "don't smoke around gasoline," to "use the proper tool for the job." The trick to avoiding injuries is to develop safe work habits and take every possible precaution.

Dos

• Do keep a fire extinguisher and first aid kit within easy reach.

• Do wear safety glasses or goggles when cutting, drilling, grinding or prying, even if you have 20-20 vision. If you wear glasses for the sake of vision, wear safety goggles over your regular glasses.

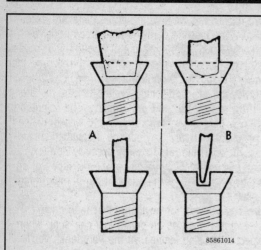

Fig. 12 Keep screwdrivers in good shape. They should fit the slot as shown in "A". If they look like those in "B", they need to be ground or replaced

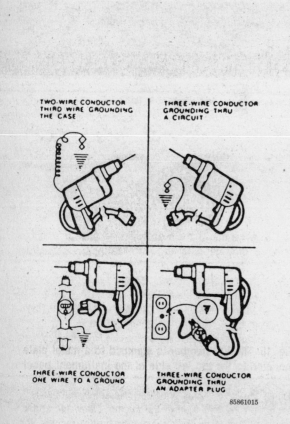

TWO-WIRE CONDUCTOR THIRD WIRE GROUNDING THE CASE

THREE-WIRE CONDUCTOR GROUNDING THRU A CIRCUIT

THREE-WIRE CONDUCTOR ONE WIRE TO A GROUND

THREE-WIRE CONDUCTOR GROUNDING THRU AN ADAPTER PLUG

Fig. 13 When using electric tools, make sure they are properly grounded

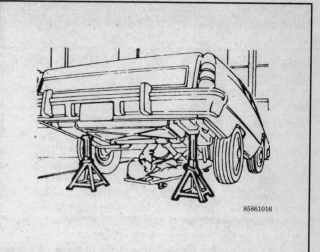

Fig. 14 NEVER work under a vehicle unless it is supported using safety stands (jackstands)

• Do shield your eyes whenever you work around the battery. Batteries contain sulfuric acid. In case of contact with the eyes or skin, flush the area with water or a mixture of water and baking soda and get medical attention immediately.

• Do use safety stands for any undercar service. Jacks are for raising vehicles; safety stands are for making sure the vehicle stays raised until you want it to come down. Whenever the car is raised, block the wheels remaining on the ground and set the parking brake.

• Do use adequate ventilation when working with any chemicals or hazardous materials. Like carbon monoxide, the asbestos dust resulting from brake lining wear can be poisonous in sufficient quantities.

• Do disconnect the negative battery cable when working on the electrical system. The secondary ignition system contains extremely high voltage. In some cases it can even exceed 50,000 volts.

• Do follow manufacturer's directions whenever working with potentially hazardous materials. Both brake fluid and antifreeze are poisonous if taken internally.

• Do properly maintain your tools. Loose hammerheads, mushroomed punches and chisels, frayed or poorly grounded electrical cords, excessively worn screwdrivers, spread wrenches (open end), cracked sockets, slipping ratchets, or faulty droplight sockets can cause accidents.

• Likewise, keep your tools clean; a greasy wrench can slip off a bolt head, ruining the bolt and often ruining your knuckles in the process.

• Do use the proper size and type of tool for the job at hand.

• Do when possible, pull on a wrench handle rather than push on it, and adjust your stance to prevent a fall.

• Do be sure that adjustable wrenches are tightly closed on the nut or bolt and pulled so that the face is on the side of the fixed jaw.

• Do select a wrench or socket that fits the nut or bolt. The wrench or socket should sit straight, not cocked.

• Do strike squarely with a hammer; avoid glancing blows.

• Do set the parking brake and block the drive wheels if the work requires a running engine.

Don'ts

• Don't run the engine in a garage or anywhere else without proper ventilation — EVER! Carbon monoxide is poisonous; it takes a long time to leave the human body and you can build up a deadly supply of it in your system by simply breathing in a little every day. You may not realize you are slowly poisoning yourself. Always use power vents, windows, fans or open the garage door.

• Don't work around moving parts while wearing a necktie or other loose clothing. Short sleeves are much safer than long, loose sleeves. Hard-toed shoes with neoprene soles protect your toes and give a better grip on slippery surfaces. Jewelry such as watches, fancy belt buckles, beads or body adornment of any kind is not safe working around a car. Long hair should be tied back under a hat or cap.

• Don't use pockets for toolboxes. A fall or bump can drive a screwdriver deep into your body. Even a wiping cloth hanging from the back pocket can wrap around a spinning shaft or fan.

• Don't smoke when working around gasoline, cleaning solvent or other flammable material.

• Don't smoke when working around the battery. When the battery is being charged, it gives off explosive hydrogen gas.

• Don't use gasoline to wash your hands; there are excellent soaps available. Gasoline contains dangerous additives which can enter the body through a cut or through your pores. Gasoline also removes all the natural oils from the skin so that bone dry hands will suck up oil and grease.

• Don't service the air conditioning system unless you are equipped with the necessary tools and training. The refrigerant, R-12, is extremely cold when compressed, and when released into the air will instantly freeze any surface it contacts, including your eyes. Although the refrigerant is normally non-toxic, R-12 becomes a deadly poisonous gas in the presence of an open flame. One good whiff of the vapors from burning refrigerant can be fatal.

• Don't use screwdrivers for anything other than driving screws! A screwdriver used as an prying tool can snap when you least expect it, causing injuries. At the very least, you'll ruin a good screwdriver.

• Don't use a bumper or emergency jack (that little ratchet, scissors, or pantograph jack supplied with the car) for anything other than changing a flat! These jacks are only intended for emergency use out on the road; they are NOT designed as a maintenance tool. If you are serious about maintaining your car yourself, invest in a hydraulic floor jack of a least 1½ ton capacity, and at least two sturdy jackstands.

SERIAL NUMBER IDENTIFICATION

Vehicle

▶ See Figures 15, 16, 17, 18, 19, 20 and 21

All models have a vehicle identification number (VIN) stamped on a plate which is attached to the left side of the instrument panel. This plate is visible through the windshield. The VIN is also stamped on a plate in the engine compartment which is usually located on the cowl.

The serial number on all 1970-80 models consists of a series identification number, followed by a 6-digit production number. The serial number on all 1981 and later models was changed to a new 17 digit format. The first three digits are the world manufacturer identification number. The next five digits are the vehicle description section (same as the series identification number used on vehicles through 1980). The remaining nine numbers are the production numbers.

Engine

▶ See Figures 22 and 23

The engine serial number consists of an engine series identification number, followed by a 6-digit production number. The location of this serial number varies slightly from one engine to

85861017

Fig. 15 The VIN number is stamped to a metal plate mounted to the top left side of the instrument panel

another. On the K-series engines (3K-C), the number is stamped on the right side of the engine, below the spark plugs. On most other engines covered by this manual, the serial number is stamped on the left side of the engine, behind the dipstick.

Fig. 16 An identification plate may also be found on the cowl

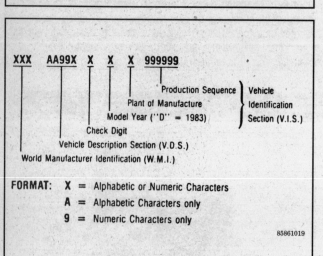

```
XXX   AA99X   X   X   X   999999
```

Production Sequence } Vehicle
Plant of Manufacture } Identification
Model Year ("D" = 1983) } Section (V.I.S.)
Check Digit
Vehicle Description Section (V.D.S.)
World Manufacturer Identification (W.M.I.)

FORMAT: X = Alphabetic or Numeric Characters
A = Alphabetic Characters only
9 = Numeric Characters only

Fig. 17 A 17 digit VIN is found on all 1981 and later vehicles covered by this manual

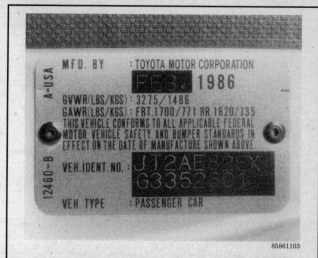

Fig. 19 A vehicle certification label is usually found on the driver's door jamb

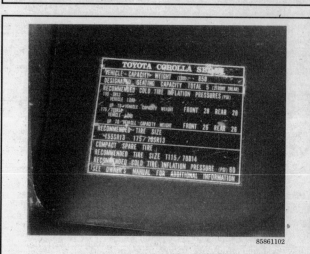

Fig. 20 A second information label (usually found in the trunk or passenger compartment) contains vehicle weight, tire size and recommended pressures

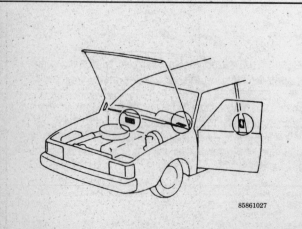

Fig. 18 Later model Toyotas have VIN plate markings at multiple locations

Chassis Identification

Model	Year	Chassis Designation
Corolla 1200	'70–'79	KE
Corolla 1600	'71–'79	TE
Corolla 1800	'80–'82	TE
Corolla (Gas Eng.)	'83–'87	AE
Corolla (Diesel Eng.)	'84–'85	CE

Fig. 21 Although early Corolla's were normally identified by there engine size, a chassis designation was also available

ENGINE IDENTIFICATION

Year	Model	Engine Displacement Cu. In. (cc)	Engine Series Identification	No. of Cylinders	Engine Type
1970	Corolla	71 (1166)	3K-C	4	OHV
1971	Corolla 1200	71 (1166)	3K-C	4	OHV
	Corolla 1600	97 (1588)	2T-C	4	OHV
1972	Corolla 1200	71 (1166)	3K-C	4	OHV
	Corolla 1600	97 (1588)	2T-C	4	OHV
1973	Corolla 1200	71 (1166)	3K-C	4	OHV
	Corolla 1600	97 (1588)	2T-C	4	OHV
1974	Corolla 1200	71 (1166)	3K-C	4	OHV
	Corolla 1600	97 (1588)	2T-C	4	OHV
1975	Corolla 1200	71 (1166)	3K-C	4	OHV
	Corolla 1600	97 (1588)	2T-C	4	OHV
1976	Corolla 1200	71 (1166)	3K-C	4	OHV
	Corolla 1600	97 (1588)	2T-C	4	OHV
1977	Corolla 1200	71 (1166)	3K-C	4	OHV
	Corolla 1600	97 (1588)	2T-C	4	OHV
1978	Corolla 1200	71 (1166)	3K-C	4	OHV
	Corolla 1600	97 (1588)	2T-C	4	OHV
1979	Corolla 1200	71 (1166)	3K-C	4	OHV
	Corolla 1600	97 (1588)	2T-C	4	OHV
1980	Corolla 1800	108 (1770)	3T-C	4	OHV
1981	Corolla 1800	108 (1770)	3T-C	4	OHV
1982	Corolla 1800	108 (1770)	3T-C	4	OHV
1983	Corolla	97 (1587)	4A-C, 4A-LC	4	SOHC
1984	Corolla	97 (1587)	4A-C, 4A-LC	4	SOHC
1985	Corolla	97 (1587)	4A-C, 4A-LC	4	SOHC
	Corolla	97 (1587)	4A-GE	4	DOHC
1986	Corolla	97 (1587)	4A-C, 4A-LC	4	SOHC
	Corolla	97 (1587)	4A-GE	4	DOHC
1987	Corolla	97 (1587)	4A-C, 4A-LC	4	SOHC
	Corolla	97 (1587)	4A-GE	4	DOHC

85861023

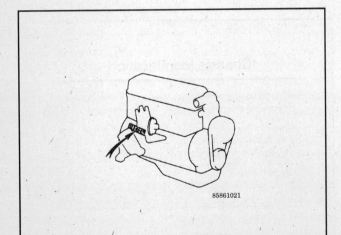

Fig. 22 Engine serial number location — K-series engines (3K-C)

85861021

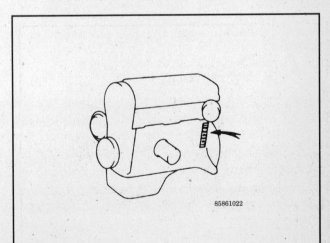

Fig. 23 Engine serial number location — except K-series engines

85861022

ROUTINE MAINTENANCE

Air Cleaner

▶ **See Figures 24, 25, 26, 27, 28, 29 and 30**

The air cleaner has a dual purpose. It not only filters the air going to the carburetor or throttle body, but also acts as a flame arrester if the engine should backfire. The engine should never be run without the air cleaner installed unless an engine maintenance procedure specifically requires the temporary removal of the air cleaner. Operating a car without its air cleaner may result in some throaty sounds giving the impression of increased power but will only cause trouble. Unfiltered air will eventually result in a dirty, inefficient carburetor or throttle body and an inefficient engine. A dirty carburetor increases the chances of carburetor backfire and, without the protection of an air cleaner, an underhood fire becomes a very real danger.

Because the air filter is used to keep dust present in the air out of the engine, proper element maintenance is vital. A clogged element not only restricts the air flow and thus the power, but can also cause premature engine wear. A severely worn element may begin disintegrating an actually pollute the engine with the very dust the element had protected the engine from earlier.

The filter element should be cleaned and inspected every 7,500 miles, or more often if the car is driven under dry, dusty conditions. Remove the filter element and carefully blow dirt out from the inside using low pressure compressed air.

➡ **The filter element used on Toyota vehicles is of the dry, disposable type. It should never be washed, soaked or oiled.**

The filter element should be replaced every 18,000 miles, (1970-72); every 24,000 miles, (1973-74); every 25,000 miles, (1975-77); and every 30,000 miles, (1978 and later). But, once again, these intervals should be shortened as necessary if the vehicle is operated under dry, dusty conditions. Be sure to use the correct element; all Toyota elements are of the same type but they come in a variety of sizes. To remove or replace the element:

1. Unfasten the wing nut(s) and/or clips that retain the element cover.
2. Remove the cover for access to the element.
3. Lift out the air filter element and clean or replace it, as necessary.
4. Before installing the air cleaner element, carefully wipe our any remaining dust or dirt in the air cleaner housing using a damp cloth.
5. During installation make sure the element is properly seated inside the housing.

Fuel Filters

There are two basic types of fuel filters used by these vehicles: The cartridge type (disposable element) which is removed from a reusable housing or the fully disposable (throwaway)

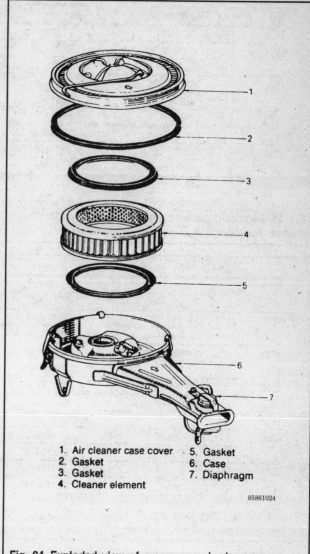

1. Air cleaner case cover
2. Gasket
3. Gasket
4. Cleaner element
5. Gasket
6. Case
7. Diaphragm

85861024

Fig. 24 Exploded view of a common air cleaner assembly — carbureted engines

composite element/housing type. A third type can be found in the fuel tank on some late model carbureted vehicles and all fuel injected vehicles. The third type is a disposable "sock" type filter used to prevent debris which may be located in the tank from entering the fuel system.

The fuel filter should be replaced a minimum of every 25,000-30,000 miles, but sooner if it seems dirty or clogged. The removal and installation procedures differ slightly for certain years.

✳✳CAUTION

DO NOT smoke or have open flame near the car when working on the fuel system.

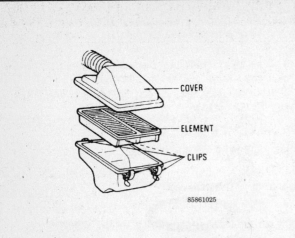

Fig. 25 Replacing the air cleaner element — diesel engines (gasoline fuel injected engines similar)

Fig. 26 When only slightly dirty (not clogged) the air cleaner element may be carefully cleaned with low pressure compressed air

Fig. 27 Loosen and remove the fastener(s), in this case a wing nut, from the air cleaner cover

Fig. 28 If equipped, release the cover retaining clamps

Fig. 29 Remove the air cleaner housing cover for access to the filter element

Fig. 30 Remove the filter element from the housing

REMOVAL & INSTALLATION

Cartridge Type Filter Element

▶ **See Figure 31**

The cartridge type filter is located in the fuel line. To replace the element, proceed as follows:

1. Loosen and remove the nut on the filter bowl.
2. Withdraw the bowl, element spring, element, and gasket.
3. Wash the parts in solvent and examine them for damage.
4. Install a new filter element and bowl gasket.
5. Install the components in the reverse order of their removal. Do not fully tighten the bail nut.
6. Seat the bowl by turning it slightly. Tighten the bail nut fully and check for leaks.

The above service should be performed if the clear glass bowl fills up with gasoline or at normal routine maintenance intervals.

➡ **Be sure to specify engine and model when buying the element replacement kit. The kits come in several different sizes.**

Throwaway Type Filter Assembly

The throwaway (disposable filter element/housing) fuel filter is located in the fuel line. The filter may be located by tracing the fuel line backwards from the engine or forward from the fuel tank. On most vehicles covered by this manual, the filter will be found in the engine compartment, often on the left strut tower.

No service is possible on these filters except replacement. The filter must be completely removed from the fuel line in order to replace it.

1971-74 GASOLINE ENGINES

▶ **See Figure 32**

1. Unfasten the fuel intake hose. Use a wrench to loosen the attachment nut and another wrench on the opposite side to keep the filter body from turning (except 1973-74 vehicles).

2. On 2T-C engines, slip the flexible fuel line off the neck on the other side of the filter. On 1973-74 vehicles, remove the fuel lines from both sides of the filter by loosening the clamp and slipping the rubber hose off.

3. If equipped, unfasten the attaching screws from the filter bracket and remove the filter from the vehicle.

4. Install a completely new fuel filter assembly in the reverse order of removal.

1975 AND LATER GASOLINE ENGINES

▶ **See Figures 33, 34 and 35**

1. If applicable on fuel injected engines, unbolt and remove the protective shield.

➡ **Before disengaging any fuel line connections, place a drain pan under the fitting to catch any escaping fuel.**

2. On carbureted vehicles, loosen and remove the hose clamps from the inlet and outlet hoses. If spring clamps are used, squeeze the tabs to release the clamps. The clamps should be repositioned further back on the hoses, past the filter inlet and outlet necks. Work the hoses off of the filter necks.

➡ **Most fuel injected engines use fuel fittings instead of clamped hoses. Because the fuel injection system operates under pressure, wrap a shop rag around the fitting before attempting to disconnect it. With the shop rag in place, SLOWLY loosen the fitting and allow the pressure bleed off.**

3. On fuel injected vehicles, carefully loosen and remove the fuel line fittings and/or union bolts from the filter.

4. Snap the filter out of its bracket and replace it with a new one. The filters on some later model vehicles may be secured to the retaining bracket using a bolt or clamp.

➡ **The arrow on the fuel filter must always point toward the carburetor.**

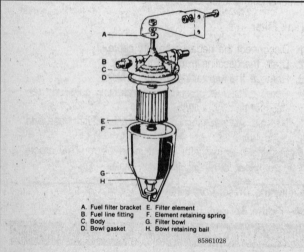

A. Fuel filter bracket **E.** Filter element
B. Fuel line fitting **F.** Element retaining spring
C. Body **G.** Filter bowl
D. Bowl gasket **H.** Bowl retaining bail

85861028

Fig. 31 Exploded view of the cartridge type fuel filter mounting

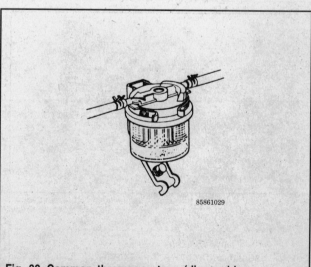

85861029

Fig. 32 Common throwaway type (disposable element/housing) fuel filter

5. Installation of the remaining components is in the reverse order of removal.

➡When tightening the fuel line bolts to the filter on fuel injected engines, you must use a torque wrench and a crow's foot adapter. The tightening torque is very important as under or over tightening may cause fuel leakage. Insure that there is no fuel line interference and that there is sufficient clearance between it and any other parts.

6. On fuel injected engines, coat the flare nut, union nut and bolt threads with clean engine oil. Connect and hand-tighten the fuel lines, then use a torque wrench to tighten the fitting/union bolts to specification. Tighten the inlet bolt to 23-33 ft. lbs. (31-45 Nm), then tighten the fuel delivery pipe to 18-25 ft. lbs. (24-34 Nm). If supplied with the replacement filter, be sure to replace any O-rings or gaskets.

7. Run the engine for a few minutes and check the filter for any leaks.

8. If applicable, install the protective shield.

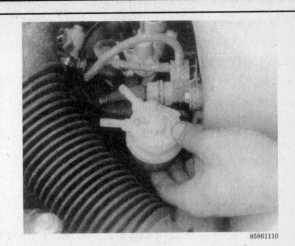

Fig. 35 Remove the filter from the retaining bracket and from the vehicle (note that the arrow points at the fuel line running to the engine)

1C-L DIESEL ENGINE

▶ See Figure 36

1. Disconnect the fuel level warning switch connector at the lower end of the filter.

2. Drain water and fuel from the filter. For details, please refer to the procedure found later in this section.

3. Loosen the two mounting bolts and remove the filter/bracket assembly.

4. Remove the water level warning switch from the filter housing and then unscrew the filter from the housing. An oil filter strap wrench may come in handy when removing the filter.

To install:

5. Install the water level warning switch using a new O-ring.

6. Coat the filter gasket lightly with diesel fuel and then screw it in hand-tight. DO NOT use a wrench to tighten the fuel filter.

7. Mount the filter assembly, tighten the bolts and connect the warning switch.

8. Using the priming pump on top of the filter, fill the filter with fuel and check for leaks.

In-Tank Filter

1. Disconnect the negative battery cable.

2. Drain the gasoline from the fuel tank.

3. Remove the fuel tank from the vehicle.

4. Remove the fuel pump bracket retaining bolts and remove the fuel pump bracket.

5. Remove the retaining clip from the fuel filter hose and remove the fuel filter.

6. Install a new fuel filter and reverse the removal procedure to complete the installation procedure.

Draining the Diesel Fuel Filter

▶ See Figure 37

❋❋CAUTION

When the fuel filter warning light or buzzer comes on, the water in the fuel filter must be drained immediately.

Fig. 33 Loosen the fuel line clamp and position it back on the hose, past the raised portion of the filter nipple

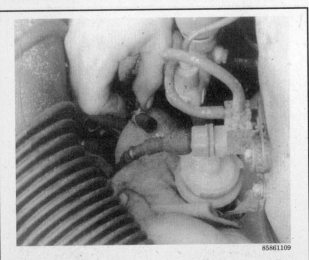

Fig. 34 Position a rag to catch any escaping fuel, then disconnect the lines from the filter

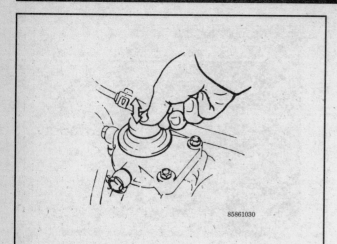

Fig. 36 Whenever the fuel filter is drained or replaced, the filter must be filled with fuel using the priming pump BEFORE attempting to start the engine

1. Raise the hood and position a small pan or jar underneath the drain plug to catch the water which is about to be released.

2. Reach under the fuel filter and turn the drain plug counterclockwise about 2-2½ turns.

➡**Loosening the drain plug more than the suggested amount will cause water to ooze from around the threads of the plug.**

3. Depress the priming pump on top of the filter housing until fuel is the only substance being forced out.

4. Retighten the drain plug by hand only, do not use a wrench.

PCV Valve

▶ **See Figure 38**

Most gasoline engines covered by this manual are equipped with a Positive Crankcase Ventilation (PCV) valve. The PCV valve regulates crankcase ventilation during various engine op-

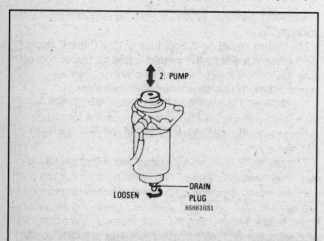

Fig. 37 Turn the drain plug counterclockwise in order to drain water from the filter

erating conditions. At high vacuum (idle speed and partial load range) it will open slightly and at low vacuum (full throttle) it will open fully. This causes vapor to be removed from the crankcase by the engine vacuum and then sucked into the combustion chamber where it is dissipated.

➡**On models with fuel injection there is no PCV valve. Vapor passage in the ventilation lines is controlled by two orifices. To check the PCV system on these models, inspect the hoses for cracks, leaks or other damage. Blow through the orifices to make sure they are not blocked. Replace all components as necessary.**

REMOVAL, INSTALLATION & INSPECTION

▶ **See Figures 39, 40, 41 and 42**

1. Check the ventilation hoses for leaks or clogging. Clean or replace as necessary.

2. Locate the PCV valve in the cylinder head cover or in the manifold-to-crankcase line. Carefully separate the hose(s), then remove the valve from the grommet (if mounted in the cylinder head cover).

3. Blow into the crankcase end of the valve. There should be a free passage of air through the valve.

4. Blow into the intake manifold end of the valve. There should be little or no passage of air through the valve.

5. If the PCV valve failed either of the preceding two checks, it will require replacement.

6. When installing the valve, make sure the hose(s), valve and grommet (if used) are all properly seated.

Evaporative Canister and System

SERVICING

▶ **See Figures 43, 44 and 45**

Most gasoline engine vehicles covered by this manual are equipped with a fuel vapor evaporative canister. The purpose

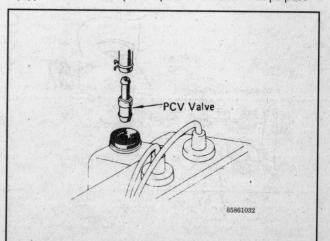

Fig. 38 Common PCV valve installation — the valve is usually mounted to a rubber grommet in the cylinder head (valve/camshaft) cover

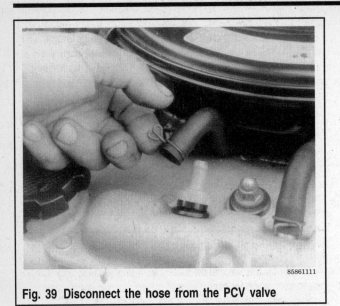

Fig. 39 Disconnect the hose from the PCV valve

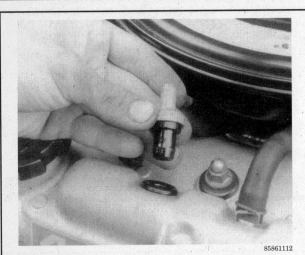

Fig. 40 Remove the valve from the grommet in the cylinder head (camshaft/valve) cover

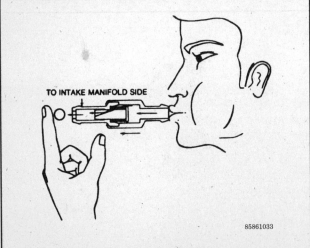

Fig. 41 Air should pass through the PCV valve when blowing in from the crankcase side

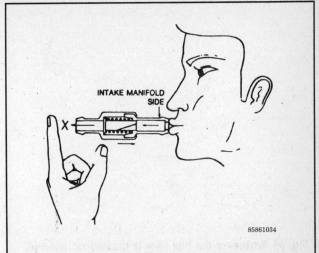

Fig. 42 No air should pass the the valve when blowing from the intake manifold side

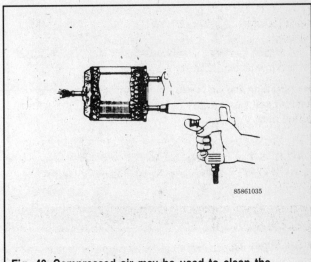

Fig. 43 Compressed air may be used to clean the charcoal canister

of the canister and system is to capture and store fuel vapors which would otherwise evaporate from the tank causing pollution.

The system should be checked every 15,000 miles. Inspect the fuel/vapor lines and the vacuum hoses for proper connections and correct routing, as well as condition. Replace clogged, damaged or deteriorated parts as necessary.

If the charcoal canister is clogged, it may be cleaned using low pressure compressed air. The entire canister should be replaced every 5 years/50,000 miles (60,000 miles for 1978 and later cars).

The canister is removed by tagging and unfastening the various hoses from the canister, then removing the mounting bolts from the mounting bracket or loosening the mounting clamp and removing the canister. It is always wise to tag the vapor hoses before disconnecting them, as improper connections will cause pollution and could interfere with proper engine operation. For more information on the evaporative emission system, please refer to Section 4 of this manual.

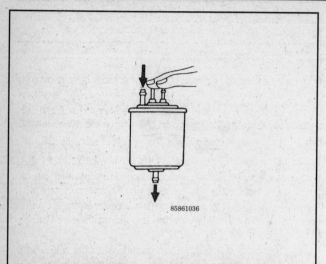

Fig. 44 When cleaning a late model canister, blow air into the outer vent pipe while plugging the other 2

Fig. 45 The evaporative canister is normally located in the engine compartment (in this case, just below the master cylinder)

Battery

FLUID LEVEL/SPECIFIC GRAVITY

Except Maintenance-Free Batteries

▶ **See Figures 46, 47 and 48**

Most vehicles covered by this manual were originally equipped with an unsealed, serviceable battery. These batteries require periodic inspection and service to assure proper operation. Check the battery fluid level on all serviceable batteries at least once a month, more often in hot weather or during extended periods of travel. The electrolyte level should be between the indicator lines on the side of the see-through battery casing. If no marks can be found on the battery, the electrolyte level should be even with the bottom of each cell's split ring. Be sure to check all 6 battery cells, not just one or

two of them. If necessary, add distilled water to the battery in order to raise the electrolyte level in any cell which is low.

The specific gravity should be checked at least once a year using a hydrometer (an inexpensive tool available from many sources, including auto parts stores). The hydrometer has a squeeze bulb at one end and a nozzle at the other. Battery electrolyte is sucked into the hydrometer until the float is lifted from its seat. The specific gravity is then read by noting the position of the float. Generally, if after charging, the specific gravity between any two cells varies more than 50 points (0.050), the battery is bad and should be replaced. Most batteries should read between 1.20-1.26 at room temperature.

After checking the specific gravity, clean and tighten the clamps, then apply a thin coat of petroleum jelly to the terminals. This will help to retard corrosion. The terminals can be cleaned with a stiff wire brush or with an inexpensive terminal cleaner designed for this purpose.

If distilled water is added during freezing weather, the car should be driven several miles to allow the electrolyte and water to mix. Otherwise the battery could freeze.

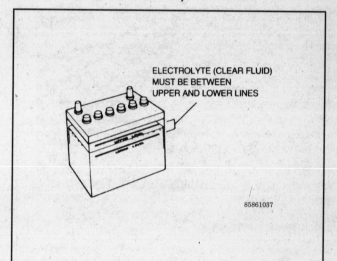

ELECTROLYTE (CLEAR FLUID)
MUST BE BETWEEN
UPPER AND LOWER LINES

Fig. 46 On most batteries check the fluid level using indicator lines located on the side of the battery casing

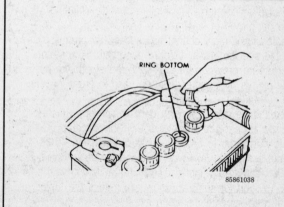

RING BOTTOM

Fig. 47 If no indicator lines are provided, electrolyte level for each cell should be even with the bottom of the split ring

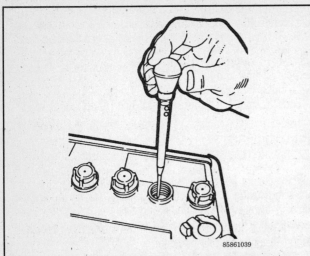

Fig. 48 On all serviceable batteries, a simple float type hydrometer may be used to check specific gravity

If the battery becomes corroded, a solution of baking soda and water will neutralize the corrosion, then the solution should be rinsed from the battery using cold water. Before applying the solution, make sure that the fluid caps are securely in place in order to prevent contaminating the electrolyte.

Some batteries were equipped with a felt terminal washer. This should be saturated with engine oil approximately every 6,000 miles. This will help to retard corrosion.

If a fast charger is used while the battery is in the car, disconnect the battery before connecting the charger.

➡**Keep flame or sparks away from the battery, especially when charging it; the battery gives off explosive hydrogen gas.**

Maintenance-Free Batteries

Some vehicles may be equipped with a maintenance-free battery. These batteries are especially popular with the aftermarket and any car whose battery has been replaced may wind up with one. Sealed maintenance-free batteries do not require normal attention as far as fluid level checks are concerned. However, the terminals require periodic cleaning, which should be performed at least once a year.

The sealed top battery cannot be checked for charge by checking the specific gravity using a hand-held hydrometer since there is no provision for access to the electrolyte. Instead, the built-in hydrometer must be used in order to determine the current state of charge.

Sealed batteries usually have a decal which gives instructions on how to read the indicator eye. If this decal is present on refer to it in order to determine battery condition. If the decal is not present, a few general rules may be followed. For most sealed batteries a light eye indicates a battery with sufficient fluid (though for some a yellow eye means the battery is in need of a charge while a green eye indicates a sufficient electrical charge). If the eye is dark, the electrolyte fluid is probably too low and the battery should be replaced. Many automotive parts stores that specialize in replacement batteries are also equipped to test the battery and will be happy to double check your findings.

CABLES AND CLAMPS

▶ **See Figures 49, 50, 51 and 52**

➡**In order to avoid the possibility of accidentally grounding the car's electrical system always remove the negative battery cable first. Failure to do so could allow a spark to occur exploding battery gasses and cause personal injury.**

Once a year, the battery terminals and the cable clamps should be cleaned. Loosen the clamps and remove the cables, negative cable first. On batteries with posts on top, the use of a puller specially made for this purpose is recommended. These are inexpensive, and are usually available in auto parts stores. Side terminal battery cables are secured with a bolt.

Clean the cable clamps and the battery terminals with a wire brush, until all corrosion, grease, etc. is removed and the metal is shiny. It is especially important to clean the inside of the clamp thoroughly, since a small deposit of foreign material or oxidation will prevent a sound electrical connection and could inhibit both starting or charging. Special tools are available for cleaning these parts, one type for conventional batteries and another type for side terminal batteries.

Before installing the cables, loosen the battery hold-down clamp or strap, remove the battery and check the battery tray. Clear it of any debris, and check it for soundness. Rust should be wire brushed away, and the metal given a coat of anti-rust paint. Reposition the battery and tighten the hold-down clamp or strap securely, but be careful not to overtighten the retainer and crack the battery case.

After the clamps and terminals are clean, reinstall the cables, negative cable last. Never hammer on the clamps to install. Tighten the clamps securely, but do not distort them. Give the clamps and terminals a thin external coat of grease after installation, to retard corrosion.

Check the cables at the same time that the terminals are cleaned. If the cable insulation is cracked or broken, or if the

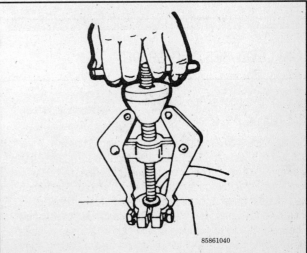

Fig. 49 A puller will make clamp removal easier on post battery terminals

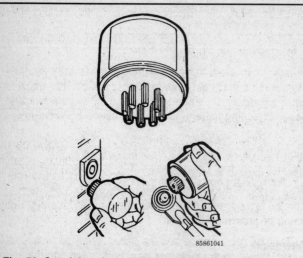

Fig. 50 Special tools are also available to clean the battery terminals and clamps on side terminal batteries

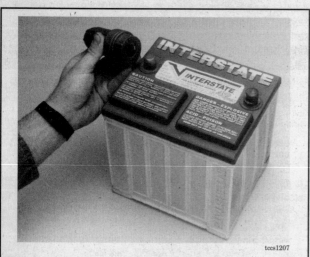

Fig. 51 The underside of this special battery tool has a wire brush to clean post terminals

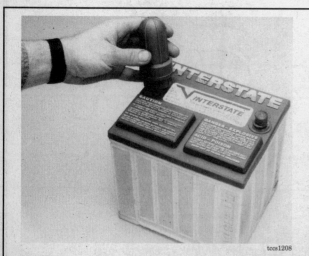

Fig. 52 Place the tool over the terminals and twist to clean the post

ends are frayed, the cable should be replaced using a new part of the same length and gauge.

➡**Keep flame or sparks away from the battery; it gives off explosive hydrogen gas. Battery electrolyte contains sulfuric acid. If you should splash any on your skin or in your eyes, flush the affected area with plenty of clean water; if it lands in your eyes, get medical help immediately.**

REPLACEMENT

When battery replacement becomes necessary, select a battery with a rating equal to or greater than the one which was originally installed. Deterioration and aging of the battery cables, starter motor, and associated wires makes the battery's job harder in successive years. The slow increase in electrical resistance over time makes it prudent to install a new battery with a greater capacity then the old. Details on the role the battery plays in the vehicle's electrical systems are covered in Section 3 of this manual.

1. Carefully disconnect the negative battery cable from the battery terminal.

✳✳CAUTION

Always use caution when working on or near the battery. Never allow a tool to bridge the gap between the negative and positive battery terminals. Also, be careful not to allow a tool to provide a ground between the positive cable/terminal and any metal component on the vehicle. Either of these conditions will cause a short leading to sparks and possibly, personal injury.

2. Make sure the ignition switch is **OFF**. On vehicles equipped with fuel injection or feedback carburetors, the computer control module could be seriously damaged or destroyed if the battery is disconnected with the ignition **ON**.

3. With the negative battery cable disconnected and out of the way, carefully disconnect the positive cable from the battery terminal.

4. Loosen the nut and/or bolt retaining the battery retainer strap or clamp. Remove or reposition the battery retainer.

5. Wearing an old pair of work gloves or using a battery lifting tool, carefully lift the battery out of the vehicle and place it in a safe location. Be sure to keep the battery away from open flame and to protect surrounding areas from acid. Be carefully when handling the battery not to spill any of the acid.

➡**Spilled acid can be neutralized with a baking soda and water solution. If you somehow get acid into your eyes, flush it out with lots of clean water or a solution of water and baking soda, then get to a doctor IMMEDIATELY.**

To install:
6. Inspect the battery tray and cables for damage or corrosion. As necessary, clean or repair the tray and cables.

7. Thoroughly clean the battery terminals and the cable clamps. For details, please refer to cables and clamps earlier in this section.

8. Carefully lower the battery into position in the tray, making sure not to allow the terminals to short on any bare metal during installation.

9. Position and secure the battery retainer strap or clamp.

10. Connect the positive battery cable to the battery terminal.

➡ **When connecting the cables to the battery terminals, DO NOT hammer them into place. Also, after they are secured, the terminals should be coated with grease to prevent corrosion.**

11. Make sure the ignition switch is **OFF**, then connect the negative battery cable to the battery terminal.

✳✳CAUTION

Make absolutely sure that the battery is connected properly before you turn the ignition switch ON. Reversed polarity can burn out your alternator and regulator in a matter of seconds.

Belts

▶ **See Figure 53**

The condition of the drive belts should be visually checked whenever the hood is opened. The benefit of catching a damaged belt before it breaks will more than even the additional time it takes to quickly check the belts. Belt tension should be checked and adjusted every 15,000 miles.

1. When checking and adjusting the belts, look for signs of glazing or cracking. A glazed belt will be perfectly smooth from slippage, while a good belt will have a slight texture of fabric visible. Cracks will usually start at the inner edge of the belt and run outward. Replace the belt at the first sign of cracking or if the glazing is severe.

2. Belt tension does not refer to play or droop. Check tension midway between 2 pulleys (the two which are furthest apart for that belt) using your thumb, it should be possible to depress the belt ¼-½ inch. If any of the belts can be depressed more than this, or cannot be depressed this much, adjust the tension. Inadequate tension will result in slippage

and wear, while excessive tension will damage bearings and cause belts to fray and crack.

3. All drive belts should be replaced every 60,000 miles regardless of their condition.

ADJUSTMENT

▶ **See Figures 54, 55, 56, 57 and 58**

➡**Belt adjustment is usually obtained by one of two methods. Either a component is pivoted in its mounting bracket (this could be any 1 component when a drive belt is run on 3 or more pulleys) or an adjusting bolt is used to change the position of the component/pulley, thereby tightening or loosening the belt.**

Alternator

To adjust the tension of the alternator drive belt on all models, loosen the pivot and mounting bolts on the alternator. Using a wooden hammer handle, a broomstick, or your hand, move the alternator one way or the other until the proper tension is achieved.

✳✳CAUTION

Do not use a screwdriver or any other metal device such as a pry bar, as a lever or damage may occur to the alternator housing or other engine components.

Tighten the mounting bolts securely. If a new belt has been installed, recheck the tension after about 200 miles of driving.

Air Conditioning Compressor

On most vehicles A/C compressor belt tension can be adjusted by turning the tension adjusting bolt which is located on the compressor tensioner bracket. Turn the bolt clockwise to tighten the belt and counterclockwise to loosen it.

If not equipped with an adjusting bolt, usually the AIR pump may be pivoted to adjust belt tension.

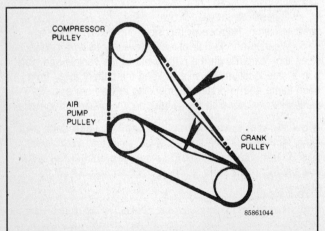

Fig. 53 Belt tension should be checked mid-way between 2 pulleys on the belt's longest stretch — These examples are of AIR pump belts on vehicles with and without A/C

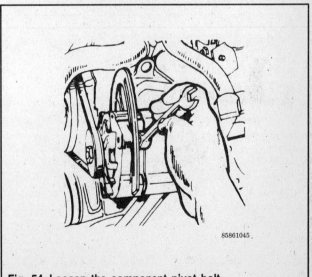

Fig. 54 Loosen the component pivot bolt

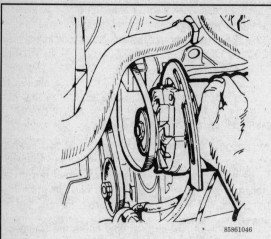

Fig. 55 Push the component to loosen the drive belt (usually this means pushing the component inwards towards the engine)

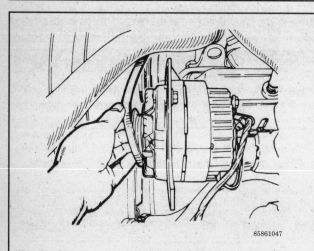

Fig. 56 Slip the old belt off and the new one on the pulley, making sure the belt is properly seated and routed

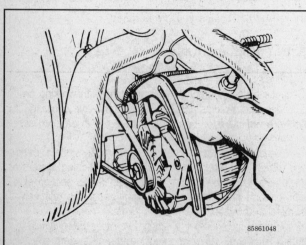

Fig. 57 Pull the component (usually outwards) to adjust the belt tension and hold while the pivot bolt is tightened

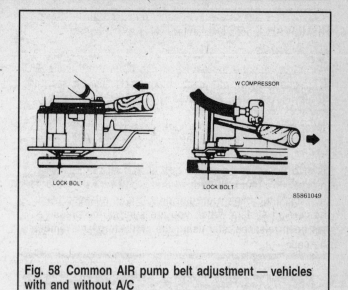

Fig. 58 Common AIR pump belt adjustment — vehicles with and without A/C

Air Pump

To adjust the tension of the air pump drive belt, loosen the adjusting lever bolt and the pivot bolt. Move the pump in or out until the desired tension is felt.

➡The tension should be checked between the air pump and the crankshaft pulley on cars without air conditioning. On cars with A/C, the tension should be checked between the A/C compressor and the crankshaft pulley.

Power Steering Pump

Tension on the power steering belt is usually adjusted by means of an idler pulley. Loosen the lock bolt and turn the adjusting bolt on the idler pulley until the desired tension is felt, then tighten the lock bolt.

Hoses

Upper and lower radiator hoses along with the heater hoses should be checked for deterioration, leaks and loose hose clamps at least every 15,000 miles. It is also wise to check the hoses periodically in early spring and at the beginning of the fall or winter when you are performing other maintenance. A quick visual inspection could discover a weakened hose which might have left you stranded if it had remained unrepaired.

Whenever you are checking the hoses, make sure the engine and cooling system is cold. Visually inspect for cracking, rotting or collapsed hoses, replace as necessary. Run your hand along the length of the hose. If a weak or swollen spot is noted when squeezing the hose wall, the hose should be replaced.

REMOVAL & INSTALLATION

1. Remove the radiator pressure cap.

❄❄CAUTION

Never remove the pressure cap while the engine is running or personal injury from scalding hot coolant or steam may result. If possible, wait until the engine has cooled to remove the pressure cap. If this is not possible, wrap a thick cloth around the pressure cap and turn it slowly to the stop. Step back while the pressure is released from the cooling system. When you are sure all the pressure has been released, still using the cloth, turn and remove the cap.

2. Position a clean container under the radiator and/or engine drain cock or plug, then open the drain and allow the cooling system to drain to an appropriate level. For some upper hoses only a little coolant must be drained. To remove hoses positioned lower on the engine, such as a lower radiator hose, the entire cooling system must be drained.

❄❄CAUTION

When draining coolant, keep in mind that cats and dogs are attracted by ethylene glycol antifreeze, and are quite likely to drink any that is left in an uncovered container or in puddles on the ground. This will prove fatal in sufficient quantity. Always drain the coolant into a sealable container. Coolant may be reused unless it is contaminated or several years old.

3. Loosen the hose clamps at each end of the hose requiring replacement. Clamps are usually either of the spring tension type (which require pliers to squeeze the tabs and loosen) or of the screw tension type (which require screw or hex drivers to loosen). Pull the clamps back on the hose away from the connection.

4. Twist, pull and slide the hose off the fitting taking care not to damage the neck of the component from which the hose is being removed.

➡**If the hose is stuck at the connection, do not try to insert a screwdriver or other sharp tool under the hose end in an effort to free it, as the connection and/or hose may become damaged. Heater connections especially may be easily damaged by such a procedure. If the hose is to be replaced, use a single-edged razor blade to make a slice along the portion of the hose which is stuck on the connection, perpendicular to the end of the hose. Do not cut deep so as to prevent damaging the connection. The hose can then be peeled from the connection and discarded.**

5. Clean both hose mounting connections. Inspect the condition of the hose clamps and replace them, if necessary.

To install:

6. Dip the ends of the new hose into clean engine coolant to ease installation.

7. Slide the hose clamps over the replacement hose and slide the hose ends over the connections into position.

8. Position and secure the clamps at least ¼ in. (6.35mm) from the ends of the hose. Make sure they are located inside the raised bead of the connector.

9. Close the radiator or engine drains and properly refill the cooling system with the clean drained engine coolant or a suitable 50/50 mixture of ethylene glycol coolant and water.

10. If available, install a pressure tester and check for leaks.

11. Leave the radiator cap off, then start and run the engine to normal operating temperature. When the engine is at operating temperature and the thermostat has opened, continue to fill the radiator until the level stabilizes just below the filler neck.

12. Install the radiator pressure cap and check the clamped hose ends for leaks.

13. Shut the engine **OFF** and allow the engine to cool. Once the engine has cooled, check for proper coolant level and add, as necessary.

Air Conditioning

Regular maintenance for the air conditioning system includes periodic checks of the drive belt tension. In addition, the system should be operated for at least five minutes every month (yes, in the winter too!). This ensures an adequate supply of lubricant to the bearings and also helps to prevent the seals and hoses from drying out. To do this comfortably in the winter, turn the air conditioning ON, the temperature control lever to WARM or HI and turn on the blower to the highest setting. This will engage the compressor, circulating lubricating oils within the system, but preventing the discharge of cold air. The system should also be checked for proper refrigerant charge using the refrigerant level check procedure located later in this section.

➡**Before touching your A/C system, check with your local authorities. In many areas it is illegal for you to service the system unless you are a certified A/C system technician. Also, it may be impossible to purchase the necessary refrigerant unless you are certified.**

SAFETY PRECAUTIONS

Because of the inherent dangers involved with working on air conditioning systems and R-12 refrigerant, the following safety precautions must be strictly adhered to in order to service the system safely.

1. Avoid contact with a charged refrigeration system, even when working on another part of the air conditioning system or vehicle. If a heavy tool comes into contact with a section of tubing or a heat exchanger, it can easily cause the relatively soft material to rupture.

2. When it is necessary to apply force to a fitting which contains refrigerant, as when checking that all system couplings are securely tightened, be sure to use a wrench on both parts of the fitting involved whenever possible. This will avoid putting torque on refrigerant tubing. (It is advisable, when pos-

sible, to use tube or line wrenches when tightening flare nut fittings.)

➡R-12 refrigerant is a chlorofluorocarbon which, when released into the atmosphere, can contribute to the depletion of the ozone layer in the upper atmosphere. Ozone filters out harmful radiation from the sun.

3. Do not attempt to discharge the system by merely loosening a fitting, or removing the service valve caps and cracking these valves. Precise control is possible only when using the service gauges and a proper A/C refrigerant recovery station. Wear protective gloves when connecting or disconnecting service gauge hoses.

➡Be sure to consult the laws in your area before servicing the air conditioning system. In some states, it is illegal to perform repairs involving refrigerant unless the work is performed by a certified technician.

4. Discharge the system only in a well ventilated area, as high concentrations of the gas which might accidentally escape can exclude oxygen and act as an anesthetic. When leak testing or soldering, this is particularly important, as toxic gas is formed when R-12 contacts any flame.

5. Never start a system without first verifying that both service valves are properly installed, and that all fittings throughout the system are snugly connected.

6. Avoid applying heat to any refrigerant line or storage vessel. Charging may be aided by using water heated to less than 125°F (50°C) to warm the refrigerant container. Never allow a refrigerant storage container to sit out in the sun, or near any other source of heat, such as a radiator.

7. Always wear goggles to protect your eyes when working on a system. If refrigerant contacts the eyes, it is advisable in all cases to see a physician as soon as possible.

8. Frostbite from liquid refrigerant should be treated by first gradually warming the area with cool water, and then gently applying petroleum jelly. A physician should be consulted.

9. Always keep refrigerant drum fittings capped when not in use. If the container is equipped with a safety cap to protect the valve, make sure the cap is in place when the can is not being used. Avoid sudden shock to the drum, which might occur from dropping it, or from banging a heavy tool against it. Never carry a drum in the passenger compartment of a car.

10. Always completely discharge the system into a suitable recovery unit before painting the vehicle (if the paint is to be baked on), or before welding anywhere near refrigerant lines.

11. When servicing the system, minimize the time that any refrigerant line or fitting is open to the air in order to prevent moisture or dirt from entering the system. Contaminants such as moisture or dirt can damage internal system components. Always replace O-rings on lines or fittings which are disconnected. Prior to installation coat, but do not soak, replacement O-rings with suitable compressor oil.

GENERAL SERVICING PROCEDURES

➡It is recommended, and possibly required by law, that a qualified technician perform the following services.

The most important aspect of air conditioning service is the maintenance of a pure and adequate charge of refrigerant in the system. A refrigeration system cannot function properly if a significant percentage of the charge is lost. Leaks are common because the severe vibration encountered underhood in an automobile can cause cracking or loosening of the air conditioning fittings; allowing, the extreme operating pressures of the system to force refrigerant out.

The problem can be understood by considering what happens to a common A/C system when it is operated with a continuous leak. Because the expansion valve regulates the flow of refrigerant to the evaporator, the level of refrigerant located there is fairly constant. The receiver/drier stores any excess of refrigerant, and so a loss will first appear there as a reduction in the level of liquid. As this level nears the bottom of the vessel, some refrigerant vapor bubbles will begin to appear in the stream of liquid supplied to the expansion valve. This vapor decreases the capacity of the expansion valve very little as the valve opens to compensate for its presence. As the quantity of liquid in the condenser decreases, the operating pressure will drop there and throughout the high side of the system. As the R-12 continues to be expelled, the pressure available to force the liquid through the expansion valve will continue to decrease, and, eventually, the valve's orifice will prove to be too much of a restriction for adequate flow even with the needle fully withdrawn.

At this point, low side pressure will start to drop, and severe reduction in cooling capacity, marked by freeze-up of the evaporator coil, will result. Eventually, the operating pressure of the evaporator will be lower than the pressure of the atmosphere surrounding it, and air will be drawn into the system wherever there are leaks in the low side.

Because all atmospheric air contains at least some moisture, water will enter the system and mix with the R-12 and the oil. Trace amounts of moisture will cause sludging of the oil, and corrosion of the system. Saturation and clogging of the filter/drier, and freezing of the expansion valve orifice will eventually result. As air fills the system to a greater and greater extent, it will interfere more and more with the normal flows of refrigerant and heat.

From this description, you may conclude that much of the repairman's time will be spent detecting leaks, repairing them, and then restoring the purity and quantity of the refrigerant charge. A list of general rules should be followed in addition to all safety precautions:

1. Keep all tools as clean and dry as possible.

2. Thoroughly purge the service gauges/hoses of air and moisture before connecting them to the system. Keep them capped when not in use.

3. Thoroughly clean any refrigerant fitting before disconnecting it, in order to minimize the entrance of dirt into the system.

4. Plan any operation that requires opening the system beforehand, in order to minimize the length of time it will be exposed to open air. Cap or seal the open ends to minimize the entrance of foreign material.

5. When adding oil, pour it through an extremely clean and dry tube or funnel. Keep the oil capped whenever possible. Do not use oil that has not been kept tightly sealed.

6. Use only R-12 refrigerant. Purchase refrigerant intended for use only in automatic air conditioning systems. Avoid the use of R-12 that may be packaged for other purposes, such as cleaning, or powering a horn, as it is impure.

7. Completely evacuate any system that has been opened to replace a component, or that has leaked sufficiently to draw in moisture and air. This requires evacuating air and moisture with a good vacuum pump for at least one hour. If a system has been open for a considerable length of time it may be advisable to evacuate the system for up to 12 hours (overnight).

8. Use a wrench on both halves of a fitting that is to be disconnected, so as to avoid placing torque on any of the refrigerant lines.

9. When overhauling a compressor, pour some of the oil into a clean glass and inspect it. If there is evidence of dirt or metal particles, or both, flush all refrigerant components with clean refrigerant before evacuating and recharging the system. In addition, if metal particles are present, the compressor should be replaced.

10. Schrader valves may leak only when under full operating pressure. Therefore, if leakage is suspected but cannot be located, operate the system with a full charge of refrigerant and look for leaks from all Schrader valves. Replace any faulty valves.

Additional Preventive Maintenance Checks

ANTIFREEZE

In order to prevent heater core freeze-up during A/C operation, it is necessary to maintain permanent type antifreeze protection of +15°F, or lower. A reading of -15°F is ideal since this protection also supplies sufficient corrosion inhibitors for the protection of the engine cooling system.

➡**The same antifreeze should not be used longer than the manufacturer specifies.**

RADIATOR CAP

For efficient operation of an air conditioned car's cooling system, the radiator cap should have a holding pressure which meets manufacturer's specifications. A cap which fails to hold these pressures should be replaced.

CONDENSER

Any obstruction of or damage to the condenser configuration will restrict the air flow which is essential to its efficient operation. It is therefore a good rule to keep this unit clean and in proper physical shape.

➡**Bug screens are regarded as obstructions.**

CONDENSATION DRAIN TUBE

Usually a single molded drain tube expels the condensation, which accumulates on the bottom of the evaporator housing, into the engine compartment. If this tube is obstructed, the air conditioning performance can be restricted and condensation buildup can spill over onto the vehicle's floor.

AIR CONDITIONING TOOLS AND GAUGES

Test Gauges

Most of the service work performed in air conditioning requires the use of a set of two gauges, one for the high (head)

pressure side of the system, the other for the low (suction) side.

The low side gauge records both pressure and vacuum. Vacuum readings are usually calibrated from 0 to 30 inches and the pressure graduations read from 0 to no less than 60 psi (414kPa).

The high side gauge measures pressure from 0 to at least 600 psi (4140kPa).

Both gauges are threaded into a manifold that contains two hand shut-off valves. Proper manipulation of these valves and the use of the attached test hoses allow the user to perform the following services:

1. Test high and low side pressures.
2. Remove air, moisture, and contaminated refrigerant.

The manifold valves are designed so they have no direct effect on gauge readings, but serve only to provide for the flow or cut-off of refrigerant through the manifold. During all testing and hook-up operations, the valves are kept in a closed position to avoid disturbing the refrigeration system. The valves are opened only to purge the system of refrigerant or to charge it.

Usually, when purging the system, the center hose is attached to a recovery station at the lower end, and both valves are cracked open slightly. This allows refrigerant pressure to force the entire contents of the system out through the center hose and into a suitable recovery station. During charging, the valve on the high side of the manifold is closed, and the valve on the low side is cracked open. Under these conditions, the low pressure in the evaporator will draw refrigerant from the relatively warm refrigerant storage container into the system.

Service Valves

For the user to diagnose an air conditioning system, he or she must gain "entrance" to the system in order to observe the pressures. There are two types of terminals for this purpose, the hand shut off type and the familiar Schrader valve.

The Schrader valve is similar to a tire valve stem and the process of connecting the test hoses is the same as threading a hand pump outlet hose to a bicycle tire. As the test hose is threaded to the service port the valve core is depressed, allowing the refrigerant to enter the test hose outlet. Removal of the test hose automatically closes the system.

Extreme caution must be observed when removing test hoses from the Schrader valves as some refrigerant will normally escape, usually under high pressure. (Observe safety precautions.)

Using the Manifold Gauges

The following is a common guide to correct gauge usage.

1. Wear goggles or a face shield during all testing operations.
2. Remove caps from high and low side service ports. Make sure both gauge valves are closed.
3. Connect low side test hose to the low side service valve (usually this valve is on the line between the evaporator outlet and the compressor).
4. Attach high side test hose to the high side service valve (usually this valve is located on the line that leads to the condenser).
5. Start engine and allow for warm-up. All testing and charging of the system should be done after engine and sys-

tem have reached normal operation temperatures (unless the recovery/charging station's manufacturer instructs otherwise).

6. Adjust air conditioner controls to maximum cold.

7. Observe gauge readings. When the gauges are not being used it is a good idea to:

a. Keep both valves in the closed position.

b. Attach both ends of the high and low service hoses to the manifold, if extra outlets are present on the manifold, or plug them if not. Also, keep the center charging hose attached to an empty refrigerant can. This extra precaution will reduce the possibility of moisture entering the gauges. If air and moisture have gotten into the gauges, purge the hoses by supplying refrigerant under pressure to the center hose with both gauge valves open and all openings unplugged.

SYSTEM INSPECTION

➡R-12 refrigerant is a chlorofluorocarbon which, when released into the atmosphere, can contribute to the depletion of the ozone layer in the upper atmosphere. Ozone filters out harmful radiation from the sun.

The easiest and often most important check for the air conditioning system consists of a visual inspection of the system components. Visually inspect the air conditioning system for refrigerant leaks, damaged compressor clutch, compressor drive belt tension and condition, plugged evaporator drain tube, blocked condenser fins, disconnected or broken wires, blown fuses, corroded connections and poor insulation.

A refrigerant leak will usually appear as an oily residue at the leakage point in the system. The oily residue soon picks up dust or dirt particles from the surrounding air and appears greasy. Through time, this will build up and appear to be a heavy dirt impregnated grease. Most leaks are caused by damaged or missing O-ring seals at the component connections, damaged charging valve cores or missing service gauge port caps.

For a thorough visual and operational inspection, check the following:

1. Check the surface of the radiator and condenser for dirt, leaves or other material which might block air flow.

2. Check for kinks in hoses and lines. Check the system for leaks.

3. Make sure the drive belt is under the proper tension. When the air conditioning is operating, make sure the drive belt is free of noise or slippage.

4. Make sure the blower motor operates at all appropriate positions, then check for distribution of the air from all outlets with the blower on HIGH.

➡Keep in mind that under conditions of high humidity, air discharged from the A/C vents may not feel as cold as expected, even if the system is working properly. This is because the vaporized moisture in humid air retains heat more effectively than does dry air, making the humid air more difficult to cool.

5. Make sure the air passage selection lever is operating correctly. Start the engine and warm it to normal operating temperature, then make sure the hot/cold selection lever is operating correctly.

REFRIGERANT LEVEL CHECKS

♦ **See Figure 59**

✳✳CAUTION

Do not attempt to charge or discharge the refrigerant system unless you have access to a recovery station and are thoroughly familiar with both the system's operation and the hazards involved. The compressed refrigerant used in the air conditioning system expands and evaporates (boils) into the atmosphere at a temperature of -21.7°F (-29.8°C) or less. This will freeze any surface that it comes in contact with, including your eyes. In addition, the refrigerant decomposes into a poisonous gas in the presence of flame.

Factory installed Toyota air conditioners are equipped with a sight glass for checking the refrigerant charge. The sight glass is on top of the receiver/drier which is located in the front of the engine compartment, on the right or left side of the radiator depending upon the year and model of your car.

➡If your car is equipped with an aftermarket air conditioner, the following system check may not apply. Contact the manufacturer of the unit for instructions on system checks.

This test works best if the outside air temperature is warm (above 70°F).

1. Place the automatic transmission in Park or the manual transmission in Neutral. Set the parking brake and block the drive wheels.

2. With the help of a friend, run the engine at a fast idle (about 1500 rpm).

3. Set the controls for maximum cold with the blower on high.

4. Look at the sight glass on top of the receiver/drier. If a steady stream of bubbles is present in the sight glass, the system is low on charge. If so, it is very likely that there is a leak in the system.

5. If no bubbles are present, the system is either fully charged or empty. Feel the high and low pressure lines at the compressor, if no appreciable temperature difference is felt, the system is empty, or nearly so.

6. If one hose is warm (high pressure) and the other is cold (low pressure), the system may be OK. However, you are probably making these tests because there is something wrong with the air conditioning, so proceed to the next step.

7. Either disconnect the compressor clutch wire or have an assistant in the car turn the fan control On and Off to operate the compressor clutch. Watch the sight glass.

8. If bubbles appear when the clutch is disengaged and disappear when it is engaged, the system is properly charged.

9. If the refrigerant takes more than 45 seconds to bubble when the clutch is disengaged, the system is most likely overcharged. This will usually result in poor cooling at low speeds.

➡If it is determined that the system has a leak, or requires charging, it should be serviced as soon as possible. Leaks may allow moisture to enter the system, causing an expensive rust problem.

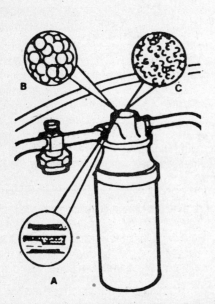

Oil streaks (A), constant bubbles (B) or foam (C) indicate there is not enough refrigerant in the system. Occasional bubbles during initial operation is normal. A clear sight glass indicates a proper charge of refrigerant or no refrigerant at all, which can be determined by the presence of cold air at the outlets in the car. If the glass is clouded with a milky white substance, have the receiver/drier checked professionally

85861050

Fig. 59 The sight glass in the receiver/drier may be used to check refrigerant charge

LEAK TESTING THE SYSTEM

Whenever a refrigerant leak is suspected, begin by checking for leaks at the fittings and valves. There are several methods of detecting leaks in an air conditioning system; among them, the two most popular are (1) halide leak-detection or the "open flame method," and (2) electronic leak-detection. Use of an electronic leak detector, if available is preferable for ease and safety of operation.

The halide leak detector is a torch like device which produces a yellow-green color when refrigerant is introduced into the flame at the burner. A purple or violet color indicates the presence of large amounts of refrigerant at the burner.

An electronic leak detector is a small portable electronic device with an extended probe. With the unit activated the probe is passed along those components of the system which contain refrigerant. If a leak is detected, the unit will sound an alarm signal or activate a display signal depending on the manufacturer's design. Follow the manufacturer's instructions carefully. Move the detector probe at approximately 1 in.

(25.4mm) per second in the suspected leak area. When escaping refrigerant gas is located, the ticking/beeping signal from the detector will increase in ticks/beeps per second. If the gas is relatively concentrated, the signal will be a constant shrill.

✳✳CAUTION

Care should be taken to operate either type of detector in well ventilated areas, so as to reduce the chance of personal injury, which may result from coming in contact with poisonous gases produced when R-12 is exposed to flame or electric spark.

If a tester is not available, perform a visual inspection and apply a soap solution to the questionable fitting or area. Bubbles will form to indicate a leak. Make sure to rinse the solution from the fitting before attempting repairs.

Windshield Wipers

REFILL (ELEMENT) REPLACEMENT

▶ See Figures 60, 61 and 62

For maximum effectiveness and longest element life, the windshield and wiper blades should be kept clean. Dirt, tree sap, road tar and so on will cause streaking, smearing and blade deterioration if left on the glass. It is advisable to wash the windshield carefully with a commercial glass cleaner at least once a month. Wipe off the rubber blades with the wet rag afterwards. Do not attempt to move the wipers back and forth by hand; damage to the motor and drive mechanism will result.

If the blades are found to be cracked, broken or torn, they should be replaced immediately. Replacement intervals will vary with usage, although ozone deterioration usually limits blade life to about one year. If the wiper pattern is smeared or streaked, or if the blade chatters across the glass, the blades should be replaced. It is easiest and most sensible to replace them in pairs.

There are basically three different types of wiper blade refills, which differ in their method of replacement. One type has two release buttons, approximately 1/3 of the way up from the ends of the blade frame. Pushing the buttons down releases a lock and allows the rubber blade to be removed from the frame. The new blade slides back into the frame and locks into place.

The second type of refill has two metal tabs which are unlocked by squeezing them together. The rubber blade can then be withdrawn from the frame jaws. A new one is installed by inserting it into the front frame jaws and sliding it rearward to engage the remaining frame jaws. There are usually four jaws; when installing, be certain that the refill is engaged in all of them. At the end of its travel, the tabs will lock into place on the front jaws of the wiper blade frame.

The third type is a refill made from polycarbonate. The refill has a simple locking device at one end which flexes downward out of the groove into which the jaws of the holder fit, allowing easy release. By sliding the new refill through all the jaws and pushing through the slight resistance when it reaches the end of its travel, the refill will lock into position.

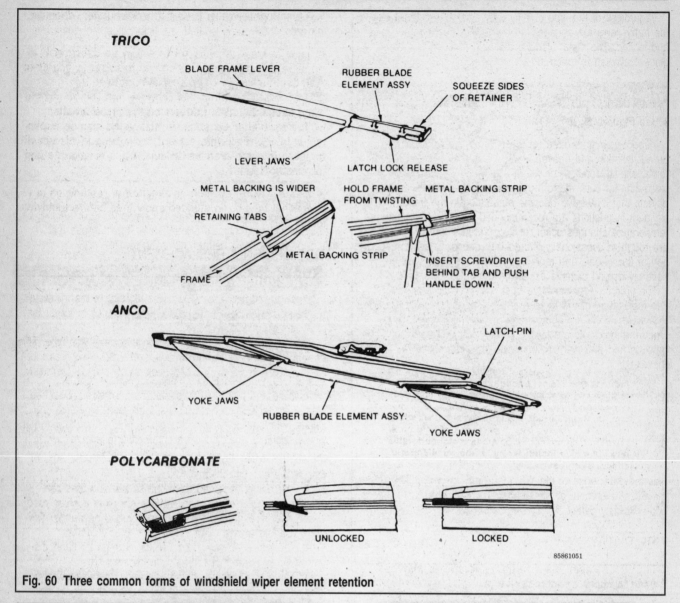

TRICO

BLADE FRAME LEVER

RUBBER BLADE
ELEMENT ASSY

SQUEEZE SIDES
OF RETAINER

LEVER JAWS

LATCH LOCK RELEASE

METAL BACKING IS WIDER

RETAINING TABS

FRAME

METAL BACKING STRIP

HOLD FRAME
FROM TWISTING

METAL BACKING STRIP

INSERT SCREWDRIVER
BEHIND TAB AND PUSH
HANDLE DOWN.

ANCO

LATCH-PIN

YOKE JAWS

RUBBER BLADE ELEMENT ASSY.

YOKE JAWS

POLYCARBONATE

UNLOCKED

LOCKED

85861051

Fig. 60 Three common forms of windshield wiper element retention

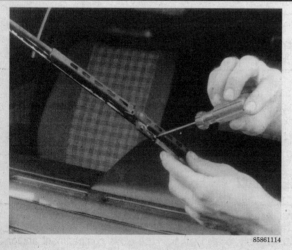

85861114

Fig. 61 If necessary, the entire wiper blade refill and retainer may be removed

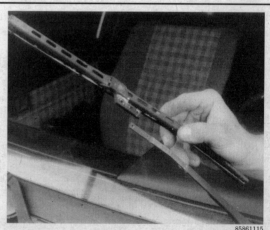

85861115

Fig. 62 Once the fasteners are removed/released, the blade and retainer assembly is separated from the wiper arm

Regardless of the type of refill used, make sure that all of the frame jaws are engaged as the refill is pushed into place and locked. The metal blade holder and frame will scratch the glass if allowed to touch it.

Tires

▶ **See Figures 63, 64, 65 and 66**

Inspect your tires often (at least weekly) for signs of improper inflation and uneven wear, which may indicate a need for balancing, rotation, or wheel alignment. Check the tires frequently for cuts, stone bruises, abrasions, blisters and for objects that may have become embedded in the tread. More frequent inspections are recommended when rapid or extreme temperature changes occur, or if operated where road surfaces are rough or occasionally littered with debris. Check the condition of the wheels and replace any that are bent, cracked, severely dented or have excessive run-out.

The tires on your car have built-in wear indicators molded into the bottom of the tread grooves. The indicators will begin to appear as the tire approaches replacement tread depth. Once the indicators are visible across 2 or more adjacent grooves and at 3 or more locations, the tires should be replaced.

Wear that occurs only on certain portions of the tire may indicate a particular problem, which when corrected or avoided, may significantly extend tire life. Wear that occurs only in the center of the tire indicates either overinflation or heavy acceleration on a drive wheel. Wear occurring at the outer edges of the tire and not at the center may indicate underinflation, excessively hard cornering or a lack of rotation. If wear occurs at only the outer edge of the tire, there may be a problem with the wheel alignment or the tire, when constructed, contained a non-uniformity defect.

TIRE ROTATION

▶ **See Figure 67**

Tire rotation is recommended every 6,000 miles or so, to obtain maximum tire wear. The pattern you use depends on whether or not your car has a full-sized usable spare or an undersized "donut" spare. Because the compact or donut spare tire is designed for limited emergency use, it should not be included in normal tire rotation.

Due to their design, radial tires tend to wear faster in the shoulder area, particularly in the front positions. Radial tires in non-drive locations, may develop an irregular wear pattern that can generate tire noise. It was originally thought the radial tires should not be cross-switched (from one side of the car to the other); because of their wear patterns and that they would last longer if their direction of rotation is not changed. Today, most manufacturers recommend rotating even radial tires using a cross-switching pattern to allow for more uniform tire wear. Toyota however, still tends to recommend not switching rotational direction on radial tires. You will have to make up your own mind what is better for your vehicle and use. If in doubt, check with a reputable tire supplier for advice or follow

Toyota's recommendations, after all their engineers designed the car.

➡**Some specialty aftermarket tires may be directional, meaning they may only be mounted to rotate in one direction. Some snow tires and special performance tires/wheels will fall into this category and will be marked with directional rotation arrows on the tire sidewalls. NEVER switch the direction of rotation on tires so marked or poor performance/tire damage could occur. This should be taken into consideration in choosing a rotation pattern for directional tires.**

➡**Mark the wheel position or direction of rotation on any directional tires or on studded snow tires before removing them.**

TIRE DESIGN & REPLACEMENT

When buying new tires, give some thought to the following points, especially if you are considering a switch to larger tires or a different profile series:

1. All four tires must be of the same construction type. This rule cannot be violated, radial, bias, and bias-belted tires must not be mixed or vehicle handling and safety may be seriously jeopardized.

2. The wheels should be the correct width for the tire. Tire dealers have charts of tire and rim compatibility. A miss-match will cause sloppy handling and rapid tire wear. The tread width should match the rim width (inside bead to inside bead) within an inch (25.4mm). For radial tires, the rim should be 80% or less of the tire (not tread) width.

3. The height (mounted diameter) of the new tires can change speedometer accuracy, engine speed at a given road speed, fuel mileage, acceleration, and ground clearance. Tire manufacturers furnish full measurement specifications.

4. The spare tire should be usable, at least for short distance and low speed operation, with the new tires.

5. There shouldn't be any vehicle body interference when loaded, on bumps, or in turns. If the tire hits the wheel-well under load, wear and the possibility of a blow-out will be significantly increased.

STORAGE

Store the tires at the proper inflation pressure if they are mounted on wheels. Keep them in a cool dry place, laid on their sides. If the tires are stored in the garage or basement, do not let them stand on a concrete floor; set them on strips of wood.

INFLATION

Tires should be checked weekly for proper air pressure. A chart, usually located either in the glove compartment and/or on one of the vehicle's doors or door jambs, gives the recommended inflation pressures. Maximum fuel economy and tire life will result if the pressure is maintained at the highest figure given on the chart. Pressures should be checked with the tires

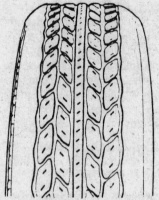
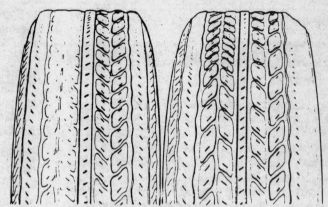

- ● Hard Cornering
- ● Under Inflation
- ● Lack of Rotation

- ● Incorrect Wheel Alignment
- ● Tire Construction Non-Uniformity
- ● Rear Wheel Heavy Acceleration

Tire Wear Diagnosis

TIRE DIAGNOSIS

Irregular and/or Premature Wear

Irregular and premature wear has many causes. Some of them are: incorrect inflation pressures, lack of tire rotation, driving habits, improper alignment.

If the following conditions are noted, rotation is in order:

1. Front tire wear is different from rear.

2. Uneven wear exists across the tread of any tire.

3. Left front and right front tire wear is unequal.

4. Left rear and right rear tire wear is unequal.

5. There is cupping, flat spotting etc.

A wheel alignment check is in order if the following conditions are noted:

1. Left front and right front tire wear is unequal.

2. Wear is uneven across the tread of any front tire.

3. Front tire treads have scuffed appearance with "feather" edges on one side of tread ribs or blocks.

Wear Indicators

The original equipment tires have built-in tread wear indicators to show when tires need replacement. These indicators will appear as 12.70 mm (1/2") wide bands when the tire tread depth becomes 1.59 mm (1/16 of an inch). When the indicators appear in 2 or more grooves at 3 locations, tire replacement is recommended.

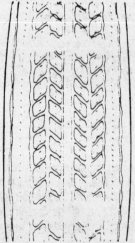

Tire Wear Indicator

85861052

Fig. 63 Uneven tire wear can be caused by variables from tire/vehicle condition to driving style

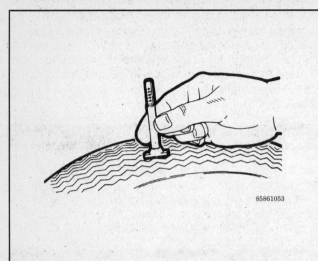

Fig. 64 Tread depth can be checked using an inexpensive gauge

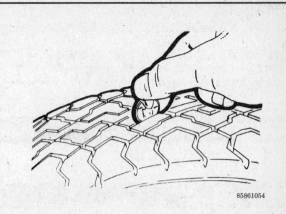

Fig. 65 If a gauge is not available, a penny may be used to check for tire tread depth; when the top of Lincoln's head is visible, it is probably time for a new tire

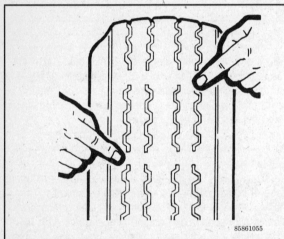

Fig. 66 If tires a used beyond the point of tread life, built-in wear indicators will begin to appear as lines perpendicular to the tread

cold before driving 1 mile or more since pressure can increase as much as six pounds Per Square Inch (psi) due to heat buildup as the tire is warmed. It is a good idea to have your own accurate pressure gauge, because many gauges on service station air pumps cannot be trusted. When checking pressures, do not neglect the spare tire. Note that some spare tires require pressures considerably higher than those used in the other tires.

While you are about the task of checking air pressure, inspect the tire treads for cuts, bruises and other damage. Check the air valves to be sure that they are tight. Replace any missing valve caps. Dirt and moisture gathering in the valve stem could lead to an early demise of the stem and a subsequent flat tire.

Check the tires for uneven wear that might indicate the need for front end alignment or tire rotation. Tires should be replaced when tread wear indicators appears as solid bands across the tread.

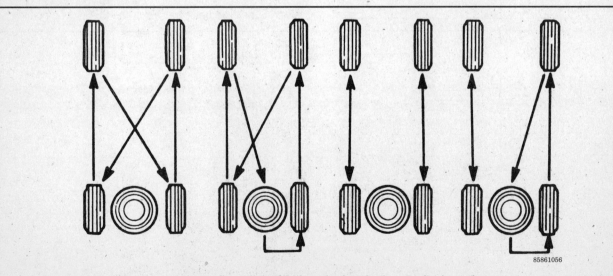

Fig. 67 Acceptable tire rotation patterns for radial and bias ply tires in 4 or 5 wheel rotations

CARE OF ALUMINUM WHEELS

If your car is equipped with aluminum wheels such as from an aftermarket application, they are normally coated to preserve their appearance. To clean the aluminum wheels, use a mild soap/water solution and rinse thoroughly with clean water. If you want to use one of the commercially available wheel cleaners, make sure the label indicates that the cleaner is safe for coated wheels. Never use steel wool or any cleaner that contains an abrasive. Also, never use strong detergents that contain high alkaline or caustic agents, as they will damage your wheels.

FLUIDS AND LUBRICANTS

▶ See Figures 68, 69, 70 and 71

Fluid Disposal

Used fluids such as engine oil, transmission/transaxle fluid, antifreeze and brake fluid are hazardous wastes and must be disposed of properly. Before draining any fluids, consult with the local authorities; in many areas, waste oil, etc. is accepted as a part of recycling programs. A number of service stations and auto parts stores are also accepting waste fluids for recycling.

Be sure of the recycling center's policies before draining any fluids, as many will not accept different fluids that have been mixed together, such as oil and antifreeze.

Oil and Fuel Recommendations

OIL

▶ See Figure 72

The Society of Automotive Engineers (SAE) grade number indicates the viscosity of the engine oil and thus its ability to lubricate at a given temperature. The lower the SAE grade number, the lighter the oil; the lower the viscosity, the easier it is to crank the engine in cold weather.

Oil viscosities should be chosen from those oils recommended for the lowest anticipated temperatures during the oil change interval.

Multi-viscosity oils (10W-30, 20W-50, etc.) offer the important advantage of being adaptable to temperature extremes. They allow easy starting at low temperatures, yet they give good protection at high speeds and engine temperatures. This is a decided advantage in changeable climates or in long distance touring.

The American Petroleum Institute (API) designation indicates the classification of engine oil used under certain given operating conditions. Only oils designated for use Service SF or Service SG should be used. Oils of the SF/SG type perform a

Fig. 68 View of the a late model FWD Corolla gasoline engine compartment

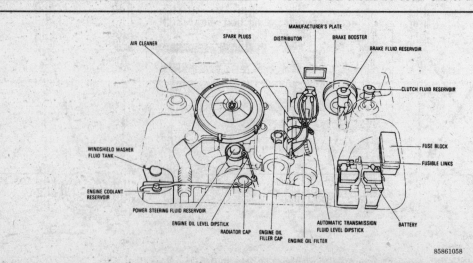

Fig. 69 Fluid and basic maintenance locations in the engine compartment — late model RWD Corolla with gasoline engine

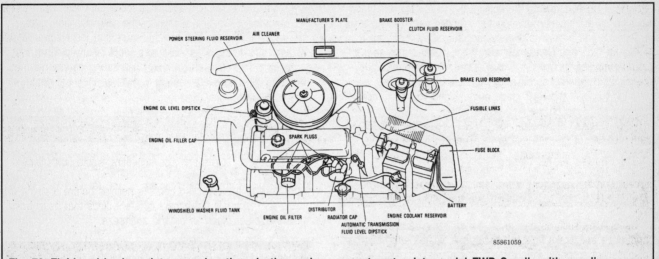

Fig. 70 Fluid and basic maintenance locations in the engine compartment — late model FWD Corolla with gasoline engine

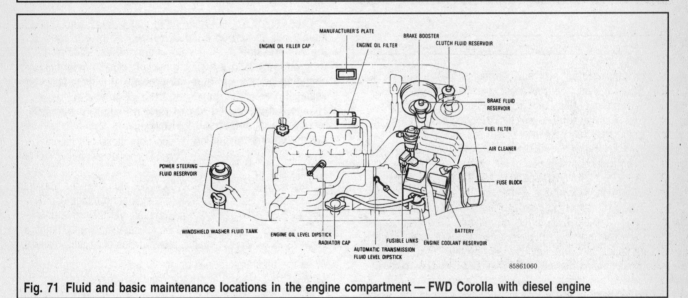

Fig. 71 Fluid and basic maintenance locations in the engine compartment — FWD Corolla with diesel engine

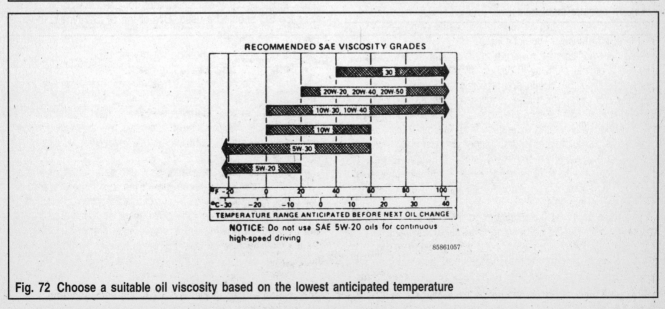

Fig. 72 Choose a suitable oil viscosity based on the lowest anticipated temperature

variety of functions inside the engine in addition to their basic function as a lubricant. Through a balanced system of metallic detergents and polymeric dispersants, the oil prevents the formation of high and low temperature deposits and also keeps sludge and particles of dirt in suspension. Acids, particularly sulfuric acid, as well as other by-products of combustion, are neutralized. Both the SAE grade number and the API designation can be found on the side of the bottle.

Diesel engines also require SF or SG engine oil. In addition, the oil must qualify for a CC rating. The API has a number of different diesel engine ratings, including CB, CC, and CD. Any of these other oils are fine as long as the designation CC appears on the can along with them. Do not use oil labeled only SF/SG or only CC. Both designations must always appear together.

❊❊CAUTION

Non-detergent or straight mineral oils should not be used in your car.

SYNTHETIC OIL

There are excellent synthetic and fuel-efficient oils available that, under the right circumstances, can help provide better fuel mileage and better engine protection. However, these advantages come at a price, which can be more than the price per quart of conventional motor oils.

Before pouring any synthetic oils into your car's engine, you should consider the condition of the engine and the type of driving you do. It is also wise to check the vehicle manufacturer's position on synthetic oils.

Generally, it is best to avoid the use of synthetic oil in both brand new and older, high mileage engines. New engines require a proper break-in, and some people feel that the synthetics are so slippery that they may impede this; most manufacturers recommend that you wait at least 5,000 miles before switching to a synthetic oil. Conversely, older engines are looser and tend to use more oil; synthetics will slip past worn parts more readily than regular oil, and will be used up faster. If your car already leaks oil (due to bad seals or gaskets), it may leak more with a synthetic inside.

Consider your type of driving. If most of your accumulated mileage is on the highway at higher, steadier speed, a synthetic oil will reduce friction and probably help deliver better fuel mileage. Under such ideal highway conditions, the oil change interval can be extended, as long as the oil filter will operate effectively for the extended life of the oil. If the filter can't do its job for this extended period, dirt and sludge will build up in your engine's crankcase, sump, oil pump and lines, no matter what type of oil is used. If using synthetic oil in this manner, you should continue to change the oil filter at the recommended intervals.

Cars used under harder, stop-and-go, short hop circumstances should always be serviced more frequently, and for these cars synthetic oil may not be a wise investment. Because of the necessary shorter change interval needed for this type of driving, you cannot take advantage of the long recommended change interval of most synthetic oils.

FUEL

Most 1970-76 Corollas were designed to operate on regular grade fuel. The 1975-76 Corollas which were built for use in California, and all models made in 1977 and later are designed to run on unleaded fuel ONLY. The use of leaded fuel in a car requiring unleaded fuel will plug the catalytic converter, rendering it inoperative. It will increase exhaust backpressure to the point where engine output will be severely reduced. In all cases, the minimum octane rating of the fuel used must be at least 87. All unleaded fuels sold in the U.S. are required to meet this minimum octane rating.

The use of a fuel too low in octane (a measurement of anti-knock quality) will result in spark knock. Since many factors, such as altitude, terrain, air temperature and humidity affect operating efficiency, knocking may result even though the recommended fuel is being used. If persistent knocking occurs, it may be necessary to switch to a higher grade of fuel. Continuous or heavy knocking may result in engine damage.

➡**Your engine's fuel requirement can change with time, mainly due to carbon buildup, which will in turn change the compression ratio. If your engine pings, knocks or runs on, switch to a higher grade of fuel. Sometimes just changing brands will cure the problem. If it becomes necessary to retard the timing from specifications, don't change it more than a few degrees. Retarded timing will reduce power output and fuel mileage, in addition to making the engine run hotter.**

Corolla Diesels require the use of diesel fuel (obviously). At no time should gasoline be substituted. Two grades of diesel fuel are manufactured, #1 and #2, although #2 grade is generally more available. Better fuel economy results from the use of #2 grade fuel. In some northern parts of the U.S. and in most parts of Canada, #1 grade fuel is available in the winter or a winterized blend of #2 grade is supplied in winter months. When the temperature falls below 20°F (-7°C), #1 grade or winterized #2 grade fuel are the only fuels that can be used. Cold temperatures cause unwinterized #2 to thicken (it actually gels), blocking the fuel lines and preventing the engine from running. There are a few cautions to keep in mind when dealing with diesel fuel:

• Do not use home heating oil in your car.

• Do not use ether or starting assist fluids in your car.

• Do not use any fuel additives recommended for use in gasoline engines.

• Do not thin your fuel with gasoline in cold weather. The lighter gasoline, which is more explosive, will cause rough running at the very least, and may cause extensive damage if enough is used.

• Remember that diesel fuel also acts as a lubricant to the fuel system. Using the wrong fuel in the fuel system is akin to using the wrong engine oil in the crankcase.

It is normal that the engine noise level is louder during the warm-up period in winter. It is also normal that whitish-blue smoke may be emitted from the exhaust after starting and during warm-up. The amount of smoke depends upon the outside temperature.

Engine

OIL LEVEL CHECK

▶ See Figures 73, 74 and 75

✳✳CAUTION

Prolonged and repeated skin contact with used engine oil may be harmful, especially if no effort is made to remove the oil. Always follow these simple precautions when handling used motor oil.

- Avoid prolonged skin contact with used motor oil.
- Remove oil from skin by washing thoroughly with soap and water or waterless hand cleaner. Do not use gasoline, thinners or other solvents.
- Avoid prolonged skin contact with oil-soaked clothing.

Every time you stop for fuel, check the engine oil making sure the engine has fully warmed and the vehicle is parked on a level surface. Because it takes a few minutes for all the oil to drain back to the oil pan, you should wait a few minutes before checking your oil. If you are doing this at a fuel stop, first fill the fuel tank, then open the hood and check the oil, but don't get so carried away as to forget to pay for the fuel. Most station attendants won't believe that you forgot.

1. Park the car on a level surface.
2. When checking the oil level it is best for the engine to be at operating temperature, but keep in mind that checking the oil immediately after stopping will lead to a false reading. Wait a few minutes after turning the engine **OFF** in order to allow the oil to drain back into the crankcase.

Fig. 73 Locate the dipstick (towards the rear of the engine compartment) and withdraw it from the guide tube

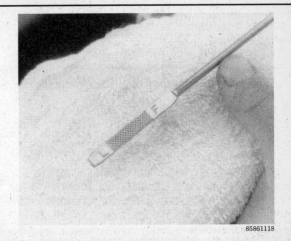

Fig. 74 Wipe oil from the dipstick using a clean rag, then fully reinsert it into the guide tube in order to check the level

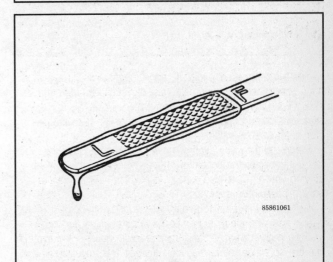

Fig. 75 A properly filled crankcase is indicated by oil just up to the top of the F or full mark on the dipstick

3. Open the hood and locate the dipstick. Pull the dipstick from its tube, wipe it clean and reinsert it.
4. Pull the dipstick out again and, holding is horizontally, read the oil level. The oil should be between the **F** and **L** or high and low marks on the dipstick. If the oil is below the **L** or low mark, add oil of the proper viscosity through the capped opening on the top of the cylinder head cover. Please refer to the oil recommendation information found earlier in this section for the proper viscosity and rating of oil to use.
5. Replace the dipstick and check the oil level again after adding any oil. Be careful not to overfill the crankcase. Approximately one quart of oil will raise the level from the **L** or low mark to the **F** or high mark. Excess oil will generally be consumed at an accelerated rate.

OIL AND FILTER CHANGE

▶ See Figures 76, 77, 78, 79, 80, 81, 82, 83, 84, 85 and 86

✳✳CAUTION

Prolonged and repeated skin contact with used engine oil, with no effort to remove the oil, may be harmful. Always follow these simple precautions when handling used motor oil:

- **Avoid prolonged skin contact with used motor oil.**
- **Remove oil from skin by washing thoroughly with soap and water or waterless hand cleaner. Do not use gasoline, thinners or other solvents.**
- **Avoid prolonged skin contact with oil-soaked clothing.**

If the vehicle is operated on a daily or semi-daily basis and most trips are for several miles (allowing the engine to properly warm-up), the oil should be changed a minimum of every 12 months or 10,000 miles whichever comes first.

If however, the vehicle is used to tow a trailer, is made to idle for extended periods of time (such as in heavy daily traffic) or if used as a service vehicle (police, taxi, delivery) or the vehicle is used for only short trips in below freezing temperature, the oil change interval should be shortened. Likewise, if your vehicle is used under dusty, polluted or off-road conditions, the oil should be changed more frequently. Under these circumstances oil has a greater chance of building up sludge and contaminants which could damage your engine. If your vehicle use fits into these circumstance, as most do, it is suggested that the oil and filter be changed every 5,000 miles or 6 months, whichever comes first.

Oil should always be changed after the engine has been running long enough to bring it up to normal operating temperature. Hot oil will flow easier and more contaminants will be removed along with the oil than if it were drained cold. The oil drain plug is located on the bottom, rear of the oil pan (bottom of the engine, underneath the car).

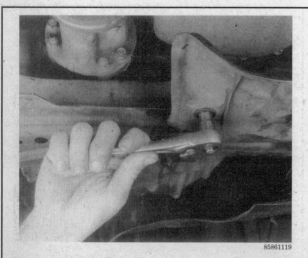

Fig. 76 If equipped it may be necessary to remove the splash shield(s) for access to the drain plug/filter

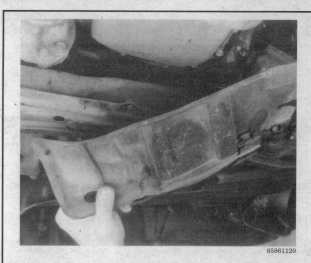

Fig. 77 After the retainers are removed, carefully lower the splash shield(s) from the vehicle

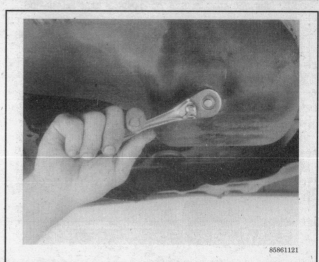

Fig. 78 Loosen the oil pan drain plug using an appropriate socket or box wrench

Fig. 79 Unthread the drain plug, then withdraw the plug while moving your hand away from the hot oil

Fig. 80 Allow the oil to completely drain from the crankcase

Fig. 83 Coat the new oil filter gasket with clean engine oil

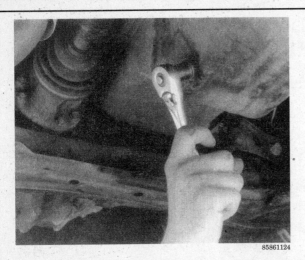

Fig. 81 Install the drain plug and tighten being careful not to overtighten and strip the plug

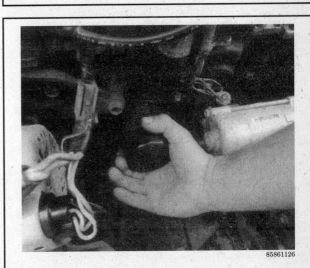

Fig. 84 Install the new filter BY HAND, do not use a filter wrench

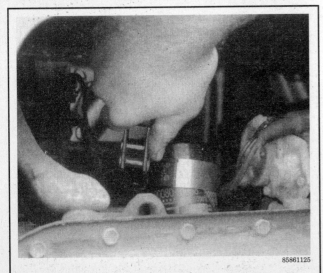

Fig. 82 Loosen the oil filter using a strap wrench

Fig. 85 Twist and remove the cover from the oil fill (usually found on the cylinder head cover)

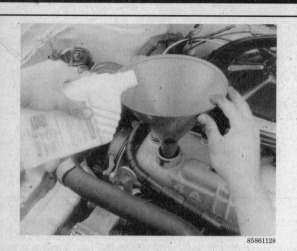

Fig. 86 After the plug and new filter is installed, add clean engine oil IMMEDIATELY. Waiting is only taking the risk that you might forget

Except California Diesel Engines

▶ See Figure 87

1. Run the engine until it reaches normal operating temperature.
2. Raise the front of the vehicle and support it safely using a suitable pair of jackstands.

➡Some vehicles may be equipped with a splash shield which must be removed in order to access the drain plug.

3. Slide a drain pan of a least 6 quarts capacity under the oil pan. Wipe the drain plug and surrounding area clean using an old rag. hand, using a rag to shield your fingers from the hot oil. By keeping an inward pressure on the plug as you unscrew it, oil won't escape past the threads and you can remove it without being burned by hot oil.
4. Quickly withdraw the plug and move your hands out of the way. Allow the oil to drain completely in the pan, then install and carefully tighten the drain plug. Do not overtighten the drain plug, otherwise you'll be buying a new pan or a replacement plug for stripped threads.

➡Although some manufacturers have at times recommended changing the oil filter every other oil change, we recommend the filter be replaced each time you change your oil. The added benefit of clean oil is quickly lost if the old filter is clogged. The added protection to your engine far outweighs the few dollars saved by using an old filter.

5. Move the drain pan under the oil filter. Use a strap-type or cap-type filter wrench to loosen and remove the oil filter from the engine block. Keep in mind that it's holding a significant amount of dirty, hot oil.
6. Empty the old filter into the drain pan and properly dispose of the filter.
7. Using a clean rag, wipe off the filter adapter on the engine block. Be sure that the rag doesn't leave any lint which could clog an oil passage.
8. Coat the rubber gasket on the filter with fresh oil, then spin it onto the engine by hand; when the gasket touches the

adapter surface, give it another 1/2-1/3 turn. No more, or you may squash the gasket causing it to leak.

9. Remove the jackstands and carefully lower the vehicle. IMMEDIATELY refill the engine with the correct amount of fresh oil. Refilling it right away will help prevent the possibility of someone accidentally attempting to start a dry engine. Please refer to the Capacities chart at the end of this section.

10. Check the oil level on the dipstick. It is normal for the level to be a bit above the full mark. Start the engine and allow it to idle for a few minutes.

❉❉CAUTION

Do not run the engine above idle speed until it has built up oil pressure, as indicated when the oil light goes out and/or the gauge moves up (out of the warning zone).

11. Shut off the engine and allow the oil to flow back to the crankcase for a few minutes, then recheck the oil level. Check around the filter and drain plug for any leaks, and correct as necessary.

California Diesel Engines

▶ See Figures 88 and 89

1. Run the engine until it reaches normal operating temperature.
2. Raise the front of the vehicle and support it safely using a suitable pair of jackstands.

➡Some vehicles may be equipped with a splash shield which must be removed in order to access the drain plug.

3. Slide a drain pan of a least 6 quarts capacity under the oil pan. Wipe the drain plug and surrounding area clean using an old rag.
4. Loosen the drain plug using a ratchet, short extension and socket or a box-wrench. Turn the plug out by hand, using a rag to shield your fingers from the hot oil. By keeping an inward pressure on the plug as you unscrew it, oil won't escape past the threads and you can remove it without being burned by hot oil.

Fig. 87 On most engines, oil is added through the opening in the cylinder head (valve/camshaft) cover

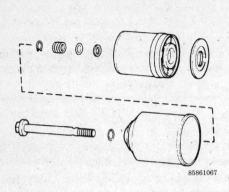

Fig. 88 Exploded view of the oil filter assembly found on California diesel engines

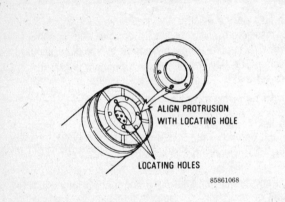

ALIGN PROTRUSION
WITH LOCATING HOLE

LOCATING HOLES

85861068

Fig. 89 Always may sure the protrusion on the new gasket algins with one of the locating holes on the filter — California diesel engine oil filter assembly

5. Quickly withdraw the plug and move your hands out of the way. Allow the oil to drain completely in the pan, then install and carefully tighten the drain plug. Do not overtighten the drain plug, otherwise you'll be buying a new pan or a replacement plug for stripped threads.

➡Although some manufacturers have at times recommended changing the oil filter every other oil change, we recommend the filter be replaced each time you change your oil. The added benefit of clean oil is quickly lost if the old filter is clogged. The added protection to your engine far outweighs the few dollars saved by using a old filter.

6. Loosen and remove the oil filter case retaining bolt, then carefully remove the oil filter case.

7. Lift off the rubber gasket, then withdraw the filter element.

✳✳CAUTION

Be careful not to lose the rubber washer, washer spring, snapring and O-ring from inside the oil filter case when removing the filter element.

8. Position a new rubber gasket on the oil filter element so that the gasket tab aligns with the hole in the element.
9. Install the snapring washer and new rubber washer into the filter case and then install the new filter element and gasket.
10. Coat the rubber gasket with clean engine oil, then install the entire oil filter assembly onto the engine block.
11. Remove the jackstands and carefully lower the vehicle. IMMEDIATELY refill the engine with the correct amount of fresh oil. Refilling it right away will help prevent the possibility of someone accidentally attempting to start a dry engine. Please refer to the Capacities chart at the end of this section.
12. Check the oil level on the dipstick. It is normal for the level to be a bit above the full mark. Start the engine and allow it to idle for a few minutes.

✳✳CAUTION

Do not run the engine above idle speed until it has built up oil pressure, as indicated when the oil light goes out and/or the gauge moves up (out of the warning zone).

13. Shut off the engine and allow the oil to flow back to the crankcase for a few minutes, then recheck the oil level. Check around the filter and drain plug for any leaks, and correct as necessary.

Transmission/Transaxle

FLUID LEVEL CHECK

Manual
◆ **See Figures 90 and 91**

The oil in the manual transmission/transaxle should be checked at least every 15,000 miles and replaced every 25,000-30,000 miles. Be sure to use only API GL-4/GL-5 or SAE 80W-90 gear oil in most gasoline vehicles covered by this manual. Toyotas equipped with a manual transmission (RWD) may also use SAE 75W-90 gear oil.

➡MOST diesel engine Corollas are equipped with a manual transaxle which requires the use of Dexron®II automatic transmission/transaxle fluid.

1. Either with the car parked on a level surface (with the parking brake firmly set) or with the vehicle raised and supported safely using jackstands at 4 points so it is LEVEL, remove the filler plug from the side of the transmission housing.
2. If the lubricant begins to trickle out of the hole, there is enough. Otherwise, carefully insert your finger (watch out for

sharp threads) and check to see if the oil is up to the edge of the hole.

3. If necessary, add oil through the hole until the level is at the hole's edge. Most gear lubricants come in a plastic squeeze bottle with a nozzle, making additions simple and some will come equipped with a small hand-pump attachment. You can also use a common everyday kitchen baster.

4. Install the filler plug.

Automatic

♦ **See Figures 92 and 93**

Check the automatic transmission/transaxle fluid level at least every 15,000 miles, though it is a wise idea to check it more often under severe usage (excessive stop and go traffic, towing a trailer, dusty conditions, freezing temperatures . . .). Level is checked using the dipstick which is usually located toward the rear of the engine compartment.

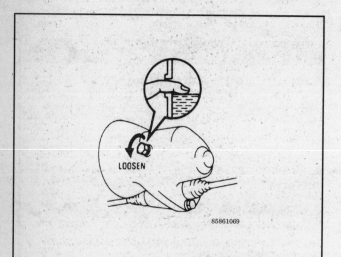

Fig. 90 Check the oil level using your finger (but watching for sharp burrs on the threads)

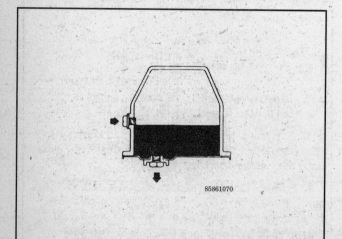

Fig. 91 A cross sectional view of a properly filled transmission/transaxle case — oil level is up to the bottom of the filler hole

2-SPEED TOYOGLIDE

Start the car cold and allow the engine to idle for a few minutes. Set the handbrake and apply the service brakes. Move the gear selector through all of the ranges.

✳✳CAUTION

Do not overfill the transmission.

With the engine still running, the parking brake on, and the selector in Neutral (N), remove and clean the transmission dipstick. Insert the dipstick fully, remove it and take a reading. The fluid level should fall between the L and F marks. If the level is below L, add type F fluid to the filler tube until the fluid level is up to the F mark.

✳✳CAUTION

Never use type A, DEXRON® or DEXRON®II fluid or gear oil in the 2-speed Toyoglide transmission. Do not use engine oil supplements either.

The fluid on the dipstick should always be a bright in color. If it is discolored (brown or black), or smells burnt, serious transmission troubles, probably due to overheating, should be suspected. The transmission should be inspected by a qualified service technician to locate the cause of the burnt fluid.

EXCEPT 2-SPEED TOYOGLIDE

The fluid level should be checked only when the transmission/transaxle is hot (normal operating temperature). The transmission is considered hot after about 20 miles of highway driving.

1. Park the car on a level surface with the engine idling. Shift the transmission into Neutral, firmly set the parking brake and, if possible, block the drive wheels. If the drive wheels cannot be blocked, you may want for a friend to sit in the car and apply the brakes.

2. Remove the dipstick and wipe it clean, then reinsert it firmly. Be sure that it has been pushed all the way in. Remove the dipstick and check the fluid level while holding it horizontally. With the engine running, the fluid level should be be-

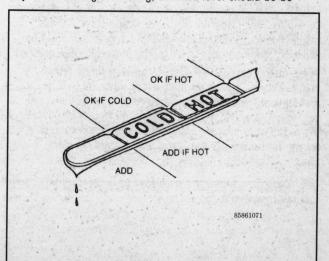

Fig. 92 Common automatic transmission/transaxle dipstick — except 2-speed Toyoglide

Fig. 93 Fluid is normally added to automatic transmissions/transaxles through the dipstick guide tube — a flexible funnel can be especially helpful here

tween the second and third notches on the dipstick (the hot level area).

➡ **The dipstick is often labelled to indicate the proper type of fluid required by the transmission/transaxle assembly.**

3. If the fluid level is below the second notch, add the required type of transmission fluid until the proper level is reached. This is easily done through the dipstick guide tube with the aid of a funnel. Check the level often as you are filling the transmission. Be extremely careful not to overfill it. Overfilling will cause slippage, seal damage and overheating. Approximately one pint of transmission fluid will raise the level from one notch to the other.

✳✳CAUTION

Use Type F automatic transmission fluid in all transmissions EXCEPT the A55, A41, A130L and A131L models. The A55, A41, A130L and A131L (along with ALL 1985-87 Corollas) use only DEXRON II (Never use Type F in these units). Check your vehicle owner's manual to be sure.

The fluid on the dipstick should always be a bright red color. If it is discolored (brown or black), or smells burnt, serious transmission troubles, probably due to overheating, should be suspected. The transmission should be inspected by a qualified service technician to locate the cause of the burnt fluid.

DRAIN AND REFILL

Manual
▶ **See Figures 94, 95 and 96**

The manual transmission/transaxle oil should be changed at least every 25,000-30,000 miles.
1. The oil must be hot before it is drained. If the car is driven until the engine is at normal operating temperature, the oil should be hot enough.
2. Remove the filler plug to provide a vent.

3. The drain plug is normally located on the bottom of the transmission/transaxle housing. Place large container underneath the transmission and remove the plug.
4. Allow the oil to drain completely. Clean off the plug and replace it. Tighten it until it is just snug.
5. Fill the transmission with a suitable gear oil or transmission/transaxle fluid, depending on the application. For more information, please refer to the fluid level checking located earlier in this section.
6. The oil level should come up to the top of the filler hole.
7. Replace the filler plug, drive the car for a few minutes, stop, and check for any leaks.

Automatic
▶ **See Figures 97, 98 and 99**

The automatic transmission fluid should be changed at least every 25,000-30,000 miles. If the car is normally used in severe service, such as stop-and-go driving, trailer towing or the like, the interval should be halved. The fluid should be hot

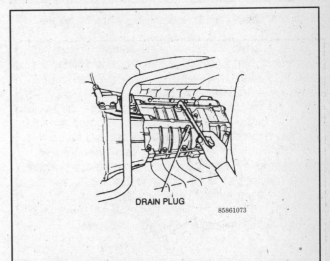

Fig. 94 Common manual transmission/transaxle drain and filler plug locations

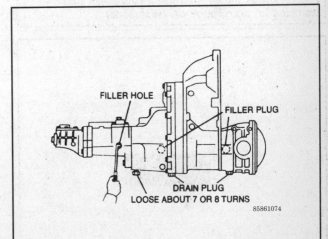

Fig. 95 Drain and filler plug locations for the 4wd transaxle

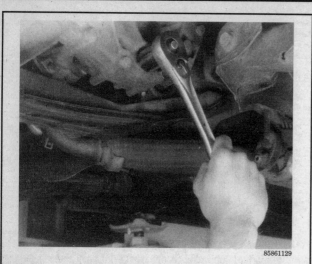

Fig. 96 Loosen and remove the drain plug using a socket or box wrench

before it is drained; a 20 minute drive will accomplish this nicely.

Toyota automatic transmissions are normally equipped with a drain plug so that if you are in a hurry, you can simply remove the plug, drain the fluid, replace the plug and then refill the transmission. BUT keep in mind that a "fluid only" change is rarely recommended. As with engine oil changes, the benefit of fresh fluid is quickly lost if the fluid filter is clogged and not operating properly. To change both the fluid and filter:

1. Remove the plug and drain the fluid. When the fluid stops coming out of the drain hole, loosen the pan retaining screws until the pan can be pulled down at one corner. Lower a corner of the pan and allow any remaining fluid to drain out.

2. After the pan has drained completely, remove the pan retaining screws, then remove the pan and gasket.

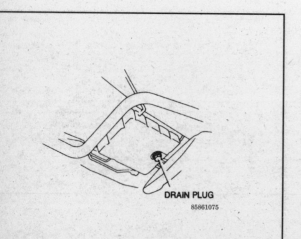

Fig. 97 Most Toyota automatic transmissions/transaxles are equipped with a fluid drain plug

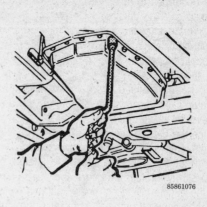

Fig. 98 Loosen the bolts in order to remove the fluid pan and access the filter

3. With the pan removed, the transaxle filter (strainer) is visible. Remove the bolts holding the filter, then remove the filter and, if equipped, the filter gasket.

➡On some models the filter retaining bolts may be different lengths and MUST BE reinstalled in their correct locations. If equipped with bolts of various lengths, take great care not to interchange them.

4. Clean the mating surfaces for the oil pan and the filter; make sure all traces of the old gasket material is removed.

5. Clean the pan thoroughly and allow it to air dry. If you wipe it out with a rag you run the risk of leaving bits of lint in the pan which could clog the tiny hydraulic passages in the transmission.

To install:

6. Install the new filter assembly (some models use a gasket under the oil filter). Install the retaining bolts in their correct locations and tighten evenly.

7. Install the pan (with the magnet or magnets correctly positioned in the oil pan, if so equipped) using a new gasket. Carefully tighten the retaining bolts in progressive steps.

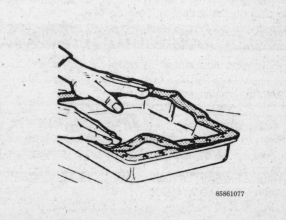

Fig. 99 Always replace the gasket when installation the transmission/transaxle fluid pan

8. Install and carefully tighten the drain plug.

9. It is a good idea to measure the amount of fluid drained from the transmission to determine the correct amount of fresh fluid to add. This is because some parts of the transmission may not drain completely and using the dry refill amount specified in the capacities chart could lead to overfilling as it is intended to show the total amount of fluid held by the component. Fluid is normally added through the dipstick tube. Use the proper automatic transmission fluid as specified earlier under the level checking procedure..

10. Replace the dipstick after filling. Start the engine and allow it to idle. DO NOT race the engine.

11. After the engine has idled for a few minutes, shift the transmission slowly through the gears and then return it to Park. With the engine still idling, check the fluid level on the dipstick. If necessary, add more fluid to raise the level to where it is supposed to be.

Differential

FLUID LEVEL CHECK

▶ **See Figures 100, 101 and 102**

The oil in the differential should be checked at least every 15,000 miles and replaced every 25,000-30,000 miles. On FWD vehicles, the differential is part of the transaxle assembly. On some early model vehicles the internal components of the transaxle and the differential may be isolated so separate fluids may be used. Check for 2 sets of drain and filler plugs to see if a separate differential fluid is used. On most later model FWD vehicles the differential and transaxle components share fluid and only one set of drain and filler plugs are necessary. On housings with shared fluids, be SURE to only add the proper fluid as directed under the transmission information earlier in this section.

1. Either park the vehicle on a level surface and firmly set the parking brake or raise and support it safely using jackstands at 4 points, but making sure the vehicle is LEVEL. Remove the filler plug from the back of the differential (rear differential) or the side (front differential).

➡ **The plug on the bottom is the drain plug.**

❊❊CAUTION

On FWD components where the transaxle and differential do not share fluid DO NOT confuse the differential filler plug with the transaxle filler plug.

2. If oil begins to trickle out of the hole, there is enough. Otherwise, carefully insert your finger into the hole (watch for sharp threads) and check to see if the oil is up to the bottom edge of the filler hole.

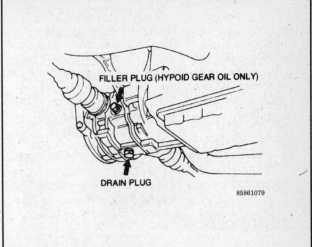

Fig. 100 Common filler and drain plug locations on a FWD differential housing

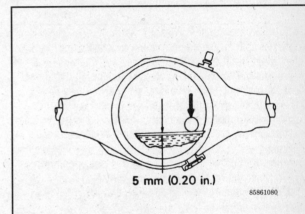

Fig. 101 Cross-sectional view of the fluid level in relation to the differential housing — rear housing shown

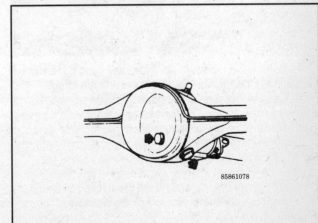

Fig. 102 Filler (upper) and drain plug locations — rear differential housing

3. If not, add oil through the hole until the level is at the edge of the hole. Most gear oils come in a plastic squeeze bottle with a nozzle, making additions simple. Some gear oils may even come equipped with a small hand operated pump. You can also use a common everyday kitchen baster. Check your owner's manual for the proper fluid in your differential. Most RWD vehicles, 4WD and some early FWD vehicles use standard API GL-5 hypoid type gear oil, SAE 80W-90. Some later model FWD vehicles use Dexron®II automatic transmission/transaxle fluid.

➡**Take note of the fluid which is drained from the housing. When in doubt of what type to use consult your owner's manual or local Toyota dealer. Keep in mind that gear oil is a thick, dark, greenish fluid which smells very earthy, while Dexron®II is thinner, reddish fluid (which has its own unique smell).**

4. Replace the filler plug and run the engine for a while. Turn off the engine and check for leaks.

DRAIN AND REFILL

The gear oil in the differential should be changed at least every 25,000-30,000 miles.
1. Either park the vehicle on a level surface and firmly set the parking brake or raise and support it safely using jackstands at 4 points, but making sure the vehicle is LEVEL.
2. Remove the filler (upper) plug. Place a container which is large enough to catch all of the differential oil, under the drain plug.
3. Remove the drain (lower) plug and, if equipped, the gasket. Allow all of the oil to drain into the container.
4. Install the drain plug. Tighten it so that it will not leak, but do not overtighten.
5. Refill with the proper grade and viscosity of axle lubricant. Please refer to the fluid level checking procedure located earlier in this section.
6. Install the filler plug and check for leakage.

Cooling System

▶ See Figure 103

✳✳CAUTION

Never remove the radiator cap under any conditions while the engine is hot! Failure to follow these instructions could result in damage to the cooling system, engine and/or personal injury. To avoid having scalding hot coolant or steam blow out of the radiator, use extreme care whenever you are removing the radiator cap. Wait until the engine has cooled, then wrap a thick cloth around the radiator cap and turn it slowly to the first stop. Step back while the pressure is released from the cooling system. When you are sure the pressure has been released, press down on the radiator cap (still have the cloth in position), turn and remove the radiator cap.

Dealing with the cooling system can be a dangerous matter unless the proper precautions are observed. It is best to check the coolant level in the radiator when the engine is cold. On early models this is accomplished by carefully removing the radiator cap and checking that the coolant is within ¾ in. (19mm) of the bottom of the filler neck. Most vehicles covered by this manual should be equipped with a coolant recovery tank. If the coolant level is at or near the ADD/FULL COLD line (engine cold) or the FULL HOT line (engine hot), the level is satisfactory. Always be certain that the filler caps on both the radiator and the recovery tank are closed tightly.

In the event that the coolant level must be checked when the engine is hot and the vehicle is not equipped with a coolant recovery tank, place a thick rag over the radiator cap and slowly turn the cap counterclockwise until it reaches the first detent. Allow all hot steam to escape through the vent. This will allow the pressure in the system to drop gradually, preventing an explosion of hot coolant. When the hissing noise stops, carefully remove the cap the rest of the way.

If the coolant level is found to be low, add a 50/50 mixture of ethylene glycol-based antifreeze and clean water. On older models, coolant must be added through the radiator filler neck. On newer models with the recovery tank, coolant may be added either through the filler neck on the radiator or directly into the recovery tank.

✳✳CAUTION

Never add coolant to a hot engine unless it is running. If it is not running you run the risk of cracking the engine block.

Although the fluid level should be checked often, it is wise to pressure check the cooling system at least once per year. If the coolant level is chronically low or rusty, the system should be thoroughly flushed and checked for leaks.

Check the freezing protection rating at least once a year, preferably just before the winter sets in. This can be done with an antifreeze tester (most service stations will have one on hand and will probably check it for you (once your engine cools). If not, they are available at an auto parts store). Maintain a protection rating of at least -20°F (-29°C) to prevent engine damage as a result of freezing and to assure the proper engine operating temperature.

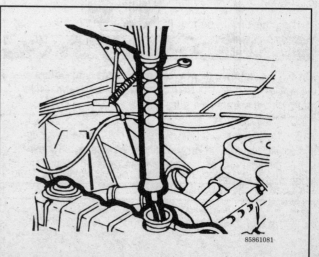

85861081

Fig. 103 Coolant protection can be easily checked using a float-type hydrometer tester

At least once every 2 years, the engine cooling system should be inspected, flushed, and refilled with fresh coolant. If the coolant is left in the system too long, it loses its ability to prevent rust and corrosion. If the coolant has too much water, it won't protect against freezing.

The pressure cap should be examined for signs of age or deterioration. The fan belt and other drive belts should be inspected and adjusted to the proper tension. (See checking belt tension).

Hose clamps should be tightened, and soft or cracked hoses replaced. Damp spots, or accumulations of rust or dye near hoses, water pump or other areas, indicate possible leakage, which must be corrected before filling the system with fresh coolant.

FLUID RECOMMENDATION

When adding or changing the fluid in the system, create a 50/50 mixture of high quality ethylene glycol antifreeze and water.

LEVEL CHECK

▶ **See Figures 104 and 105**

On most late model vehicles, the fluid level may be checked by observing the fluid level marks of the recovery tank. The level should be near the ADD or FULL COLD mark, as applicable, when the system is cold. At normal operating temperatures, the level should be above the ADD/FULL COLD mark or, if applicable, between the ADD/FULL COLD and the FULL HOT/FULL marks. Only add coolant to the recovery tank as necessary to bring the system up to a proper level.

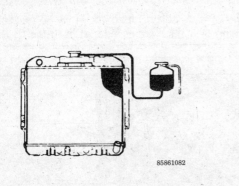

85861082

Fig. 104 If equipped, the coolant recovery/overflow tank is used to check coolant level

85861130

Fig. 105 When equipped, coolant should be added through the recovery tank (unless performing a dry refill)

❊❊CAUTION

Should it be necessary to remove the radiator cap, make sure that the system has had time to cool, reducing the internal pressure.

On any vehicle that is not equipped with a coolant recovery or overflow tank, the level must be checked by removing the radiator cap. This should only be done when the cooling system has had time to sufficiently cool after the engine has been run. The coolant level should be within ¾ in. (19mm) of the base of the radiator filler neck. If necessary, coolant can then be added directly to the radiator.

COOLING SYSTEM INSPECTION

Checking the Radiator Cap Seal
▶ **See Figure 106**

While you are checking the coolant level, check the radiator cap for a worn or cracked gasket. It the cap doesn't seal properly, fluid will be lost and the engine will overheat.

Worn caps should be replaced with a new one.

Checking the Radiator for Debris
▶ **See Figure 107**

Periodically clean any debris — leaves, paper, insects, etc. — from the radiator fins. Pick the large pieces off by hand. The smaller pieces can be washed away with water pressure from a hose.

Carefully straighten any bent radiator fins with a pair of needle nose pliers. Be careful — the fins are very soft. Don't wiggle the fins back and forth too much. Straighten them once and try not to move them again.

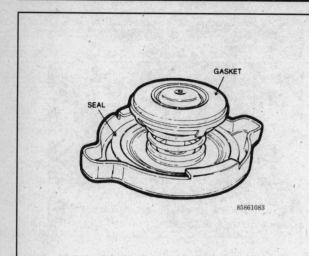

Fig. 106 Check the radiator cap seal and gasket condition whenever it is removed

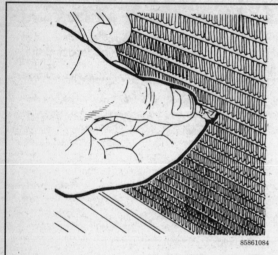

Fig. 107 Clean the radiator fins of any debris which might impede air flow

DRAINING AND REFILLING THE SYSTEM

▶ See Figures 108, 109 and 110

1. Make sure the engine is cool and the vehicle is parked on a level surface, then remove the radiator neck cap and, if equipped, the recovery tank cap in order to relieve system pressure.

2. Position a large drain pan under the vehicle, then drain the existing antifreeze and coolant by opening the radiator petcock and/or removing the engine block drain plug. It its also possible to drain the system by disconnecting the lower radiator hose, from the bottom radiator outlet.

✳✳CAUTION

When draining coolant, keep in mind that cats and dogs are attracted by ethylene glycol antifreeze, and are quite likely to drink any that is left in an uncovered container or in puddles on the ground. This will prove fatal in sufficient quantity. Always drain the coolant into a sealable container. Ethylene glycol coolant should be reused unless it is contaminated or several years old at which point it should be returned to a coolant recycling or hazardous waste disposal sight. Check your local laws for proper disposal methods.

3. Close the radiator/engine drains or reconnect the lower hose, as applicable.

4. Determine the capacity of your coolant system (see capacities specifications). Through the radiator filler neck, add a 50/50 mix of quality antifreeze (ethylene glycol) and water to provide the desired protection.

5. Leave the radiator pressure cap off, then start and run the engine until the thermostat heats up and opens, this will allow air to bleed from the system and provide room for additional coolant to be added to the radiator.

6. Add additional coolant to the radiator, as necessary, until the level is within ¾ in. (19mm) of the radiator's filler neck base.

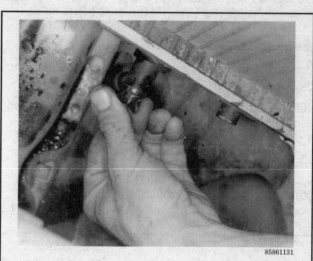

Fig. 108 The radiator drain cock may be reached by leaning over the radiator support (with the hood raised)

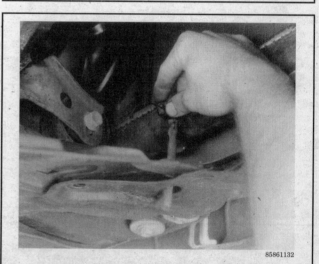

Fig. 109 If the vehicle is raised and supported, the drain cock may be reached from underneath

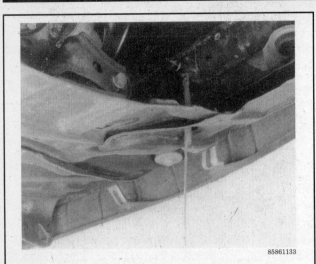

Fig. 110 Loosen the drain a few turns and allow the coolant to drain into a suitable container

7. Stop the engine and check the coolant level.

8. Check the level of protection with an antifreeze tester, then install the radiator pressure cap.

9. If equipped with a coolant recovery/overflow tank, add coolant to the tank, as necessary to achieve the proper level.

10. Start and run the engine to normal operating temperature, then check the system for leaks.

FLUSHING AND CLEANING THE SYSTEM

The cooling system should be drained, thoroughly flushed and refilled at least every 30,000 miles or 24 months. These operations should be done with the engine cold, especially if a backpressure flushing kit is being used. Completely draining, flushing and refilling the cooling system at least every two years will remove accumulated rust, scale and other deposits. Coolant in late model vehicles is a 50/50 mixture of ethylene glycol and water for year round use. Use a good quality antifreeze with water pump lubricants, rust inhibitors and other corrosion inhibitors along with acid neutralizers.

There are many products available for cooling system flushing. If a backpressure flushing kit is used, it is recommended that the thermostat be temporarily removed in order to allow free flow to the system with cold water. Always follow the kit or cleaner manufacturer's instructions and make sure the product is compatible with your vehicle.

1. Make sure the engine is cool and the vehicle is parked on a level surface, then remove the radiator neck cap and, if equipped the recovery tank cap in order to relieve system pressure.

2. Position a large drain pan under the vehicle, then drain the existing antifreeze and coolant by opening the radiator petcock and/or engine drains. It is also possible to drain the system by disconnecting the lower radiator hose, from the bottom radiator outlet.

3. Close the radiator/engine drains or reconnect the lower hose, as applicable then fill the system with water.

4. Add a can of quality radiator flush.

5. Idle the engine until the upper radiator hose gets hot and the thermostat has opened. This will allow the solution to fully circulate through the system.

6. Drain the system again.

7. Repeat this process until the drained water is clear and free of scale.

8. Close all drains and connect all the hoses.

9. If equipped with a coolant recovery system, flush the reservoir with water and leave empty.

10. Determine the capacity of your coolant system (see capacities specifications). Through the radiator filler neck, add a 50/50 mix of quality antifreeze (ethylene glycol) and water to provide the desired protection.

11. Leave the radiator pressure cap off, then start and run the engine until the thermostat heats up and opens, this will allow air to bleed from the system and provide room for additional coolant to be added to the radiator.

12. Add additional coolant to the radiator, as necessary, until the level is within 2 in. (51mm) of the radiator's filler neck base.

13. Stop the engine and check the coolant level.

14. Check the level of protection with an antifreeze tester, then install the radiator pressure cap.

15. If equipped with a coolant recovery/overflow tank, add coolant to the tank, as necessary to achieve the proper level.

16. Start and run the engine to normal operating temperature, then check the system for leaks.

Brake and Clutch Master Cylinders

FLUID LEVEL CHECK

▶ **See Figures 111, 112, 113, 114, 115, 116, 117 and 118**

The brake and clutch master cylinders are located under the hood, in the left rear section of the engine compartment. They are made of translucent plastic so that the levels may be checked without removing the tops. The fluid level in both reservoirs should be checked at least every 15,000 miles. The fluid level should be maintained at the upper most mark on the side of the reservoir. Any sudden decrease in the level indicates a possible leaks in the system and should be checked out immediately.

➡**Some early models may have two separate reservoirs for the brake master cylinder, but most will only have one. All Corollas with a manual transmission will also utilize a clutch master cylinder which is located close to the brake master cylinder.**

When making additions of brake fluid to the brake or clutch master cylinders use only fresh, uncontaminated brake fluid meeting or exceeding DOT 3 standards. Be careful not to spill any brake fluid on painted surfaces, as it eats the paint. Do not allow the brake fluid container or the master cylinder reservoir to remain open any longer than necessary; brake fluid absorbs moisture from the air, reducing its effectiveness and causing corrosion in the lines.

➡**ALWAYS clean the cylinder reservoir cover before removal. This will help prevent the possibility of allowing dirt to enter the system as the cover is removed.**

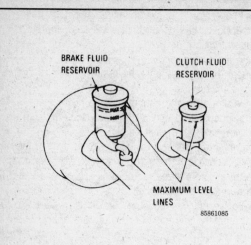

Fig. 111 Common brake and clutch master cylinder reservoirs — late model RWD shown

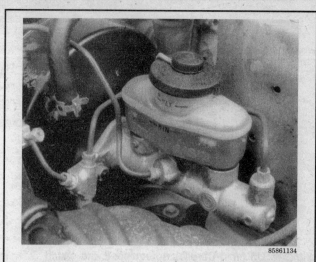

Fig. 114 Most transparent master cylinder reservoirs are equipped with MAX/MIN fill lines to ease level checking

Fig. 112 When adding fluid to the reservoir, pour slowly so as to minimize formation of air bubbles

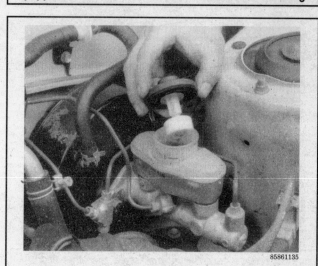

Fig. 115 If adding fluid is necessary, clean and remove the cover from the top of the reservoir

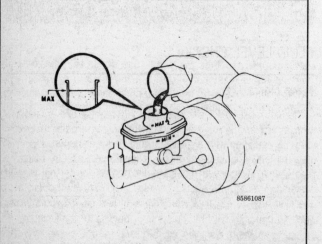

Fig. 113 Adding fluid to a common early model master cylinder reservoir — late model FWD vehicles similar

Fig. 116 Add a sufficient amount of fluid to bring the level to the MAX line

Fig. 117 On most Corollas so equipped, the clutch master cylinder reservoir is located at the firewall, near the brake master cylinder

Fig. 118 Always clean the cap before removal to prevent system contamination

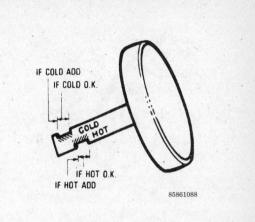

Fig. 119 Late model power steering pump reservoir cap and dipstick

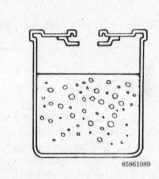

Fig. 120 Foaming or emulsification indicates air in the system

Power Steering Pump

FLUID LEVEL CHECK

▶ **See Figures 119 and 120**

The fluid level in the power steering reservoir should be checked at least every 15,000 miles. The vehicle should be parked on level ground, with the engine warm and running at normal idle. Remove the filler cap and check the level on the dipstick; it should be in between the edges of the cross-hatched area on older models or within the HOT area of the dipstick on newer models. If the level is low, add Dexron®II type ATF until the proper level is achieved.

Steering Gear

FLUID LEVEL CHECK

▶ **See Figure 121**

Though most vehicles covered by this manual are equipped with a rack and pinion steering assembly, some early models may be equipped with a steering gear. If so equipped, the gear oil level should be checked at least every 15,000 miles. The filler plug on these models is located on top of the gear housing. The oil level should be kept even with the bottom of the filler hole or slightly lower. Use standard GL-4 hypoid type gear oil SAE 90.

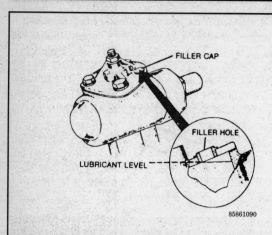

Fig. 121 On models equipped with a steering gear (instead of rack and pinion steering), fill the gear to the bottom of the filler hole

Fig. 122 The washer pump reservoir is usually located at the side of the engine compartment

Windshield Washer Pump

FLUID RECOMMENDATIONS AND LEVEL CHECK

▶ **See Figure 122**

The windshield washer pump fluid reservoir is a plastic container usually found on the side of the engine compartment, near the wiper motor. The reservoir should be filled using a wiper fluid solution which can be found at most automotive stores. Do not further dilute the solution (unless it is sold in concentrate, then follow the manufacturer's instructions), as this will adversely affect its ability to keep from freezing at low temperatures. Also, never place another fluid, such as ethylene glycol antifreeze in the reservoir as other fluids could damage pump seals.

Chassis Greasing

Chassis lubrication for these models is limited to greasing the front ball joints every 25,000-30,000 miles.

1. Remove the screw plug from the ball joint. Install a grease nipple.
2. Using a hand-operated grease gun, lubricate the ball joint with NLGI #1 or NLGI #2 molybdenum-disulfide lithium-based grease.
3. Remove the nipple and reinstall the screw plug.
4. Repeat for the other ball joint(s).

Body Lubrication

There is no set period recommended by Toyota for body lubrication. However, it is a good idea to lubricate the following body points at least once a year, especially in the fall before cold weather.

Use engine oil on the following points:
- Door lock latches.
- Door lock rollers.
- Door, hood and hinge pivots.

Use Lubriplate® (or an equivalent lubricating compound) here:
- Trunk lid latch and hinge.
- Glove box door latch.
- Front seat slides

Use silicone spray at these locations:
- All rubber weather stripping.
- Hood stops.

When you are finished lubricating any body part, be sure that all the excess lubricant has been wiped off, especially in the areas of the car which may come in contact with clothing.

Wheel Bearings

The front wheel bearings should be repacked every 24,000 miles on 1970-74 vehicles, 25,000 miles on 1975-77 vehicles, and 30,000 miles on 1978 and later vehicles, or every 24 months, whichever occurs first. For removal, repacking and installation procedures, please refer either to Section 7 or Section 8 depending on the application.

TRAILER TOWING

General Recommendations

Your car was primarily designed to carry passengers and cargo. It is important to remember that towing a trailer will place additional loads on your vehicle's engine, drive train, steering, braking and other systems. However, if you find it necessary to tow a trailer, using the proper equipment is a must.

Local laws may require specific equipment such as trailer brakes or fender mounted mirrors. Check with your local authorities.

Trailer Weight

The weight of the trailer is the most important factor. A good weight-to-horsepower ratio is about 35:1, 35 lbs. of GCW (Gross Combined Weight) for every horsepower your engine develops. Multiply the engine's rated horsepower by 35 and subtract the weight of the car passengers and luggage. The result is the approximate ideal maximum weight you should tow, although a numerically higher axle ratio can help compensate for heavier weight. For most models, Toyota recommends that the total trailer weight (trailer plugs its cargo) should NOT exceed 1500 lbs. (660 kg). Exceeding this weight limit is dangerous.

Another point to consider when determining a proper trailer weight is the Gross Vehicle Weight Rating (GVWR) which can be found on the vehicle certification plate (usually mounted on the driver's door jamb). The GVWR is the MAXIMUM allowable weight which can be handled by the vehicle. It is the sum of all weights, including the unloaded vehicle, driver, passengers, luggage, hitch and trailer tongue load. DO NOT exceed the GVWR. Generally speaking, about 60 percent of the trailer cargo weight should be located on the front half of the trailer, while the remaining 40 percent should be distributed on the rear half. NEVER place more weight on the rear half of the trailer, than on the front half.

Hitch (Tongue) Weight

▶ See Figure 123

Figure the hitch weight to select a proper hitch. Hitch weight is usually 9-11% of the trailer gross weight and should be measured with the trailer loaded. Hitches fall into various categories: those that mount on the frame or rear bumper and the bolt-on or weld-on distribution type used for larger trailers. Axle mounted or clamp-on bumper hitches should never be used.

Check the gross weight rating of your trailer. Tongue weight is usually figured as 10% of gross trailer weight. Therefore, a trailer with a maximum gross weight of 2,000 lbs. will have a maximum tongue weight of 200 lbs. Class I trailers fall into this category. For the limited towing capabilities of the Toyota Corolla, a Class I hitch is all you should ever need. Class II trailers are those with a gross weight rating of 2,000-3,500 lbs., while Class III trailers fall into the 3,500-6,000 lbs. category. Class IV trailers are those over 6,000 lbs. and are for use with fifth wheel trucks/trailers, only.

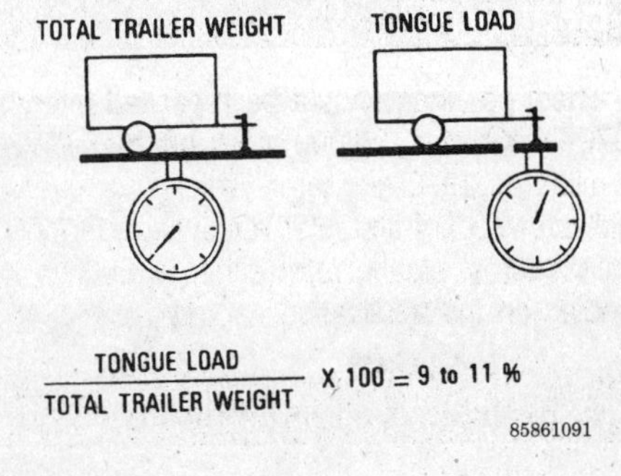

When you've determined the hitch that you'll need, follow the manufacturer's installation instructions, exactly, especially when it comes to fastener torques. The hitch will subjected to a lot of stress and good hitches come with hardened bolts. Never substitute an inferior bolt for a hardened bolt.

Cooling

ENGINE

One of the most common, if not THE most common problems associated with trailer towing is engine overheating. If you have an early model standard cooling system, without an expansion tank, you'll definitely need to get an aftermarket expansion tank kit, preferably one with at least a 2 quart capacity. These kits are easily installed on the radiator's overflow hose, and come with a pressure cap designed for expansion tanks.

Aftermarket engine oil coolers are helpful for prolonging engine oil life and reducing overall engine temperatures. Both of these factors increase engine life. While not absolutely necessary in towing Class I and some Class II trailers, they are recommended for heavier Class II and all Class III towing. Engine oil cooler systems consist of an adapter, screwed on in place of the oil filter, a remote filter mounting and a multi-tube, finned heat exchanger, which is mounted in front of the radiator or air conditioning condenser.

TRANSMISSION/TRANSAXLE

An automatic transmission/transaxle is usually recommended for trailer towing. Modern automatics have proven reliable and, of course, easy to operate, in trailer towing. The increased load of a trailer, however, causes an increase in the temperature of the automatic transmission fluid. Heat is the worst enemy of an automatic transmission. As the temperature of the fluid increases, the life of the fluid decreases.

It is essential, therefore, that you install an automatic transmission cooler. The cooler, which consists of a multi-tube, finned heat exchanger, is usually installed in front of the radiator or air conditioning compressor, and hooked in-line with the transmission cooler tank inlet line. Follow the cooler manufacturer's installation instructions.

Select a cooler of at least adequate capacity, based upon the combined gross weights of the car and trailer.

Cooler manufacturers recommend that you use an aftermarket cooler in addition to, and not instead of, the present cooling tank in your radiator. If you do want to use it in

Fig. 123 Calculating tongue weight

place of the radiator cooling tank, get a cooler at least two sizes larger than normally necessary.

➡**A transmission cooler can, sometimes, cause slow or harsh shifting in the transmission during cold weather, until the fluid has a chance to come up to normal operating temperature. Some coolers can be purchased with or retrofitted with a temperature bypass valve which will allow fluid flow through the cooler only when the fluid has reached above a certain operating temperature.**

PUSHING AND TOWING

Push Starting

This is the least recommended method of starting a car and should be used only in an extreme case. If necessary, any vehicle equipped with a manual transmission/transaxle can probably be push started, although more than one car has received a dented fender or bumper from this operation. To push start the car, turn the ignition switch to the **ON** position, push in the clutch pedal, put the gear shift lever in second or third gear and partially depress the gas pedal. As the car begins to pick up momentum while being pushed, release the clutch pedal and give it gas. If another driver is using a vehicle is push your car, you should instruct them to brake and allow your car to roll away slightly. You should NOT attempt to let out the clutch and start your vehicle until there is some distance between you and the push car.

❋❋CAUTION

Never attempt to push start the car while it is in reverse.

Because of the basic principles of operation for automatic transmissions/transaxles, Toyotas that are equipped with an automatic can not be push started no matter how far or how fast they are pushed.

Towing

To state it simply, towing a vehicle using a flat bed or a total car trailer is BY FAR the most preferable method of transporting your car. But because this is not always possible,

Handling A Trailer

Towing a trailer with ease and safety requires a certain amount of experience. It's a good idea to learn the feel of a trailer by practicing turning, stopping and backing in an open area such as an empty parking lot.

most vehicles covered by this manual may be towed using other methods.

Cars with a manual transmission can be towed with the front end up in the air or with all four wheels on the ground. You must only remember that the transmission must be in Neutral, the parking brake must be off and the ignition switch must be in the **ACC** position.

➡**For most vehicles covered by this manual Toyota recommends that the car NOT be towed with the rear end up in the air UNLESS the front wheels are resting on a support dolly.**

Cars with an automatic transmission have a few more restrictions when it comes to towing. The transmission must always be in Neutral, the parking brake must be off and the ignition switch must be in the **ACC** position.

With the exception of 1974-77 models, when towing RWD and 4WD Toyotas with the front wheels in the air, be sure cover distances of no more than 50 miles at speeds no greater than 30 mph. Anything more than this will require disconnecting the driveshaft. The same restriction applies when the car is being flat-towed on all 4-wheels.

1974-77 Toyotas should not be towed with the rear wheels on the ground regardless of the circumstances. If the front end must be raised, either put dollies under the rear wheels or disconnect the driveshaft. The only way that the car can be flat-towed is if the driveshaft has been disconnected.

➡**Most Toyotas are equipped with tow hooks at the front and back of the car. If the car is to be flat-towed, use the hooks. Don't use an unsuspecting suspension member or the bumper.**

JUMP STARTING A DEAD BATTERY

▸ **See Figure 124**

Whenever a vehicle is jump started, precautions must be followed in order to prevent the possibility of personal injury. Remember that batteries contain a small amount of explosive hydrogen gas which is a by-product of battery charging. Sparks should always be avoided when working around batter-

ies, especially when attaching jumper cables. To minimize the possibility of accidental sparks, follow the procedure carefully.

❋❋CAUTION

NEVER hook the batteries up in a series circuit or the entire electrical system will go up in smoke, especially the starter!

Cars equipped with a diesel engine may utilize two 12 volt batteries. If so, the batteries are connected in a parallel circuit (positive terminal to positive terminal, negative terminal to negative terminal). Hooking the batteries up in parallel circuit increases battery cranking power without increasing total battery

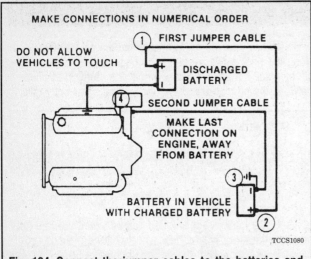

MAKE CONNECTIONS IN NUMERICAL ORDER

DO NOT ALLOW VEHICLES TO TOUCH

① FIRST JUMPER CABLE

DISCHARGED BATTERY

④ SECOND JUMPER CABLE

MAKE LAST CONNECTION ON ENGINE, AWAY FROM BATTERY

③

BATTERY IN VEHICLE WITH CHARGED BATTERY

②

TCCS1080

Fig. 124 Connect the jumper cables to the batteries and engine in the order shown

voltage output. Output remains at 12 volts. On the other hand, hooking two 12 volt batteries up in a series circuit (positive terminal to negative terminal, positive terminal to negative terminal) increases total battery output to 24 volts (12 volts plus 12 volts).

Jump Starting Precautions

- Be sure that both batteries are of the same voltage. Vehicles covered by this manual and most vehicles on the road today utilize a 12 volt charging system.
- Be sure that both batteries are of the same polarity (have the same terminal, in most cases NEGATIVE grounded).
- Be sure that the vehicles are not touching or a short could occur.
- On serviceable batteries, be sure the vent cap holes are not obstructed.
- Do not smoke or allow sparks anywhere near the batteries.
- In cold weather, make sure the battery electrolyte is not frozen. This can occur more readily in a battery that has been in a state of discharge.
- Do not allow electrolyte to contact your skin or clothing.

Jump Starting Procedure

1. Make sure that the voltages of the 2 batteries are the same. Most batteries and charging systems are of the 12 volt variety.
2. Pull the jumping vehicle (with the good battery) into a position so the jumper cables can reach the dead battery and that vehicle's engine. Make sure that the vehicles do NOT touch.
3. Place the transmissions of both vehicles in **NEUTRAL** or **PARK**, as applicable, then firmly set their parking brakes.

➡**If necessary for safety reasons, the hazard lights on both vehicles may be operated throughout the entire procedure without significantly increasing the difficulty of jumping the dead battery.**

4. Turn all lights and accessories off on both vehicles. Make sure the ignition switches on both vehicles are turned to the **OFF** position.
5. Cover the battery cell caps with a rag, but do not cover the terminals.
6. Make sure the terminals on both batteries are clean and free of corrosion or proper electrical connection will be impeded. If necessary, clean the battery terminals before proceeding.
7. Identify the positive (+) and negative (-) terminals on both battery posts.
8. Connect the first jumper cable to the positive (+) terminal of the dead battery, then connect the other end of that cable to the positive (+) terminal of the booster (good) battery.
9. Connect one end of the other jumper cable to the negative (-) terminal on the booster battery and the other cable clamp to an engine bolt head, alternator bracket or other solid, metallic point on the engine with the dead battery. Try to pick a ground on the engine that is positioned away from the battery in order to minimize the possibility of the 2 clamps touching should one loosen during the procedure. DO NOT connect this clamp to the negative (-) terminal of the bad battery.

✳✳CAUTION

Be very careful to keep the jumper cables away from moving parts (cooling fan, belts, etc.) on both engines.

10. Check to make sure that the cables are routed away from any moving parts, then start the donor vehicle's engine. Run the engine at moderate speed for several minutes to allow the dead battery a chance to receive some initial charge.
11. With the donor vehicle's engine still running slightly above idle, try to start the vehicle with the dead battery. Crank the engine for no more than 10 seconds at a time and let the starter cool for at least 20 seconds between tries. If the vehicle does not start in 3 tries, it is likely that something else is also wrong or that the battery needs additional time to charge.
12. Once the vehicle is started, allow it to run at idle for a few seconds to make sure that it is operating properly operating.
13. Turn on the headlights, heater blower and, if equipped, the rear defroster of both vehicles in order to reduce the severity of voltage spikes and subsequent risk of damage to the vehicles' electrical systems when the cables are disconnected. This step is especially important to late model vehicles equipped with computer control modules.
14. Carefully disconnect the cables in the reverse order of connection. Start with the negative cable that is attached to the engine ground, then the negative cable on the donor battery. Disconnect the positive cable from the donor battery and finally, disconnect the positive cable from the formerly dead battery. Be careful when disconnecting the cables from the positive terminals not to allow the alligator clips to touch any metal on either vehicle or a short and sparks will occur.

JACKING

▶ **See Figures 125, 126 and 127**

If you plan to service your vehicle on a regular bassis, it would be wise to obtain a hydraulic floor jack. These are easier to use and you will probably find the convenience well worth the price. Always protect the undercoating of your vehicle by placing a small block of wood or a sturdy rubber pad between the jack/jackstand and the vehicle frame/body rails.

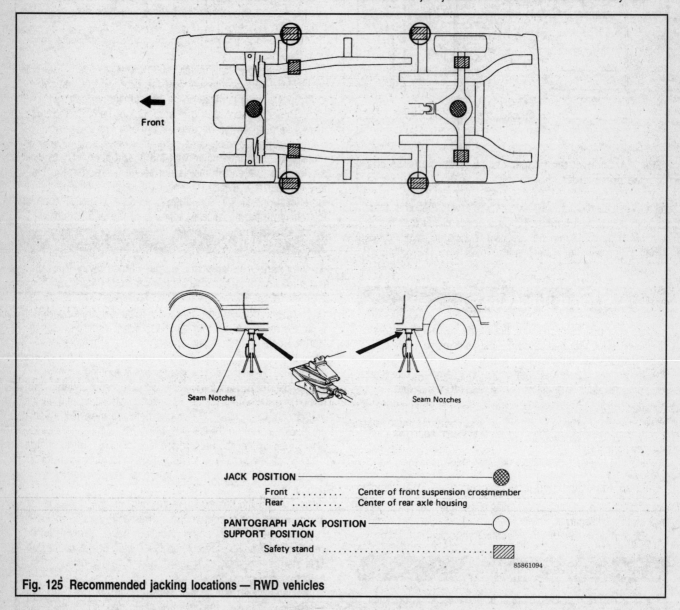

Front

Seam Notches   Seam Notches

JACK POSITION ──────────────────────
Front . . . . Center of front suspension crossmember
Rear . . . . Center of rear axle housing

PANTOGRAPH JACK POSITION ────────────────
SUPPORT POSITION

Safety stand . . . .

85861094

Fig. 125 Recommended jacking locations — RWD vehicles

ALWAYS follow these safety precautions when jacking the vehicle:
• Always raise the car on a level surface.
• Firmly set the parking brake (if the front wheels are being raised), and block wheels which remain on the ground. This is EXTREMELY important to keep the vehicle from rolling of the jack.

➡ **The tool kit supplied with many Toyotas includes a wheel block.**

• If the vehicle is being raised in order to work underneath it (EVEN, if it is only for a moment such as to check for a leak or a loose wire), support the vehicle using jackstands or ramps. Do not place the jackstands against sheet metal panels beneath the car or the underbody will be damaged.

❊❊CAUTION

NEVER work beneath a vehicle supported only by a jack.

• Do not use a bumper jack to raise the vehicle; the bumpers are not designed for this purpose.
• NEVER use cinder blocks to support a vehicle, they may crumble without warning causing severe personal injury.

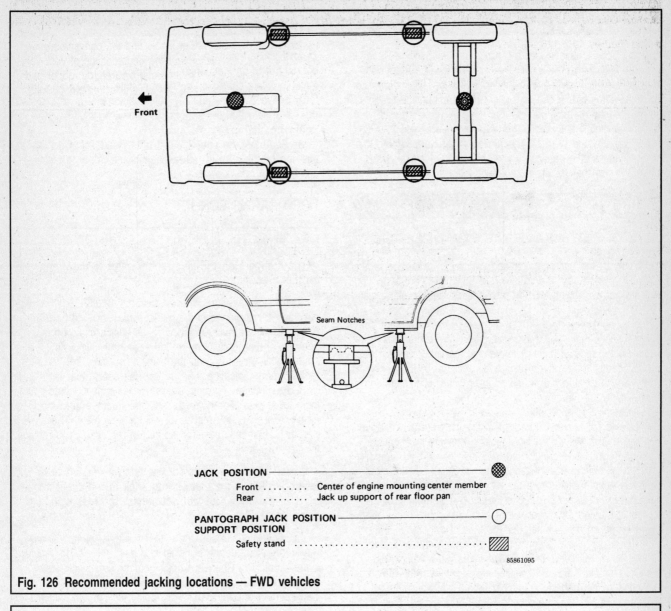

Fig. 126 Recommended jacking locations — FWD vehicles

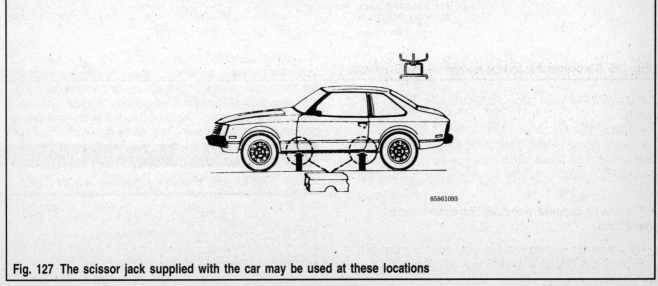

Fig. 127 The scissor jack supplied with the car may be used at these locations

HOW TO BUY A USED CAR

Many people believe that a two or three year old used car is a better buy than a new car. This may be true as most new cars suffer the heaviest depreciation in the first two years and, at three years old, a car is usually not old enough to present a lot of costly repair problems. But keep in mind, when buying a non-warranted automobile, there are no guarantees. Whatever the age of the used car you might want to buy, this section and a little patience should increase your chances of selecting one that is safe and dependable.

TIPS

1. First decide what model you want, and how much you want to spend.

2. Check the used car lots and your local newspaper ads. Privately owned cars are usually less expensive, however, you will not get a warranty that, in many cases, comes with a used car purchased from a lot. Of course, many aftermarket warranties may not be worth the extra money, so this is a point you will have to debate and consider based on your priorities.

3. Never shop at night. The glare of the lights make it easy to miss faults on the body caused by accident or rust repair.

4. Try to get the name and phone number of the previous owner. Contact him/her and ask about the car. If the owner of a lot refuses this information, look for a car somewhere else.

A private seller can tell you about the car and maintenance. But remember, there's no law requiring honesty from private citizens selling used cars. There is a law that forbids tampering with or turning back the odometer mileage. This includes both the private citizen and the lot owner. The law also requires that the seller or anyone transferring ownership of the car must provide the buyer with a signed statement indicating the mileage on the odometer at the time of transfer.

5. You may wish to contact the National Highway Traffic Safety Administration (NHTSA) to find out if the vehicle has ever been included in an manufacturer's recalls. Write down the year, model and serial number before you buy the car, then contact NHTSA, there should be 1-800 number that your phone companies information line can supply. If the vehicle was listed for a recall, make sure the needed repairs were made.

6. Refer to the Used Car Checklist in this section and check all the items on the car you are considering. Some items are more important than others. Only you know how much money you can afford for repairs, and depending on the price of the car, may consider performing any needed work yourself. Beware, however, of trouble in areas that will affect operation, safety or emission. Problems in the Used Car Checklist break down as follows:

- Numbers 1-8: Two or more problems in these areas indicate a lack of maintenance. You should beware.
- Numbers 9-13: Problems here tend to indicate a lack of proper care, however, these can usually be corrected with a tune-up or relatively simple parts replacement.
- Numbers 14-17: Problems in the engine or transmission can be very expensive. Unless you are looking for a project, walk away from any car with problems in 2 or more of these areas.

7. If you are satisfied with the apparent condition of the car, take it to an independent diagnostic center or mechanic for a complete check. If you have a state inspection program, have it inspected immediately before purchase, or specify on the bill of sale that the sale is conditional on passing state inspection.

8. Road test the car — refer to the Road Test Checklist in this section. If your original evaluation and the road test agree — the rest is up to you.

USED CAR CHECKLIST

▶ **See Figure 128**

➡**The numbers on the illustrations refer to the numbers on this checklist.**

1. Mileage: Average mileage is about 12,000-15,000 miles per year. More than average mileage may indicate hard usage or could indicate many highway miles (which could be less detrimental than half as many tough around town miles).

2. Paint: Check around the tailpipe, molding and windows for overspray indicating that the car has been repainted.

3. Rust: Check fenders, doors, rocker panels, window moldings, wheelwells, floorboards, under floormats, and in the trunk for signs of rust. Any rust at all will be a problem. There is no way to permanently stop the spread of rust, except to replace the part or panel.

➡**If rust repair is suspected, try using a magnet to check for body filler. A magnet should stick to the sheet metal parts of the body, but will not adhere to areas with large amounts of filler.**

4. Body appearance: Check the moldings, bumpers, grille, vinyl roof, glass, doors, trunk lid and body panels for general overall condition. Check for misalignment, loose hold-down clips, ripples, scratches in glass, welding in the trunk, severe misalignment of body panels or ripples, any of which may indicate crash work.

5. Leaks: Get down and look under the car. There are no normal leaks, other than water from the air conditioner condenser.

6. Tires: Check the tire air pressure. A common trick is to pump the tire pressure up to make the car roll easier. Check the tread wear, open the trunk and check the spare too. Uneven wear is a clue that the front end may need an alignment.

7. Shock absorbers: Check the shock absorbers by forcing downward sharply on each corner of the car. Good shocks will not allow the car to bounce more than once after you let go.

8. Interior: Check the entire interior. You're looking for an interior condition that agrees with the overall condition of the car. Reasonable wear is expected, but be suspicious of new seatcovers on sagging seats, new pedal pads, and worn armrests. These indicate an attempt to cover up hard use. Pull back the carpets and look for evidence of water leaks or flooding. Look for missing hardware, door handles, control knobs, etc. Check lights and signal operations. Make sure all accessories (air conditioner, heater, radio, etc.) work. Check windshield wiper operation.

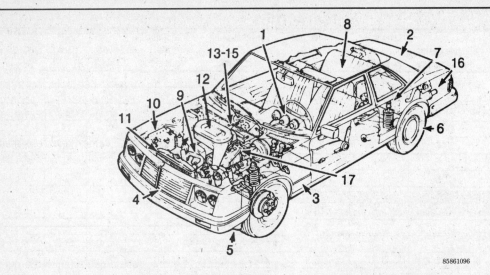

85861096

Fig. 128 Each of the numbered items should be checked when purchasing a used car

9. Belts and Hoses: Open the hood, then check all belts and hoses for wear, cracks or weak spots.

10. Battery: Low electrolyte level, corroded terminals and/or cracked case indicate a lack of maintenance.

11. Radiator: Look for corrosion or rust in the coolant indicating a lack of maintenance.

12. Air filter: A severely dirty air filter would indicate a lack of maintenance.

13. Ignition wires: Check the ignition wires for cracks, burned spots, or wear. Worn wires will have to be replaced.

14. Oil level: If the oil level is low, chances are the engine uses oil or leaks. Beware of water in the oil (cracked block or bad head gasket), excessively thick oil (used to quiet a noisy engine), or thin, dirty oil with a distinct gasoline smell (internal engine problems).

15. Automatic Transmission: Pull the transmission dipstick out when the engine is running. The level should read Full, and the fluid should be clear or bright red. Dark brown or black fluid that has distinct burnt odor, indicates a transmission in need of repair or overhaul.

16. Exhaust: Check the color of the exhaust smoke. Blue smoke indicates, among other problems, worn rings. Black smoke can indicate burnt valves or carburetor problems. Check the exhaust system for leaks; it can be expensive to replace.

17. Spark Plugs: Remove one or all of the spark plugs (the most accessible will do, though all are preferable). An engine in good condition will show plugs with a light tan or gray deposit on the firing tip. Please refer to Section 2 of this manual for more information on spark plug diagnosis.

ROAD TEST CHECK LIST

1. Engine Performance: The car should be peppy whether cold or warm, with adequate power and good pickup. It should respond smoothly through the gears.

2. Brakes: They should provide quick, firm stops with no noise, pulling or brake fade.

3. Steering: Sure control with no binding harshness, or looseness and no shimmy in the wheel should be expected. Noise or vibration from the steering wheel when turning the car means trouble.

4. Clutch (Manual Transmission/Transaxle): Clutch action should give quick, smooth response with easy shifting. The clutch pedal should have about 1-1½ in. (25-38mm) of free-play before it disengages the clutch. Start the engine, set the parking brake, put the transmission in first gear and slowly release the clutch pedal. The engine should begin to stall when the pedal is ½-¾ of the way up.

5. Automatic Transmission/Transaxle: The transmission should shift rapidly and smoothly, with no noise, hesitation, or slipping.

6. Differential: No noise or thumps should be present. Differentials have no normal leaks.

7. Driveshaft, Universal Joints: Vibration and noise could mean driveshaft problems. Clicking at low speed or coast conditions means worn U-joints.

8. Suspension: Try hitting bumps at different speeds. A car that bounces has weak shock absorbers. Clunks mean worn bushings or ball joints.

9. Frame/Body: Wet the tires and drive in a straight line. Tracks should show two straight lines, not four. Four tire tracks indicate a frame/body bent by collision damage. If the tires can't be wet for this purpose, have a friend drive along behind you and see if the car appears to be traveling in a straight line.

CAPACITIES

Year	Model	Engine Series Identification	Crankcase (qts.) With Filter	Crankcase (qts.) Without Filter	Transmission (qts.) Manual	Transmission (qts.) Automatic	Drive Axle (pts.)	Fuel Tank (gals.)	Cooling System (qts.)
1970	Corolla	3K-C	3.7	2.9	4S-1.8, 5S-2.6	2.6	2.2	12	5.1
1971	Corolla 1200	3K-C	3.7	2.9	4S-1.8, 5S-2.6	2.6	2.2	12	5.1
	Corolla 1600	2T-C	4.6	3.7	1.6	2.5	2.4	13.2	8.8
1972	Corolla 1200	3K-C	3.7	2.9	4S-1.8, 5S-2.6	2.6	2.2	12	5.1
	Corolla 1600	2T-C	4.6	3.7	1.6	2.5	2.4	13.2	8.8
1973	Corolla 1200	3K-C	3.7	2.9	4S-1.8, 5S-2.6	2.6	2.2	12	5.1
	Corolla 1600	2T-C	4.6	3.7	1.6	2.5	2.4	13.2	8.8
1974	Corolla 1200	3K-C	3.7	2.9	4S-1.8, 5S-2.6	2.6	2.2	12	5.1
	Corolla 1600	2T-C	4.6	3.7	1.6	2.5	2.4	13.2	8.8
1975	Corolla 1200	3K-C	3.7	2.9	4S-1.8, 5S-2.6	2.6	2.2	12	5.1
	Corolla 1600	2T-C	4.6	3.7	1.6	2.5	2.4	13.2	8.8
1976	Corolla 1200	3K-C	3.7	2.9	4S-1.8, 5S-2.6	2.6	2.2	12	5.1
	Corolla 1600	2T-C	4.6	3.7	1.6	2.5	2.4	13.2	8.8
1977	Corolla 1200	3K-C	3.7	2.9	4S-1.8, 5S-2.6	2.6	2.2	12	5.1
	Corolla 1600	2T-C	4.6	3.7	1.6	2.5	2.4	13.2	8.8
1978	Corolla 1200	3K-C	3.7	2.9	4S-1.8, 5S-2.6	2.6	2.2	12	5.1
	Corolla 1600	2T-C	4.6	3.7	1.6	2.5	2.4	13.2	8.8
1979	Corolla 1200	3K-C	3.7	2.9	4S-1.8, 5S-2.6	2.6	2.2	12	5.1
	Corolla 1600	2T-C	4.6	3.7	1.6	2.5	2.4	13.2	8.8
1980	Corolla 1800	3T-C	4	3.5	1.8	2.4	1.1	13.2	NA
1981	Corolla 1800	3T-C	4	3.5	1.8	2.4	1.1	13.2	NA
1982	Corolla 1800	3T-C	4	3.5	1.8	2.4	1.1	13.2	NA
1983	Corolla	4A-C, 4A-LC	3.5	3.2	4S-1.8, 5S-2.6	2.5	2.2	13.2	5.2
1984	Corolla	4A-C, 4A-LC	3.5	3.2	4S-1.8, 5S-2.6	2.5	2.2	13.2	5.2
1985	Corolla	4A-C, 4A-LC	3.5	3.2	4S-1.8, 5S-2.6	2.5	2.2	13.2	5.2
	Corolla	4A-GE	3.9	3.5	1.8	2.5	2.8	13.2	5.9
1986	Corolla	4A-C, 4A-LC	3.5	3.2	4S-1.8, 5S-2.6	2.5	2.2	13.2	5.2
	Corolla	4A-GE	3.9	3.5	1.8	2.5	2.8	13.2	5.9
1987	Corolla	4A-C, 4A-LC	3.5	3.2	4S-1.8, 5S-2.6	2.5	2.2	13.2	5.2
	Corolla	4A-GE	3.9	3.5	1.8	2.5	2.8	13.2	5.9

NOTE: All capacities on this chart are approximate. Add fluid gradually, checking the level often.

85861097

2

ENGINE PERFORMANCE AND TUNE-UP

TUNE-UP PROCEDURES

In order to extract the full measure of performance and economy from your engine it is essential that it be properly tuned at regular intervals. A regular tune-up will keep your Toyota's engine running smoothly and will prevent the annoying minor breakdowns and poor performance associated with an untuned engine.

➤ **All Toyota models covered by this manual through 1974 use a conventional breaker points ignition. In 1975 Toyota switched to a transistorized ignition system. This ignition was much like the previous system with one basic difference; instead of the breaker points switching the primary current to the coil on and off, they triggered a transistor which did it for them. In 1977, certain Toyotas sold in California came equipped with a fully transistorized electronic ignition system (no points). In 1978, this system became standard on all models.**

A complete tune-up should be performed every 15,000 miles or twelve months, whichever comes first. This interval should be halved if the car is operated under severe conditions such as trailer towing, prolonged idling, continual stop and start driving, or if starting or running problems are noticed. It is assumed that the routine maintenance described in Section 1 has been kept up, as this will have a decided effect on the results of a tune-up. All of the applicable steps of a tune-up should be followed in order, as the result is a cumulative one. Any adjustment made to the engine is normally performed only when it will not be affected by other adjustments that are yet to be made during the tune-up.

If the specifications on the underhood tune-up sticker in the engine compartment of your car disagree with the Tune-Up Specifications chart in this Section, the figures on the sticker must be used. The sticker often reflects changes made during the production run or revised information that apply to the particular systems in that vehicle.

Spark Plugs

▸ **See Figure 1**

Spark plugs are used to ignite the air and fuel mixture in the cylinder as the piston reaches the top of the compression stroke. The controlled explosion that results forces the piston down, turning the crankshaft and the rest of the drive train.

A typical spark plug consists of a metal shell surrounding a ceramic insulator. A metal electrode extends downward through the center of the insulator and protrudes a small distance. Located at the end of the plug and attached to the side of the outer metal shell is the side electrode. The side electrode bends in at a 90 degree angle so that its tip is just past and parallel to the tip of the center electrode. The distance between these two electrodes (measured in thousandths of an inch or hundredths of a millimeter) is called the spark plug gap. The spark plug does not produce a spark but instead provides a gap across which the current can arc. The transistorized ignition coil (used on some later model vehicle covered by this manual) produces produces considerably more voltage than the standard (breaker point) type, approximately 50,000 volts, which travels through the wires to the spark

plugs. The current passes along the center electrode and jumps the gap to the side electrode, and in doing so, ignites the fuel/air mixture in the combustion chamber. All plugs should have a resistor built into the center electrode to reduce interference to any nearby radio and television receivers. The resistor also cuts down on erosion of plug electrodes caused by excessively long sparking. Resistor spark plug wiring is original equipment on all models.

Spark plug life and efficiency depend upon condition of the engine and the temperatures to which the plug is exposed. Combustion chamber temperatures are affected by many factors such as compression ratio of the engine, fuel/air mixtures, exhaust emission equipment, and the type of driving you do. Spark plugs are designed and classified by number according to the heat range at which they will operate most efficiently. The amount of heat that the plug absorbs is determined by the length of the lower insulator. The longer the insulator (it extends farther into the engine), the hotter the plug will operate; the shorter it is, the cooler it will operate. A plug that has a short path for heat transfer and remains too cool will quickly accumulate deposits of oil and carbon since it is not hot enough to burn them off. This leads to plug fouling and consequently to misfiring. A plug that has a long path of heat transfer will have no deposits but, due to the excessive heat, the electrodes will burn away quickly and, in some instances, pre-ignition may result. Pre-ignition takes place when plug tips get so hot that they glow sufficiently to ignite the fuel/air mixture before the spark does. This early ignition will usually cause a pinging during low speeds and heavy loads. In severe cases, the heat may become enough to start the fuel/air mixture burning throughout the combustion chamber rather than just to the front of the plug as in normal operation. At this time, the piston is rising in the cylinder making its compression stroke. The burning mass is compressed and an explosion results producing tremendous pressure. Something has to give, and it does; pistons are often damaged. Obviously, this detonation (explosion) is a destructive condition that can be avoided by installing a spark plug designed and specified for your particular engine.

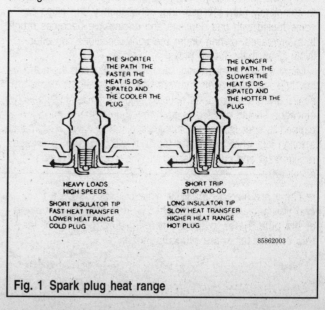

THE SHORTER THE PATH THE FASTER THE HEAT IS DISSIPATED AND THE COOLER THE PLUG

THE LONGER THE PATH, THE SLOWER THE HEAT IS DISSIPATED AND THE HOTTER THE PLUG

HEAVY LOADS
HIGH SPEEDS

SHORT INSULATOR TIP
FAST HEAT TRANSFER
LOWER HEAT RANGE
COLD PLUG

SHORT TRIP
STOP-AND-GO

LONG INSULATOR TIP
SLOW HEAT TRANSFER
HIGHER HEAT RANGE
HOT PLUG

85862003

Fig. 1 Spark plug heat range

A set of spark plugs usually requires replacement after about 15,000 miles (point type ignitions) or about 30,000 miles (electronic ignitions). The electrode on a new spark plug has a sharp edge but, with use, this edge becomes rounded by erosion causing the plug gap to increase. In normal operation, plug gap increases about 0.001 in. (0.0254mm) for every 1,000-2,000 miles. As the gap increases, the plug's voltage requirement also increases. It requires a greater voltage to jump the wider gap and about 2-4 times as much voltage to fire a plug at high speed and acceleration than at idle.

The higher voltage produced by the electronic transistorized ignition coil is one of the primary reasons for the prolonged replacement interval for spark plugs in late model cars. A consistently hotter spark prevents the fouling of plugs for much longer than could normally be expected; this spark is also able to jump across a larger gap more efficiently than a spark from a conventional system. However, even plugs used with these systems wear after time in the engine.

When you remove the spark plugs, check their condition. They are a good indicator of the condition of the engine. It is a good idea to remove the spark plugs every 6,000 miles to keep an eye on the mechanical state of the engine. A small deposit of light tan or gray material (or rust red with unleaded fuel) on a spark plug that has been used for any period of time is to be considered normal. Any other color or abnormal amounts of deposit, indicates that there is something amiss in the engine.

When a spark plug is functioning normally or, more accurately, when the plug is installed in an engine that is functioning properly, the plugs can be taken out, cleaned, gapped, and reinstalled without doing the engine any harm. But, if a plug fouls, causing misfire, you will have to investigate, correct the cause of the fouling, and either clean or replace the plug.

Worn or fouled plugs become obvious during acceleration. Voltage requirement is greatest during acceleration and a plug with an enlarged gap (or that is fouled) may require more voltage than the coil is able to produce. As a result, the engine misses and sputters until acceleration is reduced. Reducing acceleration reduces the plug's voltage requirement and the engine runs smoother. Slow, city driving is hard on plugs. The long periods of idle experienced in traffic creates an overly rich gas mixture. The engine does not run fast enough to completely burn the gas and, consequently, the plugs become fouled with gas deposits and engine idle becomes rough. In many cases, driving under the right conditions can effectively clean these fouled plugs.

Many shops have a spark plug sandblaster and there are a few inexpensive models that are designed for home use and available from aftermarket sources. After sandblasting, the electrode should be filed to a sharp, square shape and then gapped to specifications. Gapping a plug too close will produce a rough idle while gapping it too wide will increase its voltage requirement and cause missing at high speed and during acceleration.

➡**There are several reasons why a spark plug will foul and you can usually learn what is at fault by just looking at the plug. Refer to the spark plug diagnosis figure in this section for spark plug diagnosis.**

In most cases the factory recommended heat range is correct; it is chosen to perform well under a wide range of operating conditions. However, if most of your driving is long distance, high speed travel, you may want to install a spark plug one step colder than standard. If most of your driving is of the short trip variety, when the engine may not always reach operating temperature, a hotter plug may help burn off the deposits normally accumulated under those conditions.

REMOVAL

▶ **See Figures 2, 3, 4 and 5**

✳✳WARNING

The cylinder heads on most vehicles covered by this manual are cast aluminum. To prevent possible damage to the cylinder head threads ONLY remove the spark plugs once the engine has sufficiently cooled.

When you're removing spark plugs, you should work on one at a time. Don't start by removing the plug wires all at once because unless you number them, they are going to get mixed up. On some models though, it will be more convenient for you to remove all the wires before you start to work on the plugs. If this is necessary, take a minute before you begin and number the wires with tape before you disconnect them. The time you spend doing this will pay off later when it comes time to reconnect the wires to the plugs.

1. Disconnect the negative battery cable.
2. Tag the spark plug wires to assure proper installation.
3. Twist the spark plug boot slightly in either direction to break loose the seal, then remove the boot from the plug. You may also use a plug wire removal tool designed especially for this purpose. Do not pull on the wire itself or you may separate the plug connector from the end of the wire. When the wire has been removed, take a wire brush and clean the area around the plug. An evaporative spray cleaner such as those designed for brake applications will also work well. Make sure

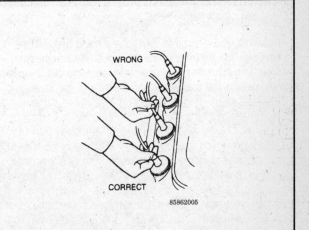

Fig. 2 When disconnecting the spark plug wire, always grasp it by the rubber boot

that all the foreign material is removed so that none will enter the cylinder after the plug has been removed.

➡️ **If you have access to a compressor, use the air hose to blow all material away from the spark plug bores before loosening the plug. Always protect your eyes with safety glasses when using compressed air.**

4. Remove the plug using the proper size socket, extensions, and universals as necessary. Be careful to hold the socket or the extension close to the plug with your free hand as this will help lessen the possibility of applying a shear force which might snap the spark plug in half.

5. If removing the plug is difficult, drip some penetrating oil on the plug threads, allow it to work, then remove the plug. Also, be sure that the socket is straight on the plug, especially on those hard to reach plugs. Again, if the socket is cocked to 1 side a shear force may be applied to the plug and could snap the plug in half.

Fig. 3 Disconnect the wire from the spark plug

Fig. 4 Loosen the spark plug using a socket

Fig. 5 Unthread and remove the spark plug from the cylinder head

INSPECTION

▶️ **See Figures 6 and 7**

Check the plugs for deposits and wear. If they are not going to be replaced, clean the plugs thoroughly. Remember that any kind of deposit will decrease the efficiency of the plug. Plugs can be cleaned on a spark plug cleaning machine, which can sometimes be found in service stations, or you can do an acceptable job of cleaning with a stiff brush. If the plugs are cleaned, the electrodes must be filed flat. Use an ignition points file, not an emery board or the like, which will leave deposits. The electrodes must be filed perfectly flat with sharp edges; rounded edges reduce the spark plug voltage by as much as 50%.

Check and adjust the spark plug gap immediately before installation. The ground electrode (the L-shaped one connected to the body of the plug) must be parallel to the center electrode and the specified size gauge (see Tune-Up Specifications) should pass through the gap with a slight drag. Always check the gap on new plugs, too; since they are not always set correctly at the factory.

⁑CAUTION

Never adjust the gap or attempt to clean a used platinum tipped spark plug.

Do not use a flat feeler gauge when measuring the gap on used plugs, because the reading may be inaccurate. The ground electrode on a used plug is often rounded on the face closest to the center electrode. A flat gauge will not be able to accurately measure this distance as well as a wire gauge. Most gapping tools usually have a bending tool attached. This tool may be used to adjust the side electrode until the proper distance is obtained. Never attempt to move or bend the center electrode or spark plug damage will likely occur. Also, be careful not to bend the side electrode too far or too often; if it is overstressed it may weaken and break off within the engine, requiring removal of the cylinder head to retrieve it.

Tracking Arc
High voltage arcs between a fouling deposit on the insulator tip and spark plug shell. This ignites the fuel/air mixture at some point along the insulator tip, retarding the ignition timing which causes a power and fuel loss.

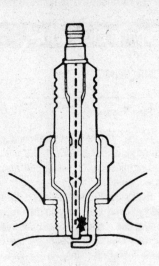

Wide Gap
Spark plug electrodes are worn so that the high voltage charge cannot arc across the electrodes. Improper gapping of electrodes on new or "cleaned" spark plugs could cause a similar condition. Fuel remains unburned and a power loss results.

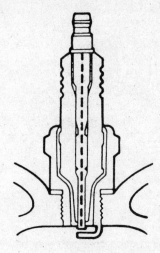

Flashover
A damaged spark plug boot, along with dirt and moisture, could permit the high voltage charge to short over the insulator to the spark plug shell or the engine. AC's buttress insulator design helps prevent high voltage flashover.

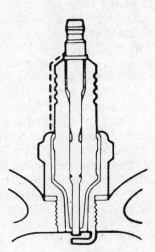

Fouled Spark Plug
Deposits that have formed on the insulator tip may become conductive and provide a "shunt" path to the shell. This prevents the high voltage from arcing between the electrodes. A power and fuel loss is the result.

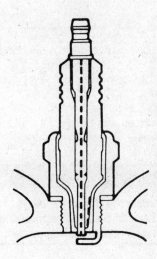

Bridged Electrodes
Fouling deposits between the electrodes "ground out" the high voltage needed to fire the spark plug. The arc between the electrodes does not occur and the fuel air mixture is not ignited. This causes a power loss and exhausting of raw fuel.

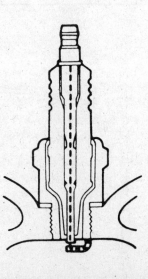

Cracked Insulator
A crack in the spark plug insulator could cause the high voltage charge to "ground out." Here, the spark does not jump the electrode gap and the fuel air mixture is not ignited. This causes a power loss and raw fuel is exhausted.

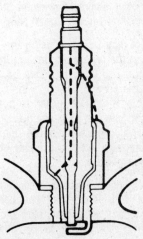

85862004

Fig. 6 Spark plug diagnosis

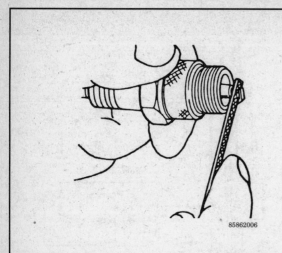

Fig. 7 Spark plugs that are in good condition may be filed and re-used

INSTALLATION

1. Inspect the spark plugs and clean or replace, as necessary. Inspect the spark plug boot for tears or damage. If a damaged boot is found, the spark plug wire must be replaced.

2. Using a feeler gauge, check and adjust the spark plug gap to specification. When using a gauge, the proper size should pass between the electrodes with a slight drag. The next larger size should not be able to pass while the next smaller size should pass freely.

✳✳CAUTION

Do not use the spark plug socket to thread the plugs. Always thread the plug by hand to prevent the possibility of cross-threading and damaging the cylinder head bore.

3. Lubricate the spark plug threads with a drop of clean engine oil, then carefully start the spark plugs by hand and tighten a few turns until a socket is needed to continue tightening the spark plug. Do not apply the same amount of force you would use for a bolt; just snug them in. If a torque wrench is available, tighten the plugs to 11-15 ft. lbs. (15-20 Nm).

➡**A spark plug threading tool may be made using the end of an old spark plug wire. Cut the wire a few inches from the top of the spark plug boot. The boot may then be used to hold the plug while the wire is turned to thread it. Because the wire is so flexible, it may be turned to bend around difficult angles and, should the plug begin to crossthread, the resistance should be sufficient to bend the wire instead of forcing the plug into the cylinder head, thus preventing serious thread damage.**

4. Apply a small amount of silicone dielectric compound to the end of the spark plug lead or inside the spark plug boot to prevent sticking, then install the boot to the spark plug and push until it clicks into place. The click may be felt or heard, then gently pull back on the boot to assure proper contact.

5. Connect the spark plug wires as tagged during removal.

6. Connect the negative battery cable.

Spark Plug Wires

CHECKING

▶ **See Figure 8**

At every tune-up, visually inspect the spark plug cables for burns, cuts, or breaks in the insulation. Check the boots and the nipples on the distributor cap and coil. Replace any damaged wiring.

Every 36,000 miles or so, the resistance of the wires should be checked with an ohmmeter. Wires with excessive resistance will cause misfiring, and may make the engine difficult to start in damp weather. Generally the useful life of the cables is 36,000-50,000 miles.

To check resistance, remove the distributor cap, leaving the wires attached. Connect one lead of an ohmmeter to an electrode within the cap; connect the other lead to the corresponding spark plug terminal (remove it from the plug for this test). Replace any wire which shows a resistance over 25,000 ohms. Test the high tension lead from the coil by connecting the ohmmeter between the center contact in the distributor cap and either of the primary terminals of the coil. If resistance is more than 25,000 ohms, remove the cable from the coil and check the resistance of the cable alone. Anything over 15,000 ohms is cause for replacement. It should be remembered that resistance is also a function of length; the longer the cable, the greater the resistance. Thus, if the cables on your car are longer than the factory originals, resistance will be higher, quite possibly outside these limits.

When installing new cables, replace them one at a time to avoid mix-ups. Start by replacing the longest one first. Install the boot firmly over the spark plug. Route the wire over the same path as the original. Insert the nipple firmly into the tower on the cap or the coil. Be sure to apply silicone dielectric compound to the spark plug wire boots and tower connectors prior to installation.

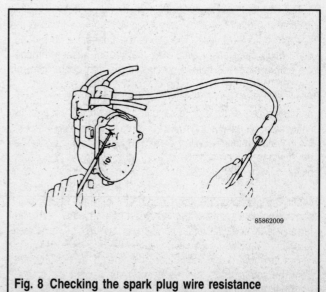

Fig. 8 Checking the spark plug wire resistance

FIRING ORDERS

▶ See Figures 9 and 10

➡To avoid confusion, spark plug wires should be replaced one at a time. Distributor terminal position may differ slightly from that which is illustrated.

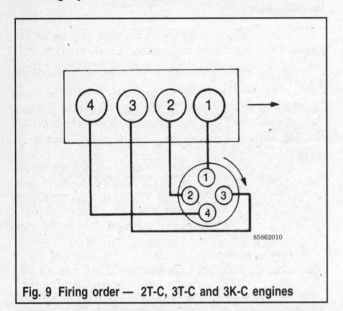

Fig. 9 Firing order — 2T-C, 3T-C and 3K-C engines

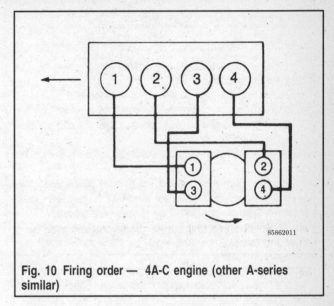

Fig. 10 Firing order — 4A-C engine (other A-series similar)

CONVENTIONAL & TRANSISTORIZED POINT IGNITION SYSTEMS

Breaker Points and Condenser

The points function as a circuit breaker for the primary circuit of the ignition system. The ignition coil must boost the 12 volts of electrical pressure supplied by the battery to as much as 25,000 volts in order to fire the plugs. To do this, the coil depends on the points and the condenser to make a clean break in the primary circuit.

The coil has both primary and secondary circuits. When the ignition is turned **ON**, the battery supplies voltage through the coil and onto the points. The points are connected to ground, completing the primary circuit. As the current passes through the coil, a magnetic field is created in the iron center core of the coil. When the cam in the distributor turns, the points open, breaking the primary circuit. The magnetic field in the primary circuit of the coil then collapses and cuts through the secondary circuit windings around the iron core. Because of the physical principle called electromagnetic induction, the battery voltage is increased to a level sufficient to fire the spark plugs.

When the points open, the electrical charge in the primary circuit tries to jump the gap created between the two open contacts of the points. If this electrical charge were not transferred elsewhere, the metal contacts of the points would start to change rapidly.

The function of the condenser is to absorb excessive voltage from the points when they open and thus prevent the points from becoming pitted or burned.

If you have ever wondered why it is necessary to tune your engine occasionally, consider the fact that the ignition system must complete the above cycle each time spark plug fires. On a 4-cylinder, 4-cycle engine, two of the four plugs must fire once for ever engine revolution. If the idle speed of your engine is 800 revolutions per minute (800 rpm), the breaker points open and close 1,600 times (2 x 800 = 1,600). And that is just at idle. What about at 60 mph?

There are two ways to check breaker point gap; with a feeler gauge or with a dwell meter. Either way you set the points, you are adjusting the amount of time (in degrees of distributor rotation) that the points will remain open. If you adjust the points with a feeler gauge, you are setting the maximum amount the points will open when the rubbing block on the points is on a high point of the distributor cam. When you adjust the points with a dwell meter, you are measuring the number of degrees (of distributor cam rotation) that the points will remain closed before they start to open as a high point of the distributor cam approaches the rubbing block of the points.

If you still do not understand how the points function, take a friend, go outside, and remove the distributor cap from your engine. Have your friend operate the starter (make sure that the transmission is not in gear) as you look at the exposed parts of the distributor.

There are two rules that should always be followed when adjusting or replacing points. The points and condenser are a matched set (non transistorized point ignitions); never replace one without replacing the other. If you change the point gap or dwell of the engine, you also change the ignition timing. Therefore, if you adjust the points, you must also adjust the timing.

INSPECTION AND CLEANING

The breaker points should be inspected and cleaned at 6,000 mile intervals.

1. Disconnect the high tension lead from the coil.

2. Unsnap the two distributor cap retaining clips and lift the cap straight up. Leave the leads connected to the cap and position it out of the way.

3. Remove the rotor and dust cover by pulling them straight up.

4. Place a screwdriver against the breaker points and carefully pry them open. Examine their condition. If they are excessively worn, burned, or pitted, they should be replaced.

5. Polish the points with a point file. Do not use emery cloth or sandpaper; these may leave particles on the points causing them to arc.

6. Clean the distributor cap and rotor with alcohol. Inspect the cap terminals for looseness and corrosion. Check the rotor tip for excessive burning. Inspect both cap and rotor for cracks. Replace either if they show any of the above signs of wear or damage.

7. Check the operation of the centrifugal advance mechanism by turning the rotor clockwise. Release the rotor; it should return to its original position. If it doesn't, check for binding parts.

8. Check the vacuum advance unit, by removing the plastic cap and pressing on the octane selector. It should return to its original position. Check for binding if it doesn't.

9. If the points do not require replacement, proceed with the adjustment procedure, otherwise perform the point and condenser replacement procedures. Both are located later in this section.

POINT REPLACEMENT

The points should be replaced every 12,000 miles (24,000 miles with transistorized ignition since the points do not carry as much current and do not wear as quickly), or any time they are found to be badly pitted, worn, or burned.

1. Disconnect the high tension lead from the coil.

2. Unsnap the two distributor cap retaining clips and lift the cap straight up. Leave the leads connected to the cap and position it out of the way.

3. Remove the rotor and dust cover by pulling them straight up.

4. Unfasten the point lead connector.

5. Remove the point retaining clip and unfasten the point hold-down screw(s). It is a good idea to use a magnetic or locking screwdriver to remove the small screws inside the dis-

tributor, since they are almost impossible to find once they have been dropped.

6. Lift out the points set.

7. Install the new point set in the reverse order of removal. After completing installation, adjust the points as detailed later in this section.

CONDENSER REPLACEMENT

Vehicles Through 1974

Replace the condenser whenever the points are replaced, or if it is suspected of being defective. On Toyota passenger cars the condenser is located on the outside of the distributor.

1. Carefully remove the nut and washer from the condenser lead terminal.

2. Use a magnetic or locking screwdriver to remove the condenser mounting screw. The magnetic or locking screwdriver is used to help prevent loss of the small fastener.

3. Remove the condenser.

4. Installation of a new condenser is performed in the reverse order of removal.

ADJUSTMENT

Perform the gap adjustment procedure whenever new points are installed, or as part of routine maintenance. If you are adjusting an old set of points, you must check the dwell as well, since the feeler gauge is really only accurate with a new point set. The points on all 1975-77 models are adjusted in a slightly different manner than you may be familiar with so make sure that you follow the correct adjustment procedure.

Vehicles Through 1974

▶ **See Figures 11 and 12**

1. Rotate the engine by hand (or by using a remote starter switch), so that the edge of the point set rubbing block is on the high point of the distributor cam lobe.

2. Insert a 0.018 in. (0.46mm) feeler gauge between the points; a slight drag should be felt.

3. If no drag is felt or if the feeler gauge cannot be inserted at all, loosen, but do not remove, the point hold-down screw.

4. Insert a screwdriver into the adjustment slot. Rotate the screwdriver until the proper point gap is attained. The point gap is increased by rotating the screwdriver counterclockwise and decreased by rotating it clockwise.

5. Tighten the point hold-down screw.

➡**Lubricate the cam lobes, breaker arm, rubbing block, arm pivot, and distributor shaft with special high temperature distributor grease.**

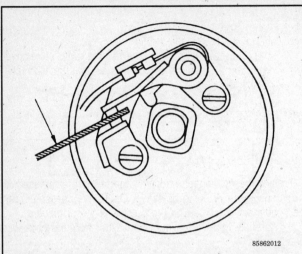

Fig. 11 The arrow indicates the feeler gauge being used to check the point gap — vehicles through 1974

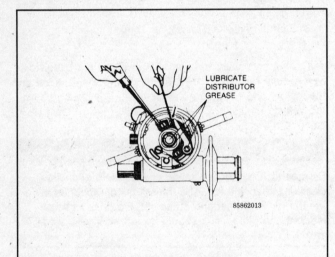

LUBRICATE DISTRIBUTOR GREASE

Fig. 12 Adjustment of the points and lubricant distribution — vehicles through 1974

1975-77 Transistorized Point Vehicles

▶ **See Figure 13**

The point set on this ignition system is covered by a piece of protective plastic shielding. Because of this, the gap must be checked between the point rubbing block and the distributor cam lobe instead of between the two point tips. Do not try to remove the plastic shielding as it will damage the point set.

1. Using your hands or a remote starter switch, rotate the engine so that the rubbing block is resting on the low point (flat side) of the cam lobe.

2. Insert a 0.018 in. (0.46mm) flat feeler gauge between the rubbing block and the cam lobe; a slight drag should be felt.

3. If no drag can be felt or if the feeler gauge cannot be inserted at all, loosen, but do not remove, the point hold-down screw.

4. Insert a screwdriver into the point adjustment slot. Rotate the screwdriver until the proper gap is achieved. The gap is increased by rotating the screwdriver counterclockwise and decreased by rotating it clockwise.

5. Tighten the point hold-down screw. Lubricate the cam lobes, breaker arm, rubbing block, arm pivot and distributor shaft with special high temperature distributor grease.

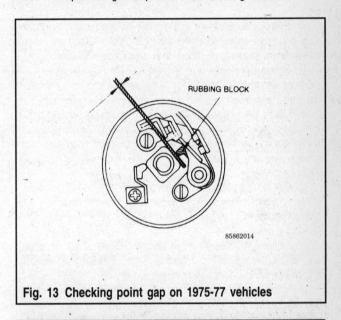

RUBBING BLOCK

Fig. 13 Checking point gap on 1975-77 vehicles

Dwell Angle

▶ **See Figure 14**

The dwell angle is the number of degrees of distributor cam rotation through which the points remain closed (conducting electricity). Increasing the point gap decreases dwell, while decreasing the gap increases dwell.

The dwell angle may be checked with the distributor cap and rotor installed and the engine running, or with the cap and rotor removed and the engine cranking at starter speed. The meter gives a constant reading with the engine running. With the engine cranking, the meter will fluctuate between 0 dwell and the maximum figure for that setting. Never attempt to adjust the points when the ignition is **ON**, or you may receive a shock.

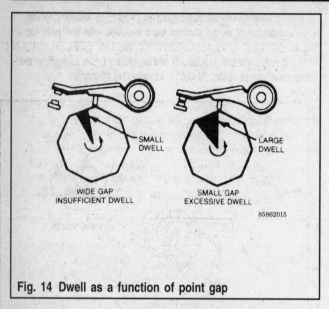

Fig. 14 Dwell as a function of point gap

➡On cars with a fully transistorized electronic ignition (1978 and later vehicles without points), the dwell is pre-set at the factor and is not adjustable.

ADJUSTMENT WITH A DWELL METER

▶ See Figure 15

1. Connect a dwell meter to the ignition system, according to the tool manufacturer's instructions but keeping in mind the following points:

   a. When checking the dwell on a conventional ignition system, connect one meter lead (usually black) to a metallic part of the car to ground the meter; the other lead (usually red) is connected to the coil primary post (the one with the small lead which runs to the distributor body);

   b. When checking dwell on a model with transistorized ignition, ground one meter lead (usually black) to a metallic part of the car; hook up the other lead (usually red) to the negative (-) coil terminal. Under no circumstances should the meter be connected to the distributor or the positive (+) side of the coil. (Please refer to the preceding service precautions).

Fig. 15 Dwell meter connections with a transistorized point ignition

2. If the dwell meter has a set line, adjust the needle until it rests on the line.

3. Start the engine. It should be warmed up and running at the specified idle speed.

➡It is not necessary to check the dwell on the transistorized system for certain 1977 California models. It is set at the factory and requires no adjustment. If in doubt, check the Vehicle Emission Control Information (VECI) label located in the engine compartment.

✳✳CAUTION

Be sure to keep fingers, tools, clothes, hair, and wires clear of the engine fan. The transmission should be in Neutral (or Park), parking brake set, the drive wheels blocked and the vehicle should be in a well ventilated area.

4. Check the reading on the dwell meter. If your meter doesn't have a 4-cylinder scale, multiply the 8-cylinder reading by two.

5. If the meter reading is within specification (refer to the Tune-Up Specifications chart), shut the engine **OFF** and disconnect the dwell meter.

6. If the dwell is not within specifications, shut the engine **OFF** and adjust the point gap as previously outlined. Increasing the point gap decreases the dwell angle and vice versa.

7. Adjust the points until dwell is within specifications, then disconnect the dwell meter. Adjust the timing as detailed in the following section.

ELECTRONIC IGNITION

General Information

▶ See Figure 16

A fully electronic transistorized ignition system is used on some later model vehicles covered by this manual. Electronic ignition systems offer many advantages over the conventional breaker point ignition system. By eliminating the points mainte-

nance requirements are greatly reduced. An electronic ignition system is capable of producing much higher voltage, which in turn aids in starting, reduces spark plug fouling and provides better emission control.

In 1977, certain Corollas made for California came equipped with electronic ignition. In 1978, Toyota decided to make electronic ignition standard equipment on all models and the same basic system is still used today.

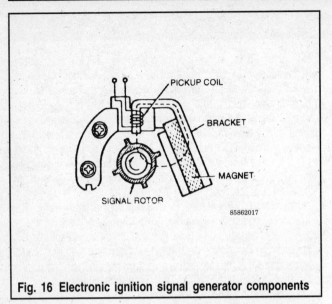

Fig. 16 Electronic ignition signal generator components

The system Toyota uses consists of a distributor with a signal generator, an ignition coil and an electronic igniter. The signal generator is used to activate the electronic components of the igniter. It is located in the distributor and consists of three main components; the signal rotor, the pick-up coil and the permanent magnet. The signal rotor (not to be confused with the normal rotor) revolves with the distributor shaft, while the pickup coil and the permanent magnet are stationary. As the signal rotor spins, the teeth on it pass a projection leading from the pickup coil. When this happens, voltage is allowed to flow through the system, firing the spark plugs. There is no physical contact and no electrical arcing, hence no need to replace burnt or worn parts.

Service consists of inspection of the distributor cap, rotor and the ignition wires; replacing them as necessary. In addition, the air gap between the signal rotor and the projection on the pickup coil should be checked periodically.

Air Gap

ADJUSTMENT

▶ **See Figures 17 and 18**

1. Disconnect the negative battery cable.
2. Unsnap the distributor cap retaining clips and lift the cap straight up. Leave the leads connected to the cap and position it out of the way. If it is necessary to disconnect any of the spark plug wiring leads ALWAYS tag them before removal.
3. Inspect the cap for cracks, carbon tracks or a worn center contact. Replace it if necessary, transferring the wires one at a time from the old cap to the new one.
4. Pull the ignition rotor (not the signal rotor) straight up and remove it. Replace it if the contacts are worn, burned or pitted. Do not file the contacts.
5. Turn the engine over (you may use a socket wrench on the front pulley bolt to do this) until the projection on the pickup coil is directly opposite the signal rotor tooth.

6. Obtain a non-ferrous (paper, brass, or plastic) feeler gauge of 0.012 in. (0.30mm), and insert it into the pick-up air gap. DO NOT USE AN ORDINARY METAL FEELER GAUGE! The gauge should just touch either side of the gap. The permissible range is 0.008-0.016 in. (0.20-0.40mm).

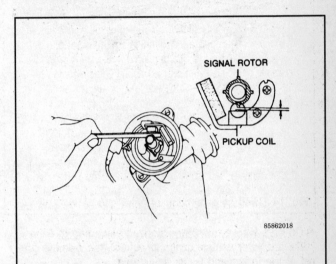

Fig. 17 Checking the air gap on all engines except the 1983 and later A-series engines

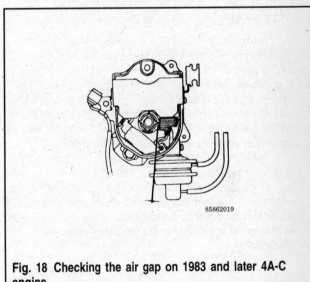

Fig. 18 Checking the air gap on 1983 and later 4A-C engine

➡The air gap on 1983 and later 4A-C and most A-series engines is NOT adjustable. If the gap is not within specifications, the pick-up coil (igniter) must be replaced.

7. If the gap is either too wide or too narrow, loosen the Phillips screws (usually 2) mounting the pickup coil onto the distributor base plate. Then, wedge a screwdriver between the notch in the pickup coil assembly and the two dimples on the base plate, and turn the screwdriver back and forth until the pickup gap is correct.
8. Tighten the screws and recheck gap, readjusting if necessary.
9. After adjustment, install the distributor cap and connect the negative battery cable.

IGNITION TIMING

General Information

Ignition timing is the measurement, in degrees of crankshaft rotation, of the point at which the spark plugs fire in each of the cylinders. It is measured in degrees before or after Top Dead Center (TDC) of the compression stroke and is usually set according to TDC of the No. 1 piston. Ignition timing is adjusted by loosening the distributor locking device and turning the distributor in the engine.

Ideally, the air/fuel mixture in the cylinder will be ignited (by the spark plug) and just begin its rapid expansion as the piston passes top dead center (TDC) of the compression stroke. If this happens, the piston will be start the power stroke just as the compressed (by the movement of the piston) and ignited air/fuel mixture starts to expand. The expansion of the air/fuel mixture will then force the piston down on the power stroke and turn the crankshaft.

Because it takes a fraction of a second for the spark plug to ignite the mixture in the cylinder, the spark plug must fire a little before the piston reaches TDC. Otherwise, the mixture will not be completely ignited as the piston passes TDC and the full power of the explosion will not be used by the engine.

The timing measurement is given in degrees of crankshaft rotation before the piston reaches TDC (BTDC). If the setting for the ignition timing is 5 degrees BTDC, the spark plug must fire 5 degrees before each piston reaches TDC. This only holds true, however, when the engine is at idle speed.

As the engine speed increases, the pistons go faster. The spark plugs have to ignite the fuel even sooner if it is to be completely ignited when the piston reaches TDC. To do this, distributors have various means of advancing the spark timing as the engine speed increases.

The distributor in your Toyota probably has one or two means of advancing the ignition timing. One is called centrifugal advance and is actuated by weights in the distributor. The other is called vacuum advance and is controlled by that larger circular housing on the side of the distributor (models so equipped).

In addition, some distributors have a vacuum/retard mechanism which is contained in the same housing on the side of the distributor as the vacuum advance. The function of this mechanism is to retard the timing of the ignition spark under certain engine conditions. This causes more complete burning of the air/fuel mixture in the cylinder and consequently lower exhaust emissions.

Because these mechanisms change ignition timing, it is necessary to disconnect and plug the one or two vacuum lines from the distributor when setting the basic ignition timing. (Consult the emissions sticker under the hood of your vehicle. Follow those instructions if they differ from the ones listed here).

If ignition timing is set too far advanced (BTDC), the ignition and expansion of the air/fuel mixture in the cylinder will try to force the piston down the cylinder while it is still traveling upward. This causes engine ping, a sound which resembles marbles being dropped into an empty tin can. If the ignition timing is too far retarded (after, or ATDC), the piston will have already passed TDC and started on its way down when the fuel is ignited. This will cause the piston to be forced down for only a portion of its trave, resulting in poor engine performance and lack of power.

Ignition timing adjustment is checked with a timing light. This instrument is usually connected to the number one (No. 1) spark plug of the engine (see the equipment manufacturer's instructions). The timing light flashes every time an electrical current is sent from the distributor, through the No. 1 spark plug wire, to the spark plug. The crankshaft pulley and the front cover of the engine are marked with a timing pointer and a timing scale. When the timing pointer is aligned with the 0 mark on the timing scale, the piston in the No. 1 cylinder is at TDC of its compression stroke. With the engine running, and the timing light aimed at the timing pointer and timing scale, the stroboscopic flashes from the timing light will allow you to check the ignition timing setting of the engine. The timing light flashes every time the spark plug in the No. 1 cylinder of the engine fires. Since the flash from the timing light makes the crankshaft pulley seem stationary for a moment, you will be able to read the exact position of the piston in the No. 1 cylinder on the timing scale.

There are three basic types of timing light available. the first is a simple neon bulb with two wire connections (one for the spark plug and one for the plug wire, connecting the light in series). This type of light is quite dim, and must be held closely to the marks to be seen, but it is inexpensive. The second type of light operates from the car battery. Two alligator clips connect to the batter terminals, while a third wire connects to the spark plug with an adaptor. This type of light is more expensive, but the xenon bulb provides a nice bright flash which can even be seen in sunlight. the third type replaces the battery source with 110 volt house current. Some timing lights have other functions built into them, such as dwell meters, tachometers, or remote starting switches. These are convenient, in that they reduce the tangle of wires under the hood, but may duplicate the functions of tools you already have.

If your Toyota has electronic ignition, you should use a timing light with an inductive pickup. This pickup simple clamps onto the No. 1 plug wire, eliminating the adaptor. It is not susceptible to crossfiring or false triggering, which may occur with a conventional light, due to the greater voltages produced by electronic ignition.

Checking and Adjustment

▶ **See Figures 19, 20, 21, 22 and 23**

SINGLE POINT AND ELECTRONIC DISTRIBUTORS

1. Warm-up the engine, then shut the ignition **OFF**.

➡**Before hooking up a tachometer to a 1975-77 car with a transistorized ignition system, refer to the preceding service precautions located under the point and transistorized point type ignition system information earlier in this section. On all models equipped with a transistorized point or fully electronic ignition, hook the dwell meter or tachometer to the negative (-) side of the coil, not to the distributor primary lead; damage to the transistorized switch or ignition control unit will result.**

2. Connect a tachometer (following the tool manufacturer's instructions) and check the engine idle speed to be sure that it is set to specification.

➡**1983 and later A-series engines require a special type of tachometer which hooks up to the service connector wire coming out of the distributor. As many tachometers are not compatible with this hook-up, we recommend that you consult with the manufacturer before purchasing a certain type.**

3. If the timing marks are difficult to see, use a dab of paint or chalk to make them more visible.

4. Connect a timing light according to the tool manufacturer's instructions.

5. Disconnect the vacuum line(s) from the distributor vacuum unit. Plug each disconnected line using a pencil or golf tee.

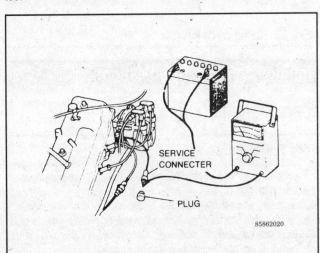

Fig. 19 1983 and later A-series engines will require a special tachometer hook-up

6. Be sure that the timing light wires are clear of the fan, then start the engine.

✳✳CAUTION

Keep fingers, clothes, tools, hair, and leads clear of the spinning engine fan. Be sure that you are running the engine in a well ventilated area.

7. Allow the engine to run at the specified idle speed with the gearshift in Neutral (manual transmission) or Drive "D" (automatic transmission).

✳✳CAUTION

Be sure that the parking brake is set and that the drive wheels are blocked to prevent the car from rolling forward, especially when Drive is selected with an automatic.

8. Point the timing light at the marks indicated in the chart and illustrations. With the engine at idle, timing should be at the specification given in the specifications chart located earlier in this section.

9. If the timing is not at the specification, loosen the pinch bolt at the base of the distributor just sufficiently so that the distributor can be turned. Rotate the distributor to advance or retard the timing as required. Once the proper marks aligned (as seen with the timing light), ignition timing is correct.

10. Stop the engine and tighten the pinch bolt. Start the engine and recheck the timing to be sure it did not change while the bolt was tightened.

11. Stop the engine; disconnect the tachometer and timing light. Connect the vacuum line(s) to the distributor vacuum unit.

DUAL POINT DISTRIBUTOR

A dual point distributor is offered as an option on some Corolla models (sold outside of California for 1975-77). To adjust the dual point system, proceed as follows:

1. Adjust the timing for the main set of points as previously outlined in the Single Point section.

2. Use a jumper wire to ground the terminal on the thermoswitch connector after removing the connector from the thermoswitch. The thermoswitch is threaded into the intake manifold and is connected to the dual point system relay. Be careful not to confuse it with any of the emission control system switches which are connected to the computer.

3. Check the timing with a light as described earlier under the single point procedure, the timing should be approximately 22 degrees before top dead center (BTDC).

4. If the timing is off, connect a dwell meter to the negative side of the coil, and adjust the sub-points so that the dwell angle is 52 degrees. The sub-points are adjusted in the same manner as the main points.

5. Remove the test equipment and reconnect the thermoswitch.

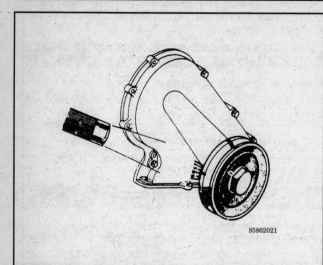

Fig. 20 Timing mark location — 3K-C and 2T-C engines

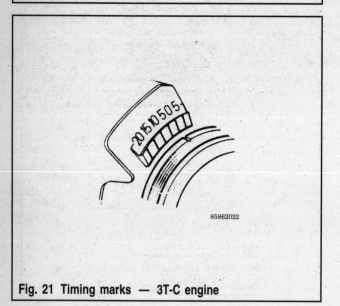

Fig. 21 Timing marks — 3T-C engine

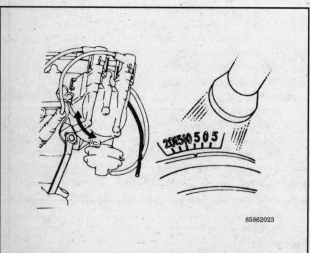

Fig. 22 Setting timing on the 4A-C engine (note the disconnected vacuum line, it should be plugged)

Fig. 23 Timing mark location — 4A-GE

Ignition System Troubleshooting

POINT TYPE IGNITION

▶ **See Figure 24**

To easily diagnose problems with your point type ignition, use the following chart.

The points should be replaced every 12,000 miles (24,000 miles with transistorized ignition since the points do not carry as much current and do not wear as quickly), or any time they are found to be badly pitted, worn, or burned.

Replace the condenser whenever the points are replaced, or if it is suspected of being defective. On Toyota passenger cars the condenser is located on the outside of the distributor.

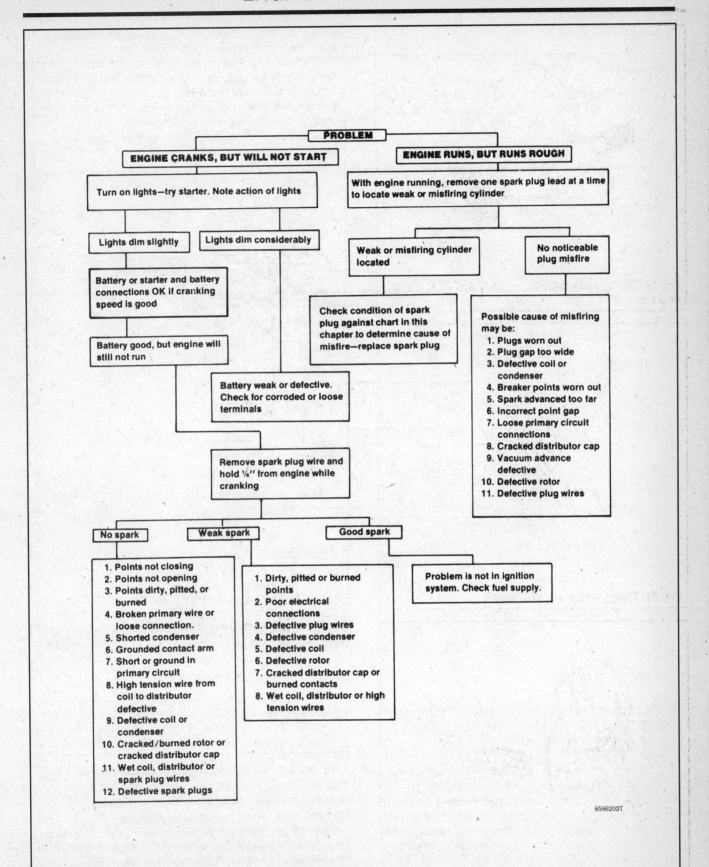

PROBLEM

ENGINE CRANKS, BUT WILL NOT START

Turn on lights—try starter. Note action of lights

Lights dim slightly

Lights dim considerably

Battery or starter and battery connections OK if cranking speed is good

Battery good, but engine will still not run

Battery weak or defective. Check for corroded or loose terminals

Remove spark plug wire and hold ¼" from engine while cranking

No spark

1. Points not closing
2. Points not opening
3. Points dirty, pitted, or burned
4. Broken primary wire or loose connection.
5. Shorted condenser
6. Grounded contact arm
7. Short or ground in primary circuit
8. High tension wire from coil to distributor defective
9. Defective coil or condenser
10. Cracked/burned rotor or cracked distributor cap
11. Wet coil, distributor or spark plug wires
12. Defective spark plugs

Weak spark

1. Dirty, pitted or burned points
2. Poor electrical connections
3. Defective plug wires
4. Defective condenser
5. Defective coil
6. Defective rotor
7. Cracked distributor cap or burned contacts
8. Wet coil, distributor or high tension wires

Good spark

Problem is not in ignition system. Check fuel supply.

ENGINE RUNS, BUT RUNS ROUGH

With engine running, remove one spark plug lead at a time to locate weak or misfiring cylinder

Weak or misfiring cylinder located

No noticeable plug misfire

Check condition of spark plug against chart in this chapter to determine cause of misfire—replace spark plug

Possible cause of misfiring may be:

1. Plugs worn out
2. Plug gap too wide
3. Defective coil or condenser
4. Breaker points worn out
5. Spark advanced too far
6. Incorrect point gap
7. Loose primary circuit connections
8. Cracked distributor cap
9. Vacuum advance defective
10. Defective rotor
11. Defective plug wires

85862027

Fig. 24 Point Type Ignition Problem Diagnosis

ELECTRONIC IGNITION

▶ **See Figure 25**

Troubleshooting this system is easy, but you must have an accurate ohmmeter and voltmeter. The numbers in the diagram correspond to the numbers of the following troubleshooting steps. Be sure to perform each step in order.

1. Check for a spark at the spark plugs by hooking up a timing light in the usual manner. If the light flashes, it can be assumed that voltage is reaching the plugs, which should then be inspected, along with the fuel system. If no flash is generated, go on to the following ignition checks.

2. Check all wiring and plastic connectors for tight and proper connections.

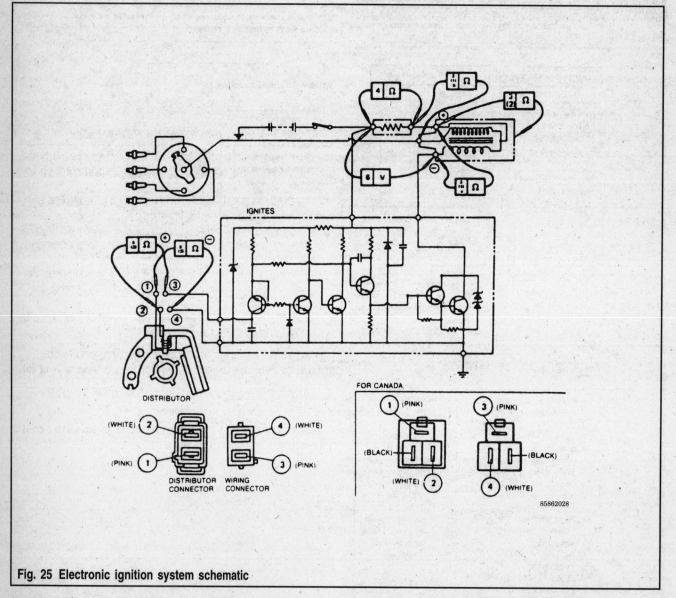

Fig. 25 Electronic ignition system schematic

3. (1) With an ohmmeter, check between the positive (+) and negative (-) primary terminals of the ignition coil. The resistance (cold) should be 1.3-1.7 ohms. Between the primary terminal and the high tension terminal, the resistance (cold) should be 12-16k ohms. (2) The insulation resistance between the (+) primary terminal and the ignition coil case should be infinite.

4. The resistor wire (brown and yellow) resistance should be 1.2 ohms (cold). To measure, disengage the plastic connector at the igniter and connect one wire of the ohmmeter to the yellow wire and one to the brown.

5. Remove the distributor cap and ignition rotor. (1) Check the air gap between the timing rotor spoke and the pick-up coil. When aligned, the air gap should be 0.008-0.016 in. (0.20-0.40mm). You will probably have to bump the engine around with the starter to line up the timing rotor. (2) Unplug the distributor connector at the distributor. Connect one wire of the ohmmeter to the white wire, and one wire to the pink wire. The resistance of the signal generator should be 130-190 ohms.

6. Check the igniter last; connect the (-) voltmeter wire to the (-) ignition coil primary terminal, and the (+) voltmeter wire

to the yellow resistor wire at the connector unplugged in Step 4. With the ignition switch turned on **On** (not Start) the voltage should measure 12 volts.

7. Check the voltage between the (-) ignition coil primary terminal and the yellow resistor wire again, but this time use the ohmmeter as resistance. Using the igniter end of the distributor connector unplugged in Step 5, connect the positive (+) ohmmeter wire to the pink distributor wire, and the negative (-) ohmmeter wire to the white wire.

✳✳CAUTION

Do not intermix the (+) and (-) terminals of the ohmmeter.

Select either the 1 ohms or 10 ohms range of the ohmmeter. With the voltmeter connected as in Step 6 (1), and the ignition switch turned to **On** (not Start), the voltage should measure nearly zero.

Octane Selector

Adjustment

▶ **See Figures 26 and 27**

The octane selector is used as a fine adjustment to match the vehicle's ignition timing to the grade of gasoline being used. It is located near the distributor vacuum unit (on models so equipped), beneath a plastic dust cover. Normally the octane selector should not require periodic attention, however should adjustment become necessary:

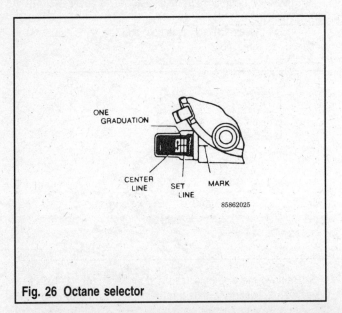

Fig. 26 Octane selector

Octane Selector Test Speeds	
Engine Type	**Test Speed (mph)**
3K-C	19 – 21
2T-C	16 – 22

85862026

Fig. 27 Figures shown are actual road speeds

1. Align the setting line with the threaded end of the housing and then align the center line with the setting mark on the housing.

2. Drive the car to the specified speed for the octane selector test in High gear on a level road.

3. Depress the accelerator pedal all the way to the floor. A slight pinging sound should be heard. As the car accelerates, the sound should gradually go away.

4. If the pinging sound is low or if it fails to disappear as the vehicle speed increases, retard the timing by turning the knob toward **R** (Retard).

5. If there is no pinging sound at all, advance the timing by turning the knob toward **A** (Advance).

➡**On 1973-79 models, do not turn the octane selector more than ½ turn toward R. Do not turn it toward A at all.**

6. When the adjustment is completed, install the plastic dust cover.

➡**One graduation of the octane selector is equal to about 10 degrees of crankshaft angle.**

VALVE LASH

Valve lash is one factor which determines how far the intake and exhaust valves will open into the cylinder. All vehicles covered by this manual are equipped with mechanical valve lifters, which must be adjusted at the factory recommended intervals (1970-77, every 12,000 miles; 1978-84, every 15,000 miles; 1985-87, every 30,000 miles).

If the valve clearance is too large, part of the camshaft lift will be used to remove the excessive clearance, thus the valves will not be open sufficiently. This condition has two effects, the valve train components will emit a tapping noise as excessive clearance is taken up, and the engine will perform poorly, since the less the intake valve opens, the smaller amount of air/fuel mixture is admitted to the cylinder. The less the exhaust valves open, the greater the back-pressure in the cylinder which prevents the proper air/fuel mixture from entering even if the intake valve did open properly.

If the valve clearance is too small, the intake and exhaust valves will not fully seat on the cylinder head when they close. When a valve seats on the cylinder head it accomplishes two things, it seals the combustion chamber so none of the gases in the cylinder can escape and it cools itself by transferring some of the heat it absorbed from the combustion process through the cylinder head and into the engine cooling system. Therefore, if the valve clearance is too small, the engine will run poorly (due to gases escaping from the combustion chamber), and the valves will overheat and warp (since they cannot transfer heat efficiently unless they are touching the seat in the cylinder head).

➡ **While all valve adjustments must be as accurate as possible, it is better to have the valve adjustment slightly loose than slightly tight, as burnt valves may result form overly tight adjustments.**

Adjustment

ALL ENGINES EXCEPT 1C-L AND 4A-GE

▶ **See Figures 28, 29, 30, 31, 32, 33, 34, 35, 36, 37, 38 and 39**

1. Start the engine and run it until it reaches normal operating temperature.
2. Stop the engine, then remove the air cleaner assembly.
3. Remove any other hoses, cables, etc. which are attached to, or in the way of the, cylinder head (camshaft/valve) cover. Remove the cylinder head cover.

✳✳CAUTION

Be careful when removing components as the engine will be hot.

4. Turn the crankshaft until the pointer or notch on the pulley aligns with the **O** or **T** mark on the timing scale. This will insure that the engine is at TDC.

➡**Check that the rocker arms on the No. 1 cylinder are loose and those on the No. 4 cylinder are tight. If not, turn the crankshaft one complete revolution (360 degrees). When the engine is at No. 1 TDC the cylinder is ready for the spark plug to fire; meaning the valves should be closed.**

5. Retighten the cylinder head bolts on all 3K-C engines to the proper torque specifications (please refer to the torque specifications information in Section 3 of this manual). Also on the 3K-C, retighten the valve rocker support bolts to 13-17 ft. lbs. (18-23 Nm).

✳✳CAUTION

Tighten all of the bolts in Step 4 in the proper sequence and stages (please refer to Section 3 of this manual for details).

6. Using a flat feeler gauge, check the clearance between the bottom of the rocker arm and the top of the valve stem. This measurement should correspond to the one given in the tune-up specifications chart (located earlier in this chapter). Check only the valves listed under "**First**" in the accompanying valve arrangement illustrations for your particular engine.
7. If the clearance is not within specifications, the valves will require adjustment. Loosen the locknut on the other end (A-series engines usually have the locknut on the same end) of the rocker arm and, still holding the nut with an open end wrench, turn the adjustment screw to achieve the correct clearance.
8. Once the correct valve clearance is achieved, keep the adjustment screw from turning using your screwdriver and tighten the locknut. Recheck the valve clearances.
9. Turn the engine one complete revolution (360 degrees so the paired opposite cylinder to No. 1 is at TDC and No. 1 is on its exhaust stroke) and adjust the remaining valves. Repeat the necessary steps of this procedures and use the valve arrangement illustration marked "**Second.**"
10. Instal the cylinder head (camshaft/valve) cover using a new gasket.
11. Install the air cleaner assembly and the remaining hoses or wiring, as removed.

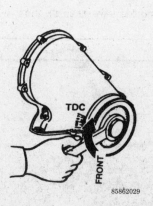

Fig. 28 Turn the crankshaft to align the timing marks and set the engine at No. 1 TDC

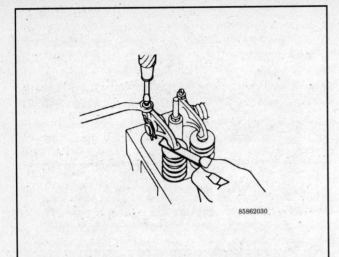

Fig. 29 Checking the valve lash — all engines except A-series

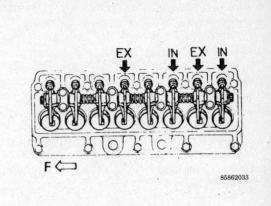

Fig. 32 Adjust these valves SECOND on the 3K-C engine

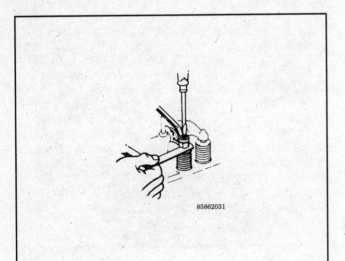

Fig. 30 Checking the valve lash on most A-series engines

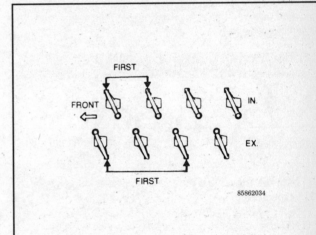

Fig. 33 Adjust these valves FIRST on the 2T-C and 3T-C engines

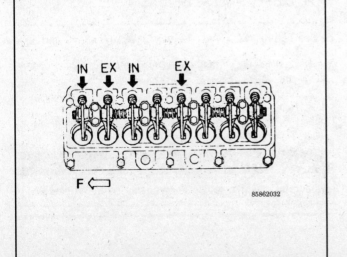

Fig. 31 Adjust these valves FIRST on the 3K-C engine

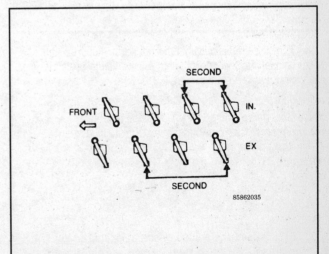

Fig. 34 Adjust these valves SECOND on the 2T-C and 3T-C engines

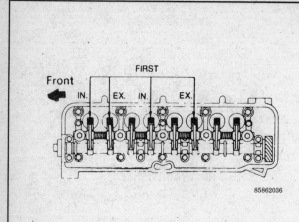

Fig. 35 Adjust these valves FIRST on A-series engines (except 4A-GE)

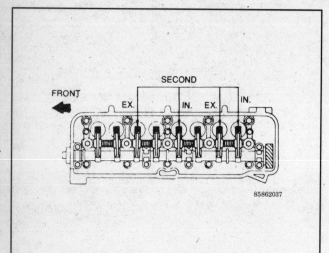

Fig. 36 Adjust these valves SECOND on A-series engines (except 4A-GE)

Fig. 37 Loosen the adjusting screw locknut (note: you should use a driver to keep the screw from turning while loosening the nut in order to preserve present adjustment)

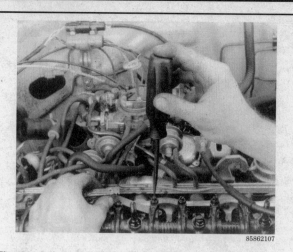

Fig. 38 Adjust the valve lash using a screwdriver to turn the adjusting screw and a feeler gauge to check clearance

Fig. 39 Keep the adjusting screw from turning and tighten the locknut to secure the adjustment

1C-L DIESEL AND 4A-GE GASOLINE ENGINES

▶ See Figures 40, 41, 42, 43, 44, 45, 46, 47, 48, 49 and 50

1. Start the engine and run it until it reaches normal operating temperature.
2. Stop the engine, then remove the air cleaner assembly.
3. Remove any other hoses, cables, etc. which are attached to, or in the way of, the, cylinder head (camshaft/valve) cover. Remove the cylinder head cover.

✳✳CAUTION

Be careful when removing components as the engine will be hot.

4. Use a wrench and turn the crankshaft until the notch in the pulley aligns with the timing pointer in the front cover. This will insure that the engine is at TDC.

➡**Check that the valve lifters on the No. 1 cylinder are loose and that those on the No. 4 cylinder are tight. If not, turn the crankshaft one complete revolution (360 degrees) and then realign the marks. When the engine is at No. 1 TDC the cylinder is ready for the spark plug to fire; meaning the valves should be closed.**

5. Using a flat feeler gauge, measure the clearance between the camshaft lobe and the valve lifter. This measurement should correspond to the specification provided earlier in this section on the tune-up chart. Check only the valves listed under "**First**" in the accompanying valve arrangement illustrations for your particular engine.

➡**If the measurement is within specifications, go on to the next step. If not, record the measurement taken for each individual valve.**

6. Turn the crankshaft one complete revolution and realign the timing marks as previously described.

7. Measure the clearance of the valves shown in the valve arrangement illustration marked "**Second.**"

➡**If the measurement for this set of valves (and also the previous one) is within specifications, you need go no further, the procedure is finished. If not, record the measurements and continue.**

8. Turn the crankshaft to position the intake camshaft lobe of the cylinder to be adjusted, upward.

9. Using a small screwdriver, turn the valve lifter so that the notch is easily accessible.

10. Install SST #09248-64010 (Diesel) or SST 09248-70012 (4A-GE) or equivalent, between the two camshaft lobes and then turn the handle so that the tool presses down both (intake and exhaust) valve lifters evenly. On the 4A-GE engine, the tool will work on only one lifter at a time.

11. Using a small screwdriver and a magnet, remove the valve shims.

12. Measure the thickness of the old shim with a micrometer. Locate that particular measurement in the Installed Shim Thickness column of the accompanying chart, then locate the already recorded measurement for that valve in the Measured Clearance column of the chart. Index the two columns to arrive at the proper replacement shim thickness.

➡**On Diesel engines, replacement shims are available in 25 sizes, in increments of 0.050mm (0.0020 in.), from 2.200mm (0.00866 in.) to 3.400mm (0.1399 in.). On the 4A-GE engine, shims are available from 2.500mm (0.984 in.) to 3.300mm (0.1299 in.).**

13. Install the new shim, remove the special tool and then recheck the valve clearance.

14. Installation of the remaining components is in the reverse order of removal. Check both the ignition timing and the idle speed after installation is complete and, if necessary, adjust.

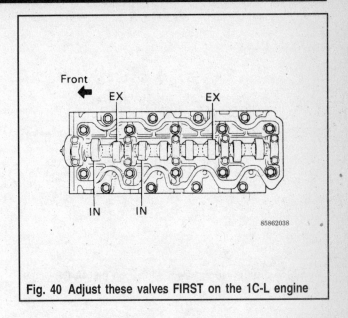

Fig. 40 Adjust these valves FIRST on the 1C-L engine

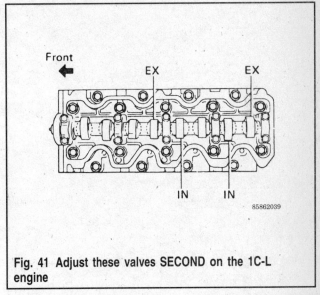

Fig. 41 Adjust these valves SECOND on the 1C-L engine

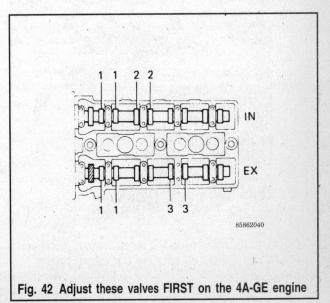

Fig. 42 Adjust these valves FIRST on the 4A-GE engine

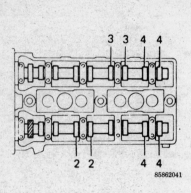

Fig. 43 Adjust these valves SECOND on the 4A-GE engine

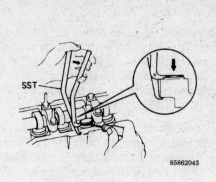

Fig. 45 Depressing the valve lifters in order to remove the shims — 4A-GE

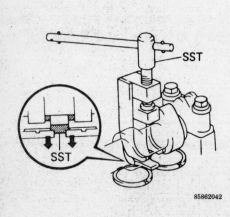

Fig. 44 A special tool must be used to depress the valve lifters — 1C-L shown

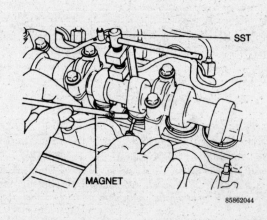

Fig. 46 Use a magnet and a screwdriver to remove the old valve shims

Intake

	Installed Shim Thickness (mm)																																															
Measured Clearance (mm)	2.200	2.225	2.250	2.275	2.300	2.325	2.350	2.375	2.400	2.425	2.450	2.475	2.500	2.525	2.550	2.575	2.600	2.625	2.650	2.675	2.700	2.725	2.750	2.775	2.800	2.825	2.850	2.875	2.900	2.925	2.950	2.975	3.000	3.025	3.050	3.075	3.100	3.125	3.150	3.175	3.200	3.225	3.250	3.275	3.300	3.325	3.350	3.375	3.400
0.000-0.025									01	01	01	03	03	05	05	07	07	09	09	11	11	13	13	15	15	17	17	19	19	21	21	23	23	25	25	27	27	29	29	31	31	33	33	35	35	37	37	39	39
0.026-0.050								01	01	01	03	03	05	05	07	07	09	09	11	11	13	13	15	15	17	17	19	19	21	21	23	23	25	25	27	27	29	29	31	31	33	33	35	35	37	37	39	39	41
0.051-0.075							01	01	01	03	03	05	05	07	07	09	09	11	11	13	13	15	15	17	17	19	19	21	21	23	23	25	25	27	27	29	29	31	31	33	33	35	35	37	37	39	39	41	41
0.076-0.100						01	01	01	03	03	05	05	07	07	09	09	11	11	13	13	15	15	17	17	19	19	21	21	23	23	25	25	27	27	29	29	31	31	33	33	35	35	37	37	39	39	41	41	43
0.101-0.125					01	01	01	03	03	05	05	07	07	09	09	11	11	13	13	15	15	17	17	19	19	21	21	23	23	25	25	27	27	29	29	31	31	33	33	35	35	37	37	39	39	41	41	43	43
0.126-0.150				01	01	01	03	03	05	05	07	07	09	09	11	11	13	13	15	15	17	17	19	19	21	21	23	23	25	25	27	27	29	29	31	31	33	33	35	35	37	37	39	39	41	41	43	43	45
0.151-0.175			01	01	01	03	03	05	05	07	07	09	09	11	11	13	13	15	15	17	17	19	19	21	21	23	23	25	25	27	27	29	29	31	31	33	33	35	35	37	37	39	39	41	41	43	43	45	45
0.176-0.199		01	01	01	03	03	05	05	07	07	09	09	11	11	13	13	15	15	17	17	19	19	21	21	23	23	25	25	27	27	29	29	31	31	33	33	35	35	37	37	39	39	41	41	43	43	45	45	47
0.200-0.300																																																	
0.301-0.325	03	05	05	07	07	09	09	11	11	13	13	15	15	17	17	19	19	21	21	23	23	25	25	27	27	29	29	31	31	33	33	35	35	37	37	39	39	41	41	43	43	45	45	47	47	49	49	49	
0.326-0.350	05	05	07	07	09	09	11	11	13	13	15	15	17	17	19	19	21	21	23	23	25	25	27	27	29	29	31	31	33	33	35	35	37	37	39	39	41	41	43	43	45	45	47	47	49	49	49		
0.351-0.375	05	07	07	09	09	11	11	13	13	15	15	17	17	19	19	21	21	23	23	25	25	27	27	29	29	31	31	33	33	35	35	37	37	39	39	41	41	43	43	45	45	47	47	49	49	49			
0.376-0.400	07	07	09	09	11	11	13	13	15	15	17	17	19	19	21	21	23	23	25	25	27	27	29	29	31	31	33	33	35	35	37	37	39	39	41	41	43	43	45	45	47	47	49	49	49				
0.401-0.425	07	09	09	11	11	13	13	15	15	17	17	19	19	21	21	23	23	25	25	27	27	29	29	31	31	33	33	35	35	37	37	39	39	41	41	43	43	45	45	47	47	49	49	49					
0.426-0.450	09	09	11	11	13	13	15	15	17	17	19	19	21	21	23	23	25	25	27	27	29	29	31	31	33	33	35	35	37	37	39	39	41	41	43	43	45	45	47	47	49	49	49						
0.451-0.475	09	11	11	13	13	15	15	17	17	19	19	21	21	23	23	25	25	27	27	29	29	31	31	33	33	35	35	37	37	39	39	41	41	43	43	45	45	47	47	49	49	49							
0.476-0.500	11	11	13	13	15	15	17	17	19	19	21	21	23	23	25	25	27	27	29	29	31	31	33	33	35	35	37	37	39	39	41	41	43	43	45	45	47	47	49	49	49								
0.501-0.525	11	13	13	15	15	17	17	19	19	21	21	23	23	25	25	27	27	29	29	31	31	33	33	35	35	37	37	39	39	41	41	43	43	45	45	47	47	49	49	49									
0.526-0.550	13	13	15	15	17	17	19	19	21	21	23	23	25	25	27	27	29	29	31	31	33	33	35	35	37	37	39	39	41	41	43	43	45	45	47	47	49	49	49										
0.551-0.575	13	15	15	17	17	19	19	21	21	23	23	25	25	27	27	29	29	31	31	33	33	35	35	37	37	39	39	41	41	43	43	45	45	47	47	49	49	49											
0.576-0.600	15	15	17	17	19	19	21	21	23	23	25	25	27	27	29	29	31	31	33	33	35	35	37	37	39	39	41	41	43	43	45	45	47	47	49	49	49												
0.601-0.625	15	17	17	19	19	21	21	23	23	25	25	27	27	29	29	31	31	33	33	35	35	37	37	39	39	41	41	43	43	45	45	47	47	49	49	49													
0.626-0.650	17	17	19	19	21	21	23	23	25	25	27	27	29	29	31	31	33	33	35	35	37	37	39	39	41	41	43	43	45	45	47	47	49	49	49														
0.651-0.675	17	19	19	21	21	23	23	25	25	27	27	29	29	31	31	33	33	35	35	37	37	39	39	41	41	43	43	45	45	47	47	49	49	49															
0.676-0.700	19	19	21	21	23	23	25	25	27	27	29	29	31	31	33	33	35	35	37	37	39	39	41	41	43	43	45	45	47	47	49	49	49																
0.701-0.725	19	21	21	23	23	25	25	27	27	29	29	31	31	33	33	35	35	37	37	39	39	41	41	43	43	45	45	47	47	49	49	49																	
0.726-0.750	21	21	23	23	25	25	27	27	29	29	31	31	33	33	35	35	37	37	39	39	41	41	43	43	45	45	47	47	49	49	49																		
0.751-0.775	21	23	23	25	25	27	27	29	29	31	31	33	33	35	35	37	37	39	39	41	41	43	43	45	45	47	47	49	49	49																			
0.776-0.800	23	23	25	25	27	27	29	29	31	31	33	33	35	35	37	37	39	39	41	41	43	43	45	45	47	47	49	49	49																				
0.801-0.825	23	25	25	27	27	29	29	31	31	33	33	35	35	37	37	39	39	41	41	43	43	45	45	47	47	49	49	49																					
0.826-0.850	25	25	27	27	29	29	31	31	33	33	35	35	37	37	39	39	41	41	43	43	45	45	47	47	49	49	49																						
0.851-0.875	25	27	27	29	29	31	31	33	33	35	35	37	37	39	39	41	41	43	43	45	45	47	47	49	49	49																							
0.876-0.900	27	27	29	29	31	31	33	33	35	35	37	37	39	39	41	41	43	43	45	45	47	47	49	49	49																								
0.901-0.925	27	29	29	31	31	33	33	35	35	37	37	39	39	41	41	43	43	45	45	47	47	49	49	49																									
0.926-0.950	29	29	31	31	33	33	35	35	37	37	39	39	41	41	43	43	45	45	47	47	49	49	49																										
0.951-0.975	29	31	31	33	33	35	35	37	37	39	39	41	41	43	43	45	45	47	47	49	49	49																											
0.976-1.000	31	31	33	33	35	35	37	37	39	39	41	41	43	43	45	45	47	47	49	49	49																												
1.001-1.025	31	33	33	35	35	37	37	39	39	41	41	43	43	45	45	47	47	49	49	49																													
1.026-1.050	33	33	35	35	37	37	39	39	41	41	43	43	45	45	47	47	49	49	49																														
1.051-1.075	33	35	35	37	37	39	39	41	41	43	43	45	45	47	47	49	49	49																															
1.076-1.100	35	35	37	37	39	39	41	41	43	43	45	45	47	47	49	49	49																																
1.101-1.125	35	37	37	39	39	41	41	43	43	45	45	47	47	49	49	49																																	
1.126-1.150	37	37	39	39	41	41	43	43	45	45	47	47	49	49	49																																		
1.151-1.175	37	39	39	41	41	43	43	45	45	47	47	49	49	49																																			
1.176-1.200	39	39	41	41	43	43	45	45	47	47	49	49	49																																				
1.201-1.225	39	41	41	43	43	45	45	47	47	49	49	49																																					
1.226-1.250	41	41	43	43	45	45	47	47	49	49	49																																						
1.251-1.275	41	43	43	45	45	47	47	49	49	49																																							
1.276-1.300	43	43	45	45	47	47	49	49	49																																								
1.301-1.325	43	45	45	47	47	49	49	49																																									
1.320-1.350	45	45	47	47	49	49	49																																										
1.351-1.375	45	47	47	49	49	49																																											
1.376-1.400	47	47	49	49	49																																												
1.401-1.425	47	49	49	49																																													
1.426-1.450	49	49	49																																														
1.451-1.475	49	49																																															
1.476-1.500	49																																																

Intake Valve Clearance (cold): 0.20 – 0.30 mm (0.008 – 0.012 in.)

Example: 2.700 mm (0.1063 in.) shim installed
Measured clearance is 0.350 mm (0.0138 in.).
Replace 2.700 mm (0.1063 in.) shim with shim No. 25.

Shim Thickness

Shim No.	Thickness mm (in.)	Shim No.	Thickness mm (in.)
01	2.20 (0.0866)	27	2.85 (0.1122)
03	2.25 (0.0886)	29	2.90 (0.1142)
05	2.30 (0.0906)	31	2.95 (0.1161)
07	2.35 (0.0925)	33	3.00 (0.1181)
09	2.40 (0.0945)	35	3.05 (0.1201)
11	2.45 (0.0965)	37	3.10 (0.1220)
13	2.50 (0.0984)	39	3.15 (0.1240)
15	2.55 (0.1004)	41	3.20 (0.1260)
17	2.60 (0.1024)	43	3.25 (0.1280)
19	2.65 (0.1043)	45	3.30 (0.1299)
21	2.70 (0.1063)	47	3.35 (0.1319)
23	2.75 (0.1083)	49	3.40 (0.1339)
25	2.80 (0.1102)		

85862045

Fig. 47 Valve shim selection chart — 1C-L engine (In)

Exhaust

Measured Clearance (mm)	Installed Shim Thickness (mm)																																																
	2.200	2.225	2.250	2.275	2.300	2.325	2.350	2.375	2.400	2.425	2.450	2.475	2.500	2.525	2.550	2.575	2.600	2.625	2.650	2.675	2.700	2.725	2.750	2.775	2.800	2.825	2.850	2.875	2.900	2.925	2.950	2.975	3.000	3.025	3.050	3.075	3.100	3.125	3.150	3.175	3.200	3.225	3.250	3.275	3.300	3.325	3.350	3.375	3.400
0.000-0.025											01	01	01	03	03	05	05	07	07	09	09	11	11	13	13	15	15	17	17	19	19	21	21	23	23	25	25	27	27	29	29	31	31	33	33	35	35	37	37
0.026-0.050										01	01	01	03	03	05	05	07	07	09	09	11	11	13	13	15	15	17	17	19	19	21	21	23	23	25	25	27	27	29	29	31	31	33	33	35	35	37	37	39
0.051-0.075									01	01	01	03	03	05	05	07	07	09	09	11	11	13	13	15	15	17	17	19	19	21	21	23	23	25	25	27	27	29	29	31	31	33	33	35	35	37	37	39	39
0.076-0.100								01	01	01	03	03	05	05	07	07	09	09	11	11	13	13	15	15	17	17	19	19	21	21	23	23	25	25	27	27	29	29	31	31	33	33	35	35	37	37	39	39	41
0.101-0.125							01	01	01	03	03	05	05	07	07	09	09	11	11	13	13	15	15	17	17	19	19	21	21	23	23	25	25	27	27	29	29	31	31	33	33	35	35	37	37	39	39	41	41
0.126-0.150						01	01	01	03	03	05	05	07	07	09	09	11	11	13	13	15	15	17	17	19	19	21	21	23	23	25	25	27	27	29	29	31	31	33	33	35	35	37	37	39	39	41	41	43
0.151-0.175					01	01	01	03	03	05	05	07	07	09	09	11	11	13	13	15	15	17	17	19	19	21	21	23	23	25	25	27	27	29	29	31	31	33	33	35	35	37	37	39	39	41	41	43	43
0.176-0.200				01	01	01	03	03	05	05	07	07	09	09	11	11	13	13	15	15	17	17	19	19	21	21	23	23	25	25	27	27	29	29	31	31	33	33	35	35	37	37	39	39	41	41	43	43	45
0.201-0.225			01	01	01	03	03	05	05	07	07	09	09	11	11	13	13	15	15	17	17	19	19	21	21	23	23	25	25	27	27	29	29	31	31	33	33	35	35	37	37	39	39	41	41	43	43	45	45
0.226-0.249		01	01	01	03	03	05	05	07	07	09	09	11	11	13	13	15	15	17	17	19	19	21	21	23	23	25	25	27	27	29	29	31	31	33	33	35	35	37	37	39	39	41	41	43	43	45	45	47
0.250-0.350																																																	
0.351-0.375	03	05	05	07	07	09	09	11	11	13	13	15	15	17	17	19	19	21	21	23	23	25	25	27	27	29	29	31	31	33	33	35	35	37	37	39	39	41	41	43	43	45	45	47	47	49	49	49	
0.376-0.400	05	05	07	07	09	09	11	11	13	13	15	15	17	17	19	19	21	21	23	23	25	25	27	27	29	29	31	31	33	33	35	35	37	37	39	39	41	41	43	43	45	45	47	47	49	49	49		
0.401-0.425	05	07	07	09	09	11	11	13	13	15	15	17	17	19	19	21	21	23	23	25	25	27	27	29	29	31	31	33	33	35	35	37	37	39	39	41	41	43	43	45	45	47	47	49	49	49			
0.426-0.450	07	07	09	09	11	11	13	13	15	15	17	17	19	19	21	21	23	23	25	25	27	27	29	29	31	31	33	33	35	35	37	37	39	39	41	41	43	43	45	45	47	47	49	49	49				
0.451-0.475	07	09	09	11	11	13	13	15	15	17	17	19	19	21	21	23	23	25	25	27	27	29	29	31	31	33	33	35	35	37	37	39	39	41	41	43	43	45	45	47	47	49	49	49					
0.476-0.500	09	09	11	11	13	13	15	15	17	17	19	19	21	21	23	23	25	25	27	27	29	29	31	31	33	33	35	35	37	37	39	39	41	41	43	43	45	45	47	47	49	49	49						
0.501-0.525	09	11	11	13	13	15	15	17	17	19	19	21	21	23	23	25	25	27	27	29	29	31	31	33	33	35	35	37	37	39	39	41	41	43	43	45	45	47	47	49	49	49							
0.526-0.550	11	11	13	13	15	15	17	17	19	19	21	21	23	23	25	25	27	27	29	29	31	31	33	33	35	35	37	37	39	39	41	41	43	43	45	45	47	47	49	49	49								
0.551-0.575	11	13	13	15	15	17	17	19	19	21	21	23	23	25	25	27	27	29	29	31	31	33	33	35	35	37	37	39	39	41	41	43	43	45	45	47	47	49	49	49									
0.576-0.600	13	13	15	15	17	17	19	19	21	21	23	23	25	25	27	27	29	29	31	31	33	33	35	35	37	37	39	39	41	41	43	43	45	45	47	47	49	49	49										
0.601-0.625	13	15	15	17	17	19	19	21	21	23	23	25	25	27	27	29	29	31	31	33	33	35	35	37	37	39	39	41	41	43	43	45	45	47	47	49	49	49											
0.626-0.650	15	15	17	17	19	19	21	21	23	23	25	25	27	27	29	29	31	31	33	33	35	35	37	37	39	39	41	41	43	43	45	45	47	47	49	49	49												
0.651-0.675	15	17	17	19	19	21	21	23	23	25	25	27	27	29	29	31	31	33	33	35	35	37	37	39	39	41	41	43	43	45	45	47	47	49	49	49													
0.676-0.701	17	17	19	19	21	21	23	23	25	25	27	27	29	29	31	31	33	33	35	35	37	37	39	39	41	41	43	43	45	45	47	47	49	49	49														
0.701-0.725	17	19	19	21	21	23	23	25	25	27	27	29	29	31	31	33	33	35	35	37	37	39	39	41	41	43	43	45	45	47	47	49	49	49															
0.726-0.750	19	19	21	21	23	23	25	25	27	27	29	29	31	31	33	33	35	35	37	37	39	39	41	41	43	43	45	45	47	47	49	49	49																
0.751-0.775	19	21	21	23	23	25	25	27	27	29	29	31	31	33	33	35	35	37	37	39	39	41	41	43	43	45	45	47	47	49	49	49																	
0.776-0.800	21	21	23	23	25	25	27	27	29	29	31	31	33	33	35	35	37	37	39	39	41	41	43	43	45	45	47	47	49	49	49																		
0.801-0.825	21	23	23	25	25	27	27	29	29	31	31	33	33	35	35	37	37	39	39	41	41	43	43	45	45	47	47	49	49	49																			
0.826-0.850	23	23	25	25	27	27	29	29	31	31	33	33	35	35	37	37	39	39	41	41	43	43	45	45	47	47	49	49	49																				
0.851-0.875	23	25	25	27	27	29	29	31	31	33	33	35	35	37	37	39	39	41	41	43	43	45	45	47	47	49	49	49																					
0.876-0.900	25	25	27	27	29	29	31	31	33	33	35	35	37	37	39	39	41	41	43	43	45	45	47	47	49	49	49																						
0.901-0.925	25	27	27	29	29	31	31	33	33	35	35	37	37	39	39	41	41	43	43	45	45	47	47	49	49	49																							
0.926-0.950	27	27	29	29	31	31	33	33	35	35	37	37	39	39	41	41	43	43	45	45	47	47	49	49	49																								
0.951-0.975	27	29	29	31	31	33	33	35	35	37	37	39	39	41	41	43	43	45	45	47	47	49	49	49																									
0.976-1.000	29	29	31	31	33	33	35	35	37	37	39	39	41	41	43	43	45	45	47	47	49	49	49																										
1.001-1.025	29	31	31	33	33	35	35	37	37	39	39	41	41	43	43	45	45	47	47	49	49	49																											
1.026-1.050	31	31	33	33	35	35	37	37	39	39	41	41	43	43	45	45	47	47	49	49	49																												
1.051-1.075	31	33	33	35	35	37	37	39	39	41	41	43	43	45	45	47	47	49	49	49																													
1.076-1.100	33	33	35	35	37	37	39	39	41	41	43	43	45	45	47	47	49	49	49																														
1.101-1.125	33	35	35	37	37	39	39	41	41	43	43	45	45	47	47	49	49	49																															
1.126-1.150	35	35	37	37	39	39	41	41	43	43	45	45	47	47	49	49	49																																
1.151-1.175	35	37	37	39	39	41	41	43	43	45	45	47	47	49	49	49																																	
1.176-1.200	37	37	39	39	41	41	43	43	45	45	47	47	49	49	49																																		
1.201-1.225	37	39	39	41	41	43	43	45	45	47	47	49	49	49																																			
1.226-1.250	39	39	41	41	43	43	45	45	47	47	49	49	49																																				
1.251-1.275	39	41	41	43	43	45	45	47	47	49	49	49																																					
1.276-1.300	41	41	43	43	45	45	47	47	49	49	49																																						
1.301-1.325	41	43	43	45	45	47	47	49	49	49																																							
1.326-1.350	43	43	45	45	47	47	49	49	49																																								
1.351-1.375	43	45	45	47	47	49	49	49																																									
1.376-1.400	45	45	47	47	49	49	49																																										
1.401-1.425	45	47	47	49	49	49																																											
1.426-1.450	47	47	49	49	49																																												
1.451-1.475	47	49	49	49																																													
1.476-1.500	49	49	49																																														
1.501-1.525	49	49																																																
1.526-1.550	49																																																	

Exhaust Valve Clearance (cold): 0.25 – 0.35 mm (0.0010 – 0.014 in.)

Example: 2.700 mm (0.1063 in.) shim installed
Measured clearance is 0.450 mm (0.0177 in.).
Replace 2.700 mm (0.1063 in.) shim with shim No. 27.

Shim Thickness

Shim No.	Thickness mm (in.)	Shim No.	Thickness mm (in.)
01	2.20 (0.0866)	27	2.85 (0.1122)
03	2.25 (0.0886)	29	2.90 (0.1142)
05	2.30 (0.0906)	31	2.95 (0.1161)
07	2.35 (0.0925)	33	3.00 (0.1181)
09	2.40 (0.0945)	35	3.05 (0.1201)
11	2.45 (0.0965)	37	3.10 (0.1220)
13	2.50 (0.0984)	39	3.15 (0.1240)
15	2.55 (0.1004)	41	3.20 (0.1260)
17	2.60 (0.1024)	43	3.25 (0.1280)
19	2.65 (0.1043)	45	3.30 (0.1299)
21	2.70 (0.1063)	47	3.35 (0.1319)
23	2.75 (0.1083)	49	3.40 (0.1339)
25	2.80 (0.1102)		

85862046

Fig. 48 Valve shim selection chart — 1C-L engine (Ex)

Intake

Installed shim thickness (mm)

Measured clearance (mm)	2.500	2.525	2.550	2.575	2.600	2.625	2.650	2.675	2.700	2.725	2.750	2.775	2.800	2.825	2.850	2.875	2.900	2.925	2.950	2.975	3.000	3.025	3.050	3.075	3.100	3.125	3.150	3.175	3.200	3.225	3.250	3.275	3.300
0.000–0.025							02	02	02	04	04	06	06	08	08	10	10	12	12	14	14	16	16	18	18	20	20	22	22	24	24	26	26
0.026–0.050						02	02	02	04	04	06	06	08	08	10	10	12	12	14	14	16	16	18	18	20	20	22	22	24	24	26	26	28
0.051–0.075					02	02	02	04	04	06	06	08	08	10	10	12	12	14	14	16	16	18	18	20	20	22	22	24	24	26	26	28	28
0.076–0.100				02	02	02	04	04	06	06	08	08	10	10	12	12	14	14	16	16	18	18	20	20	22	22	24	24	26	26	28	28	30
0.101–0.125			02	02	02	04	04	06	06	08	08	10	10	12	12	14	14	16	16	18	18	20	20	22	22	24	24	26	26	28	28	30	30
0.126–0.149		02	02	02	04	04	06	06	08	08	10	10	12	12	14	14	16	16	18	18	20	20	22	22	24	24	26	26	28	28	30	30	32
0.150–0.250																																	
0.251–0.275	04	06	06	08	08	10	10	12	12	14	14	16	16	18	18	20	20	22	22	24	24	26	26	28	28	30	30	32	32	34	34	34	
0.276–0.300	06	06	08	08	10	10	12	12	14	14	16	16	18	18	20	20	22	22	24	24	26	26	28	28	30	30	32	32	34	34	34		
0.301–0.325	06	08	08	10	10	12	12	14	14	16	16	18	18	20	20	22	22	24	24	26	26	28	28	30	30	32	32	34	34	34			
0.326–0.350	08	08	10	10	12	12	14	14	16	16	18	18	20	20	22	22	24	24	26	26	28	28	30	30	32	32	34	34	34				
0.351–0.375	08	10	10	12	12	14	14	16	16	18	18	20	20	22	22	24	24	26	26	28	28	30	30	32	32	34	34	34					
0.376–0.400	10	10	12	12	14	14	16	16	18	18	20	20	22	22	24	24	26	26	28	28	30	30	32	32	34	34	34						
0.401–0.425	10	12	12	14	14	16	16	18	18	20	20	22	22	24	24	26	26	28	28	30	30	32	32	34	34	34							
0.426–0.450	12	12	14	14	16	16	18	18	20	20	22	22	24	24	26	26	28	28	30	30	32	32	34	34	34								
0.451–0.475	12	14	14	16	16	18	18	20	20	22	22	24	24	26	26	28	28	30	30	32	32	34	34	34									
0.476–0.500	14	14	16	16	18	18	20	20	22	22	24	24	26	26	28	28	30	30	32	32	34	34	34										
0.501–0.525	14	16	16	18	18	20	20	22	22	24	24	26	26	28	28	30	30	32	32	34	34	34											
0.526–0.550	16	16	18	18	20	20	22	22	24	24	26	26	28	28	30	30	32	32	34	34	34												
0.551–0.575	16	18	18	20	20	22	22	24	24	26	26	28	28	30	30	32	32	34	34	34													
0.576–0.600	18	18	20	20	22	22	24	24	26	26	28	28	30	30	32	32	34	34	34														
0.601–0.625	18	20	20	22	22	24	24	26	26	28	28	30	30	32	32	34	34	34															
0.626–0.650	20	20	22	22	24	24	26	26	28	28	30	30	32	32	34	34	34																
0.651–0.675	20	22	22	24	24	26	26	28	28	30	30	32	32	34	34	34																	
0.676–0.700	22	22	24	24	26	26	28	28	30	30	32	32	34	34	34																		
0.701–0.725	22	24	24	26	26	28	28	30	30	32	32	34	34	34																			
0.726–0.750	24	24	26	26	28	28	30	30	32	32	34	34	34																				
0.751–0.775	24	26	26	28	28	30	30	32	32	34	34	34																					
0.776–0.800	26	26	28	28	30	30	32	32	34	34	34																						
0.801–0.825	26	28	28	30	30	32	32	34	34	34																							
0.826–0.850	28	28	30	30	32	32	34	34	34																								
0.851–0.875	28	30	30	32	32	34	34	34																									
0.876–0.900	30	30	32	32	34	34	34																										
0.901–0.925	30	32	32	34	34	34																											
0.926–0.950	32	32	34	34	34																												
0.951–0.975	32	34	34	34																													
0.976–1.000	34	34	34																														
1.001–1.025	34	34																															
1.026–1.050	34																																

Intake valve clearance (cold):
0.15 – 0.25 mm (0.006 – 0.010 in.)

Example: **2.800 mm installed is**
Measured clearance is 0.450 mm
Replace 2.800 mm shim with
shim No. 24 (3.050 mm).

Shim thickness mm (in.)

Shim No.	Thickness	Shim No.	Thickness
02	2.500 (0.0984)	20	2.950 (0.1161)
04	2.550 (0.1004)	22	3.000 (0.1181)
06	2.600 (0.1024)	24	3.050 (0.1201)
08	2.650 (0.1043)	26	3.100 (0.1220)
10	2.700 (0.1063)	28	3.150 (0.1240)
12	2.750 (0.1083)	30	3.200 (0.1260)
14	2.800 (0.1102)	32	3.250 (0.1280)
16	2.850 (0.1122)	34	3.300 (0.1299)
18	2.900 (0.1142)		

85862047

Fig. 49 Valve shim selection chart — 4A-GE (In)

Exhaust

Measured clearance (mm) \ Installed shim thickness (mm)	2.500	2.525	2.550	2.575	2.600	2.625	2.650	2.675	2.700	2.725	2.750	2.775	2.800	2.825	2.850	2.875	2.900	2.925	2.950	2.975	3.000	3.025	3.050	3.075	3.100	3.125	3.150	3.175	3.200	3.225	3.250	3.275	3.300
0.000—0.025									02	02	02	04	04	06	06	08	08	10	10	12	12	14	14	16	16	18	18	20	20	22	22	24	24
0.026—0.050								02	02	02	04	04	06	06	08	08	10	10	12	12	14	14	16	16	18	18	20	20	22	22	24	24	26
0.051—0.075							02	02	02	04	04	06	06	08	08	10	10	12	12	14	14	16	16	18	18	20	20	22	22	24	24	26	26
0.076—0.100						02	02	02	04	04	06	06	08	08	10	10	12	12	14	14	16	16	18	18	20	20	22	22	24	24	26	26	28
0.101—0.125					02	02	02	04	04	06	06	08	08	10	10	12	12	14	14	16	16	18	18	20	20	22	22	24	24	26	26	28	28
0.126—0.150				02	02	02	04	04	06	06	08	08	10	10	12	12	14	14	16	16	18	18	20	20	22	22	24	24	26	26	28	28	30
0.151—0.175			02	02	02	04	04	06	06	08	08	10	10	12	12	14	14	16	16	18	18	20	20	22	22	24	24	26	26	28	28	30	30
0.176—0.199		02	02	02	04	04	06	06	08	08	10	10	12	12	14	14	16	16	18	18	20	20	22	22	24	24	26	26	28	28	30	30	32
0.200—0.300																																	
0.301—0.325	04	06	06	08	08	10	10	12	12	14	14	16	16	18	18	20	20	22	22	24	24	26	26	28	28	30	30	32	32	34	34	34	
0.326—0.350	06	06	08	08	10	10	12	12	14	14	16	16	18	18	20	20	22	22	24	24	26	26	28	28	30	30	32	32	34	34	34		
0.351—0.375	06	08	08	10	10	12	12	14	14	16	16	18	18	20	20	22	22	24	24	26	26	28	28	30	30	32	32	34	34	34			
0.376—0.400	08	08	10	10	12	12	14	14	16	16	18	18	20	20	22	22	24	24	26	26	28	28	30	30	32	32	34	34	34				
0.401—0.425	08	10	10	12	12	14	14	16	16	18	18	20	20	22	22	24	24	26	26	28	28	30	30	32	32	34	34	34					
0.426—0.450	10	10	12	12	14	14	16	16	18	18	20	20	22	22	24	24	26	26	28	28	30	30	32	32	34	34	34						
0.451—0.475	10	12	12	14	14	16	16	18	18	20	20	22	22	24	24	26	26	28	28	30	30	32	32	34	34	34							
0.476—0.500	12	12	14	14	16	16	18	18	20	20	22	22	24	24	26	26	28	28	30	30	32	32	34	34	34								
0.501—0.525	12	14	14	16	16	18	18	20	20	22	22	24	24	26	26	28	28	30	30	32	32	34	34	34									
0.526—0.550	14	14	16	16	18	18	20	20	22	22	24	24	26	26	28	28	30	30	32	32	34	34	34										
0.551—0.575	14	16	16	18	18	20	20	22	22	24	24	26	26	28	28	30	30	32	32	34	34	34											
0.576—0.600	16	16	18	18	20	20	22	22	24	24	26	26	28	28	30	30	32	32	34	34	34												
0.601—0.625	16	18	18	20	20	22	22	24	24	26	26	28	28	30	30	32	32	34	34	34													
0.626—0.650	18	18	20	20	22	22	24	24	26	26	28	28	30	30	32	32	34	34	34														
0.651—0.675	18	20	20	22	22	24	24	26	26	28	28	30	30	32	32	34	34	34															
0.676—0.700	20	20	22	22	24	24	26	26	28	28	30	30	32	32	34	34	34																
0.701—0.725	20	22	22	24	24	26	26	28	28	30	30	32	32	34	34	34																	
0.726—0.750	22	22	24	24	26	26	28	28	30	30	32	32	34	34	34																		
0.751—0.775	22	24	24	26	26	28	28	30	30	32	32	34	34	34																			
0.776—0.800	24	24	26	26	28	28	30	30	32	32	34	34	34																				
0.801—0.825	24	26	26	28	28	30	30	32	32	34	34	34																					
0.826—0.850	26	26	28	28	30	30	32	32	34	34	34																						
0.851—0.875	26	28	28	30	30	32	32	34	34	34																							
0.876—0.900	28	28	30	30	32	32	34	34	34																								
0.901—0.925	28	30	30	32	32	34	34	34																									
0.926—0.950	30	30	32	32	34	34	34																										
0.951—0.975	30	32	32	34	34	34																											
0.976—1.000	32	32	34	34	34																												
1.001—1.025	32	34	34	34																													
1.026—1.050	34	34	34																														
1.051—1.075	34	34																															
1.076—1.100	34																																

Exhaust valve clearance (cold):
0.20 – 0.30 mm (0.008 – 0.012 in.)

Example: **2.800 mm Installed is**
Measured clearance is 0.450 mm
Replace 2.800 mm shim with
shim No. 22 (3.000 mm).

Shim thickness mm (in.)

Shim No.	Thickness	Shim No.	Thickness
02	2.500 (0.0984)	20	2.950 (0.1161)
04	2.550 (0.1004)	22	3.000 (0.1181)
06	2.600 (0.1024)	24	3.050 (0.1201)
08	2.650 (0.1043)	26	3.100 (0.1220)
10	2.700 (0.1063)	28	3.150 (0.1240)
12	2.750 (0.1083)	30	3.200 (0.1260)
14	2.800 (0.1102)	32	3.250 (0.1280)
16	2.850 (0.1122)	34	3.300 (0.1299)
18	2.900 (0.1142)		

85862048

Fig. 50 Valve shim selection chart — 4A-GE (Ex)

IDLE SPEED AND MIXTURE ADJUSTMENTS

Carburetor/Fuel Injection

This section contains only adjustments as they normally apply to engine tune-up. Descriptions of the carburetor or fuel injection systems and other procedures can be found in Section 5 of this manual.

GENERAL INFORMATION

When the engine in your Toyota is running, air/fuel mixture from the carburetor is being drawn into the engine by a partial vacuum which is created by the downward movement of the pistons on the intake stroke of the 4-stroke cycle of the engine. The amount of air/fuel mixture that enters the engine is controlled by throttle plates in the bottom of the carburetor. When the engine is not running the throttle plates are closed, blocking off the bottom of the carburetor from the inside of the engine. The throttle plates are connected, through the throttle linkage, to the gas pedal in the passenger compartment of the car. After you start the engine and put the transmission in gear, you depress the gas pedal to start the car moving. What you actually are doing when you depress the gas pedal is opening the throttle plate in the carburetor to admit more of the air/fuel mixture to the engine. The further you open the throttle plates in the carburetor, the higher the engine speed becomes.

As previously stated, when the engine is not running, the throttle plates in the carburetor are closed. But, in order for the engine to idle, it is necessary to open the throttle plates slightly. To prevent having to keep your foot on the gas pedal when the engine is idling, an idle speed adjusting screw was added to the carburetor. This screw has the same effect as keeping your foot slightly depressed on the gas pedal. The idle speed adjusting screw contacts a lever (the throttle lever) on the outside of the carburetor. When the screw is turned in, it opens the throttle plate on the carburetor, raising the idle speed of the engine. This screw is called the curb idle adjusting screw, and the procedures in this section will tell you how to adjust it.

Fuel injected engines function in a similar manner. Vacuum is used to draw the air/fuel mixture into the engine, but fuel injectors are used to introduce this fuel just upstream from the appropriate intake valve. The throttle plate is still used to control engine speed by the amount of air allowed into the engine, then the computer control module will regulator fuel delivery based on input from various sensors (including the throttle position). Again, an idle speed screw is used to set the curb idle speed.

On carbureted engines, it is difficult for the engine to draw the air/fuel mixture from the carburetor with the small amount of throttle plate opening that is present when the engine is idling. Because of this, an idle mixture passage is provided in the bottom of the carburetor below the throttle plates. This idle mixture passage contains an adjusting screw which restricts the amount of air/fuel mixture that enters the engine at idle. the procedure given in this section will tell how to set the idle mixture adjusting screw.

ADJUSTMENTS

1970-74

◗ See Figures 51 and 52

➡Perform the following adjustments with the air cleaner in place. When adjusting the idle speed and mixture, the gear selector should be placed in Drive (D) on 1970-73 models equipped with an automatic transmission. Be sure to set the parking brake and block the drive wheels. On all cars equipped with manual transmissions and all 1974 automatics, adjust the idle speed with the gearshift in Neutral (N).

1. Run the engine until it reaches normal operating temperature, then stop the engine.
2. Connect a tachometer to the engine as detailed in the manufacturer's instructions, but keeping the following in mind:
    a. On models equipped with a conventional ignition system, one lead (usually black) goes to a good chassis ground. The other lead (usually red) goes to the distributor primary side of the coil (the terminal with small wire running to the distributor body);
    b. On models with transistorized ignition, connect one lead (usually black) of the tachometer to a good chassis ground. Connect the other lead (usually red) to the negative (-) coil terminal; NOT to the distributor or positive (+) side. Connecting the tach to the wrong side will damage the switching transistor.
3. Remove the plug and install a vacuum gauge in the manifold vacuum port by using a suitable metric adaptor.
4. Start the engine and allow it to stabilize at idle.
5. Turn the idle speed screw until the engine runs smoothly at the lowest possible engine speed without stalling.
6. Turn the idle speed screw until the vacuum gauge indicates the highest specified reading (please refer to the vacuum at idle chart) at the specified idle speed. (For idle speed infor-

Vacuum at Idle
(in. Hg)

Year	Engine	Transmission	Minimum Vacuum Gauge Reading
1970-72	3K-C	All	16.9
	2T-C	All	16.9
1973	3K-C	MT	16.5
	2T-C	MT	16.9
		AT	14.1
1974	3K-C	MT	16.5
	2T-C ①	All	16.9
	2T-C ②	All	15.7

MT—anual transmission
AT—Automatic transmission
① All US cars except California
② California only

85862050

mation, please refer to the tune-up specifications chart located earlier in this section.)

7. Tighten the idle speed screw to the point just before the engine rpm and vacuum readings drop off.

8. Remove the tachometer and the vacuum gauge. Install the plug back in the manifold vacuum port. Road test the vehicle.

9. In some states, emission inspection is required. In such cases, you should take your car to a diagnostic center which has an HC/CO meter, and have the idle emission level checked to be sure that it is in accordance with state regulations. Starting 1974, CO levels at idle are normally provided on the engine tune-up decal under the hood.

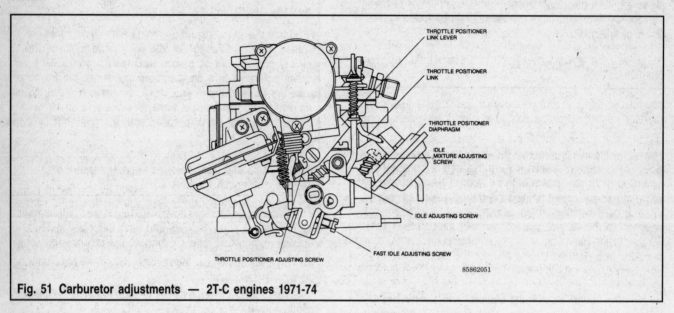

Fig. 51 Carburetor adjustments — 2T-C engines 1971-74

85862051

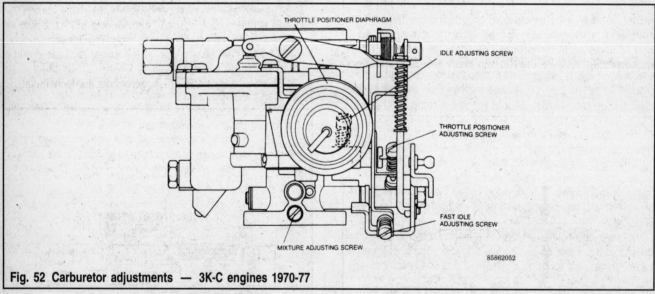

Fig. 52 Carburetor adjustments — 3K-C engines 1970-77

85862052

1975 and Later (Except 1C-L Diesel)

▶ **See Figures 53, 54, 55, 56, 57, 58 and 59**

The idle speed and mixture should be adjusted under the following conditions: the air cleaner must be installed, the choke fully opened, the transmission should be in Neutral (N), all accessories should be turned off, all vacuum lines should be connected, and the ignition timing should be set to specification. Be sure to firmly set the parking brake and block the drive wheels for additional safety.

1. Start the engine and allow it to reach normal operating temperature (180°).

2. Check the float setting; the fuel level should be just about even with the spot on the sight glass. If the fuel level is too high or low, adjust the float level. For details, please refer to Section 5 of this manual.

➡**1983 and later A-series engines require a special type of tachometer which hooks up to the service connector wire coming out of the distributor. As many tachometers are not compatible with this hook-up, we recommend that you consult with the manufacturer before purchasing a certain type.**

3. Connect a tachometer in accordance with the manufacturer's instructions. However, connect the tachometer positive (+) lead to the coil. Negative (-) terminal. Do NOT hook it up to the distributor or positive (+) side; damage to the transistorized ignition will result.

➡**On 1980 and later models, all of which have tamperproof idle mixture screws, merely turn the idle speed adjusting screw until the proper idle speed is obtained (for specifications refer to the tune-up chart earlier in this sec-**

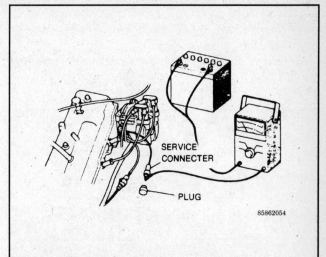

Fig. 54 1983 and later A-series engines require a special tachometer hook-up

tion). Disregard the steps following idle speed adjustment, as they do not apply to 1980 and later vehicles. Instead, shut the engine OFF and disconnect the tachometer.

4. Turn the idle speed adjusting screw to obtain the correct curb idle speed.

5. Turn the idle mixture adjusting screw to increase the idle speed as much as is possible.

6. Turn the idle speed screw to again obtain the correct curb idle speed, then if possible, turn the idle mixture screw to increase the idle speed again. Keep repeating this step until the idle mixture adjusting screw will no longer increase the idle speed.

7. Shut the engine OFF, then disconnect the tachometer.

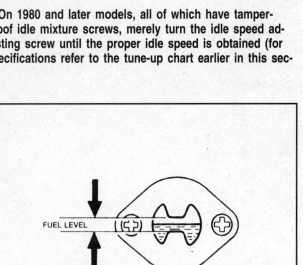

Fig. 53 Check the fuel level in the float bowl through the site glass

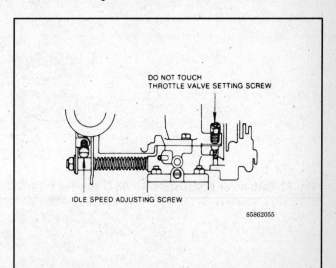

Fig. 55 Carburetor adjustments for 1978 and later 3K-C engine

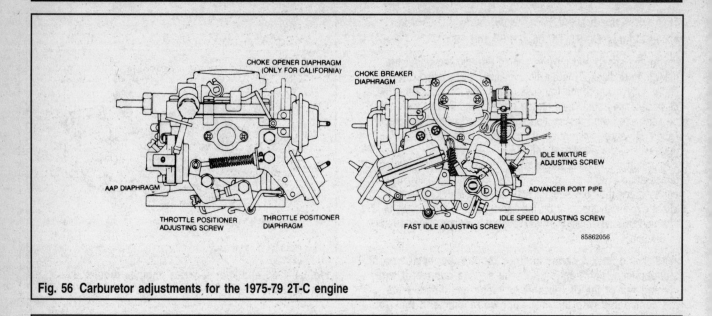

Fig. 56 Carburetor adjustments for the 1975-79 2T-C engine

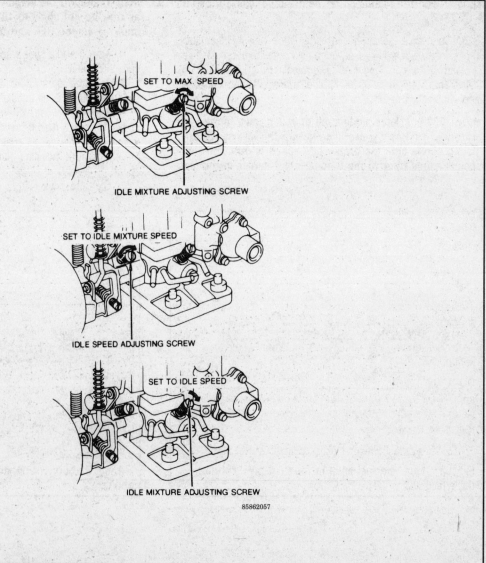

Fig. 57 Carburetor adjustment points — 3T-C engine

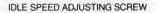
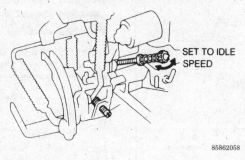

IDLE SPEED ADJUSTING SCREW

SET TO IDLE
SPEED

85862058

Fig. 58 Idle speed adjustment on the 4A-C engine

85862109

Fig. 59 The idle speed adjusting screw on many late model engines (such as the 4A-C) utilizes a thumb knob to ease adjustment

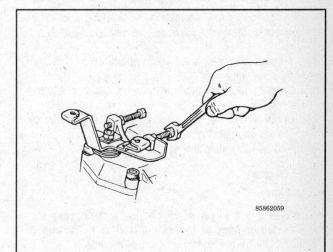

85862059

Fig. 60 Adjusting the idle speed on the 1C-L diesel engine

1C-L Diesel Engine

▶ **See Figures 60, 61 and 62**

1. Run the engine until it reaches normal operating temperature.

➡**The air cleaner should be in place, all accessories should be turned off and the transmission should be in Neutral. Be sure to firmly set the parking brake and block the drive wheels.**

2. Install a tachometer that is compatible with diesel engines.

3. Disconnect the accelerator cable from the injection pump and then check that the idle speed is within specifications. If not, adjust it using the adjustment screw on the injection pump.

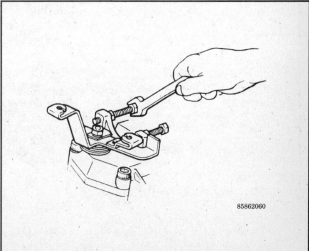

85862060

Fig. 61 Adjusting the maximum speed on the diesel engine

Fig. 62 After adjustments, connect the accelerator cable and adjust so there is no slack

4. With the tachometer still connected, check the engine maximum speed by fully depressing the adjusting lever on the injection pump. Maximum speed should be approximately 5,100 rpm.

5. If maximum speed is not within specifications, turn the adjusting screw until it is.

6. Connect the accelerator cable and adjust it so that there is no slack.

7. Check to see that the adjusting lever is stopped by the maximum speed adjusting screw when the accelerator pedal is depressed all the way to the floor.

4A-GE Engine

▶ See Figure 63

➡ **Idle speed is the only service adjustment possible for fuel injected engines as the air/fuel mixture is controlled electronically by the computer control module.**

1. Connect a tachometer (follow the tachometer manufacturer's directions) to the engine. Run the engine until the normal operating temperature is reached. Make sure that the air cleaner is installed, all pipes and hoses of the air intake system are installed and all vacuum hoses are connected.

❊❊CAUTION

When running the engine, MAKE SURE the parking brake is firmly set and the drive wheels are blocked.

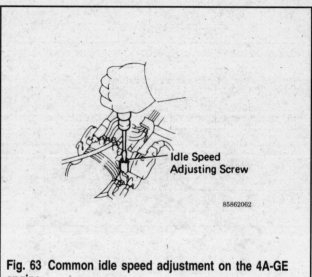

Idle Speed
Adjusting Screw

Fig. 63 Common idle speed adjustment on the 4A-GE engine

2. Check that all electrical connectors are fastened and tight. Switch off all accessories.

3. Run the engine up to 2,500 rpm for about two minutes. Allow the engine to return to the normal idle speed. Adjust the speed as necessary by turning the curb idle speed screw (rear upper side of unit).

GASOLINE ENGINE TUNE-UP SPECIFICATIONS

Year	Model	Engine Series Identification	Spark Plug Gap (in.)	Distributor Points Dwell (deg.)	Distributor Points Gap (in.)	Ignition Timing (deg.) MT	Ignition Timing (deg.) AT	Fuel[1] Pump (psi)	Idle Speed (rpm) MT	Idle Speed (rpm) AT	Valve Clearance (in.) In.	Valve Clearance (in.) Ex.
1970	Corolla	3K-C	0.031	52	0.018	5	—	2.8–4.3	750	—	0.008	0.012
1971	Corolla 1200	3K-C	0.031	52	0.018	5	—	2.8–4.3	750	—	0.008	0.012
	Corolla 1600	2T-C	0.031	52	0.018	5	5	2.8–4.3	750	650	0.007	0.013
1972	Corolla 1200	3K-C	0.031	52	0.018	5	—	2.8–4.3	750	—	0.008	0.012
	Corolla 1600	2T-C	0.031	52	0.018	5	5	2.8–4.3	750	650	0.007	0.013
1973	Corolla 1200	3K-C	0.031	52	0.018	5	—	2.8–4.3	750	—	0.008	0.012
	Corolla 1600	2T-C	0.031	52	0.018	5	5	2.8–4.3	750	650	0.007	0.013
1974	Corolla 1200	3K-C	0.031	52	0.018	5	—	2.8–4.3	750	—	0.008	0.012
	Corolla 1600	2T-C	0.031	52	0.018	5	5	2.8–4.3	750	650	0.007	0.013
1975	Corolla 1200	3K-C	0.031	52	0.018	5	—	2.8–4.3	750	—	0.008	0.012
	Corolla 1600	2T-C	0.03	52[2]	0.018	10[3]	10[3]	2.8–4.3	850	850	0.008	0.013
1976	Corolla 1200	3K-C	0.031	52	0.018	5	—	2.8–4.3	750	—	0.008	0.012
	Corolla 1600	2T-C	0.03	52[2]	0.018	10[3]	10[3]	2.8–4.3	850	850	0.008	0.013
1977	Corolla 1200	3K-C	0.031	52	0.018	5	—	2.8–4.3	750	—	0.008	0.012
	Corolla 1600	2T-C	0.03	52[2]	0.018	10[3]	10[3]	2.8–4.3	850	850	0.008	0.013
1978	Corolla 1200	3K-C	0.031	[4]	[5]	8	8	3.0–4.5	750	750	0.008	0.012
	Corolla 1600	2T-C	0.03	[4]	[5]	10	10	3.0–4.5	850	850	0.008	0.013
1979	Corolla 1200	3K-C	0.031	[4]	[5]	8	8	3.0–4.5	750	750	0.008	0.012
	Corolla 1600	2T-C	0.03	[4]	[5]	10	10	3.0–4.5	850	850	0.008	0.013
1980	Corolla 1800	3T-C	0.043	[4]	[5]	10	10	NA	700[6]	750[6]	0.008	0.013
1981	Corolla 1800	3T-C	0.043	[4]	[5]	11[7]	11[7]	NA	650[8]	750[8]	0.008	0.013
1982	Corolla 1800	3T-C	0.043	[4]	[5]	11[7]	11[7]	NA	650[8]	750[8]	0.008	0.013
1983	Corolla	4A-C, 4A-LC	0.043	[4]	[5]	5	5	2.5–3.5	800[9]	900[9]	0.008	0.012
1984	Corolla	4A-C, 4A-LC	0.043	[4]	[5]	5	5	2.5–3.5	650[9]	800[9]	0.008	0.012
1985	Corolla	4A-C, 4A-LC	0.043[12]	[4]	[5]	5	5	2.5–3.5	650[10]	800[10]	0.008	0.012
	Corolla	4A-GE	0.043	[4]	—	10	10	33–39	800	800	[11]	[11]
1986	Corolla	4A-C, 4A-LC	0.043[12]	[4]	[5]	5	5	2.5–3.5	650[13]	800[13]	0.008	0.012
	Corolla	4A-GE	0.043	[4]	—	10	10	33–39	800	800	[11]	[11]
1987	Corolla	4A-C, 4A-LC	0.043[12]	[4]	[5]	5	5	2.5–3.5	650[13]	800[13]	0.008	0.012
	Corolla	4A-GE	0.043	[4]	—	10	10	33–39	800	800	[11]	[11]

[1] Fuel pressure for 1975–77 California models with electric fuel pump: 2.4–3.8
[2] Dual point models: main—57, sub—52
[3] Dual point models: main—12B, sub—19–25B
[4] Electronic ignition; dwell is set automatically
[5] Distributor air gap: 0.008–0.016
[6] With power steering: 850
[7] Canada: 10B
[8] With power steering: 850; Canada MT without power steering: 700
[9] With power steering: MT—650, AT—800
[10] Specification is for FWD, RWD: MT w/o PS-700 or w/PS-800 & AT w/o PS-800 or w/PS-900
[11] In: 0.006–0.010, Ex.: 0.008–0.012
[12] Specification is US, Canada 0.031
[13] Specification is for FWD, RWD: MT w/o PS-700 or w/PS-750 & AT w/o PS-800 or w/PS-850

DIESEL ENGINE TUNE-UP SPECIFICATIONS

Model	Engine Type	Warm Valve Clearance (in.)		Intake Valve Opens (deg.)	Injection Pump Setting (deg.)	Injection Nozzle Pressure (psi)		Idle Speed (rpm)	Compression Pressure (psi)
		In.	Ex.			New	Used		
Corolla	1C-L	0.008–0.012	0.010–0.014	NA	25–30B	2062–2205	2062–2205	700	356–427

85862002

3

ENGINE AND ENGINE OVERHAUL

UNDERSTANDING BASIC ELECTRICITY

Understanding the basic theory of electricity makes electrical troubleshooting much easier. Several gauges are used in electrical troubleshooting to see inside the circuit being tested. Without a basic understanding, it will be difficult to understand testing procedures.

Electricity is the flow of electrons, hypothetical particles thought to constitute the basic substance of electricity. In a comparison with water flowing in a pipe, the electrons would be the water. As the flow of water can be measured, the flow of electricity can be measured. The unit of measurement is amperes, frequently abbreviated amps. An ammeter will measure the actual amount of current flowing in the circuit.

Just as the water pressure is measured in units such as pounds per square inch, electrical pressure is measured in volts. When a voltmeter's two probes are placed on two live portions of an electrical circuit with different electrical pressures, current will flow through the voltmeter and produce a reading which indicates the difference in electrical pressure between the two parts of the circuit.

While increasing the voltage in a circuit will increase the flow of current, the actual flow depends not only on voltage, but on the resistance of the circuit. The standard unit for measuring circuit resistance is an ohm, measured by an ohmmeter. The ohmmeter is somewhat similar to an ammeter, but incorporates its own source of power so that a standard voltage is always present.

An actual electric circuit consists of four basic parts. These are: the power source, such as a generator or battery; a hot wire, which conducts the electricity under a relatively high voltage to the component supplied by the circuit; the load, such as a lamp, motor, resistor, or relay coil; and the ground wire, which carries the current back to the source under very low voltage. In such a circuit the bulk of the resistance exists between the point where the hot wire is connected to the load, and the point where the load is grounded. In an automobile, the vehicle's frame, which is made of steel, is used as a part of the ground circuit for many of the electrical devices.

Remember that, in electrical testing, the voltmeter is connected in parallel with the circuit being tested (without disconnecting any wires) and measures the difference in voltage between the locations of the two probes; but an ammeter is connected in series with the load (the circuit is separated at one point and the ammeter inserted so it becomes a part of the circuit); and the ohmmeter is self-powered, so that all the power in the circuit should be off and the portion of the circuit to be measured is contacted by one of the meter probes at either end.

For any electrical system to operate, it must make a complete circuit, meaning the power flow from the battery must make a circle. When an electrical component is operating, power flows from the battery to the component, passes through the component causing it to perform its function (for example lighting a light) and then returns to the battery through the ground of the circuit. This ground is usually (but not always) the metal part of the car on which the electrical component is mounted.

Perhaps the easiest way to visualize this is to think of connecting a light bulb (with two wires attached) to your car battery. The battery in your car has two posts (negative and positive). If one of the two wires attached to the light bulb was attached to the negative post of the battery and the other wire was attached to the positive post of the battery, you would have a complete circuit. Current from the battery would flow out one post, through the wire attached to it and then to the light bulb, where it would pass through causing it to light. It would then leave the light bulb, travel through the other wire, and return to the other post of the battery.

➡ **Many times a bad battery ground on the engine or chassis can cause electrical problems which may appear to make the battery, alternator or starter/solenoid to act as if they are faulty. The first check in all electrical diagnosis should be the condition and connections of the battery and battery cables.**

The normal automotive circuit differs from this simple example in two ways. First, instead of having a return wire from the bulb to the battery, the light bulb usually returns the current to the battery through the chassis of the vehicle. Since the negative battery cable is attached to the chassis and the chassis is made of electrically conductive metal, the chassis of the vehicle can serve as a ground wire to complete the circuit. Secondly, most automotive circuits contain switches to turn components on and off.

Some electrical components which require a large amount of current to operate also have a relay in their circuit. Since these circuits carry a large amount of current, the thickness of the wire in the circuit (gauge size) is also greater. If this large wire were connected from the component to the control switch on the instrument panel, and then back to the component, a voltage drop would occur in the circuit. To prevent this potential drop in voltage, an electromagnetic switch (relay) is used. The large wires in the circuit are connected from the car battery to one side of the relay, and from the opposite side of the relay to the component. The relay is normally open, preventing current from passing through the circuit. An additional, smaller, wire is connected from the relay to the control switch for the circuit. When the control switch is turned on, it grounds the smaller wire from the relay and completes the circuit.

If you were to disconnect the light bulb (from the previous example) from the wires and touch the two wires together (please take our word for this; don't try it), the result will be a shower of sparks. A similar thing happens (on a smaller scale) when the power supply wire to a component or the electrical component itself becomes grounded before the normal ground connection for the circuit. To prevent damage to the system, the fuse blows to interrupt the circuit, protecting the components from damage. Because grounding a wire from a power source makes a complete circuit, less the required component to use the power, the phenomenon is called a short circuit. The most common causes of short circuits are: the rubber insulation on a wire breaking, melting or rubbing through to expose the current carrying core of the wire to a metal part of the car, or a shorted switch.

Some electrical systems on the car are protected by a circuit breaker which is, basically, a self-repairing fuse. When a short circuit or excessive load is placed on a circuit breaker protected system, the breaker opens the circuit the same way as a blown fuse. However, when either the short is removed from the circuit or the surge subsides, the circuit breaker resets itself and does not have to be replaced.

Another protective device in the chassis electrical system is a fusible link. A fuse link is a wire that acts as a fuse. It is most commonly found between the starter relay and the main wiring harness for the car. This connection is under the hood, very near a similar fuse link which protects the engine electrical system. Since the fuse link protects all the chassis electrical components, it is the probable cause of trouble when none of the electrical components function, unless the battery is disconnected or dead.

Electrical problems generally fall into one of three areas:
- The component that is not functioning is not receiving current.
- The component itself is not functioning.
- The component is not properly grounded.

Problems that fall into the first category are by far the most complicated. It is the current supply system to the component which contains all the switches, relays, fuses, etc.

The electrical system can be checked using a test light and a jumper wire or a voltmeter. A test light is a device that looks like a pointed screwdriver with a wire attached to it. It has a light bulb in its handle. A jumper wire is a piece of insulated wire with an alligator clip attached to each end.

If a light bulb is not working, you must follow a systematic plan to determine which of the three causes is the villain.

1. Disconnect the power supply wire from the bulb.
2. Attach the ground wire on the test light to a good metal ground.
3. Turn on the switch that controls the inoperable bulb.
4. Touch the probe end of the test light to the end of the power supply wire that was disconnected from the bulb. If the bulb is receiving current, the test light will go on.

➡**If the bulb is one which works only when the ignition key is turned ON (such as a turn signal), make sure the key is turned ON.**

If the test light does not go on, then the problem is in the circuit between the battery and the bulb. As mentioned before, this includes all the switches, fuses, and relays in the system. Turn to the wiring diagram and find the bulb, then follow the wire that runs back to the battery in order to find the difficulty.

➡**Never substitute the jumper wire for the bulb, as the bulb is the component required to use the power from the power source.**

5. If the bulb in the test light goes on, then current is getting to the bulb that is not working in the car. This eliminates the first of the three possible causes. Reconnect the power supply wire and connect a jumper wire from the bulb to a good metal ground. Do this with the switch which controls the bulb turned on, and also the ignition switch turned on if it is required for the light to work. If the bulb works with jumper wire installed, then it has a bad ground. This is usually caused when the metal area on which the bulb mounts to the car becomes coated with some type of foreign matter.

6. If neither test located the source of the trouble, then the light bulb itself is defective.

The theory behind this test procedure can be applied to any of the components of the chassis electrical system by substituting the component that is not working for the light

bulb. Remember that for any electrical system to work, all connections must be clean and tight.

Battery and Starting System

The battery is the first link in the chain of mechanisms which work together to provide cranking of the automobile engine. In most modern cars, the battery is a lead-acid electrochemical device consisting of six 2 volt (2V) subsections connected in series so the unit is capable of producing approximately 12V of electrical current. Each subsection, or cell, consists of a series of positive and negative plates held a short distance apart in a solution of sulfuric acid and water. The two types of plates are of dissimilar metals. This causes a chemical reaction to be set up, and it is this reaction which produces current flow from the battery when its positive and negative terminals are connected to an electrical appliance such as a lamp or motor. The continued transfer of electrons would eventually convert the sulfuric acid in the electrolyte to water, and make the two plates identical in chemical composition. As electrical energy is removed from the battery, its voltage output tends to drop. Thus, measuring battery voltage and battery electrolyte composition are two ways of checking the ability of the unit to supply power. During engine start-up, electrical energy is removed from the battery. However, if the charging circuit is in good condition and the operating conditions are normal, the power removed from the battery will be replaced by the alternator which will force electrons back through the battery, reversing the normal flow, and restoring the battery to its original chemical state.

The battery and starting motor are linked by very heavy electrical cables designed to minimize resistance to the flow of current. Generally, the major power supply cable that leaves the battery goes directly to the starter, while other electrical system needs are supplied by a smaller cable. During starter operation, power flows from the battery to the starter, while it is grounded through the car's frame and the battery's negative ground strap.

The starting motor is a specially designed, direct current electric motor capable of producing a very great amount of power for its size. One thing that allows the motor to produce a great deal of power is its tremendous rotating speed. It drives the engine through a tiny pinion gear (attached to the starter's armature), which drives the very large flywheel ring gear at a greatly reduced speed. Another factor allowing it to produce so much power is that only intermittent operation is required of it. Thus, little allowance for air circulation is required, and the windings can be built into a very small space.

The starter solenoid is a magnetic device which employs the small current supplied by the starting switch circuit of the ignition switch. The magnetic action moves a plunger which mechanically engages the starter and electrically closes the heavy switch which connects it to the battery. The starting circuit consists of the starting switch contained within the ignition switch, a transmission neutral safety switch or clutch pedal switch, and the wiring necessary to connect these with the starter solenoid or relay.

A pinion, which is a small gear, is mounted to a one-way drive clutch. This clutch is splined to the starter armature shaft. When the ignition switch is moved to the **START** position, the solenoid plunger slides the pinion toward the flywheel ring gear via a collar and spring. If the teeth on the pinion and flywheel match properly, the pinion will engage the flywheel immediately. If the gear teeth butt one another, the spring will compress and force the gears to mesh as soon as the starter turns far enough to allow them to do so. As the solenoid plunger reaches the end of its travel, it closes the contacts that connect the battery and starter and the engine is cranked.

As soon as the engine starts, the flywheel ring gear begins turning fast enough to drive the pinion at an extremely high rate of speed. At this point, the one-way clutch begins allowing the pinion to spin faster than the starter shaft so that the starter will not operate at excessive speed. When the ignition switch is released from the starter position, the solenoid is de-energized. At this point, a spring contained within the solenoid assembly pulls the gear out of mesh and interrupts the current flow to the starter.

Some starters employ a separate relay, mounted away from the starter, to switch the motor solenoid current on and off. The relay thus replaces the solenoid electrical switch, but does not eliminate the need for a solenoid mounted on the starter used to mechanically engage the starter drive gears. The relay is used to reduce the amount of current the starting switch must carry.

The Charging System

The automobile charging system provides electrical power for operation of the vehicle's ignition system, starting system and all the electrical accessories. The battery serves as an electrical surge or storage tank, storing (in chemical form) the energy originally produced by the belt driven alternator. The system also provides a means of regulating alternator output to protect the battery from being overcharged and to avoid excessive voltage to the accessories.

The storage battery is a chemical device incorporating parallel lead plates in a tank containing a sulfuric acid-water solution. Adjacent plates are slightly dissimilar, and the chemical reaction of the two dissimilar plates produces electrical energy when the battery is connected to a load such as the starter motor. The chemical reaction is reversible, so that when the alternator is producing a voltage greater then that produced by the battery, electricity is forced into the battery, and the battery is returned to its fully charged state.

The vehicle's alternator is driven mechanically, through a V-belt (or serpentine belt depending upon the application), by the engine crankshaft. It consists of two coils of fine wire, one stationary (the stator), and one movable (the rotor). The rotor may also be known as the armature and consists of fine wire wrapped around an iron core which is mounted on a shaft. The electricity which flows through the two coils of wire (provided initially by the battery in some cases) creates an intense magnetic field around both rotor and stator, and the interaction between the two fields creates voltage, allowing the alternator to power the accessories and charge the battery.

There are generally 2 types of alternators; the earlier of the 2 (often known as a generator) is the direct current (DC) type. The DC generator voltage is produced in the armature and carried off the spinning armature by stationary brushes contacting the commutator. The commutator is a series of smooth metal contact plates on the end of the armature. The

commutator plates, which are separated from one another by a very short gap, are connected to the armature circuits so that current will flow in one direction only in wires carrying the generator output. The generator stator consists of two stationary coils of wire which draw some of the output current of the generator to form a powerful magnetic field and create the interaction of fields which generates the voltage. The generator field is wired in series with the regulator.

Newer automobiles use alternating current generators or alternators because they are more efficient, can be rotated at higher speeds, and have fewer brush problems, In an alternator, the field rotates while all the current produced passes only through the stator windings. The brushes bear against continuous slip rings rather than a commutator. This causes the current produced to periodically reverse the direction of its flow. Diodes (electrical one-way switches) block the flow of current which is prevented from traveling in the wrong direction. A series of diodes is wired together to permit the alternating flow of the stator to be converted to a pulsating, but unidirectional, flow of current from traveling in the wrong direction. The alternator's field is wired in series with the voltage regulator.

The regulator consist of several circuits. Each circuit has a core, or magnetic coil of wire, which operates a switch. Each switch is connected to ground through one or more resistors. The coil of wire responds directly to system voltage. When the voltage reaches the required level, the magnetic field created by the winding of wire closes the switch and inserts a resistance into the generator field circuit, thus reducing the output. The contacts of the switch cycle open and close many times each second to precisely control voltage.

While alternators are self-limiting as far as maximum current is concerned, DC generators employ a current regulating circuit which responds directly to the total amount of current flowing through the generator circuit rather than to the output voltage. The current regulator is similar to the voltage regulator except all system current must flow through the energizing coil on its way to the various accessories.

SAFETY PRECAUTIONS

Observing these precautions will help avoid damage to the vehicle's electrical system and ensure safe handling of the system components:

• Be absolutely sure of the polarity of a booster battery before making connections. Connect the cables positive to positive, and negative to a good ground. Connect positive cables first and then make the last connection to ground on the body of the booster vehicle so that arcing cannot ignite hydrogen gas that may have accumulated near the battery. Remember, even momentary connection of a booster battery with the polarity reversed will damage alternator diodes.

• Disconnect both vehicle battery cables before attempting to charge a battery.

• Never ground the alternator/generator output or battery terminal. Be cautious when using metal tools around a battery to avoid creating a short circuit between the terminals.

• Never ground the field circuit between the generator and regulator.

• Never run an alternator or generator without load unless the field circuit is disconnected.

- Never attempt to polarize an alternator.
- Keep the regulator cover in place when taking voltage and current limiter readings.
- Use insulated tools when adjusting the regulator.
- Whenever DC generator-to-regulator wires have been disconnected, the generator must be repolarized. To do this

with an externally grounded, light duty generator, momentarily place a jumper wire between the battery terminal and the generator terminal of the regulator. With an internally grounded heavy duty unit, disconnect the wire to the regulator field terminal and touch the regulator battery terminal with it.

ENGINE ELECTRICAL

Ignition Coil

PRIMARY RESISTANCE CHECK

▶ **See Figures 1 and 2**

In order to check the coil primary resistance, you must first disconnect all wires from the ignition coil terminals. Using an ohmmeter, check the resistance between the positive and the negative terminals on the coil. The resistance should be:
- 2T-C: 1.3-1.6 ohms.
- 3K-C w/o igniter: 1.2-1.5 ohms; w/igniter: 1.3-1.6 ohms.
- 1980 3T-C Federal and Canada: 0.4-0.5 ohms; California: 0.8-1.0 ohms.
- 1981-82 3T-C: 0.8-1.0 ohms.
- 4A-C and 4A-LC US: 0.4-0.5 ohms; Canada: 1.2-1.5 ohms.
- 4A-GE: 0.5-0.7 ohms.

If the resistance is not within these tolerances, the coil will require replacement.

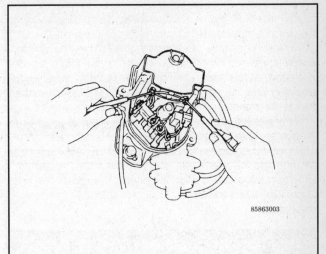

Fig. 2 Checking the coil primary resistance — 1983 and later A-series engines

SECONDARY RESISTANCE CHECK

▶ **See Figures 3 and 4**

In order to check the coil secondary resistance, you must first disconnect all wires from the ignition coil terminals. Using an ohmmeter, check the resistance between the negative terminal and the coil wire terminal. The resistance should be:
- 2T-C: 10,200-13,800 ohms.
- 3K-C-w/o igniter: 8,000-12,000 ohms; w/igniter: 10,000-15,000 ohms.
- 1980 3T-C: 8,500-11,500 ohms; California: 11,500-15,500 ohms.
- 1981-82 3T-C: 11,500-15,500 ohms.
- 4A-C and 4A-LC: 7,700-10,400 ohms.
- 4A-GE: 11,000-16,000 ohms.

If the resistance is not within these tolerances, the coil will require replacement.

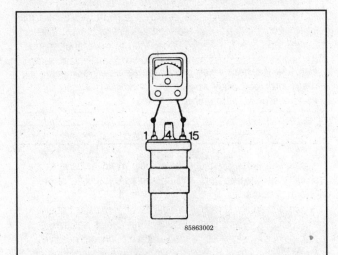

Fig. 1 Checking the coil primary resistance — all except 1983 and later A-series engines

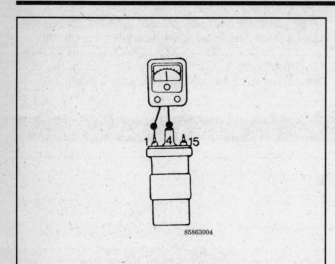

Fig. 3 Checking the coil primary resistance — all except 1983 and later A-series engines

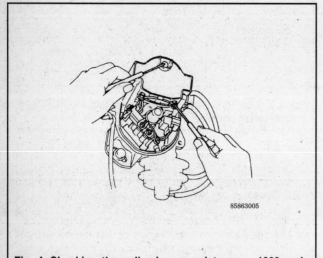

Fig. 4 Checking the coil primary resistance — 1983 and later A-series engines

Distributor

REMOVAL

▶ **See Figures 5, 6, 7, 8, 9, 10, 11, 12, 13, 14, 15, 16, 17, 18 and 19**

Except 1983 and Later A-Series Engines

1. Disconnect the negative battery cable.
2. Unfasten the retaining clips or loosen the retainers and lift the distributor cap straight up. It will be easier to install the distributor if the wiring is left connected to the cap. If the wires must be removed from the cap, be sure to mark their positions in order to aid in installation.
3. Remove the dust cover and mark the position of the rotor relative to the distributor body; then mark the position of the body relative to the engine.

4. Disconnect the coil primary wire and the vacuum line(s). If the distributor vacuum unit has two vacuum lines, be sure to tag them to assure proper installation.
5. Remove the pinch bolt and lift the distributor straight up or out, away from the engine. The rotor will turn as the distributor is removed, be sure to mark the final position of the rotor for timing purposes. The rotor and body markings will assure that the distributor and rotor can be returned to the position from which they were removed. To preserve ignition timing, DO NOT turn or disturb the engine (unless absolutely necessary, such as for engine rebuilding/repair), after the distributor has been removed.

1983 and Later A-Series Engines

1. Disconnect the negative battery cable.
2. Disengage the two electrical leads at the distributor.

Fig. 5 If the plug wires are being removed from the distributor cap, they should be marked or tagged to assure proper installation

Fig. 6 If the distributor cap is being removed, release the fasteners

Fig. 7 In most cases the cap should be removed in order to matchmark the rotor

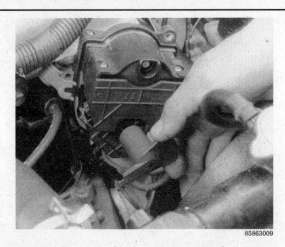

Fig. 8 If necessary the rotor may be replaced with the cap off, but don't do this now if the distributor is being removed from the engine

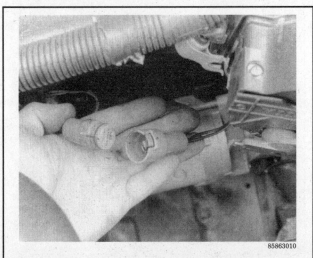

Fig. 9 Disengage the electrical wiring from the distributor assembly

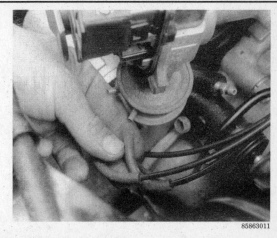

Fig. 10 Disconnect the vacuum hose(s) from the distributor, if there are 2 hoses, be sure to tag them for proper installation

Fig. 11 Matchmark the distributor housing to the engine (and the rotor to the housing)

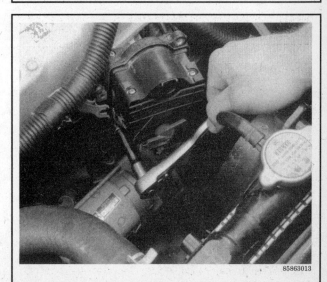

Fig. 12 Loosen the distributor hold-down bolt

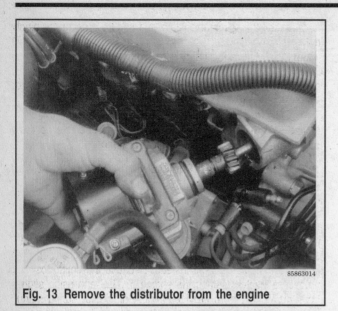

Fig. 13 Remove the distributor from the engine

Fig. 14 If coil replacement is necessary on distributors equipped with an internal coil, remove the protective cover

Fig. 15 Disconnect the coil wiring

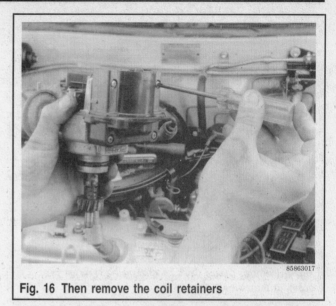

Fig. 16 Then remove the coil retainers

Fig. 17 If equipped, be sure not to lose the rubber seal

Fig. 18 Remove the coil from the distributor assembly

Fig. 19 Check condition of the distributor shaft O-ring and replace, if damaged or worn

3. Grasp each spark plug wire by its rubber boot and remove it from the spark plug or from the distributor cap, whichever is preferable.

➡**Don't forget to tag each spark plug wire before removal.**

4. Tag and disconnect the vacuum advance hose(s).
5. If the engine will not be disturbed while the distributor is out, remove the distributor cap and matchmark the rotor to the distributor housing. Also, matchmark the housing to the engine. When the distributor is removed, the rotor will turn slightly, be sure to mark that position as well. All marks are made for reference during installation in order to preserve engine timing.

➡**Because the distributors used on these engines are equipped with TDC alignment marks, it is not absolutely necessary to matchmark the rotor during removal. However, if only the distributor is being replaced, or the engine is not being disturbed, it may be less hassle to make your own alignment marks, rather than having to set the engine to TDC during distributor installation.**

6. Remove the distributor hold-down (pinch) bolt and lift out the distributor.

INSTALLATION — TIMING NOT DISTURBED

Except 1983 and Later A-Series Engines
▶ See Figures 20, 21 and 22

1. Insert the distributor in the block while aligning the matchmarks made during removal. Begin with the rotor aligned to the last mark made (after removal), then while inserting the distributor, the rotor should turn and align with the first mark. Make sure the distributor housing-to-engine mark is properly aligned as well.
2. Make sure the distributor driven gear is properly engaged with the distributor drive.

3. Install the distributor clamp and secure it using the pinch bolt.
4. Install the cap, primary wire, and vacuum line(s).
5. Install the spark plug leads. Consult the marks made during removal to be sure that the proper leads are connected. Install the high tension wire if it was removed.
6. Start the engine. Check and adjust the timing and/or octane selector, as necessary. For details, please refer to the procedures located in Section 2 of this manual.

1983 and Later A-Series Engines
▶ See Figure 23

If alignment marks were made during removal, this procedure may be used to install the distributor into the engine and preserve ignition timing. However, if the engine was disturbed after removal, the procedure found later in this section for timing lost should be used instead. Because the timing lost procedure involves setting the engine to TDC and using alignment marks which are provided on the distributor during manufacture, that procedure may be followed even if timing is not disturbed.

1. Insert the distributor in the block while aligning the matchmarks made during removal. Begin with the rotor aligned to the last mark made (after removal), then while inserting the distributor, the rotor should turn and align with the first mark. Make sure the distributor housing-to-engine mark is properly aligned as well.
2. Secure the distributor using the hold-down (pinch) bolt.
3. Install the distributor cap.
4. Connect the vacuum advance hose(s).
5. Connect the spark plug wiring.
6. Connect the two electrical leads at the distributor.
7. Connect the negative battery cable, then check and adjust the ignition timing, as necessary. For details, please refer to Section 2 of this manual.

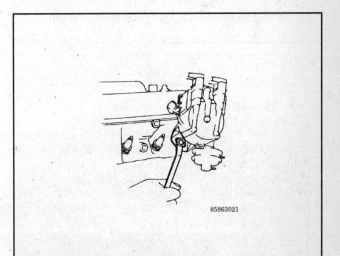

Fig. 20 Once the distributor is properly installed, tighten the retaining (pinch) bolt

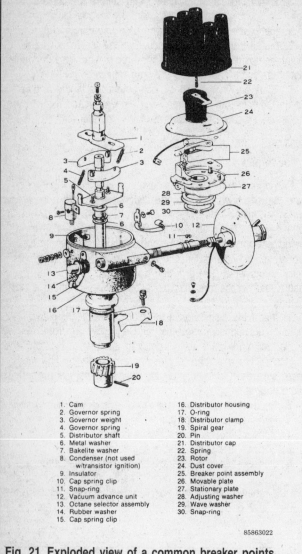

1. Cam
2. Governor spring
3. Governor weight
4. Governor spring
5. Distributor shaft
6. Metal washer
7. Bakelite washer
8. Condenser (not used w/transistor ignition)
9. Insulator
10. Cap spring clip
11. Snap-ring
12. Vacuum advance unit
13. Octane selector assembly
14. Rubber washer
15. Cap spring clip
16. Distributor housing
17. O-ring
18. Distributor clamp
19. Spiral gear
20. Pin
21. Distributor cap
22. Spring
23. Rotor
24. Dust cover
25. Breaker point assembly
26. Movable plate
27. Stationary plate
28. Adjusting washer
29. Wave washer
30. Snap-ring

85863022

Fig. 21 Exploded view of a common breaker points distributor assembly

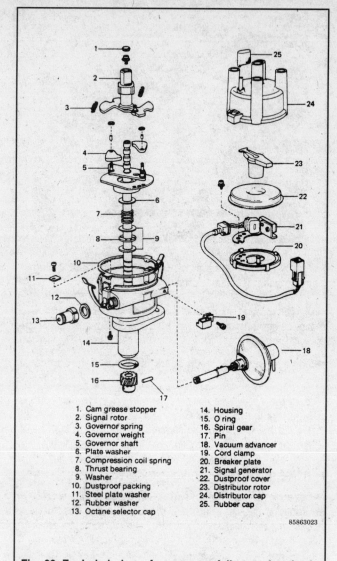

1. Cam grease stopper
2. Signal rotor
3. Governor spring
4. Governor spring
5. Governor shaft
6. Plate washer
7. Compression coil spring
8. Thrust bearing
9. Washer
10. Dustproof packing
11. Steel plate washer
12. Rubber washer
13. Octane selector cap
14. Housing
15. O ring
16. Spiral gear
17. Pin
18. Vacuum advancer
19. Cord clamp
20. Breaker plate
21. Signal generator
22. Dustproof cover
23. Distributor rotor
24. Distributor cap
25. Rubber cap

85863023

Fig. 22 Exploded view of a common fully transistorized ignition distributor

INSTALLATION — TIMING LOST

Except 1983 and Later A-Series Engines
▶ See Figure 24

If the engine has been cranked, dismantled, or the timing otherwise lost, proceed as follows:

1. Determine Top Dead Center (TDC) of the No. 1 cylinder's compression stroke by removing the spark plug from the No. 1 cylinder and placing your finger or a compression gauge over the spark plug hole.

✳✳CAUTION

On engines which have the spark plugs buried under the exhaust manifold, use a compression gauge or a tool handle to feel for compression if the manifold is still hot.

2. Crank the engine until compression pressure starts to build up. Continue cranking the engine until the timing marks indicate TDC or **0**. Make sure the timing marks are aligned

ONLY on a stroke when compression is felt, this is important because the timing marks will also line up when the cylinder is on its exhaust stroke, but this would leave the ignition timing 180 degrees off.

3. Next align the timing marks to specification, by turning the engine back slightly or by cranking the engine again, but remember, if the engine is turned over only 1 additional revolution, timing will be incorrect as No. 1 will be on its exhaust stroke. If the engine is cranked forward to align the timing marks, turn the crankshaft almost 2 complete revolutions.

4. Temporarily install the rotor in the distributor without the dust cover. Turn the distributor shaft so that the rotor is pointing toward the No. 1 terminal in the distributor cap. The points should just be about to open. On A-series engines, alignment marks are provided so the distributor cap may remain in position when installing the distributor at TDC.

➡On 1980-82 A-series models: align the drilled mark on the driven gear (not the driven gear straight pin) with the center of the No. 1 terminal on the distributor cap and then align the stationary flange center with the bolt hole center. This will set the distributor to No. 1 TDC.

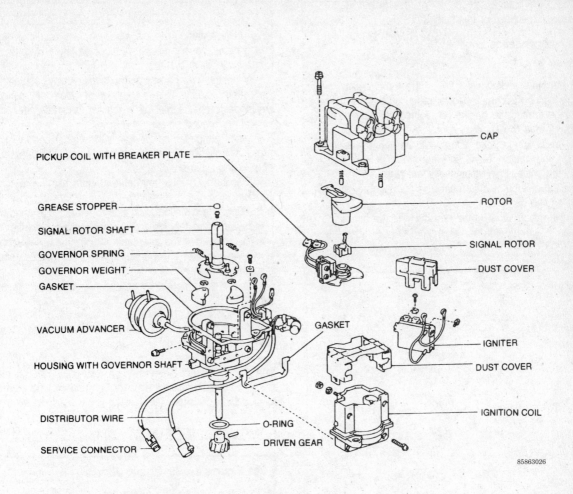

Fig. 23 Exploded view of a late model A-series electronic distributor

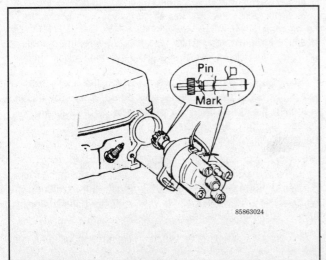

Fig. 24 Distributor alignment marks — 1980-82 A-series engines

5. Use a small screwdriver to align the slot on the distributor drive (oil pump driveshaft) with the key on the bottom of the distributor shaft.

6. Align the matchmarks on the distributor body and the block which were made during the removal. Install the distributor in the block by rotating it slightly (no more than one gear tooth in either direction) until the driven gear meshes with the drive.

➡ **Oil distributor spiral gear and the oil pump driveshaft end before distributor installation.**

7. Except for A-series engines, rotate the distributor, once it is installed, so that the points are just about to open or the projection on the pickup coil is almost opposite the signal rotor tooth. Temporarily tighten the pinch bolt.

8. If applicable, remove the rotor and install the dust cover. Replace the rotor and the distributor cap.

9. Install the primary wire and the vacuum line(s).

10. Install the No. 1 spark plug. Connect the spark plug cables using the marks made during removal. Install the high tension lead if it was removed.

11. Start the engine, then check and adjust the ignition timing along with the octane selector, as necessary. For details, please refer to Section 2 of this manual.

1983 and Later A-Series Engines
▶ See Figure 25

1. Set the No. 1 cylinder to TDC of the compression stroke. This can be accomplished by removing the No. 1 spark plug and then turning the engine (crankshaft) by hand while your thumb is over the spark plug hole. As the No. 1 piston comes up on its firing stroke, you should be able to feel the pressure on your thumb. Make sure the timing pointer is at the 0 mark on the scale, then install the spark plug.

2. Coat the distributor drive gear and the governor shaft tip with clean engine oil.

3. Align the protrusion on the housing with the pin of the spiral driven drill mark side and then align the center of the flange with the center of the bolt hole in the cylinder head.

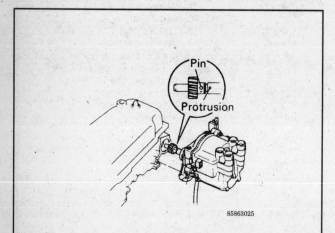

85863025

Fig. 25 Distributor mark alignment — 1983 and later A-series engines

4. Tighten the hold-down bolt.

5. Install the spark plug wires and the vacuum hose(s), as tagged or marked during removal.

6. Engage the electrical leads and the negative battery cable.

7. Start the engine and check the ignition timing. Adjust if necessary.

Alternator

▶ See Figures 26, 27 and 28

All models covered in this manual use a 12 volt alternator. Amperage ratings vary according to the year and model. All 1970-79 models utilize a separate, adjustable regulator, while 1980 and later models come equipped with either a separate, adjustable regulator or a transistorized, non-adjustable IC regulator, integral with the alternator.

ALTERNATOR PRECAUTIONS

To prevent damage to the alternator and regulator, the following precautionary measures must be taken when working with the electrical system.

• Never reverse battery connections. Always visually check the battery polarity. This is to be done before any connections are made to ensure that all of the connections correspond to the battery ground polarity of the car.

• When jump-starting the car with another battery, make sure that only like terminals are connected. This also applies when using a battery charger.

• Disconnect the battery cables before using a fast charger; the charger has a tendency to force current through the diodes in the opposite direction for which they were designed.

• Never use a fast charger as a booster for starting the car.

• Never operate the alternator with the battery disconnected or otherwise on an uncontrolled open circuit. Double check to see that all connections are tight.

• Do not short across or ground any alternator/regulator terminals.

• Do not attempt to polarize the alternator.

• Disconnect the battery cables and remove the alternator before using an electric arc welder on the car.

• Protect the alternator from excessive moisture. If the engine is to be steam cleaned, cover or remove the alternator.

• Always disconnect the battery ground cable before disconnecting the alternator lead.

REMOVAL & INSTALLATION

▶ See Figures 29, 30, 31 and 32

➡On some models the alternator is mounted very low on the engine. On these models it may be necessary to remove the gravel/splash shield and work from underneath the car in order to gain access to the alternator.

1. Disconnect the negative battery cable.

2. Unfasten the starter-to-battery cable at the battery end.

3. If necessary, remove the air cleaner to gain access to the alternator.

4. Unfasten the bolts which attach the adjusting link to the alternator. Remove the alternator drive belt.

➡On some late model vehicles on which the alternator belt also drives the power steering pump, it may be easier to loosen the power steering pump and pivot it inward to release tension from the belt, then remove the belt from the alternator pulley.

5. Unfasten the alternator wiring connections.

➡Diesel engine alternators are equipped with a vacuum pump. Before removal, two oil lines and a vacuum hose must first be disconnected.

6. Remove the alternator attaching bolt(s) then withdraw the alternator from its bracket.

7. Installation is performed in the reverse order of removal. After installing the alternator, adjust the belt tension as detailed in Section 1 of this manual.

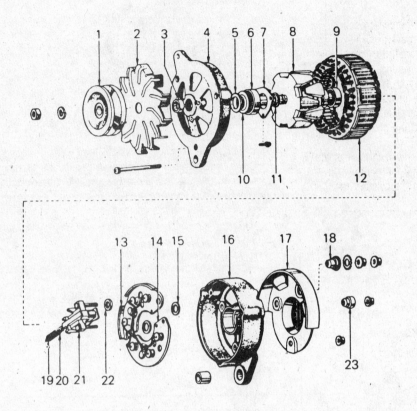

1. Pulley
2. Fan
3. Spacer collar
4. Drive end frame
5. Felt ring
6. Bearing
7. Bearing retainer
8. Rotor
9. Bearing
10. Felt cover
11. Spacer ring
12. Stator assembly
13. (+) Rectifier holder
14. (−) Rectifier holder
15. Insulator
16. Rear end frame
17. Rear end cover
18. Insulator
19. Brush
20. Brush spring
21. Brush holder
22. Insulator
23. Insulator

85863027

Fig. 26 Exploded view of a common early model (1970-79) alternator

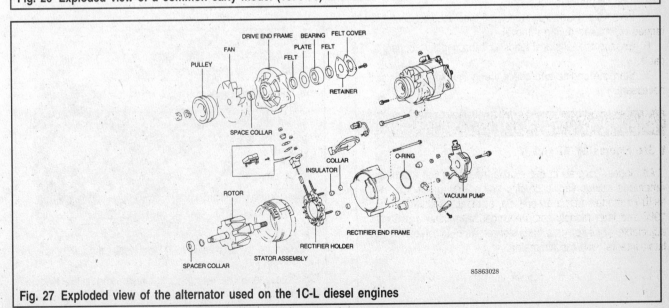

85863028

Fig. 27 Exploded view of the alternator used on the 1C-L diesel engines

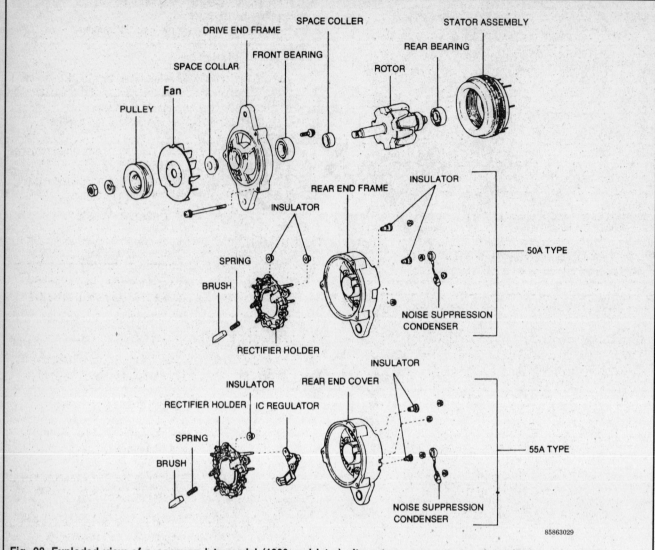

Fig. 28 Exploded view of a common late model (1980 and later) alternator — separate regulator (50A type) and IC regulator (55A type)

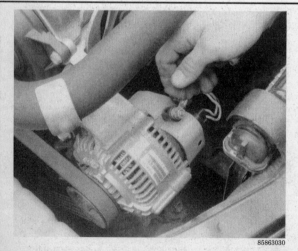

Fig. 29 Pull back the rubber boot to expose alternator wiring

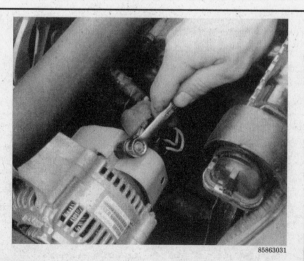

Fig. 30 Loosen the retaining nut and remove the ring terminal

Fig. 31 If equipped, remove the multi-pin wiring connector from the back of the alternator

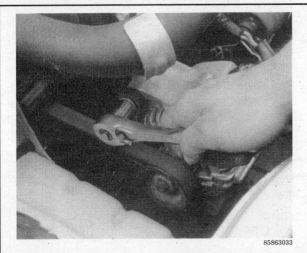

Fig. 32 Loosen and remove the alternator retaining bolt(s)

Regulator

All 1970-79 models are equipped with a separate, adjustable regulator. All 1980 and later models are either equipped with an external, adjustable regulator (like the earlier vehicles) or a transistorized regulator which is attached to the brush assembly on the side of the alternator housing. If faulty, the internal regulator must be replaced; there are no adjustments which can be made.

REMOVAL & INSTALLATION

External (Separate From Alternator)

1. Disconnect the negative battery cable.
2. Disengage the wiring harness connector at the back of the regulator.

3. Remove the regulator mounting bolts.
4. Remove the regulator.
5. Installation is in the reverse order of removal.

IC (Mounted In Alternator)

1. Remove the alternator as detailed earlier in this section.
2. Remove the two screws on the back of the alternator housing, then remove the regulator end cover.
3. Underneath the end cover there are three terminal screws, remove them.
4. Remove the two regulator mounting screws, then remove the regulator.
5. Using a suitable tool, carefully pry out the plastic housing and the rubber seal around the regulator terminals.
6. Installation is in the reverse order of removal.

ADJUSTMENT

➡Only regulators which are separate from the alternator are adjustable. Internally mounted IC regulators are NOT adjustable.

Voltage

1. Connect a voltmeter to the battery terminals. Negative (black) lead to the negative (-) terminal; positive (red) lead to positive (+) terminal.
2. Start the engine and gradually increase its speed to about 1,500 rpm.
3. At this speed, the voltage reading should fall within the range specified in the alternator and regulator specifications chart found later in this section.
4. If the voltage does not fall within the specifications, remove the cover from the regulator and adjust it by bending the adjusting arm.
5. Repeat Steps 2 and 3. If the voltage cannot be brought to specification, proceed with the mechanical adjustments found in this section.

Mechanical

➡Perform the voltage adjustment outlined earlier in this section, before beginning the mechanical adjustments.

FIELD RELAY

▶ See Figure 33

1. Remove the cover from the regulator assembly.
2. Use a feeler gauge to check the amount that the contact spring is deflected while the armature is being depressed.
3. If the measurement is not within specifications (refer to the alternator and regulator specifications chart found in this section), adjust the regulator by bending the point holder P2 (please see the illustration).
4. Check the point gap with a feeler gauge against the specifications in the chart.
5. Adjust the point gap, as required, by bending the point holder P1 (see the illustration).
6. Clean off the points with emery cloth if they are dirty and wash them with solvent.

VOLTAGE REGULATOR

▶ See Figure 34

1. Use a feeler gauge to measure the air (armature) gap. If it is not within the specifications (refer to the alternator and regulator specifications chart), adjust it by bending the low speed point holder (please see the illustration).

2. Check the point gap with a feeler gauge. If it is not within specifications, adjust it by bending the high speed point holder (please see the illustration). Clean the points with emery cloth and wash them off with solvent.

3. Check the amount of contact spring deflection while depressing the armature. The specification should be the same as that for the contact spring on the field relay. If the amount of deflection is not within specification, replace, do not adjust, the voltage regulator. Go back and perform the steps outlined under Voltage Adjustment. If the voltage cannot be brought within specifications, replace the voltage regulator. If the voltage still fails to come within specifications, the alternator is probably defective and should be replaced.

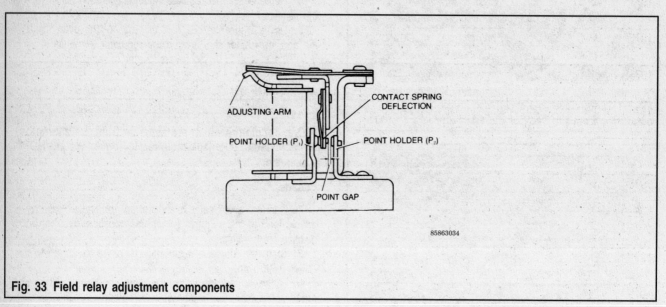

Fig. 33 Field relay adjustment components

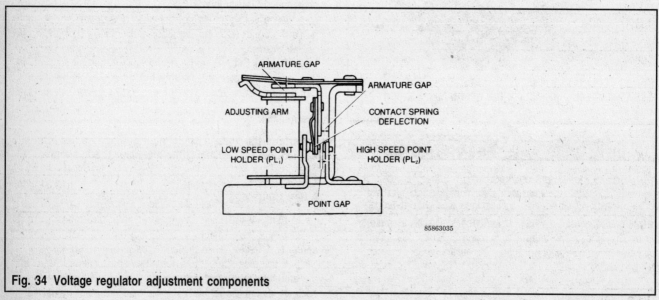

Fig. 34 Voltage regulator adjustment components

ALTERNATOR AND REGULATOR SPECIFICATIONS

Year	Engine Series Identification	Alternator Output (amps)	Alternator Manufacturer	Manufacturer	Field Relay Contact Spring Deflection (in.)	Field Relay Point Gap (in.)	Field Relay Volts to Close	Regulator Air Gap (in.)	Regulator Point Gap (in.)	Volts
1970	3K-C	25	Nippondenso	Nippondenso	0.008–0.024	0.016–0.047	4.5–5.8	0.012	0.010–0.018	13.8–14.8
1971	3K-C	25	Nippondenso	Nippondenso	0.008–0.024	0.016–0.047	4.5–5.8	0.012	0.010–0.018	13.8–14.8
	2T-C	40①	Nippondenso	Nippondenso	0.008–0.024	0.016–0.047	4.5–5.8	0.012	0.010–0.018	13.8–14.8
1972	3K-C	25	Nippondenso	Nippondenso	0.008–0.024	0.016–0.047	4.5–5.8	0.012	0.010–0.018	13.8–14.8
	2T-C	40①	Nippondenso	Nippondenso	0.008–0.024	0.016–0.047	4.5–5.8	0.012	0.010–0.018	13.8–14.8
1973	3K-C	25	Nippondenso	Nippondenso	0.008–0.024	0.016–0.047	4.5–5.8	0.012	0.010–0.018	13.8–14.8
	2T-C	40①	Nippondenso	Nippondenso	0.008–0.024	0.016–0.047	4.5–5.8	0.012	0.010–0.018	13.8–14.8
1974	3K-C	25	Nippondenso	Nippondenso	0.008–0.024	0.016–0.047	4.5–5.8	0.012	0.010–0.018	13.8–14.8
	2T-C	40①	Nippondenso	Nippondenso	0.008–0.024	0.016–0.047	4.5–5.8	0.012	0.010–0.018	13.8–14.8
1975	3K-C	25	Nippondenso	Nippondenso	0.008–0.024	0.016–0.047	4.5–5.8	0.012	0.010–0.018	13.8–14.8
	2T-C	40①	Nippondenso	Nippondenso	0.008–0.024	0.016–0.047	4.5–5.8	0.012	0.010–0.018	13.8–14.8
1976	3K-C	25	Nippondenso	Nippondenso	0.008–0.024	0.016–0.047	4.5–5.8	0.012	0.010–0.018	13.8–14.8
	2T-C	40①	Nippondenso	Nippondenso	0.008–0.024	0.016–0.047	4.5–5.8	0.012	0.010–0.018	13.8–14.8
1977	3K-C	25	Nippondenso	Nippondenso	0.008–0.024	0.016–0.047	4.5–5.8	0.012	0.010–0.018	13.8–14.8
	2T-C	40①	Nippondenso	Nippondenso	0.008–0.024	0.016–0.047	4.5–5.8	0.012	0.010–0.018	13.8–14.8
1978	3K-C	50	Nippondenso	Nippondenso	0.008–0.024	0.016–0.047	4.5–5.8	0.012	0.010–0.018	13.8–14.8
	2T-C	40①	Nippondenso	Nippondenso	0.008–0.024	0.016–0.047	4.5–5.8	0.012	0.010–0.018	13.8–14.8
1979	3K-C	50	Nippondenso	Nippondenso	0.008–0.024	0.016–0.047	4.5–5.8	0.012	0.010–0.018	13.8–14.8
	2T-C	40①	Nippondenso	Nippondenso	0.008–0.024	0.016–0.047	4.5–5.8	0.012	0.010–0.018	13.8–14.8
1980	3T-C	50	Nippondenso	Nippondenso	0.008–0.024	0.016–0.047	4.5–5.8	0.012	0.010–0.018	13.8–14.8
	3T-C	55	Nippondenso	Nippondenso	IC Regulator Is Not Adjustable					14.0–14.7
1981	3T-C	50	Nippondenso	Nippondenso	0.008–0.024	0.016–0.047	4.5–5.8	0.012	0.010–0.018	13.8–14.4
	3T-C	55	Nippondenso	Nippondenso	IC Regulator Is Not Adjustable					14.0–14.7
1982	3T-C	50	Nippondenso	Nippondenso	0.008–0.024	0.016–0.047	4.5–5.8	0.012	0.010–0.018	13.8–14.4
	3T-C	55	Nippondenso	Nippondenso	IC Regulator Is Not Adjustable					14.0–14.7
1983	4A-C, 4A-LC	50	Nippondenso	Nippondenso	0.008–0.024	0.016–0.047	4.5–5.8	0.012	0.010–0.018	13.8–14.8
	4A-C, 4A-LC	55	Nippondenso	Nippondenso	IC Regulator Is Not Adjustable					13.8–14.4
1984	4A-C, 4A-LC	50	Nippondenso	Nippondenso	0.008–0.024	0.016–0.047	4.5–5.8	0.012	0.010–0.018	13.8–14.8
	1C-L	②	Nippondenso	Nippondenso	Not Adjustable					13.8–14.4
	4A-C, 4A-LC	55	Nippondenso	Nippondenso	IC Regulator Is Not Adjustable					③
1985	4A-C, 4A-LC	55	Nippondenso	Nippondenso	IC Regulator Is Not Adjustable					13.5–14.3
	4A-C, 4A-LC	60	Nippondenso	Nippondenso	IC Regulator Is Not Adjustable					④
	1C-L	②	Nippondenso	Nippondenso	Not Adjustable					13.8–14.4
	4A-GE	60	Nippondenso	Nippondenso	IC Regulator Is Not Adjustable					13.5–14.3
1986	4A-C, 4A-LC	55	Nippondenso	Nippondenso	IC Regulator Is Not Adjustable					13.5–14.3
	4A-C, 4A-LC	60	Nippondenso	Nippondenso	IC Regulator Is Not Adjustable					13.9–15.1
	4A-GE	60	Nippondenso	Nippondenso	IC Regulator Is Not Adjustable					13.5–14.3
1987	4A-C, 4A-LC	55	Nippondenso	Nippondenso	IC Regulator Is Not Adjustable					13.5–14.3
	4A-C, 4A-LC	60	Nippondenso	Nippondenso	IC Regulator Is Not Adjustable					13.9–15.1
	4A-GE	60	Nippondenso	Nippondenso	IC Regulator Is Not Adjustable					13.5–14.3

① 50 amp optional ② 55 or 60 amp ③ Rwd: 13.8–14.4; Fwd: 14.0–15.1 ④ Rwd: 13.5–14.3, Fwd: 13.9–15.1

85863036

Starter

REMOVAL & INSTALLATION

▶ **See Figures 35, 36, 37 and 38**

1. Disconnect the negative battery cable.
2. Disconnect the cable which runs from the starter to the battery at the battery end.
3. If necessary, remove the air cleaner assembly in order to gain access to the starter.

➡ **On some models with automatic transmissions, it may be necessary to unfasten the throttle linkage connecting rod.**

4. On Corolla 1200 models, disconnect the manual choke cable and the accelerator cable from the carburetor. Unfasten the front exhaust pipe flange from the manifold and then remove the complete manifold assembly.

➡ **Radiator removal will facilitate starter removal on diesel engines.**

5. On Corollas with gasoline engines and automatic transmissions, remove the transmission oil filler tube.
6. Disconnect all of the wiring at the starter. If necessary, tag the wiring to assure proper installation.
7. Unfasten the starter retainers and withdraw the starter assembly from the engine.
8. Installation is in the reverse order of removal.

OVERHAUL

▶ **See Figures 39 and 40**

Direct Drive Type

SOLENOID REPLACEMENT

1. Remove the starter from the vehicle.

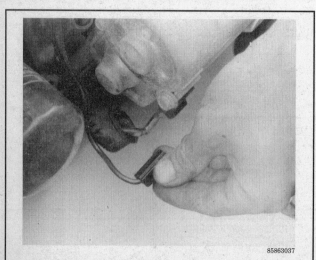

Fig. 35 Disengage any wiring connectors from the starter assembly

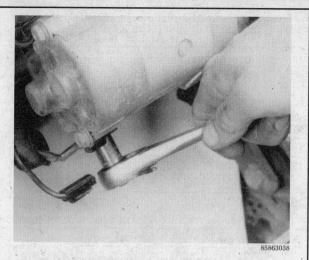

Fig. 36 If equipped, loosen the retaining nut and remove the ring terminal connector

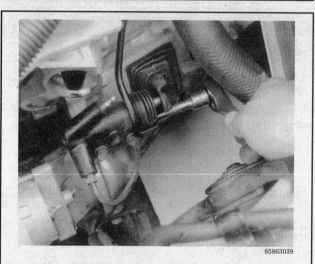

Fig. 37 Loosen the starter retainers, in most cases a long extension will be helpful here

Fig. 38 Separate the starter from the engine and remove it from the vehicle

2. Unscrew the two solenoid switch (magnetic switch) retaining screws.

3. Remove the solenoid. In order to unhook the solenoid from the starter drive lever, lift it up at the same time that you are pulling it out of the starter housing.

4. Installation is in the reverse order of removal. Make sure that the solenoid switch is properly engaged with the drive lever before tightening the mounting screws.

BRUSH REPLACEMENT

1. Remove the starter from the vehicle.
2. Remove the solenoid (magnetic switch).
3. Remove the two end frame cap mounting bolts and remove the end frame cap.
4. Remove the O-ring and the lock plate from the armature shaft groove then slide the shims off the shaft.
5. Unscrew the two long housing screws (they are found at the front of the starter) and carefully pull off the end plate.
6. Using a screwdriver, separate the brushes and the brush springs then remove the brushes from the brush holder.
7. Slide the brush holder off of the armature shaft.

8. Crush the old brushes off of the copper braid and file away any remaining solder.

9. Fit the new brushes to the braid and spread the braid slightly.

➡ **You will need a soldering iron of at least 250 watts.**

10. Using radio solder, solder the brush to the braid. Grip the copper braid with flat pliers to prevent the solder from flowing down its length.

11. File off any extra solder and then repeat the procedure for the remaining three brushes.

12. Installation is in the reverse order of removal.

➡ **When installing the brush holder, make sure that the brushes line up properly.**

STARTER DRIVE REPLACEMENT

1. Remove the starter from the vehicle.
2. Remove the solenoid (magnetic switch).
3. Remove the two end frame cap mounting bolts and remove the cap.

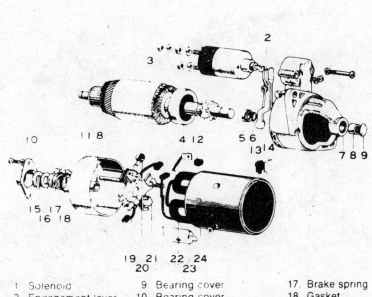

1. Solenoid	9. Bearing cover	17. Brake spring
2. Engagement lever	10. Bearing cover	18. Gasket
3. Armature	11. Commutator end frame	19. Brush
4. Overrunning clutch	12. Rubber bushing	20. Brush spring
5. Clutch stop	13. Rubber grommet	21. Brush holder
6. Snap-ring	14. Plate	22. Field coil
7. Drive housing	15. Lockplate	23. Pole shoes
8. Bushing	16. Washer	24. Field yoke

85863041

Fig. 39 Exploded view of a common direct-drive starter motor assembly

4. Remove the O-ring and the lock plate from the armature shaft groove, then slide the shims off the shaft.

5. Unscrew the two long housing screws (they are found at the front of the starter) and carefully pull off the end plate.

6. Using a screwdriver, separate the brushes and the brush springs then remove the brushes from the holder.

7. Slide the brush holder off of the armature shaft.

8. Pull the field frame away from the drive housing and remove it.

9. Remove the drive lever pivot bolt from the drive housing.

10. Pull the armature from the drive housing.

11. Take a 14mm socket and slide it over the armature shaft until it rests on the stop collar.

12. Tap the stop collar down with a hammer.

13. Pry off the exposed stopring and then remove the stop collar from the shaft.

14. Remove the starter drive clutch assembly.

15. Installation is in the reverse order of removal.

Reduction Gear Type

BRUSH REPLACEMENT

1. Remove the starter from the vehicle.

2. Disconnect the lead from the solenoid (magnetic switch) terminal.

3. Unscrew the two mounting bolts and remove the field frame assembly from the solenoid housing.

4. Remove the O-ring and the felt seal.

5. Unthread the mounting screws and remove the starter housing from the solenoid housing.

6. Pull out the clutch assembly, then remove the pinion and idler gears.

7. Remove the steel ball from the clutch shaft hole.

8. Using a screwdriver, separate the brushes and the brush springs and then remove the brushes from the holder.

9. Slide the brush holder off of the armature shaft.

10. Crush the old brushes off of the copper braid and file away any remaining solder.

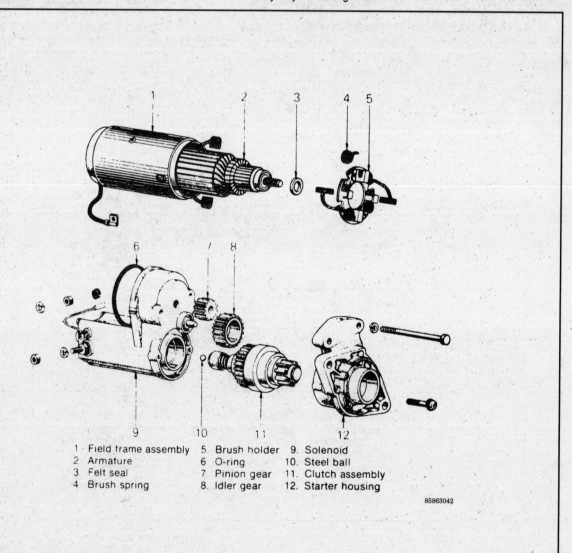

1 Field frame assembly	5. Brush holder	9. Solenoid
2 Armature	6 O-ring	10. Steel ball
3 Felt seal	7. Pinion gear	11. Clutch assembly
4 Brush spring	8. Idler gear	12. Starter housing

85863042

Fig. 40 Exploded view of a common gear reduction starter motor

11. Fit the new brushes to the braid and spread the braid slightly.

➡️ **You will need a soldering iron of at least 250 watts.**

12. Using radio solder, solder the brush to the braid. Grip the copper braid with flat pliers to prevent the solder from flowing down its length.

13. File off any extra solder and then repeat the procedure for the remaining three brushes.

14. Installation is in the reverse order of removal.

➡️ **When installing the brush holder, make sure that the brushes line up properly.**

BATTERY AND STARTER SPECIFICATIONS

Year	Engine Series Identification	Ampere Hour Capacity	Volts	Terminal Grounded	Load Test Amps	Load Test Volts	Torque (ft. lbs.)	No Load Test Amps	No Load Test Volts	RPM	Minimum Brush Tension (oz.)	Minimum Brush Length (in.)
1970	3K-C	48	12	Negative	450	8.5	8	55	11	3,500	21	0.51
1971	3K-C	48	12	Negative	450	8.5	8	55	11	3,500	21	0.51
	2T-C	50	12	Negative	Not Recommended			①	11.5	3,500	52.8	0.55
1972	3K-C	48	12	Negative	450	8.5	8	55	11	3,500	21	0.51
	2T-C	50	12	Negative	Not Recommended			①	11.5	3,500	52.8	0.55
1973	3K-C	48	12	Negative	450	8.5	8	55	11	3,500	21	0.51
	2T-C	50	12	Negative	Not Recommended			①	11.5	3,500	52.8	0.55
1974	3K-C	48	12	Negative	450	8.5	8	55	11	3,500	21	0.51
	2T-C	50	12	Negative	Not Recommended			①	11.5	3,500	52.8	0.55
1975	3K-C	48	12	Negative	450	8.5	8	55	11	3,500	21	0.51
	2T-C	50	12	Negative	Not Recommended			①	11.5	3,500	52.8	0.55
1976	3K-C	48	12	Negative	450	8.5	8	55	11	3,500	21	0.51
	2T-C	50	12	Negative	Not Recommended			①	11.5	3,500	52.8	0.55
1977	3K-C	50	12	Negative	600	7	13	50	11	5,000	21	0.47
	2T-C	60	12	Negative	Not Recommended			90	11.5	4,000	-21	0.33
1978	3K-C	50	12	Negative	600	7	13	50	11	5,000	21	0.47
	2T-C	60	12	Negative	Not Recommended			90	11.5	4,000	21	0.33
1979	3K-C	50	12	Negative	600	7	13	50	11	5,000	21	0.47
	2T-C	60	12	Negative	Not Recommended			90	11.5	4,000	21	0.33
1980	3T-C	50, 60, 110	12	Negative	Not Recommended			90	11.5	3,500	31.6	0.57
1981	3T-C	50, 60, 110	12	Negative	Not Recommended			90	11.5	3,500	31.6	0.57
1982	3T-C	50, 60, 110	12	Negative	Not Recommended			90	11.5	3,500	31.6	0.57
1983	4A-C, 4A-LC	50, 60, 110	12	Negative	Not Recommended			90	11.5	3,500	31.6	0.57
1984	4A-C, 4A-LC	50, 60, 110	12	Negative	Not Recommended			90	11.5	3,500	31.6	0.57
	1C-L	50, 60, 110	12	Negative	Not Recommended			90	11.5	3,500	31.6	0.57
1985	4A-C, 4A-LC	50, 60, 110	12	Negative	Not Recommended			90	11.5	3,500	31.6	0.57
	1C-L	50, 60, 110	12	Negative	Not Recommended			90	11.5	3,500	31.6	0.57
	4A-GE	50, 60, 110	12	Negative	Not Recommended			90	11.5	3,500	31.6	0.57
1986	4A-C, 4A-LC	50, 60, 110	12	Negative	Not Recommended			90	11.5	3,500	31.6	0.57
	4A-GE	50, 60, 110	12	Negative	Not Recommended			90	11.5	3,500	31.6	0.57
1987	4A-C, 4A-LC	50, 60, 110	12	Negative	Not Recommended			90	11.5	3,500	31.6	0.57
	4A-GE	50, 60, 110	12	Negative	Not Recommended			90	11.5	3,500	31.6	0.57

① Less than 90 amps

85863043

ENGINE MECHANICAL

Understanding the Engine

The basic piston engine is a metal block containing a series of chambers. The upper engine block is usually an iron or aluminum alloy casting, consisting of outer walls, which form hollow jackets around the cylinder walls. The lower block of most engines provides a number of rigid mounting points for the bearings which hold the crankshaft in place, and is known as the crankcase. The hollow jackets of the upper block add to the rigidity of the engine and contain the liquid coolant which carries the heat away from the cylinders and other engine parts. The block of an air cooled engine (through these are rarely seen in automotive applications today) consists of a crankcase which provides for the rigid mounting of the crankshaft and for studs which hold the cylinders in place. The cylinders are individual, single-wall castings, finned for cooling, and are usually bolted to the crankcase, rather than cast integrally with the block. In a water-cooled engine, only the cylinder head is bolted to the top of the block. The water pump is usually mounted directly to the block.

The crankshaft is a long, iron or steel shaft mounted rigidly in the bottom of the crankcase, at a number of points (usually 4-7). The crankshaft is free to turn and contains a number of counterweighted crankpins (one for each cylinder) that are offset several inches from the center of the crankshaft and turn in a circle as the crankshaft turns. The crankpins are centered under each cylinder. Pistons, equipped with circular rings to seal the small space between the pistons and wall of the cylinders, are connected to the crankpins by steel connecting rods. The rods connect the pistons at their upper ends to the crankpins at their lower ends.

When the crankshaft spins, the pistons move up and down in the cylinder. Two openings in each cylinder head (above the cylinders) allow the intake of the air/fuel mixture and the exhaust of the burned gases. The volume of the combustion chamber must be variable. This allows the engine to compress the fuel charge before combustion, to make use of the expansion of the burning gases and to exhaust the burned gases (in order to take in a fresh fuel mixture). As the pistons are forced downward by the expansion of burning fuel, the connecting rods convert the reciprocating (up and down) motion of the pistons into rotary (turning) motion of the crankshaft. A round flywheel at the rear of the crankshaft provides a large, stable mass to smooth out the rotation.

The cylinder head forms a tight cover for the tops of the cylinders and contains machined chambers into which the fuel mixture is forced as it is compressed by the pistons reaching the upper limit of their travel. Each combustion chamber contains at least one intake valve, one exhaust valve and one spark plug per cylinder. Some modern engines are equipped with multiple intake and/or exhaust valves. The spark plugs are screwed into holes in the cylinder head so that the tips protrude into the combustion chambers. The valve in each opening is opened and closed by the action of the camshaft. The camshaft is driven by the crankshaft through a chain or belt at $\frac{1}{2}$ crankshaft speed (the camshaft gear is twice the size of the crankshaft gear). The valves are operated through a valve train which may take various forms. Many older engines utilize lifters, pushrods and rocker arms. Overhead camshaft engines may utilize rockers arms (with or without adjustment shim tappets) or may actuate the valves directly through lifters or shims.

Lubricating oil is stored in a pan at the bottom of the engine and is force fed to all parts of the engine by a gear type pump, driven from the crankshaft. The oil lubricates the entire engine and also seals the piston rings, giving good compression.

Engine Overhaul Tips

Most engine overhaul procedures are fairly standard. In addition to specific parts replacement procedures and specifications for your individual engine, this section is also a guide to acceptable rebuilding procedures. Examples of standard rebuilding practice are shown and should be used along with specific details concerning your particular engine.

In most instances it is more profitable for the do-it-yourself mechanic to remove, clean and inspect the component, buy the necessary parts and deliver these to a shop for actual machine work. Competent and accurate machine shop services will ensure maximum performance, reliability and engine life.

On the other hand, much of the rebuilding work (crankshaft, block, bearings, piston rods, and other components) is well within the scope of the do-it-yourself mechanic's tools and abilities. You will have to decide for yourself the depth of involvement you desire in an engine repair or rebuild.

TOOLS

The tools required for an engine overhaul or parts replacement will depend on the depth of your involvement. With a few exceptions, they will be the tools found in a mechanic's tool kit (see Section 1 of this manual). More in-depth work will require some or all of the following:
- a dial indicator (reading in thousandths) mounted on a universal base
- micrometers and telescope gauges
- jaw and screw-type pullers
- scraper
- valve spring compressor
- ring groove cleaner
- piston ring expander and compressor
- ridge reamer
- cylinder hone or glaze breaker
- Plastigage®
- engine stand

The use of most of these tools is found in this section. Many can be rented for a one-time use from a local parts jobber or tool supply house specializing in automotive work.

Occasionally, the use of special tools is called for. See the information on special tools and the safety notice in the front of this book before substituting another tool.

INSPECTION TECHNIQUES

Procedures and specifications are given in this section for inspecting, cleaning and assessing the wear limits of most major components. Other procedures such as Magnaflux® and Zyglo® can be used to locate material flaws and stress cracks. Magnaflux® is a magnetic process applicable only to ferrous materials. The Zyglo® process coats the material with a fluorescent dye penetrant and can be used on any material. Checking for suspected surface cracks can be more readily made using spot check dye. The dye is sprayed onto the suspected area, wiped off and the area then sprayed with a developer. Cracks will show up brightly.

OVERHAUL TIPS

Aluminum has become extremely popular for use in engines, due to its low weight. Observe the following precautions when handling aluminum parts:
• Never hot tank aluminum parts (the caustic hot tank solution will eat the aluminum.
• Remove all aluminum parts (identification tag, etc.) from engine parts prior to the tanking.
• Always coat threads lightly with engine oil or anti-seize compounds before installation, to prevent seizure.
• Never overtorque bolts or spark plugs especially in aluminum threads.
• If you are unsure if a part is aluminum check it using a magnet. The magnet will not stick to aluminum.
Stripped threads in any component can be repaired using any of several commercial repair kits (Heli-Coil®, Microdot®, Keenserts®, etc.).

When assembling the engine, any parts that will be exposed to frictional contact must be prelubed to provide lubrication at initial start-up. Any product specifically formulated for this purpose can be used, but engine oil is not recommended as a prelube in most cases, unless the engine will be run immediately after assembly.

When semi-permanent (locked, but removable) installation of bolts or nuts is desired, threads should be cleaned and coated with Loctite® or other similar, commercial non-hardening sealant.

REPAIRING DAMAGED THREADS

▶ **See Figures 41, 42, 43, 44 and 45**

Several methods of repairing damaged threads are available. Heli-Coil® (shown here), Keenserts® and Microdot® are among the most widely used. All involve basically the same principle — drilling out stripped threads, tapping the hole and installing a prewound insert — making welding, plugging and oversize fasteners unnecessary.

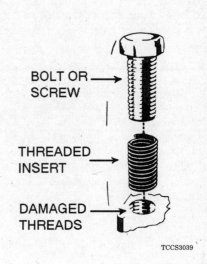

Fig. 41 Damaged bolt hole threads can be replaced with thread repair inserts

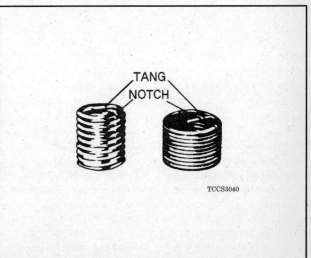

Fig. 42 Standard thread repair insert (left), and spark plug thread insert

Two types of thread repair inserts are usually supplied: a standard type for most Inch Coarse, Inch Fine, Metric Course and Metric Fine thread sizes and a spark lug type to fit most spark plug port sizes. Consult the individual manufacturer's catalog to determine exact applications. Typical thread repair kits will contain a selection of prewound threaded inserts, a tap (corresponding to the outside diameter threads of the insert) and an installation tool. Spark plug inserts usually differ because they require a tap equipped with pilot threads and a combined reamer/tap section. Most manufacturers also supply blister-packed thread repair inserts separately or in a master kit containing a variety of taps and inserts plus installation tools.

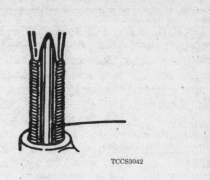

Fig. 44 Using the kit, tap the hole in order to receive the thread insert. Keep the tap well oiled and back it out frequently to avoid clogging the threads.

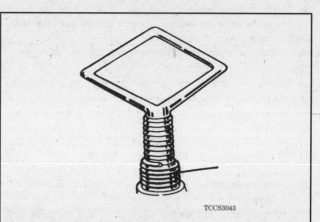

Fig. 45 Screw the threaded insert onto the installer tool until the tang engages the slot. Thread the insert into the hole until it is ¼ or ½ turn below the top surface, then remove the tool and break off the tang using a punch.

Before repairing to a threaded hole, remove any snapped, broken or damaged bolt/studs. Penetrating oil can be used to free frozen threads. The offending item can be removed with locking pliers or with a screw/stud extractor. After the hole is clear, the thread can be repaired, as shown in the series of accompanying illustrations and in the kit manufacturer's instructions.

Fig. 43 Drill out the damaged threads with the specified drill. Be sure to drill completely through the hole or to the bottom of a blind hole

GENERAL ENGINE SPECIFICATIONS

Year	Engine Series Identification	Engine Displacement Cu. In. (cc)	Fuel System Type	Net Horsepower @ rpm	Net Torque @ rpm (ft. lbs.)	Bore × Stroke (in.)	Compression Ratio
1970	3K-C	71 (1166)	2 bbl	73 @ 6000	70 @ 4200	2.95 × 2.60	9.0:1
1971	3K-C	71 (1166)	2 bbl	73 @ 6000	70 @ 4200	2.95 × 2.60	9.0:1
	2T-C	97 (1588)	2 bbl	102 @ 6000	101 @ 3800	3.35 × 2.76	8.5:1
1972	3K-C	71 (1166)	2 bbl	65 @ 6000	67 @ 3800	2.95 × 2.60	9.0:1
	2T-C	97 (1588)	2 bbl	88 @ 6000	98 @ 3800	3.35 × 2.76	8.5:1
1973	3K-C	71 (1166)	2 bbl	65 @ 6000	67 @ 3800	2.95 × 2.60	9.0:1
	2T-C	97 (1588)	2 bbl	88 @ 6000	98 @ 3800	3.35 × 2.76	8.5:1
1974	3K-C	71 (1166)	2 bbl	65 @ 6000	67 @ 3800	2.95 × 2.60	9.0:1
	2T-C	97 (1588)	2 bbl	88 @ 6000	98 @ 3800	3.35 × 2.76	8.5:1
1975	3K-C	71 (1166)	2 bbl	65 @ 6000	67 @ 3800	2.95 × 2.60	9.0:1
	2T-C	97 (1588)	2 bbl	75 @ 5800	83 @ 3800	3.35 × 2.76	9.0:1
1976	3K-C	71 (1166)	2 bbl	65 @ 6000	67 @ 3800	2.95 × 2.60	9.0:1
	2T-C	97 (1588)	2 bbl	75 @ 5800	83 @ 3800	3.35 × 2.76	9.0:1
1977	3K-C	71 (1166)	2 bbl	65 @ 6000	67 @ 3800	2.95 × 2.60	9.0:1
	2T-C	97 (1588)	2 bbl	75 @ 5800	83 @ 3800	3.35 × 2.76	9.0:1
1978	3K-C	71 (1166)	2 bbl	58 @ 5800	63 @ 3800	2.95 × 2.60	9.0:1
	2T-C	97 (1588)	2 bbl	75 @ 5400	85 @ 2800	3.35 × 2.76	9.0:1
1979	3K-C	71 (1166)	2 bbl	58 @ 5800	63 @ 3800	2.95 × 2.60	9.0:1
	2T-C	97 (1588)	2 bbl	75 @ 5400	85 @ 2800	3.35 × 2.76	9.0:1
1980	3T-C	108 (1770)	2 bbl	75 @ 5000 ①	95 @ 2600 ②	3.35 × 3.07	9.0:1
1981	3T-C	108 (1770)	2 bbl	75 @ 5000 ①	95 @ 2600 ②	3.35 × 3.07	9.0:1
1982	3T-C	108 (1770)	2 bbl	70 @ 4600	93 @ 2400	3.35 × 3.07	9.0:1
1983	4A-C, 4A-LC	97 (1587)	2 bbl	70 @ 4800	85 @ 2800	3.19 × 3.03	9.0:1
1984	4A-C, 4A-LC	97 (1587)	2 bbl	70 @ 4800	85 @ 2800	3.19 × 3.03	9.0:1
	1C-L	112 (1839)	DFI	56 @ 4500	76 @ 3000	3.27 × 3.35	22.5:1
1985	4A-C, 4A-LC	97 (1587)	2 bbl	70 @ 4800	85 @ 2800	3.19 × 3.03	9.0:1
	4A-GE	97 (1587)	EFI	112 @ 6600	97 @ 4800	3.19 × 3.03	9.4:1
	1C-L	112 (1839)	DFI	56 @ 4500	76 @ 3000	3.27 × 3.35	22.5:1
1986	4A-C, 4A-LC	97 (1587)	2 bbl	74 @ 5200	86 @ 2800	3.19 × 3.03	9.0:1
	4A-GE	97 (1587)	EFI	112 @ 6600	97 @ 4800	3.19 × 3.03	9.4:1
1987	4A-C, 4A-LC	97 (1587)	2 bbl	74 @ 5200	86 @ 2800	3.19 × 3.03	9.0:1
	4A-GE	97 (1587)	EFI	112 @ 6600	97 @ 4800	3.19 × 3.03	9.4:1

2 bbl—2 barrel carburetor
EFI—Electronic Fuel Injection
DFI—Diesel Fuel Injection
① California: 73 @ 5000
② California: 90 @ 2600

85863049

VALVE SPECIFICATIONS

Year	Engine Series Identification	Engine Displacement Cu. In. (cc)	Seat Angle (deg.)	Face Angle (deg.)	Spring Pressure (lbs.)	Spring Installed Height (in.)	Stem-to-Guide Clearance (in.)		Stem Diameter (in.)	
							Intake	Exhaust	Intake	Exhaust
1970	3K-C	71 (1166)	45	44.5	70.1	1.512	0.0010–0.0020	0.0021–0.0030	0.3140	0.3140
1971	3K-C	71 (1166)	45	44.5	70.1	1.512	0.0010–0.0020	0.0021–0.0030	0.3140	0.3140
	2T-C	97 (1588)	45	44.5	58.4	1.484	0.0012–0.0020	0.0012–0.0024	0.3410	0.3410
1972	3K-C	71 (1166)	45	44.5	70.1	1.512	0.0010–0.0020	0.0021–0.0030	0.3140	0.3140
	2T-C	97 (1588)	45	44.5	58.4	1.484	0.0012–0.0020	0.0012–0.0024	0.3410	0.3410
1973	3K-C	71 (1166)	45	44.5	70.1	1.512	0.0010–0.0020	0.0021–0.0030	0.3140	0.3140
	2T-C	97 (1588)	45	44.5	58.4	1.484	0.0012–0.0020	0.0012–0.0024	0.3410	0.3410
1974	3K-C	71 (1166)	45	44.5	70.1	1.512	0.0010–0.0020	0.0021–0.0030	0.3140	0.3140
	2T-C	97 (1588)	45	44.5	58.4	1.484	0.0012–0.0020	0.0012–0.0024	0.3410	0.3410
1975	3K-C	71 (1166)	45	44.5	70.1	1.512	0.0010–0.0020	0.0021–0.0030	0.3140	0.3140
	2T-C	97 (1588)	45	44.5	58.4	1.484	0.0012–0.0020	0.0012–0.0024	0.3410	0.3410
1976	3K-C	71 (1166)	45	44.5	70.1	1.512	0.0010–0.0020	0.0021–0.0030	0.3140	0.3140
	2T-C	97 (1588)	45	44.5	58.4	1.484	0.0012–0.0020	0.0012–0.0024	0.3410	0.3410
1977	3K-C	71 (1166)	45	44.5	70.1	1.512	0.0010–0.0020	0.0021–0.0030	0.3140	0.3140
	2T-C	97 (1588)	45	44.5	58.4	1.484	0.0012–0.0020	0.0012–0.0024	0.3410	0.3410
1978	3K-C	71 (1166)	45	44.5	70.1	1.512	0.0012–0.0026	0.0014–0.0028	0.3140	0.3140
	2T-C	97 (1588)	45	44.5	57.9	1.484	0.0012–0.0020	0.0012–0.0024	0.3410	0.3410
1979	3K-C	71 (1166)	45	44.5	70.1	1.512	0.0012–0.0026	0.0014–0.0028	0.3140	0.3140
	2T-C	97 (1588)	45	44.5	57.9	1.484	0.0012–0.0020	0.0012–0.0024	0.3410	0.3410
1980	3T-C	108 (1770)	45	44.5	57.9	1.484	0.0010–0.0024	0.0012–0.0026	0.3139	0.3139
1981	3T-C	108 (1770)	45	44.5	57.9	1.484	0.0010–0.0024	0.0012–0.0026	0.3139	0.3139
1982	3T-C	108 (1770)	45	44.5	57.9	1.484	0.0010–0.0024	0.0012–0.0026	0.3139	0.3139

85863050

VALVE SPECIFICATIONS

Year	Engine Series Identification	Engine Displacement Cu. In. (cc)	Seat Angle (deg.)	Face Angle (deg.)	Spring Pressure (lbs.)	Spring Installed Height (in.)	Stem-to-Guide Clearance (in.)		Stem Diameter (in.)	
							Intake	Exhaust	Intake	Exhaust
1983	4A-C, 4A-LC	97 (1587)	45	44.5	52	1.520	0.0010–0.0024	0.0012–0.0026	0.2744–0.2750	0.2742–0.2748
1984	4A-C, 4A-LC	97 (1587)	45	44.5	52	1.520	0.0010–0.0024	0.0012–0.0026	0.2744–0.2750	0.2742–0.2748
1984	4A-C, 4A-LC	97 (1587)	45	44.5	52	1.520	0.0010–0.0024	0.0012–0.0026	0.2744–0.2750	0.2742–0.2748
	1C-L	112 (1839)	45	44.5	53	1.587	0.0008–0.0022	0.0014–0.0028	0.3140–0.3146	0.3134–0.3140
1985	4A-C, 4A-LC	97 (1587)	45	44.5	52	1.520	0.0010–0.0024	0.0012–0.0026	0.2744–0.2750	0.2742–0.2748
	4A-GE	97 (1587)	45	44.5	35.9	1.366	0.0010–0.0024	0.0012–0.0026	0.2350–0.2356	0.2348–0.2354
	1C-L	112 (1839)	45	44.5	53	1.587	0.0008–0.0022	0.0014–0.0028	0.3140–0.3146	0.3134–0.3140
1986	4A-C, 4A-LC	97 (1587)	45	44.5	52	1.520	0.0010–0.0024	0.0012–0.0026	0.2744–0.2750	0.2742–0.2748
	4A-GE	97 (1587)	45	44.5	35.9	1.366	0.0010–0.0024	0.0012–0.0026	0.2350–0.2356	0.2348–0.2354
1987	4A-C, 4A-LC	97 (1587)	45	44.5	52	1.520	0.0010–0.0024	0.0012–0.0026	0.2744–0.2750	0.2742–0.2748
	4A-GE	97 (1587)	45	44.5	35.9	1.366	0.0010–0.0024	0.0012–0.0026	0.2350–0.2356	0.2348–0.2354

8586305A

CAMSHAFT SPECIFICATIONS

All measurements given in inches.

Year	Engine Series Identification	Engine Displacement Cu. In. (cc)	Journal Diameter					Lobe Lift		Bearing Clearance	Camshaft End Play
			1	2	3	4	5	In.	Ex.		
1970	3K-C	71 (1166)	1.7011–1.7018	1.6911–1.6917	1.6813–1.6819	1.6716–1.6722	—	NA	NA	①	0.0030–0.0060
1971	3K-C	71 (1166)	1.7011–1.7018	1.6911–1.6917	1.6813–1.6819	1.6716–1.6722	—	NA	NA	①	0.0030–0.0060
	2T-C	97 (1588)	1.8291–1.8297	1.8292–1.8199	1.8094–1.8100	1.7996–1.8002	1.7897–1.7904	NA	NA	0.0010–0.0026	0.0030–0.0060
1972	3K-C	71 (1166)	1.7011–1.7018	1.6911–1.6917	1.6813–1.6819	1.6716–1.6722	—	NA	NA	①	0.0030–0.0060
	2T-C	97 (1588)	1.8291–1.8297	1.8292–1.8199	1.8094–1.8100	1.7996–1.8002	1.7897–1.7904	NA	NA	0.0010–0.0026	0.0030–0.0060
1973	3K-C	71 (1166)	1.7011–1.7018	1.6911–1.6917	1.6813–1.6819	1.6716–1.6722	—	NA	NA	①	0.0030–0.0060
	2T-C	97 (1588)	1.8291–1.8297	1.8292–1.8199	1.8094–1.8100	1.7996–1.8002	1.7897–1.7904	NA	NA	0.0010–0.0026	0.0030–0.0060
1974	3K-C	71 (1166)	1.7011–1.7018	1.6911–1.6917	1.6813–1.6819	1.6716–1.6722	—	NA	NA	①	0.0030–0.0060
	2T-C	97 (1588)	1.8291–1.8297	1.8292–1.8199	1.8094–1.8100	1.7996–1.8002	1.7897–1.7904	NA	NA	0.0010–0.0026	0.0030–0.0060
1975	3K-C	71 (1166)	1.7011–1.7018	1.6911–1.6917	1.6813–1.6819	1.6716–1.6722	—	NA	NA	①	0.0030–0.0060
	2T-C	97 (1588)	1.8291–1.8297	1.8292–1.8199	1.8094–1.8100	1.7996–1.8002	1.7897–1.7904	NA	NA	0.0010–0.0026	0.0030–0.0060
1976	3K-C	71 (1166)	1.7011–1.7018	1.6911–1.6917	1.6813–1.6819	1.6716–1.6722	—	NA	NA	①	0.0030–0.0060
	2T-C	97 (1588)	1.8291–1.8297	1.8292–1.8199	1.8094–1.8100	1.7996–1.8002	1.7897–1.7904	NA	NA	0.0010–0.0026	0.0030–0.0060
1977	3K-C	71 (1166)	1.7011–1.7018	1.6911–1.6917	1.6813–1.6819	1.6716–1.6722	—	NA	NA	①	0.0030–0.0060
	2T-C	97 (1588)	1.8291–1.8297	1.8292–1.8199	1.8094–1.8100	1.7996–1.8002	1.7897–1.7904	NA	NA	0.0010–0.0026	0.0030–0.0060
1978	3K-C	71 (1166)	1.7011–1.7018	1.6911–1.6917	1.6813–1.6819	1.6716–1.6722	—	NA	NA	①	0.0030–0.0060
	2T-C	97 (1588)	1.8291–1.8297	1.8292–1.8199	1.8094–1.8100	1.7996–1.8002	1.7897–1.7904	NA	NA	0.0010–0.0026	0.0030–0.0060
1979	3K-C	71 (1166)	1.7011–1.7018	1.6911–1.6917	1.6813–1.6819	1.6716–1.6722	—	NA	NA	①	0.0030–0.0060
	2T-C	97 (1588)	1.8291–1.8297	1.8292–1.8199	1.8094–1.8100	1.7996–1.8002	1.7897–1.7904	NA	NA	0.0010–0.0026	0.0030–0.0060
1980	3T-C	108 (1770)	1.8291–1.8297	1.8292–1.8199	1.8094–1.8100	1.7996–1.8002	1.7897–1.7904	1.5295–②1.5335	1.5059–③1.5098	0.0010–0.0026	0.0030–0.0060
1981	3T-C	108 (1770)	1.8291–1.8297	1.8292–1.8199	1.8094–1.8100	1.7996–1.8002	1.7897–1.7904	1.5295–②1.5335	1.5059–③1.5098	0.0010–0.0026	0.0030–0.0060
1982	3T-C	108 (1770)	1.8291–1.8297	1.8292–1.8199	1.8094–1.8100	1.7996–1.8002	1.7897–1.7904	1.5295–②1.5335	1.5059–③1.5098	0.0010–0.0026	0.0030–0.0060

85863051

CAMSHAFT SPECIFICATIONS

All measurements given in inches.

Year	Engine Series Identification	Engine Displacement Cu. In. (cc)	Journal Diameter					Lobe Lift		Bearing Clearance	Camshaft End Play
			1	2	3	4	5	In.	Ex.		
1983	4A-C	97 (1587)	1.1015–1.1022	1.1015–1.8199	1.1015–1.8100	1.1015–1.8002	—	1.5528–1.5531	1.5528–1.5531	0.0015–0.0029	0.0031–0.0071
	4A-LC	97 (1587)	1.1015–1.1022	1.1015–1.8199	1.1015–1.8100	1.1015–1.8002	—	1.5528–1.5531	1.5528–1.5531	0.0015–0.0029	0.0031–0.0071
1984	4A-C	97 (1587)	1.1015–1.1022	1.1015–1.8199	1.1015–1.8100	1.1015–1.8002	—	1.5528–1.5531	1.5528–1.5531	0.0015–0.0029	0.0031–0.0071
	4A-LC	97 (1587)	1.1015–1.1022	1.1015–1.8199	1.1015–1.8100	1.1015–1.8002	—	1.5528–1.5531	1.5528–1.5531	0.0015–0.0029	0.0031–0.0071
	1C-L	112 (1839)	1.1015–1.1022	1.1015–1.8199	1.1015–1.8100	1.1015–1.8002	—	1.8474 MIN	1.8478 MIN	0.0015–0.0029	0.0031–0.0071
1985	4A-C	97 (1587)	1.1015–1.1022	1.1015–1.8199	1.1015–1.8100	1.1015–1.8002	—	1.5528–1.5531	1.5528–1.5531	0.0015–0.0029	0.0031–0.0071
	4A-LC	97 (1587)	1.1015–1.1022	1.1015–1.8199	1.1015–1.8100	1.1015–1.8002	—	1.5528–1.5531	1.5528–1.5531	0.0015–0.0029	0.0031–0.0071
	4A-GE	97 (1587)	1.0610–1.0616	1.0610–1.0616	1.0610–1.0616	1.0610–1.0616	—	1.3998–1.4002	1.3998–1.4002	0.0014–0.0028	0.0031–0.0075
	1C-L	112 (1839)	1.1015–1.1022	1.1015–1.8199	1.1015–1.8100	1.1015–1.8002	—	1.8474 MIN	1.8478 MIN	0.0015–0.0029	0.0031–0.0071
1986	4A-C	97 (1587)	1.1015–1.1022	1.1015–1.8199	1.1015–1.8100	1.1015–1.8002	—	1.5528–④ 1.5531	1.5528–④ 1.5531	0.0015–0.0029	0.0031–0.0071
	4A-LC	97 (1587)	1.1015–1.1022	1.1015–1.8199	1.1015–1.8100	1.1015–1.8002	—	1.5528–④ 1.5531	1.5528–④ 1.5531	0.0015–0.0029	0.0031–0.0071
	4A-GE	97 (1587)	1.0610–1.0616	1.0610–1.0616	1.0610–1.0616	1.0610–1.0616	—	1.3998–1.4002	1.3998–1.4002	0.0014–0.0028	0.0031–0.0075
1987	4A-C	97 (1587)	1.1015–1.1022	1.1015–1.8199	1.1015–1.8100	1.1015–1.8002	—	1.5528–④ 1.5531	1.5528–④ 1.5531	0.0015–0.0029	0.0031–0.0071
	4A-LC	97 (1587)	1.1015–1.1022	1.1015–1.8199	1.1015–1.8100	1.1015–1.8002	—	1.5528–④ 1.5531	1.5528–④ 1.5531	0.0015–0.0029	0.0031–0.0071
	4A-GE	97 (1587)	1.0610–1.0616	1.0610–1.0616	1.0610–1.0616	1.0610–1.0616	—	1.3998–1.4002	1.3998–1.4002	0.0014–0.0028	0.0031–0.0075

① Nos. 1 & 4: 0.0010–0.0026, Nos. 2 & 3: 0.0014–0.0028
② Specification is for USA, Canada: 1.5102–1.5142
③ Specification is for USA, Canada: 1.5059–1.5098
④ Specification is for RWD, FWD: 1.5508–1.5547

8586305B

CRANKSHAFT AND CONNECTING ROD SPECIFICATIONS

Year	Engine Series Identification	Engine Displacement Cu. In. (cc)	Crankshaft				Connecting Rod		
			Main Brg. Journal Dia.	Main Brg. Oil Clearance	Shaft End-play	Thrust on No.	Journal Diameter	Oil Clearance	Side Clearance
1970	3K-C	71 (1166)	1.9675–1.9685	0.0005–0.0015	0.0020–0.0090	3	1.6525–1.6535	0.0006–0.0015	0.0040–0.0080
1971	3K-C	71 (1166)	1.9675–1.9685	0.0005–0.0015	0.0020–0.0090	3	1.6525–1.6535	0.0006–0.0015	0.0040–0.0080
	2T-C	97 (1588)	2.2827–2.2834	0.0012–0.0024	0.0030–0.0070	3	1.8889–1.8897	0.0008–0.0020	0.0063–0.0102
1972	3K-C	71 (1166)	1.9675–1.9685	0.0005–0.0015	0.0020–0.0090	3	1.6525–1.6535	0.0006–0.0015	0.0040–0.0080
	2T-C	97 (1588)	2.2827–2.2834	0.0012–0.0024	0.0030–0.0070	3	1.8889–1.8897	0.0008–0.0020	0.0063–0.0102
1973	3K-C	71 (1166)	1.9675–1.9685	0.0005–0.0015	0.0020–0.0090	3	1.6525–1.6535	0.0006–0.0015	0.0040–0.0080
	2T-C	97 (1588)	2.2827–2.2834	0.0012–0.0024	0.0030–0.0070	3	1.8889–1.8897	0.0008–0.0020	0.0063–0.0102
1974	3K-C	71 (1166)	1.9675–1.9685	0.0005–0.0015	0.0020–0.0090	3	1.6525–1.6535	0.0006–0.0015	0.0040–0.0080
	2T-C	97 (1588)	2.2827–2.2834	0.0012–0.0024	0.0030–0.0070	3	1.8889–1.8897	0.0008–0.0020	0.0063–0.0102
1975	3K-C	71 (1166)	1.9675–1.9685	0.0005–0.0015	0.0020–0.0090	3	1.6525–1.6535	0.0006–0.0015	0.0040–0.0080
	2T-C	97 (1588)	2.2827–2.2834	0.0012–0.0024	0.0030–0.0070	3	1.8889–1.8897	0.0008–0.0020	0.0063–0.0102
1976	3K-C	71 (1166)	1.9675–1.9685	0.0005–0.0015	0.0020–0.0090	3	1.6525–1.6535	0.0006–0.0015	0.0040–0.0080
	2T-C	97 (1588)	2.2827–2.2834	0.0012–0.0024	0.0030–0.0070	3	1.8889–1.8897	0.0008–0.0020	0.0063–0.0102
1977	3K-C	71 (1166)	1.9675–1.9685	0.0005–0.0015	0.0020–0.0090	3	1.6525–1.6535	0.0006–0.0015	0.0040–0.0080
	2T-C	97 (1588)	2.2827–2.2834	0.0012–0.0024	0.0030–0.0070	3	1.8889–1.8897	0.0008–0.0020	0.0063–0.0102
1978	3K-C	71 (1166)	1.9675–1.9685	0.0005–0.0015	0.0016–0.0087	3	1.6525–1.6535	0.0009–0.0019	0.0043–0.0084
	2T-C	97 (1588)	2.2827–2.2834	0.0009–0.0019	0.0010–0.0090	3	1.8889–1.8897	0.0008–0.0020	0.0063–0.0102
1979	3K-C	71 (1166)	1.9675–1.9685	0.0005–0.0015	0.0016–0.0087	3	1.6525–1.6535	0.0009–0.0019	0.0043–0.0084
	2T-C	97 (1588)	2.2827–2.2834	0.0009–0.0019	0.0010–0.0090	3	1.8889–1.8897	0.0008–0.0020	0.0063–0.0102
1980	3T-C	108 (1770)	2.2825–2.2835	0.0009–0.0019	0.0008–0.0087	3	1.8889–1.8897	0.0009–0.0019	0.0063–0.0102
1981	3T-C	108 (1770)	2.2825–2.2835	0.0009–0.0019	0.0008–0.0087	3	1.8889–1.8897	0.0009–0.0019	0.0063–0.0102
1982	3T-C	108 (1770)	2.2825–2.2835	0.0009–0.0019	0.0008–0.0087	3	1.8889–1.8897	0.0009–0.0019	0.0063–0.0102

CRANKSHAFT AND CONNECTING ROD SPECIFICATIONS

Year	Engine Series Identification	Engine Displacement Cu. In. (cc)	Crankshaft Main Brg. Journal Dia.	Main Brg. Oil Clearance	Shaft End-play	Thrust on No.	Connecting Rod Journal Diameter	Oil Clearance	Side Clearance
1983	4A-C	97 (1587)	1.8892–1.8898	0.0005–0.0019	0.0008–0.0073	3	1.5742–1.5748	0.0008–0.0020	0.0059–0.0098
	4A-LC	97 (1587)	1.8891–1.8898	0.0006–0.0013	0.0008–0.0087	3	1.5742–1.5748	0.0008–0.0020	0.0059–0.0098
1984	4A-C	97 (1587)	1.8892–1.8898	0.0005–0.0019	0.0008–0.0073	3	1.5742–1.5748	0.0008–0.0020	0.0059–0.0098
	4A-LC	97 (1587)	1.8891–1.8898	0.0006–0.0013	0.0008–0.0087	3	1.5742–1.5748	0.0008–0.0020	0.0059–0.0098
	1C-L	112 (1839)	2.2435–2.2441	0.0013–0.0026	0.0016–0.0094	3	1.9877–1.9882	0.0014–0.0025	0.0031–0.0118
1985	4A-C	97 (1587)	1.8892–1.8898	0.0005–0.0019	0.0008–0.0073	3	1.5742–1.5748	0.0008–0.0020	0.0059–0.0098
	4A-LC	97 (1587)	1.8891–1.8898	0.0006–0.0013	0.0008–0.0087	3	1.5742–1.5748	0.0008–0.0020	0.0059–0.0098
	4A-GE	97 (1587)	1.8891–1.8898	0.0006–0.0013	0.0008–0.0087	3	1.5742–1.5748	0.0008–0.0020	0.0059–0.0098
	1C-L	112 (1839)	2.2435–2.2441	0.0013–0.0026	0.0016–0.0094	3	1.9877–1.9882	0.0014–0.0025	0.0031–0.0118
1986	4A-C	97 (1587)	1.8892–1.8898	0.0005–0.0019	0.0008–0.0073	3	1.5742–1.5748	0.0008–0.0020	0.0059–0.0098
	4A-LC	97 (1587)	1.8891–1.8898	0.0006–0.0013	0.0008–0.0087	3	1.5742–1.5748	0.0008–0.0020	0.0059–0.0098
	4A-GE	97 (1587)	1.8891–1.8898	0.0006–0.0013	0.0008–0.0087	3	1.5742–1.5748	0.0008–0.0020	0.0059–0.0098
1987	4A-C	97 (1587)	1.8892–1.8898	0.0005–0.0019	0.0008–0.0073	3	1.5742–1.5748	0.0008–0.0020	0.0059–0.0098
	4A-LC	97 (1587)	1.8891–1.8898	0.0006–0.0013	0.0008–0.0087	3	1.5742–1.5748	0.0008–0.0020	0.0059–0.0098
	4A-GE	97 (1587)	1.8891–1.8898	0.0006–0.0013	0.0008–0.0087	3	1.5742–1.5748	0.0008–0.0020	0.0059–0.0098

8586305C

PISTON AND RING SPECIFICATIONS

All measurements are given in inches.

Year	Engine Series Identification	Engine Displacement Cu. In. (cc)	Piston Clearance	Ring Gap			Ring Side Clearance		
				Top Compression	Bottom Compression	Oil Control	Top Compression	Bottom Compression	Oil Control
1970	3K-C	71 (1166)	0.0010–0.0020	0.0006–0.0014	0.0006–0.0014	0.0006–0.0014	0.0011–0.0027	0.0007–0.0023	0.0006–0.0023
1971	3K-C	71 (1166)	0.0010–0.0020	0.0006–0.0014	0.0006–0.0014	0.0006–0.0014	0.0011–0.0027	0.0007–0.0023	0.0006–0.0023
	2T-C	97 (1588)	0.0024–0.0031	0.0008–0.0016	0.0004–0.0012	0.0004–0.0012	0.0008–0.0024	0.0008–0.0024	0.0008–0.0024
1972	3K-C	71 (1166)	0.0010–0.0020	0.0006–0.0014	0.0006–0.0014	0.0006–0.0014	0.0011–0.0027	0.0007–0.0023	0.0006–0.0023
	2T-C	97 (1588)	0.0024–0.0031	0.0008–0.0016	0.0004–0.0012	0.0004–0.0012	0.0008–0.0024	0.0008–0.0024	0.0008–0.0024
1973	3K-C	71 (1166)	0.0010–0.0020	0.0006–0.0014	0.0006–0.0014	0.0006–0.0014	0.0011–0.0027	0.0007–0.0023	0.0006–0.0023
	2T-C	97 (1588)	0.0024–0.0031	0.0008–0.0016	0.0004–0.0012	0.0004–0.0012	0.0008–0.0024	0.0008–0.0024	0.0008–0.0024
1974	3K-C	71 (1166)	0.0010–0.0020	0.0006–0.0014	0.0006–0.0014	0.0006–0.0014	0.0011–0.0027	0.0007–0.0023	0.0006–0.0023
	2T-C	97 (1588)	0.0024–0.0031	0.0008–0.0016	0.0004–0.0012	0.0004–0.0012	0.0008–0.0024	0.0008–0.0024	0.0008–0.0024
1975	3K-C	71 (1166)	0.0010–0.0020	0.0006–0.0014	0.0006–0.0014	0.0006–0.0014	0.0011–0.0027	0.0007–0.0023	0.0006–0.0023
	2T-C	97 (1588)	0.0024–0.0031	0.0008–0.0016	0.0004–0.0012	0.0004–0.0012	0.0008–0.0024	0.0008–0.0024	0.0008–0.0024
1976	3K-C	71 (1166)	0.0010–0.0020	0.0006–0.0014	0.0006–0.0014	0.0006–0.0014	0.0011–0.0027	0.0007–0.0023	0.0006–0.0023
	2T-C	97 (1588)	0.0024–0.0031	0.0008–0.0016	0.0004–0.0012	0.0004–0.0012	0.0008–0.0024	0.0008–0.0024	0.0008–0.0024
1977	3K-C	71 (1166)	0.0010–0.0020	0.0006–0.0014	0.0006–0.0014	0.0006–0.0014	0.0011–0.0027	0.0007–0.0023	0.0006–0.0023
	2T-C	97 (1588)	0.0024–0.0031	0.0008–0.0016	0.0004–0.0012	0.0004–0.0012	0.0008–0.0024	0.0008–0.0024	0.0008–0.0024
1978	3K-C	71 (1166)	0.0010–0.0020	0.0004–0.0011	0.0004–0.0011	0.0008–0.0035	0.0011–0.0027	0.0010–0.0030	0.0006–0.0023
	2T-C	97 (1588)	0.0024–0.0031	0.0006–0.0011	0.0008–0.0013	0.0008–0.0028	0.0008–0.0024	0.0006–0.0022	0.0008–0.0035
1979	3K-C	71 (1166)	0.0010–0.0020	0.0004–0.0011	0.0004–0.0011	0.0008–0.0035	0.0011–0.0027	0.0010–0.0030	0.0006–0.0023
	2T-C	97 (1588)	0.0024–0.0031	0.0006–0.0011	0.0008–0.0013	0.0008–0.0028	0.0008–0.0024	0.0006–0.0022	0.0008–0.0035
1980	3T-C	108 (1770)	0.0020–0.0028	0.0039–0.0098	0.0059–0.0118	0.0079–0.0276	0.0008–0.0024	0.0006–0.0022	snug
1981	3T-C	108 (1770)	0.0020–0.0028	0.0039–0.0098	0.0059–0.0118	0.0079–0.0276	0.0008–0.0024	0.0006–0.0022	snug
1982	3T-C	108 (1770)	0.0020–0.0028	0.0039–0.0098	0.0059–0.0118	0.0079–0.0276	0.0008–0.0024	0.0006–0.0022	snug

85863053

PISTON AND RING SPECIFICATIONS

All measurements are given in inches.

Year	Engine Series Identification	Engine Displacement Cu. In. (cc)	Piston Clearance	Ring Gap			Ring Side Clearance		
				Top Compression	Bottom Compression	Oil Control	Top Compression	Bottom Compression	Oil Control
1983	4A-C	97 (1587)	0.0039–0.0047	0.0098–① 0.0138	0.0059–0.0118	0.0079–② 0.0276	0.0016–0.0031	0.0012–0.0028	snug
	4A-LC	97 (1587)	0.0035–0.0043	0.0098–① 0.0138	0.0059–0.0165	0.0078–② 0.0276	0.0016–0.0031	0.0012–0.0028	snug
1984	4A-C	97 (1587)	0.0039–0.0047	0.0098–③ 0.0173	0.0059–④ 0.0154	0.0079–⑤ 0.0311	0.0016–0.0031	0.0012–0.0028	snug
	4A-LC	97 (1587)	0.0035–0.0043	0.0098–0.0138	0.0059–0.0165	0.0078–0.0276	0.0016–0.0031	0.0012–0.0028	snug
	1C-L	112 (1839)	0.0016–0.0024	0.0098–0.0193	0.0079–0.0173	0.0079–0.0193	0.0079–0.0081	0.0079–0.0081	snug
1985	4A-C	97 (1587)	0.0039–0.0047	0.0098–0.0185	0.0059–0.0165	0.0118–0.0402	0.0016–⑥ 0.0031	0.0012–⑦ 0.0028	snug
	4A-LC	97 (1587)	0.0035–0.0043	0.0098–0.0138	0.0059–0.0165	0.0078–0.0276	0.0016–0.0031	0.0012–0.0028	snug
	4A-GE	97 (1587)	0.0039–0.0047	0.0098–0.0138	0.0078–0.0118	0.0078–0.0276	0.0016–0.0031	0.0012–0.0028	snug
	1C-L	112 (1839)	0.0016–0.0024	0.0098–0.0193	0.0079–0.0173	0.0079–0.0193	0.0079–0.0081	0.0079–0.0081	snug
1986	4A-C	97 (1587)	0.0039–⑧ 0.0047	0.0098–0.0185	0.0059–0.0165	0.0118–0.0402	0.0016–0.0031	0.0012–0.0028	snug
	4A-LC	97 (1587)	0.0035–0.0043	0.0098–0.0138	0.0059–0.0165	0.0078–0.0276	0.0016–0.0031	0.0012–0.0028	snug
	4A-GE	97 (1587)	0.0039–0.0047	0.0098–0.0138	0.0078–0.0118	0.0078–0.0276	0.0016–0.0031	0.0012–0.0028	snug
1987	4A-C	97 (1587)	0.0039–⑧ 0.0047	0.0098–⑨ 0.0135	0.0059–⑩ 0.0118	0.0078–0.0276	0.0016–0.0031	0.0012–0.0028	snug
	4A-LC	97 (1587)	0.0035–0.0043	0.0098–0.0138	0.0059–0.0165	0.0078–0.0276	0.0016–0.0031	0.0012–0.0028	snug
	4A-GE	97 (1587)	0.0039–0.0047	0.0098–0.0138	0.0078–0.0118	0.0078–0.0276	0.0016–0.0031	0.0012–0.0028	snug

① Specification is for TP, Riken: 0.0079–0.0138
② Specification is for TP, Riken: 0.0118–0.0354
③ Specification is for RWD, FWD:
  TP: 0.0098–0.0138 or Riken: 0.0079–0.0138
④ Specification is for RWD, FWD: 0.0059–0.0118
⑤ Specification is for RWD-TP, Riken: 0.0118–0.0390;
  RWD, TP: 0.0079–0.0276 or Riken: 0.0079–0.0138
⑥ Specification is for RWD, FWD: 0.0012–0.0028
⑦ Specification is for RWD, FWD: 0.0008–0.0024
⑧ Specification is for RWD, FWD: 0.0035–0.0043
⑨ Specification is for RWD, FWD: 0.0098–0.0138
⑩ Specification is for RWD, FWD: 0.0059–0.0165

8586305D

TORQUE SPECIFICATIONS
All readings in ft. lbs.

Year	Engine Series Identification	Engine Displacement Cu. In. (cc)	Cylinder Head Bolts	Main Bearing Bolts	Rod Bearing Bolts	Crankshaft Pulley Bolts	Flywheel Bolts	Manifold Intake	Manifold Exhaust
1970	3K-C	71 (1166)	39–48	39–48	29–38	29–43	39–48	14–22	14–22
1971	3K-C	71 (1166)	39–48	39–48	29–38	29–43	39–48	14–22	14–22
	2T-C	97 (1599)	52–64	52–64	30–36	30–43	42–48	7–12	7–12
1972	3K-C	71 (1166)	39–48	39–48	29–38	29–43	39–48	14–22	14–22
	2T-C	97 (1599)	52–64	52–64	30–36	30–43	42–48	7–12	7–12
1973	3K-C	71 (1166)	39–48	39–48	29–38	29–43	39–48	14–22	14–22
	2T-C	97 (1599)	52–64	52–64	30–36	30–43	42–48	7–12	7–12
1974	3K-C	71 (1166)	39–48	39–48	29–38	29–43	39–48	14–22	14–22
	2T-C	97 (1599)	52–64	52–64	30–36	30–43	42–48	7–12	7–12
1975	3K-C	71 (1166)	39–48	39–48	29–38	29–43	39–48	14–22	14–22
	2T-C	97 (1599)	52–64	52–64	30–36	43–51	58–64	7–12	7–12
1976	3K-C	71 (1166)	39–48	39–48	29–38	29–43	39–48	14–22	14–22
	2T-C	97 (1599)	52–64	52–64	30–36	116–145	58–64	7–12	7–12
1977	3K-C	71 (1166)	39–48	39–48	29–38	33–40	39–48	14–22	14–22
	2T-C	97 (1599)	62–69	52–64	30–36	116–145	58–64	7–12	7–12
1978	3K-C	71 (1166)	39–48	39–48	29–38	33–40	39–48	14–22	14–22
	2T-C	97 (1599)	62–69	52–64	30–36	116–145	58–64	14–18	22–32
1979	3K-C	71 (1166)	39–48	39–48	29–38	33–40	39–48	14–22	14–22
	2T-C	97 (1599)	62–69	52–64	30–36	116–145	58–64	14–18	22–32
1980	3T-C	108 (1770)	62–68	53–63	29–36	47–61	42–47	14–18	22–32
1981	3T-C	108 (1770)	62–68	53–63	29–36	47–61	42–47	14–18	22–32
1982	3T-C	108 (1770)	62–68	53–63	29–36	47–61	42–47	14–18	22–32
1983	4A-C, 4A-LC	97 (1587)	40–47	40–47	32–40①	80–94	55–61	15–21	15–21
1984	4A-C, 4A-LC	97 (1587)	40–47	40–47	32–40①	80–94②	55–61	15–21	15–21
	1C-L	112 (1839)	60–65	75–78	45–50	70–75	63–68	10–15	32–36
1985	4A-C, 4A-LC	97 (1587)	40–47	40–47	32–40①	80–94②	55–61	15–21	15–21
	4A-GE	97 (1587)	40–47	40–47	32–40	100–110	50–58	15–21	15–21
	1C-L	112 (1839)	60–65	75–78	45–50	70–75	63–68	10–15	32–36
1986	4A-C, 4A-LC	97 (1587)	40–47	40–47	32–40①	80–94②	55–61	15–21	15–21
	4A-GE	97 (1587)	40–47	40–47	32–40	100–110	50–58	15–21	15–21
1987	4A-C, 4A-LC	97 (1587)	40–47	40–47	32–40①	80–94②	55–61	15–21	15–21
	4A-GE	97 (1587)	40–47	40–47	32–40	100–110	50–58	15–21	15–21

① Specification is for 4A-LC, 4A-C is 26–32,
except for connecting rods purchased after
2/15/84 which are 34–39
② Specification is for 4A-LC, 4A-C: 55–61

85863054

Engine

▶ See Figures 46 and 47

✳✳CAUTION

Please refer to Section 1 before discharging the compressor or disconnecting air conditioning lines. Damage to the air conditioning system or personal injury could result. Consult your local laws concerning refrigerant discharge and recycling. In many areas it may be illegal for anyone but a certified technician to service the A/C system. Always use an approved recovery station when discharging the air conditioning.

Removal & Installation

3K-C

1. Drain the entire cooling system. Remove any emissions systems hoses which are in the way, but mark them beforehand so that you'll know where to put them back.
2. Disconnect the negative battery cable, then unfasten the cable which runs from the battery to the starter at the battery terminal.
3. Scribe marks on the hood and hinges to aid in hood alignment during assembly. Remove the hood.
4. Unfasten the headlight bezel retaining screws and remove the bezels. Remove the radiator grille attachment screws and remove the grille.
5. Remove the hood lock assembly after detaching the release cable.
6. Unfasten the nuts from the horn retainers and disconnect the wiring. Withdraw the horn assembly.
7. Remove the air cleaner from its bracket after unfastening the hoses from it.
8. Remove the windshield washer tank from its bracket but first drain its contents into a clean container.
9. Remove both the upper and lower radiator hoses from the engine after loosening the hose clamps.

➡**On models with automatic transmissions, disconnect and plug the oil line from the oil cooler.**

10. Detach the radiator mounting bolts and remove the radiator.
11. Remove the accelerator cable from its support on the cylinder head cover. Unfasten the cable at the carburetor throttle arm. Unfasten the choke cable from the carburetor.
12. Detach the water hose retainer from the cylinder head.
13. Disconnect the by-pass and heater hoses at the water pump. Disconnect the other end of the heater hose from the water valve. Remove the heater control cable from the wiring harness multi-connectors.
14. Detach the exhaust pipe from the exhaust manifold.
15. Detach the wires from the water temperature and oil pressure sending units.
16. Remove the nut from the front left hand engine mount.
17. Remove the fuel line from the fuel pump.
18. Detach the battery ground cable from the cylinder block.
19. Remove the nut from the front right hand engine mount.

20. Remove the clip and detach the cable from the clutch release lever.
21. Remove the primary and high tension wires from the coil.
22. Detach the back-up light switch wire at its connector on the right side of the extension housing.
23. If equipped with a manual transmission, remove the carpet from the transmission tunnel, then remove the boots from the shift lever. Remove the snapring from the gearshift selector lever base and withdraw the selector lever assembly.
24. If equipped with an automatic transmission:
    a. Disconnect the accelerator linkage torque rod at the carburetor.
    b. Disconnect the throttle linkage connecting rod from the bellcrank lever.
    c. Drain the oil from the transmission oil pan.
    d. Detach the transmission gear selector shift rod from the control shaft.
25. Raise the rear wheels of the car and support safely using jackstands.

✳✳CAUTION

Be sure that the car is supported securely; remember, you will be working underneath it!

26. Disconnect the driveshaft from the transmission.

➡**Drain the oil from the manual transmission before removing the driveshaft, this will help prevent it from leaking out.**

27. Detach the exhaust pipe support bracket from the extension housing.
28. Remove the insulator bolt from the rear engine mount.
29. Place a jack under the transmission and remove the four bolts from the rear (engine support) crossmember.
30. Install lifting hooks on the engine lifting brackets. Attach a suitable hoist.
31. Lift the engine slightly; then move it toward the front of the car. Bring the engine the rest of the way out at an angle.

✳✳CAUTION

Use care not to damage other parts of the automobile.

32. Engine installation is the reverse order of removal. Adjust all transmission and carburetor linkages, as detailed in the appropriate section of this manual.
33. Install and adjust the hood.
34. Refill the engine, radiator, and transmission fluids to capacity, as detailed in Section 1 of this manual.

2T-C, 3T-C and 4A-C (RWD)

1. Drain the radiator, cooling system, transmission, and engine oil.
2. Disconnect the battery-to-starter cable at the positive battery terminal after first disconnecting the negative cable.
3. Scribe marks on the hood and its hinges to aid in alignment during installation.
4. Disconnect the hood supports from the body. Remove the hood.

➡**Do not remove the supports from the hood.**

5. Unfasten the headlight bezel retaining screws and remove the bezels. Remove the radiator grille attachment screws and remove the grille.

6. Remove the hood lock assembly after detaching the release cable.

7. Unfasten the nuts from the horn retainers and disconnect the wiring. Withdraw the horn assembly.

8. Detach both the upper and lower hoses from the radiator. On cars with automatic transmissions, disconnect and plug the lines from the oil cooler. Remove the radiator.

9. Unfasten the clamps and remove the heater and by-pass hoses from the engine. Remove the heater control cable from the water valve.

10. Remove the wiring from the coolant temperature and oil pressure sending units.

11. Remove the air cleaner from its bracket, complete with its hoses.

12. Unfasten the accelerator torque rod from the carburetor. On models equipped with automatic transmissions, remove the transmission linkage as well.

13. Remove the emission control system hoses and wiring, as necessary (mark them to aid in installation).

14. Remove the clutch hydraulic line support bracket.

15. Unfasten the high tension and primary wires from the coil.

16. Mark the spark plug cables and remove them from the distributor.

17. Detach the right hand front engine mount.

18. Remove the fuel line at the pump (or at the filter on 1975-76 models with electric pumps).

19. Detach the downpipe from the exhaust manifold.

20. Detach the left hand front engine mount.

21. Disconnect all of the wiring harness multi-connectors.

22. On cars equipped with manual transmissions, remove the shift lever boot and the shift lever cap boot.

23. Unfasten the four gear selector lever cap retaining screws, remove the gasket and withdraw the gear selector lever assembly from the top of the transmission.

➡On all Corolla 5-speed models, the floor console must be removed in order to access the gear selector lever.

24. Lift the rear wheels of the car off the ground and support the car with jackstands.

✳✳CAUTION

Be sure that the car is securely supported!

25. On cars equipped with automatic transmissions, disconnect the gear selector control rod.

26. Detach the exhaust pipe support bracket.

27. Disconnect the driveshaft from the rear of the transmission.

28. Unfasten the speedometer cable from the transmission. Disconnect the wiring from the back-up light switch and the neutral safety switch (automatic only).

29. Detach the clutch release cylinder assembly, complete with hydraulic lines. Do not disconnect the lines.

30. Unbolt the rear support member mounting insulators.

31. Support the transmission and detach the rear support member retaining bolts. Withdraw the support member from under the car.

32. Install lifting hooks on the engine lifting brackets. Attach a suitable hoist to the engine.

33. Remove the jack from under the transmission.

34. Raise the engine and move it toward the front of the car. Use care to avoid damaging components which remain on the car.

35. Support the engine on a workstand.

36. Install the engine by following the removal steps in reverse order. Adjust all of the linkages as detailed in the appropriate sections of this manual.

37. Install the hood and adjust it. Replenish the fluid levels in the engine, radiator, and transmission as detailed in Section 1 of this manual.

4A-GE Series (RWD)

1. Disconnect the battery cables (negative cable first), then remove the battery.

2. Remove the hood and the engine undercover splash shield.

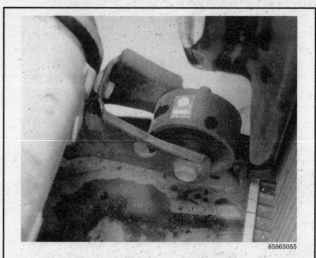

Fig. 46 In essence, the engine is retained to the vehicle by the engine mounts and the transaxle bolts

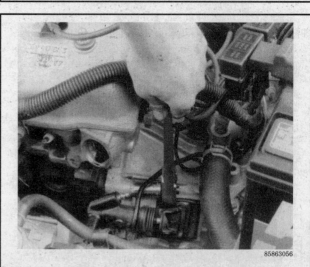

Fig. 47 On FWD vehicles, the transaxle is usually unbolted before the engine is removed

3. Remove the No. 2 air cleaner hose. Disconnect the actuator and accelerator cables from their bracket on the cylinder head.

4. From inside the vehicle; remove the center console, lift up the shift boot and remove the shifter.

5. Drain the engine oil and transmission fluid. On automatic transmission equipped vehicles, disconnect the two cooler lines from the radiator.

6. Drain the radiator and engine coolant. Remove the radiator hoses then remove the radiator and shroud.

7. Remove the air cleaner assembly.

8. Remove the power steering pump and the pump mounting bracket.

9. Loosen the water pump pulley set nuts, remove the drive belt adjusting bolt and remove the drive belt.

10. Remove the set nuts, then remove the fluid coupling with the fan and water pump pulley.

11. Remove the air conditioning compressor and its mounting bracket. DO NOT DISCONNECT THE TWO HOSES. Position the compressor (with the hoses connected) to the side and out of the way. Wire the compressor to the frame so it can not slip, and so there is no tension on the hoses.

12. Remove the spark plug wires from the plugs and cover mounting brackets. Disconnect the coil wire. Matchmark and remove the distributor.

13. Remove the exhaust pipe bracket from the pipe and clutch housing.

14. Disconnect, and separate, the exhaust pipe from the exhaust manifold.

15. Disconnect the starter wire harness.

16. Remove the fuel hose from the pulsation damper and pressure regulator

17. Remove the cold start injector pipe. Remove the PCV hose from the intake manifold.

18. Tag and disconnect all related vacuum hoses: Brake booster hose; Charcoal canister hose from the intake manifold; VSV hose from the air valve; Two air valve hoses from the vacuum pipe; and the Vacuum sensing hose from the pressure regulator.

19. Remove the wiring harness and the vacuum pipe from the No. 3 timing cover.

20. Tag and disconnect all the related wires: Two igniter connections; Oil pressure sender gauge connector; Noise filter connector; Relay block connector; Ground strap (between the oil filter retainer and the body); Ground strap connector; Solenoid resistor connector; Four injector connectors; Ground strap from the intake manifold; Ground strap (between the cylinder head and body); Water temperature sender gauge connector; VSV connector; and the Throttle position sensor connector. Position the harness to one side without disconnecting it from the engine.

21. Raise and safely support the front of the vehicle using jackstands.

22. Remove the engine mounting bolts on either side of the engine.

23. Unbolt the clutch release cylinder without disconnecting the hydraulic line and position it out of the way.

24. Disconnect the driveshaft. Tag and disconnect the speedometer cable and the back-up switch connector. Remove the O-ring.

25. Disconnect the bond cables from the clutch and extension housings. Remove the jackstands and carefully lower the vehicle.

26. Attach a suitable engine sling and hoist to the lift bracket on the engine. Support the engine rear mounting on a jack. Remove the rear mounting bolts. Carefully raise the engine and transmission then remove them from the vehicle.

27. Remove the starter, the two stiffener plates and then separate the transmission from the engine.

28. Install the engine and transmission in the reverse order of removal.

4A-C and 4A-LC (FWD)

1. Disconnect the negative battery cable.

2. Matchmark and remove the hood.

3. Remove the air cleaner and all necessary lines attached to it.

4. Drain the radiator.

5. Cover both driveshaft boots with a shop towel.

6. Remove the solenoid valve connector, water temperature switch connector, and the electric fan connector.

7. Remove the exhaust support plate bolts, and the exhaust pipe.

8. Remove the top radiator support.

9. Remove the top and bottom radiator hoses, then remove the radiator with the fan.

➡On cars equipped with automatic transmissions remove the coolant lines before removing the radiator.

10. Remove the windshield washer tank.

11. Remove the heater hoses and the lines to the fuel pump.

12. Remove the accelerator cable, choke cable, and the ground strap.

13. Remove the brake booster vacuum lines.

14. Remove the coil wire and unplug the alternator.

15. Remove the clutch release cable.

16. Remove the wires on the starter.

17. Remove the temperature sending and oil pressure switch connectors.

18. Remove the battery ground strap from the block.

19. Jack up your vehicle and support it safely using jackstands.

20. Remove the engine mounting bolts and the engine shock absorbers.

21. Support the differential with a jack.

22. Remove the transaxle-to-engine mounting bolts.

➡It is probably easier to remove these bolts from underneath the car.

23. Tie the bell housing to the cowl to keep support on the transaxle.

24. Remove the engine from the vehicle. If your vehicle is equipped with an automatic transmission refer to the additional steps located immediately after this procedure.

➡The grille may be removed, if necessary, to give better leverage when removing the engine.

25. Installation is the reverse of removal. Adjust all linkages as covered in the appropriate sections of this manual. Refill all

fluids to the proper levels, please refer to Section 1 for details. Tighten transaxle bolts 37-57 ft. lbs. (50-77 Nm).

26. **On cars with automatic transmissions, the following procedures are necessary.**

  a. Remove the starter.

  b. Remove the cooling lines from the transmission.

  c. Support the transmission with a jack.

  d. Remove the transaxle mounting bolts.

  e. Remove the torque converter mounting bolts.

➡️**In order to turn the converter, place a wrench on the crankshaft pulley and turn it until you see a bolt appear in the area where the starter was. Loosen and remove the converter-to-flywheel bolts.**

  f. While the engine is suspended from your hoist, pull it forward about 2 in.

  g. Insert a pry bar in this opening and gently separate the torque converter from the engine.

27. Installation is the reverse of removal.

28. Confirm that the converter contact surface is 1.02 in. from the housing. Install a guide bolt in one of the mounting bolt holes. Remove the engine mounting insulator (left side) and the mounting bracket (right side). To secure the transaxle to the engine temporarily install the top two mounting bolts. This will ease engine installation.

4A-GE Series (FWD)

1. Remove the battery and hood. Disconnect the negative cable first when removing the battery. Scribe the hood hinge outline on the underhood to help with installation alignment.

2. Remove the under engine splash shields. Drain the engine oil.

3. Drain the engine coolant from the radiator. If the vehicle is equipped with automatic transaxle, drain the transaxle fluid.

4. Remove the air cleaner assembly. Remove the coolant reservoir tank.

5. Remove the radiator and electric cooling fan assembly. Disconnect the heater hoses from the heater inlet housing.

6. Disconnect the fuel hose from the inlet of the fuel filter. Disconnect the heater and air hoses from the air valve, then disconnect the fuel return line from the pressure regulator.

7. If the vehicle is equipped with a manual transaxle, remove the clutch release cylinder from the transaxle case.

8. Disconnect the charcoal canister vacuum hose. Disconnect the transaxle control cables from the shift levers.

9. Disconnect the speedometer cable from the transaxle case. Disconnect the accelerator link and cruise control cable. Remove the cruise control actuator.

10. Remove the ignition coil.

11. Disconnect the main engine wire by:

  a. Remove the right cowl panel.

  b. Disconnect the No. 4 junction block connectors.

  c. Remove the Electronic Control Unit (ECU) cover, then disengage the ECU connectors.

  d. Pull out the engine main wire to the engine compartment.

12. Disconnect the following:

  a. No. 2 junction block connectors.

  b. Starter cable from the battery positive post terminal (if not already disconnected).

  c. Washer charge valve connector.

  d. Cruise control vacuum pump connector.

  e. Cruise control vacuum switch connector.

  f. Solenoid resistor connector.

13. Disconnect the brake booster vacuum line.

14. Disconnect the AC compressor and vane pump by:

  a. Remove the vane pump pulley nut and loosen the pulley.

  b. Loosen the idler pulley adjusting bolt and pulley bolt, remove the drive belt.

  c. Remove the four compressor mounting bolts and move the compressor WITH THE LINES ATTACHED to the side and secure out of the way.

  d. Loosen the bolts mounting the compressor bracket.

  e. Disconnect the oil pressure connector.

  f. Loosen the vane pump lock bolt and pivot bolts.

  g. Remove the vane pump with its mounting bracket and secure it out of the way.

15. Remove the oxygen sensor.

16. Disconnect the oil cooler lines.

17. Raise and support the front of the vehicle safely using jackstands.

18. Disconnect the exhaust pipe from the exhaust manifold.

19. Disconnect the front and rear mounting from the crossmember by removing the two hole covers, then removing the two bolts from each mounting.

20. Remove the front mounting bolt and mount.

21. Remove the center engine mounting crossmember.

22. Disconnect the drive axle shafts from the transaxle.

23. Remove the jackstands and carefully lower the front of the vehicle.

24. Attach an engine hoist to the engine.

25. Remove the right hand mounting bracket. Remove the left hand mounting bracket from the transaxle bracket.

26. Carefully lift the engine from the vehicle.

27. Service as required. Install in the reverse order of removal.

1C-L Diesel

1. Drain the engine coolant.

2. Matchmark and remove the hood.

3. Remove the battery, disconnecting the negative cable first.

4. Tag and disconnect all cables attached to the various engine parts.

5. Tag and disconnect all electrical wires attached to the various engine parts.

6. Tag and disconnect all vacuum liens connected to the various engine parts.

7. Remove the cruise control actuator and bracket.

8. Disconnect the radiator and heater hoses.

9. Disconnect the automatic transmission cooler lines at the radiator.

10. Unbolt the two radiator supports and lift out the radiator.

11. Remove the air cleaner assembly.

12. Disconnect all wiring and linkage at the transmission.

13. Pull out the injection system wiring harness and secure to the right side fender apron.

14. Disconnect the fuel lines at the fuel filter and return pipes.

15. Disconnect the speedometer cable at the transmission.

16. Remove the clutch release cylinder without disconnecting the fluid line.

17. Unbolt the air conditioning compressor and secure it out of the way.

18. Raise and support the car safely using jackstands.

19. Drain the transaxle fluid.

20. While someone holds the brake pedal depressed, unbolt both axle shafts. It's a good idea to wrap the boots with shop towels to prevent grease loss and help protect the boots from damage.

21. Unbolt the power steering pump and secure it out of the way.

22. Disconnect the exhaust pipe from the manifold.

23. Disconnect the front and rear engine mounts at the frame member.

24. Lower the vehicle.

25. Attach an engine crane at the lifting eyes.

26. Take up the engine weight with the crane, then remove the right and left side engine mounts.

27. Slowly and carefully, remove the engine and transaxle assembly.

28. Installation is the reverse of removal. Torque the engine mount bolts to 29 ft. lbs. (40 Nm). Torque the axle shaft bolts to 27 ft. lbs. (37 Nm). Torque the fuel line connectors to 22 ft. lbs. (30 Nm).

Cylinder Head (Camshaft/Valve) Cover

REMOVAL & INSTALLATION

▶ **See Figures 48, 49, 50, 51, 52, 53, 54 and 55**

1. Remove the air clean, its assorted hoses and lines. Be sure to tag all connections to assure proper installation.

2. Tag and disconnect any wires, hoses or lines which might interfere with the cylinder head cover removal. If necessary, remove the retaining bolts from the wiring harness brackets.

➡**On some vehicles, the accelerator cable is routed through a cover mounted bracket, slip the cable from the bracket so the cover may be removed.**

3. If equipped with a camshaft cover mounted PCV valve, disengage the hose from the valve or remove the valve from the cover, whichever is easier.

4. Unscrew the retaining screws/bolts and then lift off the cylinder head cover. On some engines, the timing belt cover

may be bolted to the end of the camshaft cover, if so, these bolts must be removed as well.

➡**If the cylinder head cover is stuck, tap it lightly with a rubber mallet to loosen it. DO NOT attempt to pry it off.**

5. Using a new gasket and, if necessary, silicone sealant, replace the cylinder head cover and tighten the bolts down until they are snug — BUT not too tight!

Installation of the remaining components is in the reverse order of removal.

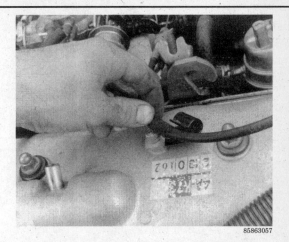

Fig. 48 On some vehicles the accelerator cable is routed through a bracket mounted on the camshaft cover

Fig. 49 Disengage the hose from the PCV valve, or remove the valve from the cover

Fig. 50 If the timing belt cover is bolted to the camshaft cover, loosen and remove the retainers

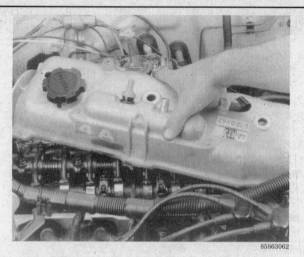

Fig. 53 Carefully lift the camshaft cover from the cylinder head

Fig. 51 Loosen and remove the camshaft cover retainers

Fig. 54 If equipped, check the condition of the rubber seal at the rear of the cylinder head

Fig. 52 If equipped, remove the grommet washers so they are not lost when the camshaft cover is removed

Fig. 55 Remove the old gasket from the sealing lip of the camshaft cover

Rocker Arms

REMOVAL & INSTALLATION

▶ See Figures 56, 57, 58, 59 and 60

➡ The diesel engine (1C-L) uses no rocker arms as the valves are operated directly by the camshaft.

Most vehicles covered by this manual are equipped with rocker arms which are mounted on shaft assemblies. In order to remove or replace a rocker arm, the entire shaft assembly must be unbolted from the top of the cylinder head and disassembled. Be sure to use the proper bolt removal/torque sequence when removing or installing the rocker arm shaft retainers.

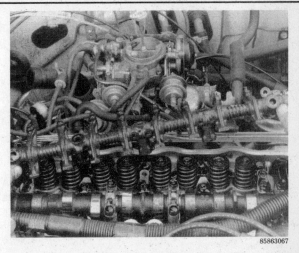

Fig. 58 Once the retainers are removed, carefully lift the shaft assembly from the engine

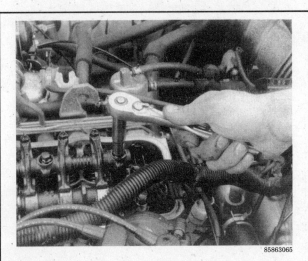

Fig. 56 Loosen and remove the rocker arm shaft retainers using the proper sequence

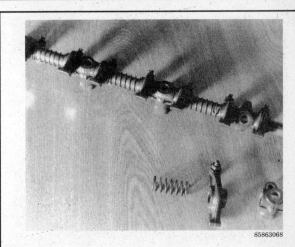

Fig. 59 If disassembly is necessary, be sure to tag or arrange ALL components to assure installation in the proper locations

Fig. 57 On A-series engines, DON'T forget the bolts mounted on the shaft lower flanges

Fig. 60 Inspect the rocker arms, shafts and other components for wear or damage

A-Series and K-Series Engines

▶ **See Figures 61, 62, 63, 64, 65, 66, 67 and 68**

1. Remove the cylinder head cover. For details, please refer to the procedure located earlier in this section.

2. Loosen the valve rocker arm shaft bolts little-by-little, using 3 steps of the proper sequence (moving from the outer to the inner bolts). Carefully lift the rocker arm assembly from the engine.

3. Inspect the valve contacting surface of each rocker arm for wear. Inspect the rocker arm. If movement is felt, disassemble and inspect.

4. Disassemble the rocker shaft assembly by carefully pulling the components from the shaft. Note how each component is oriented on the shaft. Also, BE SURE to tag or arrange all components to assure installation in their original locations.

5. If the valve contacting surface of the rocker arm is worn, resurface it with a valve refacer or an oil stone.

6. Measure the oil clearance between the rocker arms and the shaft. It should be no more than 0.0024 in. (0.061mm), if the clearance is greater, replace the rocker arms.

To install:

7. When assembling the rocker shaft components on the 4A-C engine, face the oil holes in the rocker shaft to the right, left and bottom.

8. After assembly, install the rocker arm and shaft assembly using the retaining bolts. Tighten the retaining bolts gradually, using 3 passes in the reverse order of removal.

➡**Tighten the rocker support bolts to 14-17 ft. lbs. (19-23 Nm).**

9. Check the valve clearances. If clearance should be checked hot, temporarily install the camshaft cover so the engine may be warmed.

➡**On most vehicles, unless the rocker arms were replaced or the adjustment screws were turned, adjustment should not be necessary. BUT, it is always wiser to check adjustment now, then to damage the valve train later.**

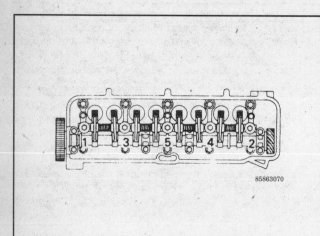

Fig. 61 Rocker arm shaft retainer loosening sequence for A-series engines — NOTE that there are usually Two bolts at locations "1", "5" and "2".

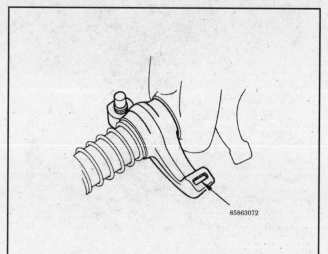

Fig. 63 Once the shaft is removed, inspect the valve contacting surface of each rocker arm

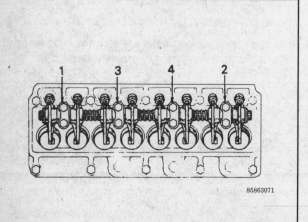

Fig. 62 Rocker arm shaft bolt loosening sequence — K-series engines

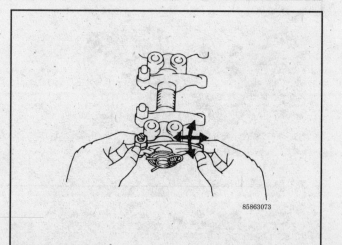

Fig. 64 Check the rocker arm-to-shaft clearance by attempting to rock the arms while they are installed on the shaft

10. Once the valve clearance has be checked and/or adjusted, install the camshaft cover to the engine.

T-Series Engines
▶ **See Figures 63, 64, 65, 66 and 69**

1. Remove the cylinder head cover. For details, please refer to the procedure located earlier in this section.

2. Loosen the valve rocker arm shaft bolts little-by-little, using 3 steps of the proper sequence (moving from the outer to the inner bolts). Carefully lift the rocker arm assembly from the engine.

3. Inspect the valve contacting surface of each rocker arm for wear. Inspect the rocker arm. If movement is felt, disassemble and inspect.

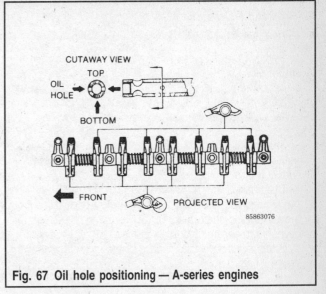

Fig. 67 Oil hole positioning — A-series engines

4. To disassemble the rocker shaft assembly, remove the retaining clips from the ends of each shaft, then carefully slide the supports, springs and rocker arms off of each shaft.

5. If the valve contacting surface of the rocker arm is worn, resurface it with a valve refacer or an oil stone.

6. Measure the oil clearance between the rocker arms and the shaft. It should be no more than 0.0024 in. (0.061mm), if the clearance is greater, replace the rocker arms.

To install:

7. When assembling the rocker arms and shafts:

a. Face the holes in the intake and exhaust shafts toward the front.

b. There are three (3) types of rocker supports, install them on the shafts in the order noted during removal.

c. Face the side of the rocker support with an F toward the front.

d. The short rocker arms are for the intake (right) side and the long ones are for the exhaust (left) side.

e. Align the hole in the rocker support with the groove in the rocker shaft, then install the bolt to keep the shaft from turning.

8. After assembly, install the rocker arm and shaft assembly using the retaining bolts. Tighten the retaining bolts gradually, using 3 passes in the reverse order of removal.

➡**As the rocker support bolts are also the cylinder head bolts, make sure that they are properly torqued to specification.**

9. Check the valve clearances. If clearance is to be checked hot, temporarily install the camshaft cover so the engine may be warmed.

➡**On most vehicles, unless the rocker arms were replaced or the adjustment screws were turned, adjustment should not be necessary. BUT, it is always wiser to check adjustment now, then to damage the valve train later.**

10. Once the valve clearance has be checked and/or adjusted, install the camshaft cover to the engine.

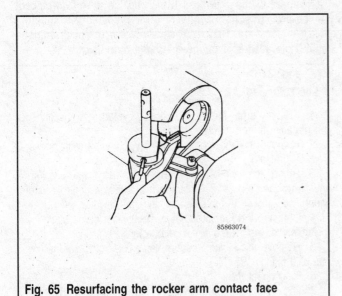

Fig. 65 Resurfacing the rocker arm contact face

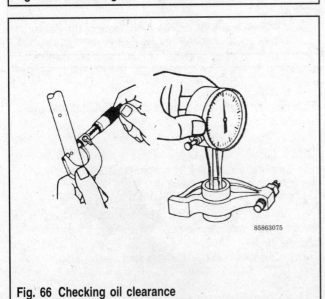

Fig. 66 Checking oil clearance

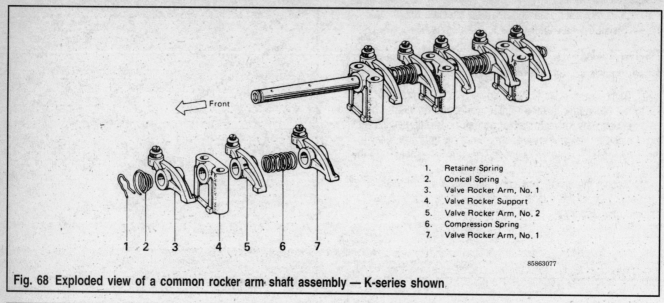

1. Retainer Spring
2. Conical Spring
3. Valve Rocker Arm, No. 1
4. Valve Rocker Support
5. Valve Rocker Arm, No. 2
6. Compression Spring
7. Valve Rocker Arm, No. 1

85863077

Fig. 68 Exploded view of a common rocker arm shaft assembly — K-series shown

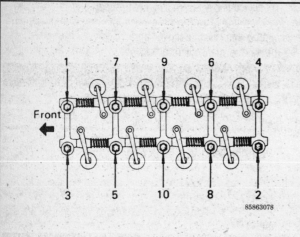

85863078

Fig. 69 Rocker arm shaft bolts loosening sequence — T-series engines

Intake Manifold

REMOVAL & INSTALLATION

1C-L

1. Disconnect the negative battery cable.
2. Drain the engine coolant.
3. Remove the air cleaner assembly.
4. Tag and disconnect all wires, hoses and cables which are in the way of manifold removal.
5. Remove the coolant bypass pipe.
6. Unbolt and remove the manifold.

7. Installation is in the reverse order of removal.

2T-C and 3T-C

▶ See Figure 70

1. Properly drain the engine cooling system and disconnect the negative battery cable.
2. Remove the air cleaner assembly, complete with hoses, from its bracket.
3. Remove the choke stove hoses, fuel lines, and vacuum lines from the carburetor. Unfasten the emission control system wiring, hoses, and the accelerator linkage from it.
4. Unfasten the four nuts which secure the carburetor to the manifold, then remove the carburetor.
5. Remove the mixture control valve line from its intake manifold fitting (1971-74).
6. Disconnect the PCV hose.
7. Disconnect the water by-pass hose from the intake manifold.
8. Unbolt and remove the manifold.
9. Installation is performed in the reverse order of removal. Remember to use new gaskets. Tighten the intake manifold bolts to the figures given in the torque specification chart found in this section.

➡**Tighten the bolts, in several stages, working from the inside out.**

4A-GE

1. Properly relieve the fuel system pressure, then disconnect the negative battery cable.
2. Remove the air cleaner assembly and drain the coolant.
3. Tag and remove all wires, hoses or cables in the way of intake manifold removal. Remove the intake manifold stay (bracket).
4. If necessary, remove the cold start injector pipe.

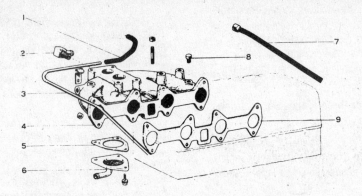

1. Choke stove intake hose
2. Elbow
3. Choke stove intake
4. Intake manifold
5. Gasket
6. Water by-pass outlet
7. Choke stove outlet
8. Plug
9. Intake manifold gasket

85863079

Fig. 70 Exploded view of the intake manifold assembly mounting — T-series engines

5. Disengage the electrical connectors, then remove the fuel delivery pipe (fuel rail) and injectors. During removal, be careful not to drop the injectors.

❊❊CAUTION

The fuel system is under pressure. Release pressure slowly and contain spillage. Observe no smoking/no open flame precautions. Have a Class B-C (dry powder) fire extinguisher within arm's reach at all times.

6. Remove the intake manifold retaining bolts. Remove the intake manifold from the vehicle.

To install:

7. Clean the gasket mating surfaces, being careful not to damage them. Check the mating surfaces for warpage with a straightedge.

8. Compare the old gasket with the new one for an exact match. Use a new gasket when installing the manifold, tighten the bolts evenly and in several passes from the center outward to specification. Install the intake manifold stay (bracket).

9. Install the fuel rail and injector assembly, then engage the injector wiring.

10. If removed, install the cold start injector pipe.

11. Install all necessary wires, hoses or cables. Install the air cleaner assembly.

12. Refill the cooling system. Connect the negative battery cable. Start the engine. Check for leaks and road test for proper operation.

Exhaust Manifold

REMOVAL & INSTALLATION

▶ See Figure 71

1C-L

1. Disconnect the negative battery cable.
2. Raise and support the vehicle safely using jackstands.
3. Remove the gravel shield from underneath the engine.

4. Remove the downpipe support bracket.
5. Unscrew the bolts from the exhaust flange, then detach the downpipe from the manifold.
6. Loosen the manifold retaining bolts.

❊❊CAUTION

Always remove and tighten the manifold bolts in two or three stages, starting from the inside and working out.

7. Installation is in the reverse order of removal. Always use a new gasket and tighten the retaining bolts to the proper specifications.

2T-C and 3T-C
▶ See Figure 72

❊❊CAUTION

Do not perform this operation on a warm or hot engine!

1. Detach the manifold heat stove intake pipe.

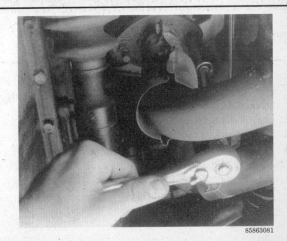

85863081

Fig. 71 Exhaust pipe retainers tend to rust; spray them with a penetrating lubricant then use a deep socket when attempting to loosen them

2. Unfasten the nut on the stove outlet pipe union.

3. Remove the wiring from the emission control system thermosensor.

4. Unfasten the U-bolt from the downpipe bracket.

5. Unfasten the downpipe flange from the manifold.

6. In order to remove the manifold, unfasten the retaining bolts.

➡**Remove the bolts in two or three stages and starting from the inside working out.**

7. Installation of the manifold is performed in the reverse order of removal. Remember to use a new gasket. Please refer to the torque specifications chart for the proper installation torque.

4A-GE Series

1. Disconnect the negative battery cable.

2. Raise and safely support the vehicle safely using jackstands.

3. Remove the right side gravel shield.

4. Disconnect the exhaust pipe from the manifold after removing the support bracket. Disengage the oxygen sensor connector.

5. Lower the vehicle (if necessary) for underhood access, then remove the mounting bolts and exhaust manifold.

6. Install in the reverse order of removal. Torque the manifold retainers (from center outwards) to 18 ft. lbs. (24 Nm).

Combination Manifold

REMOVAL & INSTALLATION

▶ **See Figure 73**

✳✳CAUTION

Do not perform this procedure on a warm engine!

3K-C

1. Remove the air cleaner assembly, complete with hoses.

2. Disconnect the accelerator and choke linkages from the carburetor, along with the fuel and vacuum lines as well.

3. Remove, or move aside, any of the emission control system components which are in the way.

4. Unfasten the retaining bolts and remove the carburetor from the manifold.

5. Loosen the manifold retaining nuts, working form the inside out, in two or three stages.

6. Remove the intake/exhaust manifold assembly from the cylinder head as a complete unit.

7. Installation is performed in the reverse order of removal. Always use new gaskets. Tighten the bolts, working from the inside out, to the specifications given in the torque specifications chart.

➡**Always tighten the bolts in two or three stages in order to prevent cracking or warping the manifold.**

4A-C and 4A-LC

1. Disconnect the negative battery cable.

2. Remove the air cleaner and all necessary hoses.

3. Disconnect all of the carburetor linkages.

4. Remove the carburetor.

➡**Cover the carburetor with a clean towel to prevent dirt from entering it.**

5. Disconnect the exhaust manifold pipe.

6. Loosen the retainers and remove the manifold.

7. Installation is the reverse of removal. Tighten the manifold bolts to 15-21 ft. lbs. (20-28 Nm).

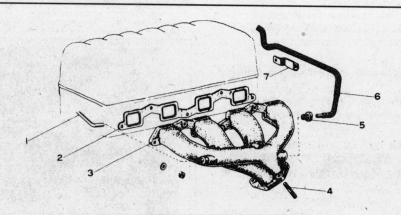

1. Automatic choke stove intake pipe
2. Exhaust manifold gasket
3. Exhaust manifold
4. Stud
5. Union
6. Automatic choke stove outlet
7. Clamp

85863080

Fig. 72 Exploded view of the exhaust manifold mounting — T-series engines

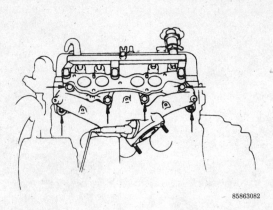

Fig. 73 Common bolt locations for combination manifold mounting

Cylinder Head

REMOVAL & INSTALLATION

▶ See Figures 74, 75, 76, 77, 78, 79, 80, 81, 82 and 83

3K-C

▶ See Figures 84, 85 and 86

✳✳CAUTION

Do not perform this operation on a warm engine!

1. Disconnect the battery and drain the cooling system.
2. Remove the air cleaner assembly from its bracket, complete with its hoses.
3. Disconnect the hoses from the air injection system (1970-71) or the vacuum switching valve (1972-74).
4. Detach the accelerator cable from its support on the cylinder head cover and also from the carburetor throttle arm.
5. Remove the choke cable and fuel lines from the carburetor.
6. Remove the water hose bracket from the cylinder head cover.
7. Unfasten the water hose clamps, then remove the hoses from the water pump and the water valve. Detach the heater temperature control cable from the water valve.
8. Disconnect the PCV line from the cylinder head cover.
9. Unbolt and remove the valve cover.
10. Remove the valve rocker support securing bolts and nuts. Lift out the valve rocker assembly.
11. Withdraw the pushrods from their bores.

✳✳CAUTION

Keep the pushrods in their original order.

12. Unfasten the hose clamps and remove the upper radiator hose from the water outlet.
13. Tag and disconnect the wires from the spark plugs.

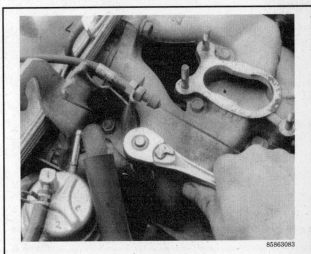

Fig. 74 Remove all necessary cables and brackets from the manifolds and the cylinder head

Fig. 75 If the manifold is being removed, loosen the manifold retainers

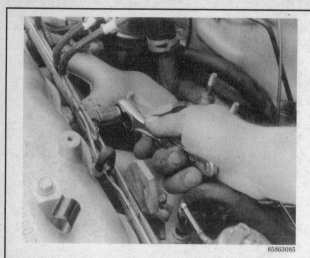

Fig. 76 Here, the combination manifold of the 4A-C is unbolted from the side of the cylinder head

Fig. 78 Loosen and remove the cylinder head bolts (using several passes of the proper loosening sequence

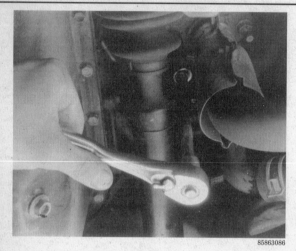

Fig. 77 Disconnect the exhaust pipe from the manifold flange

Fig. 79 Carefully lift the cylinder head from the engine block — note than an assistant not only makes this easier, but helps keep you from hurting yourself

14. Disconnect the wiring and the fluid line from the windshield washer assembly. Remove the assembly.

➡Use a clean container to catch the fluid from the windshield washer reservoir when disconnecting its fluid line. Another alternative is to have a short length of plugged hose handy to install on the reservoir in order to keep the fluid from draining.

15. Unfasten the exhaust pipe flange from the exhaust manifold.

16. Remove the head assembly retaining bolts and remove the head from the engine.

➡Remove the head bolts using 2 or 3 passes of the illustrated sequence (working from the outer toward the inner bolts).

17. Place the cylinder head on wooden blocks to prevent damage to it.

Fig. 80 The old gasket and all traces of gasket material must be cleaned from the engine block's cylinder head mating surface

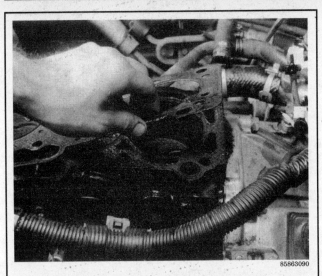

Fig. 81 Lift the old gasket from the engine block

Fig. 82 Use a scraper to remove traces of material, BUT cover the cylinder bores to minimize the amount of material which must be cleaned from the pistons

Fig. 83 During installation, a torque wrench MUST be used to assure proper bolt tightening

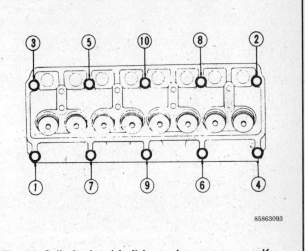

Fig. 84 Cylinder head bolt loosening sequence — K-series engines

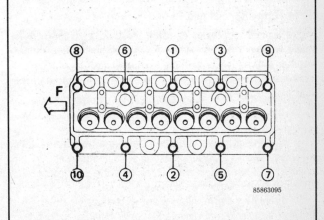

Fig. 85 Cylinder head bolt torque sequence — K-series engines

18. Installation is essentially the reverse order of removal. Clean both the cylinder head and block gasket mounting surfaces. Always use a new head gasket.

➡Be sure that the top side of the gasket is facing upward. When installing the head on the block, be sure to tighten the bolts using several passes of the proper torque sequence (working from the inner towards the outer bolts) until the proper torque specification is reached. The valve clearances should be adjusted to specification, please refer to Section 2 of this manual for details.

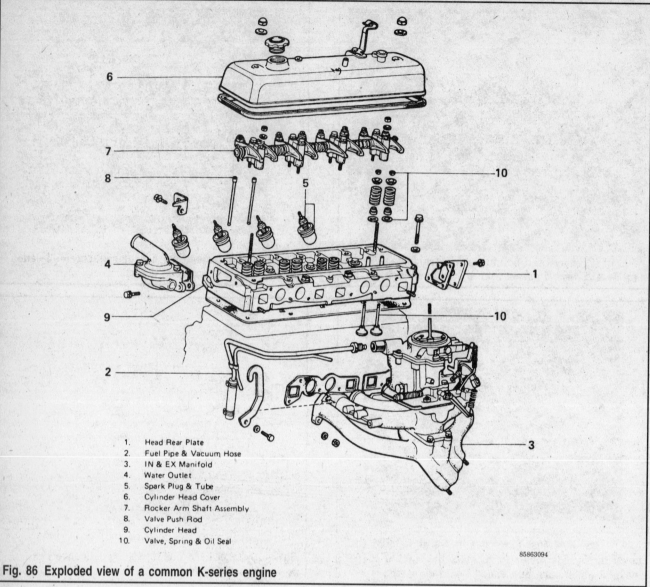

1. Head Rear Plate
2. Fuel Pipe & Vacuum Hose
3. IN & EX Manifold
4. Water Outlet
5. Spark Plug & Tube
6. Cylinder Head Cover
7. Rocker Arm Shaft Assembly
8. Valve Push Rod
9. Cylinder Head
10. Valve, Spring & Oil Seal

85863094

Fig. 86 Exploded view of a common K-series engine

2T-C and 3T-C

◆ See Figures 87, 88 and 89

✳✳CAUTION

Do not perform this operation on a warm engine!

1. Disconnect the battery and drain the cooling system.
2. Remove the air cleaner assembly from its bracket, complete with its hoses.
3. Disconnect the vacuum lines which run from the vacuum switching valve to the various emission control devices mounted on the cylinder head. Disconnect the air injection system lines on engines so equipped.
4. Disconnect the mixture control valve hose which runs to the intake manifold and remove the valve from its mounting bracket (1971-74).
5. Unfasten the water hose clamps, then remove the hoses from the water pump and the water valve. Detach the heater temperature control cable from the water valve.

6. Detach the water temperature sender wiring.
7. Remove the choke stove pipe and its intake pipe.
8. Remove the PCV hose from the intake manifold.
9. Disconnect the fuel and vacuum lines from the carburetor.
10. Remove the clutch hydraulic line bracket from the cylinder head.
11. Raise the car and support it with jackstands. Unfasten the exhaust pipe clamp. Remove the exhaust manifold from the cylinder head.
12. Label and disconnect the spark plug leads. Remove the valve cover.
13. Loosen and remove the cylinder head bolts using several passes of the illustrated sequence.

✳✳CAUTION

Remove the bolts in stages; not one at a time.

14. Remove the valve rocker support securing bolts and nuts. Lift out the valve rocker assembly.

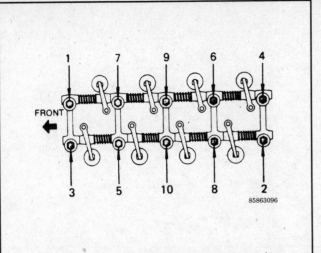

Fig. 87 Cylinder head bolt loosening sequence — T-series engines

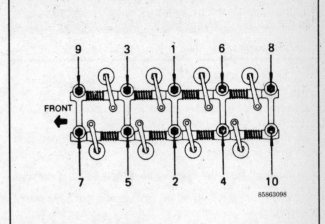

Fig. 89 Cylinder head bolt torque sequence — T-series engines

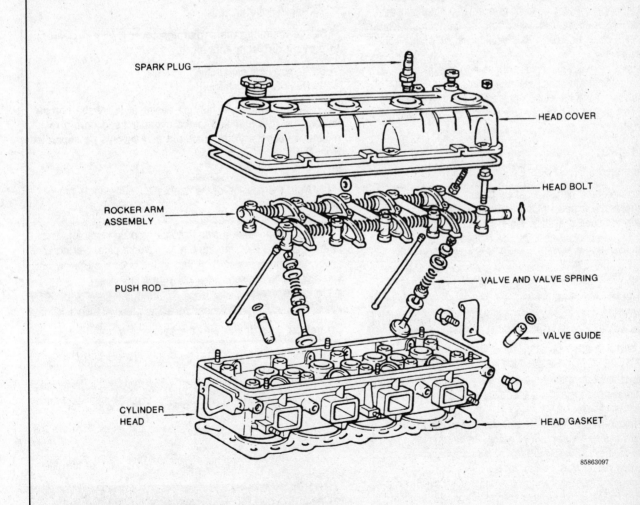

Fig. 88 Exploded view of the cylinder head for the 3T-C engine (2T-C similar)

15. Withdraw the pushrods from their bores.

❋❋CAUTION

Keep the pushrods in their original order.

16. Remove the cylinder head, complete with the intake manifold.
17. Separate the intake manifold from the cylinder head.

Install the cylinder head in the following order:

18. Clean the gasket mounting surfaces of the cylinder head and the block completely.

➡ **Remove oil from the cylinder head bolt holes, if present.**

19. Place a new gasket on the block and install the head assembly.

❋❋CAUTION

Do not slide the cylinder head across the block, as there are locating pins on the block!

20. Install the pushrods and the valve rocker assembly.
21. Tighten the cylinder head bolts evenly, in stages, using the proper torque sequence. Please refer to the torque specifications chart located earlier in this section for the proper tightening torque.
22. Install the intake manifold, using a new gasket and tighten the retainers to specifications.
23. The rest of the installation procedure is the reversal of removal. Remember to properly check and adjust the valve clearances.

4A-C and 4A-LC

◗ **See Figures 90, 91, 92 and 93**

1. Disconnect the negative battery cable.
2. Remove the exhaust pipe from the manifold.
3. Drain the cooling system. Unless it is contaminated or too old, save the coolant as it can be reused.
4. Remove the air cleaner and all necessary hoses.
5. Mark all vacuum lines for easy installation and then remove them.

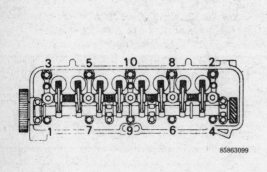

Fig. 90 Cylinder head bolt loosening sequence — SOHC A-series engines

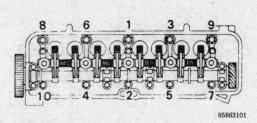

Fig. 91 Cylinder head bolt torque sequence — SOHC A-series engines

6. Remove all linkage from the carburetor, fuel lines, etc., from the head and manifold.
7. Remove the fuel pump.

➡ **Before removing the carburetor cover it with a clean rag to prevent dirt from entering it.**

8. Remove the carburetor.
9. Remove the manifold.

➡ **On some vehicles, it may be easier to leave the combination manifold installed to the cylinder head during removal. If necessary, the manifold may always be separated from the head after removal.**

10. Remove the valve cover.
11. Note the position of the spark plug wires and remove them.
12. Remove the spark plugs.
13. Set the engine on No. 1 cylinder top dead center. This is accomplished by removing the No.1 spark plug, placing your finger over the hole and then turning the crankshaft pulley until you feel pressure exerted against your finger.

❋❋CAUTION

Do not put your finger into the spark plug hole!

14. Remove the crankshaft pulley with an appropriate puller.
15. Remove the water pump pulley.
16. Remove the top and bottom timing chain cover.
17. Matchmark the camshaft pulley and timing belt for reassembly.
18. Loosen the belt tensioner.
19. Remove the water pump.
20. Remove the timing belt. Do not bend, twist, or turn the belt inside out.

➡ **Check the belt for wear, cracks, or glazing. Once the belt is removed it is usually a good idea to replace a used belt with a new one even though it is not necessary.**

21. Remove the rocker arm shaft bolts, then remove the rocker arm and shaft assembly.
22. Remove the camshaft as detailed later in this section.

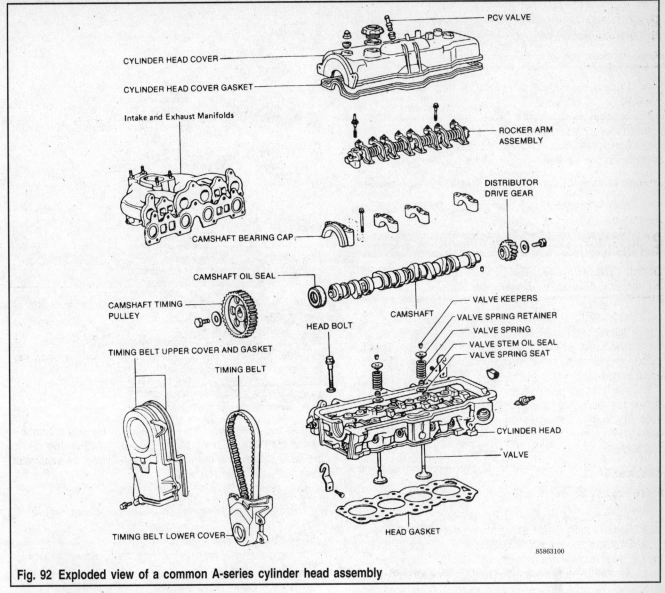

Fig. 92 Exploded view of a common A-series cylinder head assembly

85863100

23. Loosen the head bolts using several passes of the proper sequence to prevent warping of the head.

24. Lift the head directly up. Do not attempt to slide it off.

25. Installation is the reverse of removal.

➡️**When replacing the head, always use a new gasket. Also replace the camshaft seal, making sure to grease the lip before installation. The following torques are needed for installation: cam bearing caps 8-10 ft. lbs. (1114 Nm), cam sprocket 29-39 ft. lbs. (39-53 Nm), crankshaft pulley 55-61 ft. lbs. (75-83 Nm), manifold bolts 15-21 ft. lbs. (20-28 Nm), rocker arm bolts 17-19 ft. lbs. (23-26 Nm), timing gear idler bolt 22-32 ft. lbs. (30-43 Nm), belt tension 0.24-0.28 in. (6.1-7.1mm). Adjust the valves to the proper clearances.**

1C-L Diesel Engine

▶ **See Figures 94, 95, 96 and 97**

1. Disconnect the negative battery cable.

2. Drain the coolant. If you are on a tight budget, you'll probably want to save and reuse the old coolant, unless it is dirty or otherwise contaminated.

3. Remove the engine undercover, then drain the oil — you shouldn't save this for reuse no matter how tight your budget.

4. Disconnect the exhaust pipe from the manifold.

5. Disconnect the air inlet hose.

6. On models equipped with an automatic transmission, disconnect the accelerator and throttle cables from the injection pump.

7. Disconnect the water inlet hose, then remove the inlet pipe.

8. Disconnect the two heater hoses.

9. Remove the EGR valve and its pipe.

10. Tag and disconnect all wires and cables which might interfere with cylinder head removal.

11. Disconnect the water bypass hose from the cylinder head union.

12. Disconnect the fuel hoses from the fuel pipe.

13. Remove the clamp and then disconnect the injection pipe.

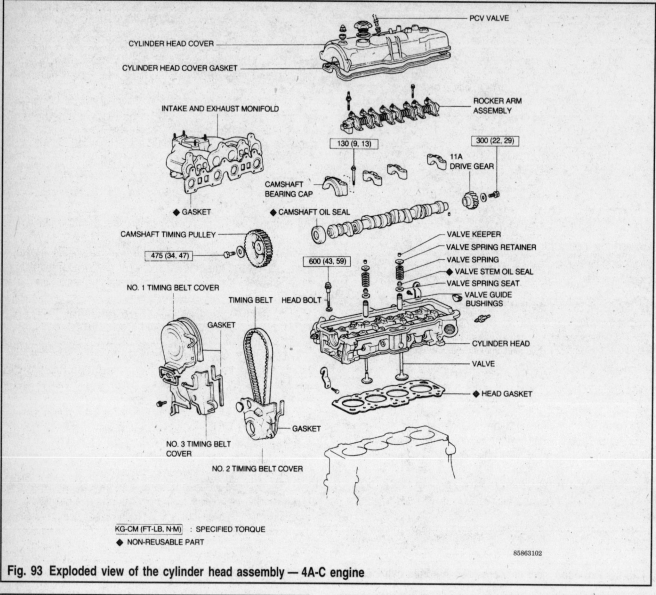

Fig. 93 Exploded view of the cylinder head assembly — 4A-C engine

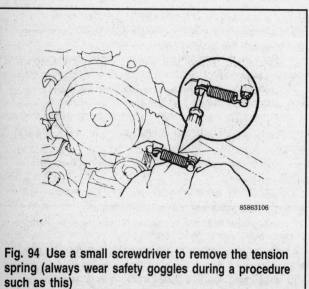

Fig. 94 Use a small screwdriver to remove the tension spring (always wear safety goggles during a procedure such as this)

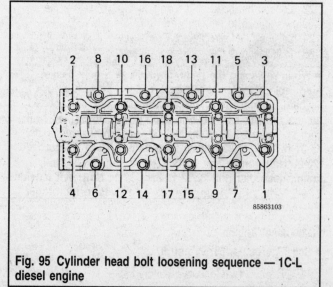

Fig. 95 Cylinder head bolt loosening sequence — 1C-L diesel engine

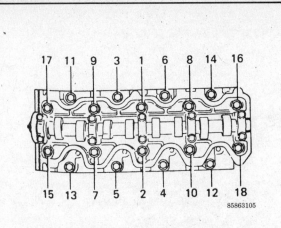

Fig. 96 Cylinder head bolt torque sequence — 1C-L diesel engine

14. Disconnect the fuel return hose at the injection pump. Remove the four locknuts, then remove the return pipe.

15. Remove the current sensor, then remove the glow plugs.

16. Use special tool 09268064010 to remove the injectors. Don't lose the injection seats and gaskets.

➡**Arrange the injector holders in the proper order.**

17. Remove the No. 2 timing belt cover and its gasket.

18. Turn the crankshaft clockwise and set the No. 1 cylinder at TDC of the compression stroke. Place matchmarks on the camshaft timing pulley, the injection pump pulley and the timing belt.

19. Remove the tension spring. Loosen the No. 1 idler pulley mounting bolt and push it aside. Remove the timing belt from the gear.

❋❋CAUTION

DO NOT pinch the tension spring with pliers or the like!

20. Loosen the mounting bolt and remove the camshaft gear.

21. Support the timing belt so it doesn't slip a tooth.

❋❋CAUTION

Be very careful not to drop anything into the timing cover. Make sure that the timing belt does not touch oil, water or dust!

22. Remove the cylinder head cover and the oil level gauge guide clamp.

23. Loosen the remove the cylinder head bolts in two or three stages, using the sequence shown in the illustration.

24. The cylinder head is positioned by means of dowels — lift it straight upward when removing it. Never attempt to slide it off the block.

25. Installation is in the reverse order of removal. Tighten the cylinder head bolts in two or three stages of the illustrated

sequence. Refer to the timing belt procedures located later in this section when installing the belt.

➡**When replacing the cylinder head, always use a new gasket. It's also a good idea to replace the camshaft oil seal, making sure to grease the lip before installation.**

26. Note the following tightening torques: Cylinder head bolts: 64 ft. lbs (87 Nm). Cylinder head cover nuts: 65 inch lbs. (7 Nm). Camshaft gear bolt: 22 ft. lbs. (30 Nm). Idler pulley set bolt: 27 ft. lbs. (37 Nm). Injectors: 47 ft. lbs (64 Nm). Glow plugs: 9 ft. lbs. (12 Nm).

4A-GE Series

▶ **See Figures 98, 99 and 100**

1. Disconnect the negative battery cable. Remove the engine undercover. Drain the coolant and engine oil.

2. Loosen the retaining clamp and then disconnect the No. 1 air cleaner hose from the throttle body. Disconnect the actuator and accelerator cables from the mounting bracket on the throttle body.

3. If the vehicle is equipped with power steering, remove the pump (with hoses attached) and the mounting bracket, then position to the side.

4. Loosen the water pump pulley set nuts. Remove the drive belt adjusting bolt and remove the drive belt. Remove the pulley set nuts and remove the fluid coupling with the fan and water pump pulley.

5. Disconnect the upper radiator hose at the water outlet on the cylinder head. Disconnect the two heater hoses at the water bypass pipe and at the cylinder head rear plate.

6. Remove the distributor. Remove the cold start injector pipe and the PCV hose from the cylinder head.

7. Remove the pulsation damper from the delivery pipe. Disconnect the fuel return hose from the pressure regulator.

8. Tag (for identification) and disconnect all vacuum hoses which may interfere with cylinder head removal. Remove the wiring harness and the vacuum pipe from the No. 3 timing cover.

9. Tag (for identification) and disconnect all wires which might interfere with cylinder head removal. Position the wiring harness to one side.

10. Disconnect the exhaust bracket from the exhaust pipe, and disconnect the exhaust pipe from the manifold.

11. Remove the vacuum tank and the VCV valve. Remove the exhaust manifold.

12. Remove the water outlet housing from the cylinder head with the No. 1 bypass pipe and gasket. Pull the bypass pipe out of the housing.

13. Remove the fuel delivery pipe along with the fuel injectors. When removing the delivery pipe, be very careful not to drop or bump the fuel injector nozzles. Do not remove the injector cover.

14. Remove the intake manifold stay bracket. Remove the intake manifold along with the air control valve.

15. Remove the cylinder head covers and gaskets. Remove the spark plugs.

16. Rotate the crankshaft until the groove on the crank pulley is aligned with the timing mark (0) on the No. 1 timing cover. Check that the valve lifters on No. 1 cylinder are loose. If not, rotate the engine, once again aligning the marks, then check the lifters. Remove the timing covers and gaskets.

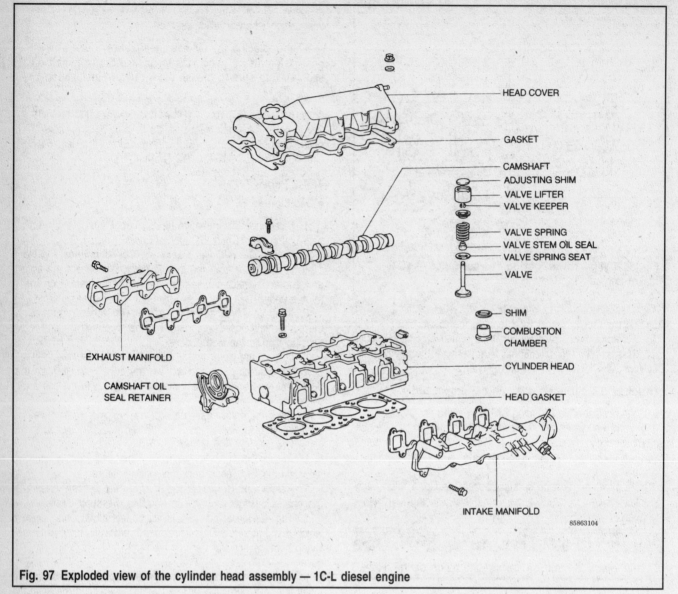

HEAD COVER

GASKET

CAMSHAFT
ADJUSTING SHIM
VALVE LIFTER
VALVE KEEPER

VALVE SPRING
VALVE STEM OIL SEAL
VALVE SPRING SEAT

VALVE

SHIM

COMBUSTION
CHAMBER

CYLINDER HEAD

HEAD GASKET

INTAKE MANIFOLD

EXHAUST MANIFOLD

CAMSHAFT OIL
SEAL RETAINER

85863104

Fig. 97 Exploded view of the cylinder head assembly — 1C-L diesel engine

17. Place matchmarks on the timing belt and two timing pulleys. Loosen the idler pulley bolts and move the pulley to the left as far as it will go. Tighten a pulley bolt to keep it in position.

18. Remove the timing belt from the camshaft pulleys. Support the belt during removal so that it does not turn the pulleys out of position. Take care not to drop anything into the timing cases. Do not allow the timing belt to come into contact with dirt or grease.

19. Lock the camshafts in position (a flat in the center of each shaft is provided for holding it in position with a suitable wrench) and remove the pulleys. Remove the No. 4 timing belt cover.

20. It is now possible to check camshaft end-play, if desired. Mount a dial indicator so that the probe is zeroed and resting against the nose of the camshaft. Move the camshaft back and forth and measure play. Maximum play allowed is 0.0118 in. (0.3mm). Replace the thrust bearing if necessary.

21. Loosen each camshaft bearing cap a little at a time starting from each end and working toward the center. Remove the caps, oil seal and camshafts.

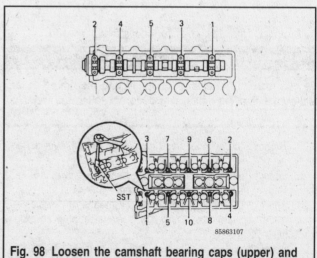

85863107

Fig. 98 Loosen the camshaft bearing caps (upper) and cylinder head bolts (lower) using the proper sequence for each — 4A-GE engine

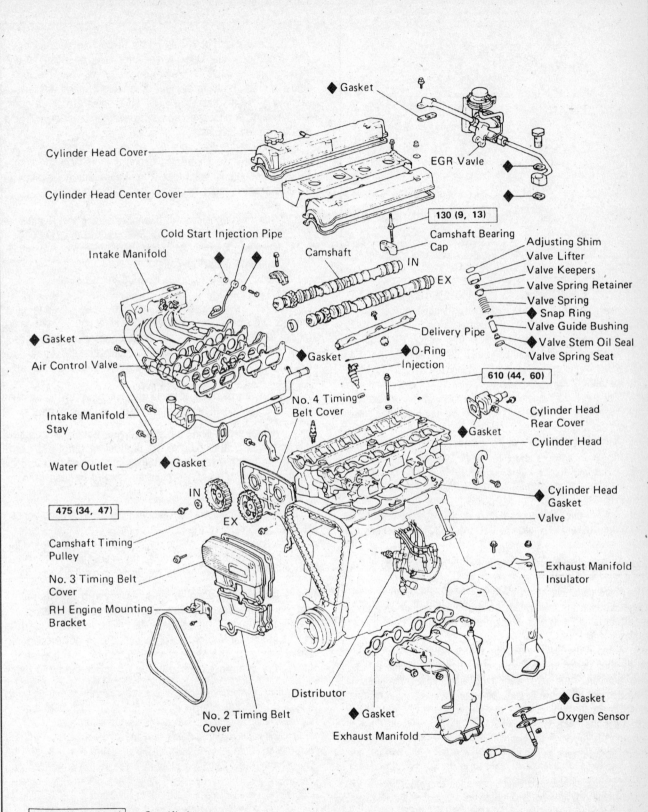

Fig. 99 Exploded view of the cylinder head assembly — 4A-GE engine

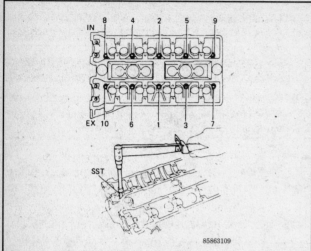

Fig. 100 Cylinder head bolt torque sequence — 4A-GE engine

22. Use a suitable socket tool (SST 09205-16010 or equivalent), and loosen the head bolts in stages, starting from the ends and working toward the center.

23. Remove the cylinder head from the vehicle. Clean all block and head gasket mounting surfaces. Service the head as required.

To install:

24. Position the cylinder head and a new gasket in position. Lightly coat the mounting bolts with engine oil. Install the short bolts on the intake side, and the long bolts on the exhaust side. Starting at the center of the cylinder head and working outward, tighten the cylinder head bolts gradually in three stages. The final torque value should be 45 ft. lbs. (61 Nm).

25. Position the camshafts on the head. Position the bearing caps over the camshaft (arrows pointing forward).

26. Tighten each bearing cap bolt in stages, starting from the center outwards. Tighten to 9 ft. lbs. (12 Nm). Recheck the end-play.

27. Use a suitable driver tool and carefully drive new oil seals into position. Install the No. 4 timing cover.

28. Install the timing pulleys onto the camshafts. Make sure the pins and matchmarks are in the correct position. Lock the camshafts in position and tighten the pulley mounting bolts to 34 ft. lbs. (46 Nm).

29. Align the matchmarks made during removal and install the timing belt. Loosen the bolt that is holding the idler pulley in position. Be sure that the pulleys have not been moved when installing the belt.

30. Rotate the engine two complete revolutions (from TDC to TDC; 0 to 0). Make sure that the matchmarks align. If not, the timing is wrong. If necessary, shift the belt to pulley meshing to correct mark misalignment. Repeat the previous step.

31. Tighten the idler pulley bolts to 27 ft. lbs. (37 Nm). Measure the timing belt deflection at the top span between the two camshaft pulleys. Deflection should be no more that 0.16 in. at 4.4 lbs. of pressure. If deflection is not correct, adjust by increasing or decreasing idler pulley pressure. Install the remaining components in the reverse order of removal.

CHECKING ENGINE COMPRESSION

A noticeable lack of engine power, excessive oil consumption and/or poor fuel mileage measured over an extended period are all indicators of internal engine wear. Worn piston rings, scored and worn cylinder bores, blown head gaskets, sticking or burnt valves and worn valve seats are all possible culprits here. A check of each cylinder's compression will help you locate the problems.

As mentioned in the tools and equipment information of Section 1, a screw-in compression gauge is more accurate than the type you simply hold against the spark plug hole, although it takes slightly longer to use (it's worth it). To check compression:

1. Warm the engine up to normal operating temperature.
2. Disconnect the fuel-cut solenoid wire on the 1C-L.
3. Remove all four spark plugs (gasoline engines) or all four glow plugs (diesel engines).
4. Disconnect the high tension wire from the ignition coil (gasoline engines only).
5. Screw the compression gauge into the No. 1 spark plug hole (or glow plug hole) until the fitting is snug. Be very careful not to cross-thread the hole, as the head is aluminum.
6. Fully open the throttle either by operating the throttle linkage by hand, or on gasoline fuel injected cars having an assistant floor the accelerator pedal.
7. Ask your assistant to crank the engine a few times using the ignition switch while you watch the compression gauge.

➡ **A cylinder's compression pressure is usually acceptable if it is not less than 80% of the highest reading. For example, if the highest reading is 150 psi, the lowest should be no lower than 120 psi. No cylinder should be less than 100 psi.**

8. Read the compression gauge at the end of each series of cranks, and record the highest of these readings. Repeat this procedure for each of the engine's cylinders. Compare the highest reading of each cylinder to the readings on the other cylinders. Readings should be similar for all of the cylinders.

➡ **For most of the gasoline engines covered by this manual the compression reading should be somewhere between 150-180 psi, though slightly lower on older engines is not abnormal, as long as one cylinder is not more than 20% lower than the highest reading. On all gasoline engines, the compression should be no lower than 100 psi.**

9. If a cylinder is unusually low, pour a tablespoon of clean engine oil into the cylinder through the spark plug hole and repeat the compression test. If the compression comes up after adding the oil, it appears that the cylinder's piston rings or bore are damaged or worn. If the pressure remains low, the valves may not be seating properly (a valve job is needed), or the head gasket may be blown near that cylinder. If compression in any two adjacent cylinders is low, and if the addition of oil doesn't help the compression, there is leakage past the head gasket. Oil and coolant water in the combustion chamber can result from this problem. There may be evidence of water droplets on the engine dipstick when a head gasket has blown.

CLEANING AND INSPECTION

▶ **See Figures 101, 102 and 103**

When the rocker assembly and valve train have been removed from the cylinder head (please refer to the information on valves and springs located later in this section), place the head on two wooden blocks on a work bench, (combustion chamber side up). Use a scraper or putty knife, and carefully scrape away any gasket material that may have stuck to the head-to-block mating surface when the head was removed. Make sure you DO NOT gouge the mating surface with the tool.

Use a wire brush chucked into your electric drill to remove the carbon in each combustion chamber. Make sure the brush is actually removing the carbon and not merely burnishing it.

Clean all the valve guides using a valve guide brush (available at most auto parts or auto tool shops) and solvent. A fine-bristled rifle bore cleaning brush also works here.

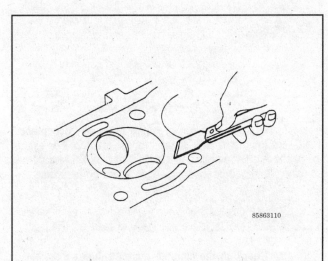

85863110

Fig. 101 DO NOT scratch the cylinder head mating surface when removing the old gasket material

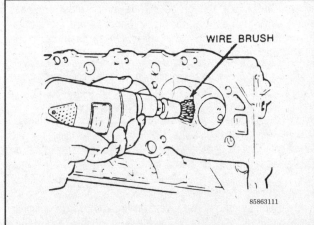

WIRE BRUSH

85863111

Fig. 102 Remove combustion chamber carbon using a wire brush — make sure the carbon is removed and not merely burnished

Inspect the threads of each spark plug hole by screwing a plug into each, making sure it screws down completely. Repair any damaged threads using a tap or Heli-coil®.

✳✳CAUTION

DO NOT hot tank the cylinder head! The head material on most engines covered by this manual is aluminum, which is ruined if subjected to the hot tank solution!

➡**Before hot-tanking any overhead camshaft cylinder head, check with the machine shop doing the work. Some cam bearings are easily damaged by the hot tank solution.**

Finally, go over the entire head with a clean shop rag soaked in solvent to remove any grit, old gasket particles, etc. Blow out the bolt holes, coolant galleys, intake and exhaust ports, valve guides and plug holes with compressed air.

RESURFACING

▶ **See Figures 104, 105, 106 and 107**

While the head is removed, check the head-to-block mating surface for straightness. If the engine has overheated and blown a head gasket, this must be done as a matter of course. A warped mating surface must be resurfaced (milled); this is done on a milling machine and is quite similar to planing a piece of wood.

Use a precision steel straightedge and a blade-type feeler gauge, and check the surface of the head across its length, width and diagonal length as shown in the illustrations. Check the intake and exhaust manifold mating surfaces. If head warpage exceeds 0.003 in. (0.76mm), in a 6 in. (152.4mm) span, or 0.006 in. (0.15mm), over the total length, the head must be milled. If warpage is highly excessive, the head must be replaced. Consult a reputable machine shop operator on head milling limitations.

CYLINDER BLOCK CLEANING

▶ **See Figure 108**

When the cylinder head is removed, the top of the cylinder block and pistons must be cleaned. Before you begin, rotate the crankshaft until one or more pistons are flush with the top of the block (on the four cylinder engines, you will either have Nos. 1 and 4 up, or Nos. 2 and 3 up). Carefully stuff clean rags into the cylinders in which the pistons are down. This will help keep grit and carbon chips out during cleaning. Use care not to gouge or scratch the block-to-head mating surface and the piston top(s), clean away any old gasket material with a wire brush and/or scraper. On the piston tops, make sure you are actually removing the carbon and not merely burnishing it.

Remove the rags from the down cylinders after you have wiped the top of the block with a solvent soaked rag. Rotate the crankshaft until the other pistons come up flush with the top of the block, and clean those pistons.

➡**Because you have rotated the crankshaft, you will have to re-time the engine following the procedure listed under the timing chain/timing belt removal.**

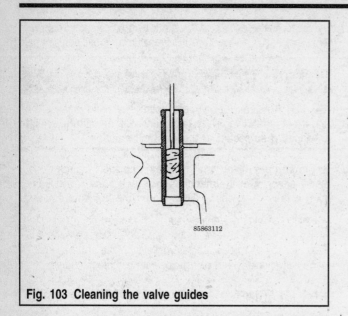

Fig. 103 Cleaning the valve guides

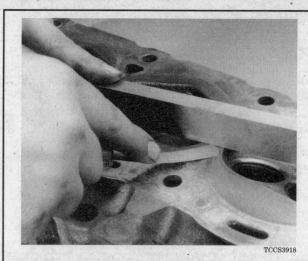

Fig. 106 Checking a cylinder head for straightness diagonally across the head surface

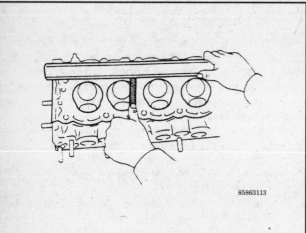

Fig. 104 Check the cylinder head mating surface for straightness using a precision straight-edge and a feeler gauge

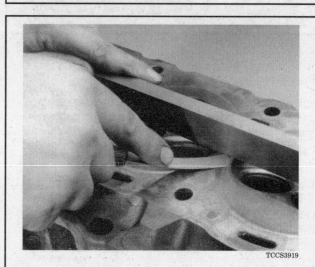

Fig. 107 Checking the cylinder head straight across the surface

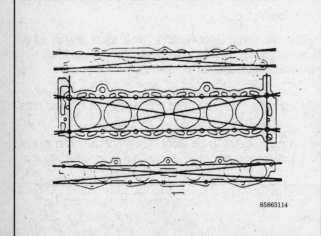

Fig. 105 Check the cylinder head across each of these planes (widthwise, lengthwise and diagonally)

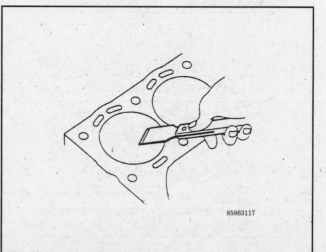

Fig. 108 When removing carbon from the piston tops, be careful NOT to scratch the pistons

Make sure you wipe out each cylinder thoroughly with a solvent soaked rag, to remove all traces of grit, before the head is reassembled to the block. Compressed air and a pair of safety goggles are also helpful here.

Valves and Springs

REMOVAL & INSTALLATION

◗ **See Figures 109, 110, 111, 112, 113, 114 and 115**

1. Remove the cylinder head and rocker arm shafts (gasoline engines only) as detailed previously in this section. For the diesel engine, remove the camshaft as detailed later in this section. Lift out the valve lifters and any accompanying shims.

➡**Always be sure to keep all valve train components in the proper order to assure installation in their original locations.**

2. Using a suitable valve spring compressor tool, compress the spring and remove the keepers.
3. Lift off the spring retainer and the spring.
4. Pull off the valve oil seal and the lower spring seat. Remove the valve through the bottom of the cylinder head.

➡**When removing the valve seal and the lower spring seat, a small screwdriver and a magnet may come in handy.**

5. Inspect the valve and spring. Clean the valve guide with a cotton swab and solvent. Inspect the valve guide and seat, then check the valve guide-to-stem clearance.
To install:
6. Lubricate the valve stem and guide with engine oil. Install the valve in the cylinder head through the bottom and position the lower spring seat.

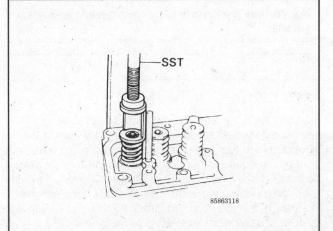

Fig. 109 Use a valve spring compressor to hold the spring while removing the keepers — gasoline engine

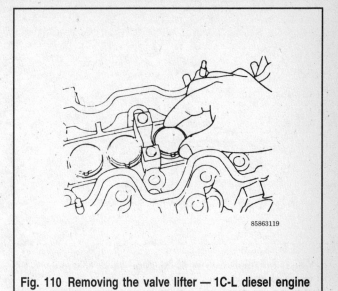

Fig. 110 Removing the valve lifter — 1C-L diesel engine

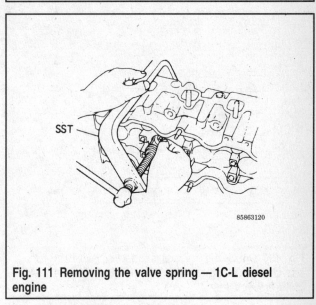

Fig. 111 Removing the valve spring — 1C-L diesel engine

7. Lubricate the valve seal with engine oil and then install it into position over the lower spring seat.

➡**When installing seals, ensure that a small amount of oil is able to pass the seal to lubricate the valve guides; otherwise, excessive wear may result.**

8. Install the valve spring and the upper spring retainer, then compress the spring using the compressor tool and install the valve keeper(s).

➡**Tap the installed valve stem lightly with a rubber mallet to ensure proper fit.**

9. Don't forget the valve lifters and shims on the diesel engine. Make sure the lifters rotate smoothly in the cylinder head.

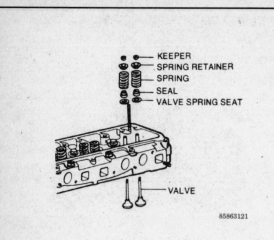

Fig. 112 Exploded view of common valve assembly components

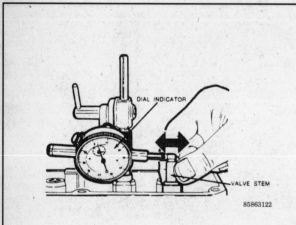

Fig. 113 Valve stem-to-guide clearance may be checked using a dial gauge

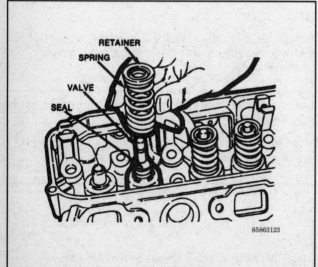

Fig. 114 Installing the valve assembly

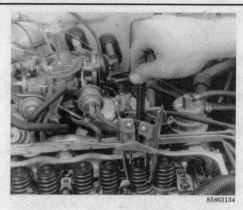

Fig. 115 On most engines, the valve springs and seals may be removed with the cylinder head installed, but ONLY if a spark plug air fitting (with a an air compressor) is used to hold the valves for that cylinder in position

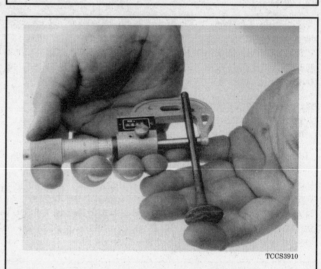

Fig. 116 Use a micrometer to measure the valve stem diameter

INSPECTION

▶ **See Figures 113, 116, 117, 118 and 119**

Inspect the valve faces and the cylinder head valve seats for pits, burned spots and other evidence of poor seating. If the valve face is in such bad shape that the head of the valve must be ground in order to true up the face, discard the valve because the sharp edge will run too hot. The correct angle for valve faces is given in the specification charts found earlier in this section. It is recommended that any reaming or resurfacing (grinding) be performed by a reputable machine shop.

Check the valve stem for scoring and/or burned spots. If not noticeably scored or damaged, clean the valve stem with a suitable solvent to remove all gum and varnish. Clean the valve guides using a suitable solvent and an expanding wire-type valve guide cleaner (generally available at a local automotive supply store). If you have access to a dial indicator for measuring valve stem-to-guide clearance, mount it so that the stem of the indicator is at a 90° angle to the valve stem and

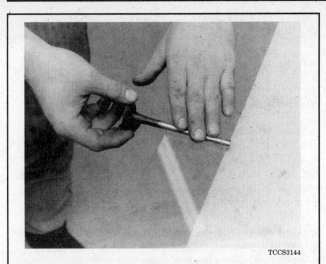

Fig. 117 Valve stems may be rolled on a flat surface to check for bends

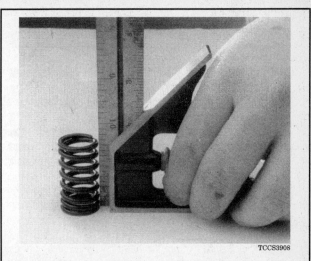

Fig. 118 Check the valve spring for squareness on a flat surface, a carpenters square can be used

as close to the valve guide as possible. Move the valve off its seat slightly and measure the valve guide-to-stem clearance by rocking the valve back and forth so that the stem actuates the dial indicator. Measure the valve stem using a micrometer, and compare to specifications in order to determine whether the stem or the guide is responsible for the excess clearance. If a dial indicator and a micrometer are not available, take the cylinder head and valves to a reputable machine shop.

Use a steel square to check the squareness of the valve spring. If the spring is out of square more than the maximum allowable (K-series: 0.063 in. or 1.6mm. A-series engines: 0.079 in. or 2mm. T-series engines: 0.075 in. or 1.9mm.), it will require replacement. Check that the spring height and strength is up to specifications. If the spring is weak, it must be replaced. If the installed height is incorrect, add shim washers between the spring pad and the spring.

➡**Use only washers designed for this purpose.**

REFACING

▶ **See Figure 120**

Valve refacing should only be handled by a reputable machine shop, as the experience and equipment needed to do the job are beyond that of the average owner/mechanic. During the course of a normal valve job, refacing is necessary in cases when simply lapping the valves into their seats will not correct the seat and face wear. When the valves are reground (resurfaced), the valve seats must also be recut, again requiring special equipment and experience.

VALVE LAPPING

▶ **See Figure 121**

The valves must be lapped into their seats after resurfacing, to ensure proper sealing. Even if the valves have not been refaced, they should be lapped into the head before reassembly.

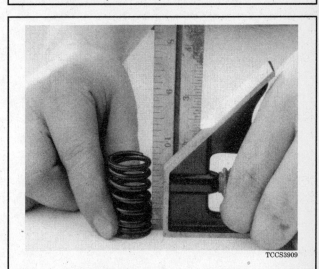

Fig. 119 The valve spring should be straight up and down when placed like this

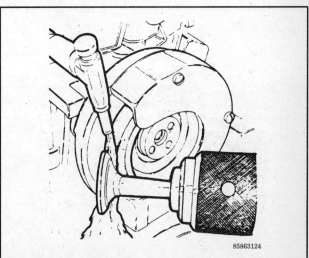

Fig. 120 Valve refacing should be handled by a reputable machine shop

Set the cylinder head on the workbench, combustion chamber side up. Rest the head on wooden blocks on either end, so there are 2-3 in. (51-76mm) between the tops of the valve guides and the bench.

1. Lightly lube the valve stem with clean engine oil. Coat the valve seat completely with valve grinding compound. Use just enough compound that the full width and circumference of the seat are covered.

2. Install the valve in its proper location in the head. Attach the suction cup end of a valve lapping tool to the valve head. It usually helps to put a small amount of saliva into the suction cup to aid it sticking to the valve.

3. Rotate the tool between your palms, changing position and lifting the tool often to prevent grooving. Lap the valve in until a smooth, evenly polished seat and valve face are evident.

4. Remove the valve from the head. Wipe away all traces of grinding compound from the valve face and seat. Wipe out the port with a solvent soaked rag, then swab out the valve guide with a piece of solvent soaked rag to make sure there are no traces of compound grit inside the guide. This cleaning is important.

5. Proceed through the remaining valves, one at a time. Make sure the valve faces, seats, cylinder ports and valve guides are clean before reassembling the valve train.

Valve Seats

The valve seats in the engines covered in this guide are all non-replaceable, and must be recut when service is required. Seat recutting requires a special tool and experience, and should be handled at a reputable machine shop. Seat concentricity should also be checked by a machinist.

Valve Guides

INSPECTION

▶ **See Figure 122**

Valve guides should be cleaned as outlined earlier, and checked when valve stem diameter and stem-to-guide clearance is checked. Generally, if the engine is using oil through the guides (assuming the valve seals are OK) and the valve stem diameter is within specification, it is the guides that are worn and need to be replaced.

Valve guides which are not excessively worn or distorted may, in some cases, be knurled rather than replaced. Knurling is a process in which metal inside the valve guide bore is displaced and raised (forming a very fine cross-hatch pattern), thereby reducing clearance. Knurling also provides excellent oil control. The possibility of knurling rather than replacing the guides should be discussed with a machinist.

REMOVAL & INSTALLATION

▶ **See Figures 123, 124 and 125**

1. Heat the cylinder head to 176-212°F (80-100 Nm), evenly, before beginning the replacement procedure.

2. On models equipped with a snapring retainer: Use a brass rod to break the valve guide off above its snapring.

➡**On the diesel engine, insert an old valve wrapped with tape into the guide. Break off the guide by rapping sharply with a hammer. Remove the guide bushing snapring.**

3. Drive out the valve guide, toward the combustion chamber using a suitable tool.

The guides are replaced using a stepped drift. Determine the height above the boss that the guide must extend, and obtain a stack of washers, their inner diameter similar to the guide's

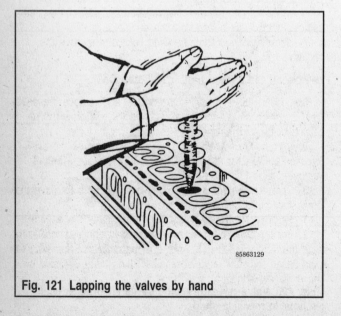

Fig. 121 Lapping the valves by hand

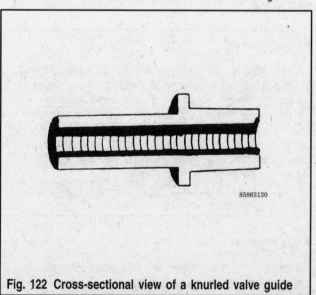

Fig. 122 Cross-sectional view of a knurled valve guide

outer diameter, of that height. Place the stack of washers on the guide, and insert the guide into the boss.

➡**Valve guides are often tapered or beveled for installation.**

4. Use the stepped installation tool and press or tap the guides into position. Ream the guides according to the size of the valve stem. Install a snapring on the new valve guide.

Engine Timing Cover (Front Cover)

Only the K-series and T-series engines covered by this manual utilize a timing chain (instead of a belt). The timing chain is run wet (oiled) and therefore the timing cover is also the engine front cover in the sense that it seals the front of the crankcase. On the 1C-L diesel engine and on all A-series engines, a timing belt is utilized. When a timing belt is used it

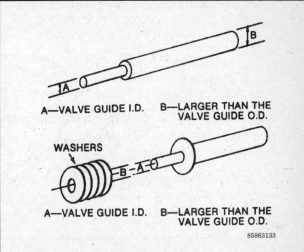

Fig. 125 Valve guide installation tool using washers to achieve proper height

is normally run dry, therefore the timing cover is NOT the seal for the front of the engine crankcase. On engines utilizing a timing belt, an oil pump body/front cover is mounted behind the timing belt and is used to seal the front of the crankcase.

REMOVAL & INSTALLATION

Except 1C-L and A-Series Engines

▶ **See Figures 126 and 127**

1. Drain the engine cooling system from the radiator, then drain the engine oil from the crankcase.

2. Disconnect the negative battery cable, then disconnect the positive cable. If necessary, remove the battery.

3. Remove the air cleaner assembly, complete with hoses, from its bracket.

4. Remove the hood latch as well as its brace and support.

5. Remove the headlight bezels and grille assembly.

6. Unfasten the upper and lower radiator hose clamps, then remove both of the hoses from the engine.

7. Unfasten the radiator securing bolts and remove the radiator.

➡**Take off the shroud first, if so equipped.**

8. Loosen the drive belt adjusting link and remove the drive belt. Unfasten the alternator multi-connector, withdraw the retaining bolts, and remove the alternator.

9. If equipped, loosen the drive belt and remove the air injection pump. Disconnect the hoses from the pump before removing it.

10. Unfasten the crankshaft pulley retaining bolt. Remove the crankshaft pulley with a gear puller.

11. Remove the gravel shield from underneath the engine.

12. For the 3K-C engine, remove the nuts and washers from both the right and left front engine mounts. Detach the exhaust pipe flange from the exhaust manifold, then raise the front of the engine slightly.

13. On 2T-C engines, remove the right hand brace plate.

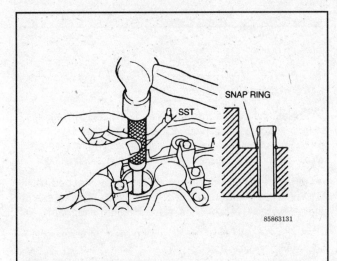

Fig. 123 If equipped, the snapring must be removed before driving out the valve guide

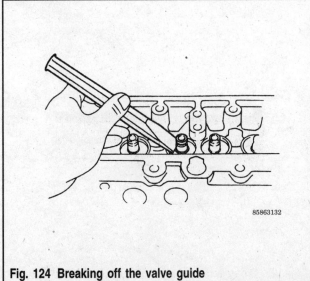

Fig. 124 Breaking off the valve guide

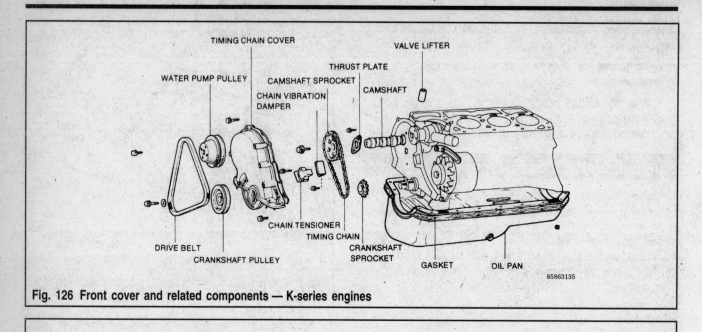

Fig. 126 Front cover and related components — K-series engines

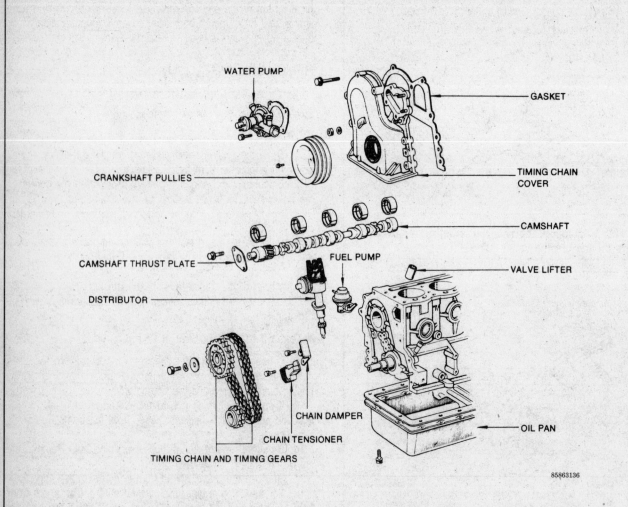

Fig. 127 Front cover and related components — T-series engines

14. Remove the front oil pan bolts, to gain access to the bottom of the timing chain cover.

➡It may be necessary to insert a thin knife between the pan and the gasket in order to break the pan loose. Use care not to damage the gasket.

Installation is basically the reverse order of removal. There are, however, several points to·remember:
• Apply sealer to the two front corners of the 2T-C engine's oil pan gasket.
• Tighten the crankshaft pulley to the figure given in the torque specifications chart.
• Adjust the drive belts as detailed in Section 1 of this manual.

4A-C (RWD)

▶ See Figure 128

1. Disconnect the negative battery cable.
2. Remove the drive belt(s).
3. Bring the engine to the top dead center timing position. Please refer to the cylinder head removal procedure for details.
4. Remove the crankshaft pulley using a suitable puller.
5. Remove the water pump pulley.
6. Remove the upper and lower timing case covers.
7. Installation is the reverse of removal. Tighten the timing belt cover fasteners to 61-99 inch lbs. (7-11 Nm).

4A-C, 4A-LC (FWD)

▶ See Figure 129

1. Disconnect the negative battery cable.
2. Remove the right side cover under the engine.
3. Loosen the water pump pulley bolts and then remove the alternator belt. Remove the power steering pump drive belt (if so equipped).
4. Remove the bolts and then disconnect the water pump pulley from the water pump.
5. Loosen the idler pulley mounting bolt. Loosen the adjusting nut and then remove the A/C drive belt. Remove the idler pulley.
6. Set the No. 1 piston to TDC of its compression stroke. Loosen the crankshaft pulley mounting bolt and then remove the pulley.

➡Before removing the pulley, check that the rockers on the No. 1 cylinder are loose, if not, turn the engine one complete revolution.

7. Remove the mounting bolts and then remove the No. 1 (lower) timing belt cover.
8. Remove the four bolts and then remove the center engine mount.
9. Place a block of wood on a floor jack and then raise the engine slightly. Remove the two bolts, then remove the right engine mount.
10. Lower the engine, then remove the No. 2 (upper) timing cover and its gasket.
11. Remove the No. 3 (center) timing cover and its gasket.

12. Installation is in the reverse order of removal. Tighten the crankshaft pulley bolt to 80-94 ft. lbs. (108-127 Nm) and the center engine mount bolts to 29 ft. lbs. (39 Nm).

1C-L Diesel Engine

▶ See Figure 130

1. Disconnect the negative battery cable.
2. Remove the cover under the engine.
3. Remove the power steering pump drive belt and pulley.
4. Remove the mounting bolts, then remove the power steering pump.
5. Remove the three clips and five bolts, then remove the No. 2 (upper) timing belt cover along with its gasket.
6. Remove the alternator drive belt.
7. Set the No. 1 piston to TDC of the compression stroke. Loosen the set bolt and remove the crankshaft pulley.
8. Remove the mounting bolts, then remove the No. 1 (lower) timing belt cover along with the gasket and belt guide.
9. Remove the four bolts, then disconnect the center engine mount.
10. Installation is in the reverse order of removal. Tighten the center engine mount bolts to 29 ft. lbs. (39 Nm) and the crankshaft pulley bolt to 72 ft. lbs. (98 Nm). Tighten the power steering pump bolts and the idler pulley nut to 29 ft. lbs. (39 Nm).

4A-GE

▶ See Figure 131

➡For additional information, please refer to the timing belt removal and installation procedures located later in this section.

1. Disconnect the negative battery cable.
2. Remove the air cleaner assembly, then remove the drive belt(s).
3. If the vehicle is equipped with cruise control, remove the actuator and bracket assembly.
4. Raise and support the vehicle safely using jackstands.
5. Remove the right side front tire and wheel, then remove the right side engine splash shield. Remove the right side mount insulator.
6. If necessary, remove the valve cover.
7. Remove the crankshaft pulley, then remove the timing cover mounting bolts and cover.
8. Install in the reverse order.

Front Cover Oil Seal

Only the K-series and T-series engines covered by this manual utilize a timing chain (instead of a belt). The timing chain is run wet (oiled) and therefore the timing cover is also the engine front cover in the sense that is seals the front of the crankcase. On the 1C-L diesel engine and on all A-series engines, a timing belt is utilized. When a timing belt is used it is normally run dry, therefore the timing cover is NOT the seal for the front of the engine crankcase. On engines utilizing a timing belt, an oil pump body/front cover is mounted behind the timing belt and is used to seal the front of the crankcase.

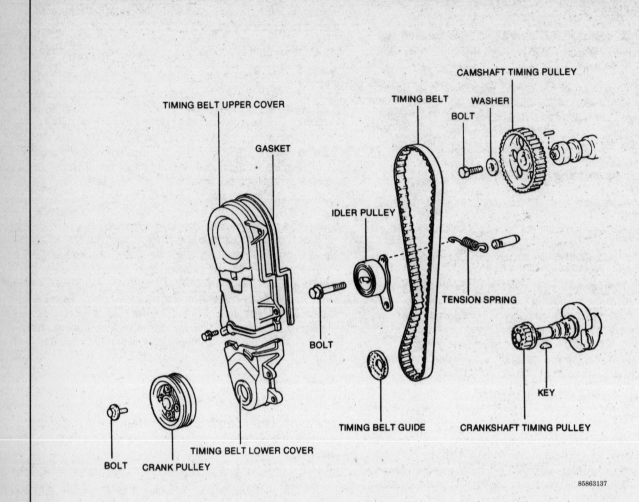

Fig. 128 Exploded view of the front cover and related components — RWD A-series engines

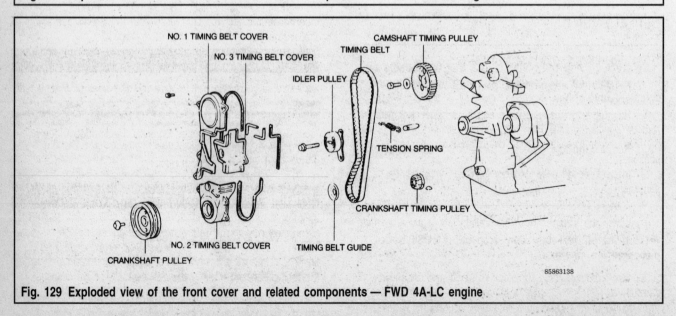

Fig. 129 Exploded view of the front cover and related components — FWD 4A-LC engine

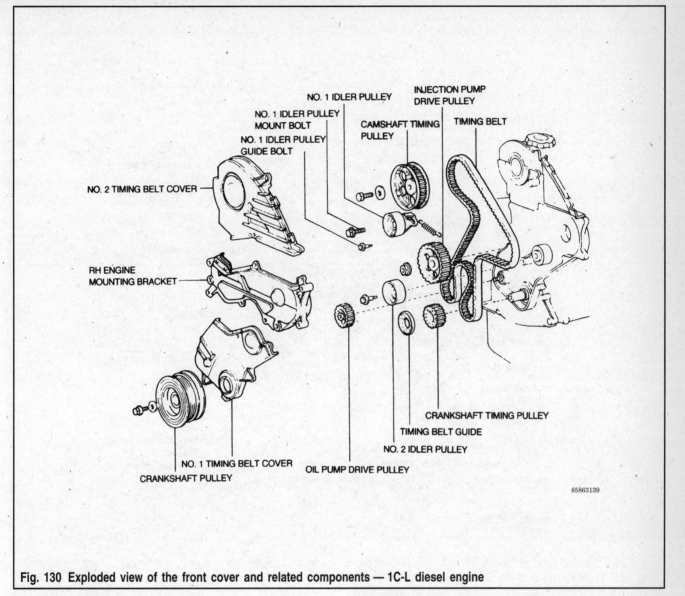

NO. 1 IDLER PULLEY

INJECTION PUMP
DRIVE PULLEY

NO. 1 IDLER PULLEY
MOUNT BOLT

CAMSHAFT TIMING
PULLEY

TIMING BELT

NO. 1 IDLER PULLEY
GUIDE BOLT

NO. 2 TIMING BELT COVER

RH ENGINE
MOUNTING BRACKET

NO. 1 TIMING BELT COVER

CRANKSHAFT PULLEY

OIL PUMP DRIVE PULLEY

NO. 2 IDLER PULLEY

TIMING BELT GUIDE

CRANKSHAFT TIMING PULLEY

85863139

Fig. 130 Exploded view of the front cover and related components — 1C-L diesel engine

REPLACEMENT

▶ **See Figures 132, 133, 134 and 135**

1. Remove the engine timing cover, as detailed earlier in this section.

2. For the 1C-L diesel engine and all A-series engines, remove the timing belt, then remove the oil pump body assembly. For details, please refer to the procedures located in this section.

3. Inspect the oil seal for signs of wear, leakage, or damage.

4. If worn, pry the oil seal out, using a suitable flat bladed tool. Remove it toward the front of the cover.

➡ **Once the oil seal has been removed, it MUST be replaced with a new one.**

5. Use a socket, pipe, or block of wood and a hammer, carefully drive the oil seal into place. Again, work from the front of the cover. Make sure whatever is used for a driver tool is approximately the same diameter as the seal and the sur-face which contacts the seal is smooth to prevent damaging the seal's lips.

❋❋CAUTION

Be extremely careful not to damage the seal or else it will leak!

6. On timing belt equipped engines, install the oil pump body assembly and the timing belt.

7. Install the engine timing cover.

Timing Chain and Tensioner

REMOVAL & INSTALLATION

▶ **See Figures 136, 137, 138, 139 and 140**

Only the K-series and T-series engines covered by this manual are equipped with a timing chain. The diesel and the A-

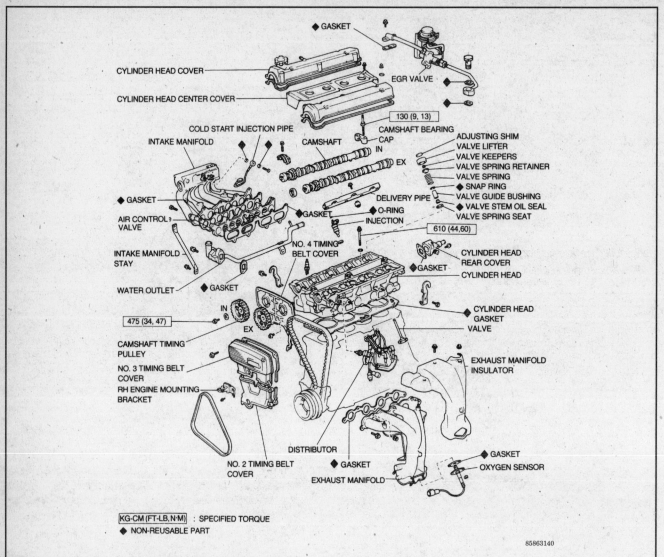

Fig. 131 Exploded view of the 4A-GE cylinder head and upper engine components showing the timing covers, gears and belt.

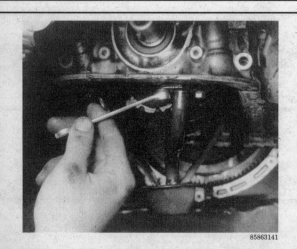

Fig. 132 On engines equipped with timing belts, the oil pump pickup must be removed from the front cover (oil pump body)

Fig. 133 Remove the retainers and remove the front crankcase sealing cover (timing cover or oil pump body, as applicable) from the engine

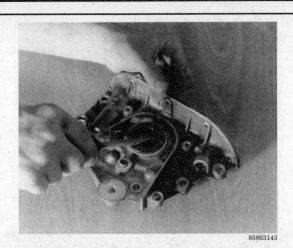

Fig. 134 Use a small prytool to carefully remove the old seal, but DO NOT score or damage the cover sealing surface

Fig. 135 Use a suitable driver to carefully install the new seal

series engines are equipped with a timing belt. For timing belt procedures, please refer to the information found later in this section.

1. Remove the drive belts.

2. Remove the crankshaft set bolt, then using a puller, remove the crankshaft pulley.

3. Remove the front cover as detailed earlier in this section.

4. On K-series engines, measure the timing chain slack using a spring scale. If the slack is more than 0.531 in. at 22 lbs. of tension, replace the chain and sprockets.

5. Remove the timing chain tensioner and vibration damper.

6. On K-series engines, remove the camshaft sprocket set bolt, then remove the timing chain and sprocket together. Use a gear puller to remove the crankshaft sprocket.

7. On T-series engines remove the chain and both sprockets at the same time.

8. Measure the timing chain length with the chain fully stretched. It should be no more than 10.7 in. for K-series engines or 11.472 in. for T-series engines in any three posi-

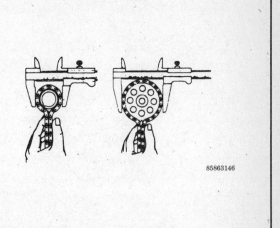

Fig. 137 Measure the outer sides of the chain rollers with a vernier caliper

tions. Wrap the chain around a sprocket. Using a vernier caliper, measure the outer sides of the chain rollers. If the measurement is less than 2.339 in. on the crankshaft sprocket or 4.480 in. around the camshaft sprocket, replace the chain and sprocket.

9. **Installation for the K-series engines is performed in the following order:**

a. Install the camshaft sprocket.

b. Set the No. 1 piston to TDC and align the camshaft dowel pin with the mark on the thrust plate.

c. Install the timing chain around the two sprockets. Make sure that the marks on the sprockets are aligned with the marks (usually bright links) on the timing chain.

d. Install the timing chain and the two sprockets onto the shafts. Make sure the timing marks are aligned with the camshaft dowel pin and the mark on the thrust plate.

e. Install the timing chain tensioner and the vibration damper.

f. Installation of the remaining components is in the reverse order of removal.

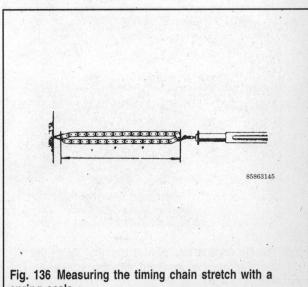

Fig. 136 Measuring the timing chain stretch with a spring scale

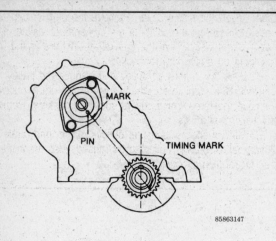

Fig. 138 Align the camshaft dowel pin and the mark on the thrust plate — K-series engines

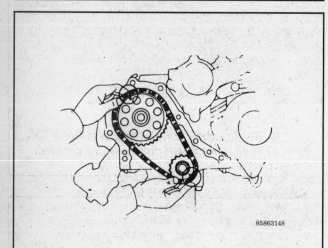

Fig. 139 Aligning the marks on the sprockets with the bright links on the chain

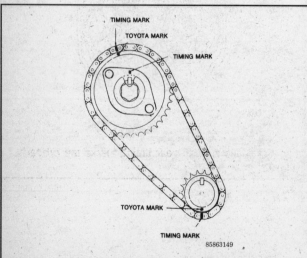

Fig. 140 Align the timing marks with the chain and sprocket — T-series engines

10. **Installation for the T-series engines is performed in the following order:**

a. Align the key in the camshaft with the mark on the thrust plate. Face the key in the crankshaft straight up.

b. Install the timing chain around the two sprockets so that the bright links line up with the timing marks on the sprockets.

c. Install the chain and gears onto the shafts.

d. Squirt oil into the cylinder in the chain tensioner, then install it to the cylinder block.

e. Install the chain damper parallel to the chain so that there is a 0.020 in. space in between.

f. Installation of the remaining components is in the reverse order of removal.

Timing Belt

REMOVAL & INSTALLATION

A-Series Engines (SOHC)
▶ **See Figures 141 and 142**

1. Remove the timing belt upper and lower covers, along with their gaskets as previously detailed.

➡ **It is always a good idea to set the engine on TDC and note the position of any pulley alignment marks before removing the timing belt.**

2. If the timing belt is to be reused, mark an arrow in the direction of engine revolution on its surface. Matchmark the belt to the pulleys using tape, a marker or a small dab of paint.

3. Loosen the idler pulley bolt, push it to the left as far as it will go, then temporarily tighten it.

4. Remove the timing belt, idler pulley bolt, idler pulley and the return spring.

➡ **Do not bend, twist, or turn the belt inside out. Do not allow grease or water to come in contact with it.**

5. Inspect the timing belt for cracks, missing teeth or overall wear. Replace as necessary.
   To install:

6. Install the return spring and idler pulley.

7. Install the timing belt. Align the marks made earlier if reusing the old belt.

8. Adjust the idler pulley so that the belt deflection is 0.24-0.28 in. at 4.5 lbs.

9. Check the valve timing. This is accomplished by rotating the engine 2 complete clockwise revolutions from No. 1 TDC to No. 1 TDC and making sure that each pulley aligns with the appropriate timing marks.

10. Installation of the remaining components is in the reverse order of removal.

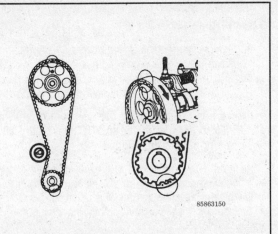

Fig. 141 Mark the timing belt before removal — A-series engines

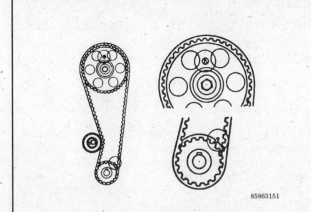

Fig. 142 Check the valve timing by turning the engine 2 complete clockwise revolutions and checking to see if the timing marks are properly aligned

4A-GE Series (DOHC)

▶ See Figures 143, 144, 145 and 146

1. Disconnect the negative battery cable. Disconnect the air cleaner hose from the throttle intake.

2. If the vehicle is equipped with power steering, remove the pump (with hoses attached) and position it out of the way.

3. Loosen the water pump pulley set nuts, remove the drive belt adjusting bolt, then remove the drive belt. Remove the set nuts, fluid coupling, fan and water pump pulley.

4. Remove the spark plugs. Rotate the crankshaft so that the timing groove on the pulley is in alignment with the timing mark (0) on the timing cover. Remove the oil filler cap and check to see that the cavity in the camshaft is visible. If the cavity is not visible, turn the crankshaft until the timing marks are lined up again, and recheck.

5. Lock the crankshaft pulley and remove the pulley mounting bolt. Use a suitable puller to remove the crank pulley. Remove the three timing covers and their gaskets. Remove the timing belt guide.

6. Matchmark the camshaft pulleys to the inner case and timing belt (if the old belt is to be reused. Also mark the old belt for rotation direction).

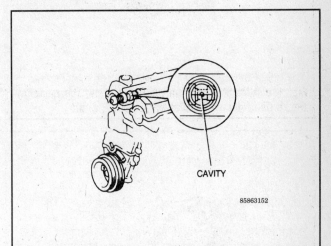

Fig. 143 When setting the 4A-GE engine to No. 1 TDC, remove the oil filler cap and check that the camshaft cavity is visible

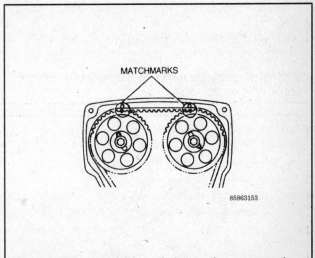

Fig. 144 Make sure all gear timing marks are properly aligned

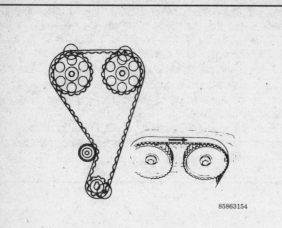

Fig. 145 If the belt is to be reused, place matchmarks on the camshaft timing pulleys and the belt (also mark the belt's direction of rotation) — 4A-GE engine

7. Loosen the idler pulley mounting bolts and move the idler pulley as far to the left as possible. Secure the pulley in the far left position. Remove the timing belt. Remove the idler pulley and the tensioner spring if servicing is required.

To install:

8. Service the engine as required.

9. Install the timing belt making sure all matchmarks and timing marks are aligned. Use care when installing the belt so that the camshaft pulleys are not moved out of position.

10. Set the idler pulley in to position so that belt deflection is 0.16 in. at 4.4 lbs. Apply more or less tension as required.

11. Turn the engine, clockwise, two complete revolutions and recheck timing mark alignment. Readjust if necessary. The idler pulley mounting bolts should be torqued to 27 ft. lbs. (37 Nm).

12. Install the remaining components in the reverse order of removal.

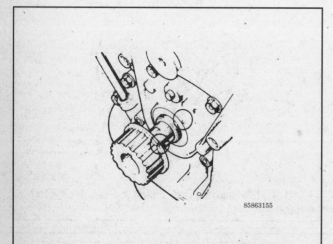

Fig. 146 When installing the crankshaft pulley, make sure the TDC marks on the oil pump body and the pulley are in alignment — 4A-GE

1C-L Diesel Engines

◗ **See Figures 147 and 148**

1. Remove the engine timing covers as previously detailed.

2. Raise the engine slightly with a jack and a block of wood. Disconnect the right engine mount from its bracket.

3. Lower the engine, then remove the right engine mount.

➡ **Before removing a timing belt or chain it is always a good idea to set the engine to TDC. Make sure all appropriate timing marks are aligned.**

4. If the timing belt is to be reused, mark an arrow in the direction of engine rotation on its surface. Matchmark the belt to the pulleys as shown in the illustration.

5. Use a screwdriver and remove the idler pulley tension spring.

✳✳CAUTION

Don't pinch the spring with pliers!

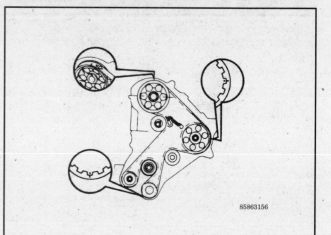

Fig. 147 If the timing belt is to be reused, matchmark it to the pulleys and mark the direction of rotation — 1C-L diesel engine

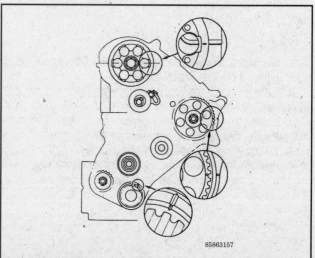

Fig. 148 During belt installation, make sure all timing marks are properly aligned

6. Loosen the idler pulley bolt, push it to the left as far as it will go, then temporarily tighten it.

7. Remove the timing belt.

❊❊CAUTION

Do not bend, twist or turn the belt inside out. Do not allow grease or water to come in contact with it!

To install:

8. Inspect the belt for cracks, missing teeth or overall wear. Replace as necessary.

9. Install the idler pulley, then install the timing belt. Make sure that the belt is aligned at all positions if new, or at all previously marked points, if it is being reused.

❊❊CAUTION

Be sure that the timing belt is securely meshed with the gear teeth; it should never be loose!

10. Install the tension spring, then turn the engine two complete revolutions (from TDC to TDC). Always turn the engine clockwise, using the crankshaft pulley bolt. All timing marks should still be in alignment; if not, remove the belt and try again.

11. Further installation is in the reverse order of removal.

Camshaft

REMOVAL & INSTALLATION

K-Series and T-Series Engines

▶ **See Figures 149 and 150**

1. Remove the cylinder head from the vehicle. For details, please refer to the procedure located earlier in this section.

2. Matchmark and remove the distributor.

3. Remove the radiator.

4. Remove the timing chain as detailed previously.

5. Remove the valve lifters in the proper sequence. Be sure to tag or arrange all valve train components in order to assure installation in their original locations.

6. Remove the fuel pump.

7. Remove the two thrust plate set bolts.

8. Screw a cylinder head bolt into the end of the camshaft. Slowly turn the camshaft and withdraw it out being careful not to damage the bearings.

To install:

9. Inspect the camshaft and bearings for damage.

10. Coat the camshaft bearings and journals lightly with oil, then carefully install the camshaft into the cylinder block.

11. Install the thrust plate in the proper position and torque the two bolts to 4-6 ft. lbs. (5-8 Nm) on K-series engines and 7-11 ft. lbs. (9-15 Nm) on T-series engines.

12. Installation of the remaining components is in the reverse order of removal.

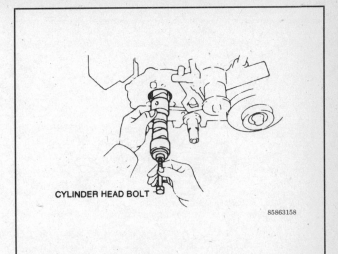

Fig. 149 Use a cylinder headbolt to remove and install the camshaft

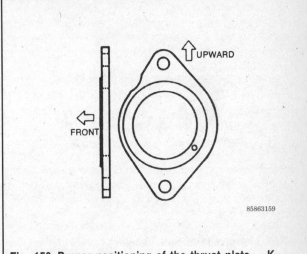

Fig. 150 Proper positioning of the thrust plate — K-series engines

A-Series Engines (SOHC)

▶ **See Figures 151, 152, 153, 154, 155, 156, 157, 158, 159 and 160**

1. Disconnect the negative battery cable.

2. Remove the cylinder head cover.

3. Remove the rocker arm and shaft assembly.

4. Loosen the bolts and pull the fuel pump back from the cylinder head. Support the fuel pump, just out of position.

➡ **Whenever the timing belt is disturbed, it is a good idea to first set the engine to No. 1 TDC in order to align the timing marks and make an easy reference for installation.**

5. Matchmark the timing belt to the camshaft timing pulley.

6. If equipped, remove the plug in the end of the timing cover for access to the camshaft pulley bolt. If not equipped with an access plug, the front timing cover must be removed.

7. Use safety wire to support the pulley in position, keeping the belt sufficiently taught in order to hold the belt teeth to the crankshaft and camshaft pulleys.

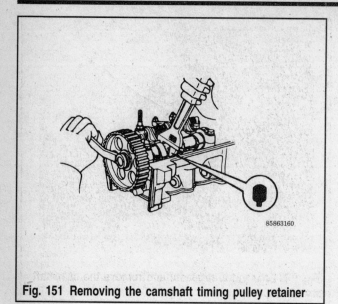

Fig. 151 Removing the camshaft timing pulley retainer

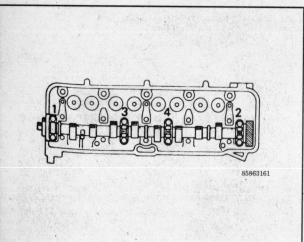

Fig. 152 Loosen the camshaft bearing caps using gradually passes of this sequence — SOHC A-series engines

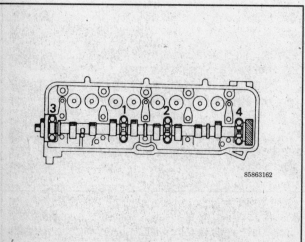

Fig. 153 Tighten the camshaft bearing caps using multiple passes of this sequence — SOHC A-series engines

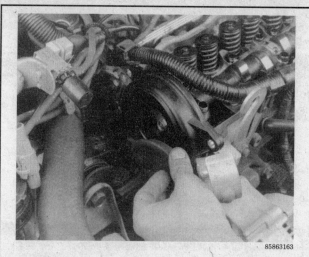

Fig. 154 If equipped, remove the end plug (access cover) from the engine timing cover

Fig. 155 Keep the camshaft from turning using a wrench or pliers on the provided flats

8. Separate the timing pulley from the camshaft. To accomplish this, hold the shaft flats with a pair of channel lock pliers and remove the bolt in the pulley end of the shaft.

➡**Never hold the camshaft on the lobes, as damage will result.**

9. If necessary, secure the camshaft with channel locks once again and loosen the distributor drive gear bolt.

10. Loosen each bearing cap bolt a little at a time using multiple passes of the proper sequence. Make sure that you keep the bearing caps in the proper order.

11. Remove the camshaft and oil seal.

12. If necessary for replacement, remove the oil seal from the end of the shaft.

To install:

13. Apply grease to the inside edge of the oil seal and liquid sealant to the outside edge, then slip the seal onto the camshaft.

➡**Be careful not to install the oil seal onto the camshaft crooked.**

14. Install the camshaft and oil seal to the cylinder head.

15. If removed, install the distributor drive gear and the plate washer with the bolt onto the camshaft.

16. Coat all bearing journals lightly with oil, then place the camshaft into position in the head.

17. Place the bearing caps Nos. 2, 3 and 4 on each journal with the arrows pointing toward the front of the engine.

18. Apply liquid sealant to the two bottom edges of the No. 1 bearing cap then install it into position.

19. Torque each bearing cap bolt a little at a time using passes in the proper sequence. Tighten to 8-10 ft. lbs. (11-14 Nm).

20. Recheck the thrust clearance, then if removed, tighten the distributor drive gear bolt to 20-23 ft. lbs. (27-31 Nm).

21. Install the timing pulley and belt to the camshaft, making sure that all marks are in alignment. The timing belt must have been kept taught to assure the belt did not jump a tooth of the crankshaft pulley.

22. Reposition and secure the fuel pump.

23. Install the access cover or the timing cover, as applicable.

24. Install the rocker arm and shaft assembly. Check and adjust the valve clearances, but remember that they must be adjusted hot. In order to do this, temporarily install the cylinder head cover and connect the negative battery cable so the engine may be run.

25. After proper valve clearance has been verified, install the cylinder head cover.

26. Connect the negative battery cable.

4A-GE Engine

▶ See Figures 161, 162, 163 and 164

1. Remove the cylinder head cover.
2. Remove the engine front covers.
3. Make certain the engine is set to TDC/compression on No.1 cylinder. Remove the timing belt following procedures outlined earlier in this section.
4. Remove the crankshaft pulley.
5. Remove the camshaft timing belt pulleys.

Fig. 157 Loosen the retainers and remove the camshaft bearing caps

Fig. 158 Lift the camshaft and, if necessary, remove the oil seal

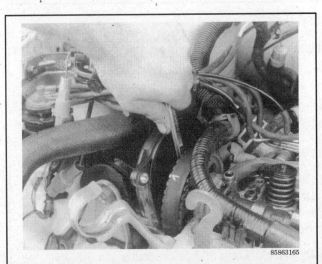

Fig. 156 Loosen and remove the pulley retaining bolt (NOTE the belt is matchmarked to a pulley tooth)

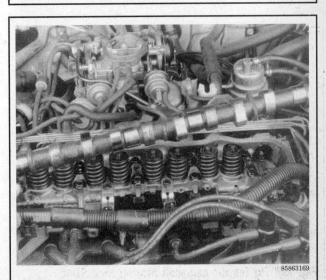

Fig. 159 Remove the camshaft from the cylinder head

Fig. 160 During installation, be sure to face the bearing cap arrows towards the front of the engine

6. Loosen and remove the camshaft bearing caps in the proper sequence. It is recommended that the bolts be loosened in two or three passes.

7. With the bearing caps removed, the camshaft(s) may be lifted clear of the head. If both cams are to be removed, label them clearly — they are not interchangeable.

➡ Handle the camshaft with care. Do not allow it to fall or hit objects, as it may break into pieces.

To install:

8. Lubricate the camshaft lobes and journals with clean engine oil.

9. Place the camshaft(s) in position on the head. The exhaust cam has the distributor drive gear on it. Observe the markings on the bearing caps and place them according to their numbered positions. The arrow should point to the front of the engine.

10. Tighten the bearing cap bolts in the correct sequence and in three passes to a final tightness of 9 ft. lbs. (12 Nm).

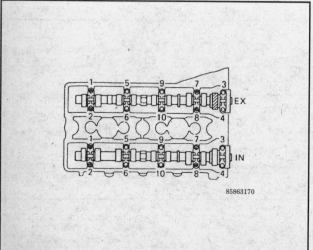

Fig. 161 Camshaft bearing cap removal sequence — 4A-GE engine

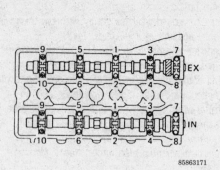

Fig. 162 Camshaft bearing cap installation sequence — 4A-GE engine

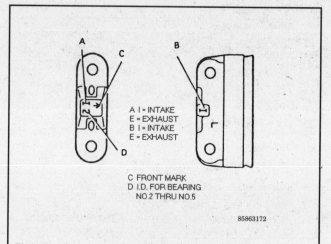

A I = INTAKE
E = EXHAUST
B I = INTAKE
E = EXHAUST

C FRONT MARK
D I.D. FOR BEARING
NO.2 THRU NO.5

Fig. 163 Examples of marking on camshaft bearing caps. Note that the bearing cap on the right is for position No. 1 only — 4A-GE engine

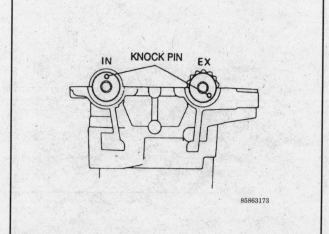

Fig. 164 Correct position of knock pins, the exhaust camshaft has the distributor drive gear — 4A-GE engine

11. Position the camshafts so that the guide pins (knock pins) are in the proper position. This step is critical to the correct valve timing of the engine.

12. Install the camshaft timing pulleys and tighten the bolts to 43 ft. lbs. (58 Nm).

13. Double check the positioning of the camshaft pulleys and the guide pin.

14. Install the crankshaft pulley. Tighten its bolt to 101 ft. lbs. (137 Nm) and double check its position to be on TDC.

15. Install the timing belt and tensioner. Adjust the belt according to procedures outlined.

16. Install the engine front timing covers.

17. Install the cylinder head cover.

1C-L Diesel

▶ **See Figure 165**

1. Perform the necessary steps of the cylinder head removal & installation procedure in order to remove the cylinder head cover, rocker arm assemblies and timing belt. If necessary, refer to the other procedures in this section for more details.

2. Remove the exhaust manifold.

3. Remove the camshaft oil seal retainer.

4. Loosen each bearing cap bolt a little at a time and in the proper sequence (starting at the ends and working inward). Make sure that the bearing caps are kept in the proper order.

5. Remove the camshaft and the half-circle plug at the rear of the head.

To install:

6. Coat the half-circle plug with adhesive and position it in the cylinder head.

7. Coat all bearing journals lightly with oil, then place the camshaft into position on the cylinder head.

8. Install the bearing caps in order. Tighten the cap bolts in two or three stages (starting at the center and working outward) until they reach a final torque of 13 ft. lbs. (18 Nm).

9. Check the thrust and oil clearances.

10. Apply adhesive to the oil seal retainer as shown, then install it onto the cylinder head.

11. Installation of the remaining components is in the reverse order of removal.

CHECKING

▶ **See Figures 166, 167, 168, 169 and 170**

1. Using a micrometer, check that the camshaft journal diameter is within specification (according to the figures listed in the camshaft specifications chart).

2. Check the bearing oil clearance:

a. On K-series and T-series engines, check the bearing bore with a cylinder micrometer. Subtract the journal diameter measurement taken in Step 1 from the bearing bore measurement. If the clearance is greater than specification, replace the bearing and/or camshaft.

b. On the 1C-L and all A-series engines, clean the bearing caps and camshaft journals. With the camshaft in position in the cylinder head, lay a strip of Plastigage® or an equivlanet gauging material; across each journal, then install the bearing caps and torque them down in the proper sequence.

➡ **Never turn the camshaft with the Plastigage® in place. Remove the bearing caps and compare the Plastigage® to the scale included in the package. If the clearance at the widest point of any strip is greater than specification, replacement of the camshaft or the cylinder head is required.**

3. Check the camshaft end-play:

a. On chain driven engines, install the thrust plate and camshaft sprocket to the camshaft. Tighten to 40-47 ft. lbs. (54-64 Nm). Using a feeler gauge, measure the clearance between the camshaft and the thrust plate. If the clearance is greater than specification, replace the thrust plate and/or sprocket.

b. On belt driven engines, attach a dial indicator to the cylinder head so that its tip is touching the end of the installed camshaft. Lever the camshaft back and forth. If the measurement is greater than specification, replace the camshaft, cylinder head or, if equipped, the thrust bearing.

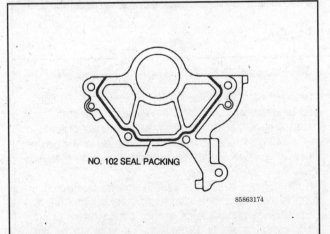

NO. 102 SEAL PACKING

85863174

Fig. 165 When installing the camshaft oil seal retainer, apply a coat of sealant to prevent leakage — 1C-L engine

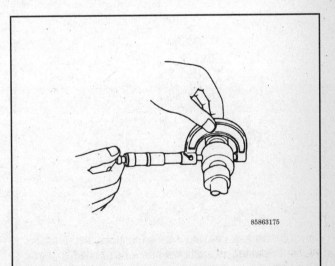

85863175

Fig. 166 Use a micrometer to measure the camshaft journal diameters

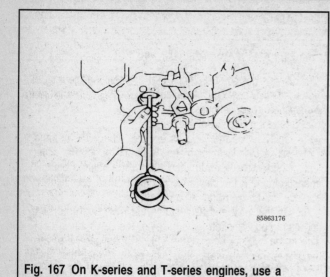

Fig. 167 On K-series and T-series engines, use a cylinder micrometer to check the bearing bore

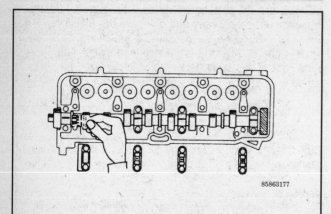

Fig. 168 On overhead camshaft engines such as the 1C-L diesel and all A-series engines, use the scale provided with the gauging material to determine bearing clearance

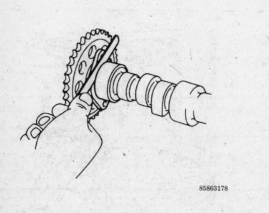

Fig. 169 On K-series and T-series engines, use a feeler gauge to determine shaft end-play when bolted to the sprocket

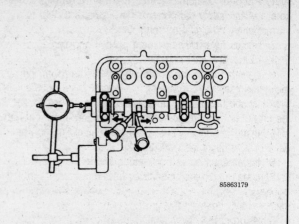

Fig. 170 On overhead camshaft engines, mount a dial gauge to read end-play when carefully prying the installed camshaft back and forth

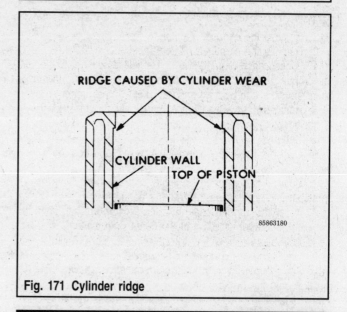

Fig. 171 Cylinder ridge

Pistons and Connecting Rods

REMOVAL

▶ **See Figures 171, 172, 173, 174, 175, 176 and 177**

Before removing the pistons, the top of the cylinder bore must be examined for a ridge. A ridge at the top of the bore is the result of normal cylinder wear; caused by the piston rings only traveling so far up the bore in the course of the piston stroke. If the ridge can be felt by hand, it must be removed before the pistons are removed.

A ridge reamer is necessary for this operation. Place the piston at the bottom of its stroke and cover it with a rag. Cut the ridge away with the ridge reamer, using extreme care to avoid cutting too deeply. Remove the rag, then remove the cuttings that remain on the piston with a magnet and a rag soaked in clean oil. Make sure the piston top and cylinder bore are absolutely clean before moving the piston.

1. Remove the engine from the vehicle.
2. Remove the cylinder head assembly.
3. Remove the oil pan.
4. If necessary, remove the oil pump assembly.
5. Matchmark the connecting rod cap to the connecting rod with a scribe; each cap must be reinstalled on its proper rod in the proper direction. Remove the connecting rod bearing cap and the rod bearing. Number the top of each piston with silver paint or a felt-tip pen for later assembly.
6. Cut lengths of ⅜ in. diameter rubber hose to use as rod bolt guides. Install the hose over the threads of the rod bolts, to prevent the bolt threads from damaging the crankshaft journals and cylinder walls when the piston is removed.
7. Squirt some clean engine oil onto the cylinder wall from above until the wall is coated. Carefully push the piston and rod assembly up and out of the cylinder by tapping on the bottom of the connecting rod with a wooden hammer handle.

8. Place the rod bearing and cap back on the connecting rod, then temporarily install the nuts. Using a number stamp or punch, stamp the cylinder number on the side of the connecting rod and cap; this will help keep the proper piston and rod assembly on the proper cylinder.

➡ **On all Toyota engines covered by this manual, the cylinders are numbered 1-4 from front to back.**

9. Remove the remaining pistons in a similar manner. When ready for reassembly, please note the following:
   a. Connecting rods/caps must be reinstalled in the same cylinder and are so marked. Make sure that the markings on the rod and cap are on the same side when reassembling.
   b. The piston pins are matched to the pistons and are not interchangeable.
   c. The arrow notch top of the piston must face forward (toward the timing chain). The oil hole in the connecting rod faces the same direction as the arrow on top of the piston.
   d. Rings are installed with the code markings upward, plain ring at the top, taper face second, and beveled oil

TCCS3916

Fig. 172 Removing the ride from the cylinder bore using a ridge cutter

USE A SHORT PIECE OF 3/8" HOSE AS A GUIDE

85863182

Fig. 174 Use lengths of rubber hose over the piston studs to protect the crankshaft journals and cylinder walls during piston removal and installation

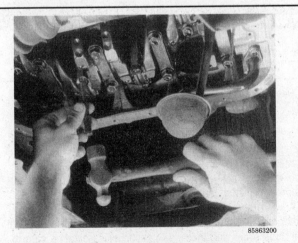

85863200

Fig. 173 If difficulty is encountered removing the bearing cap, tap upward gently on the piston stud (using a brass drift) in order to help free the cap

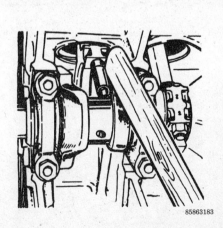

85863183

Fig. 175 Push the piston out from underneath the engine using a wooden (hammer) handle

control ring at the bottom. Offset each ring gap as illustrated later in this section.

PISTON RING AND WRIST PIN REMOVAL

▶ **See Figures 178, 179, 180, 181, 182, 183, 184 and 185**

Pistons are mounted onto the connecting rods by wrist pins. The wrist pins are retained either by circlips, or are pressed through the rod. Servicing press fitted wrist pins should be done by a machine shop. Circlip retained wrist pins are serviced by removing the circlip with a pair of circlip pliers and pushing out the pin.

A piston ring expander is necessary for removing piston rings without damaging them; any other method (screwdriver blades, pliers, etc.) usually results in the rings being bent, scratched or distorted, or the piston itself being damaged. When the rings are removed, clean the ring grooves using an appropriate ring groove cleaning tool, using care not to cut too

deeply. Thoroughly clean all carbon and varnish from the piston with solvent.

✴✴CAUTION

Do not use a wire brush or caustic solvent (acids, etc.) on pistons!

Inspect the pistons for scuffing, scoring, cracks, pitting, or excessive ring groove wear. If they are evident, the pistons must be replaced.

The piston should also be checked in relation to the cylinder diameter. Using a telescoping gauge and micrometer, or a dial gauge, measure the cylinder bore diameter perpendicular (90°) to the piston pin, 2½ in. below the cylinder block deck (surface where the block mates with the heads). Then, with the micrometer, measure the piston perpendicular to its wrist pin on the skirt. The difference between the two measurements is the piston clearance. If the clearance is within specifications or slightly below (after the cylinders have been bored or honed), finish honing is all that is necessary. If the clearance is exces-

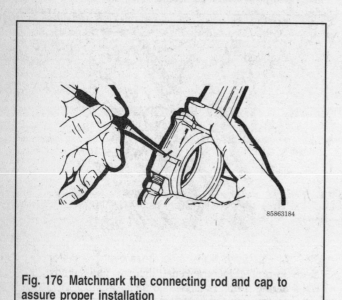

Fig. 176 Matchmark the connecting rod and cap to assure proper installation

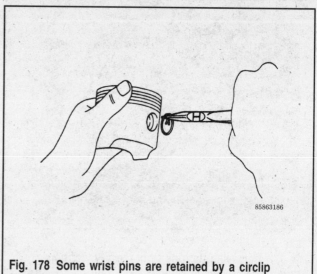

Fig. 178 Some wrist pins are retained by a circlip (snapring)

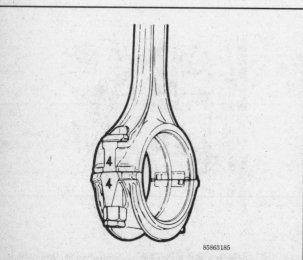

Fig. 177 A number stamp on the piston and cap will assure the assembly is installed in the proper bore

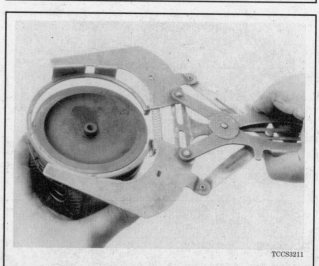

Fig. 179 Use a ring expander tool to remove or install the piston rings

Fig. 180 Clean the piston grooves using a ring groove cleaner

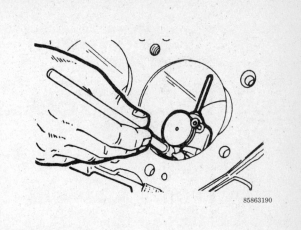

Fig. 182 The cylinder bore may be measured using a dial gauge

sive, try to obtain a slightly larger piston to bring clearance within specifications. If this is not possible, obtain the first oversize piston and hone (or if necessary, bore) the cylinder to size. Generally, if the cylinder bore is tapered 0.005 in. (0.127mm) or more, or is out-of-round 0.003 in. (0.076mm) or more, it is advisable to rebore for the smallest possible oversize piston and rings. After measuring, mark the pistons with a felt-tip pen for reference and assembly.

➡**Cylinder honing and/or boring should be performed by an authorized service technician with the proper equipment. In some cases, clean-up honing can be done with the cylinder block in the car, but most excessive honing and all cylinder boring must be done with the block stripped and removed from the car.**

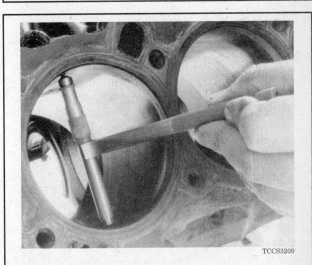

Fig. 183 A telescoping gauge may also be used to measure the cylinder bore diameter

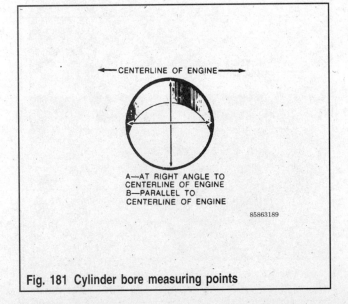

CENTERLINE OF ENGINE

A—AT RIGHT ANGLE TO CENTERLINE OF ENGINE
B—PARALLEL TO CENTERLINE OF ENGINE

Fig. 181 Cylinder bore measuring points

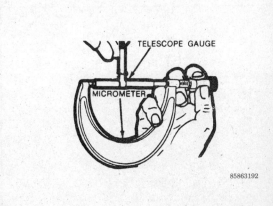

TELESCOPE GAUGE

MICROMETER

Fig. 184 Remove the telescoping gauge and measure it with a micrometer

Fig. 185 Measure the piston's outer diameter using a micrometer

PISTON RING END-GAP

▶ **See Figure 186**

Piston ring end-gap should be checked while the rings are removed from the pistons. Incorrect end-gap indicates that the wrong size rings are being used: ring breakage could occur.

Compress the piston rings to be used in a bore, one at a time, into that cylinder. Squirt clean oil into the bore, so that the rings and the top 2 in. of cylinder wall are coated. Using an inverted piston, carefully press the rings to a level approximately 1 in. below the deck of the block. Measure the ring end-gap with a feeler gauge, and compare to the specifications chart in this section. If necessary, carefully pull the ring out of the cylinder and file the ends squarely with a fine file to obtain the proper clearance.

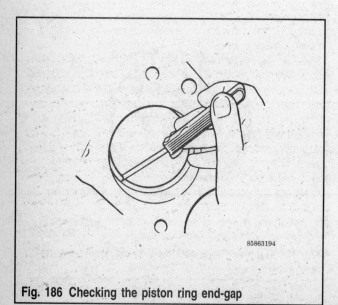

Fig. 186 Checking the piston ring end-gap

PISTON RING SIDE CLEARANCE CHECK AND INSTALLATION

▶ **See Figures 187, 188, 189, 190 and 191**

Check the pistons to see that the ring grooves and oil return holes have been properly cleaned. Slide a piston ring into its groove, and check the side clearance with a feeler gauge. Make sure that you insert the gauge between the ring and its lower land (lower edge of the groove), because any wear that occurs forms a step at the inner portion of the lower land. If the piston grooves have worn to the extent that relatively high steps exist on the lower land, the piston should be replaced, because these will interfere with the operation of the new rings and ring clearances will be excessive. Piston rings are not furnished in oversize widths to compensate for ring groove wear.

Install the rings on the piston, lowest ring first, using a piston ring expander. There is a high risk of breaking or distorting the rings, or scratching the piston, if the rings are installed by hand or other means.

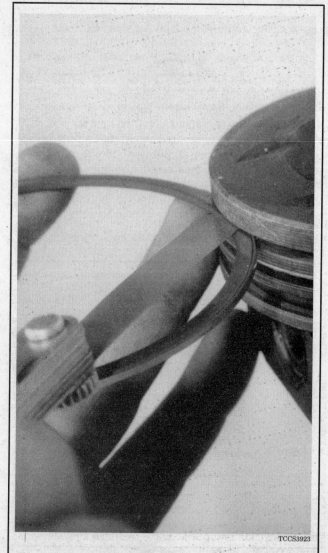

Fig. 187 Check the ring-to-piston ring groove clearance using a feeler gauge

Position the rings on the piston as illustrated; spacing of the various piston ring gaps is crucial to proper oil retention and even cylinder wear. When installing new rings, refer to the installation diagram furnished with the new parts.

➡ **For piston positioning information, please refer to Step 8 of the Piston and Connecting Rod Removal procedure in this section.**

CYLINDER BORE INSPECTION

As stated earlier under piston removal, the cylinder bore should be inspected whenever the piston is removed. Place a rag over the crankshaft journals. Wipe out each cylinder with a clean, solvent-soaked rag. Visually inspect the cylinder bores for roughness, scoring or scuffing; also check the bores by feel. Measure the cylinder bore diameter using an inside micrometer, a dial gauge, or a telescope gauge and micrometer.

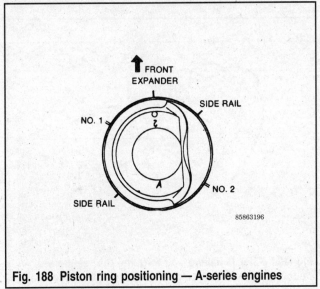

Fig. 188 Piston ring positioning — A-series engines

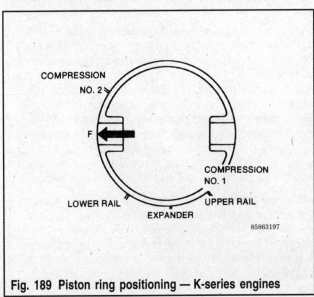

Fig. 189 Piston ring positioning — K-series engines

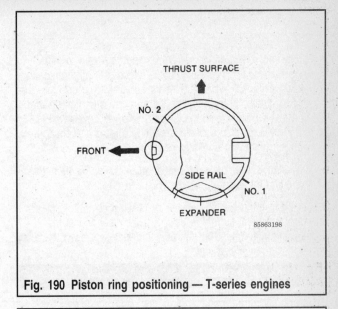

Fig. 190 Piston ring positioning — T-series engines

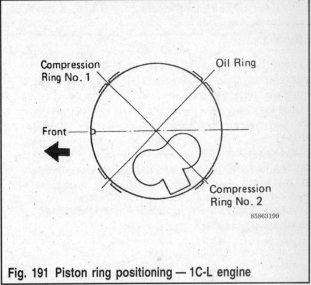

Fig. 191 Piston ring positioning — 1C-L engine

Measure the bore at points parallel and perpendicular to the engine centerline at the top (below the ridge) and bottom of the bore. Subtract the bottom measurements from the top to determine cylinder taper.

Measure the piston diameter with a micrometer; since this micrometer may not be part of your tool kit as it is necessarily large, you might want to have the pistons miked at a machine shop. Take the measurements at right angles to the wrist pin center line, about an inch down the piston skirt from the top. Compare this measurement to the bore diameter of each cylinder; the difference is the piston clearance. If the clearance is greater than that specified in the piston and ring chart (located earlier in this section), have the cylinders honed or rebored and replace the pistons with an oversize set. Piston clearance can also be checked by inverting a piston into an oiled cylinder, and sliding in a feeler gauge between the two. Keep in mind this method is least recommended as it is the least accurate and is the easiest way to score the cylinder.

CONNECTING ROD BEARINGS

Connecting rod bearings for the engines covered in this guide consist of two halves or shells which are interchangeable in the rod and cap. When the shells are placed in position, the ends extend slightly beyond the rod and cap surfaces so that when the rod bolts are torqued, the shells will be clamped tightly in place to insure positive seating and to prevent turning. A tang holds the shells in place.

➡**The ends of the bearing shells must never be filed flush with the mating surface of the rod and cap.**

If a rod bearing becomes noisy or is worn so that its clearance on the crank journal is sloppy, a new bearing of the correct undersize must be selected and installed since there is no provision for adjustment.

✳✳CAUTION

Under no circumstances should the rod end or cap be filed to adjust the bearing clearance, nor should shims of any kind be used!

Inspect the rod bearings while the rod assemblies are out of the engine. If the shells are scored or show flaking, they should be replaced. If they are in good shape check for proper clearance on the crank journal. Any scoring or ridges on the crank journal means the crankshaft must be replaced, or reground and fitted with undersized bearings. An undersize bearing is physically larger than a stock bearing, but contains a smaller inner diameter in order to compensate for the material which was removed from the crankshaft journal during grinding.

Checking Bearing Clearance and Replacing Bearings
▶ **See Figures 192, 193, 194 and 195**

Replacement bearings are available in standard size, and in undersizes for reground crankshafts. Connecting rod-to-crankshaft bearing clearance is checked using Plastigage® or an equivalent gauging material, at either the top or bottom of each crank journal. Plastigage typically has a range of 0.001-0.003 in. (0.025-0.076mm).

1. Remove the rod cap with the bearing shell. Completely clean the bearing shell and the crank journal, then blow any oil from the oil hole in the crankshaft; Plastigage® is soluble in oil.

2. Place a piece of Plastigage® lengthwise along the bottom center of the lower bearing shell, then install the cap with shell and torque the bolt or nuts to specification. DO NOT turn the crankshaft with Plastigage® in the bearing.

3. Remove the bearing cap with the shell. The flattened Plastigage® will be found sticking to either the bearing shell or crank journal. Do not remove it yet.

4. Use the scale printed on the Plastigage® envelope to measure the flattened material at its widest point. The number within the scale which most closely corresponds to the width of the Plastigage® indicates bearing clearance in thousandths of an inch.

5. Check the specifications charts located earlier in this section for the desired clearance. It is advisable in most cases

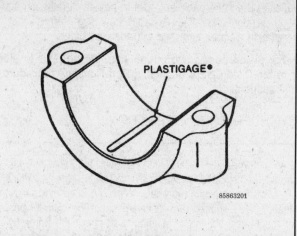

Fig. 192 Apply a strip of gauging material to the bearing shell or the crank journal

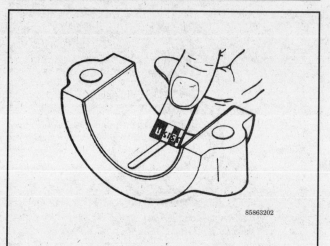

Fig. 193 After installing and torquing the retainers, remove the shell and compare the material to the scale provided with the package

to install a new bearing if clearance exceeds 0.003 in. (0.076mm); however, if the bearing is in good condition and is not being checked because of bearing noise, replacement is not necessary.

6. If you are installing new bearings, try a standard size, then each undersize in order until one is found that is within the specified limits (when checked for clearance with Plastigage®). Each undersize shell has its size stamped on it.

7. When the proper size shell is found, clean off the Plastigage®, oil the bearing thoroughly, reinstall the cap with its shell and torque the rod bolt nuts to the proper specifications.

➡**With the proper bearing selected and the nuts torqued, it should be possible to move the connecting rod back and forth freely on the crank journal as allowed by the specified connecting rod end clearance. If the rod cannot be moved, either the rod bearing is too far undersize, or a problem exists with the thrust bearing or the rod is misaligned.**

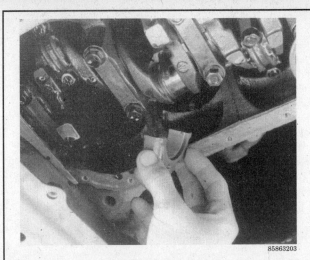

Fig. 194 Once a proper bearing size has been determined, install the bearings and cap

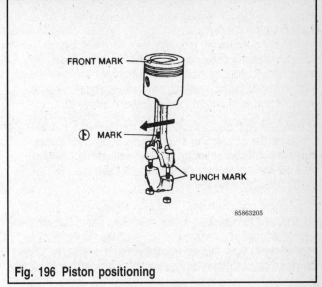

Fig. 196 Piston positioning

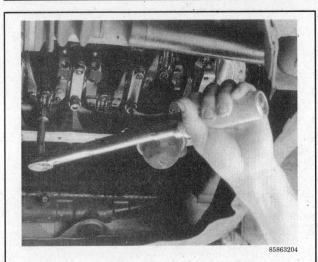

Fig. 195 Use a torque wrench to assure proper installation

Fig. 197 Installing the piston into the block using a ring compressor and a wooden tool handle

PISTON/CONNECTING ROD ASSEMBLY AND INSTALLATION

▶ See Figures 196, 197 and 198

Install the connecting rod to the piston, making sure piston installation notches and any marks on the rod are in proper relation to one another. Lubricate the wrist pin with clean engine oil, and install the pin into the rod and piston assembly, either by hand or by using a wrist pin press, as required. If equipped, install snaprings and rotate them in their grooves to make sure they are seated. To install the piston and connecting rod assembly:

1. Make sure that the connecting rod big-end bearings (including end cap) are of the correct size and properly installed.

2. Fit rubber hoses over the connecting rod bolts to protect the crankshaft journals, as done during the piston removal procedure. Coat the rod bearings with clean oil.

3. Using the proper ring compressor, insert the piston assembly into the cylinder so that the word TOP or arrow faces

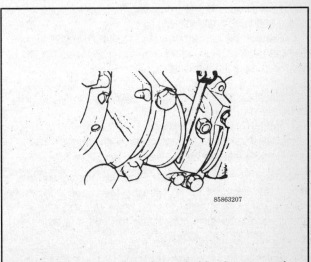

Fig. 198 Check the connecting rod side clearance using a feeler gauge

the front of the engine (this assumes that the dimples or other markings on the connecting rods are in the correct relationship).

4. From beneath the engine, coat each crank journal with clean oil. Pull the connecting rod, with the bearing shell in place, into position against the crank journal.

5. Remove the rubber hoses. Install the bearing cap and cap nuts and torque to the proper specifications.

➡**When more than one rod and piston assembly is being installed, the connecting rod cap attaching nuts should only be tightened enough to keep each rod in position until all have been installed. This will ease the installation of the remaining piston assemblies.**

6. Check the clearance between the sides of the connecting rods and the crankshaft using a feeler gauge. Spread the rods slightly using a screwdriver to insert the gauge. If clearance is below the minimum tolerance, the rod may be machined to provide adequate clearance. If clearance is excessive, substitute an unworn rod, and recheck. If clearance is still outside specifications, the crankshaft must be welded and reground, or replaced.

7. Install the oil pump, if removed, and the oil pan.

Crankshaft and Main Bearings

CRANKSHAFT REMOVAL

1. Drain the engine oil and remove the engine from the car. Mount the engine on a work stand in a suitable working area. Invert the engine, so the oil pan is facing up.
2. Remove the engine front (timing) cover.
3. Remove the timing chain/belt and gears/pulleys.
4. Remove the oil pan.
5. Remove the oil pump.
6. Stamp the cylinder number on the machined surfaces of the bolt bosses of the connecting rods and caps for identification when reinstalling. If the pistons are to be removed eventually from the connecting rod, mark the cylinder number on the pistons with silver paint or felt-tip pen for proper cylinder identification and cap-to-rod location.
7. Remove the connecting rod caps. Install lengths of rubber hose on each of the connecting rod bolts, to protect the crank journals when the crank is removed.
8. Mark the main bearing caps with a punch (preferably a number punch) so that they can be reinstalled in their original positions.
9. Remove all main bearing caps.
10. Note the position of the keyway in the crankshaft so it can be installed in the same position.

➡**To keep the connecting rods from banging against the side of the cylinders while removing the crankshaft, screw four oil pan bolts loosely into the block, then stretch a rubber band between a connecting rod bolt and an oil pan bolt for each of the pistons.**

11. Carefully lift the crankshaft out of the block. The rods will pivot to the center of the engine when the crank is removed.

MAIN BEARING INSPECTION

Like connecting rod big-end bearings, the crankshaft main bearings are shell-type inserts that do not utilize shims and cannot be adjusted. The bearings are available in various standard and oversizes; if main bearing clearance is found to be too sloppy, a new bearing (both upper and lower halves) is required.

Generally, the lower half of the bearing shell (except No. 1 bearing) shows greater wear and fatigue. If the lower half only shows the effects of normal wear (no heavy scoring or discoloration), it can usually be assumed that the upper half is also in good shape. Conversely, if the lower half is heavily worn or damaged, both halves should be replaced. Never replace one bearing half without replacing the other.

CHECKING CLEARANCE

▶ **See Figures 199 and 200**

Main bearing clearance can be checked both with the engine in the car and with the engine out of the car. If the engine block is still in the car, the crankshaft should be supported both front and rear (by the damper in front and flywheel at the rear in order to remove clearance from the upper bearing). Total clearance can then be measured between the lower bearing and journal. If the block has been removed from the car, and is inverted, the crank will rest on the upper bearings (taking up clearance) and the total clearance can be measured between the lower bearing and journal. Clearance is checked in the same manner as the connecting rod bearings, with Plastigage® or an equivalent gauging material.

➡**Crankshaft bearing caps and bearing shells should NEVER be filed flush with the cap-to-block mating surface to adjust for wear in the old bearings. Always install new bearings.**

1. If the crankshaft has been removed, install it (block removed from car). If the block is still in the car, remove the oil pan and oil pump, then be sure the crankshaft is supported to remove upper clearance. Starting with the rear bearing cap and working on one cap at a time, moving towards the front, remove the cap and wipe all oil from the crank journal and bearing.

2. Place a strip of Plastigage® the full width of the bearing, (parallel to the crankshaft), on the journal.

✳✳CAUTION

Do not rotate the crankshaft while the gauging material is between the bearing and the journal!

3. Install the bearing cap and evenly torque the cap bolts to specification.
4. Remove the bearing cap. The flattened Plastigage® will stick to either the bearing or the crankshaft journal.

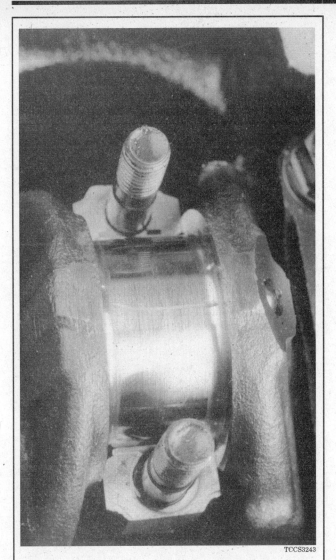

Fig. 199 Apply a strip of gauging material to the bearing or journal, then install and torque the cap

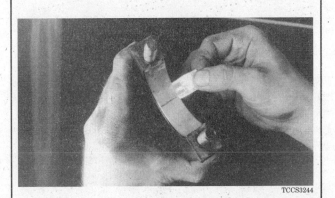

Fig. 200 As with connecting rod bearings, remove the cap and compare the gauging material to the provided scale in order to determine clearance

Fig. 201 When replacing a main bearing with the engine installed, remove the oil pan, then remove the oil pump or pickup for access

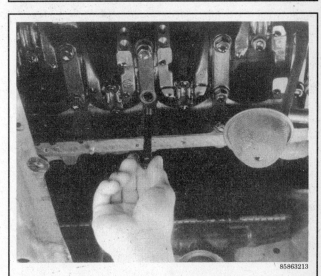

Fig. 202 Loosen and remove the bearing cap bolts

5. Use the graduated scale on the Plastigage® envelope to measure the material at its widest point.

➡If the flattened Plastigage® tapers toward the middle or ends, there is a difference in clearance indicating the bearing or journal has a taper, low spot, or other irregularity. If this is indicated, measure the crank journal with a micrometer.

6. If bearing clearance is within specifications and no scoring or damage is visible, the bearing insert is in good shape. Replace the insert if the clearance is not within specifications. Always replace both upper and lower inserts as a unit.

7. Standard, 0.001 in. (0.025mm) or 0.002 in. (0.051mm) undersize bearings should produce the proper clearance. If these sizes still produce too sloppy a fit, the crankshaft must be reground for use with the next undersize bearing. Recheck all clearances after installing new bearings.

8. Replace the rest of the bearings in the same manner. After all bearings have been checked, rotate the crankshaft to make sure there is no excessive drag.

MAIN BEARING REPLACEMENT

Engine Out of Car

1. Remove and inspect the crankshaft.

2. Remove the main bearings from the bearing saddles in the cylinder block and main bearing caps.

3. Coat the bearing surfaces of the new, correct size main bearings with clean engine oil and install them in the bearing saddles in the block and in the main bearing caps.

4. Install the crankshaft. For details, please refer to crankshaft Installation.

Engine in Car

▶ **See Figures 201, 202, 203, 204 and 205**

1. With the oil pan, oil pump or pickup and spark plugs removed, remove the cap from the main bearing needing replacement and remove the bearing from the cap.

2. Make a bearing roll-out pin, (using a bent cotter pin) as shown in the illustration. Insert the end of the pin in the oil hole in the crankshaft journal.

3. Rotate the crankshaft clockwise as viewed from the front of the engine. This will roll the upper bearing out of the block.

4. Lube the new upper bearing with clean engine oil and insert the plain (un-notched) end between the crankshaft and the indented or notched side of the block. Roll the bearing into place, making sure that the oil holes are aligned. Remove the roll pin from the oil pin.

5. Lube the new lower bearing and install the main bearing cap. Making sure it is positioned in the proper direction with the matchmarks in alignment.

6. Torque the main bearing cap bolts to the proper specification.

➡**Please refer to crankshaft installation for thrust bearing alignment.**

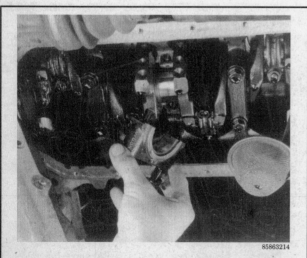

Fig. 203 Remove the cap and lower bearing from the engine

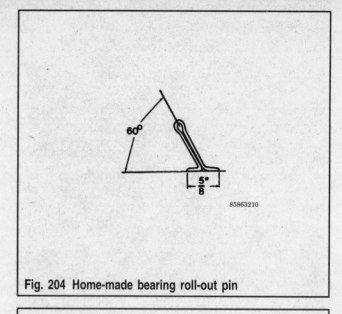

Fig. 204 Home-made bearing roll-out pin

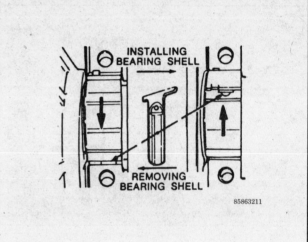

Fig. 205 Remove or install the upper bearing using the roll-out pin

CRANKSHAFT END-PLAY AND INSTALLATION

▶ **See Figures 206, 207, 208, 209, 210 and 211**

When main bearing clearance has been checked, bearings examined and/or replaced, the crankshaft can be installed. Thoroughly clean the upper and lower bearing surfaces, and lube them with clean engine oil. Install the crankshaft and main bearing caps.

Dip all main bearing cap bolts in clean oil, and torque all main bearing caps, excluding the thrust bearing cap, to specifications (please refer to the charts located in this section to determine specifications and which bearing is the thrust bearing). Finger-tighten the thrust bearing bolts. To align the thrust bearing, pry the crankshaft the extent of its axial travel several times, holding the last movement toward the front of the engine. Add thrust washers, if required for proper alignment. Torque the thrust bearing cap to specifications.

To check crankshaft end-play, pry the crankshaft to the extreme rear of its axial travel, then to the extreme front of its

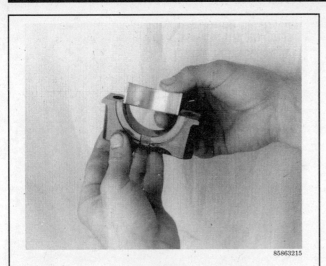

Fig. 206 Once the bearings have been selected, position them in the block and in the bearing caps

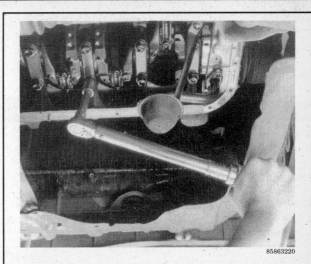

Fig. 209 Once the thrust bearing is properly aligned, tighten the thrust bearing cap retainers to specification

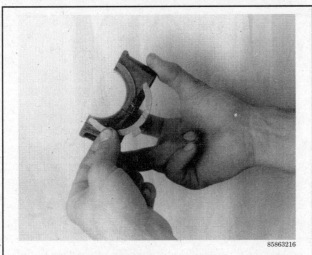

Fig. 207 The thrust bearing cap contains a cutout for the thrust washer

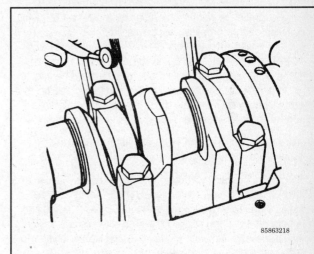

Fig. 210 Crankshaft end-play can be checked using a feeler gauge at the thrust bearing

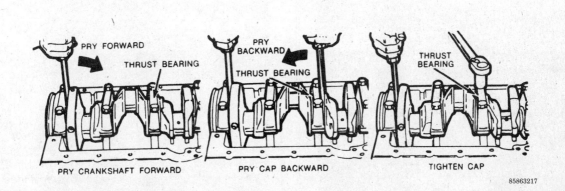

Fig. 208 Use a prybar to carefully align the thrust bearing

travel. Using a feeler gauge or a dial indicator, measure the end-play at the front of the rear main bearing. End-play may also be measured at the thrust bearing.

Install a new rear main bearing oil seal in the cylinder block and main bearing cap. Continue to reassemble the engine.

Cylinder Block

▶ **See Figures 212, 213 and 214**

Most inspection and service work on the cylinder block should be handled by a machinist or professional engine re-building shop. Included in this work are bearing alignment checks, line boring, deck resurfacing, hot-tanking and cylinder honing or boring. A block that has been checked and properly serviced will last much longer than one which has not had the proper attention when the opportunity was there for it.

Cylinder de-glazing (honing) can, however, be performed by the owner/mechanic who is careful and takes his or her time. The cylinder bores become glazed during normal operation as the rings continually ride up and down against them. This shiny glaze must be removed in order for a new set of piston rings to be able to properly seat themselves.

Cylinder hones are available at most auto tool stores and parts jobbers. With the piston and rod assemblies removed from the block, cover the crankshaft completely with a rag or cover to keep grit from the hone and cylinder material off of it. Chuck a hone into a variable-speed power drill (preferable here to a constant speed drill), and insert it into the cylinder.

➡**Make sure the drill and hone are kept square to the cylinder bore throughout the entire honing operation.**

Start the hone and move it up and down in the cylinder at a rate which will produce approximately a 60° crosshatch pattern. DO NOT extend the hone below the cylinder bore! After developing the pattern, remove the hone and recheck piston fit. Wash the cylinders with a detergent and water solution to remove the hone and cylinder grit. Wipe the bores out several times with a clean rag soaked in clean engine oil. Remove the cover from the crankshaft, and check closely to see that no grit has found its way onto the crankshaft.

Fig. 214 A properly cross-hatched cylinder bore

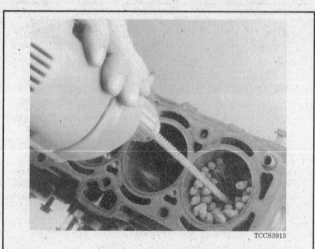
Fig. 212 Using a ball type cylinder hone is an easy way to hone the cylinder bore, BUT make sure to keep the holes square to the bore

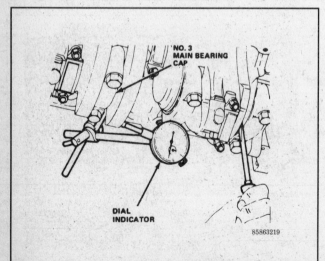
Fig. 211 End-play may also be checked using a dial indicator

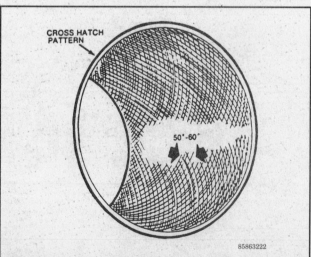
Fig. 213 Cylinders should be honed to produce approximately a 60° crosshatch pattern

Oil Pan

REMOVAL & INSTALLATION

▶ See Figures 215, 216, 217, 218, 219, 220, 221, 222, 223 and 224

1970-82 Vehicles

1. Open the engine compartment hood.

➡Leave it open for the duration of this procedure.

2. Raise the front end of the car and support it safely using jackstands.

❋❋CAUTION

Be sure that the car is securely supported. Remember, you will be working underneath it.

3. Remove the splash shield from underneath the engine.
4. Drain the engine oil.
5. Place a jack under the transmission to support it.
6. Unfasten the bolts which secure the engine rear supporting crossmember to the chassis.
7. Raise the jack under the transmission, slightly.
8. Unbolt the oil pan and work it out from underneath the engine.

➡If the oil pan does not come out easily, it may be necessary to unfasten the rear engine mounts from the crossmember.

9. Installation is performed in the reverse order of removal. On models equipped with the 2T-C engine, apply liquid sealer to the four corners of the oil pan. Tighten the oil pan securing bolts to 1.8-2.5 ft. lbs. (2.4-3.4 Nm) for the 3K-C engine or to 3.6-5.8 ft. lbs. (5-8 Nm). for 2T-C and 3T-C engines.

1983-87 Vehicles

1. Disconnect the negative battery cable.

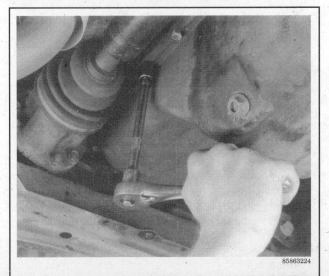

Fig. 215 Loosen and remove the oil pan retaining bolts

Fig. 216 On some vehicles, an access cover may be provided to reach certain bolts

Fig. 217 If equipped, remove the access cover and remove that pan bolt

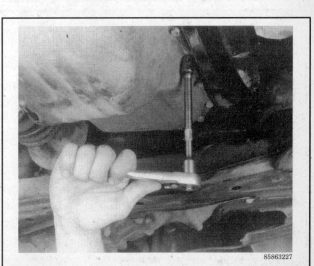

Fig. 218 A long extension may be necessary to reach certain bolts

Fig. 219 On some vehicles, the flywheel cover must also be removed for access or clearance

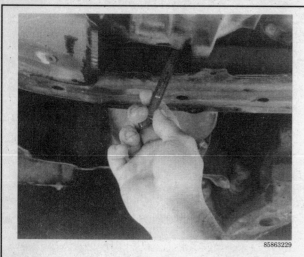

Fig. 220 An open-end or box wrench may be necessary to remove some of the flywheel cover retainers

Fig. 221 With the retainers removed, the flywheel cover may lowered from the vehicle

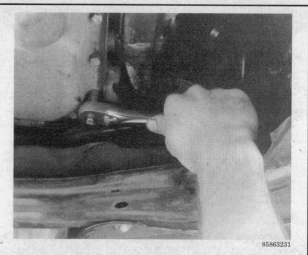

Fig. 222 Loosen and remove the remaining oil pan bolts

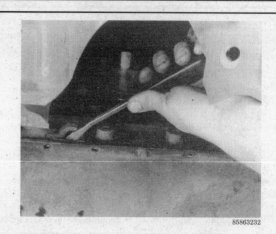

Fig. 223 If the pan is stuck, a rubber mallet is preferable to break the gasket seal, but a small prytool may be used to GENTLY pry the pan away from the block

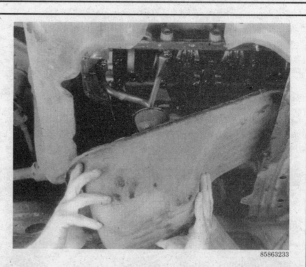

Fig. 224 Once the gasket seal is broken, lower the pan from the vehicle

2. Jack up the vehicle and support it safely using jackstands.

3. If equipped, remove the engine splash shield(s).

4. Drain the engine oil.

5. If necessary, remove the sway bar and any other necessary steering linkage parts.

6. If necessary, disconnect the exhaust pipe from the manifold.

7. On some vehicles it may be necessary to jack up the engine enough to take the weight off it, then remove the engine mounts and engine shock absorber. If so, continue to jack up the until sufficient clearance exists to remove the pan, but watch for engine contact with the cowl.

8. Remove the pan bolts and remove the pan.

➡On most FWD and some RWD vehicles it will be necessary to remove the flywheel cover in order to more easily access the rear oil pan retainers or to provide clearance for oil pan removal.

9. Installation is the reverse of removal. Always use a new pan gasket when reinstalling the pan.

Rear Main Oil Seal

REPLACEMENT

▶ See Figures 225, 226, 227, 228, 229 and 230

1. Remove the transmission from the vehicle. For details, please refer to Section 7 of this manual.

2. If equipped, remove the clutch assembly.

3. Matchmark the flywheel to the crankshaft, then unbolt and remove the flywheel.

4. If equipped, remove the dust shield from the rear of the engine.

5. Loosen and remove the oil seal retaining plate retainers, then remove the plate complete with the oil seal.

6. Use a small prytool to remove the old seal from the retaining plate. Be VERY careful not to score or damage the plate's sealing surfaces.

7. Carefully install the new seal, using a suitable seal installer, socket, or a block of wood to drive it into place. If anything other than a seal installer is used, be sure the surface touching the seal is smooth and will not tear the seal lips.

➡Do not damage the seal; a leak will result.

8. Lubricate the lips of the seal with multipurpose grease, then install the remaining components in the reverse order from removal.

Oil Pump

REMOVAL & INSTALLATION

Except Overhead Camshaft Engines

1. Remove the oil pan from the engine. For details, please refer to the procedures found earlier in this section.

Fig. 225 Matchmark the flywheel to the crankshaft before removal

Fig. 226 Loosen and remove the flywheel retainers

Fig. 227 Remove the flywheel from the engine

Fig. 228 If equipped, loosen and remove the dust seal retainers

Fig. 229 Then remove the dust seal for access to the rear main seal retainer

Fig. 230 Loosen the bolts and remove the rear main seal retainers from the engine

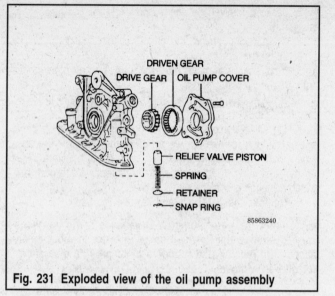

Fig. 231 Exploded view of the oil pump assembly

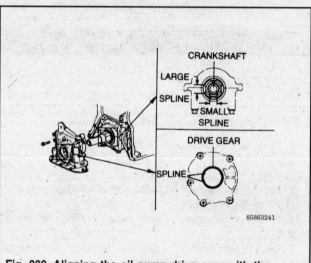

Fig. 232 Aligning the oil pump drive gear with the crankshaft gear

2. Unbolt the oil pump retainers, then remove the pump assembly.

3. Installation is the reverse of removal.

Overhead Camshaft Engines

◆ See Figures 231, 232, 233, 234, 235, 236, 237, 238, 239, 240, 241, 242, 243, 244, 245 and 246

4A-C (RWD) AND 4A-GE SERIES

1. Disconnect the negative battery cable.

2. Remove the fan shroud, then raise the front of the vehicle and support it safely using jackstands.

3. Drain the engine oil from the crankcase.

4. Remove the oil pan and the oil strainer.

5. Remove the crankshaft pulley, then remove timing belt. For details, please refer to the timing belt procedure located earlier in this section.

6. Remove the oil level gauge and guide. The guide tube is normally equipped with a small O-ring seal, check to make sure the seal is not damaged.

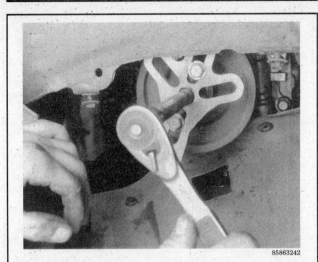

85863242

Fig. 233 Remove the crankshaft pulley using a suitable puller

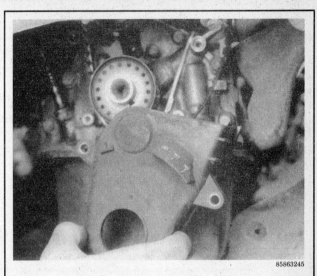

85863245

Fig. 236 Removing the timing scale lower cover

85863243

Fig. 234 View of the crankshaft pulley

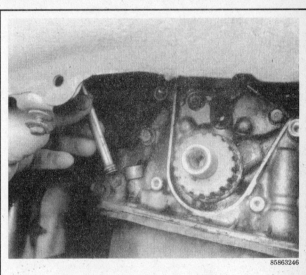

85863246

Fig. 237 Removing the oil dipstick guide

85863244

Fig. 235 Removing the timing scale lower cover mounting bolts

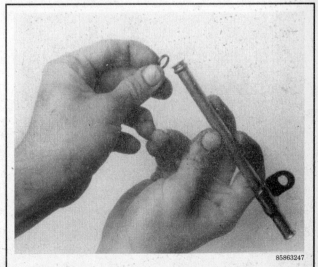

85863247

Fig. 238 Replace this O-ring on the oil dipstick guide

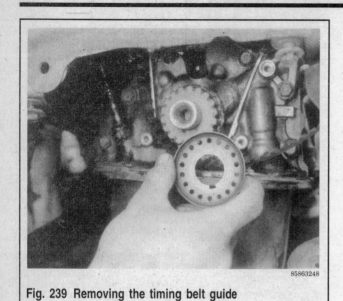

Fig. 239 Removing the timing belt guide

Fig. 242 Removing the oil pump assembly mounting gasket

Fig. 240 Removing the crankshaft timing pulley

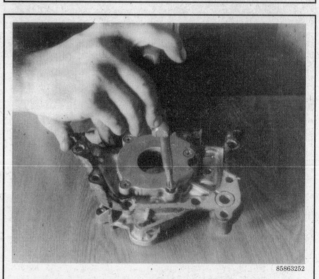

Fig. 243 Removing the oil pump assembly cover

Fig. 241 Removing the oil pump body mounting bolts

Fig. 244 With the cover removed the pump gears may be inspected or replaced

Fig. 245 View of the oil pump drive and driven gears

Fig. 246 Disassembling the oil pump assembly

7. Remove the mounting bolts, then use a rubber mallet to carefully tap the oil pump body from the cylinder block.

8. If necessary, disassemble the pump for inspection and/or service.

To install:

9. If the pump was disassembled, install the drive and driven gears, then install the pump cover.

10. Install the oil pump to the block, using a new gasket. Make sure the pump drive gear is properly aligned with the crankshaft gear.

11. Secure the pump using the mounting bolts.

12. Installation of the remaining components is in the reverse order of removal.

4A-LC (FWD) AND 1C-L DIESEL

1. Disconnect the negative battery cable.

2. Raise the front of the vehicle and support it safely using jackstands.

3. If equipped, remove the engine splash shield(s).

4. Drain the engine oil from the crankcase.

5. Remove the right tire and wheel assembly, then unbolt part of the wheel well for access.

➡At this point you will have to make a determination if this procedure will be possible with the engine in position. On most models it will be possible, just difficult. Check for clearance to remove the crankshaft damper, timing covers, timing belt and gears.

6. If it is determined that the engine must be raised or lowered.

   a. Matchmark and remove the hood.

   b. Disconnect the center engine mount.

   c. Attach an engine hoist to the two engine lifting brackets and suspend the engine. DO NOT lift the engine so far as to damage the halfshafts, wiring or other components.

7. Remove the accessory drive belt(s).

8. If necessary, remove the water pump pulley and/or the A/C idler pulley.

9. Loosen and remove the retainer, then remove the crankshaft damper using a suitable puller.

10. Remove the lower timing cover.

11. Matchmark and remove the timing belt, then remove the crankshaft timing pulley.

12. Remove the oil pan and oil strainer.

13. Remove the oil level gauge and guide. The guide tube is normally equipped with a small O-ring seal, check to make sure the seal is not damaged.

14. Remove the mounting bolts, then use a rubber mallet to carefully tap the oil pump body from the cylinder block.

15. If necessary, disassemble the pump for inspection and/or service.

To install:

16. If the pump was disassembled, install the drive and driven gears, then install the pump cover.

17. Install the oil pump to the block, using a new gasket. Make sure the pump drive gear is properly positioned over the crankshaft keyway.

18. Secure the pump using the mounting bolts.

19. Installation of the remaining components is in the reverse order of removal.

Radiator

REMOVAL & INSTALLATION

▶ See Figures 247, 248, 249, 250, 251, 252, 253 and 254

1. Drain the cooling system.

✳✳CAUTION

When draining coolant, keep in mind that cats and dogs are attracted by ethylene glycol antifreeze, and are quite likely to drink any that is left in an uncovered container or in puddles on the ground. This will prove fatal in sufficient quantity. Always drain the coolant into a sealable container. Coolant should be reused unless it is contaminated or several years old.

2. Unfasten the clamps, then remove the radiator upper and lower hoses. If equipped with an automatic transmission, remove the oil cooler lines.

3. If necessary, detach the hood lock cable and remove the hood lock from the radiator upper support.

➡**It may be necessary to remove the grille in order to gain access to the hood lock/radiator support assembly.**

4. Remove the fan shroud and electric cooling fan, if so equipped.

5. On models equipped with a coolant recovery system, disconnect the hose and remove the thermal expansion tank from its bracket.

6. Unbolt and remove the radiator upper support or upper radiator mounting clamps, as necessary.

7. Unfasten the bolts and remove the radiator.

❋❋CAUTION

Use care not to damage the radiator fins on the cooling fan!

8. Installation is performed in the reverse order of removal. Remember to check the transmission fluid level on cars with automatic transmissions.

9. Fill the radiator to the specified level.

10. Certain models are equipped with an electric, rather than a belt-driven, cooling fan. Using a radiator-mounted thermoswitch, the fan operates when the coolant temperatures reach 203°F and stops when it lowers to 190°F. It is attached to the radiator by the four radiator retaining bolts. Radiator removal is the same for this engine as all others, except for disconnecting the wiring harness and thermoswitch connector.

Electric Cooling Fan

REMOVAL & INSTALLATION

1. Drain the cooling system.
2. Remove the upper radiator hose.

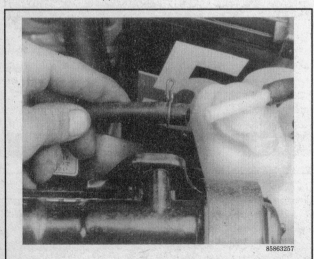
Fig. 247 Removing the overflow or coolant recovery bottle hose

Fig. 248 Removing the radiator cooling fan/shroud mounting bolts

Fig. 249 Removing the overflow or coolant recovery bottle

Fig. 250 Removing the battery hold-down bracket

Fig. 251 Removing the cooling fan and shroud assembly

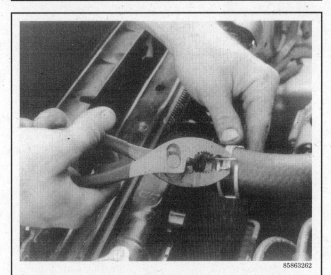

Fig. 252 Removing the upper radiator hose clamp

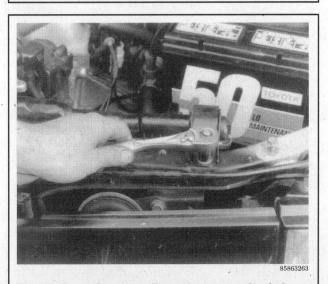

Fig. 253 Removing the radiator upper mounting bolt

Fig. 254 Removing the radiator assembly

3. Remove the coolant recovery bottle and battery hold-down clamp.

4. Disengage the electrical connector. Remove the cooling fan and shroud as an assembly.

5. Installation is the reverse order of removal. Check all fluid levels.

Water Pump

REMOVAL & INSTALLATION

▶ See Figures 255, 256 and 257

Gasoline Engines

REAR WHEEL DRIVE

➡On early models this service procedure should be modified by omitting the necessary steps.

1. Drain the cooling system.

✳✳CAUTION

When draining coolant, keep in mind that cats and dogs are attracted by ethylene glycol antifreeze, and are quite likely to drink any that is left in an uncovered container or in puddles on the ground. This will prove fatal in sufficient quantity. Always drain the coolant into a sealable container. Coolant should be reused unless it is contaminated or several years old.

2. Unfasten the fan shroud securing bolts and remove the shroud, if so equipped.

3. Loosen the alternator adjusting link bolt and remove the drive belt.

4. Remove the air and/or power steering pump drive belt, if so equipped.

5. Remove the cooling fan assembly.

❊❊CAUTION

If the fan is equipped with a fluid coupling, do not tip the fan assembly on its side, as the fluid will run out!

6. Remove the water outlet housing and by-pass pipe and hose.

7. Remove the water inlet housing and thermostat.

8. Remove the heater outlet pipe oil dipstick and oil dipstick guide.

9. Remove the lower timing belt cover.

10. Unfasten the water pump retaining bolts and remove the water pump.

11. Installation is performed in the reverse order of removal. Always use a new gasket between the pump body and its mounting. Torque the water pump mounting bolts evenly to 11 ft. lbs. (15 Nm). Remember to check for leaks after installation is completed.

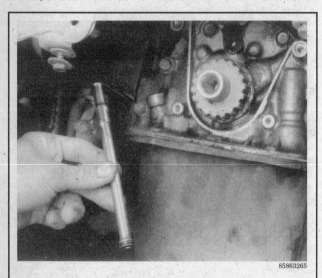

Fig. 256 Removing the oil dipstick guide

Fig. 257 Water pump assembly — front wheel drive models

FRONT WHEEL DRIVE

1. Drain the radiator.
2. Remove all drive belts.
3. Remove the water pump pulley.
4. Remove the water inlet pipe.
5. Remove the oil level gauge guide and gauge.
6. Remove the timing belt cover(s).
7. Remove the water pump. Be careful not to get coolant on the timing belt.
8. Installation is in the reverse order of removal. Place the water pump O-ring on the block and install pump. Torque the water pump mounting bolts evenly to 11 ft. lbs. (15 Nm).

Diesel Engines

1. Drain the radiator.
2. Remove the injection pump pulley as detailed in Section 5.
3. Remove the water pump.
4. Installation is in the reverse order of removal.

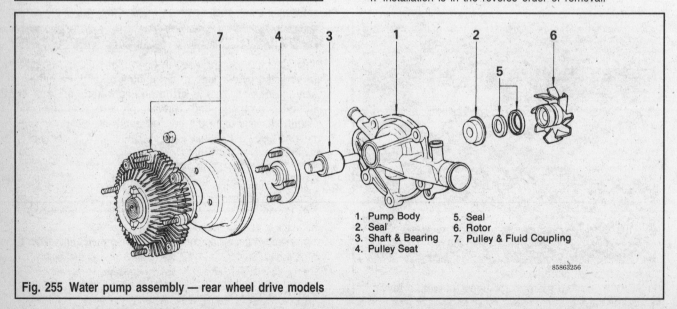

1. Pump Body
2. Seal
3. Shaft & Bearing
4. Pulley Seat
5. Seal
6. Rotor
7. Pulley & Fluid Coupling

Fig. 255 Water pump assembly — rear wheel drive models

Thermostat

REMOVAL & INSTALLATION

▶ See Figures 258, 259 and 260

1. Drain the cooling system.
2. Unfasten the clamp and remove the upper radiator hose from the water outlet elbow.
3. Unbolt and remove the water outlet (thermostat housing).
4. Withdraw the thermostat.
5. Installation is performed in the reverse order of the removal procedure. Use a new gasket on the water outlet.

✳✳CAUTION

Be sure that the thermostat is installed with the spring pointing down!

Fig. 259 Removing the thermostat

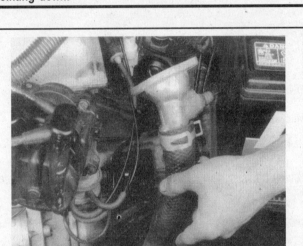

Fig. 258 Removing the water hose and thermostat housing

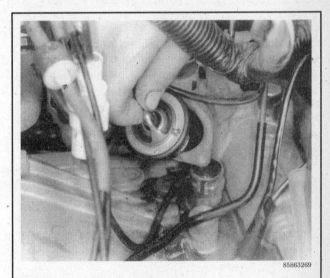

Fig. 260 Installing the thermostat

EXHAUST SYSTEM

Safety Precautions

For a number of reasons, exhaust system work can be the most dangerous type of work you can do on your car. Always observe the following precautions:

• Support the car extra securely. Not only will you often be working directly under it, but you'll frequently be using a lot of force, say, heavy hammer blows, to dislodge rusted parts. This can cause a car that's improperly supported to shift and possibly fall.

• Wear goggles. Exhaust system parts are always rusty. Metal chips can be dislodged, even when you're only turning rusted bolts. Attempting to pry pipes apart with a chisel makes the chips fly even more frequently.

• If you're using a cutting torch, keep it a GREAT distance from either the fuel tank or lines. Stop what you're doing and feel the temperature of the fuel bearing pipes or lines on the tank frequently. Even slight heat can expand and/or vaporize fuel, resulting in accumulated vapor, or even a liquid leak, near your torch.

• Watch where your hammer blows fall and make sure you hit squarely. You could easily tap a brake or fuel line when you hit an exhaust system part with a glancing blow. Inspect all lines and hoses in the area where you've been working.

✳✳CAUTION

Be very careful when working on or near the catalytic converter. External temperatures can reach 1,500°F (816°C) and more, causing severe burns. Removal or installation should be performed only on a cold exhaust system.

Special Tools

A number of special exhaust system tools can be rented from auto supply houses or local stores that rent special equipment. A common one is a tail pipe expander, designed to enable you to join pipes of identical diameter.

It may also be quite helpful to use solvents designed to loosen rusted bolts or flanges. Soaking rusted parts the night before you do the job can speed the work of freeing rusted parts considerably. Remember that these solvents are often flammable. Apply only to parts after they are cool.

The exhaust system of most engines consists of four pieces. At the front of the car, the first section of pipe connects the exhaust manifold to the catalytic converter. The catalytic converter is a sealed, non-serviceable unit which can be easily unbolted from the system and replaced if necessary.

An intermediate or center pipe containing a built-in resonator (pre-muffler) runs from the catalytic converter to the muffler at the rear of the car.

The exhaust system is attached to the body by several welded hooks and flexible rubber hangers; these hangers absorb exhaust vibrations and isolate the system from the body of the car. A series of metal heat shields runs along the exhaust piping, protecting the underbody from excess heat.

When inspecting or replacing exhaust system parts, make sure there is adequate clearance from all points on the body to avoid possible overheating of the floorpan. Check the complete system for broken, damaged, missing or poorly positioned parts. Rattles and vibrations in the exhaust system are usually caused by misalignment of parts. When aligning the system, leave all the nuts and bolts loose until everything is in its proper place, then tighten the hardware working from the front to the rear. Remember that what appears to be proper clearance during repair may change as the car moves down the road. The motion of the engine, body and suspension must be considered when replacing parts.

REMOVAL & INSTALLATION

▶ **See Figures 261 and 262**

❋❋CAUTION

DO NOT perform exhaust repairs with the engine or exhaust hot. Allow the system to cool completely before attempting any work. Also, exhaust systems are noted for sharp edges, flaking metal and rusted bolts. Gloves and eye protection are required.

➡**ALWAYS use a new gasket at each pipe joint whenever the joint is disassembled. Use new nuts, bolts and clamps to hold the joint properly. These items will serve to prevent future leaks as the system ages.**

Front Pipe

1. Raise and safely support the vehicle on jackstands.
2. Disconnect the oxygen sensor, if so equipped.
3. Remove the bolts holding the pipe to the exhaust manifold.

4. Remove the bolts holding the pipe to the catalytic converter.
5. Remove the bolts from the crossmember bracket and remove the pipe from under the car.
   To install:
6. Attach the new pipe to the crossmember bracket. Install the bolts at both the manifold and the catalyst ends, leaving them finger-tight until the pipe is correctly positioned. Make certain the gaskets are in place and straight.
7. Tighten the pipe-to-manifold bolts to 46 ft. lbs. (62 Nm).
8. Tighten the bolts at the converter to 32 ft. lbs. (43 Nm).
9. Reconnect the oxygen sensor, if so equipped.
10. Lower the vehicle to the ground, start the system and check for leaks.

Catalytic Converter

With the car safely supported on jackstands, the converter is removed simply by removing the two bolts at either end. When reinstalling the converter, install it with new gaskets and tighten the end bolts to 32 ft. lbs. (43 Nm).

Intermediate Pipe (Resonator Pipe)

1. Raise and safely support the vehicle on jackstands.
2. Remove the two bolts holding the pipe to the catalytic converter.
3. Remove the bolts holding the intermediate pipe to the muffler inlet pipe.
4. Disconnect the rubber hangers and remove the pipe.
   To install:
5. Install the new pipe by suspending it in place on the rubber hangers. Install the gaskets at each end and install the bolts finger-tight.
6. Double check the placement of the pipe and insure proper clearance to all body and suspension components.
7. Tighten the bolts holding the pipe to the catalytic converter to 32 ft. lbs. (43 Nm), then tighten the bolts to the muffler inlet pipe to 32 ft. lbs. (43 Nm).
8. Lower the car to the ground. Start the engine and check for leaks.

Muffler and Tailpipe Assembly

1. Raise and safely support the vehicle on jackstands.
2. Remove the bolts holding the muffler inlet pipe to the intermediate pipe.
3. Disconnect the forward bracket on the muffler.
4. Disconnect the rear muffler bracket and remove the muffler from under the car.
   To install:
5. When reinstalling, suspend the muffler from its front and rear hangers and check it for correct positioning under the body. If the old muffler had been rattling or hitting the body it is possible that the hangers and brackets have become bent from a light impact.
6. Attach the inlet pipe to the intermediate pipe and tighten the bolts to 32 ft. lbs. (43 Nm).
7. Lower the vehicle to the ground, start the engine and check for leaks.

Complete System

If the entire exhaust system is to be replaced, it is much easier to remove the system as a unit than remove each

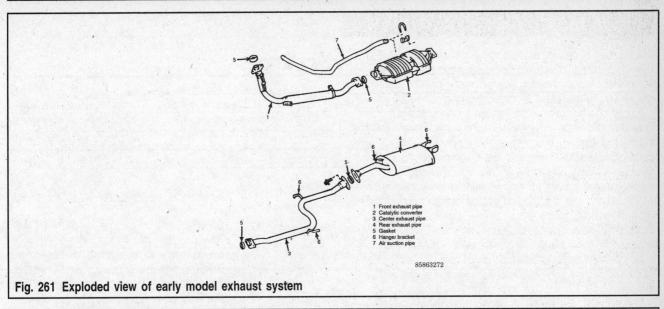

Fig. 261 Exploded view of early model exhaust system

1 Front exhaust pipe
2 Catalytic converter
3 Center exhaust pipe
4 Rear exhaust pipe
5 Gasket
6 Hanger bracket
7 Air suction pipe

85863272

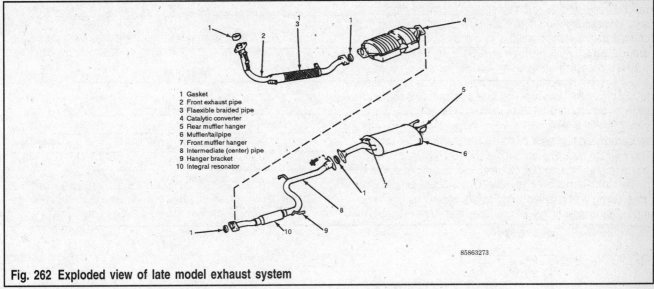

Fig. 262 Exploded view of late model exhaust system

1 Gasket
2 Front exhaust pipe
3 Flaexible braided pipe
4 Catalytic converter
5 Rear muffler hanger
6 Muffler/tailpipe
7 Front muffler hanger
8 Intermediate (center) pipe
9 Hanger bracket
10 Integral resonator

85863273

individual piece. Disconnect the first pipe at the manifold joint and work towards the rear removing brackets and hangers as you go. Remove the rear muffler bracket and slide the entire exhaust system out form under the car.

When installing the new assembly, suspend it from the flexible hangers first, then attach the fixed (solid) brackets. Check the clearance to the body and suspension and install the manifold joint bolts, tightening them to 46 ft. lbs. (62 Nm). Start the engine and check for exhaust leaks.

TORQUE SPECIFICATIONS

Component	U.S.	Metric
Camshaft bearing caps	9 ft. lbs.	13 Nm
Camshaft cover	9 ft. lbs.	13 Nm
Camshaft pulley	43 ft. lbs.	59 Nm
Cold start union bolt	18 ft. lbs.	25 Nm
Crankshaft damper bolt		
4A-GE engine	101 ft. lbs.	137 Nm
Cylinder head bolts		
1C-L engine	60–65 ft. lbs.	81–88 Nm
3K-C engine	39–47 ft. lbs.	53–64 Nm
2T-C engine	52–63 ft. lbs. ①	70–85 Nm
3T-C engine	62–68 ft. lbs.	84–92 Nm
4A-C and 4A-LC engines	40–47 ft. lbs.	54–64 Nm
4A-GE engine	40–47 ft. lbs.	54–64 Nm
Engine mount bolts	29 ft. lbs.	40 Nm
Exhaust manifold		
4A-GE engine	29 ft. lbs.	39 Nm
Flywheel bolts		
4A-GE engine	54 ft. lbs.	73 Nm
Intake manifold		
4A-GE engine	20 ft. lbs.	27 Nm
Oil pan retaining bolts	5 ft. lbs.	6.7 Nm
Rocker arm support bolts	14–17 ft. lbs.	19–23 Nm
Spark plugs	13 ft. lbs.	17 Nm
Timing belt idler pulley bolt	27 ft. lbs.	37 Nm
Transaxle mounting bolts	37–57 ft. lbs.	50–77 Nm
Water pump retaining bolts	11 ft. lbs.	14 Nm

① 1977–79: 61–68 ft. lbs. (83–92 Nm)

85863999

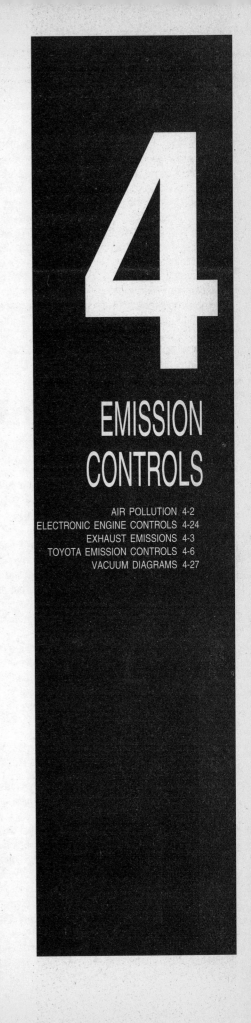

4

EMISSION CONTROLS

AIR POLLUTION

The earth's atmosphere, at or near sea level, consists approximately of 78 percent nitrogen, 21 percent oxygen and 1 percent other gases. If it were possible to remain in this state, 100 percent clean air would result. However, many varied causes allow other gases and particulates to mix with the clean air, causing the air to become unclean or polluted.

Certain of these pollutants are visible while others are invisible, with each having the capability of causing distress to the eyes, ears, throat, skin and respiratory system. Should these pollutants become concentrated in a specific area and under certain conditions, death could result due to the displacement or chemical change of the oxygen content in the air. These pollutants can also cause great damage to the environment and to the many man made objects that are exposed to the elements.

To better understand the causes of air pollution, the pollutants can be categorized into 3 separate types, natural, industrial and automotive.

Natural Pollutants

Natural pollution has been present on earth since before man appeared and continues to be a factor when discussing air pollution, although it causes only a small percentage of the overall pollution problem existing in our country today. It is the direct result of decaying organic matter, wind born smoke and particulates from such natural events as plain and forest fires (ignited by heat or lightning), volcanic ash, sand and dust which can spread over a large area of the countryside.

Such a phenomenon of natural pollution has been recently seen in the form of volcanic eruptions, with the resulting plume of smoke, steam and volcanic ash blotting out the sun's rays as it spreads and rises higher into the atmosphere. As it travels into the atmosphere the upper air currents catch and carry the smoke and ash, while condensing the steam back into water vapor. As the water vapor, smoke and ash traveled on their journey, the smoke dissipates into the atmosphere while the ash and moisture settle back to earth in a trail hundred of miles long. In some cases, lives are lost and millions of dollars of property damage result. Ironically, man can only stand by and watch it happen.

Industrial Pollution

Industrial pollution is caused primarily by industrial processes, the burning of coal, oil and natural gas, which in turn produce smoke and fumes. Because the burning fuels contain large amounts of sulfur, the principal ingredients of smoke and fumes are sulfur dioxide and particulate matter. This type of pollutant occurs most severely during still, damp and cool weather, such as at night. Even in its less severe form, this pollutant is not confined to just cities. Because of air movements, the pollutants move for miles over the surrounding countryside, leaving in its path a barren and unhealthy environment for all living things.

Working with Federal, State and Local mandated regulations and by carefully monitoring the emissions, big business has greatly reduced the amount of pollutant emitted from its industrial sources, striving to obtain an acceptable level. Because of the mandated industrial emission clean up, many land areas and streams in and around the cities that were formerly barren of vegetation and life, have now begun to move back in the direction of nature's intended balance.

Automotive Pollutants

The third major source of air pollution is automotive emissions. The emissions from the internal combustion engine were not an appreciable problem years ago because of the small number of registered vehicles and the nation's small highway system. However, during the early 1950's, the trend of the American people was to move from the cities to the surrounding suburbs. This caused an immediate problem in transportation because the majority of suburbs were not afforded mass transit conveniences. This lack of transportation created an attractive market for the automobile manufacturers, which resulted in a dramatic increase in the number of vehicles produced and sold, along with a marked increase in highway construction between cities and the suburbs. Multi-vehicle families emerged with a growing emphasis placed on an individual vehicle per family member. As the increase in vehicle ownership and usage occurred, so did pollutant levels in and around the cities, as suburbanites drove daily to their businesses and employment, returning at the end of the day to their homes in the suburbs.

It was noted that a fog and smoke type haze was being formed and at times, remained in suspension over the cities, taking time to dissipate. At first this smog, derived from the words smoke and fog, was thought to result from industrial pollution but it was determined that automobile emissions shared the blame. It was discovered that when normal automobile emissions were exposed to sunlight for a period of time, complex chemical reactions would take place.

It is now known that smog is a photo chemical layer which develops when certain oxides of nitrogen (NOx) and unburned hydrocarbons (HC) from automobile emissions are exposed to sunlight. Pollution was more severe when smog would become stagnant over an area in which a warm layer of air settled over the top of the cooler air mass, trapping and holding the cooler mass at ground level. The trapped cooler air would keep the emissions from being dispersed and diluted through normal air flows. This type of air stagnation was given the name Temperature Inversion.

Temperature Inversion

In normal weather situations, the surface air is warmed by heat radiating from the earth's surface and the sun's rays and will rise upward, into the atmosphere. Upon rising it will cool through a convection type heat exchange with the cooler upper air. As warm air rises, the surface pollutants are carried upward and dissipated into the atmosphere.

When a temperature inversion occurs, we find the higher air is no longer cooler but warmer than the surface air, causing the cooler surface air to become trapped. This warm air blanket can extend from above ground level to a few hundred or even a few thousand feet into the air. As the surface air is trapped, so are the pollutants, causing a severe smog condition. Should this stagnant air mass extend to a few thousand feet high, enough air movement with the inversion takes place to allow the smog layer to rise above ground level but the pollutants still cannot dissipate. This inversion can remain for days over an area, with the smog level only rising or lowering from ground level to a few hundred feet high. Meanwhile, the pollutant levels increase, causing eye irritation, respiratory problems, reduced visibility, plant damage and in some cases, disease.

This inversion phenomenon was first noted in the Los Angeles, California area. The city lies terrain resembling a basin and with certain weather conditions, a cold air mass is held in the basin while a warmer air mass covers it like a lid.

Because this type of condition was first documented as prevalent in the Los Angeles area, this type of trapped pollution was named Los Angeles Smog, although it occurs in other areas where a large concentration of automobiles are used and the air remains stagnant for any length of time.

Internal Combustion Engine Pollutants

Consider the internal combustion engine as a machine in which raw materials must be placed so a finished product comes out. As in any machine operation, a certain amount of wasted material is formed. When we relate this to the internal combustion engine, we find that through the input of air and fuel, we obtain power during the combustion process to drive the vehicle. The by-product or waste of this power is, in part, heat and exhaust gases with which we must dispose.

EXHAUST EMISSIONS

Composition Of The Exhaust Gases

The exhaust gases emitted into the atmosphere are a combination of burned and unburned fuel. To understand the exhaust emission and its composition, we must review some basic chemistry.

When the air/fuel mixture is introduced into the engine, we are mixing air, composed of nitrogen (78 percent), oxygen (21 percent) and other gases (1 percent) with the fuel, which is 100 percent hydrocarbons (HC), in a semi-controlled ratio. As the combustion process is accomplished, power is produced to move the vehicle while the heat of combustion is transferred to the cooling system. The exhaust gases are then composed of nitrogen, a diatomic gas (N_2), the same as was introduced in the engine, carbon dioxide (CO_2), the same gas that is used in beverage carbonation and water vapor (H_2O). The nitrogen (N_2), for the most part passes through the engine unchanged, while the oxygen (O_2) reacts (burns) with the hydrocarbons (HC) and produces the carbon dioxide (CO_2) and the water vapors (H_2O). If this chemical process would be the only process to take place, the exhaust emissions would be harmless. However, during the combustion process, other compounds are formed which are considered dangerous. These pollutants are carbon monoxide (CO), hydrocarbons (HC), oxides of nitrogen (NOx) oxides of sulfur (SOx) and engine particulates.

Heat Transfer

The heat from the combustion process can rise to over 4,000°F (2,204°C). The dissipation of this heat is controlled by a ram air effect, the use of cooling fans to cause air flow and having a liquid coolant solution surrounding the combustion area to transfer the heat of combustion through the cylinder walls and into the coolant. The coolant is then directed to a thin-finned, multi-tubed radiator, from which the excess heat is transferred to the atmosphere by 1 of the 3 heat transfer methods, conduction, convection or radiation.

The cooling of the combustion area is an important part in the control of exhaust emissions. To understand the behavior of the combustion and transfer of its heat, consider the air/fuel charge. It is ignited and the flame front burns progressively across the combustion chamber until the burning charge reaches the cylinder walls. Some of the fuel in contact with the walls is not hot enough to burn, thereby snuffing out or quenching the combustion process. This leaves unburned fuel in the combustion chamber. This unburned fuel is then forced out of the cylinder and into the exhaust system, along with the exhaust gases.

Many attempts have been made to minimize the amount of unburned fuel in the combustion chambers due to the snuffing out or quenching, by increasing the coolant temperature and lessening the contact area of the coolant around the combustion area. Design limitations within the combustion chambers prevent the complete burning of the air/fuel charge, so a certain amount of the unburned fuel is still expelled into the exhaust system, regardless of modifications to the engine.

HYDROCARBONS

Hydrocarbons (HC) are essentially fuel which was not burned during the combustion process or which has escaped into the atmosphere through fuel evaporation. The main sources of incomplete combustion are rich air/fuel mixtures, low engine temperatures and improper spark timing. The main sources of hydrocarbon emission through fuel evaporation on most cars used to be the vehicle's fuel tank and carburetor bowl.

To reduce combustion hydrocarbon emission, engine modifications were made to minimize dead space and surface area in the combustion chamber. In addition the air/fuel mixture was made more lean through the improved control which feedback carburetion and fuel injection offers and by the addition of external controls to aid in further combustion of the hydrocarbons outside the engine. Two such methods were the addition of an air injection system, to inject fresh air into the exhaust manifolds and the installation of a catalytic converter, a unit that is able to burn traces of hydrocarbons without affecting the internal combustion process or fuel economy. The vehicles covered in this manual may utilize either, both or none of these methods, depending on the year and model.

To control hydrocarbon emissions through fuel evaporation, modifications were made to the fuel tank to allow storage of the fuel vapors during periods of engine shut-down.

Modifications were also made to the air intake system so that at specific times during engine operation, these vapors may be purged and burned by blending them with the air/fuel mixture.

CARBON MONOXIDE

Carbon monoxide is formed when not enough oxygen is present during the combustion process to convert carbon (C) to carbon dioxide (CO_2). An increase in the carbon monoxide (CO) emission is normally accompanied by an increase in the hydrocarbon (HC) emission because of the lack of oxygen to completely burn all of the fuel mixture.

Carbon monoxide (CO) also increases the rate at which the photo chemical smog is formed by speeding up the conversion of nitric oxide (NO) to nitrogen dioxide (NO_2). To accomplish this, carbon monoxide (CO) combines with oxygen (O_2) and nitric oxide (NO) to produce carbon dioxide (CO_2) and nitrogen dioxide (NO_2). ($CO + O_2 + NO = CO_2 + NO_2$).

The dangers of carbon monoxide, which is an odorless and colorless toxic gas are many. When carbon monoxide is inhaled into the lungs and passed into the blood stream, oxygen is replaced by the carbon monoxide in the red blood cells, causing a reduction in the amount of oxygen being supplied to the many parts of the body. This lack of oxygen causes headaches, lack of coordination, reduced mental alertness and should the carbon monoxide concentration be high enough, death could result.

NITROGEN

Normally, nitrogen is an inert gas. When heated to approximately 2,500°F (1,371°C) through the combustion process, this gas becomes active and causes an increase in the nitric oxide (NOx) emission.

Oxides of nitrogen (NOx) are composed of approximately 97-98 percent nitric oxide (NO). Nitric oxide is a colorless gas but when it is passed into the atmosphere, it combines with oxygen and forms nitrogen dioxide (NO_2). The nitrogen dioxide then combines with chemically active hydrocarbons (HC) and when in the presence of sunlight, causes the formation of photo chemical smog.

OZONE

To further complicate matters, some of the nitrogen dioxide (NO_2) is broken apart by the sunlight to form nitric oxide and oxygen. (NO_2 + sunlight = NO + O). This single atom of oxygen then combines with diatomic (meaning 2 atoms) oxygen (O_2) to form ozone (O_3). Ozone is one of the smells associated with smog. It has a pungent and offensive odor, irritates the eyes and lung tissues, affects the growth of plant life and causes rapid deterioration of rubber products. Ozone can be formed by sunlight as well as electrical discharge into the air.

The most common discharge area on the automobile engine is the secondary ignition electrical system, especially when inferior quality spark plug cables are used. As the surge of high voltage is routed through the secondary cable, the circuit builds up an electrical field around the wire, acting upon the oxygen in the surrounding air to form the ozone. The faint glow along the cable with the engine running that may be visible on a dark night, is called the corona discharge. It is the result of the electrical field passing from a high along the cable, to a low in the surrounding air, which forms the ozone gas. The combination of corona and ozone has been a major cause of cable deterioration. Recently, different and better quality insulating materials have lengthened the life of the electrical cables.

Although ozone at ground level can be harmful, ozone is beneficial to the earth's inhabitants. By having a concentrated ozone layer called the ozonosphere, between 10 and 20 miles (16-32km) up in the atmosphere, much of the ultra violet radiation from the sun's rays are absorbed and screened. If this ozone layer were not present, much of the earth's surface would be burned, dried and unfit for human life.

There is much discussion concerning the ozone layer and its density. A feeling exists that this protective layer of ozone is slowly diminishing and corrective action must be directed to this problem. Much experimentation is presently being conducted to determine if a problem exists and if so, the short and long term effects of the problem and how it can be remedied.

OXIDES OF SULFUR

Oxides of sulfur (SOx) were initially ignored in the exhaust system emissions, since the sulfur content of gasoline as a fuel is less than $\frac{1}{10}$ of 1 percent. Because of this small amount, it was felt that it contributed very little to the overall pollution problem. However, because of the difficulty in solving the sulfur emissions in industrial pollutions and the introduction of catalytic converter to the automobile exhaust systems, a change was mandated. The automobile exhaust system, when equipped with a catalytic converter, changes the sulfur dioxide (SO_2) into the sulfur trioxide (SO_3).

When this combines with water vapors (H_2O), a sulfuric acid mist (H_2SO_4) is formed and is a very difficult pollutant to handle since it is extremely corrosive. This sulfuric acid mist that is formed, is the same mist that rises from the vents of an automobile battery when an active chemical reaction takes place within the battery cells.

When a large concentration of vehicles equipped with catalytic converters are operating in an area, this acid mist will rise and be distributed over a large ground area causing land, plant, crop, paints and building damage.

PARTICULATE MATTER

A certain amount of particulate matter is present in the burning of any fuel, with carbon constituting the largest percentage of the particulates. In gasoline, the remaining particulates are the burned remains of the various other compounds used in its manufacture. When a gasoline engine is in good internal condition, the particulate emissions are low but as the engine wears internally, the particulate emissions increase. By visually inspecting the tail pipe emissions, a determination can be made as to where an engine defect may exist. An engine with light gray or blue smoke emitting from the tail pipe normally indicates an increase in the oil consumption through burning due to internal engine wear. Black smoke would indicate a defective fuel delivery system, causing the engine to operate in a rich mode. Regardless of the color of the smoke, the internal part of the engine or the fuel delivery system should be repaired to prevent excess particulate emissions.

Diesel and turbine engines emit a darkened plume of smoke from the exhaust system because of the type of fuel used. Emission control regulations are mandated for this type of emission and more stringent measures are being used to prevent excess emission of the particulate matter. Electronic components are being introduced to control the injection of the fuel at precisely the proper time of piston travel, to achieve the optimum in fuel ignition and fuel usage. Other particulate after-burning components are being tested to achieve a cleaner emission.

Good grades of engine lubricating oils should be used, which meet the manufacturers specification. Cut-rate oils can contribute to the particulate emission problem because of their low flash or ignition temperature point. Such oils burn prematurely during the combustion process causing emissions of particulate matter.

The cooling system is an important factor in the reduction of particulate matter. With the cooling system operating at a temperature specified by the manufacturer, the optimum of combustion will occur. The cooling system must be maintained in the same manner as the engine oiling system, as each system is required to perform properly in order for the engine to operate efficiently for a long time.

Other Automobile Emission Sources

Before emission controls were mandated on the internal combustion engines, other sources of engine pollutants were discovered, along with the exhaust emission. It was determined the engine combustion exhaust produced 60 percent of the total emission pollutants, fuel evaporation from the fuel tank and carburetor vents produced 20 percent, with the another 20 percent being produced through the crankcase as a by-product of the combustion process.

CRANKCASE EMISSIONS

Crankcase emissions are made up of water, acids, unburned fuel, oil fumes and particulates. The emissions are classified as hydrocarbons (HC) and are formed by the small amount of unburned, compressed air/fuel mixture entering the crankcase from the combustion area during the compression and power strokes, between the cylinder walls and piston rings. The head of the compression and combustion help to form the remaining crankcase emissions.

Since the first engines, crankcase emissions were allowed into the atmosphere through a road draft tube, mounted on the lower side of the engine block. Fresh air came in through an open oil filler cap or breather. The air passed through the crankcase mixing with blow-by gases. The motion of the vehicle and the air blowing past the open end of the road draft tube caused a low pressure area at the end of the tube.

Crankcase emissions were simply drawn out of the road draft tube into the air.

To control the crankcase emission, the road draft tube was deleted. A hose and/or tubing was routed from the crankcase to the intake manifold so the blow-by emission could be burned with the air/fuel mixture. However, it was found that intake manifold vacuum, used to draw the crankcase emissions into the manifold, would vary in strength at the wrong time and not allow the proper emission flow. A regulating type valve was needed to control the flow of air through the crankcase.

Testing, showed the removal of the blow-by gases from the crankcase as quickly as possible, was most important to the longevity of the engine. Should large accumulations of blow-by gases remain and condense, dilution of the engine oil would occur to form water, soots, resins, acids and lead salts, resulting in the formation of sludge and varnishes. This condensation of the blow-by gases occur more frequently on vehicles used in numerous starting and stopping conditions, excessive idling and when the engine is not allowed to attain normal operating temperature through short runs.

FUEL EVAPORATIVE EMISSIONS

Gasoline fuel is a major source of pollution, before and after it is burned in the automobile engine. From the time the fuel is refined, stored, pumped and transported, again stored until it is pumped into the fuel tank of the vehicle, the gasoline gives off unburned hydrocarbons (HC) into the atmosphere. Through redesigning of the storage areas and venting systems, the pollution factor was diminished, but not eliminated, from the refinery standpoint. However, the automobile still remained the primary source of vaporized, unburned hydrocarbon (HC) emissions.

Fuel pumped from an underground storage tank is cool but when exposed to a warmer ambient temperature, will expand. Before controls were mandated, an owner would fill the fuel tank with fuel from an underground storage tank and park the vehicle for some time in warm area, such as a parking lot. As the fuel would warm, it would expand and should no provisions or area be provided for the expansion, the fuel would spill out the filler neck and onto the ground, causing hydrocarbon (HC) pollution and creating a severe fire hazard. To correct this condition, the vehicle manufacturers added overflow plumbing and/or gasoline tanks with built in expansion areas or domes.

However, this did not control the fuel vapor emission from the fuel tank. It was determined that most of the fuel evaporation occurred when the vehicle was stationary and the engine not operating. Most vehicles carry 5-25 gallons (19-95 liters) of gasoline. Should a large concentration of vehicles be parked in one area, such as a large parking lot, excessive fuel vapor emissions would take place, increasing as the temperature increases.

To prevent the vapor emission from escaping into the atmosphere, the fuel system is designed to trap the fuel vapors while the vehicle is stationary, by sealing the fuel system from the atmosphere. A storage system is used to collect and hold the fuel vapors from the carburetor and the fuel tank when the engine is not operating. When the engine is started, the storage system is then purged of the fuel vapors, which are drawn into the engine and burned with the air/fuel mixture.

TOYOTA EMISSION CONTROLS

Due to varying state, federal, and provincial regulations, specific emission control equipment may vary by area of sale. The U.S. emission equipment is divided into two categories: California and Federal. In this section, the term California applies only to cars originally built to be sold in California. Some California emissions equipment are not shared with equipment installed on cars built to be sold in the other states. Models built to be sold in Canada also have specific emissions equipment, although in many cases the Federal and Canadian equipment are the same.

Both carbureted and fuel injected cars require an assortment of systems and devices to control emissions. Newer cars rely more heavily on computer (ECM) management of many of the engine controls. This eliminates many of the vacuum hoses and linkages around the engine. Remember that not every component is found on every car.

Positive Crankcase Ventilation

▶ See Figure 1

A closed, positive crankcase ventilation system is used on all models. This system cycles incompletely burned fuel which works its way past the piston rings back into the intake manifold for reburning with the fuel/air mixture. The oil filler cap is sealed and the air is drawn from the top of the crankcase into the intake manifold through a valve with a variable orifice.

This valve (commonly known as the PCV valve) regulates the flow of air into the manifold according to the amount of manifold vacuum.

A plugged valve or hose may cause a rough idle, stalling or low idle speed, oil leaks in the engine and/or sludging and oil deposits within the engine and air cleaner.

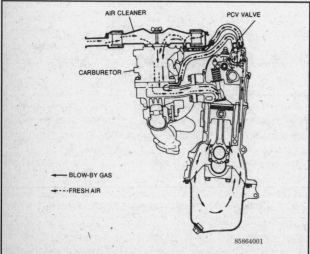

Fig. 1 PCV valve system on a carbureted engine — most engines similar

REMOVAL & INSTALLATION

Remove the PCV valve from the valve cover or camshaft cover. Remove the hose from the valve. Take note of which end of the valve was in the manifold. While the valve is removed, the hoses should be checked for splits, kinks and blockages. Check the vacuum port (that the hoses connect to) for any clogging.

TESTING

➡**A leaking valve or hose could cause an erratic idle or stalling.**

Check the PCV system hoses and connections, to ensure that there are no leaks; then replace or tighten, as necessary.

To check the valve, remove it and blow through both of its ends. When blowing from the side which goes toward the intake manifold, very little air should pass through it. When blowing from the crankcase (valve cover) side, air should pass through freely. An alternative method may be to remove the PCV valve from the cover and shake it end to end, listening for the rattle of the needle inside the valve. If no rattle is heard, the needle is jammed. Replace the valve with a new one, if the valve fails to function as outlined.

➡**Do not attempt to clean or adjust the valve; replace it with a new one.**

Evaporative Emission Control System

To prevent hydrocarbon emissions from entering the atmosphere, all vehicles use evaporative emission control (EEC or EVAP) systems. Models produced between 1970 and 1971 use a case storage system, while later models use a charcoal canister storage system.

The major components of the case storage system are a purge control or vacuum switching valve, a fuel vapor storage case, an air filter, a thermal expansion tank, and a special fuel tank.

When the vehicle is stopped or the engine is running at a low speed, the purge control or vacuum switching valve is closed; fuel vapor travels only as far as the case where it is stored.

When the engine is running at a high speed (cruising speed), the purge control valve is opened by pressure from the air pump or else the vacuum switching valve opens, depending upon the type of emission control system used. This allows the vapor stored in the case to be drawn into the intake manifold along with fresh air which is drawn in from the filter.

The charcoal canister storage system functions in a similar manner to the case system, except that the fuel vapors are stored in a canister filled with activated charcoal, rather than in a case, and that all models use a vacuum switching valve to purge the system. The air filter is not external as it is on the case system; rather it is an integral part of the charcoal canister.

REMOVAL & INSTALLATION

Removal and installation of the various evaporative emission control system components consists of unfastening hoses, loosening securing screws, and removing the part which is to be replaced from its mounting bracket. Installation is the reverse of removal.

➡**When replacing any EEC system hoses, always use hoses that are fuel-resistant or are marked EVAP.**

CHECKING THE FILLER CAP

▶ **See Figure 2**

Check that the filler cap seals effectively. Remove the filler cap and pull the safety valve outward to check for smooth operation. Replace the filler cap if the seal is defective or if it is not operating properly.

CHECKING THE PURGE CONTROL VALVE

1970-71

➡**This valve is used only on 1970-71 engines which are also equipped with an air injection system.**

1. Disconnect the line which runs from the storage case to the valve, at the valve end.
2. Connect a tachometer to the engine in accordance with the manufacturer's instructions.
3. Start the engine and slowly increase its speed until the tachometer reads 2,500 rpm (transmission in Neutral).
4. Place a finger over the hose fitting (storage case-to-valve) on the valve.

5. If there is no suction, check the air pump for a malfunction. If the air pump is not defective, replace the valve.

INSPECTING THE CHARCOAL CANISTER AND CHECK VALVES

▶ **See Figures 3 and 4**

Remove the charcoal canister from the engine compartment and visually inspect it for cracks or other damage.

Check for stuck check valves. All models from 1972-78 have one check valve in the line between the fuel tank and the charcoal canister. It is located in the trunk. To check:

1. Remove the check valve from the line.

➡**Mark which end goes toward the fuel tank and which end goes toward the charcoal canister.**

2. Blow into the fuel tank end. A slight resistance should be felt at first.
3. Blow through the other end. No resistance should be felt at all.
4. If your results differ from those above, the check valve will require replacement.

Later models have two or three check valves, all are located in the charcoal canister. To check:

5. Using low pressure compressed air, blow into the tank pipe. The air should flow from the other pipes without resistance.
6. If the air flow is incorrect, the check valve will require replacement. Before installing the canister, clean the filter. Blow compressed air into the purge pipe while keeping the others blocked with your fingers.

➡**Do not attempt to wash the charcoal canister. While cleaning the canister, under no circumstances should any activated charcoal be removed.**

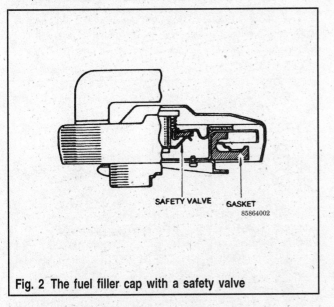

Fig. 2 The fuel filler cap with a safety valve

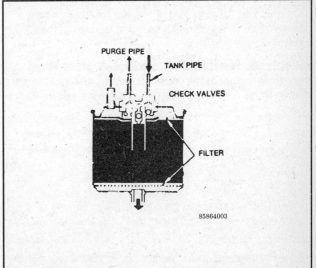

Fig. 3 Testing the charcoal canister check valves

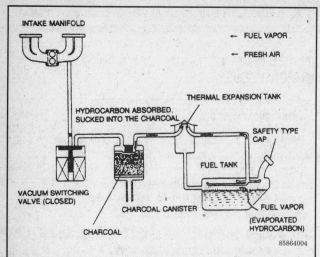

Fig. 4 Schematic of a charcoal canister vapor storage system

TESTING

EEC System Troubleshooting

➡**Before embarking on component removal or extensive diagnosis, perform a complete visual check of the system. Every vacuum line should be inspected for cracking, loose clamps and obstructions.**

There are several things which may be checked if a malfunction of the evaporative emission control system is suspected.

1. Leaks may be traced by using a hydrocarbon tester or equivalent type tester. Run the test probe along the lines and connections. The meter will indicate the presence of a leak by a high hydrocarbon (HC) reading.

2. Leaks may be caused by any of the following: Defective or worn hoses; Disconnected or pinched hoses; Improperly routed hoses; A defective filler cap or safety valve (sealed cap system).

➡**If it becomes necessary to replace any of the hoses used in the evaporative emission control system, use only hoses which are fuel-resistant or are marked EVAP.**

3. If the fuel tank, storage case, or thermal expansion tank collapses, it may be the fault of clogged or pinches vent lines, a defective vapor separator, or a plugged or incorrect filler cap.

4. To test the filler cap (if it is the safety valve type), clean it and place it against the mount. Blow into the relief valve housing. If the cap passes pressure with light blowing or if it fails to release with hard blowing, it is defective and must be replaced.

➡**Use the proper cap for the type of system used; either a sealed cap or safety valve cap, as required.**

Outer Vent Control Valve

1. Disconnect the hoses from the valve.
2. Check that the valve is open when the ignition switch is turned **OFF**.

3. Check that the valve is closed when the ignition switch is in the **ON** position.
4. If the valve doesn't operate properly, check the fuse and wiring, if OK, replace the valve.

Thermoswitch

1. Drain the radiator and save the coolant.
2. Remove the thermoswitch from the intake manifold. Cool the switch to below 109°F (43°C).
3. Use an ohmmeter and check for continuity; it should exist.
4. Heat the switch with hot water to a temperature above 131°F (55°C). There should be no continuity.
5. Apply liquid sealer to the threads of the switch and then reinstall it in the manifold.
6. Refill the coolant.

Dual Diaphragm Distributor

▶ **See Figure 5**

Some models are equipped with a dual diaphragm distributor unit. This distributor has a retard diaphragm, as well as a diaphragm for advance.

Retarding the timing helps to reduce exhaust emissions, as well as making up for the lack of engine braking on models equipped with a throttle positioner.

TESTING

1. Connect a timing light to the engine. Check the ignition timing.

➡**Before proceeding with the tests, disconnect any spark control devices, distributor vacuum valves, etc. If these are left connected, inaccurate results may be obtained.**

2. Remove the retard hose from the distributor and plug it. Increase the engine speed. The timing should advance. If it fails to do so, then the vacuum unit is faulty and must be replaced.

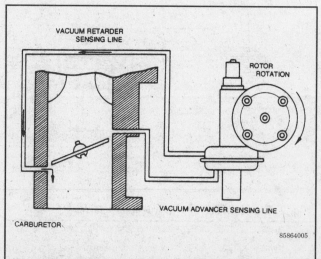

Fig. 5 Dual diaphragm distributor with vacuum switching valve

3. Check the timing with the engine at normal idle speed. Unplug the retard hose and connect it to the vacuum unit. The timing should instantly be retarded. If this does not occur, the retard diaphragm has a leak and the vacuum unit must be replaced.

Engine Modifications System

▶ **See Figure 6**

Toyota also uses an assortment of engine modifications to regulate exhaust emissions. Most of these devices fall into the category of engine vacuum controls. There are three principal components used on the engine modifications system, as well as a number of smaller parts. The three major components are: a speed sensor; a computer (speed marker); and a vacuum switching valve.

The vacuum switching valve and computer circuit operates most of the emission control components. Depending upon year and engine usage, the vacuum switching valve and computer may operate the purge control for the evaporative emission control system; the transmission controlled spark (TCS) or speed controlled spark (SCS); the dual diaphragm distributor, the throttle positioner system, the EGR system, the catalyst protection system, etc.

The functions of the evaporative emissions control system, the throttle positioner, and the dual diaphragm distributor are described in detail in this section. However, a word is necessary about the functions of the TCS and SCS systems before discussing the operation of the vacuum switching valve/computer circuit.

The major difference between the transmission controlled spark and speed controlled spark systems is the manner in which system operation is determined. Toyota TCS systems use a mechanical switch to determine which gear is selected; SCS systems use a speed sensor built into the speedometer cable.

Below a predetermined speed, or any gear other than Fourth, the vacuum advance unit on the distributor is rendered inoperative or the timing retarded. By changing the distributor advance curve in this manner, it is possible to reduce emissions of oxides of nitrogen (NOx).

➡ **Some engines are equipped with a thermosensor so that the TCS or SCS system only operates when the coolant temperature is 140-212°F.**

Aside from determining the preceding conditions, the vacuum switching valve computer circuit operates other devices in the emission control system (EGR, Catalytic converter, etc.).

The computer acts as a speed marker; at certain speeds it sends a signal to the vacuum switching valve which acts as a gate, opening and closing the emission control system vacuum circuits.

The vacuum switching valve on all 1970 and some 1971 engines is a simple affair; a single solenoid operates a valve which uncovers certain vacuum ports at the same time others are covered.

The valve used on all 1972-81 and some 1971 engines contains several solenoid and valve assemblies so that different combinations of opened and closed vacuum ports are possible. This allows greater flexibility of operation for the emission control system.

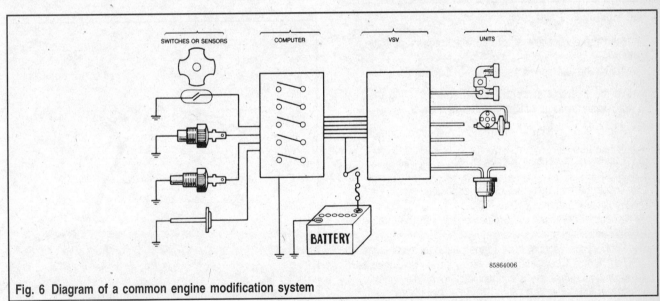

Fig. 6 Diagram of a common engine modification system

SYSTEM CHECKS

Due to the complexity of the components involved, about the only engine modification system checks which can be made, are the following:

1. Examine the vacuum lines to ensure that they are not clogged, pinched, or loose.

2. Check the electrical connections for tightness and corrosion.

3. Be sure that the vacuum sources for the vacuum switching valve are not plugged.

4. On models equipped with speed controlled spark, a broken speedometer cable could also render the system inoperative. Beyond these checks, servicing the engine modifications system is best left to an authorized service facility.

Throttle Positioner

▶ **See Figure 7**

On vehicles with an engine modification system, a throttle positioner is included to reduce exhaust emissions during deceleration. The positioner prevents the throttle from closing completely. Vacuum is reduced under the throttle valve which, in turn, acts on the retard chamber of the distributor vacuum unit. This compensates for the loss of engine braking caused by the partially opened throttle.

Once the vehicle drops below a predetermined speed, the vacuum switching valve provides vacuum to the throttle positioner diaphragm; the throttle positioner retracts allowing the throttle valve to close completely, The distributor also is returned to normal operation.

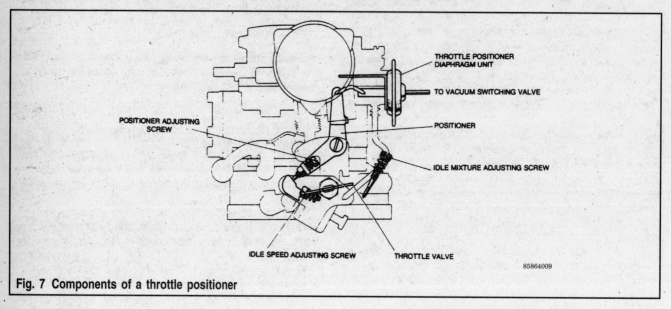

Fig. 7 Components of a throttle positioner

ADJUSTMENT

▶ **See Figures 8, 9 and 10**

1. Start the engine and allow it to reach normal operating temperature.
2. Adjust the idle speed as detailed in Section 2.

➡ **Leave the tachometer connected after completing the idle adjustments, as it will be needed in Step 5.**

3. Detach the vacuum line from the positioner diaphragm unit and plug the line up.
4. Accelerate the engine slightly to set the throttle positioner in place.
5. Check the engine speed with a tachometer when the throttle positioner is set.
6. If necessary, adjust the engine speed, with the throttle positioner adjusting screw.
7. Connect the vacuum hose to the positioner diaphragm.
8. The throttle lever should be freed from the positioner as soon as the vacuum hose is connected. Engine idle should return to normal.
9. If the throttle positioner fails to function properly, check its linkage, and vacuum diaphragm. If there are no defects in either of these, the fault probably lies in the vacuum switching valve or the speed marker unit.

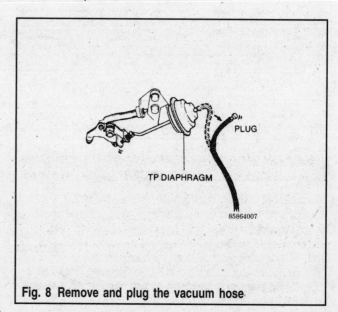

Fig. 8 Remove and plug the vacuum hose

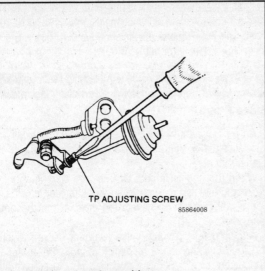

Fig. 9 Adjusting the throttle positioner

TP ADJUSTING SCREW

85864008

Throttle Positioner Setting
(rpm)

Year	Engine	Engine rpm (Positioner Set)
1975–77 ①	2T-C	1500 MT 1400 AT ①
	3K-C	1500 (Canada)
1978–82	2T-C	1400 MT 1200 AT
	3T-C	1600 MT 1300 AT ②
1980–82	1A-C, 3A 3A-C	1700 MT 1400 AT
1983–84	3A-C, 4A-C	1400 ③
1981–82	4K-C	2000

① 1977: 1200
② Calif.: 1400
③ Canadian 3A/MT: 1700
AT Automatic transmission
MT Manual transmission

85864010

Fig. 10 Throttle positioner setting specifications chart

Carburetor Auxiliary Slow System

A carburetor auxiliary slow system is used on 1970-71 3K-C engines. It provides uniform combination during deceleration. The components of the auxiliary slow system consist of a vacuum operated valve, a fresh air intake, and a fuel line which is connected to the carburetor float chamber.

During deceleration, manifold vacuum acts on the valve which opens it, causing additional air/fuel mixture to flow into the intake manifold. The additional mixture aids in more complete combustion.

REMOVAL & INSTALLATION

1. Remove the hoses from the auxiliary slow system unit.
2. Unfasten the recessed screws and withdraw the system as a complete unit. Installation is performed in the reverse order.

TESTING

♦ See Figure 11

1. Start the engine, allow it to reach normal operating temperature, and run it at normal idle speed.
2. Remove the rubber cap from the diaphragm assembly and place your finger over the opening. There should be no suction at idle speed. If there is, the diaphragm is defective and the unit must be replaced.
3. Pinch the air intake hose which runs from the air cleaner to the auxiliary slow system. There should be no change in engine idle with the hose pinched.
4. Disconnect the air intake hose at the auxiliary slow system. Race the engine. Place your finger over the air intake. Release the throttle; suction should be felt at the air intake.
5. If any of the tests indicate a defective auxiliary slow system, replace it as a unit.

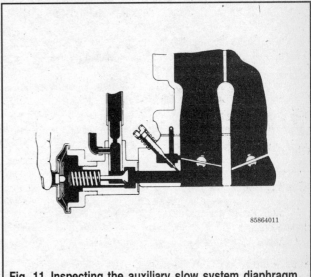

85864011

Fig. 11 Inspecting the auxiliary slow system diaphragm

Mixture Control (MC) System

The mixture control valve, used on certain engines, aids in combustion of unburned fuel during periods of deceleration. The mixture control valve is operated by the vacuum switching valve during periods of deceleration to admit additional fresh air into the intake manifold. The extra air allows more complete combustion of the fuel, thus reducing hydrocarbon emissions.

REMOVAL & INSTALLATION

1. Unfasten the vacuum switching valve line from the mixture control valve.
2. Remove the intake manifold hose from the valve.
3. Remove the valve from its engine mounting. Installation is performed in the reverse order of removal.

TESTING

1. Start the engine and allow it idle (warmed up).
2. Place your hand over the air intake at the bottom of the valve.

✳✳CAUTION

Keep your fingers clear of the engine fan!

3. Increase the engine speed and then release the throttle.
4. Suction should be felt at the air intake only while the engine is decelerating. Once the engine has returned to idle, no suction should be felt. If the above test indicates a malfunction, proceed with the next step; if not, the mixture control valve is functioning properly and requires no further adjustment.
5. Disconnect the vacuum line from the mixture control valve. If suction can be felt underneath the valve with the engine at idle, the valve seat is defective and must be replaced.
6. Reconnect the vacuum line to the valve. Disconnect the other end of the line from the vacuum switching valve and place it in your mouth.
7. With the engine idling, suck on the end of the vacuum line to duplicate the action of the vacuum switching valve.
8. Suction at the valve air intake should only be felt for an instant. If air cannot be drawn into the valve at all, or if it is

continually drawn in, replace the mixture control valve. If the mixture control valve is functioning properly, and all of the hose and connections are in good working order, the vacuum switching valve is probably at fault.

Auxiliary Enrichment System

▶ **See Figure 12**

An auxiliary enrichment system, which Toyota calls an Auxiliary Accelerator Pump (AAP) System, is used on all models, starting in 1975.

When the engine is cold, an auxiliary enrichment circuit in the carburetor is operated to squirt extra fuel into the acceleration circuit in order to prevent the mixture from becoming too lean.

A thermostatic vacuum valve (warm-up valve), which is threaded into the intake manifold, controls the operation of the enrichment circuit. Below a specified temperature, the valve is opened and manifold vacuum is allowed to act on a diaphragm in the carburetor. The vacuum pulls the diaphragm down, allowing fuel to flow into a special chamber above it.

Under sudden acceleration manifold vacuum drops momentarily, allowing the diaphragm to be pushed up by spring tension. This in turn forces the fuel from the chamber through a passage and out the accelerator pump jet.

When the coolant temperature goes above specification, the thermostatic vacuum valve closes, preventing the vacuum from reaching the diaphragm which makes the enrichment system inoperative.

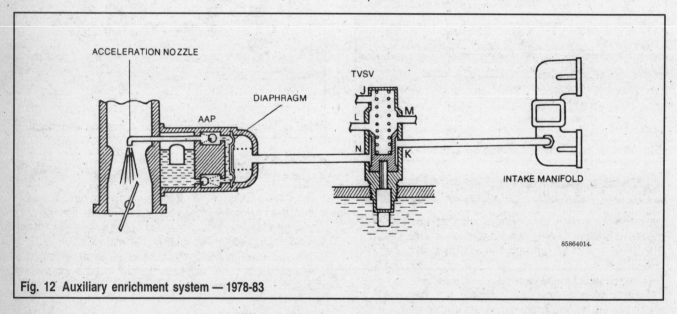

Fig. 12 Auxiliary enrichment system — 1978-83

TESTS

1974-77
▶ See Figure 13

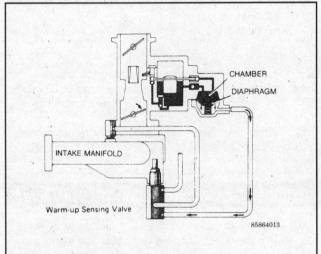

Fig. 13 Components of the auxiliary enrichment system — 1974-77

1. Check for clogged, pinched, disconnected, or misrouted vacuum lines.
2. With the engine cold (below 75°F), remove the top of the air cleaner, and allow the engine to idle.
3. Disconnect the vacuum line from the carburetor AAP unit. Gasoline should squirt out the accelerator pump jet.
4. If gas doesn't squirt out of the jet, check for vacuum at the AAP vacuum line with the engine idling. If there is no vacuum and the hose are in good shape, the thermostatic vacuum valve is defective and must be replaced.
5. If the gas doesn't squirt out and vacuum is present at the vacuum line in Step 4, the AAP unit is defective and must be replaced.
6. Repeat Step 3 with the engine at normal operating temperature. If gasoline squirts out of the pump jet, the thermostatic vacuum valve is defective and must be replaced.
7. Reconnect all of the vacuum lines and install the top of the air cleaner.

1978-83
▶ See Figure 14

1. The engine must be completely cold for this test.
2. Remove the air cleaner cover and start the engine.
3. Pinch the AAP hose and then have a helper turn off the engine while you continue pinching the hose.
4. With the engine off, release the hose. Gasoline should squirt out of the accelerator nozzle inside the carburetor.

5. Run the engine until it reaches normal operating temperature. Repeat Steps 3-4 and check that gasoline does not squirt out of the nozzle.

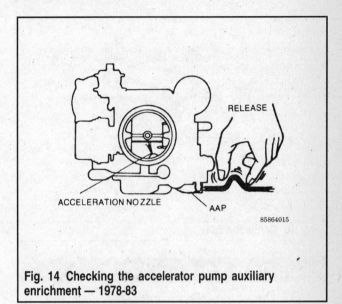

Fig. 14 Checking the accelerator pump auxiliary enrichment — 1978-83

Inspect the AAP diaphragm.
▶ See Figures 15 and 16

1. Start the engine and disconnect the hose from the diaphragm.
2. Apply and release the vacuum directly to the diaphragm at idle.
3. Check that the engine rpm changes when you release vacuum.
4. Reconnect the AAP hose. If a problem is found, replace the diaphragm.

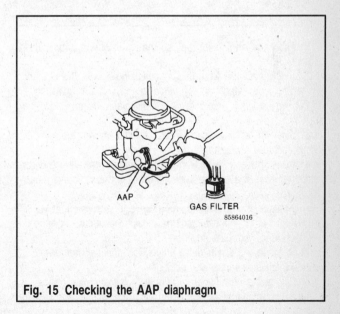

Fig. 15 Checking the AAP diaphragm

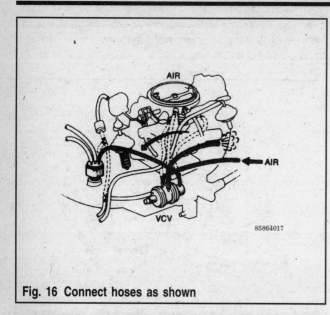

AIR

AIR

VCV

85864017

Fig. 16 Connect hoses as shown

Spark Delay Valve

Starting 1975, non-California models have a spark delay valve (SDV) in the distributor vacuum line. The valve has a small orifice in it, which slows down the vacuum flow to the vacuum advance unit on the distributor. By delaying the vacuum to the distributor, a reduction in HC and CO emissions is possible.

When the coolant temperature is below 95°F, a coolant temperature operated vacuum control valve is opened, allowing the distributor to receive undelayed, ported vacuum through a separate vacuum line. Above 95°F, this line is blocked and all ported vacuum must go through the spark delay valve.

TESTING

1. Allow the engine to cool, so that the coolant temperature is below 95°F.
2. Disconnect the vacuum line which runs from the coolant temperature operated vacuum valve to the vacuum advance unit at the advance unit end. Connect a vacuum gauge to this line.
3. Start the engine. Increase the engine speed; the gauge should indicate a vacuum.
4. Allow the engine to warm-up to normal operating temperature. Increase the engine speed; this time the vacuum gauge should read zero.
5. Replace the coolant temperature operated vacuum valve, if it fails either of these tests. Disconnect the vacuum gauge and reconnect the vacuum lines.
6. Remove the spark delay valve from the vacuum lines, noting which side faces the distributor.
7. Connect a hand operated vacuum pump which has a built-in vacuum gauge to the carburetor side of the spark delay valve.

8. Connect a vacuum gauge to the distributor side of the valve.
9. Operate the hand pump to create a vacuum. The vacuum gauge on the distributor side should show a hesitation before registering.
10. The gauge reading on the pump side should drop slightly, taking several seconds for it to balance with the reading on the other gauge.
11. If Steps 9 and 10 are negative, replace the spark delay valve.
12. Remove the vacuum gauge from the distributor side of the valve. Cover the distributor side of the valve with your finger and operate the pump to create a vacuum of 15 in.Hg.
13. The reading on the pump gauge should remain steady. If the gauge reading drops, replace the valve.
14. Remove your finger; the reading of the gauge should drop slowly. If the reading goes to zero rapidly, replace the valve.

Exhaust Gas Recirculation (EGR) Valve

Most engines, except for early 2T-C engines, use EGR system. In all cases, the EGR valve is controlled by the same computer and vacuum switching valve which is used to operate other emission control system components. On all engines there are several conditions, determined by the computer which permit exhaust gas recirculation to take place:

1. Vehicle speed.
2. Engine coolant temperature.
3. EGR valve temperature.
4. Carburetor flange temperature.

EGR VALVE CHECK

1974-78

▶ See Figure 17

1. Allow the engine to warm up and remove the top from the air cleaner.

➡ **Do not remove the entire air cleaner assembly.**

2. Disconnect the hose (white tape coded), which runs from the vacuum switching valve to the EGR valve, at its EGR valve end.
3. Remove the intake manifold hose (red coded) from the vacuum switching valve and connect it to the EGR valve. When the engine is at idle, a hollow sound should be heard coming from the air cleaner.
4. Disconnect the hose from the EGR valve; the hollow sound should disappear.
5. If the sound doesn't vary, the EGR valve is defective and must be replaced.
6. Reconnect the vacuum hoses as they were originally found. Install the top on the air cleaner.

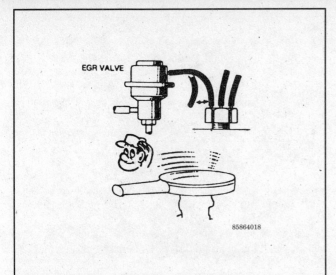

Fig. 17 Checking the EGR valve — 1974-78

After 1979

▶ **See Figure 18**

1. Start the engine.
2. Disconnect the vacuum hose leading from the EGR valve.
3. Disconnect the hose coming from the intake manifold and connect it to the empty pipe on the EGR valve.
4. When applying vacuum directly to the EGR valve, the engine should stall, if not, the EGR valve will probably require replacement.

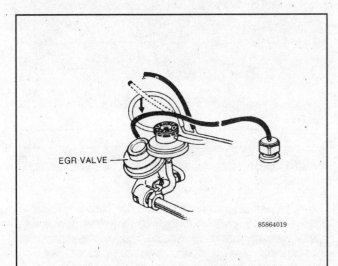

Fig. 18 Checking the EGR valve — 1979 and later

EGR VALVE THERMOSENSOR

1. Disconnect the electrical lead which runs to the EGR valve thermosensor.
2. Remove the thermosensor from the side of the EGR valve.

3. Heat the thermosensor in a pan of water to the following temperature: 260°F.
4. Connect an ohmmeter, in series with a 10 ohms resistor, between the thermosensor terminal and case.
5. With the ohmmeter the following reading should be obtained: 2.55 kilo ohms.
6. Replace the thermosensor if the ohmmeter readings vary considerably from those specified.
7. To install the thermosensor on the EGR valve, tighten it to 15-21 ft. lbs. (20-28 Nm)

➡**Do not tighten the thermosensor with an impact wrench.**

CHECKING THE EGR VACUUM MODULATOR

▶ **See Figure 19**

1. Tag and disconnect all hoses leading from the vacuum modulator.
2. Remove the vacuum modulator.
3. Unscrew the vented top plate and remove the filter.
4. Check the filter for any contamination or other damage.
5. Clean the filter using compressed air.
6. Installation is in the reverse order of removal.

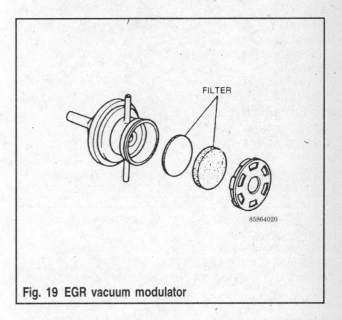

Fig. 19 EGR vacuum modulator

SYSTEM CHECK

If, after having completed the above tests, the EGR system still doesn't work right and everything else checks out OK, the fault may probably lie in the computer. If this is the case, it is best to have the car checked out by a test facility which has the necessary Toyota emission system test equipment.

REMOVAL & INSTALLATION

▶ **See Figures 20, 21, 22 and 23**

Exhaust emission control equipment is generally simple to work on and easy to get to on the engine. The air cleaner assembly will need to be removed. Always label each vacuum hose before removing it — they must be replaced in the correct position.

Most of the valves and solenoids are made of plastic, particularly at the vacuum ports. Be very careful during removal not to break or crack the ports; you have **NO** chance of regluing a broken fitting. Remember that the plastic has been in a hostile environment (heat and vibration); the fittings become brittle and less resistant to abuse or accidental impact.

The EGR valve is held in place by mounting bolts. The bolts can be difficult to remove due to corrosion. Remove the air cleaner assembly and all necessary components for access to the EGR valve mounting bolts. Once the EGR is off the engine, clean the bolts and the bolt holes of any rust or debris. Always replace the gasket any time the EGR valve is removed.

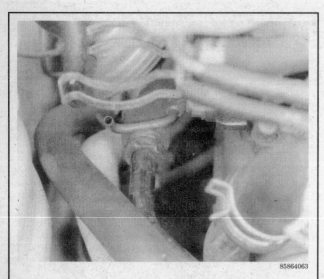

Fig. 20 Removing vacuum line from the EGR valve

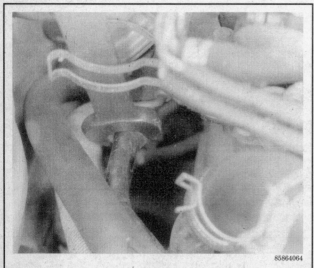

Fig. 21 Removing the tube from the EGR valve

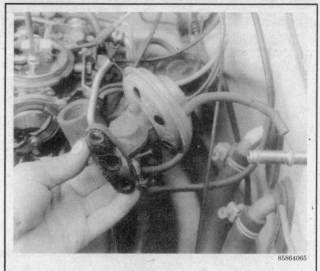

Fig. 22 Removing the EGR valve

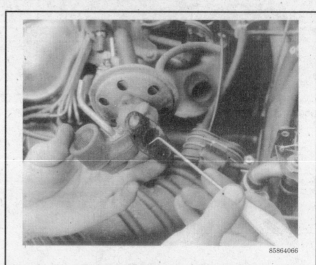

Fig. 23 Cleaning the EGR valve — always replace the gasket

Air Injection System

▶ See Figures 24 and 25

A belt driven air pump supplies air to an injection manifold which has nozzles in each exhaust port. Injection of air at this point causes combustion of unburned hydrocarbons in the exhaust manifold rather than allowing them to escape into the atmosphere. An anti-backfire valve controls the flow of air from the pump to prevent backfiring which results from an overly. rich mixture under closed throttle conditions. There are two types of anti-backfire valve used on Toyota models: 1970-71 models use gulp valves; Later models use air by-pass valves.

A check valve prevents hot exhaust gas backflow into the pump and hoses, in case of a pump failure, or when the anti-backfire valve is not working. In addition late model engines have an air switching valve (ASV). On engines without catalytic converters, the ASV is used to stop air injection under a constant heavy engine load condition.

On engines with catalytic converters, the ASV is also used to protect the catalyst from overheating, by blocking the in-jected air necessary for the operation of the converter. On late model engines, the pump relief valve is built into the ASV.

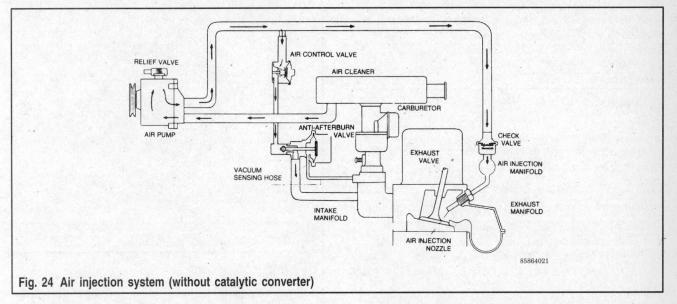

Fig. 24 Air injection system (without catalytic converter)

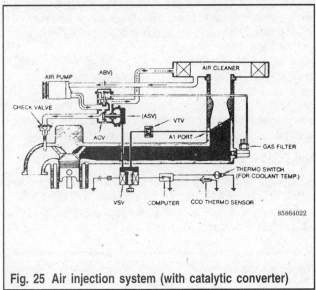

Fig. 25 Air injection system (with catalytic converter)

REMOVAL & INSTALLATION

Air Pump

1. Disconnect air hoses from the pump.
2. Loosen the bolt on the adjusting link and remove the drive belt.
3. Remove the mounting bolts and withdraw the pump.

➡**Do not pry on the pump housing; it may be distorted.**

4. Installation is in the reverse order of removal. Adjust the drive belt tension after installation. Belt deflection should be ½-¾ inch with 22 lbs. pressure.

Anti-backfire Valve and Air Switching Valve

1. Detach the air hoses from the valve, and electrical leads.
2. Remove the valve securing bolt.

3. Withdraw the valve. Installation is performed in the re-verse order of removal.

Check Valve

1. Detach the intake hose from the valve.
2. Use an open-end wrench to remove the valve from its mounting. Installation is the reverse of removal.

Relief Valve

1. Remove the air pump from the vehicle.
2. Support the pump so that it cannot rotate.

➡**Never clamp the pump in a vise; the aluminum case will be distorted.**

3. Use a bridge to remove the relief valve from the top of the pump.
4. Position the new relief valve over the opening in the pump.

➡**The air outlet should be pointing toward the left.**

5. Gently tap the relief valve home, using a block of wood and a hammer.
6. Install the pump on the engine, as outlined above.

➡**For 1975-77 models with ASV-mounted relief valves, re-place the entire ASV/relief valve as an assembly.**

Air Injection Manifold

1. Remove the check valve, as previously outlined.
2. Loosen the air injection manifold attachment nuts and withdraw the manifold. Installation is in the reverse order of removal.

Air Injection Nozzles

1. Remove the air injection manifold as previously outlined.
2. Remove the cylinder head, as detailed in Section 3.
3. Place a new nozzle on the cylinder head.
4. Install the air injection manifold over it.

5. Install the cylinder head on the engine block.

Air Control Valve

The air control valve is used only on the 3K-C engine. It is removed by simply unfastening the hoses from it.

TESTING

▶ See Figure 26

Air Pump

➡Do not hammer, pry, or bend the pump housing while tightening the drive belt or testing the pump.

BELT TENSION AND AIR LEAKS

1. Before proceeding with the tests, check the pump drive belt tension to ensure that it is within specifications.
2. Turn the pump by hand. If it has seized, the belt will slip, making a noise. Disregard any chirping, squealing, or rolling sounds from inside the pump; these are normal when it is turned by hand.
3. Check the hoses and connections for leaks. Hissing or a blast of air is indicative of a leak. Soapy water, applied lightly around the area in question, is a good method for detecting leaks.

AIR OUTPUT

▶ See Figure 27

1. Disconnect the air supply hose at the anti-backfire valve.
2. Connect a vacuum gauge, using a suitable adaptor, to the air supply hose.

➡If there are two hoses, plug the second one.

3. With the engine at normal operating temperature, increase the idle speed and watch the vacuum gauge.
4. The airflow from the pump should be steady and fall between 2-6 psi. If it is unsteady or falls below this, the pump is defective and must be replaced.

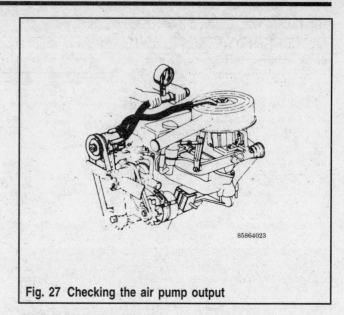

85864023

Fig. 27 Checking the air pump output

PUMP NOISE DIAGNOSIS

The air pump is normally noisy; as engine speed increases, the noise of the pump will rise in pitch. The rolling sound the pump bearings make is normal. But if this sound becomes objectionable at certain speeds, the pump may be defective and will have to be replaced.

A continual hissing sound from the air pump pressure relief valve at idle, indicates a defective valve. Replace the relief valve.

If the pump rear bearing fails, a continual knocking sound will be heard. Since the rear bearing is not separately replaceable, the pump will have to be replaced as an assembly.

Anti-backfire Valve Tests

There are two different types of anti-backfire valve used with air injection systems. A bypass valve is used on 1972 and later engines, while 1970-71 engines use a gulp type of anti-backfire valve. Test procedures for both types are given below.

Air Injection System Diagnosis Chart

Problem	Cause	Cure
1. Noisy drive belt	1a Loose belt 1b Seized pump	1a Tighten belt 1b Replace
2. Noisy pump	2a Leaking hose 2b Loose hose 2c Hose contacting other parts 2d diverter or check valve failure 2e Pump mounting loose 2f Defective pump	2a Trace and fix leak 2b Tighten hose clamp 2c Reposition hose 2d Replace 2e Tighten securing bolts 2f Replace
3. No air supply	3a Loose belt 3b Leak in hose or at fitting 3c Defective antibackfire valve 3d Defective check valve 3e Defective pump 3f Defective ASV	3a Tighten belt 3b Trace and fix leak 3c Replace 3d Replace 3e Replace 3f Replace
4. Exhaust backfire	4a Vacuum or air leaks 4b Defective antibackfire valve 4c Sticking choke 4d Choke setting rich	4a Trace and fix leak 4b Replace 4c Service choke 4d Adjust choke

85864026

Fig. 26 Checking the air injection system

GULP VALVE

1. Detach the air supply hose which runs between the pump and the gulp valve.

2. Connect a tachometer and run the engine to 1,500-2,000 rpm.

3. Allow the throttle to snap shut. This should produce a loud sucking sound from the gulp valve.

4. Repeat this operation several times. If no sound is present, the valve is not working or else the vacuum connections are loose.

5. Check the vacuum connections. If they are secure, replace the gulp valve.

BY-PASS VALVE

1. Detach the hose, which runs from the by-pass valve to the check valve, at the by-pass valve hose connection.

2. Connect a tachometer to the engine. With the engine running at normal idle speed, check to see that air is flowing from the by-pass valve hose connection.

3. Speed up the engine so that it is running at 1,5000-2,000 rpm. Allow the throttle to snap shut. The flow of air from the by-pass valve at the check valve hose connection should stop momentarily and air should then flow from the exhaust port on the valve body or the silencer assembly.

4. Repeat Step 3 several times. If the flow of air is not diverted into the atmosphere from the valve exhaust port or if it fails to stop flowing from the hose connection, check the vacuum lines and connections. If these are tight, the valve is defective and requires replacement.

5. A leaking diaphragm will cause the air to flow out both the hose connection and the exhaust port at the same time. If this happens, replace the valve.

Check Valve Test — 1974-78

1. Before starting the test, check all of the hoses and connections for leaks.

2. Detach the air supply hose from the check valve.

3. Insert a suitable probe into the check valve and depress the plate. Release it; the plate should return to its original position against the valve seat. If binding is evident, replace the valve.

4. With the engine running at normal operating temperature, gradually increase its speed to 1,500 rpm. Check for exhaust gas leakage. If any is present, replace the valve assembly.

➡**Vibration and flutter of the check valve at idle speed is a normal condition and does not mean that the valve should be replaced.**

Check Valve Test — 1979-82

▶ **See Figure 28**

1. Remove the check valve from the air injection manifold.

2. Blow into the manifold side (large side) and check that the valve is closed.

3. Blow into the ASV side (small side) and check that the valve is open.

4. If the valve is not operating properly it will probably require treatment.

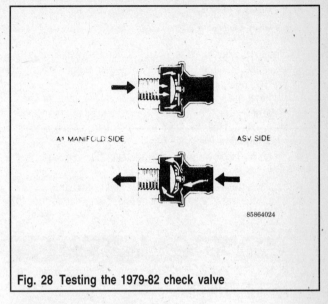

A' MANIFOLD SIDE   ASV SIDE

85864024

Fig. 28 Testing the 1979-82 check valve

Air Switching Valve (ASV) Tests

1975-81 2T-C ENGINE

▶ **See Figure 29**

1. Start the engine and allow it to reach normal operating temperature and speed.

2. At curb idle, the air from the by-pass valve should be discharged through the hose which runs to the ASV.

3. When the vacuum line to the ASV is disconnected, the air from the by-pass valve should be diverted out through the ASV-to-air cleaner hose. Reconnect the vacuum line.

4. Disconnect the ASV-to-check valve hose and connect a pressure gauge to it.

5. Increase the engine speed. The relief valve should open when the pressure gauge registers 2.7-6.5 psi.

6. If the ASV fails any of the above tests, replace it. Reconnect all hoses.

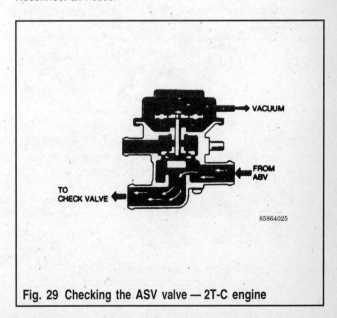

VACUUM

FROM ABV

TO CHECK VALVE

85864025

Fig. 29 Checking the ASV valve — 2T-C engine

Vacuum Delay Valve Test

1975-81 2T-C ENGINES

The vacuum delay valve is located in the line which runs from the intake manifold to either the vacuum surge tank or to the ASV. To check it, proceed as follows:

1. Remove the vacuum delay valve from the vacuum line. Be sure to note which end points toward the intake manifold.

2. When air is blown in from the ASV (surge tank) side, it should pass through the valve freely.

3. When air is blown in from the intake manifold side, a resistance should be felt.

4. Replace the valve if it fails either of the above tests.

5. Install the valve in the vacuum line, being careful not to install it backward.

Air Suction (AS) System

INSPECTING THE AS SYSTEM

▶ See Figures 30, 31 and 32

1. Visually check all hoses and tubes for cracks, kinks, loose connections or other damage.

2. Check the AS valve:

   a. On all Federal models, start the engine and check that air is being drawn into the inlet pipe while idling.

   b. On California models, disconnect and plug the vacuum hose from the AS valve. Remove the air cleaner cover and start the engine. Reconnect the vacuum hose and check that a bubbling noise is heard from the AS valve inlet within 6 seconds.

   c. On all Canadian models, remove the air cleaner cover and with the engine idling, check that a bubbling noise is heard from the AS valve inlet.

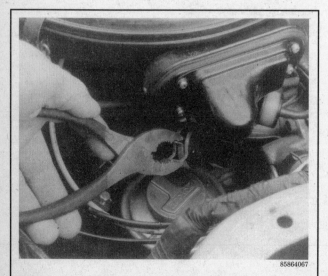

Fig. 30 Removing the hose from the AS valve

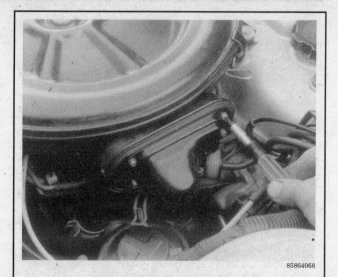

Fig. 31 Removing the AS valve retaining screws

Fig. 32 Removing the AS valve from the air cleaner

INSPECTION OF THE AS VALVE

Federal and Canada

▶ See Figure 33

1. Remove the valve from the air cleaner on Canadian models.

2. Disconnect the valve from the AS filter on Federal models.

3. Blow into the valve. There should be no passage of air through the valve.

4. Suck out of the valve. There should be passage of air.

5. Reinstall the valve.

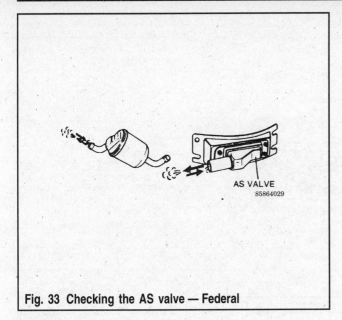

Fig. 33 Checking the AS valve — Federal

California

▶ See Figure 34

1. Remove the AS filter and valve from the air cleaner. Clean the filter.

2. Apply vacuum to the diaphragm and check that air flows from the filter side but not from the outlet pipe side.

3. Release the vacuum and check that hardly any air flows from the filter side to the outlet pipe side.

4. Reinstall the AS valve and filter.

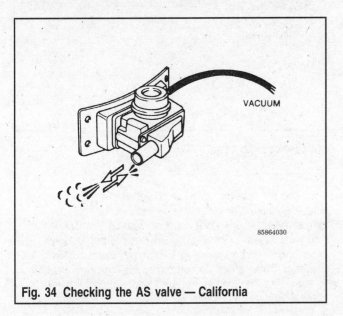

Fig. 34 Checking the AS valve — California

Catalytic Converter

▶ See Figures 35 and 36

The catalytic converter is a muffler-like container built into the exhaust system to aid in the reduction of exhaust emissions. The catalytic element consists of individual pellets coated with a noble metal such as platinum, palladium, rhodium or a combination. When the exhaust gases come into contact with the catalyst, a chemical reaction occurs which will reduce the pollutants into harmless substances like water and carbon dioxide.

There are essentially two types of catalytic converters: an oxidizing type and a three-way type. The oxidizing catalytic converter is used on most late model vehicles. It requires the addition of oxygen to spur the catalyst into reducing the engine's HC and CO emissions into H_2O and CO_2.

An air injection system is used to supply air to the exhaust system to aid in the reaction. A thermosensor, inserted into the converter, shuts off the air supply if the temperature of the catalyst becomes excessive.

The same sensor circuit will also cause an instrument panel warning light labeled **EXH TEMP** to come on when the catalyst temperature gets too high.

➡ **It is normal for the light to come on temporarily if the car is being driven downhill for long periods of time (such as descending a mountain).**

The light will come on and stay on if the air injection system is malfunctioning or if the engine is misfiring.

The oxidizing catalytic converter, while effectively reducing HC and CO emissions, does little, if anything, in the way of reducing NOx emissions. Thus, the three-way catalytic converter.

The three-way converter, unlike the oxidizing type, is capable of reducing HC, CO and NOx emissions; all at the same time. In theory, it seems impossible to reduce all three pollutants in one system since the reduction of HC and CO requires the addition of oxygen, while the reduction of NOx calls for the removal of oxygen. In actuality, the three-way system really can reduce all three pollutants, but only if the amount of oxygen in the exhaust system is precisely controlled. Due to this precise oxygen control requirement, the three-way converter system is used only in cars equipped with an oxygen sensing system.

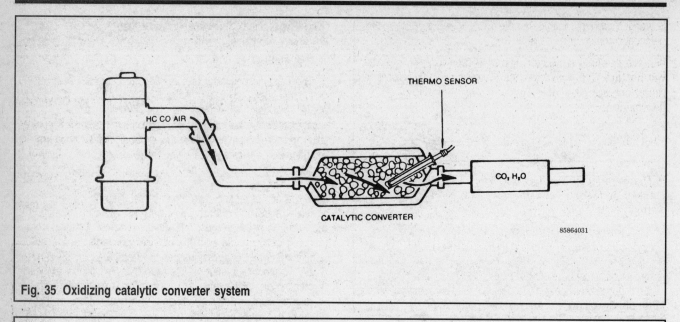

THERMO SENSOR

HC CO AIR

CO, H_2O

CATALYTIC CONVERTER

85864031

Fig. 35 Oxidizing catalytic converter system

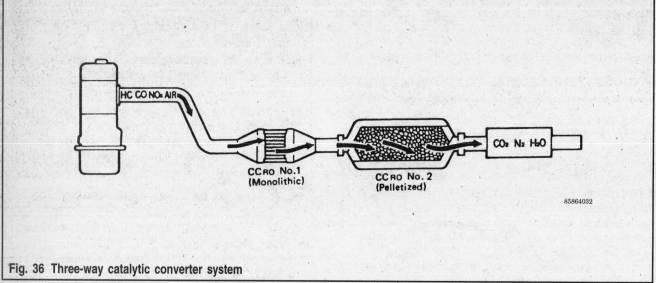

HC CO NOx AIR

CC ro No.1
(Monolithic)

CC ro No. 2
(Pelletized)

CO_2 N_2 H_2O

85864032

Fig. 36 Three-way catalytic converter system

PRECAUTIONS

1. Use only unleaded fuel.
2. Avoid prolonged idling; the engine should run no longer than 20 minutes at curb idle, nor longer than 10 minutes at fast idle.
3. Reduce the fast idle speed, by quickly depressing and releasing the accelerator pedal, as soon as the coolant temperature reaches 120°F.
4. Do not disconnect any spark plug leads while the engine is running.
5. Make engine compression checks as quickly as possible.
6. Do not dispose of the catalyst in a place where anything coated with grease, gas or oil is present; spontaneous combustion could result.

CATALYST TESTING

Testing the catalytic converter operation in the field is a difficult problem. The most reliable test is a 12 hour and 40 min. soak test (CVS) which must be done in a laboratory.

In most cases an infrared HC/CO tester is not sensitive enough to measure the higher tailpipe emissions from a failing converter. Thus, a bad converter may allow enough emissions to escape so that the vehicle is no longer in compliance with Federal or state stands, but will still not cause the needle on a tester to move off zero.

The chemical reactions which occur inside a catalytic converter generate a great deal of heat. Most converter problems can be traced to fuel or ignition system problems which cause unusually high emissions. As a result of the increased intensity of the chemical reactions, the converter literally burns itself up.

As long as you avoid severe overheating and the use of leaded fuels it is reasonably safe to assume that the converter is working properly. If you are in doubt, take the vehicle to a diagnostic center that has a tester.

➡️**If the catalytic converter becomes blocked the engine will not run. The converter has 5 year or 50,000 mile warranty; contact your local Toyota dealer for more information.**

WARNING LIGHT CHECKS

➡️**The warning light comes on while the engine is being cranked, to test its operation, just like any of the other warning light.**

1. If the warning light comes on and stays on, check the components of the air injection system as previously outlined. If these are not defective, check the ignition system for faulty leads, plugs, points, or control box.

2. If no problems can be found in Step 1, check the wiring for the light for shorts or opened circuits.

3. If nothing else can be found wrong in Steps 1 and 2, check the operation of the emission control system vacuum switching valve or computer, either by substitution of new unit, or by taking it to a service facility which has Toyota's special emission control system checker.

Oxygen Sensor System

The three way catalytic converter, which is capable of reducing HC, CO and NOx into CO_2, H_2O, O_2 and N_2, can only function as long as the fuel/air mixture is kept within a critically precise range. The oxygen sensor system is what keeps the oxygen range in control.

Basically, the oxygen sensor system works like this: As soon as the engine warms up, the computer begins to work. The oxygen sensor, located in the exhaust manifold, senses the oxygen content of the exhaust gases. The amount of oxygen in the exhaust varies according to the fuel/air mixture. The O_2 sensor produces a small voltage that varies depending on the amount of oxygen in the exhaust at the time. This voltage is picked up by the computer. The computer works together with the fuel distributor and together and together they will vary the amount of fuel which is delivered to the engine at any given time.

If the amount of oxygen in the exhaust system is low, which indicates a rich mixture, the sensor voltage will be high. The higher the voltage signal sent to the computer, the more it will reduce the amount of fuel supplied to the engine. The amount of fuel is reduced until the amount of oxygen in the exhaust system increases, indicating a lean mixture. When the mixture is lean, the sensor will send a low voltage signal to the computer. The computer will then increase the quantity of fuel until the sensor voltage increases again and then the cycle will start all over.

OXYGEN SENSOR REPLACEMENT

▶ **See Figure 37**

1. Disconnect the negative battery cable.
2. Unplug the wiring connector leading from the O_2 sensor.

➡️**Be careful not to bend the waterproof hose as the oxygen sensor will not function properly if the air passage is blocked.**

3. Unscrew the two nuts and carefully pull out the sensor.
4. Installation is in the reverse order of removal. Please note the following: Always use a new gasket; Tighten the nuts to 13-16 ft. lbs. (17-21 Nm)

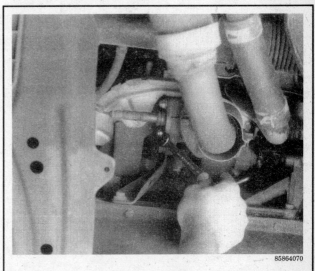
85864070

Fig. 37 Removing the oxygen sensor retaining bolts

OXYGEN SENSOR WARNING LIGHT

Many models are equipped with an oxygen sensor warning light on the instrument panel. The light may go on when the car is started, then it should go out. If the light stays on, check your odometer. The light is hooked up to an elapsed mileage counter which goes off every 30,000 miles. This is your signal that it is time to replace the oxygen sensor and have the entire system checked out. After replacement of the sensor, the elapsed mileage counter must be reset. To rest:

1. Locate the counter. If can be found under the left side of the instrument panel, on the brake pedal bracket.
2. Unscrew the mounting bolt, disconnect the wiring connector and remove the counter.
3. Remove the bolt on top of the counter.
4. Lift off the counter cover and push the reset switch.

➡️**The warning light on the instrument panel must go out at this time.**

5. Installation is in the reverse order of removal.

ELECTRONIC ENGINE CONTROLS

Check Engine Light and Diagnostic Codes

◗ See Figures 38, 39, 40 and 41

GENERAL INFORMATION

4A-GE Engine

The Check Engine light is the device which provides communication between the Electronic Control Module (ECM) and the driver. The ECM controls the electronic fuel injection, the electronic spark control, the diagnostic function and the fail-safe or default function. The module receives signals from various sensors indicating the constantly changing engine operat-

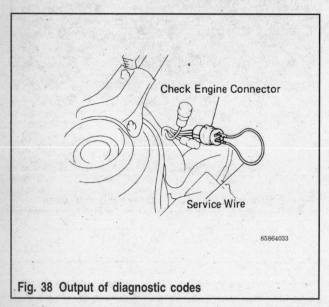

Fig. 38 Output of diagnostic codes

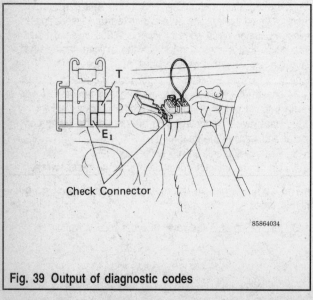

Fig. 39 Output of diagnostic codes

ing conditions. These signals are utilized by the ECM to determine the injection duration (amount of time each injector stays open) in order to maintain the optimum air/fuel ratio under all conditions. Conditions which affect the injector duration are:

- Exhaust gas oxygen content
- Intake air mass
- Intake air temperature
- Coolant temperature
- Engine rpm
- Acceleration/deceleration
- Electrical load
- Air conditioning on/off

The ECM is programmed with data for optimum ignition timing under any and all operating conditions. Using data provided by the sensors, the ECM triggers the spark within each cylinder at precisely the right instant for the existing conditions.

The ECM also performs self-diagnostics in order to detect any malfunctions or abnormalities in the sensor network. When this occurs the module will illuminate the Check Engine light on the dash panel. At the same time the trouble is identified by circuit and a diagnostic (or trouble) code is recorded within the ECM. This diagnostic code can be read by counting the number of blinks of the instrument light when both check engine terminals are shorted under the hood.

In the event of an internal computer malfunction, the ECM is programmed with back-up or default values. This allows the car to run on a fixed set of rules for engine operation. Driveability may suffer since the driving conditions cannot be dealt with by the faulty computer. This back-up programming allows the computer to fail with out stranding the car, hence the nickname fail-safe. Although no computer is completely protected from failure, a back-up system helps make the best of the situation.

FAULT CODES AND THEIR MEANING

4A-GE Engine

The following procedure may be used in order to read ECM trouble codes.

1. These initial conditions must be met or the code will not be transmitted from the ECM:

    a. Battery voltage above 11 volts

    b. Throttle plate fully closed — keep your foot off the accelerator

    c. Transmission selector in neutral

    d. All accessory switches off

2. Turn the ignition switch **ON**, but DO NOT start the engine.

3. Use a service (jumper) wire to short both terminals of the engine check connector, located under the hood near the wiper motor. Refer to the illustrations.

4. The diagnosis code(s) will be indicated by the number of flashes of the Check Engine light.

If the system is normal, the light will blink repeatedly every $\frac{1}{2}$ second. This indication is displayed when no codes are stored in the ECM. It serves as a confirmation the the ECM has nothing to tell you — all is well.

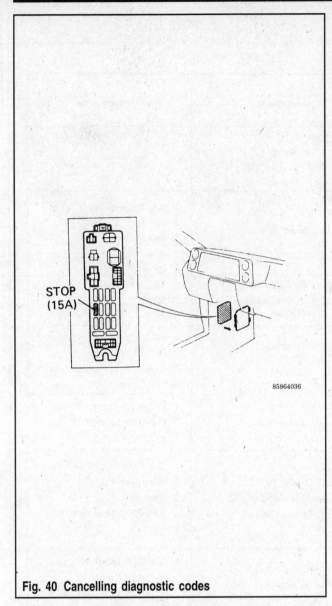

Fig. 40 Cancelling diagnostic codes

STOP
(15A)

85864036

If a fault code is stored, its two digit code will be indicated in the pattern of the flashing. For example, code 21 would be indicated by two flashes, a pause, and one flash. There will be a 1½ second pause between the first and second digit of a code. If more than one code is stored, the next will be transmitted after a 2½ second pause. Once all the codes have been flashed, the system will wait 4½ seconds and repeat the entire series. It will continue sending the fault codes as long as the initial conditions are met and the engine check connector is shorted across terminal **T** and **E1**

➡ **If more than one code is stored, they will be delivered in numerical order from the lowest to the highest, regardless of which code occurred first. The order of the codes DOES NOT indicate the order of occurrence.**

5. After the code(s) have been read and recorded, turn the ignition switch to **OFF** and disconnect the jumper wire.

✳✳WARNING

Disconnecting the wire with the ignition ON may cause severe damage to the ECM.

RESETTING THE CHECK ENGINE LIGHT

Once the codes have been read and recorded, the memory on the ECM may be cleared of any stored codes by removing the power to the ECM for at least 1 minute. This is most easily done by removing the STOP fuse from the fuse box for the necessary period of time.

✳✳WARNING

The ignition MUST be OFF when the fuse is removed and reinstalled. Serious and disabling damage may occur if this precaution is not followed.

Remember that the codes are there to indicate a problem area. Don't clear the code just to get the dashboard light off find the problem and fix it for keeps. If you erase the code and ignore the problem, the code will reset (when the engine is restarted) if the problem is still present.

The necessary time to clear the computer increases as the temperature drops. To be safe, remove the fuse for a full minute under all conditions. The system can also be cleared by disconnecting the negative battery cable, but this will require resetting other memory devices such as the clock and/or radio. If for any reason the memory does not clear, any stored codes will be retained. Any time the ECM is cleared, the car should be driven and then re-checked to confirm a normal signal from the ECM.

➡ **In the event of any mechanical work requiring the disconnection of the negative battery cable, the ECM should be interrogated for stored codes before removing the cable. Once the cable is removed, the codes will be lost almost immediately. Always check for stored codes before beginning any other diagnostic work.**

DIAGNOSTIC CODES

Code No.	Number of blinks "CHECK ENGINE"	System	Diagnosis	Trouble area
1	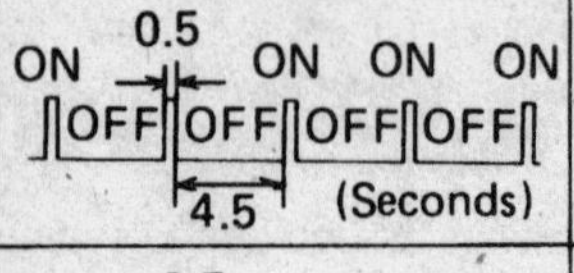 ON 0.5 ON ON ON / OFF OFF OFF OFF / 4.5 (Seconds)	Normal	This appears when none of the other codes (2 thru 11) are identified	–
2	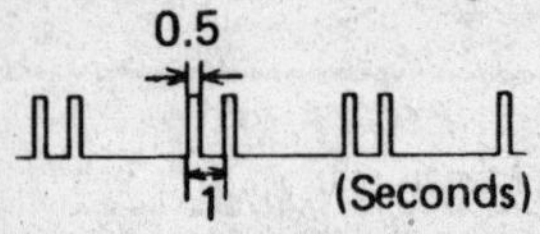 0.5 / 1 (Seconds)	Air flow meter signal	• Open circuit in V_c, V_s, V_B or E_2. • Short circuit in V_c.	1. Air flow meter circuit 2. Air flow meter 3. ECU
3	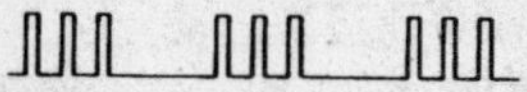	Ignition signal	No signal from igniter four times in succession.	1. Ignition circuit (+B, IGf) 2. Igniter 3. ECU
4		Water temp. sensor signal	Open or short circuit in coolant temperature sensor signal.	1. Coolant Temp. sensor circuit 2. Coolant Temp. sensor 3. ECU
5		Oxygen sensor signal	Open circuit in oxygen sensor signal (only lean indication)	1. Oxgen sensor circuit 2. Oxygen sensor 3. ECU
6		RPM signal	No Ne, G signal to ECU within several seconds after engine is cranked.	1. Distributor circuit 2. Distributor 3. Igniter 4. Starter signal circuit 5. ECU
7	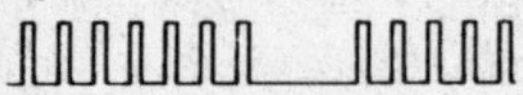	Throttle position sensor signal	Open or short circuit in throttle position sensor signal.	1. Throttle position sensor circuit 2. Throttle position sensor 3. ECU
8	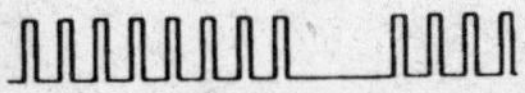	Intake air temp. sensor signal	Open or short circuit in intake air temperature sensor.	1. Air temp. sensor circuit 2. ECU
10	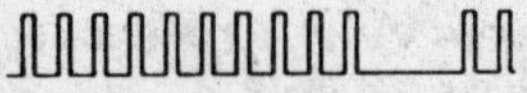	Starter signal	No STA signal to ECU when vehicle is stopped and engine is running over 800 rpm.	1. Starter relay circuit 2. IG switch circuit (starter) 3. IG Switch 4. ECU
11		Switch signal	Air conditioner switch ON or idle switch OFF during diagnosis check.	1. Air con. S/W 2. ECU 3. Idle S/W

NOTE: • There is no diagnosis code No. 9.
• Diagnosis code No. 10 will be indicated if the vehicle is push started.

85864035

Fig. 41 Diagnostic codes — 4A-GE engine

VACUUM DIAGRAMS

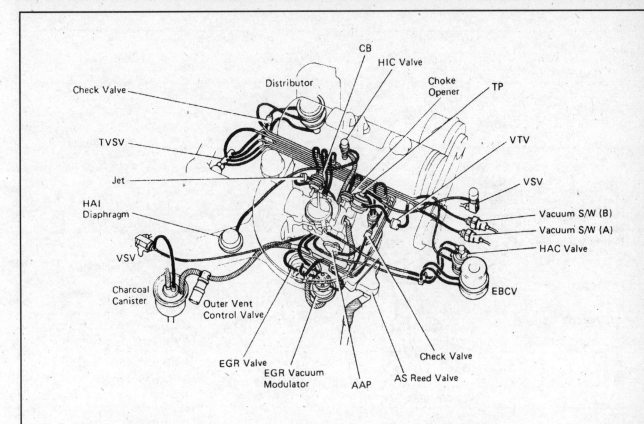

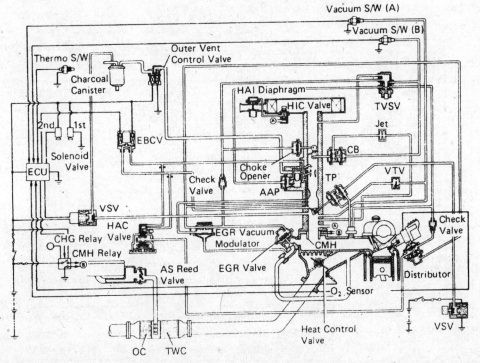

Fig. 42 Component layout and schematic drawing — 1984-85 Corolla (FWD)

85864040

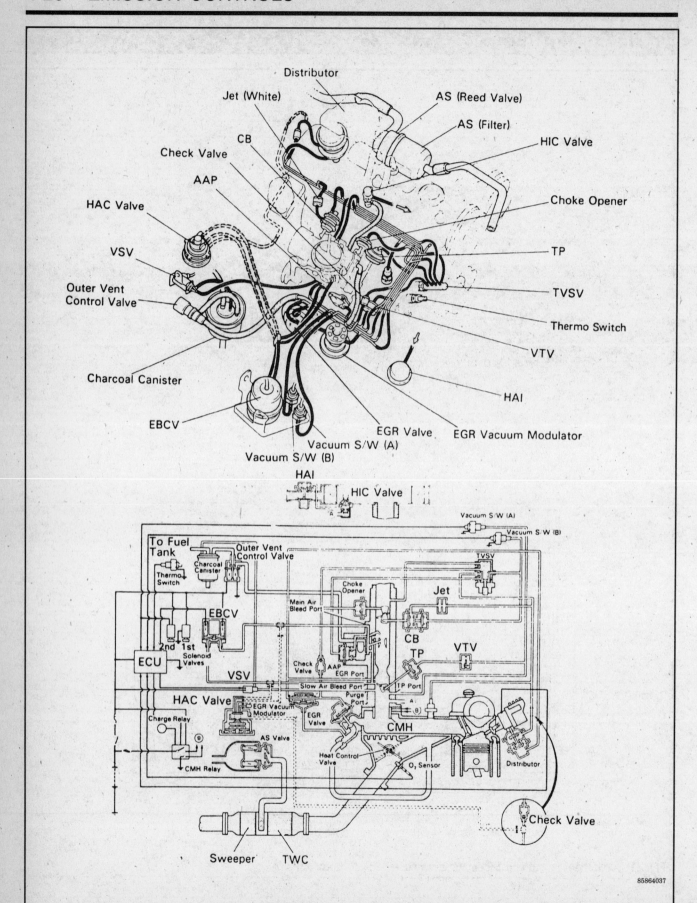

Fig. 43 Component layout and schematic drawing — 1983-84 Corolla (Federal)

85864037

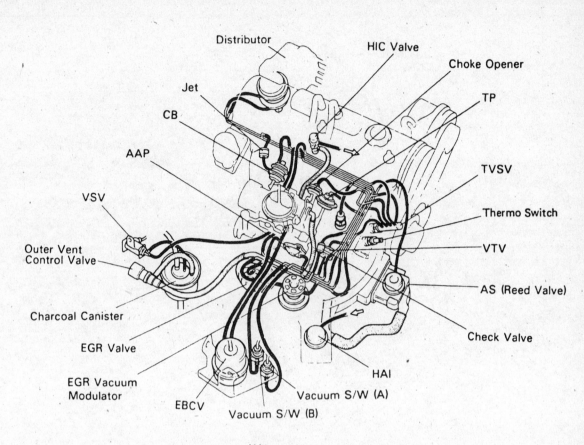

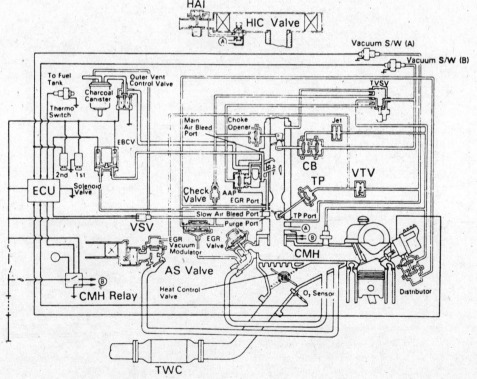

Fig. 44 Component layout and schematic drawing — 1983-84 Corolla (California)

85864038

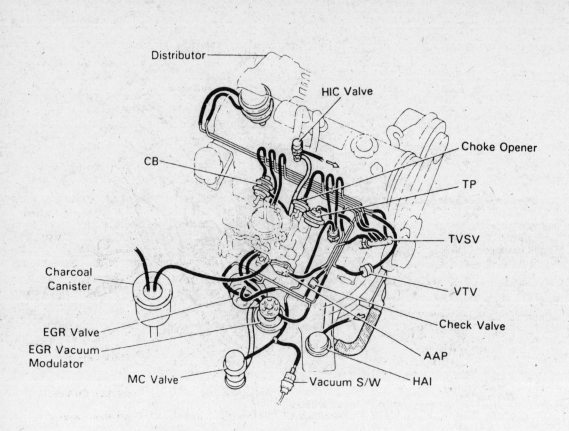

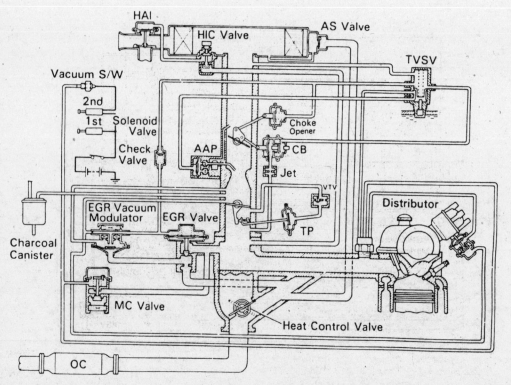

Fig. 45 Component layout and schematic drawing — 1983-84 Corolla (Canada)

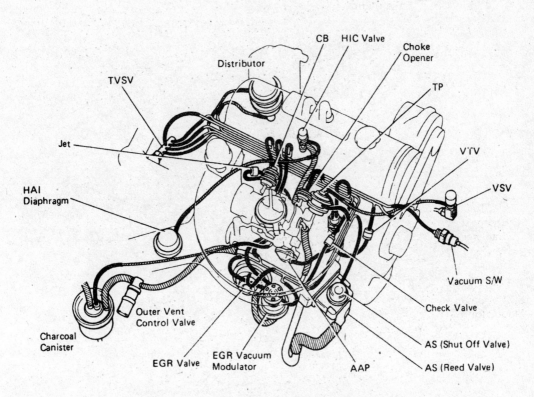

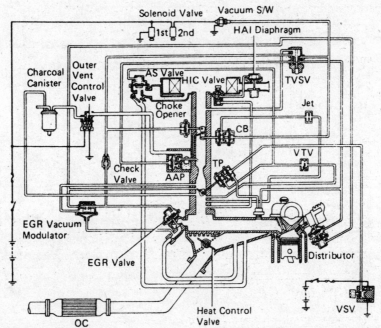

Fig. 46 Component layout and schematic drawing — 1984-85 Corolla (FWD)

85864041

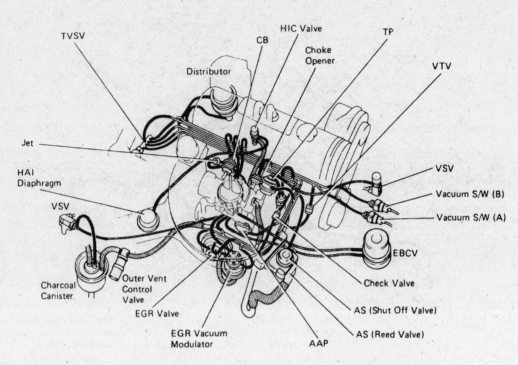

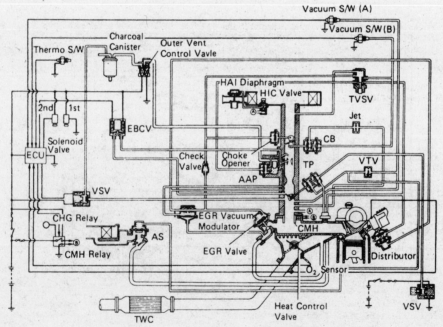

Fig. 47 Component layout and schematic drawing — 1984-85 Corolla (FWD)

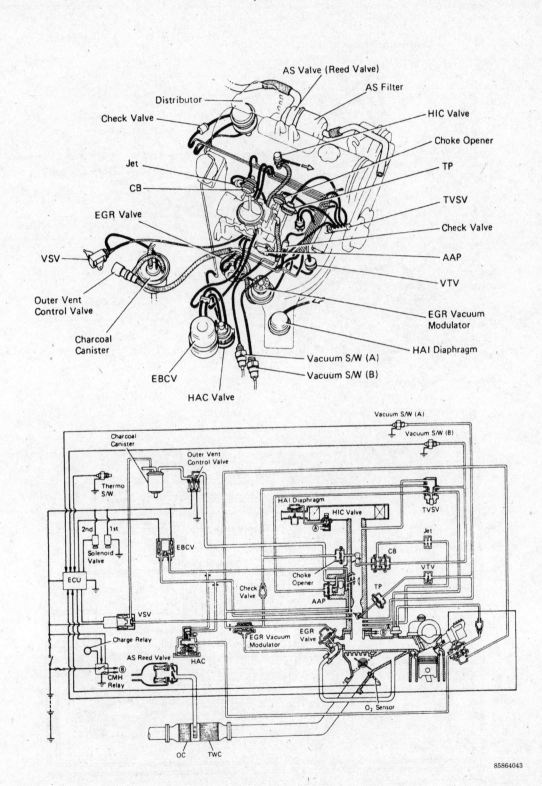

Fig. 48 Component layout and schematic drawing — 1984-85 Corolla (RWD)

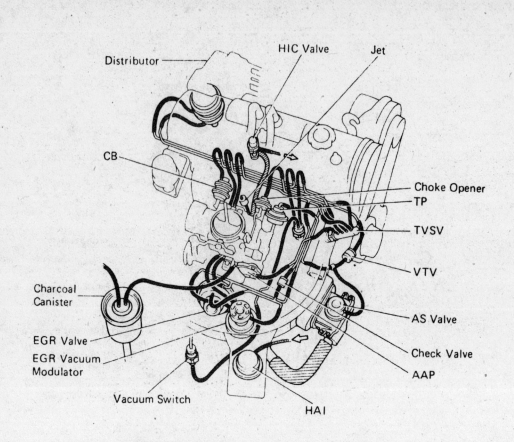

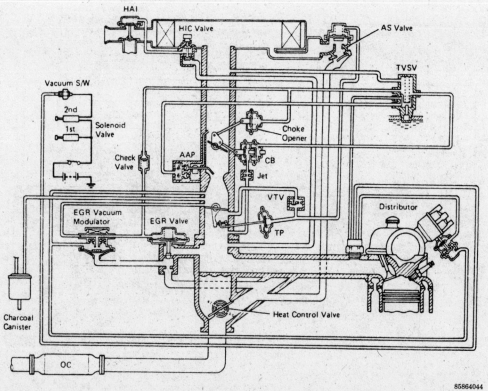

Fig. 49 Component layout and schematic drawing — 1984-85 Corolla (RWD)

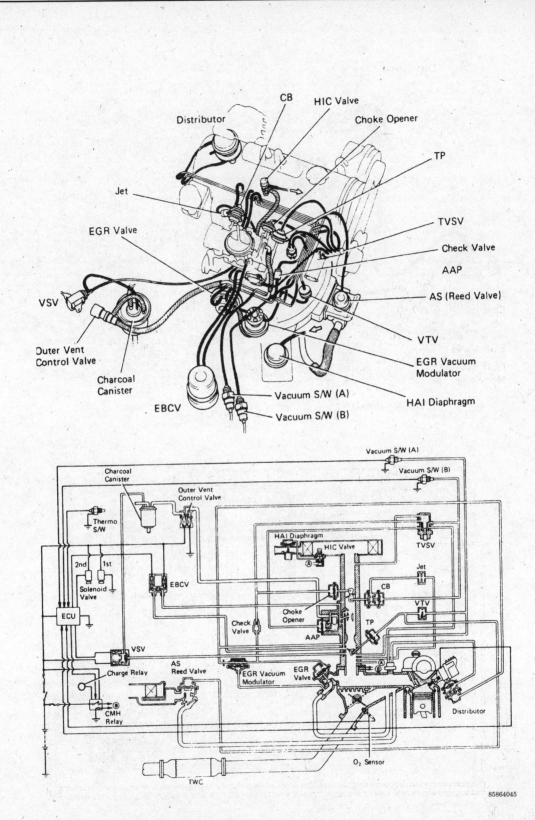

Fig. 50 Component layout and schematic drawing — 1984-85 Corolla (RWD)

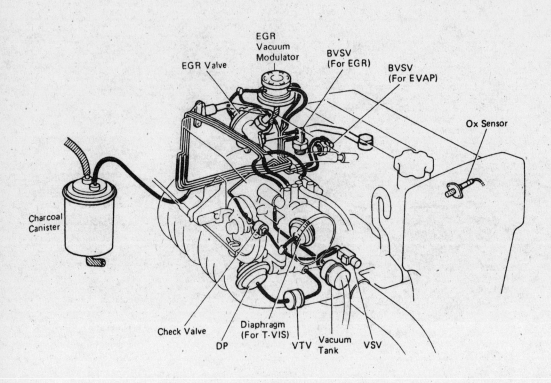

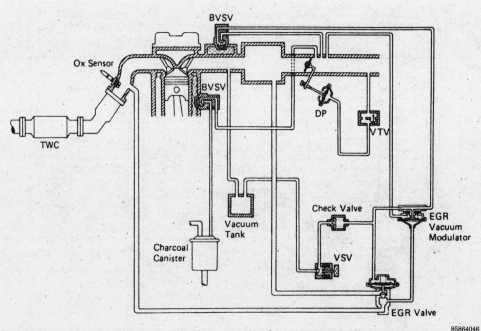

Fig. 51 Component layout and schematic drawing — 1985 Corolla (RWD 4A-GE engine)

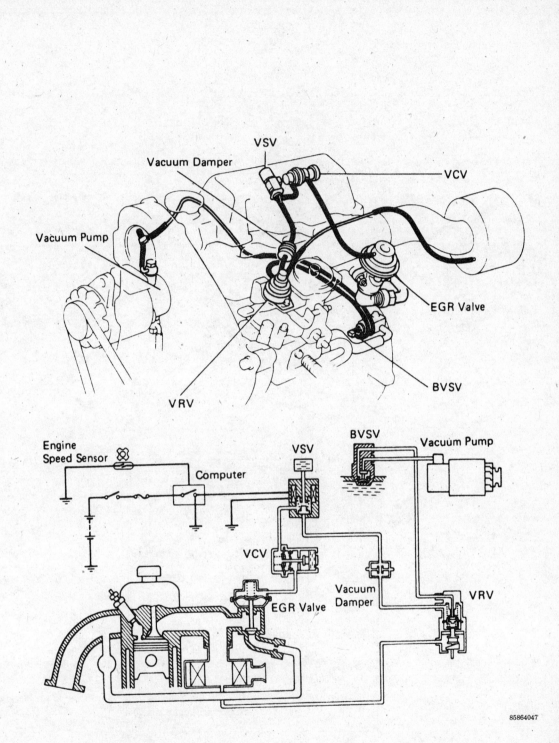

Fig. 52 Component layout and schematic drawing — 1984-85 Corolla (FWD 1C diesel engine)

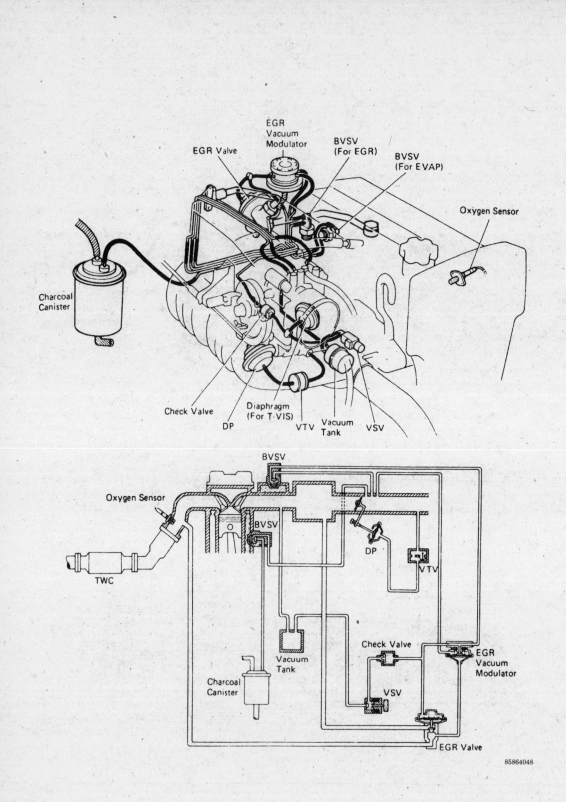

Fig. 53 Component layout and schematic drawing — 1986 Corolla (RWD 4A-GE engine)

85864048

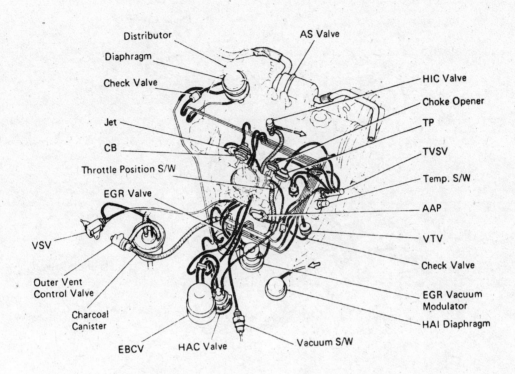

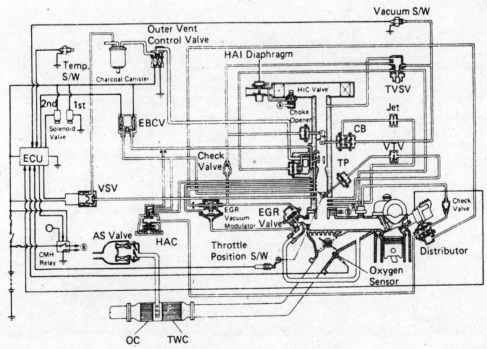

Fig. 54 Component layout and schematic drawing — 1986 Corolla (RWD 4A-C engine)

85864049

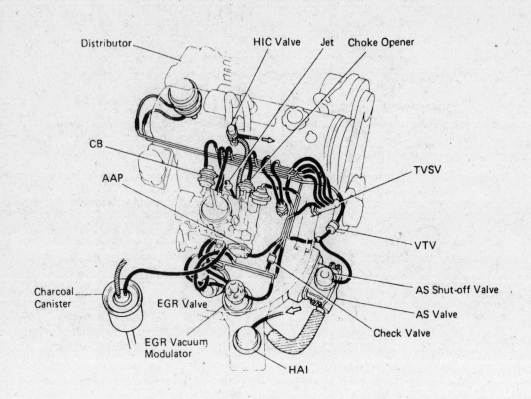

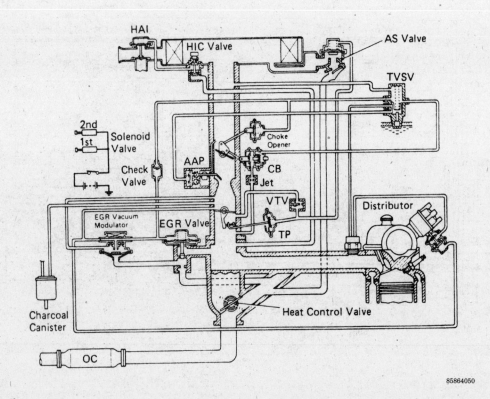

Fig. 55 Component layout and schematic drawing — 1986 Corolla (RWD 4A-C engine)

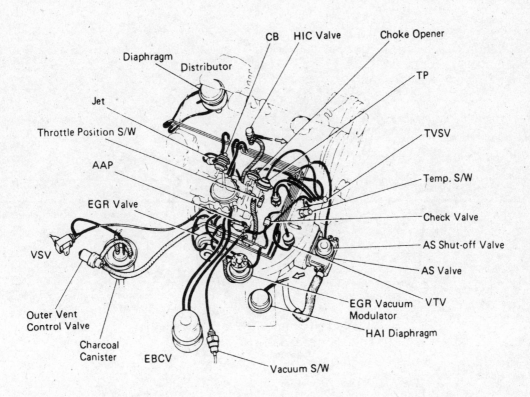

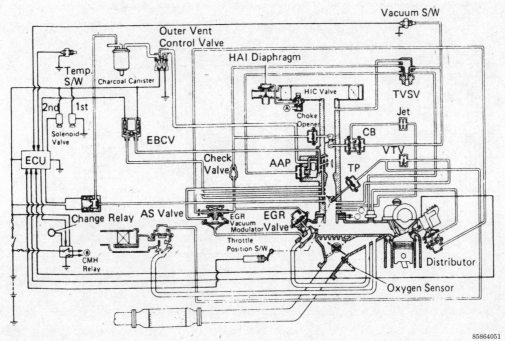

Fig. 56 Component layout and schematic drawing — 1986 Corolla (RWD 4A-C engine)

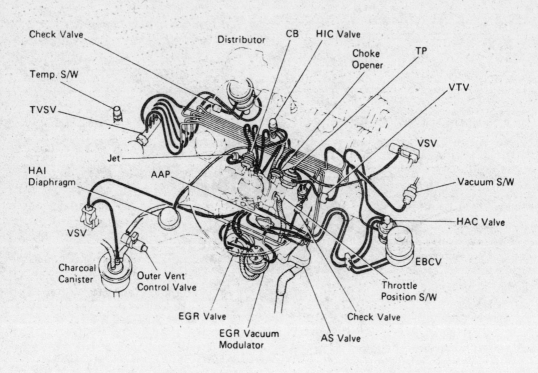

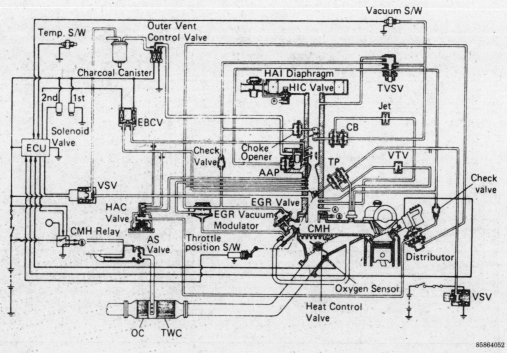

Fig. 57 Component layout and schematic drawing — 1986 Corolla (FWD 4A-C engine)

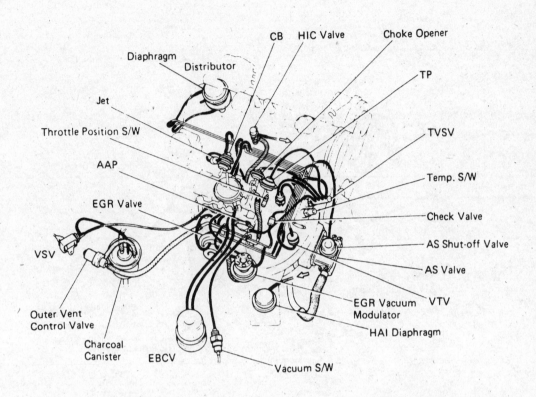

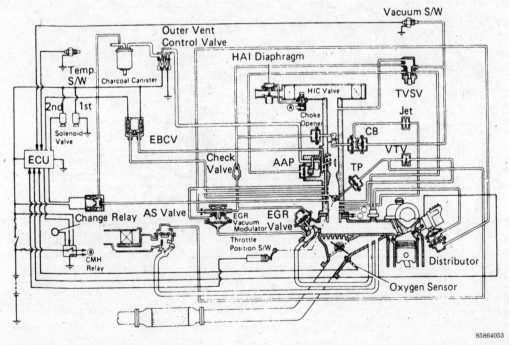

Fig. 58 Component layout and schematic drawing — 1986 Corolla (FWD 4A-GE engine)

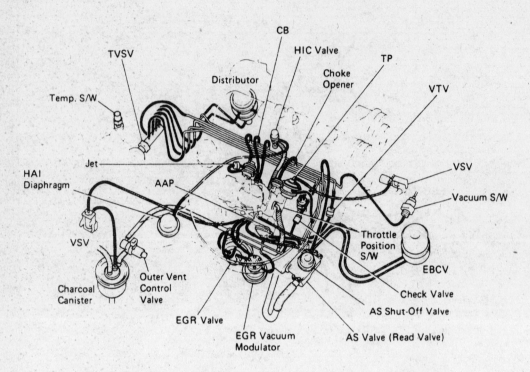

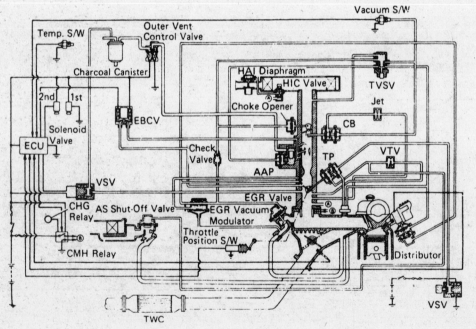

Fig. 59 Component layout and schematic drawing — 1986 Corolla (FWD 4A-GE engine)

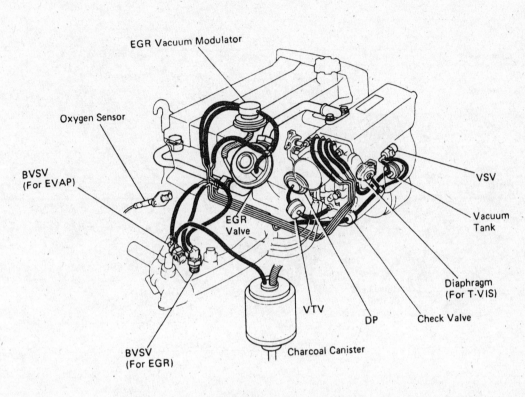

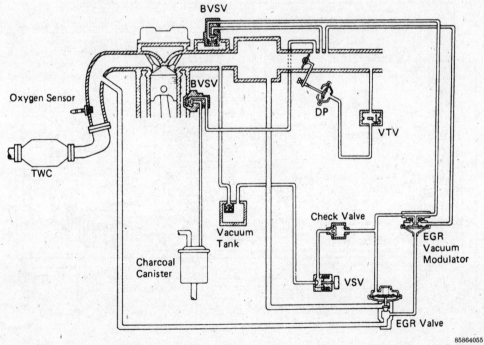

Fig. 60 Component layout and schematic drawing — 1987 Corolla (FWD 4A-GE engine)

85864055

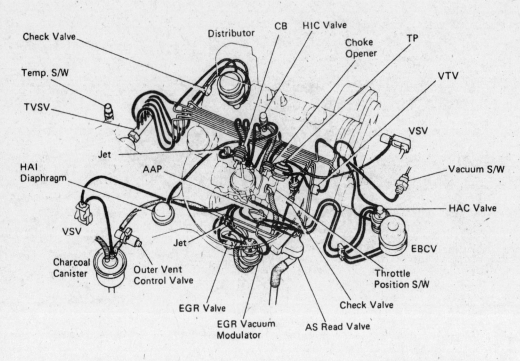

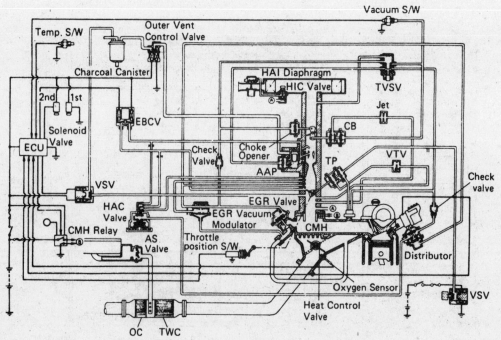

Fig. 61 Component layout and schematic drawing — 1987 Corolla (FWD 4A-C engine)

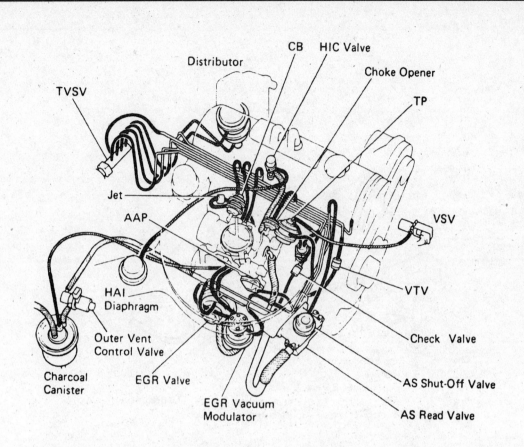

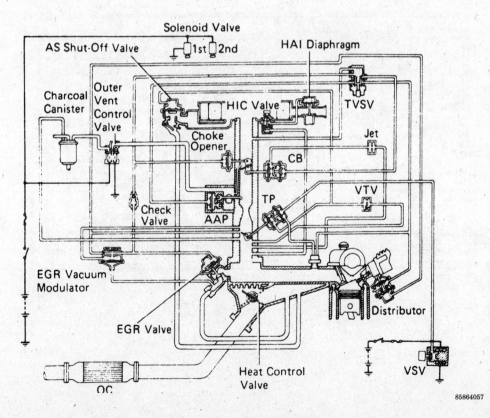

Fig. 62 Component layout and schematic drawing — 1987 Corolla (FWD 4A-C engine)

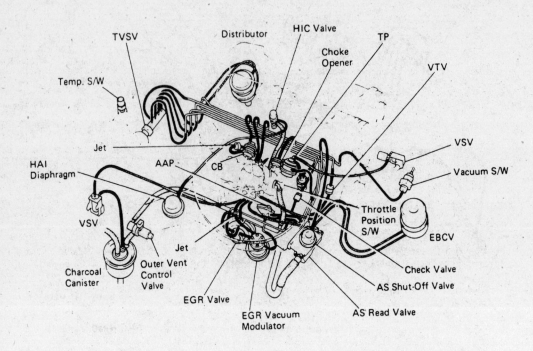

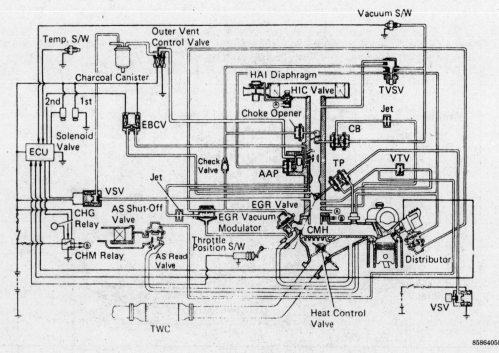

Fig. 63 Component layout and schematic drawing — 1987 Corolla (FWD 4A-C engine)

85864058

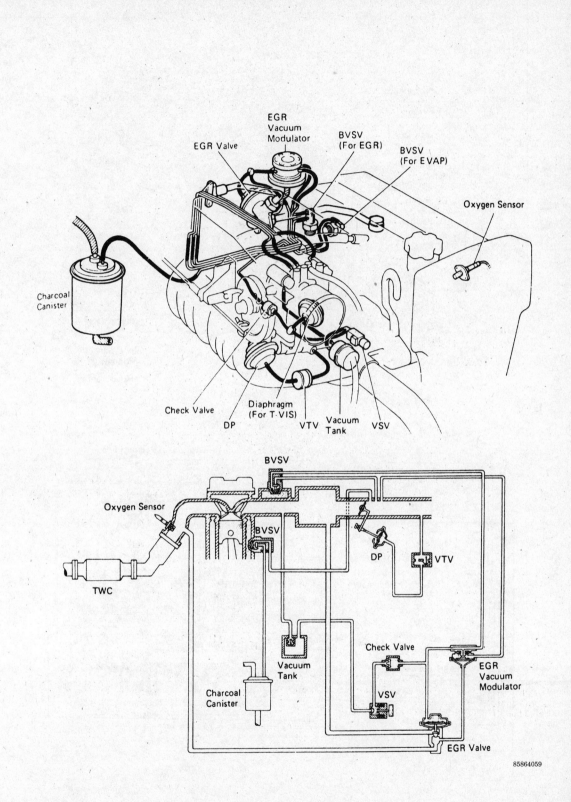

Fig. 64 Component layout and schematic drawing — 1987 Corolla (RWD 4A-GE engine)

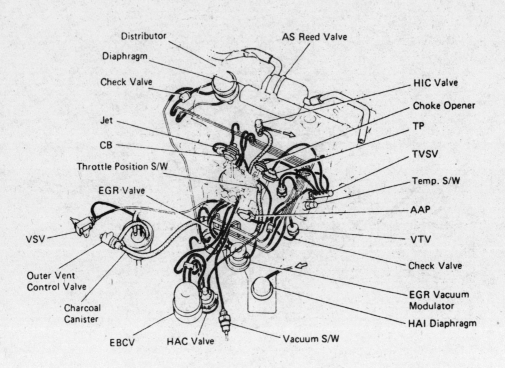

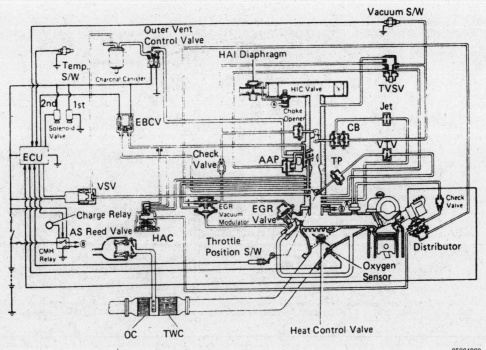

Fig. 65 Component layout and schematic drawing — 1987 Corolla (RWD 4A-C engine)

85864060

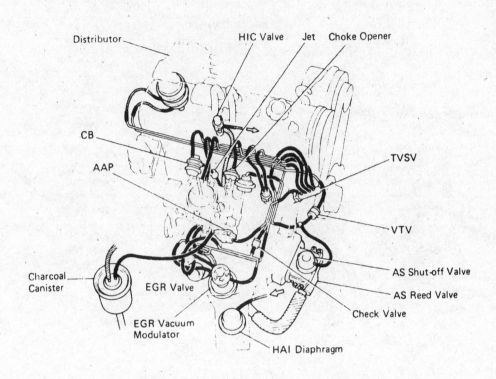

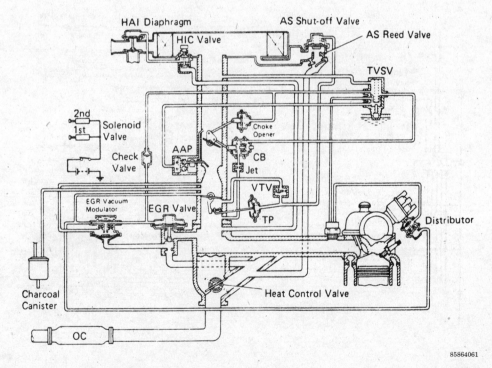

Fig. 66 Component layout and schematic drawing — 1987 Corolla (RWD 4A-C engine)

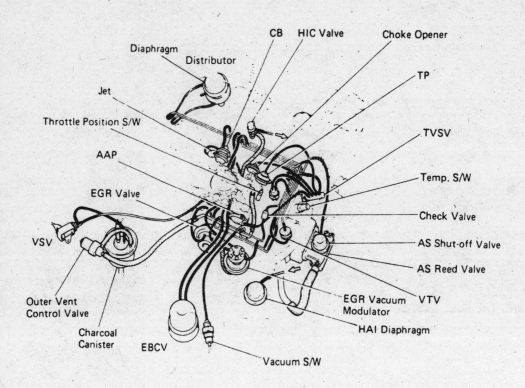

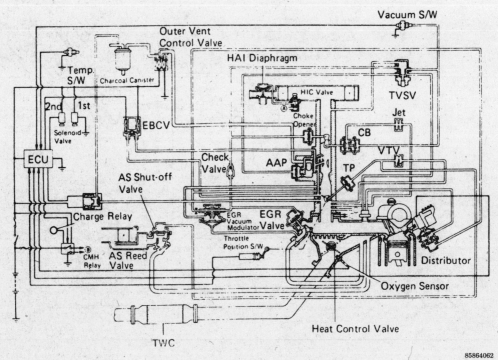

Fig. 67 Component layout and schematic drawing — 1987 Corolla (RWD 4A-GE engine)

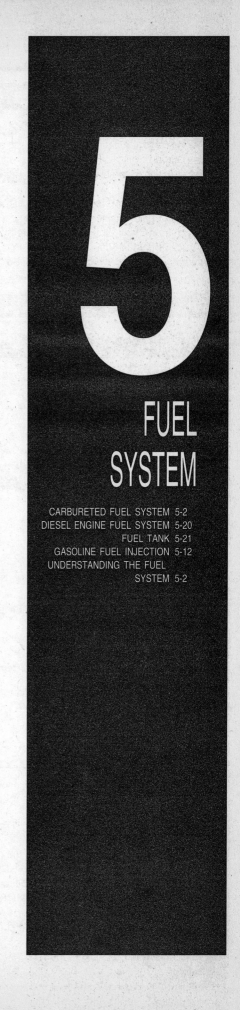

5

FUEL SYSTEM

UNDERSTANDING THE FUEL SYSTEM

An automotive fuel system consists of everything between the fuel tank and the carburetor or fuel injection unit. This includes the tank itself, all the lines, one or more fuel filters, a fuel pump (mechanical, electric, or both), and the carburetor or fuel injection unit.

With the exception of the carburetor or fuel injection unit, the fuel system is quite simple in operation. Fuel is drawn or pumped from the tank through the fuel line by the fuel pump, which forces it through the fuel filter, and from there to the carburetor/injection unit where it is distributed to the cylinders.

Basic Fuel System Diagnosis

When there is a problem starting or driving a vehicle, two of the most important checks involve the ignition and the fuel systems. The questions most mechanics attempt to answer first, "is there spark?" and "is there fuel?" will often lead to solving most basic problems. For ignition system diagnosis and testing, please refer to Section 2 of this manual. If the ignition system checks out (there is spark), then you must determine if fuel system is operating properly (is there fuel?).

CARBURETED FUEL SYSTEM

Fuel Filters

REMOVAL & INSTALLATION

For fuel filter replacement procedures, please refer to Section 1 of this manual.

Mechanical Fuel Pump

REMOVAL & INSTALLATION

▶ See Figures 1, 2, 3, 4 and 5

1. Disconnect the negative battery cable. Remove the air cleaner assembly, if necessary.
2. Disconnect and plug both of the fuel lines form the fuel pump (some models have 3 lines).
3. Unscrew and remove the two fuel pump mounting bolts.
4. Withdraw the fuel pump assembly from the engine block.
5. Installation is in the reverse order of removal.

➡ Always use a new gasket when installing the fuel pump.

6. Start the engine and check the pump for any leaks.

TESTING

➡ Some vehicles with a carburetor may use an electric, external mount type fuel pump.

Fuel pumps should always be tested on the vehicle. The larger line between the pump and tank is the suction side of the system and the smaller line, between the pump and carburetor, is the pressure side. A leak in the pressure side would be apparent because of dripping fuel. A leak in the suction side is usually only apparent because of a reduced volume of fuel delivered to the pressure side.

1. Tighten any loose line connections and look for any kinks or restrictions.
2. Disconnect the fuel line at the carburetor. Disconnect the distributor-to-coil primary wire. Place a container at the end of the fuel line and crank the engine a few revolutions. If little or

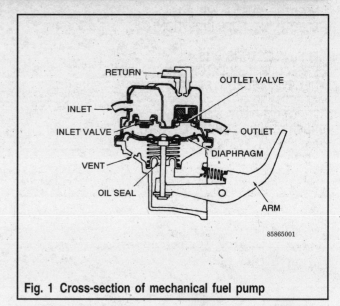

Fig. 1 Cross-section of mechanical fuel pump

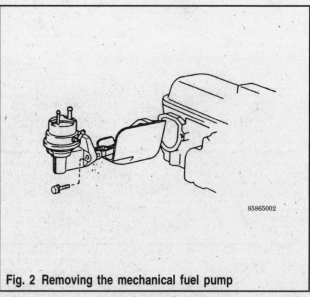

Fig. 2 Removing the mechanical fuel pump

no fuel flows from the line, either the fuel pump is inoperative or the line is plugged. Blow through the lines with compressed air and try the test again. Reconnect the line.

3. If fuel flows in good volume, check the fuel pump pressure to be sure the pump is operating properly.

4. Attach a pressure gauge to the pressure side of the fuel line. On cars equipped with a vapor return system, squeeze off the return hose.

5. Run the engine at idle and note the reading on the gauge. Stop the engine and compare the reading with the specifications listed in the Tune-Up Specifications chart found in Section 2 of this manual. If the pump is operating properly, the pressure will be as specified and will be constant at idle speed. If pressure varies sporadically or is too high/low, the pump should be replaced.

6. Remove the pressure gauge.

7. The following flow test can also be performed:

   a. Disconnect the fuel line from the carburetor. Run the fuel line into a suitable measuring container.

   b. Run the engine at idle until there is one pint of fuel in the container. One pint should be pumped in 30 seconds or less.

   c. If the flow is below minimum, check for a restriction in the line. The only way to check fuel pump pressure is by connecting an accurate pressure gauge to the fuel line at the carburetor level. Never replace a fuel pump without performing this simple test. If the engine seems to be starving for fuel, check the ignition system first. Also check for a plugged fuel filter or a restricted fuel line before replacing the pump.

Electric Fuel Pump

REMOVAL & INSTALLATION

External Mount Type

1. Disconnect the negative battery cable.
2. Unplug the fuel pump wiring connector inside the trunk.
3. Unscrew the four bolts and remove the service hole cover.
4. Disconnect and plug the fuel pump inlet hose.
5. Remove the bolt at the fuel pump bracket.

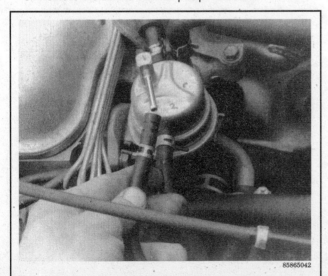

Fig. 3 Remove the fuel lines from the fuel pump

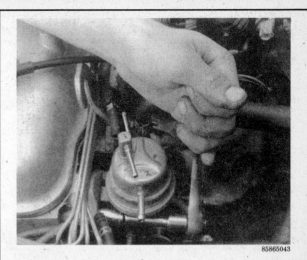

Fig. 4 The fuel pump is attached to the engine using bolts

Fig. 5 Once the bolts are removed, carefully separate the fuel pump from the engine — always replace the gasket upon installation

6. Raise the rear of the car and support it with jackstands.

7. Remove the fuel pipe bracket. Slowly loosen and then disconnect the fuel pump outlet hose.

8. Unscrew the two remaining fuel pump bracket bolts and then remove the pump.

9. Installation is in the reverse order of removal.

10. Start the engine and check for any leaks.

Carburetor

The carburetor is the most complex part of the entire fuel system. Carburetors vary greatly in construction, but they all operate basically the same way; their job is to supply the correct mixture of fuel and air to the engine in response to varying conditions.

Despite their complexity in operation, carburetors function because of a simple physical principle (the venturi principle). Air is drawn into the engine by the pumping action of the pistons. As the air enters the top of the carburetor, it passes through a venturi, which is nothing more than a restriction in the throttle bore. The air speeds up as it passes through the venturi, causing a slight drop in pressure. This pressure drop pulls fuel from the float bowl through a nozzle into the throttle bore. Once in the bore it mixes with the air and forms a fine mist, which is distributed to the cylinders through the intake manifold.

There are six different systems (fuel/air circuits) in a carburetor that make it work:

- Float system
- Main Metering system
- Idle and Low-Speed system
- Accelerator Pump system
- Power system
- Choke system

The way these systems are arranged in the carburetor determines the carburetor's size and shape. It's hard to believe that the little single-barrel carburetor used on many 4 cylinder engines has all the same basic systems as the enormous 4-barrels used on V8 engines. Of course, the 4-barrels have more throttle bores (barrels) and a lot of other hardware you won't find on the little single-barrels. But, basically, all carburetors are similar, and if you understand a simple single-barrel, you can use that knowledge to understand a 4-barrel. If you'll study the explanations of the various systems, you'll discover that carburetors aren't as tricky as you thought they were. In fact, they're fairly simple, considering the job they have to do.

It's important to remember that carburetors seldom give trouble during normal operation. Other than changing the fuel and air filters and making sure the idle speed and mixture are OK at every tune-up, there's not much maintenance you can perform on the average carburetor. Feedback carburettors found on late model vehicles require even less attention as the mixture is not adjustable, as part of regular service.

The carburetors used on Toyota models are conventional two-barrel, down-draft types similar to domestic carburetors. The main circuits are: primary, for normal operational requirements; secondary, to supply high-speed fuel needs; float, to supply fuel to the primary and secondary circuits; accelerator, to supply fuel for quick and safe acceleration; choke, for reliable starting in cold weather; and power valve, for fuel economy. Although slight differences in appearance may be noted, these carburetors are basically alike. Of course, different jets and settings are demanded by the different engines to which they are fitted.

ADJUSTMENTS

◆ **See Figures 6, 7, 8, 9, 10 and 11**

➡**On early model carburetors some adjustment service procedures must be modified. Use these service procedures as a general guide.**

Before making any adjustments to the carburetor, ALL of the following conditions must be met:

- All accessories switched off
- Ignition timing correctly set
- Transmission in neutral, parking brake set, wheels blocked front and rear
- Tachometer correctly connected.

85865047

Fig. 6 View of adjustment screws on a common carburetor

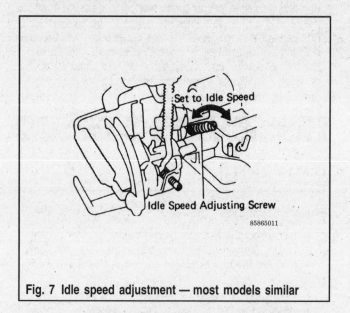

Set to Idle Speed

Idle Speed Adjusting Screw

85865011

Fig. 7 Idle speed adjustment — most models similar

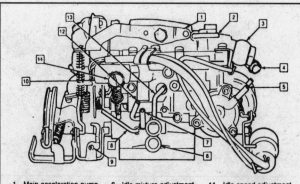

1. Main acceleration pump lever arm	6. Idle mixture adjustment screw plug	11. Idle speed adjustment screw
2. Main air bleed port to EBCV	7. EGR port to port P of EGR vacuum modulator	12. EGR R port to R port of EGR vacuum modulator
3. Fuel inlet union	8. Charcoal canister purge port from VSV	13. Slow air bleed port to EBCV
4. Bowl vent to charcoal canister	9. Fast idle adjusting screw	
5. Aux.accelerator pump-- vacuum from TVSV	10. No.1 slow cut fuel solenoid	

85865006

Fig. 8 Rear view — late model carburetor

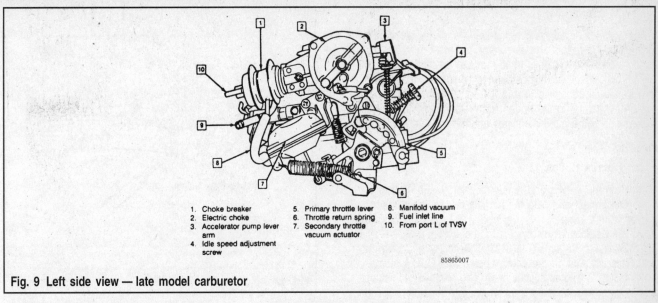

1. Choke breaker
2. Electric choke
3. Accelerator pump lever arm
4. Idle speed adjustment screw
5. Primary throttle lever
6. Throttle return spring
7. Secondary throttle vacuum actuator
8. Manifold vacuum
9. Fuel inlet line
10. From port L of TVSV

Fig. 9 Left side view — late model carburetor

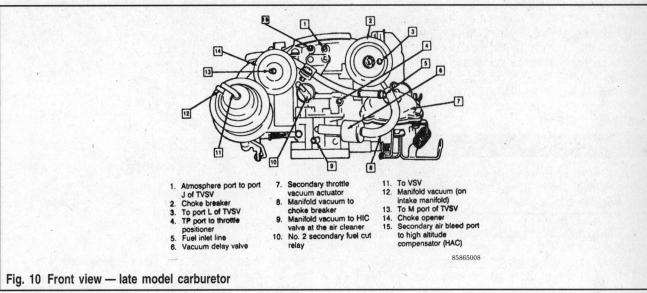

1. Atmosphere port to port J of TVSV
2. Choke breaker
3. To port L of TVSV
4. TP port to throttle positioner
5. Fuel inlet line
6. Vacuum delay valve
7. Secondary throttle vacuum actuator
8. Manifold vacuum to choke breaker
9. Manifold vacuum to HIC valve at the air cleaner
10. No. 2 secondary fuel cut relay
11. To VSV
12. Manifold vacuum (on intake manifold)
13. To M port of TVSV
14. Choke opener
15. Secondary air bleed port to high altitude compensator (HAC)

Fig. 10 Front view — late model carburetor

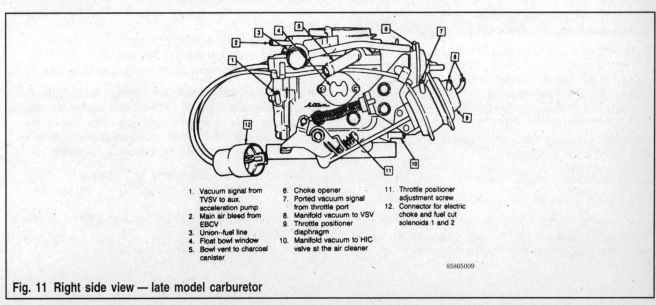

1. Vacuum signal from TVSV to aux. acceleration pump
2. Main air bleed from EBCV
3. Union--fuel line
4. Float bowl window
5. Bowl vent to charcoal canister
6. Choke opener
7. Ported vacuum signal from throttle port
8. Manifold vacuum to VSV
9. Throttle positioner diaphragm
10. Manifold vacuum to HIC valve at the air cleaner
11. Throttle positioner adjustment screw
12. Connector for electric choke and fuel cut solenoids 1 and 2

Fig. 11 Right side view — late model carburetor

Curb Idle (Warm Idle)

The curb idle is adjusted by turning the idle adjusting screw located on the rear of the carburetor. On most models, the knob has a knurled plastic head to make grasping easier. Correct idle speed for the carbureted engine is usually 650 rpm w/manual transmission and 750 rpm w/automatic transmission. Always refer to the underhood emission sticker for specifications as some models/engines may differ slightly.

Fast Idle

▶ See Figures 12 and 13

1. Stop the engine and remove the air cleaner housing.
2. Disconnect and plug the hot idle compensator hose to prevent rough idling.
3. If so equipped, disconnect the hose from the Thermovacuum Switching Valve (TVSV) port M and plug the port. This will shut off the choke opener and EGR systems.
4. Hold the throttle slightly open, (either move the linkage on the carburetor or pull lightly on the throttle cable) push the choke plate closed and hold it closed as you release the throttle.

The carburetor is now fooled into thinking it is performing a cold start — the choke is set and the various external controls are not functioning. These conditions duplicate cold start conditions.

5. Start the engine but DO NOT touch the accelerator pedal or cable. (If you do, the choke will release and Step 4 will be needed again.)

✳✳CAUTION

The engine will be running; be careful of moving parts and belts! Keep loose fitting clothes and long hair well away from the engine area!

6. The correct fast idle speed is 3000 rpm. If adjustment is necessary, turn the fast idle adjusting screw at the lower rear of the carburetor. Always refer to the underhood emission sticker for specifications as some models/engines may differ slightly.

✳✳WARNING

Do not allow the engine to run on fast idle any longer than necessary. Once the correct fast idle is achieved, release the fast idle by depressing and releasing the accelerator. Allow the engine to run at curb idle for about 30 seconds and switch the engine OFF.

7. Remove the plug and reconnect the hose to the M port of the TVSV, if so equipped.

Throttle Positioner

▶ See Figures 14, 15 and 16

1. Disconnect the hose from the Thermovacuum Switching Valve (TVSV) port M and plug the port, if so equipped. Disconnect the vacuum hose from Throttle Positioner (TP) diaphragm A.

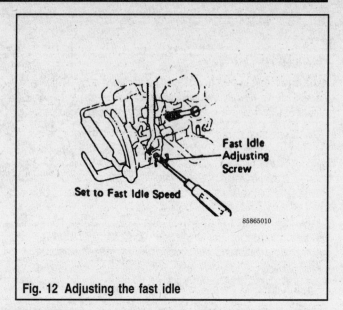

Fig. 12 Adjusting the fast idle

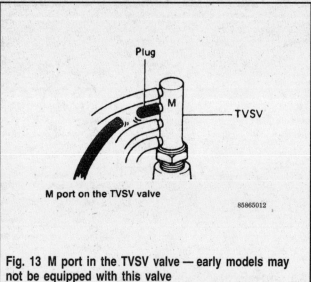

Fig. 13 M port in the TVSV valve — early models may not be equipped with this valve

2. Check that the TP is set at the first step; correct engine speed is:
- Manual transmission: 800 rpm.
- Automatic transmission: 900 rpm.

If necessary, adjust the speed with the adjusting screw.

➡**Make the adjustment with the cooling (radiator) fan OFF. Always refer to the underhood emission sticker for specifications. As some models/engines may differ slightly always follow specifications on emission sticker if none appear (the sticker is missing or damaged) follow the above.**

3. Reconnect the vacuum hose to diaphragm A.
4. Disconnect the hose from diaphragm B and plug the hose end.
5. Check that the TP is set at the second step. The correct engine speed in this position is:
- Manual transmission: 1400 rpm
- Automatic transmission: 1500 rpm

6. Reconnect the vacuum hose to diaphragm B and check that the engine returns to normal idle within 2-6 seconds.

7. Remove the plug and reconnect the vacuum hose to TVSV port M.

Float and Fuel Level

➡**In order to correct float level adjustment a rebuild kit is necessary to supply the related gaskets. Refer to the instructions in the rebuild kit for the latest specifications.**

The float level is not externally adjustable. Removal of the air horn assembly or top of the carburetor is required. The engine should be cold during this procedure. All work is performed with the engine **OFF**.

The float in the carburetor controls the entry of fuel into the bowl of the carburetor (the bowl is simply a reservoir which keeps fuel available at all times). The function of the float is to react to the level of fuel in the bowl and open or close a valve, thus maintaining the correct amount of fuel. The principle is identical to the float in a toilet tank; when the correct level is reached, the flow is shut off.

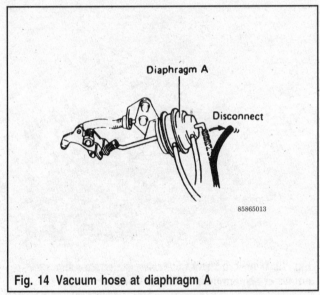

Fig. 14 Vacuum hose at diaphragm A

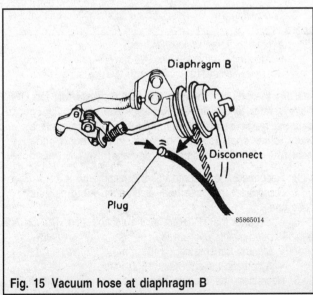

Fig. 15 Vacuum hose at diaphragm B

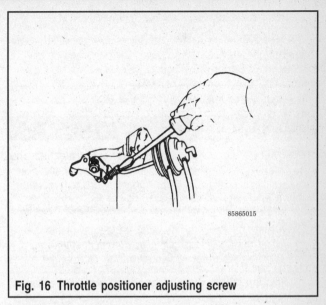

Fig. 16 Throttle positioner adjusting screw

The position of the float (and therefore the amount of fuel available) is critical to proper operation of the engine. If too little fuel is in the bowl, the engine may starve on sharp corners or on hills; too much fuel can literally lead to overflowing and flooding of the engine. To adjust the float level:

1. Remove the air cleaner assembly and disconnect the choke linkage.
2. Disconnect the accelerator pump connecting rod.
3. Remove the pump arm pivot screw and the pump arm.
4. Remove the fuel hose and union.
5. Remove the eight air horn screws. Be careful to identify and collect the external parts attached to the screws, such as wire clamps, brackets and the steel number plate.
6. Disconnect the choke link.
7. Lift the air horn with its gasket from the body of the carburetor.
8. Disconnect the wires at the connector.
9. Remove the gasket from the air horn assembly. Invert the air horn so that the float hangs down by its own weight. Check the clearance between the float tip and the air horn. Adjust the float lip by bending it gently into position.
10. Lift up the float, then check the clearance between the needle valve plunger and the float lip. If necessary, adjust the clearance by bending the outer part of the float lip.

➡**If the float has become misadjusted, it may be due to the float filling with gasoline (hole in float). Give the float a gentle shake and listen for any liquid within. If the float contains fuel replace the float and reset the levels.**

11. Install a new gasket onto the air horn.
12. Place the air horn in position on the carburetor body and install the choke link.
13. Install the eight screws. Make certain the brackets, clips and steel tag are reinstalled as well.
14. Connect the fuel hose and union.
15. Install the pump arm pivot screw and pump arm.
16. Connect the pump arm connecting rod.
17. Attach the choke linkage.
18. Install the air cleaner. Start the engine and check carefully for fuel and/or vacuum leaks. The engine may be difficult

to start; once it is running smoothly, recheck the fuel level in the sight glass.

REMOVAL & INSTALLATION

▶ See Figures 17, 18, 19, 20, 21, 22 and 23

✳✳CAUTION

The carburetor contains gasoline. Wear eye protection and contain spillage. Observe no smoking/no open flame precautions. Have a Class B-C (dry powder) fire extinguisher within arm's reach at all times.

➡**Each fuel and vacuum line must be tagged or labeled individually during disassembly for correct installation. Never tilt the carburetor assembly during removal or installation.**

Early Models

1. Disconnect the negative battery cable.
2. Loosen the radiator drain plug and drain the coolant into a suitable container.
3. Unthread the mounting screws and remove the air filter housing. Disconnect all hoses and lines leading from the air cleaner.
4. Tag and disconnect all fuel, vacuum, coolant and electrical lines or hoses leading from the carburetor.
5. Disconnect the accelerator linkage from the carburetor. On cars equipped with an automatic transmission, disconnect the throttle cable linkage running from the transmission.
6. Remove the four carburetor mounting bolts and lift off the carburetor and its gasket.

➡**Cover the manifold opening with a clean rag to prevent anything from falling into the engine.**

7. Installation is in the reverse order of removal.
8. Start the engine and check for any leaks. Check the float level.

Late Models

1. Remove the air cleaner assembly.
2. Disconnect the accelerator cable from the carburetor.
3. If equipped with automatic transmission, disconnect the throttle position cable.
4. Unplug the wiring connector.
5. Label and disconnect:
   a. Carburetor vacuum hoses
   b. Fuel inlet hoses
   c. Charcoal canister hose
6. Remove the carburetor mounting nuts.
7. Remove the cold mixture heater wire clamp and lift out the EGR vacuum modulator bracket.
8. Lift the carburetor off the engine and place it on a clean cloth on the workbench. If desired, the insulator (base gasket) may also be removed.
9. Cover the inlet area of the manifold with clean rags. This will prevent the entry of dust, dirt and loose parts.
   To install:
10. Place the insulator on the manifold, making sure it is correctly positioned.

Fig. 17 Mark all lines before carburetor removal

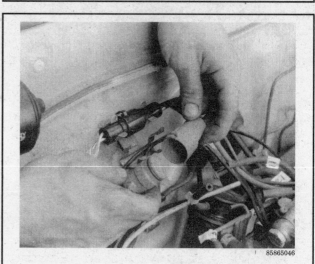

Fig. 18 Disengage any necessary wiring connectors — always align terminals before installation

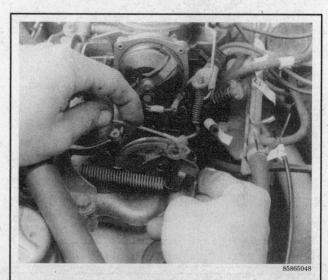

Fig. 19 Remove the gas pedal linkage cable connection

Fig. 20 Remove the carburetor return spring removal

11. Install the carburetor onto the manifold.

12. Install the EGR vacuum modulator bracket. Clamp the cold mixture heater wire into place.

13. Tighten the carburetor mounting nuts (always torque the mounting bolts evenly in steps).

14. Reconnect the fuel inlet hose, the charcoal canister hose and the vacuum hoses.

15. Engage the wiring connector.

16. Connect the accelerator cable. If equipped with automatic transmission, connect the throttle position cable.

17. Reinstall the air cleaner.

OVERHAUL

▶ **See Figures 24 and 25**

➡**A rebuild kit for a correct overhaul is necessary. Refer to the instructions in the rebuild kit for the latest specifications.**

Fig. 21 Loosen and remove the carburetor mounting bolts — a ratchet with an extension is helpful here

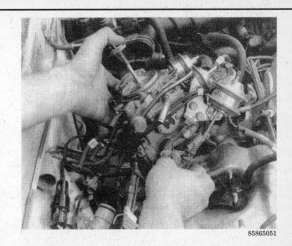

Fig. 22 When removing the carburetor, be careful not to tilt the assembly and pour gas all over or lose small parts

Fig. 23 Remove the carburetor mounting gasket

Efficient carburetion depends greatly on careful cleaning and inspection during overhaul since dirt, gum, water, or varnish in or on the carburetor parts are often responsible for poor performance.

Overhaul your carburetor in a clean, dust-free area. Carefully disassemble the carburetor, referring often to the exploded views. Keep all similar and look-alike parts segregated during disassembly and cleaning in order to avoid accidental interchange during assembly. Make a note of all jet sizes.

When the carburetor is disassembled, wash all parts (except diaphragms, electric choke units, pump plunger, and any other plastic, leather, fiber, or rubber parts) in clean carburetor solvent. Do not leave parts in the solvent any longer than is necessary to sufficiently loosen the deposits. Excessive cleaning may remove the special finish from the float bowl and choke valve bodies, leaving these parts unfit for service. Rinse all parts in clean solvent and blow them dry with compressed air or allow them to air dry. Wipe clean all cork, plastic, leather, and fiber parts with a clean, lint-free cloth.

Blow out all passages and jets with compressed air and be sure that there are no restrictions or blockages. Never use wire or similar tools to clean jets, fuel passages, or air bleeds. Clean all jets and valves separately to avoid accidental interchange.

Check all parts for wear or damage. If wear or damage is found, replace the defective parts. Especially check the following:

1. Check the float needle and seat for wear. If wear is found, replace the complete assembly.

2. Check the float hinge pin for wear and the float(s) for dents or distortion. Replace the float if fuel has leaked into it.

3. Check the throttle and choke shaft bores for wear or an out-of-round condition. Damage or wear to the throttle arm, shaft, or shaft bore will often require replacement of the throttle body. These parts require a close tolerance of fit; wear may allow air leakage, which could affect starting and idling.

➡**Throttle shafts and bushings are not included in overhaul kits. They can be purchased separately.**

4. Inspect the idle mixture adjusting needles for burrs or grooves. Any such condition requires replacement of the needle, since you will not be able to obtain a satisfactory idle.

5. Test the accelerator pump check valves. They should pass air one way but not the other. Test for proper seating by blowing and sucking on the valve. Replace the valve if necessary. If the valve is satisfactory, wash the valve again to remove breath moisture.

6. Check the bowl cover for warped surfaces with a straightedge.

7. Closely inspect the valves and seats for wear and damage, replacing as necessary.

8. After the carburetor is assembled, check the choke valve for freedom of operation.

Carburetor overhaul kits are recommended for each overhaul. These kits contain all gaskets and new parts to replace those that deteriorate most rapidly. Failure to replace all parts supplied with the kit (especially gaskets) can result in poor performance later.

Most carburetor manufacturers supply overhaul kits of 3 basic types: minor repair; major repair; and gasket kits. Basically, they contain the following:

Minor Repair Kits:
- All gaskets
- Float needle valve
- Volume control screw
- All diaphragms
- Spring for the pump diaphragm

Major Repair Kits:
- All jets and gaskets
- All diaphragms
- Float needle valve
- Volume control screw
- Pump ball valve
- Float
- Complete intermediate rod
- Intermediate pump lever
- Some cover hold-down screws and washers

Gasket Kits:
- All gaskets

After cleaning and checking all components, reassemble the carburetor, using new parts and referring to the exploded view. When reassembling, make sure that all screws and jets are tight in their seats, but do not over tighten, as the tips will be distorted. Tighten all screws gradually, in rotation. Do not tighten needle valves into their seats; uneven jetting will result. Always use new gaskets. Be sure to adjust the float level when reassembling.

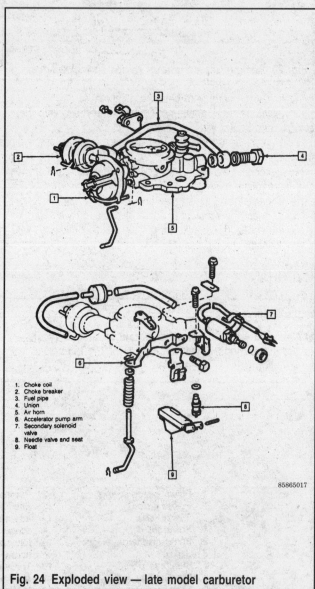

1. Choke coil
2. Choke breaker
3. Fuel pipe
4. Union
5. Air horn
6. Accelerator pump arm
7. Secondary solenoid valve
8. Needle valve and seat
9. Float

85865017

Fig. 24 Exploded view — late model carburetor

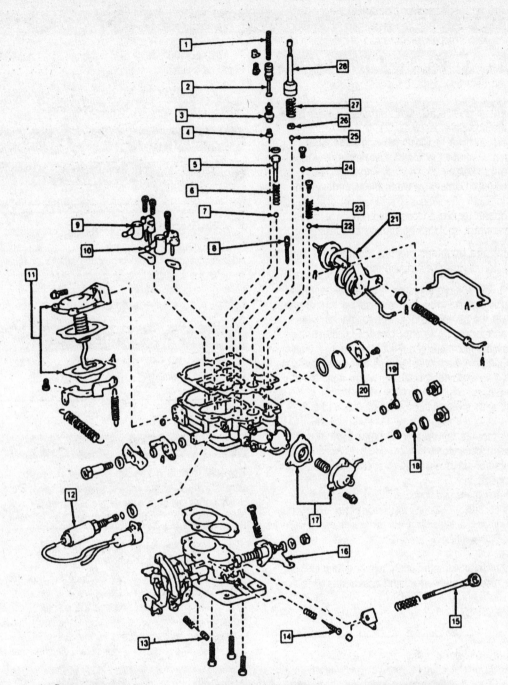

1. Power piston spring
2. Power piston
3. Power valve
4. Power jet
5. Pump discharge weight
6. Spring
7. Steel ball
8. Slow jet (idle jet)
9. Secondary small venturi
10. Primary small venturi
11. Secondary throttle valve actuator assembly
12. Primary solenoid valve
13. Fast idle adjusting screw
14. Idle mixture adjusting screw
15. Idle speed adjusting screw
16. Throttle positioner lever
17. Aux. accelerator pump
18. Primary main jet
19. Secondary main jet
20. Sight glass retainer
21. Choke breaker and throttle positioner diaphragm
22. Steel ball
23. Spring
24. Steel ball
25. Steel ball
26. Check ball retainer
27. Pump damping spring
28. Pump plunger

85865016

Fig. 25 Exploded view of a late model carburetor

GASOLINE FUEL INJECTION

Electronic Fuel Injection (EFI)

▶ See Figure 26

❋❋CAUTION

The fuel injection system is under pressure. Release pressure slowly and contain spillage. Observe no smoking/no open flame precautions. Have a Class B-C (dry powder) fire extinguisher within arm's reach at all times.

The EFI system can be broken down into three basic subsystems; the fuel system, the air induction system, and the electronic control system.

The main components of the fuel system are the fuel tank, the fuel pump and the fuel injectors. The electric fuel pump supplies fuel from the tank, under a constant pressure, to the EFI fuel injectors. These injectors in turn dispense a metered quantity of fuel into the intake manifold in accordance with signals given by the Electronic Control Unit (ECU). Each injector is opened, at the same time, to introduce the fuel required for ideal combustion with each engine revolution.

The air induction system consists of the air cleaner, an air flow meter, an air valve and an air intake chamber. All of these components contribute to the supply of the proper amount of air to the intake manifold as monitored by the ECU.

The main component of the electronic control system is the ECU. The computer receives signals from various sensors indicating changing engine operating conditions such as:
- Intake air volume.
- Intake air temperature.
- Coolant temperature.
- Engine load.
- Acceleration/deceleration.
- Exhaust oxygen content.

These signals are utilized by the computer to determine the injection duration necessary for an optimum air/fuel ratio.

TROUBLESHOOTING

➡ When there is a problem starting or driving a vehicle, two of the most important checks involve the ignition and the fuel systems. The questions most mechanics attempt to answer first, "is there spark?" and "is there fuel?" will often lead to solving most basic problems.

Engine troubles are not usually caused by the EFI system. When troubleshooting, always check the condition of all other related systems, first.

The most frequent cause of problems with the EFI system is a bad contact in a wiring connector, so always make sure that the connections are secure. When inspecting the connector, pay particular attention to the following points:
1. Check to see that the terminals are not bent.
2. Check to see that the connector is pushed in all the way and locked.

3. Check that there is no change in signal when the connector is tapped or wiggled.

➡ If necessary, refer to Section 4 for output of diagnosis codes and related service procedures

Relieving Fuel System Pressure

❋❋CAUTION

Perform this operation on a cold engine only!

1. Disconnect the negative battery cable.
2. If equipped with fuel filter shield, unthread the retaining screws and remove the protective shield for the vehicle.
3. Place a large pan or wrap a shop towel on or under the delivery pipe (large connection) to catch the dripping fuel and SLOWLY loosen the union bolt to bleed off the fuel pressure.

Electric Fuel Pump

REMOVAL & INSTALLATION

In-Tank Mount Type

❋❋CAUTION

The fuel injection system is under pressure. Release pressure slowly and contain spillage. Observe no smoking/no open flame precautions. Have a Class B-C (dry powder) fire extinguisher within arm's reach at all times.

1. Disconnect the negative battery cable. Relieve fuel pressure. Remove the filler cap.
2. Using a siphon or pump, drain the fuel from the tank and store it in a proper metal container with a tight cap.
3. On most models, remove the electrical connection at the top of the fuel tank assembly. If necessary remove the rear seat cushion to gain access to the electrical wiring connector.
4. Disconnect the fuel pump and sending unit wiring at the connector.
5. Raise the vehicle and safely support it on jackstands.
6. Loosen the clamp and remove the filler neck and overflow pipe from the tank.
7. Remove the supply hose from the tank. Wrap a rag around the fitting to collect escaping fuel. Disconnect the breather hose from the tank, again using a rag to control spillage.
8. Cover or plug the end of each disconnected line to keep dirt out and fuel in.
9. Support the fuel tank with a floor jack or transmission jack. Use a broad piece of wood to distribute the load. Be careful not to deform the bottom of the tank.
10. Remove the fuel tank support strap bolts.
11. Swing the straps away from the tank and lower the jack. Balance the tank with your other hand or have a helper assist

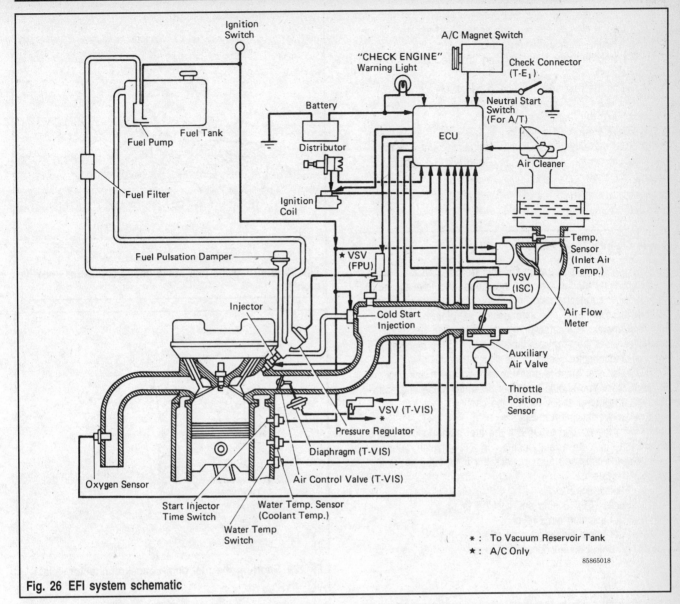

Fig. 26 EFI system schematic

you. The tank is bulky and may have some fuel left in it. If its balance changes suddenly, the tank may fall.

12. Remove the fuel filler pipe extension, the breather pipe assembly and the sending unit assembly. Keep these items in a clean, protected area away from the car.

13. To separate the electric fuel pump:

   a. Disconnect the two pump-to-harness wires.

   b. Loosen the pump outlet hose clamp at the bracket pipe.

   c. Remove the pump from the bracket and the outlet hose from the bracket pipe.

   d. Separate the outlet hose and the filter from the pump.

To install:

14. While the tank is out and disassembled, inspect it for any signs of rust, leakage or metal damage. If any problem is found, replace the tank. Clean the inside of the tank with water and a light detergent, then rinse the tank thoroughly several times.

15. Inspect all of the lines, hoses and fittings for any sign of corrosion, wear or damage to the surfaces. Check the pump outlet hose and the filter for restrictions.

16. When reassembling, ALWAYS replace the sealing gaskets with new ones. Also replace any rubber parts showing signs of deterioration.

17. Assemble the outlet hose and filter onto the pump; then attach the pump to the bracket.

18. Connect the outlet hose clamp to the bracket pipe and connect the pump wiring to the harness wire.

19. Install the fuel pump and bracket assembly onto the tank.

20. Install the sending unit assembly.

21. Connect the breather pipe assembly and the filler pipe extension.

➡**Tighten the breather pipe screw and all other attaching screws evenly.**

22. Place the fuel tank on the jack and elevate it into place within the car. Attach the straps and install the strap bolts, tightening them (in even steps) to 29 ft. lbs. (39 Nm).

23. Connect the breather hose to the tank pipe, the return hose to the tank pipe and the supply hose to its tank pipe. tighten the supply hose fitting to 21 ft. lbs. (28 Nm).

24. Connect the filler neck and overflow pipe to the tank. Make sure the clamps are properly seated and secure.

25. Lower the vehicle to the ground.

26. Connect the pump and sending unit electrical connectors to the harness.

27. Install the rear seat cushion, if necessary.

28. Using a funnel, pour the fuel that was drained from its container into the fuel filler.

29. Install the fuel filler cap.

30. Start the engine and check carefully for any sign of leakage around the tank and lines. Road test the vehicle for proper operation.

TESTING

▶ **See Figures 27, 28 and 29**

1. Turn the ignition switch **ON**, but do not start the engine.

2. On early models, remove the rubber cap from the fuel pump check connector using a jumper wire, short both terminals of the fuel pump check connector. On late models (the check connector is located under the hood near the shock tower) connect the terminals labelled FP and B+ together in the check connector. Refer to the illustrations.

3. Check that there is pressure in the hose running to the delivery pipe. You should hear fuel pressure noise and possibly hear the pump at the rear of the car.

4. Remove the jumper wire.

5. Turn the ignition to **OFF**. If the fuel pump failed to function, it may indicate a faulty pump. On EFI vehicles, before removing the tank and pump, check the following items within the pump system:
   a. Fusible link.
   b. Fuses (EFI/15 amp and IGN/7.5 amp).
   c. Fuel injection main relay.
   d. Fuel pump circuit opening relay.
   e. All wiring connections and grounds.

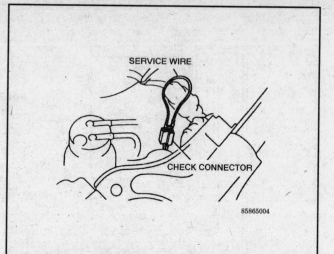

Fig. 28 Shorting the fuel pump check connector — early models

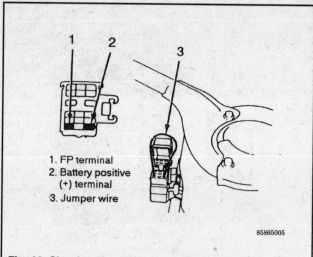

1. FP terminal
2. Battery positive (+) terminal
3. Jumper wire

Fig. 29 Shorting the fuel pump check connector — late models

Cold Start Injector

▶ **See Figures 30 and 31**

During cold engine starting, the cold start injector is used to supply additional fuel to the intake manifold in order to aid in initial start-up. The opening and closing of the injector is determined by the start injector time switch, located in the thermostat housing. When the engine coolant temperature falls below a certain point, the switch is tripped which opens the cold start injector. As the engine coolant warms up, the switch will eventually close the injector.

REMOVAL & INSTALLATION

❋❋CAUTION

Perform this operation on a cold engine only!

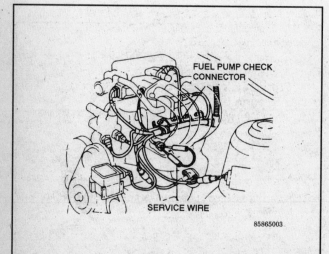

Fig. 27 Shorting the fuel pump check connector

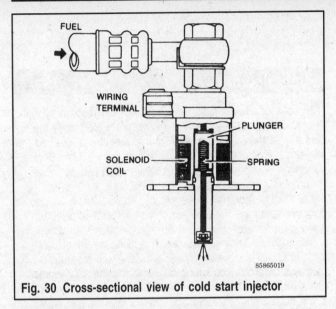

Fig. 30 Cross-sectional view of cold start injector

1. Disconnect the negative battery cable. Relieve the fuel pressure.
2. Remove the cold start injector union bolt on the delivery pipe.

➡**Before removing the union bolt, place a suitable container under it to catch any escaping fuel.**

3. Disengage the wiring connector at the injector.
4. Unscrew the two mounting bolts and then remove the cold start injector from the air intake chamber.

To install:

5. Installation is in the reverse order of removal.

➡**Always use new gaskets when reinstalling the injector.**

6. Start the engine and check for any leaks.

TESTING

▸ **See Figure 32**

1. Unplug the wiring connector and remove the cold start injector from the air intake chamber.

➡**Do not disconnect the fuel line.**

2. Remove the rubber cap from the fuel pump check terminal and short both terminals with a jumper wire.
3. Using Special Tool 09843-30011, connect one end to the injector and the other to the battery.
4. Hold the injector over a suitable container and then turn the ignition switch to the ON position. Do not start the engine.
5. Check that the fuel splash pattern is even and V-shaped.
6. Disconnect the test probes from the battery and check that the fuel does not leak from the injector tip any more than one drop per minute.
7. Remove the Special Tool and install the cold start injector.
8. Check the resistance of the injector. It should be 3-5 ohms.
9. If the cold start injector did not operate properly in any of these tests, it will require replacement.

Pressure Regulator

▸ **See Figures 33 and 34**

The pressure regulator maintains correct fuel pressure throughout the system. The regulator is vacuum controlled to provide a relatively constant pressure differential.

REMOVAL & INSTALLATION

1. Disconnect the negative battery cable. Relieve fuel pressure.
2. Place a suitable container under the union and pipe support.

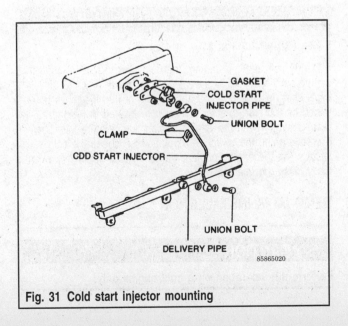

Fig. 31 Cold start injector mounting

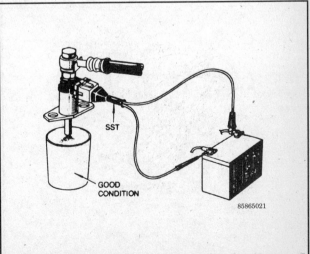

Fig. 32 Cold start injector testing — the fuel spray pattern should be even and V-shaped

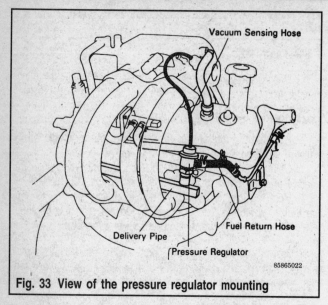

Fig. 33 View of the pressure regulator mounting

3. Disconnect the vacuum sensing hose from the top of the regulator.

4. Disconnect the fuel return hose and plug the pipe.

5. Remove the union bolt from the regulator.

6. Unscrew the two regulator mounting bolts and lift out the regulator.

7. Installation is in the reverse order of removal.

8. Start the engine and check for any leaks.

TESTING

1. Disconnect the negative battery cable.

2. Unplug the wiring connector from the cold start injector.

3. Place a suitable container under the front end of the delivery pipe and slowly remove the union bolt for the cold start injector. Drain all of the fuel in the delivery pipe.

4. Install a fuel pressure gauge in the union bolt's place, connect the battery cable and start the engine.

5. Disconnect the vacuum sensing hose from the pressure regulator and block it off.

6. Measure the fuel pressure at idle. It should be 33-38 psi. If the pressure is high, replace the regulator.

7. Installation is in the reverse order of removal.

Fuel Injectors

There is one fuel injector for each cylinder. They spray fuel in front of the intake valve. The injectors are electrically triggered valves which deliver a measured quantity of fuel into the intake manifold according to signals from the ECU. As driving conditions change, the computer signals each injector to remain open a longer or shorter period of time, thus controlling the amount of fuel introduced into the engine. Being an electric component, an injector is either on or off (open or closed); there is no variable control for an injector other than duration.

Cleanliness equals success when working on a fuel injected system. Every component must be treated with the greatest care and be protected from dust, grime and impact damage. The miniaturized and solid state circuitry is easily damaged by a jolt. Additionally, care must be used in dealing with electrical connectors. Look for and release any locking mechanisms on the connector before separating the connectors. When reattaching, make sure each pin is properly lined up and seated before pushing the connector closed.

REMOVAL & INSTALLATION

▶ **See Figures 35, 36 and 37**

1. Disconnect the negative battery cable. Relieve the fuel pressure.

2. Remove the cold start injector pipe.

➡**Be sure to have a suitable container on hand to catch any dripping fluid.**

3. Remove the air intake pipes, if necessary.

4. Disconnect the fuel inlet line from the delivery pipe. Tag and disconnect the vacuum sensing hose and the fuel return line from the pressure regulator.

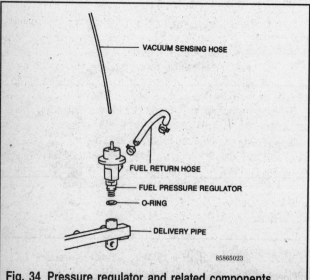

Fig. 34 Pressure regulator and related components

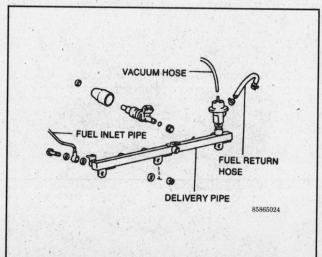

Fig. 35 Partial exploded view of the fuel rail/injector assembly

5. Remove the two plastic EFI solenoid wiring harness clamps, then tag and disconnect the wiring connectors from the tops of the fuel injectors.

6. Unscrew the three nuts, then remove the delivery pipe with the injectors attached.

➡**Be careful not to drop the injectors when removing the delivery pipe. Do not remove the cover.**

To install:

7. Insert four new insulators into the injector holes on the intake manifold.

8. Install the grommet and a new O-ring to the delivery pipe end of each injector.

9. Apply a thin coat of gasoline to the O-ring on each injector, then press them into the delivery pipe.

10. Install the injectors together with the delivery pipe to the intake manifold. Tighten the mounting bolts to 11-15 ft. lbs. (15-20 Nm).

11. Installation of the remaining components is in the reverse order of removal.

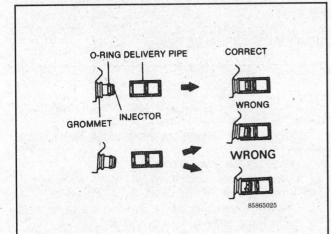

Fig. 36 Be sure to insert the injector into the fuel delivery pipe properly

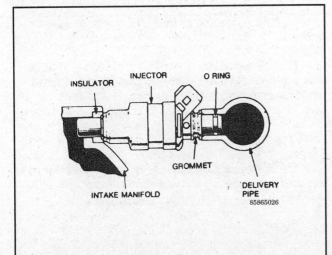

Fig. 37 View of a properly installed fuel injector

12. Start the engine and check for any fuel leaks.

TESTING

The simplest way to test the injectors is simply to listen to them with the engine running. Use either a stethoscope-type tool or the blade of a long screw driver to touch each injector while the engine is idling. You should hear or feel a distinct clicking as each injector opens and closes.

Additionally, the resistance of the injector can be easily checked. Disconnect the negative battery cable and remove the electrical connector from the injector to be tested. Use an ohmmeter to check the resistance across the terminals of the injector. Correct ohmage is approximately 13.8 ohms at 68°F (20°C); slight variations are acceptable due to temperature conditions.

Bench testing of the injectors can only be done using expensive special equipment. Generally this equipment can be found at a dealership and sometimes at a well-equipped machine or performance shop. There is no provision for field testing the injectors by the owner/mechanic. DO NOT attempt to test the injector by removing it from the engine and making it spray into a jar.

Never attempt to check a removed injector by hooking it directly to the battery. The injector runs on a much smaller voltage and the 12 volts from the battery will destroy it internally.

Air Flow Meter

Air is drawn in through the air filter to the air flow meter. The volume of air depends on the throttle plate opening as controlled by the accelerator pedal. Air volume and temperature is measured by the air flow meter which then converts the measurement to a voltage signal that is sent to the ECU.

REMOVAL & INSTALLATION

▶ **See Figure 38**

1. Disconnect the negative battery cable.
2. Unscrew the mounting bolts and remove the air cleaner inlet.
3. Remove the air cleaner element.
4. Disconnect the electrical connector from the top of the meter and remove the oxygen sensor wire from the clamp on the side of the meter.
5. Loosen the hose clamp and pull off the intake air connector.
6. Unscrew the meter support bracket bolt.
7. Unscrew the four air flow meter mounting bolts from inside the air cleaner housing and remove the meter.
8. Installation is in the reverse order of removal.

TESTING

▶ **See Figures 39 and 40**

➡**Check the air flow meter with the unit out of the car.**

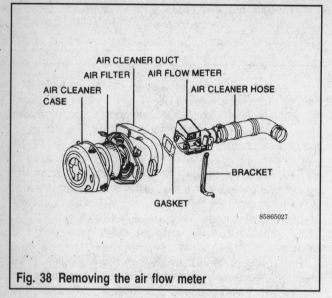

Fig. 38 Removing the air flow meter

Using an ohmmeter, check the resistance between each terminal of the electrical connector by moving the measuring plate. Resistance between E2 and Vs will be changed in accordance with the measuring plate opening.

Air Valve

During cold engine operation, the air valve is open, providing a bypass circuit past the throttle plate opening. This causes the volume of air being drawn in to increase, the increased volume is sensed by the air flow meter which in turn signals the ECU to increase the fuel flow. The results a higher idle speed during cold engine operation. As the valve gradually

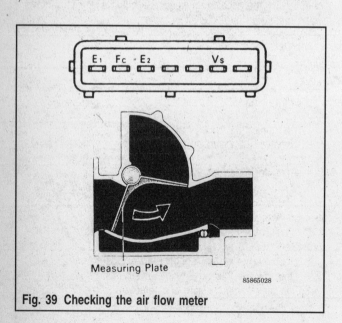

Fig. 39 Checking the air flow meter

Resistance

Between Terminals	Resistance Ω	Measuring Plate Opening
$E_1 - F_c$	Infinity	Fully closed
	Zero	Other than closed position
$E_2 - Vs$	20 – 400	Fully closed
	20 – 1000	Fully closed to Fully open position

NOTE: *Resistance between E_2 and V_s will change in accordance with the measuring plate opening.*

Fig. 40 Resistance specifications for air flow meter

closes, the air volume is reduced, thereby reducing the fuel flow.

REMOVAL & INSTALLATION

▶ **See Figure 41**

1. Disconnect the negative battery cable. Drain the engine coolant to a level below the valve.
2. Squeeze the hose clamps and remove the two air hoses from the valve.
3. Disconnect the electrical connector.
4. Unscrew the hose clamps and remove the two water hoses from the valve.
5. Unscrew the mounting bolts and remove the air valve.
6. Installation is in the reverse order of removal.

TESTING

▶ **See Figure 42**

1. Start the engine and pinch the hose between the air valve and the intake air chamber. The engine rpm should drop noticeably.
2. Run the engine until it reaches normal operating temperature and pinch the hose again. This time the engine speed should not drop more than 150 rpm.
3. After the engine has cooled off completely, restart it and remove the above hose from the air valve. You should be able to see that the valve is slightly open. If it is not, turn the adjusting screw until it is open slightly.
4. Check the heat coil resistance by removing the electrical connector and measuring across the two terminals with an ohmmeter. The resistance should be 40-60 ohms.

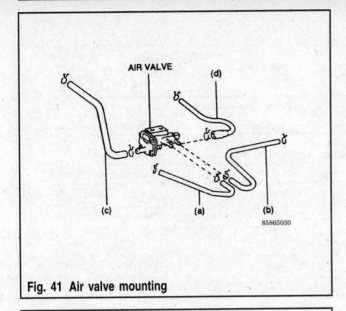

Fig. 41 Air valve mounting

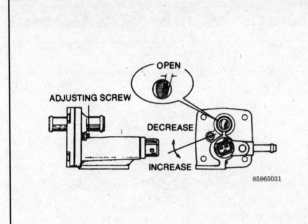

Fig. 42 Check that the air valve opens slightly at room temperature

Throttle Body

REMOVAL & INSTALLATION

⬦ **See Figure 43**

1. Disconnect the negative battery cable. Drain the engine coolant.
2. Disconnect the air intake hose. If necessary remove the air cleaner assembly.
3. Tag and disconnect all lines, hoses or wires that lead from the throttle body. Position them out of the way.
4. Unscrew the mounting bolts and remove the throttle body and gasket.
5. Installation is in the reverse order of removal.

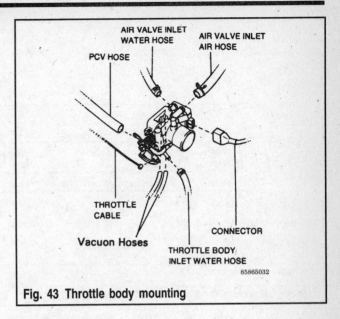

Fig. 43 Throttle body mounting

TESTING

⬦ **See Figures 44 and 45**

1. Check that the throttle linkage moves smoothly.
2. Start the engine and remove the hose from the vacuum port.
3. With your finger, check that there is no vacuum at idle and that there is vacuum at anything other than idle.
4. Unplug the electrical connector from the throttle position sensor.
5. Insert a flat feeler gauge (refer the illustration for testing the throttle body) between the throttle stop screw and the stop lever.
6. Using an ohmmeter, check the continuity between each terminal on the sensor.

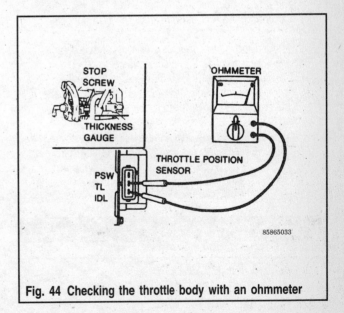

Fig. 44 Checking the throttle body with an ohmmeter

Clearance between lever and stop screw	Continuity between terminals		
	IDL–TL	Psw–TL	IDL–Psw
0.34 mm (0.0134 in.)	Continuity	No continuity	No continuity
0.70 mm (0.0276 in.)	No continuity	No continuity	No continuity
Throttle valve fully opened position	No continuity	Continuity	No continuity

85865034

Fig. 45 Specifications for testing the throttle body

DIESEL ENGINE FUEL SYSTEM

Injection Nozzle

REMOVAL & INSTALLATION

▶ See Figures 46, 47 and 48

➡Testing injection nozzles requires extensive mechanical training and elaborate testing equipment. Refer to a local machine shop for this type of repair.

1. Loosen the clamps, then remove the injection hoses from between the injection pump and pipe.
2. Disconnect both ends of the injection pipes from the pump and nozzle holders.
3. Disconnect the fuel cut off wire from the connector clamp.
4. Remove the nut, connector clamp and bond cable.
5. Unbolt and remove the injector pipes.
6. Disconnect the fuel hoses from the leakage pipes.
7. Remove the four nuts, leakage pipe and four washers.
8. Unscrew and remove the nozzles.
To install:
9. Installation is the reverse of removal. Torque the nozzles to 47 ft. lbs. (64 Nm). Always use new nozzle seat gaskets and seats. Bleed the system by loosening the pipes at the nozzles and cranking the engine until all air is expelled and fuel sprays.

Injection Pump

REMOVAL & INSTALLATION

▶ See Figure 49

1. Drain the cooling system.

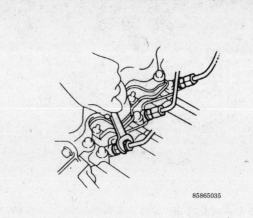

85865035

Fig. 46 The injection nozzles may be removed using an open-end wrench or crow's foot socket.

2. Disconnect the accelerator and cruise control cables from the pump.
3. Disconnect the fuel cut off wire at the pump.
4. Disconnect the fuel inlet and outlet hoses, the water by-pass hoses, the boost compensator hoses, the A/C or heater idle-up vacuum hoses and the heater hose.
5. Remove the injector pipes at the pump.
6. Remove the pump pulley.
7. Matchmark the raised timing mark on the pump flange with the block. Unbolt and remove the pump.
8. Installation is the reverse of removal. There must be no clearance between the pump bracket and stay.

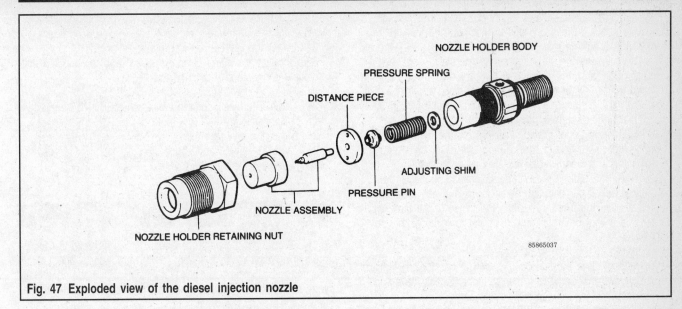

Fig. 47 Exploded view of the diesel injection nozzle

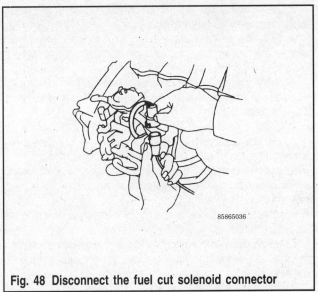

Fig. 48 Disconnect the fuel cut solenoid connector

Fig. 49 Matchmark the timing mark on the pump flange with the block

FUEL TANK

Tank Assembly

▶ See Figures 50 and 51

REMOVAL & INSTALLATION

✳✳CAUTION

The fuel injection system is under pressure. Release pressure slowly and contain spillage. Observe no smoking/no open flame precautions. Have a Class B-C (dry powder) fire extinguisher within arm's reach at all times.

1. Disconnect the negative battery cable. Relieve the fuel pressure. Remove the filler cap. Using a siphon or pump, drain the fuel from the tank and store it in a proper metal container with a tight cap. If equipped with a drain plug drain the fuel tank by removing the drain plug.

2. Remove the fuel tank pipe protector.

3. If necessary, remove the rear seat cushion to gain access to the electrical wiring.

4. Disconnect the fuel pump (only if vehicle has in-tank mounted fuel pump) and sending unit wiring at the connector.

5. Raise the vehicle and safely support it on jackstands.

6. Loosen the clamp, then remove the filler neck assembly and overflow pipe assembly from the tank.

7. Remove the supply hose from the tank. Wrap a rag around the fitting to collect escaping fuel. Disconnect the breather hose or vent tube from the tank, again using a rag to control spillage.

8. Cover or plug the end of each disconnected line to keep dirt out and fuel in.

9. Support the fuel tank with a floor jack or transmission jack. Use a broad piece of wood to distribute the load. Be careful not to deform the bottom of the tank.

10. Remove the fuel tank support strap bolts.

11. Swing the straps away from the tank and lower the jack. Balance the tank with your other hand or have a helper assist you. The tank is bulky and may have some fuel left in it. If its balance changes suddenly, the tank may fall.

12. Remove the fuel filler pipe extension, the vent pipe assembly, fuel pump and or the sending unit assembly. Keep these items in a clean, protected area away from the car.

13. While the tank is out and disassembled, inspect it for any signs of rust, leakage or metal damage. If any problem is found, replace the fuel tank. Clean the inside of the tank with water and a light detergent and rinse the tank thoroughly several times.

To install:

14. Inspect all of the lines, hoses and fittings for any sign of corrosion, wear or damage to the surfaces. Check the pump outlet hose and the filter for restrictions.

15. When reassembling, ALWAYS replace the sealing gaskets with new ones. Also replace any rubber parts showing signs of deterioration.

16. Connect the vent pipe assembly and the filler pipe extension to the fuel tank. Always use new hose clamps.

17. Install the fuel pump and bracket assembly into the tank with a NEW gasket and torque the retaining bolts to 30 inch lbs. (3 Nm) if so equipped

18. Install the fuel sending unit assembly into the tank with a NEW gasket and torque retaining bolts to 30 inch lbs. (3 Nm).

➡**Tighten the vent or breather tube screw to 17 INCH lbs. (2 Nm) and all other attaching screws to 30 INCH lbs. (3 Nm).**

19. Place the fuel tank on the jack and elevate it into place within the car. Attach the straps and install the strap bolts, tightening them to EVENLY 29 ft. lbs. (39 Nm).

➡**Make sure that fuel tank cushions are installed in the correct location before installing the fuel tank to the vehicle. The fuel tank cushions prevent vibration and noise during vehicle operation.**

20. Connect the breather hose or vent to the tank pipe, the return hose to the tank pipe and the supply hose to its tank pipe. tighten the supply hose fitting to 21 ft. lbs. (28 Nm).

21. Connect the filler neck and overflow pipe to the vehicle. Make sure the clamps are properly seated and secure.

22. Lower the vehicle to the ground.

23. Connect the pump (if so equipped) and the sending unit electrical connectors to the harness.

24. Install the rear seat cushion, if necessary.

25. Using a funnel, pour the fuel that was drained earlier, from its container into the fuel tank.

26. Install the fuel filler cap.

27. Start the engine and check carefully for any sign of leakage around the tank and lines.

Sending Unit Replacement

1. Disconnect the negative battery cable. Relieve the fuel pressure. Remove the filler cap. Using a siphon or pump, drain the fuel from the tank and store it in a proper metal container with a tight cap. If equipped with a drain plug drain the fuel tank by removing the drain plug.

2. Remove the fuel tank assembly from the vehicle. Refer to the necessary service procedures.

3. With the fuel tank drained and on a suitable work bench remove the fuel sending unit retaining screws and carefully lift the the sending unit from the fuel tank.

4. While the tank is out and disassembled, inspect it for any signs of rust, leakage or metal damage. If any problem is found, replace the tank.

To install:

5. Install the sending unit and gasket in the fuel tank assembly. Torque the retaining bolts to 30 inch lbs. (3 Nm). When reassembling, ALWAYS replace the sealing gasket with a new one. Also replace rubber parts showing any sign of deterioration.

6. Install the fuel tank assembly to the vehicle. Refer to the necessary service procedures.

7. Install drain plug if necessary. Using a funnel, pour the fuel that was drained earlier, from its container and into the fuel filler.

8. Install the fuel filler cap.

9. Start the engine and check carefully for any sign of leakage around the tank and lines.

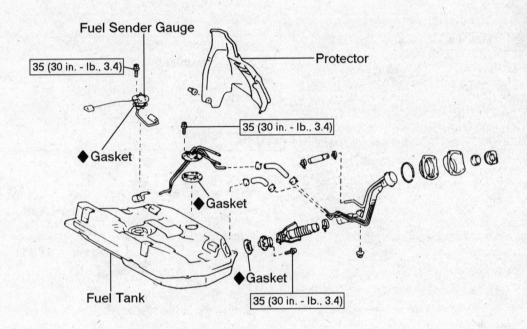

Fuel Sender Gauge

35 (30 in. - lb., 3.4)

Protector

◆ Gasket

35 (30 in. - lb., 3.4)

◆ Gasket

Fuel Tank

◆ Gasket

35 (30 in. - lb., 3.4)

85865040

kg-cm (ft-lb, N·m) : Specified torque

◆ Non- reusable part

Fig. 50 Fuel tank assembly — carburetor equipped

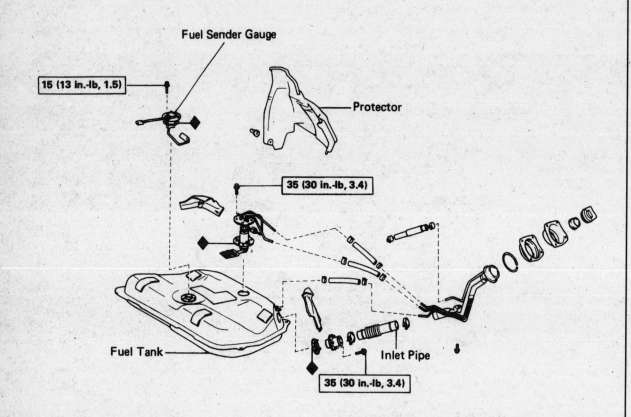

Fuel Sender Gauge

15 (13 in.-lb, 1.5)

Protector

35 (30 in.-lb, 3.4)

Fuel Tank

Inlet Pipe

35 (30 in.-lb, 3.4)

kg-cm (ft-lb, N·m) : Specified torque

◆ Non-reusable part

85865041

Fig. 51 Fuel tank assembly — EFI equipped

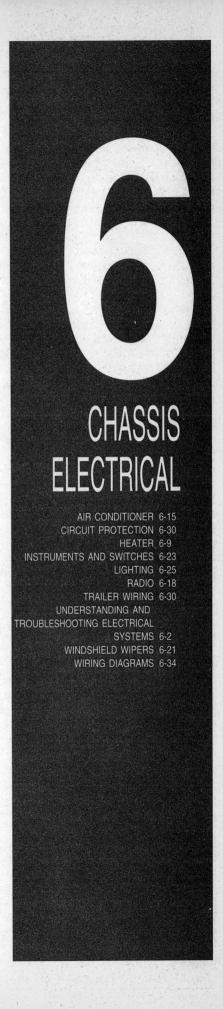

6

CHASSIS
ELECTRICAL

UNDERSTANDING AND TROUBLESHOOTING ELECTRICAL SYSTEMS

While it is true that electronic components should never wear out, in the real world malfunctions do occur. It is also true that any computer-based system is extremely sensitive to electrical voltages and cannot tolerate careless or haphazard testing or service procedures. An inexperienced individual can literally do major damage looking for a minor problem by using the wrong kind of test equipment or connecting test leads or connectors with the ignition switch **ON**. When selecting test equipment, make sure the manufacturers instructions state that the tester is compatible with whatever type of electronic control system is being serviced. Read all instructions carefully and double check all test points before installing probes or making any test connections.

The following section outlines basic diagnosis techniques for dealing with computerized automotive control systems. Along with a general explanation of the various types of test equipment available to aid in servicing modern electronic automotive systems, basic repair techniques for wiring harnesses and connectors is given. Read the basic information before attempting any repairs or testing on any computerized system, to provide the background of information necessary to avoid the most common and obvious mistakes that can cost both time and money. Although the replacement and testing procedures are simple in themselves, the systems are not, and unless one has a thorough understanding of all components and their function within a particular computerized control system, the logical test sequence that these systems demand cannot be followed. Minor malfunctions can make a big difference, so it is important to know how each component affects the operation of the overall electronic system to find the ultimate cause of a problem without replacing good components unnecessarily. It is not enough to use the correct test equipment; the test equipment must be used correctly.

Safety Precautions

❊❊CAUTION

Whenever working on or around any computer based microprocessor control system, always observe these general precautions to prevent the possibility of personal injury or damage to electronic components.

• Never install or remove battery cables with the key **ON** or the engine running. Jumper cables should be connected with the key **OFF** to avoid power surges that can damage electronic control units. Engines equipped with computer controlled systems should avoid both giving and getting jump starts due to the possibility of serious damage to components from arcing in the engine compartment when connections are made with the ignition **ON**.

• Always remove the battery cables before charging the battery. Never use a high output charger on an installed battery or attempt to use any type of (24 volt) starting aid.

• Exercise care when inserting test probes into connectors to insure good connections without damaging the connector or spreading the pins. Always probe connectors from the rear

(wire) side, NOT the pin side, to avoid accidental shorting of terminals during test procedures.

• Never remove or attach wiring harness connectors with the ignition switch **ON**, especially to an electronic control unit.

• Do not drop any components during service procedures and never apply 12 volts directly to any component (like a solenoid or relay) unless instructed specifically to do so. Some component electrical windings are designed to safely handle only 4 or 5 volts and can be destroyed in seconds if 12 volts are applied directly to the connector.

• Remove the electronic control unit if the vehicle is to be placed in an environment where temperatures exceed approximately 176°F (80°C), such as a paint spray booth or when arc or gas welding near the control unit location in the car.

ORGANIZED TROUBLESHOOTING

When diagnosing a specific problem, organized troubleshooting is a must. The complexity of a modern automobile demands that you approach any problem in a logical, organized manner. There are certain troubleshooting techniques that are standard:

1. Establish when the problem occurs. Does the problem appear only under certain conditions? Were there any noises, odors, or other unusual symptoms?

2. Isolate the problem area. To do this, make some simple tests and observations; then eliminate the systems that are working properly. Check for obvious problems such as broken wires, dirty connections or split or disconnected vacuum hoses. Always check the obvious before assuming something complicated is the cause.

3. Test for problems systematically to determine the cause once the problem area is isolated. Are all the components functioning properly? Is there power going to electrical switches and motors? Is there vacuum at vacuum switches and/or actuators? Is there a mechanical problem such as bent linkage or loose mounting screws? Doing careful, systematic checks will often turn up most causes on the first inspection without wasting time checking components that have little or no relationship to the problem.

4. Test all repairs after the work is done to make sure that the problem is fixed. Some causes can be traced to more than one component, so a careful verification of repair work is important to pick up additional malfunctions that may cause a problem to reappear or a different problem to arise. A blown fuse, for example, is a simple problem that may require more than another fuse to repair. If you don't look for a problem that caused a fuse to blow, for example, a shorted wire may go undetected.

Experience has shown that most problems tend to be the result of a fairly simple and obvious cause, such as loose or corroded connectors or air leaks in the intake system; making careful inspection of components during testing essential to quick and accurate troubleshooting. Special, hand held computerized testers designed specifically for diagnosing a system are available from a variety of aftermarket sources, as well as from the vehicle manufacturer, but care should be taken that any test equipment being used is designed to diagnose that particular computer controlled system accurately without damaging the control unit (ECU) or components being tested.

➡Pinpointing the exact cause of trouble in an electrical system can sometimes only be accomplished by the use of special test equipment. The following describes commonly used test equipment and explains how to put it to best use in diagnosis. In addition to the information covered below, the manufacturer's instructions booklet provided with the tester should be read and clearly understood before attempting any test procedures.

TEST EQUIPMENT

Jumper Wires

Jumper wires are simple, yet extremely valuable, pieces of test equipment. Jumper wires are merely wires that are used to bypass sections of a circuit. The simplest type of jumper wire is merely a length of multi-strand wire with an alligator clip at each end. Jumper wires are usually fabricated from lengths of standard automotive wire and whatever type of connector (alligator clip, spade connector or pin connector) that is required for the particular vehicle being tested. The well equipped tool box will have several different styles of jumper wires in several different lengths. Some jumper wires are made with three or more terminals coming from a common splice for special purpose testing. In cramped, hard-to-reach areas it is advisable to have insulated boots over the jumper wire terminals in order to prevent accidental grounding, sparks, and possible fire, especially when testing fuel system components.

Jumper wires are used primarily to locate open electrical circuits, on either the ground (-) side of the circuit or on the hot (+) side. If an electrical component fails to operate, connect the jumper wire between the component and a good ground. If the component operates only with the jumper installed, the ground circuit is open. If the ground circuit is good, but the component does not operate, the circuit between the power feed and component is open. You can sometimes connect the jumper wire directly from the battery to the hot terminal of the component, but first make sure the component uses 12 volts in operation. Some electrical components, such as fuel injectors, are designed to operate on about 4 volts and running 12 volts directly to the injector terminals can burn out the wiring. By inserting an inline fuse holder between a set of test leads, a fused jumper wire can be used for bypassing open circuits. Use a 5 amp fuse to provide protection against voltage spikes. When in doubt, use a voltmeter to check the voltage input to the component and measure how much voltage is being applied normally. By moving the jumper wire successively back from the lamp toward the power source, you can isolate the area of the circuit where the open is located. When the component stops functioning, or the power is cut off,

the open is in the segment of wire between the jumper and the point previously tested.

✳✳CAUTION

Never use jumpers made from wire that is of lighter gauge than used in the circuit under test. If the jumper wire is of too small gauge, it may overheat and possibly melt. Never use jumpers to bypass high resistance loads (such as motors) in a circuit. Bypassing resistances, in effect, creates a short circuit which may, in turn, cause damage and fire. Never use a jumper for anything other than temporary bypassing of components in a circuit.

12 Volt Test Light

The 12 volt test light is used to check circuits and components while electrical current is flowing through them. It is used for voltage and ground tests. Twelve volt test lights come in different styles but all have three main parts; a ground clip, a probe, and a light. The most commonly used 12 volt test lights have pick-type probes. To use a 12 volt test light, connect the ground clip to a good ground and probe wherever necessary with the pick. The pick should be sharp so that it can penetrate wire insulation to make contact with the wire, without making a large hole in the insulation. The wrap-around light is handy in hard to reach areas or where it is difficult to support a wire to push a probe pick into it. To use the wrap around light, hook the wire to probed with the hook and pull the trigger. A small pick will be forced through the wire insulation into the wire core.

✳✳CAUTION

Do not use a test light to probe electronic ignition spark plug or coil wires. Never use a pick-type test light to probe wiring on computer controlled systems unless specifically instructed to do so. Any wire insulation that is pierced by the test light probe should be taped and sealed with silicone after testing.

Like the jumper wire, the 12 volt test light is used to isolate opens in circuits. But, whereas the jumper wire is used to bypass the open to operate the load, the 12 volt test light is used to locate the presence of voltage in a circuit. If the test light glows, you know that there is power up to that point; if the 12 volt test light does not glow when its probe is inserted into the wire or connector, you know that there is an open circuit (no power). Move the test light in successive steps back toward the power source until the light in the handle does glow. When it does glow, the open is between the probe and point previously probed.

➡The test light does not detect that 12 volts (or any particular amount of voltage) is present; it only detects that some voltage is present. It is advisable before using the test light to touch its terminals across the battery posts to make sure the light is operating properly.

Self-Powered Test Light

The self-powered test light usually contains a 1.5 volt penlight battery. One type of self-powered test light is similar in design to the 12 volt test light. This type has both the battery and the light in the handle and pick-type probe tip. The second type has the light toward the open tip, so that the light illuminates the contact point. The self-powered test light is dual purpose piece of test equipment. It can be used to test for either open or short circuits when power is isolated from the circuit (continuity test). A powered test light should not be used on any computer controlled system or component unless specifically instructed to do so. Many engine sensors can be destroyed by even this small amount of voltage applied directly to the terminals.

Open Circuit Testing

To use the self-powered test light to check for open circuits, first isolate the circuit from the vehicle's 12 volt power source by disconnecting the battery or wiring harness connector. Connect the test light ground clip to a good ground and probe sections of the circuit sequentially with the test light. (start from either end of the circuit). If the light is out, the open is between the probe and the circuit ground. If the light is on, the open is between the probe and end of the circuit toward the power source.

Short Circuit Testing

By isolating the circuit both from power and from ground, and using a self-powered test light, you can check for shorts to ground in the circuit. Isolate the circuit from power and ground. Connect the test light ground clip to a good ground and probe any easy-to-reach test point in the circuit. If the light comes on, there is a short somewhere in the circuit. To isolate the short, probe a test point at either end of the isolated circuit (the light should be on). Leave the test light probe connected and open connectors, switches, remove parts, etc., sequentially, until the light goes out. When the light goes out, the short is between the last circuit component opened and the previous circuit opened.

➡**The 1.5 volt battery in the test light does not provide much current. A weak battery may not provide enough power to illuminate the test light even when a complete circuit is made (especially if there are high resistances in the circuit). Always make sure that the test battery is strong. To check the battery, briefly touch the ground clip to the probe; if the light glows brightly the battery is strong enough for testing. Never use a self-powered test light to perform checks for opens or shorts when power is applied to the electrical system under test. The 12 volt vehicle power will quickly burn out the 1.5 volt light bulb in the test light.**

Voltmeter

A voltmeter is used to measure voltage at any point in a circuit, or to measure the voltage drop across any part of a circuit. It can also be used to check continuity in a wire or circuit by indicating current flow from one end to the other. Voltmeters usually have various scales on the meter dial and a selector switch to allow the selection of different voltages. The voltmeter has a positive and a negative lead. To avoid damage to the meter, always connect the negative lead to the negative (-) side of the circuit (to ground or nearest the ground side of the circuit) and connect the positive lead to the positive (+) side of the circuit (to the power source or the nearest power source). Note that the negative voltmeter lead will always be black and that the positive voltmeter will always be some color other than black (usually red). Depending on how the voltmeter is connected into the circuit, it has several uses.

A voltmeter can be connected either in parallel or in series with a circuit and it has a very high resistance to current flow. When connected in parallel, only a small amount of current will flow through the voltmeter current path; the rest will flow through the normal circuit current path and the circuit will work normally. When the voltmeter is connected in series with a circuit, only a small amount of current can flow through the circuit. The circuit will not work properly, but the voltmeter reading will show if the circuit is complete or not.

Available Voltage Measurement

Set the voltmeter selector switch to the 20V position and connect the meter negative lead to the negative (-) post of the battery. Connect the positive meter lead to the positive (+) post of the battery and turn the ignition switch ON to provide a load. Read the voltage on the meter or digital display. A well charged battery should register over 12 volts. If the meter reads below 11.5 volts, the battery power may be insufficient to operate the electrical system properly. This test determines voltage available from the battery and should be the first step in any electrical trouble diagnosis procedure. Many electrical problems, especially on computer controlled systems, can be caused by a low state of charge in the battery. Excessive corrosion at the battery cable terminals can cause a poor contact that will prevent proper charging and full battery current flow.

Normal battery voltage is 12 volts when fully charged. When the battery is supplying current to one or more circuits it is said to be, under load. When everything is off the electrical system is under a no-load condition. A fully charged battery may show about 12.5 volts at no load; will drop to 12 volts under medium load; and will drop even lower under heavy load. If the battery is partially discharged the voltage decrease under heavy load may be excessive, even though the battery shows 12 volts or more at no load. When allowed to discharge further, the battery's available voltage under load will decrease more severely. For this reason, it is important that the battery be fully charged during all testing procedures to avoid errors in diagnosis and incorrect test results.

Voltage Drop

When current flows through a resistance, the voltage beyond the resistance is reduced (the larger the current, the greater the reduction in voltage). When no current is flowing, there is no voltage drop because there is no current flow. All points in the circuit which are connected to the power source are at the same voltage as the power source. The total voltage drop always equals the total source voltage. In a long circuit with many connectors, a series of small, unwanted voltage drops due to corrosion at the connectors can add up to a total loss of voltage which impairs the operation of the normal loads in the circuit.

INDIRECT COMPUTATION OF VOLTAGE DROPS

1. Set the voltmeter selector switch to the 20 volt position.
2. Connect the meter negative lead to a good ground.

3. Probe all resistances in the circuit with the positive meter lead.

4. Operate the circuit in all modes and observe the voltage readings.

DIRECT MEASUREMENT OF VOLTAGE DROPS

1. Set the voltmeter switch to the 20 volt position.
2. Connect the voltmeter negative lead to the ground side of the resistance load to be measured.
3. Connect the positive lead to the positive side of the resistance or load to be measured.
4. Read the voltage drop directly on the 20 volt scale.

Too high a voltage indicates too high a resistance. If, for example, a blower motor runs too slowly, you can determine if there is too high a resistance in the resistor pack. By taking voltage drop readings in all parts of the circuit, you can isolate the problem. Too low a voltage drop indicates too low a resistance. If, for example, a blower motor runs too fast in the MED and/or LOW position, the problem can be isolated in the resistor pack by taking voltage drop readings in all parts of the circuit to locate a possibly shorted resistor. The maximum allowable voltage drop under load is critical, especially if there is more than one high resistance problem in a circuit because all voltage drops are cumulative. A small drop is normal due to the resistance of the conductors.

HIGH RESISTANCE TESTING

1. Set the voltmeter selector switch to the 4 volt position.
2. Connect the voltmeter positive lead to the positive (+) post of the battery.
3. Turn on the headlights and heater blower to provide a load.
4. Probe various points in the circuit with the negative voltmeter lead.
5. Read the voltage drop on the 4 volt scale. Some average maximum allowable voltage drops are:

> FUSE PANEL — 7 volts
> IGNITION SWITCH — 5 volts
> HEADLIGHT SWITCH — 7 volts
> IGNITION COIL (+) — 5 volts
> ANY OTHER LOAD — 1.3 volts

➡**Voltage drops are all measured while a load is operating; without current flow, there will be no voltage drop.**

Ohmmeter

The ohmmeter is designed to read resistance (ohms) in a circuit or component. Although there are several different styles of ohmmeters, all will usually have a selector switch which permits the measurement of different ranges of resistance (usually the selector switch allows the multiplication of the meter reading by 10, 100, 1000, and 10,000). A calibration knob allows the meter to be set at zero for accurate measurement. Since all ohmmeters are powered by an internal battery (usually 9 volts), the ohmmeter can be used as a self-powered test light. When the ohmmeter is connected, current from the ohmmeter flows through the circuit or component being tested. Since the ohmmeter's internal resistance and voltage are known values, the amount of current flow through the meter depends on the resistance of the circuit or component being tested.

The ohmmeter can be used to perform continuity test for opens or shorts (either by observation of the meter needle or as a self-powered test light), and to read actual resistance in a circuit. It should be noted that the ohmmeter is used to check the resistance of a component or wire while there is no voltage applied to the circuit. Current flow from an outside voltage source (such as the vehicle battery) can damage the ohmmeter, so the circuit or component should be isolated from the vehicle electrical system before any testing is done. Since the ohmmeter uses its own voltage source, either lead can be connected to any test point.

➡**When checking diodes or other solid state components, the ohmmeter leads can only be connected one way in order to measure current flow in a single direction. Make sure the positive (+) and negative (-) terminal connections are as described in the test procedures to verify the one-way diode operation.**

In using the meter for making continuity checks, do not be concerned with the actual resistance readings. Zero resistance, or any resistance readings, indicate continuity in the circuit. Infinite resistance indicates an open in the circuit. A high resistance reading where there should be none indicates a problem in the circuit. Checks for short circuits are made in the same manner as checks for open circuits except that the circuit must be isolated from both power and normal ground. Infinite resistance indicates no continuity to ground, while zero resistance indicates a dead short to ground.

RESISTANCE MEASUREMENT

The batteries in an ohmmeter will weaken with age and temperature, so the ohmmeter must be calibrated or zeroed before taking measurements. To zero the meter, place the selector switch in its lowest range and touch the two ohmmeter leads together. Turn the calibration knob until the meter needle is exactly on zero.

➡**All analog (needle) type ohmmeters must be zeroed before use, but some digital ohmmeter models are automatically calibrated when the switch is turned on. Self-calibrating digital ohmmeters do not have an adjusting knob, but its a good idea to check for a zero readout before use by touching the leads together. All computer controlled systems require the use of a digital ohmmeter with at least 10 megohms impedance for testing. Before any test procedures are attempted, make sure the ohmmeter used is compatible with the electrical system or damage to the on-board computer could result.**

To measure resistance, first isolate the circuit from the vehicle power source by disconnecting the battery cables or the harness connector. Make sure the key is **OFF** when disconnecting any components or the battery. Where necessary, also isolate at least one side of the circuit to be checked to avoid reading parallel resistances. Parallel circuit resistances will always give a lower reading than the actual resistance of either of the branches. When measuring the resistance of parallel circuits, the total resistance will always be lower than the smallest resistance in the circuit. Connect the meter leads to both sides of the circuit (wire or component) and read the actual measured ohms on the meter scale. Make sure the selector switch is set to the proper ohm scale for the circuit being tested to avoid misreading the ohmmeter test value.

❋❋CAUTION

Never use an ohmmeter with power applied to the circuit. Like the self-powered test light, the ohmmeter is designed to operate on its own power supply. The normal 12 volt automotive electrical system current could damage the meter.

Ammeters

An ammeter measures the amount of current flowing through a circuit in units called amperes or amps. Amperes are units of electron flow which indicate how fast the electrons are flowing through the circuit. Since Ohms Law dictates that current flow in a circuit is equal to the circuit voltage divided by the total circuit resistance, increasing voltage also increases the current level (amps). Likewise, any decrease in resistance will increase the amount of amps in a circuit. At normal operating voltage, most circuits have a characteristic amount of amperes, called current draw which can be measured using an ammeter. By referring to a specified current draw rating, measuring the amperes, and comparing the two values, one can determine what is happening within the circuit to aid in diagnosis. An open circuit, for example, will not allow any current to flow so the ammeter reading will be zero. More current flows through a heavily loaded circuit or when the charging system is operating.

An ammeter is always connected in series with the circuit being tested. All of the current that normally flows through the circuit must also flow through the ammeter; if there is any other path for the current to follow, the ammeter reading will not be accurate. The ammeter itself has very little resistance to current flow and therefore will not affect the circuit, but it will measure current draw only when the circuit is closed and electricity is flowing. Excessive current draw can blow fuses and drain the battery, while a reduced current draw can cause motors to run slowly, lights to dim and other components to not operate properly. The ammeter can help diagnose these conditions by locating the cause of the high or low reading.

Multimeters

Different combinations of test meters can be built into a single unit designed for specific tests. Some of the more common combination test devices are known as Volt/Amp testers, Tach/Dwell meters, or Digital Multimeters. The Volt/Amp tester is used for charging system, starting system or battery tests and consists of a voltmeter, an ammeter and a variable resistance carbon pile. The voltmeter will usually have at least two ranges for use with 6, 12 and 24 volt systems. The ammeter also has more than one range for testing various levels of battery loads and starter current draw and the carbon pile can be adjusted to offer different amounts of resistance. The Volt/Amp tester has heavy leads to carry large amounts of current and many later models have an inductive ammeter pickup that clamps around the wire to simplify test connections. On some models, the ammeter also has a zero-center scale to allow testing of charging and starting systems without switching leads or polarity. A digital multimeter is a voltmeter, ammeter and ohmmeter combined in an instrument

which gives a digital readout. These are often used when testing solid state circuits because of their high input impedance (usually 10 megohms or more).

The tach/dwell meter combines a tachometer and a dwell (cam angle) meter and is a specialized kind of voltmeter. The tachometer scale is marked to show engine speed in rpm and the dwell scale is marked to show degrees of distributor shaft rotation. In most electronic ignition systems, dwell is determined by the control unit, but the dwell meter can also be used to check the duty cycle (operation) of some electronic engine control systems. Some tach/dwell meters are powered by an internal battery, while others take their power from the car battery in use. The battery powered testers usually require calibration much like an ohmmeter before testing.

Special Test Equipment

A variety of diagnostic tools are available to help troubleshoot and repair computerized engine control systems. The most sophisticated of these devices are the console type engine analyzers that usually occupy a garage service bay, but there are several types of aftermarket electronic testers available that will allow quick circuit tests of the engine control system by plugging directly into a special connector located in the engine compartment or under the dashboard. Several tool and equipment manufacturers offer simple, hand held testers that measure various circuit voltage levels on command to check all system components for proper operation. Although these testers usually are expensive, consider that the average computer control unit (or ECM) can cost just as much and the money saved by not replacing perfectly good sensors or components in an attempt to correct a problem could justify the purchase price of a special diagnostic tester the first time it's used. These computerized testers can allow quick and easy test measurements while the engine is operating or while the car is being driven. In addition, the on-board computer memory can be read to access any stored trouble codes; in effect allowing the computer to tell you where it hurts and aid trouble diagnosis by pinpointing exactly which circuit or component is malfunctioning. In the same manner, repairs can be tested to make sure the problem has been corrected. The biggest advantage these special testers have is their relatively easy hookups that minimize or eliminate the chances of making the wrong connections and getting false voltage readings or damaging the computer accidentally.

➡**It should be remembered that these testers check voltage levels in circuits; they don't detect mechanical problems or failed components if the circuit voltage falls within the pre-programmed limits stored in the tester PROM unit. Also, most of the hand held testes are designed to work only on one or two systems made by a specific manufacturer.**

A variety of aftermarket testers are available to help diagnose different computerized control systems. Owatonna Tool Company (OTC), for example, markets a device called the OTC Monitor which plugs directly into the assembly line diagnostic link (ALDL). The OTC tester makes diagnosis a simple matter of pressing the correct buttons and, by changing the internal PROM or inserting a different diagnosis cartridge, it will work on any model from full size to subcompact, over a wide range of years. An adapter is supplied with the tester to allow connection to all types of ALDL links, regardless of the number of pin terminals used. By inserting an updated PROM into the OTC tester, it can be easily updated to diagnose any new modifications of computerized control systems.

Wiring Harnesses

The average automobile contains about ½ mile of wiring, with hundreds of individual connections. To protect the many wires from damage and to keep them from becoming a confusing tangle, they are organized into bundles, enclosed in plastic or taped together and called wire harnesses. Different wiring harnesses serve different parts of the vehicle. Individual wires are color coded to help trace them through a harness where sections are hidden from view.

A loose or corroded connection or a replacement wire that is too small for the circuit will add extra resistance and an additional voltage drop to the circuit. A ten percent voltage drop can result in slow or erratic motor operation, for example, even though the circuit is complete. Automotive wiring or circuit conductors can be in any one of three forms:

1. Single strand wire
2. Multi-strand wire
3. Printed circuitry

Single strand wire has a solid metal core and is usually used inside such components as alternators, motors, relays and other devices. Multi-strand wire has a core made of many small strands of wire twisted together into a single conductor. Most of the wiring in an automotive electrical system is made up of multi-strand wire, either as a single conductor or grouped together in a harness. All wiring is color coded on the insulator, either as a solid color or as a colored wire with an identification stripe. A printed circuit is a thin film of copper or other conductor that is printed on an insulator backing. Occasionally, a printed circuit is sandwiched between two sheets of plastic for more protection and flexibility. A complete printed circuit, consisting of conductors, insulating material and connectors for lamps or other components is called a printed circuit board. Printed circuitry is used in place of individual wires or harnesses in places where space is limited, such as behind instrument panels.

WIRING REPAIR

Soldering is a quick, efficient method of joining metals permanently. Everyone who has the occasion to make wiring repairs should know how to solder. Electrical connections that are soldered are far less likely to come apart and will conduct electricity much better than connections that are only pig-tailed together. The most popular (and preferred) method of soldering is with an electrical soldering gun. Soldering irons are available in many sizes and wattage ratings. Irons with higher wattage ratings deliver higher temperatures and recover lost heat faster. A small soldering iron rated for no more than 50 watts is recommended, especially on electrical systems where excess heat can damage the components being soldered.

There are three ingredients necessary for successful soldering; proper flux, good solder and sufficient heat. A soldering flux is necessary to clean the metal of tarnish, prepare it for soldering and to enable the solder to spread into tiny crevices. When soldering, always use a resin flux or resin core solder which is non-corrosive and will not attract moisture once the job is finished. Other types of flux (acid core) will leave a residue that will attract moisture and cause the wires to corrode. Tin is a unique metal with a low melting point. In a molten state, it dissolves and alloys easily with many metals. Solder is made by mixing tin with lead. The most common proportions are 40/60, 50/50 and 60/40, with the percentage of tin listed first. Low priced solders usually contain less tin, making them very difficult for a beginner to use because more heat is required to melt the solder. A common solder is 40/60 which is well suited for all-around general use, but 60/40 melts easier, has more tin for a better joint and is preferred for electrical work.

Soldering Techniques

Successful soldering requires that the metals to be joined be heated to a temperature that will melt the solder — usually 360-460°F (182-238°C). Contrary to popular belief, the purpose of the soldering iron is not to melt the solder itself, but to heat the parts being soldered to a temperature high enough to melt the solder when it is touched to the work. Melting flux-cored solder on the soldering iron will usually destroy the effectiveness of the flux.

➡**Soldering tips are made of copper for good heat conductivity, but must be tinned regularly for quick transference of heat to the project and to prevent the solder from sticking to the iron. To tin the iron, simply heat it and touch the flux-cored solder to the tip; the solder will flow over the hot tip. Wipe the excess off with a clean rag, but be careful as the iron will be hot.**

After some use, the tip may become pitted. If so, simply dress the tip smooth with a smooth file and tin the tip again. An old saying holds that, metals well cleaned are half soldered. Flux-cored solder will remove oxides, but rust, bits of insulation and oil or grease must be removed with a wire brush or emery cloth. For maximum strength in soldered parts, the joint must start off clean and tight. Weak joints will result in gaps too wide for the solder to bridge.

If a separate soldering flux is used, it should be brushed or swabbed on only those areas that are to be soldered. Most solders contain a core of flux and separate fluxing is unnecessary. Hold the work to be soldered firmly. It is best to solder on a wooden board, because a metal vise will only rob the piece to be soldered of heat and make it difficult to melt the solder. Hold the soldering tip with the broadest face against the work to be soldered. Apply solder under the tip close to the work, using enough solder to give a heavy film between the iron and the piece being soldered, while moving slowly and making sure the solder melts properly. Keep the work level or the solder will run to the lowest part and favor the thicker parts, because these require more heat to melt the solder. If the soldering tip overheats (the solder coating on the face of the tip burns up), it should be retinned. Once the soldering is completed, let the soldered joint stand until cool. Tape and seal all soldered wire splices after the repair has cooled.

Wire Harness and Connectors

The on-board computer (ECM) wire harness electrically connects the control unit to the various solenoids, switches and sensors used by the control system. Most connectors in the engine compartment or otherwise exposed to the elements are protected against moisture and dirt which could create oxidation and deposits on the terminals. This protection is important because of the very low voltage and current levels used by the computer and sensors. All connectors have a lock which secures the male and female terminals together, with a secondary lock holding the seal and terminal into the connector. Both terminal locks must be released when disconnecting ECM connectors.

These special connectors are weather-proof and all repairs require the use of a special terminal and the tool required to service it. This tool is used to remove the pin and sleeve terminals. If removal is attempted with an ordinary pick, there is a good chance that the terminal will be bent or deformed. Unlike standard blade type terminals, these terminals cannot be straightened once they are bent. Make certain that the connectors are properly seated and all of the sealing rings in place when connecting leads. On some models, a hinge-type flap provides a backup or secondary locking feature for the terminals. Most secondary locks are used to improve the connector reliability by retaining the terminals if the small terminal lock tangs are not positioned properly.

Molded-on connectors require complete replacement of the connection. This means splicing a new connector assembly into the harness. All splices in on-board computer systems should be soldered to insure proper contact. Use care when probing the connections or replacing terminals in them as it is possible to short between opposite terminals. If this happens to the wrong terminal pair, it is possible to damage certain components. Always use jumper wires between connectors for circuit checking and never probe through weatherproof seals.

Open circuits are often difficult to locate by sight because corrosion or terminal misalignment are hidden by the connectors. Merely wiggling a connector on a sensor or in the wiring harness may correct the open circuit condition. This should always be considered when an open circuit or a failed sensor is indicated. Intermittent problems may also be caused by oxidized or loose connections. When using a circuit tester for diagnosis, always probe connections from the wire side. Be careful not to damage sealed connectors with test probes.

All wiring harnesses should be replaced with identical parts, using the same gauge wire and connectors. When signal wires are spliced into a harness, use wire with high temperature insulation only. With the low voltage and current levels found in the system, it is important that the best possible connection at all wire splices be made by soldering the splices together. It is seldom necessary to replace a complete harness. If replacement is necessary, pay close attention to insure proper harness routing. Secure the harness with suitable plastic wire clamps to prevent vibrations from causing the harness to wear in spots or contact any hot components.

➡**Weatherproof connectors cannot be replaced with standard connectors. Instructions are provided with replacement connector and terminal packages. Some wire harnesses have mounting indicators (usually pieces of colored tape) to mark where the harness is to be secured.**

In making wiring repairs, it's important that you always replace damaged wires with wires that are the same gauge as the wire being replaced. The heavier the wire, the smaller the gauge number. Wires are color-coded to aid in identification and whenever possible the same color coded wire should be used for replacement. A wire stripping and crimping tool is necessary to install solderless terminal connectors. Test all crimps by pulling on the wires; it should not be possible to pull the wires out of a good crimp.

Wires which are open, exposed or otherwise damaged are repaired by simple splicing. Where possible, if the wiring harness is accessible and the damaged place in the wire can be located, it is best to open the harness and check for all possible damage. In an inaccessible harness, the wire must be bypassed with a new insert, usually taped to the outside of the old harness.

When replacing fusible links, be sure to use fusible link wire, NOT ordinary automotive wire. Make sure the fusible segment is of the same gauge and construction as the one being replaced and double the stripped end when crimping the terminal connector for a good contact. The melted (open) fusible link segment of the wiring harness should be cut off as close to the harness as possible, then a new segment spliced in as described. In the case of a damaged fusible link that feeds two harness wires, the harness connections should be replaced with two fusible link wires so that each circuit will have its own separate protection.

➡**Most of the problems caused in the wiring harness are due to bad ground connections. Always check all vehicle ground connections for corrosion or looseness before performing any power feed checks to eliminate the chance of a bad ground affecting the circuit.**

Repairing Hard Shell Connectors

Unlike molded connectors, the terminal contacts in hard shell connectors can be replaced. Weatherproof hard-shell connectors with the leads molded into the shell have non-replaceable terminal ends. Replacement usually involves the use of a special terminal removal tool that depress the locking tangs (barbs) on the connector terminal and allow the connector to be removed from the rear of the shell. The connector shell should be replaced if it shows any evidence of burning, melting, cracks, or breaks. Replace individual terminals that are burnt, corroded, distorted or loose.

➡**The insulation crimp must be tight to prevent the insulation from sliding back on the wire when the wire is pulled. The insulation must be visibly compressed under the crimp tabs, and the ends of the crimp should be turned in for a firm grip on the insulation.**

The wire crimp must be made with all wire strands inside the crimp. The terminal must be fully compressed on the wire strands with the ends of the crimp tabs turned in to make a firm grip on the wire. Check all connections with an ohmmeter to insure a good contact. There should be no measurable resistance between the wire and the terminal when connected.

Mechanical Test Equipment

Vacuum Gauge

Most gauges are graduated in inches of mercury (in.Hg), although a device called a manometer reads vacuum in inches of water (in. H_2O). The normal vacuum reading usually varies between 18 and 22 in.Hg at sea level. To test engine vacuum, the vacuum gauge must be connected to a source of manifold vacuum. Many engines have a plug in the intake manifold which can be removed and replaced with an adapter fitting. Connect the vacuum gauge to the fitting with a suitable rubber hose or, if no manifold plug is available, connect the vacuum gauge to any device using manifold vacuum, such as EGR valves, etc. The vacuum gauge can be used to determine if enough vacuum is reaching a component to allow its actuation.

Hand Vacuum Pump

Small, hand-held vacuum pumps come in a variety of designs. Most have a built-in vacuum gauge and allow the component to be tested without removing it from the vehicle. Operate the pump lever or plunger to apply the correct amount of vacuum required for the test specified in the diagnosis routines. The level of vacuum in inches of Mercury (in.Hg) is indicated on the pump gauge. For some testing, an additional vacuum gauge may be necessary.

Intake manifold vacuum is used to operate various systems and devices on late model vehicles. To correctly diagnose and solve problems in vacuum control systems, a vacuum source is necessary for testing. In some cases, vacuum can be taken from the intake manifold when the engine is running, but vacuum is normally provided by a hand vacuum pump. These hand vacuum pumps have a built-in vacuum gauge that allow testing while the device is still attached to the component. For some tests, an additional vacuum gauge may be necessary.

HEATER

Blower Motor

The blower motor is located under the dashboard on the far right side of the car. The blower motor turns the fan, which circulates the heated, cooled or fresh air within the car. Aside from common electrical problems, the blower motor may need to be removed to clean out leaves or debris which have been sucked into the casing.

REMOVAL & INSTALLATION

▶ **See Figures 1, 2, 3 and 4**

1. Disconnect the negative battery cable.
2. Remove the glove box assembly.
3. Disconnect the wiring from the blower motor.
4. Remove the three screws holding the blower motor and remove the blower motor.
   To install:
5. With the blower motor removed, check the heater case for any debris or signs of fan contact. Inspect the fan for wear spots, cracked blades or hub, loose retaining nut or poor alignment.
6. Place the blower motor in position, making sure it is properly aligned within the case. Install the three screws and tighten them **EVENLY**.

7. Connect the wiring to the blower motor.
8. Connect the negative battery cable. Check operation of blower motor for all speeds and heater A/C system for proper operation.

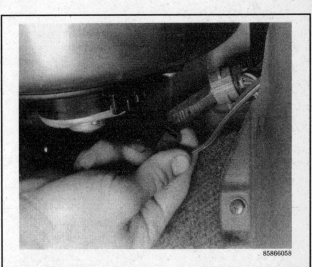

Fig. 1 Removing the electrical connection from the blower motor — most models similar

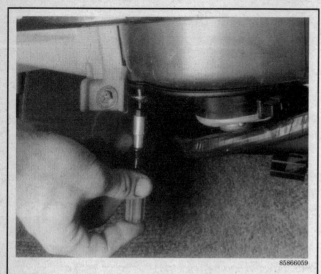

85866059

Fig. 2 Removing the blower motor retaining screws

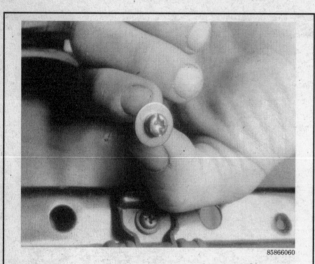

85866060

Fig. 3 View of the blower motor retaining screws/bolts — most models similar

85866061

Fig. 4 Removing the blower motor assembly — most models similar

Heater Unit

REMOVAL & INSTALLATION

1. Disconnect the negative battery cable. Drain the cooling system.

2. Remove the cooling unit, if so equipped-refer to the necessary service procedures.

3. Remove the heater hose clamps. Disconnect the heater hoses from the heater core. Remove the heater core pipe grommet.

4. Remove the instrument panel-refer to the necessary service procedure.

5. Remove the instrument panel reinforcement and bracket.

6. Remove the duct heater to register and remove the front defroster nozzle.

7. Remove the heater unit.

To install:

8. Install the heater unit in the vehicle.

9. Install the front defroster nozzle and duct heater to register.

10. Install the instrument panel reinforcement braces.

11. Install the instrument panel assembly.

12. Install the heater core pipe grommets. Push the water hoses onto the heater core pipes as far as the ridge on the pipes. Reconnect the heater hoses use NEW hose clamps if necessary.

13. Install the cooling unit assembly. Refill the cooling system.

14. Connect the negative battery cable. Check operation of heater and A/C system.

Heater Core

▶ **See Figures 5, 6, 7, 8, 9, 10, 11, 12, 13, 14, 15, 16, 17 and 18**

The heater core is simply a small heat exchanger (radiator) within the heater housing assembly in the vehicle. If the driver selects heat on the control panel, a water valve is opened allowing engine coolant to circulate through the heater core. The blower fan circulates air through the fins, picking up the heat from the engine coolant and then the heated air is ducted into the vehicle.

1. Remove the heater unit assembly-refer to the necessary service procedure.

2. Remove the screws and 2 heater core retaining clip.

3. Remove the heater core from the heater unit.

4. Installation is the reverse of the removal procedure. Push the water hoses onto the heater core pipes as far as the ridge on the pipes. Refill the cooling system. Connect the negative battery cable. Check operation of heater and A/C system.

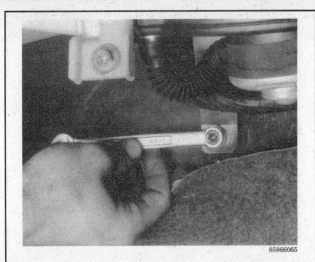

Fig. 5 Removing the heater unit assembly lower mounting bolt

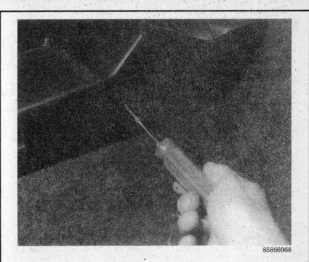

Fig. 8 Removing the retaining screw for console assembly

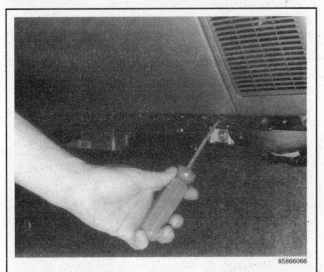

Fig. 6 Removing the dash assembly mounting screw

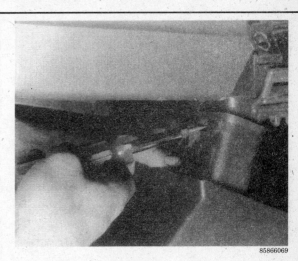

Fig. 9 Removing the heater duct from the the heater unit assembly

Fig. 7 Removing the heater unit assembly lower mounting bolt

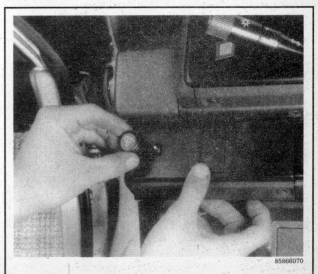

Fig. 10 Removing the dash panel

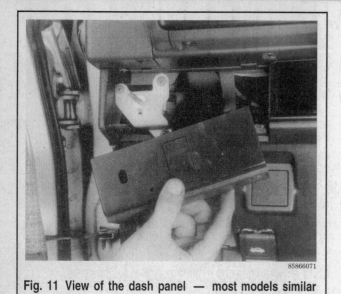

Fig. 11 View of the dash panel — most models similar

Fig. 14 Removing the heater control assembly — most models similar

Fig. 12 Removing the control cable from the control head assembly

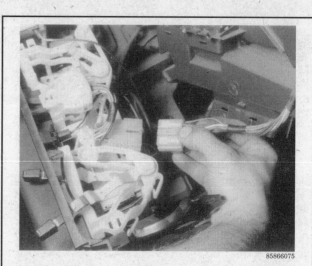

Fig. 15 Removing the electrical connection from the control head assembly

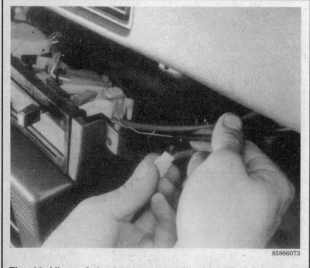

Fig. 13 View of the heater control cable clip

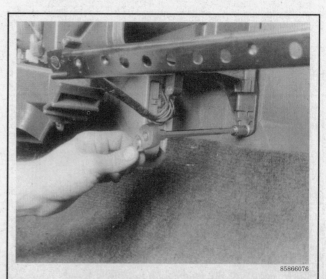

Fig. 16 Removing the lower mounting of heater unit

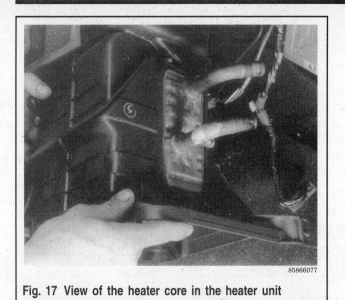

Fig. 17 View of the heater core in the heater unit

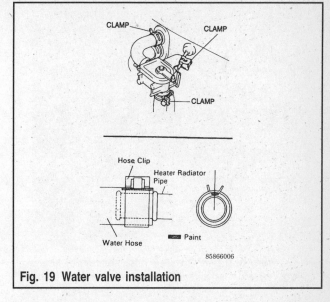

Fig. 19 Water valve installation

Fig. 18 Removing the heater core from the heater unit

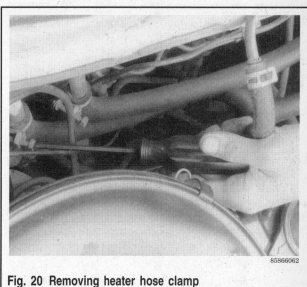

Fig. 20 Removing heater hose clamp

Heater Water Control Valve

REMOVAL & INSTALLATION

▶ See Figures 19, 20, 21 and 22

1. Disconnect the negative battery cable. Drain the cooling system.
2. Disconnect the water valve control cable.
3. Disconnect the heater hoses from the heater core and water valve.
4. Remove the water valve.
5. Installation is the reverse of the removal procedure. Push the water hose onto the heater core pipe as far as the ridge on the pipe. Refill the cooling system. Adjust control cable if necessary. Connect the negative battery cable. Check operation of the system.

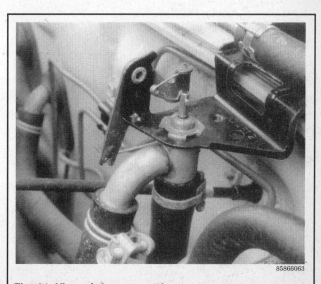

Fig. 21 View of the water valve

Fig. 22 View of water valve — note position of heater control cable

Control Assembly

REMOVAL & INSTALLATION

1. Disconnect the negative battery cable. Remove the center cluster finish lower panel and stereo opening cover.
2. Remove the center cluster finish panel and radio.
3. Disconnect the control cables from the heater unit and water valve.
4. Remove the 4 screws and the control assembly. Disconnect the air inlet control cable from the control assembly. Disconnect the blower switch connector. Remove the control assembly.
5. Installation is the reverse of the removal procedure. Adjust control cables as necessary. Connect the negative battery cable. Check operation of the system.

ADJUSTMENT

▶ See Figure 23

1. Set the air inlet damper and control lever to the **RECIRC** position, install the control cable and lock the clamp.
2. Set the mode selector damper and control lever to the **DEF** position, install the control cable and lock the clamp.
3. Set the air mix damper and control lever to the **COOL** position, install the control cable and lock the clamp.
4. Set the water valve and control lever to the **COOL** position, install the control cable and lock the clamp.

5. Move the control levers left and right and check for stiffness or binding through the full range of the levers. Test control cable operation.

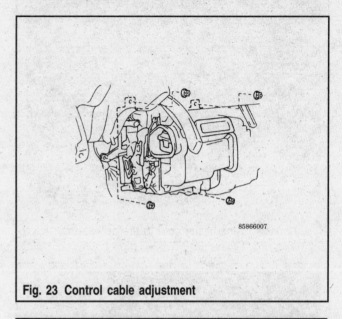

Fig. 23 Control cable adjustment

Blower Speed Control Switch

REMOVAL & INSTALLATION

1. Disconnect the negative battery cable. Remove the illumination light from the control assembly.
2. Using a tool, pry loose the clip and push out the blower speed control switch to the rear of the control assembly.
3. Installation is the reverse of the removal procedure. Connect the negative battery cable. Check operation of the system.

Blower Motor Resistor

REMOVAL & INSTALLATION

1. Disconnect the negative cable.
2. Disconnect the electrical connector from the blower resistor assembly.
3. Remove the cowl side panel and glove box assembly. Remove mounting screw and remove the blower resistor assembly from the heater case.
4. Installation is the reverse of the service removal procedure. Reconnect the negative battery cable. Check the blower motor for proper operation at all speeds after installation.

AIR CONDITIONER

Cooling Unit (Evaporator)

REMOVAL & INSTALLATION

▶ **See Figure 24**

1. Disconnect the negative battery cable. Recover refrigerant (discharge system) from refrigeration system.
2. Disconnect the suction flexible hose from the cooling unit outlet fitting.
3. Disconnect the liquid line from the cooling unit inlet fitting. Cap the open fittings immediately to keep the moisture out of the system.
4. Remove the grommets from the inlet and outlet fittings.
5. Remove the front door scuff plate and glove box assembly. Disconnect all necessary connectors and the air conditioning harness.
6. Remove the cooling unit attaching nuts and bolts. Remove the cooling unit from the vehicle.
7. Place the cooling unit on a suitable work bench and remove control amplifier, relay assemblies or power transistor assembly if so equipped.
8. Using suitable tools, remove the upper cooling unit case clamps and retaining screws. Remove thermistor with thermistor holder.
9. Remove the lower cooling unit case from the evaporator. Remove the evaporator from the cooling unit.
10. Remove the heat insulator (heat sensing tube) and the clamp from the outlet tube. Disconnect the liquid line from the inlet fitting of the expansion valve.
11. Disconnect the expansion valve from the inlet fitting of the evaporator. Remove the expansion valve.

➡ **Before installing the evaporator, check the evaporator fins for blockage. If the fins are clogged, clean them with compressed air. Never use water to clean the evaporator. Check the fittings for cracks and or scratches and replace, as necessary.**

To install:

12. Connect the expansion valve to the inlet fitting of the evaporator assembly. Be sure the O-ring is positioned on the tube fitting.
13. Connect the liquid line tube to the inlet fitting on the expansion valve.
14. Install the clamp and heat insulator (heat sensing tube) to the outlet tube.
15. Install the upper and lower cases on the evaporator. Install the thermistor. Install control amplifier, relay assemblies or power transistor assembly, if equipped.
16. Install the air conditioning wiring harness to the cooling unit and all other necessary components.
17. Install the cooling unit assembly in the vehicle. Be careful not to pinch the wiring harness while installing the cooling unit.
18. Install the glove box assembly, front door scuff plate and the grommets on the inlet and outlet fittings.

19. Connect the liquid line to the cooling unit inlet fittings and torque to 10 ft. lbs.
20. Connect the suction tube to the cooling unit outlet fitting and torque to 24 ft. lbs.
21. If the evaporator was replaced, add 2 fl. oz. of compressor oil to the compressor. Connect the negative battery cable.
22. Evacuate, charge and test the refrigeration system.

➡ **If the drain hose on the cooling unit assembly becomes clogged or blocked with debris the cooling unit will leak water on the front floor rug area.**

Expansion Valve

REMOVAL & INSTALLATION

On all vehicles, the cooling unit and evaporator assembly must be removed before the expansion valve can be replaced. Refer to the necessary service procedures.

A/C Switch

REMOVAL & INSTALLATION

▶ **See Figure 25**

1. Disconnect the negative battery cable.
2. Using a tool (tape the end of the tool before use) pry loose the clips and remove the A/C switch.
3. Installation is the reverse of the removal procedure. Connect the negative battery cable. Check operation of the A/C system.

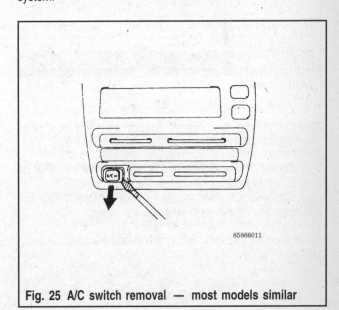

85866011

Fig. 25 A/C switch removal — most models similar

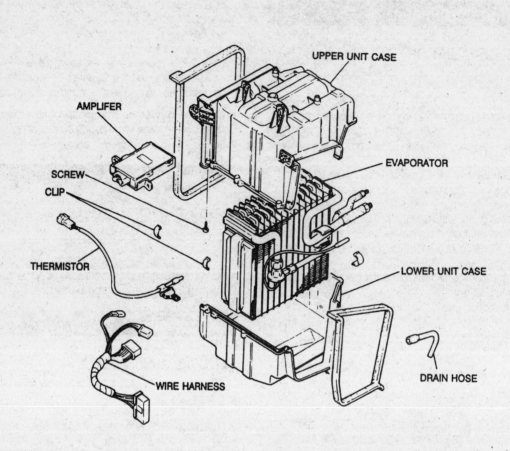

AMPLIFER

UPPER UNIT CASE

SCREW

CLIP

THERMISTOR

EVAPORATOR

LOWER UNIT CASE

DRAIN HOSE

WIRE HARNESS

85866010

Fig. 24 Exploded view of cooling unit — most models similar

Compressor

REMOVAL & INSTALLATION

▶ See Figure 26

1. Run the engine at idle with the air conditioning on for approximately 10 minutes.
2. Stop engine and disconnect the negative battery cable.
3. Remove the washer reserve tank.
4. Disconnect all electrical connection.
5. Recover refrigerant (discharge system) from refrigeration system.

6. Disconnect hoses from the compressor service valves. Cap open fittings immediately.
7. Remove engine undercover, if necessary. Loosen the compressor mounting bolts. Remove the compressor drive belt.
8. Remove the compressor mounting bolts. Remove the compressor from the vehicle.
   To install:
9. Install compressor with mounting bolts and torque retaining bolts evenly to 18 ft. lbs. (25 Nm) Install and adjust the drive belt. Install engine undercover, if necessary.
10. Reconnect hoses to the compressor service valves.
11. Reconnect all electrical connections. Install the washer reserve tank.
12. Reconnect the battery cable.
13. Evacuate, charge and test refrigerant system. Check system for leaks.

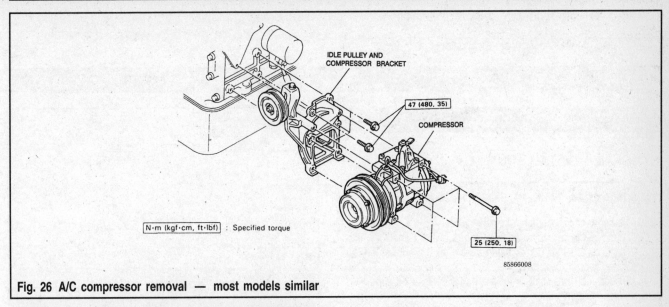

Fig. 26 A/C compressor removal — most models similar

Condenser

REMOVAL & INSTALLATION

1. Disconnect the negative battery cable.
2. Recover refrigerant (discharge system) from refrigeration system.
3. Remove the all the necessary components to gain access to condenser mounting bolts and to gain clearance for removal of condenser assembly.
4. Remove all refrigerant system connections. Remove the receiver with bracket. Cap open fittings immediately.
5. Remove the radiator support brackets. Remove the condenser mounting bolts lean the radiator back and pull out the condenser.
   To install:
6. Install the condenser assembly to the vehicle. Install radiator support brackets. Make sure all rubber cushions fit on the mounting flanges correctly.
7. Reconnect all refrigerant system connections. Install receiver with bracket. Replace O-rings, as required.
8. Install all other remaining components in reverse order of removal procedure.
9. If condenser assembly was replaced, add 2 fl. oz. of compressor oil.
10. Reconnect battery cable. Evacuate, charge and test refrigerant system. Check system for leaks.

Receiver/Drier

REMOVAL & INSTALLATION

▶ **See Figure 27**

1. Disconnect the negative battery cable.
2. Recover refrigerant (discharge system) from refrigeration system.

3. Remove the radiator grille, if necessary.
4. Disconnect lines from the receiver. Cap open fittings immediately.
5. Remove the receiver from the receiver holder assembly.
   To install:
6. Install receiver in receiver holder assembly. Reconnect lines to the receiver. Reconnect the negative battery cable.
7. Install radiator grille, if removed.
8. If receiver assembly was replaced, add 1 fl. oz. of compressor oil.
9. Evacuate, charge and test refrigerant system. Check system for leaks.

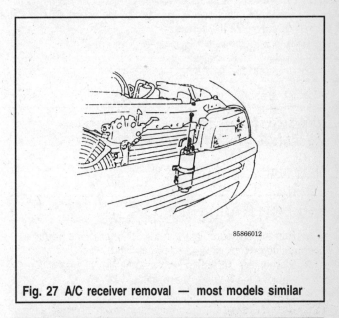

Fig. 27 A/C receiver removal — most models similar

Refrigerant Lines

REMOVAL & INSTALLATION

1. Disconnect the negative battery cable.

2. Recover refrigerant (discharge system) from refrigeration system.

3. Replace faulty line or hose. Always replace O-ring.

RADIO

Radio/Tape Player

REMOVAL & INSTALLATION

▶ See Figures 28, 29, 30, 31, 32, 33, 34, 35 and 36

1. Disconnect the negative battery cable.
2. Remove the attaching screws from the trim panel.
3. Remove the trim panel, being careful of the concealed spring clips behind the panel.
4. Disconnect the wiring from the switches if so equipped mounted in the trim panel.
5. Remove the mounting screws from the radio.
6. Remove the radio from the dash until the wiring connectors are exposed.
7. Disconnect the electrical connectors and the antenna cable from the body of the radio and remove the radio from the vehicle.

To install:

8. Reconnect all the wiring and antenna cable first, then place the radio in position within the dash.
9. Install the attaching screws.
10. Reconnect the wiring harnesses to the switches if so equipped in the trim panel and make sure the switches if so equipped are secure in the panel.
11. Install the trim panel (make sure all the spring clips engage) and install the screws.
12. Check radio system for proper operation.

4. Connect the negative battery cable. Evacuate, charge and test the refrigeration system.

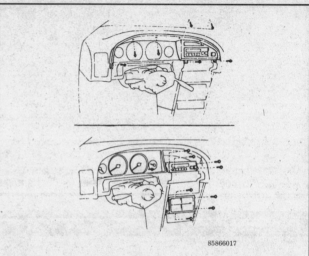

Fig. 29 Removing the radio mounting screws — radio mounted in upper dash area

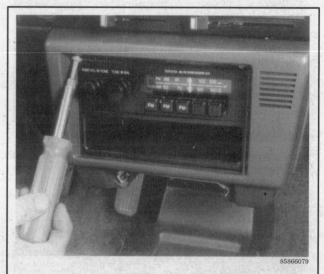

Fig. 30 Removing the radio trim panel retaining screws

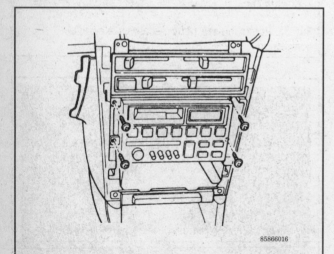

Fig. 28 Removing the radio mounting screws — radio mounted in lower console position

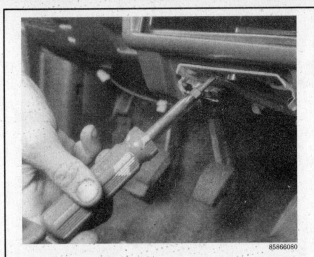

Fig. 31 Removing the radio trim panel lower retaining screws

Fig. 34 Removing the radio antenna lead

Fig. 32 Removing the radio trim panel

Fig. 35 Removing the radio assembly electrical connection

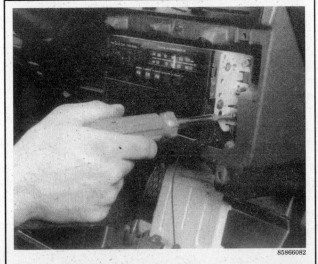

Fig. 33 Removing the radio assembly retaining screws

Fig. 36 Removing the radio assembly

Speakers

REMOVAL & INSTALLATION

▶ See Figures 37, 38, 39, 40 and 41

1. Remove the speaker cover.
2. Remove the attaching screws for the speaker. Note location of speaker wires Remove the speaker.
3. Installation is the reverse of the removal procedure. Make sure that the speaker wires are installed in the correct location. Check radio system for proper operation.

Fig. 37 Removing the speaker cover retaining screw — most models similar

Fig. 38 Removing the speaker cover

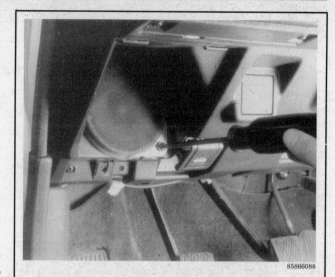

Fig. 39 Removing the speaker retaining screw

Fig. 40 Removing the speaker

Fig. 41 Removing the speaker connection

WINDSHIELD WIPERS

▶ **See Figure 42**

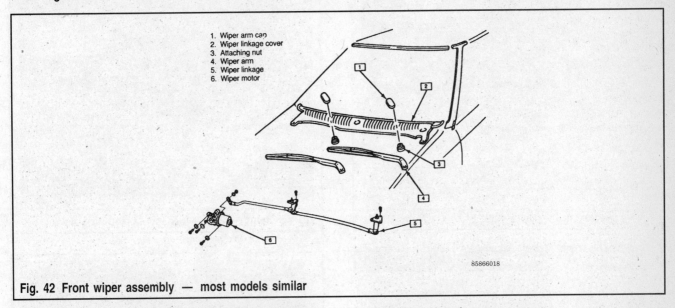

1. Wiper arm cap
2. Wiper linkage cover
3. Attaching nut
4. Wiper arm
5. Wiper linkage
6. Wiper motor

85866018

Fig. 42 Front wiper assembly — most models similar

Blade and Arm

REMOVAL & INSTALLATION

▶ **See Figures 43 and 44**

1. To remove the wiper blades lift up on the spring release tab on the wiper blade-to-wiper arm connector.

2. Pull the blade assembly off the wiper arm.

3. Press the old wiper blade insert down, away from the blade assembly, to free it from the retaining clips on the blade ends. Slide the insert out of the blade. Slide the new insert into the blade assembly and bend the insert upward slightly to engage the retaining clips.

4. To replace a wiper arm, unscrew the acorn nut (a cap covers this retaining nut at the bottom of the wiper arm) which secures it to the pivot and carefully pull the arm upward and off the pivot. Install the arm by placing it on the pivot and tightening the nut. Remember that the arm **MUST BE** reinstalled in its **EXACT** previous position or it will not cover the correct area during use.

➡If one wiper arm does not move when turned on or only moves a little bit, check the retaining nut at the bottom of the arm. The extra effort of moving wet snow or leaves off the glass can cause the nut to come loose — the pivot will turn without moving the arm.

85866091

Fig. 43 Removing the wiper arm retaining nut

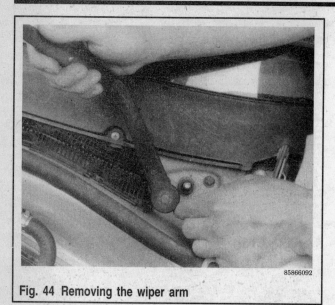

Fig. 44 Removing the wiper arm

Windshield Wiper Motor

REMOVAL & INSTALLATION

Front Wiper Assembly

 See Figures 45, 46, 47, 48 and 49

1. Disconnect the negative battery terminal.
2. Disconnect the electrical connector from the wiper motor.
3. Remove the mounting bolts and remove the motor from the firewall.
4. Remove the wiper linkage from the wiper motor assembly.
5. Installation is the reverse of removal. Check wiper system for proper operation.

Fig. 45 Removing the wiper motor electrical connection

Fig. 46 Removing the wiper motor mounting bolts

Fig. 47 On some models the ground wire may be connected to a wiper motor retaining bolt

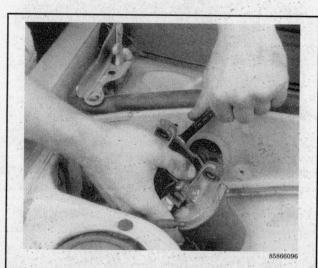

Fig. 48 Removing the wiper linkage from the wiper motor

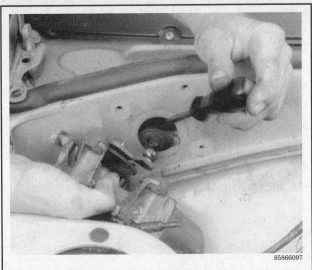

Fig. 49 Installing the wiper linkage-to-wiper motor

85866097

Rear Wiper Assembly

▶ **See Figure 50**

1. Remove the wiper arm from the pivot and remove the spacer and washer on the pivot.
2. Remove the cover (trim) panel on the inside of the hatch lock.
3. Remove the plastic cover on the wiper motor and disconnect the wiring connector from the motor.
4. Remove the mounting nuts and bolts and remove the wiper motor.

To install:

5. Position the motor and secure it in the hatch lid.
6. Connect the wiring harness and install the plastic cover.
7. Install the inner trim panel on the hatch lid.
8. Install the wiper arm with its washer and spacer, making sure the arm is correctly positioned before tightening the nut.

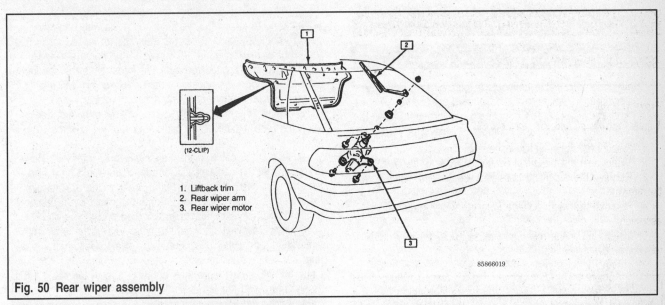

(12-CLIP)

1. Liftback trim
2. Rear wiper arm
3. Rear wiper motor

85866019

Fig. 50 Rear wiper assembly

Front Wiper Linkage

REMOVAL & INSTALLATION

1. Remove the windshield wiper motor as previously outlined.
2. Loosen the wiper arm retaining nuts and remove the arms.

INSTRUMENTS AND SWITCHES

Instrument Cluster (Combination Meter)

REMOVAL & INSTALLATION

1. Disconnect the negative battery cable.

3. Unfasten the large wiper pivot retaining nuts and remove the linkage assembly through the access hole.

To install:

4. Place the linkage through the access hole and line up the pivots in their holes.
5. Install the two large pivot retaining nuts onto the pivots. Before final tightening, make sure the linkage is aligned in all its holes.
6. Reinstall the wiper motor. Check wiper system for proper operation.

2. Remove the steering column covers. Removing the steering wheel is not required, but may make the job easier.

➡**Be careful not to damage the collapsible steering column mechanism.**

3. Remove the cluster finish panel.

4. Remove the combination meter attaching screws and pull the unit forward.

5. Disconnect the speedometer and any other electrical connections that are necessary.

6. Remove the instruments from the combination meter as required.

7. Installation is the reverse of the removal procedure.

Speedometer

REMOVAL & INSTALLATION

1. Disconnect the negative battery cable.

2. Remove the combination meter from the vehicle and disassemble the meter.

3. Remove the retaining screws and remove the speedometer from the meter lens.

4. Keep the indicator needle horizontal.

5. Remove the indicator needle without it striking the lens.

6. Installation is the reverse of the removal procedure.

Speedometer Cable

The speedometer cable connects a rotating gear within the transmission or transaxle to the dashboard speedometer/odometer assembly. The dashboard unit interprets the number of turns the made by the cable and displays the information as miles per hour and total mileage.

Assuming that the transmission or transaxle contains the correct gear for the vehicle, the accuracy of the speedometer depends primarily on tire condition and tire diameter. Badly worn tires (too small in diameter) or over-inflation (too large in diameter) can affect the speedometer reading. Replacement tires of the incorrect overall diameter (such as oversize snow tires) can also affect the readings.

Generally, manufacturers state that speedometer/odometer error of 10% is considered normal due to wear and other variables. Stated another way, if you drove the vehicle over a measured 1 mile course and the odometer showed anything between 0.9 and 1.1 miles, the error is considered normal. If you plan to do any checking, always use a measured course such as mileposts on an Interstate highway or turnpike. Never use another vehicle for comparison — the other vehicle's inherent error may further cloud your readings.

The speedometer cable can become dry or develop a kink within its case. As it turns, the ticking or light knocking noise it makes can easily lead an owner to chase engine related problems in error. If such a noise is heard, carefully watch the speedometer needle during the speed range in which the noise is heard. Generally, the needle will jump or deflect each time the cable binds.

➡The slightest bind in the speedometer cable can cause unpredictable behavior in the cruise control system. If the cruise control exhibits intermittent surging or loss of set speed symptoms, check the speedometer cable first.

REMOVAL & INSTALLATION

1. Follow the appropriate procedure given previously for removal of the instrument cluster. The cluster need not be fully removed, but only loosened to the point of being able to disconnect the speedometer cable.

2. Disconnect the speedometer cable and check that any retaining clamps or clips between the dash and the firewall are released.

3. Safely raise the vehicle and support it on jackstands.

4. Disconnect the cable fitting at the transmission or transaxle and lift the cable and case away from the transmission or transaxle.

5. Follow the cable back to the firewall, releasing any clips or retainers.

6. From inside the vehicle, work the speedometer cable through the grommet in the firewall into the engine compartment. It may be necessary to pop the grommet out of the firewall and transfer it to the new cable.

7. When reinstalling, track the new cable into position, remembering to attach the grommet to the firewall securely. Make absolutely certain that the cable is not kinked, or routed near hot or moving parts. All curves in the cable should be very gentle and not located near the ends. Note the speedometer cable inside the housing must be lubricated with the proper lubricant before installing it to the vehicle.

8. Attach any retaining clips, brackets or retainers, beginning from the middle of the cable and working towards each end.

9. Attach the cable to the transmission or transaxle. Remember that the cable has a formed, square end on it; this shaped end must fit into a matching hole in the transmission or transaxle mount. Don't try to force the cable collar (screw fitting) into place if the cable isn't seated properly.

10. Inside the vehicle, hold the other end of the cable with your fingers or a pair of tapered-nose pliers. Gently attempt to turn the cable; if it's properly seated at the other end, the cable will NOT turn more than about $\frac{1}{4}$ turn. If the cable turns freely, the other end is not correctly seated.

11. Lower the vehicle to the ground.

12. Attach the speedometer cable to the instrument cluster, again paying close attention to the fit of the square-cut end into the square hole. Don't force the cable retainer.

13. Reinstall the instrument cluster following procedures outlined previously. Road test the vehicle for proper operation.

Windshield Wiper/Washer Switch

REMOVAL & INSTALLATION

➡If the vehicle is equipped with a external mount switch (switch mounted in dashboard) remove the negative battery cable and electrical connections from switch. Remove the switch from the dashboard.

On later model vehicles, the windshield wiper/washer switch is part of the Combination Switch Assembly — refer to Turn Signal/Combination Switch services procedures in Section 8 for additional information.

Rear Window Wiper/Washer Switch

REMOVAL & INSTALLATION

1. Disconnect the negative battery cable.
2. Disconnect wiring from the switch assembly.
3. Remove the switch from the panel.
4. Installation is the reverse of the removal procedure. Check system for proper operation.

Headlight Switch

REMOVAL & INSTALLATION

➡ If the vehicle is equipped with a external mount switch (switch mounted in dashboard) remove the negative battery cable and electrical connections from switch. Remove the headlight stalk lever then remove the switch from the dashboard.

LIGHTING

Headlights

REMOVAL & INSTALLATION

Sealed Beam Type
◗ See Figure 51

➡ If vehicle is equipped with retractable headlights raise the headlights and turn the lights off with the headlights raised. Then pull out the RTR 30 AMP fuse (on early models pull out the RTR fusible link near the battery). Unless power is disconnected, headlights could suddenly retract causing injury.

1. Remove the headlight bezel (trim).
2. The sealed beam is held in place by a retainer and either 2 or 4 small screws. Identify these screws before applying any tools.

➡ DO NOT confuse the small retaining screws with the larger aiming screws! There will be two aiming screws or adjustors for each lamp. (One adjustor controls the up/down motion and the other controls the left/right motion.) Identify the adjustors and avoid them during removal. If they are not disturbed, the new head lamp will be in identical aim to the old one.

3. Using a small screwdriver (preferably magnetic) and a pair of taper-nose pliers if necessary, remove the small screws in the head lamp retainer. DON'T drop the screws.
4. Remove the retainer and the head lamp may be gently pulled free from its mounts. Detach the connector (if the con-

On later models vehicles, the headlight switch is part of the Combination Switch Assembly — refer to Turn Signal/Combination Switch services procedures in Section 8 for additional information.

Clock

REMOVAL & INSTALLATION

1. Disconnect the negative battery cable.
2. Remove all necessary trim panels-remove the clock assembly mounting screws/or push in retaining clips.
3. Disconnect the electrical connection from the rear of the clock assembly, then remove it.
4. Installation is the reverse of the removal procedure.

nector is tight wiggle it) from the back of the sealed beam unit and remove the unit from the vehicle.

To install:
5. Place the new head lamp in position (single protrusion on the glass face upward) and connect the wiring harness. Remember to install the rubber boot on the back of the new lamp — its a water seal. Make sure the headlight is right-side up.
6. Turn on the headlights and check the new lamp for proper function, checking both high and low beams before final assembly.
7. Install the retainer and the small screws that hold it.
8. Reinstall the headlight bezel.

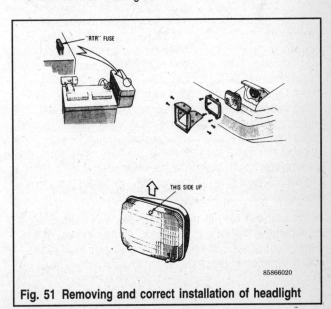

Fig. 51 Removing and correct installation of headlight

Replaceable Bulb (Semi-Sealed Beam)/Fixed Lens Type

◆ See Figures 52, 53, 54, 55 and 56

➡ This type of light is replace from behind the unit. The lens is not removed or loosened.

1. Open and support the hood.
2. Remove the wiring connector from the back the lamp. Be careful to release the locking tab completely before removal.
3. Grasp the base of the bulb holder and collar, twist it counterclockwise (as viewed from the engine compartment) and carefully remove the bulb holder and bulb from the housing.
4. Using gloves or a rag, hold the bulb and release the clip on the holder. Remove the bulb.

To install:

5. Install the new bulb in the holder and make sure the clip engages firmly.

➡ Hold the new bulb with a clean cloth or a piece of paper. DO NOT touch or grasp the bulb with your fingers. The oils from your skin will produce a hot spot on the glass envelope, shortening bulb life. If the bulb is touched accidentally, clean it with alcohol and a clean rag before installation.

6. Install the holder and bulb into the housing. Note that the holder has guides which must align with the housing. When the holder is correctly seated, turn the collar clockwise to lock the holder in place.
7. Connect the wiring harness. Turn on the headlights and check the function of the new bulb on both high and low beam.

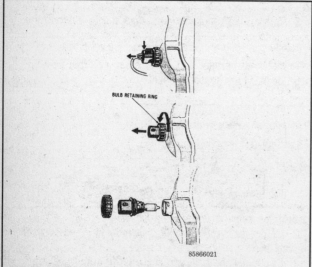

Fig. 52 Replacing semi-sealed beam headlight bulb

Fig. 53 View of the electrical connection for the headight assembly

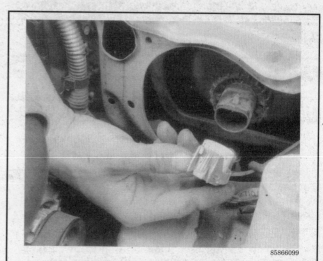

Fig. 54 Removing the electrical connection for the headight assembly

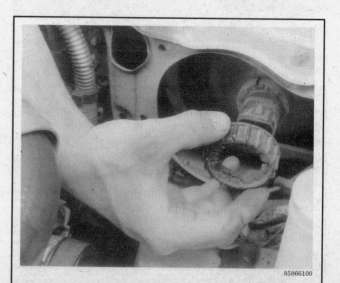

Fig. 55 Removing the bulb retaining ring for headlight

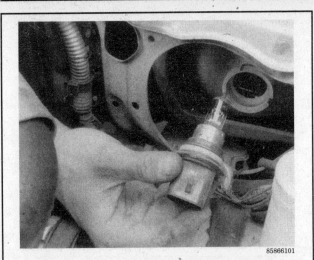

Fig. 56 Removing the headight assembly — do not touch the bulb glass

MANUAL OPERATION OF RETRACTABLE HEADLIGHTS

▶ **See Figures 57 and 58**

The retractable headlights can be manually operated if their electrical mechanism fails. To raise or lower the lights, Turn the ignition and headlight switches OFF and pull out the RTR MTR 30A fuse (on early models remove the RTR fusible link that is located near the battery). Unless the power is disconnected, there is a danger of the headlights suddenly retracting. Remove the rubber cover from the manual operation knob (under the hood next to the headlight unit) and turn the knob clockwise. Manual operation should only be used if the system has failed; be sure to check the electrical operation of the lights as soon as possible. When the headlights are retracted, they should match the silhouette of the vehicle body.

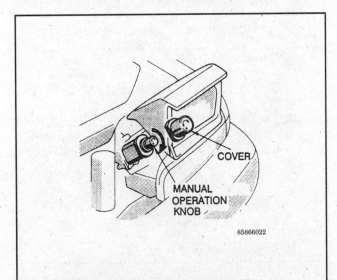

Fig. 57 Manual operation of headlight doors

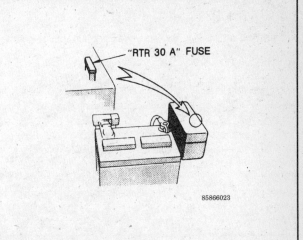

Fig. 58 On later models remove this fuse-before manual operation of headlight doors

Signal and Marker Lights

REMOVAL & INSTALLATION

Front Turn Signals

➡**This can be done with the vehicle on the ground. Access may be improved if the vehicle is safely supported on jackstands.**

1. From behind the bumper, disconnect the electrical connector.
2. Remove the two nuts from the housing.
3. Remove the turn signal lamp housing.

➡**If only the bulb is to be changed, the lens may be removed from the front.**

4. Reassemble the housing in reverse order of disassembly procedure.

Side Marker Lights (Parking Lights)
▶ **See Figures 59 and 60**

FRONT

1. Remove the retaining screws. On some models, the screws are visible at the rear corner of the lens. On other models, the screw is under the hood.
2. Gently remove the lighting assembly from the body of the vehicle.
3. Disconnect the bulb and socket(s) from the housing.
4. Reassemble in reverse order of removal procedure.

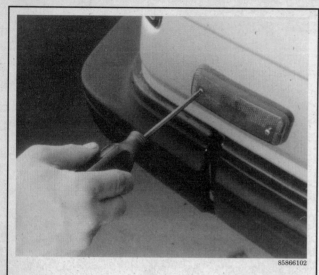

Fig. 59 Removing the side marker lens retaining screws

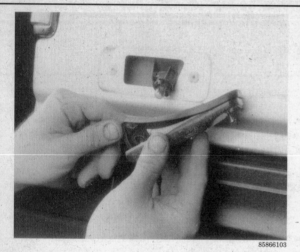

Fig. 60 Removing the side marker lens — note position of gasket on lens

REAR

1. Some models incorporates the sidelights into the taillight assemblies. Remove the two screws in the side marker lens.
2. Remove the lighting assembly from the bodywork.
3. Disconnect the bulb and socket from the lighting assembly.
4. Reassemble in reverse order of the removal procedure.

Rear Turn Signal, Brake and Parking Lights

▶ See Figures 61 and 62

1. Raise the trunk lid and remove or fold back the trunk carpeting.
2. Disconnect the wiring from the bulb holder(s).
3. If a bulb is to be changed, remove the bulb holder from the housing by pressing the tab and lifting out the holder assembly. Replace the bulb and reinsert the housing.

4. Remove the nuts holding the taillight assembly in place. Some may be difficult to reach.
5. Remove the lens assembly from the outside of the vehicle.

To install:

6. When reinstalling the lens assembly, pay close attention to the placement of the gasket. It must be correctly positioned and evenly positioned to prevent water from entering the lens or trunk area. Double check the holes through which the threaded studs pass; caulk them with sealer if needed.
7. Install the retaining nuts and tighten them evenly. Do not overtighten them or the lens may crack.
8. Install the electrical connectors. Operate the lights while you check the function at the rear of the vehicle. Replace the trunk carpet.

Fig. 61 Removing the bulb holder — most models similar

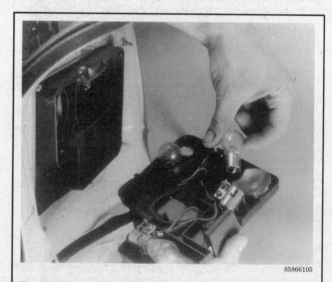

Fig. 62 Removing the bulb

Dome Light

REMOVAL & INSTALLATION

1. Remove the dome light cover.
2. Remove the bulb from holder.
3. Reassemble in reverse order of the removal procedure.

License Plate Lights

REMOVAL & INSTALLATION

1. Remove the lighting assembly from the bodywork.
2. Disconnect the bulb and socket from the lighting assembly.
3. Remove the bulb from the holder.
4. Reassemble in reverse order of the removal procedure.

High-Mount Stop Light

REMOVAL & INSTALLATION

▶ See Figures 63, 64, 65, 66 and 67

1. Remove the light cover.
2. Remove the bulb holder.
3. Remove the bulb from holder.
4. Reassemble in reverse order of the removal procedure.

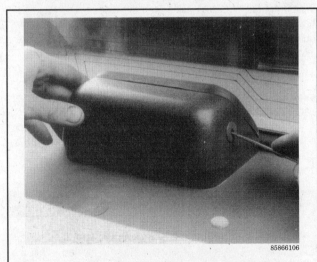

Fig. 63 Removing the high-mount stop light cover screws

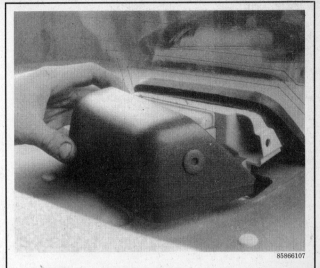

Fig. 64 Removing the high-mount stop light cover

Fig. 65 Removing the high-mount stop light bulb holder bolt

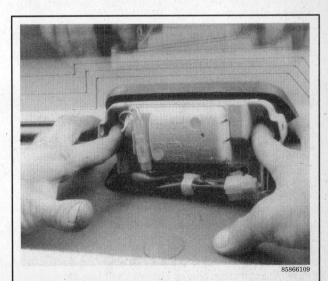

Fig. 66 Removing the high-mount stop light bulb holder

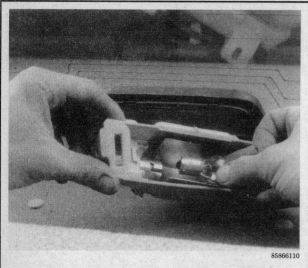

Fig. 67 Removing the high-mount stop light bulb

TRAILER WIRING

Wiring the vehicle for towing is fairly easy. There are a number of good wiring kits available and these should be used, rather than trying to design your own. All trailers will need brake lights and turn signals as well as tail lights and side marker lights. Most states require extra marker lights for overly wide trailers. Also, most states have recently required back-up lights for trailers, and most trailer manufacturers have been building trailers with back-up lights for several years.

Additionally, some trailers have electric brakes. Others can be fitted with them as an option, depending on the weight to be carried.

Add to this an accessories wire, to operate trailer internal equipment or to charge the trailer's battery, and you can have as many as seven wires in the harness.

Determine the equipment on your trailer and buy the wiring kit necessary. The kit will contain all the wires needed, plus a plug adapter set which includes the female plug, mounted on the bumper or hitch, and the male plug to be wired into the trailer harness.

When installing the kit, follow the manufacturer's instructions. The color coding of the wires is standard throughout the industry.

One point to note: some domestic vehicles, and most imported vehicles, have separate turn signals at the rear. On most domestic vehicles, the brake lights and rear turn signals operate with the same bulb. For those vehicles with separate turn signals, you can purchase an isolation unit so that the brake lights won't blink whenever the turn signals are operated.

You can also go to your local electronics supply house and buy four diodes to wire in series with the brake and turn signal bulbs. Diodes will isolate the brake and turn signals. The choice is yours. The isolation units are simple and quick to install, but far more expensive than the diodes. The diodes, however, require more work to install properly, since they require the cutting of each bulb's wire and soldering the diode into place.

The best wiring kits are those with a spring loaded cover on the vehicle mounted socket. This cover prevents dirt and moisture from corroding the terminals. Never let the vehicle socket hang loosely. Always mount it securely to the bumper or hitch. If you don't get a connector with a cover, at least put a piece of tape over the end of the connector when not in use. Most trailer lighting failures can be traced to corroded connectors and/or poor grounds.

CIRCUIT PROTECTION

Fuses And Fusible Links

REPLACEMENT

▶ See Figures 68, 69, 70, 71, 72, 73 and 74

➡Vehicle fuses, fusible links and or relays are found in relay or junction blocks. On most models, the covers for the relay or junction blocks identify each fuse, fusible link or relay.

All models have fuses, fusible links and relays found in various locations. One relay or junction block is located within the cabin of the vehicle, just under the extreme left side of the dashboard. This fuse block generally contains the fuses for body and cabin electrical circuits such as the wipers, rear defogger, ignition, cigarette lighter, etc. In addition, various relays and circuit breakers for other equipment are also mounted on or around this fuse block.

The second relay or junction block is found under the hood on the forward part of the left wheelhouse (driver's side). The fuses, fusible links and relays in this junction block generally control the engine and major electrical systems on the vehicle, such as headlights (separate fuses for left and right), air conditioning, horns, fuel injection, ECM, and fans.

Some models have an additional small panel (relay or junction block) at the right kick panel area containing a fuse (air conditioner or heater) and a relay and circuit breaker for the heater system.

Some models have another relay block near the junction block which is found under the hood. These relay blocks contain various fuses, fusible links and relays for the vehicle. The covers for the relay or junction blocks usually identify each fuse, fusible link or relay for your vehicle.

Each fuse and fusible link location is labeled on the fuse block cover identifying its primary circuit, but designations such as Engine, CDS Fan or ECU-B may not tell you what you need to know. A fuse and fusible link can control more than one circuit, so check related fuses. The sharing of fuses is necessary to conserve space and wiring.

➡**On older vehicles, a regular type or cylinder shaped glass fuse is used, both type fuses work the same way and are checked and installed in the same manner.**

Most late models, use individual fuses that are plastic or slip-fuse type. They connect into the fuse box with two small blades, similar to a household wall plug. Removing the fuse with the fingers can be difficult; there isn't a lot to grab onto. For this reason, the fuse block may contain a small plastic fuse remover which can be clipped over the back of the fuse and used as a handle to pull it free.

Once the fuse is out, view the fusible element through the clear plastic of the fuse case. An intact fuse will show a continuous horseshoe-shaped wire within the plastic. This element simply connects one blade with the other; if it's intact, power can pass. If the fuse is blown, the link inside the fuse will show a break, possibly accompanied by a small black mark. This shows that the link broke when the electrical current exceeded the wires ability to carry it.

It is possible for the link to become weakened (from age or vibration) without breaking. In this case, the fuse will look good but fail to pass the proper amount of current, causing some electrical item to not work.

Once removed, any fuse may be checked for continuity with an ohmmeter. A reliable general rule is to always replace a suspect fuse with a new one. So doing eliminates one variable in the diagnostic path and may cure the problem outright. Remember, however, that a blown fuse is rarely the cause of a problem; the fuse is opening to protect the circuit from some other malfunction either in the wiring or the component itself. Always replace a fuse or other electrical component with one of equal amperage rating; NEVER increase the ampere rating of the circuit. The number on the back of the fuse body (5, 7.5, 10, 15 ,etc.) indicates the rated amperage of the fuse.

Fig. 68 Removing the fuse block or junction block cover — most models similar

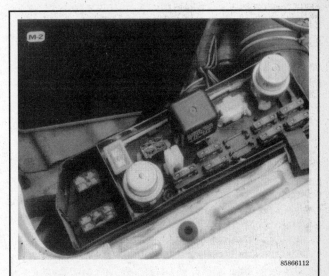

Fig. 69 View of the fuse block or junction block

Fig. 70 View of an additional junction block cover — most models similar

Fig. 71 Removing the fuse block cover near kick-panel area

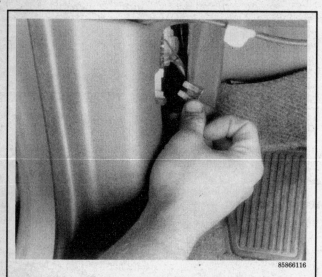

Fig. 72 Removing a fuse from the fuse block

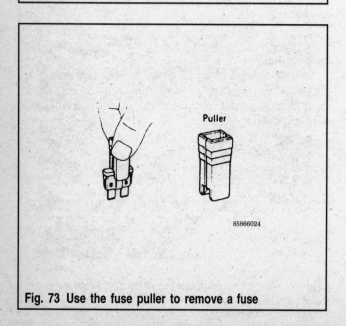

Puller

Fig. 73 Use the fuse puller to remove a fuse

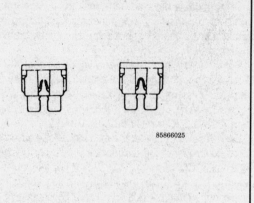

Fig. 74 A blown slip-type fuse (left) compared with an intact fuse-the fuse cannot be inspected without removing it

Circuit Breakers

REPLACEMENT

▶ **See Figures 75 and 76**

The circuit breakers found on the junction and relay blocks mount to the blocks with blades similar to the fuses. Before removing a breaker, always disconnect the negative battery cable to prevent potentially damaging electrical spikes within the system. Simply remove the breaker by pulling straight out from the block. Do not twist the circuit breaker, because damage may occur to the connectors inside the housing.

➡**Some circuit breakers do not reset automatically. Once tripped, they must be reset by hand. Use a small screwdriver or similar tool; insert it in the hole in the back of the breaker and push gently. Once the breaker is reset, either check it for continuity with an ohmmeter or reinstall it and check the circuit for function.**

Reinstall the circuit breaker by pressing it straight in to its mount. Make certain the blades line up correctly and that the circuit breaker is fully seated. Reconnect the negative battery cable and check the circuit for function.

Fig. 75 Removing a circuit breaker from the junction block

85866114

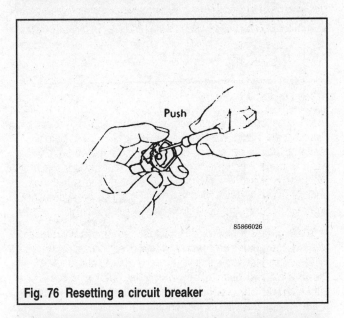

Push

85866026

Fig. 76 Resetting a circuit breaker

Turn Signal and Hazard Flasher

The combination turn signal and hazard flasher unit is located under the dash on the left side near junction block. On most later models, the flasher unit is not the classic round can shape found on many domestic vehicles. It is a small box-shaped unit easily mistaken for another relay. Depending on the year of your vehicle, the flasher may be plugged directly into the junction block (left side kick panel or dashboard area) or it may be plugged into its own connector and mounted near the junction block (left side kick panel or dashboard area). The flasher unit emits the familiar ticking sound when the signals are in use and may be identified by touching the case and feeling the click as the system functions.

The flasher unit simply unplugs from its connector and a replacement may be installed. Assuming that all the bulbs on the exterior of the vehicle are working properly, the correct rate of flash for the turn signals or hazard lights is about 60-75 flashes per minute. Very rapid flashing on one side only or no flashing on one side generally indicates a failed bulb rather than a failed flasher.

Communication and Add-On Electrical Equipment

The electrical system in your vehicle is designed to perform under reasonable operating conditions without interference between components. Before any additional electrical equipment is installed, it is recommended that you consult your Toyota dealer or a reputable repair facility familiar with the vehicle and its systems.

If the vehicle is equipped with mobile radio equipment and or mobile telephone it may have an effect upon the operation of the ECM. Radio frequency interference (RFI) from the communications system can be picked up by the vehicle's wiring harnesses and conducted into the ECM, giving it the wrong messages at the wrong time. Although well shielded against RFI, the ECM should be further protected through the following steps:

1. Install the antenna as far as possible from the ECM. Since the ECM is located behind the center console area, the antenna should be mounted at the rear of the vehicle.

2. Keep the antenna wiring a minimum of eight inches away from any wiring running to the ECM and from the ECM itself. NEVER wind the antenna wire around any other wiring.

3. Mount the equipment as far from the ECM as possible. Be very careful during installation not to drill through any wires or short a wire harness with a mounting screw.

4. Insure that the electrical feed wire(s) to the equipment are properly and tightly connected. Loose connectors can cause interference.

5. Make certain that the equipment is properly grounded to the vehicle. Poor grounding can damage expensive equipment.

6. Make sure the antenna is trimmed or adjusted for optimum function.

WIRING DIAGRAMS

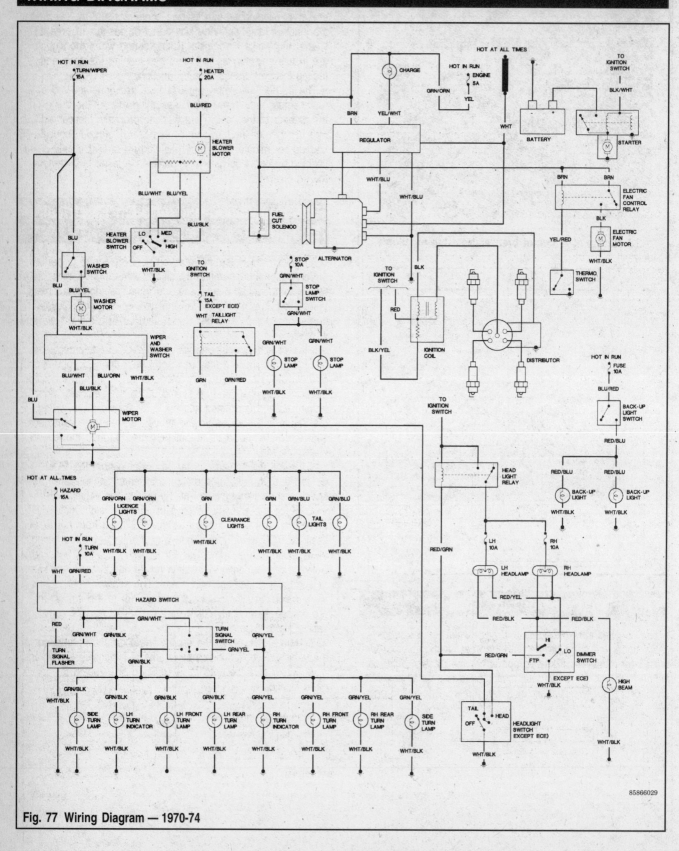

Fig. 77 Wiring Diagram — 1970-74

85866029

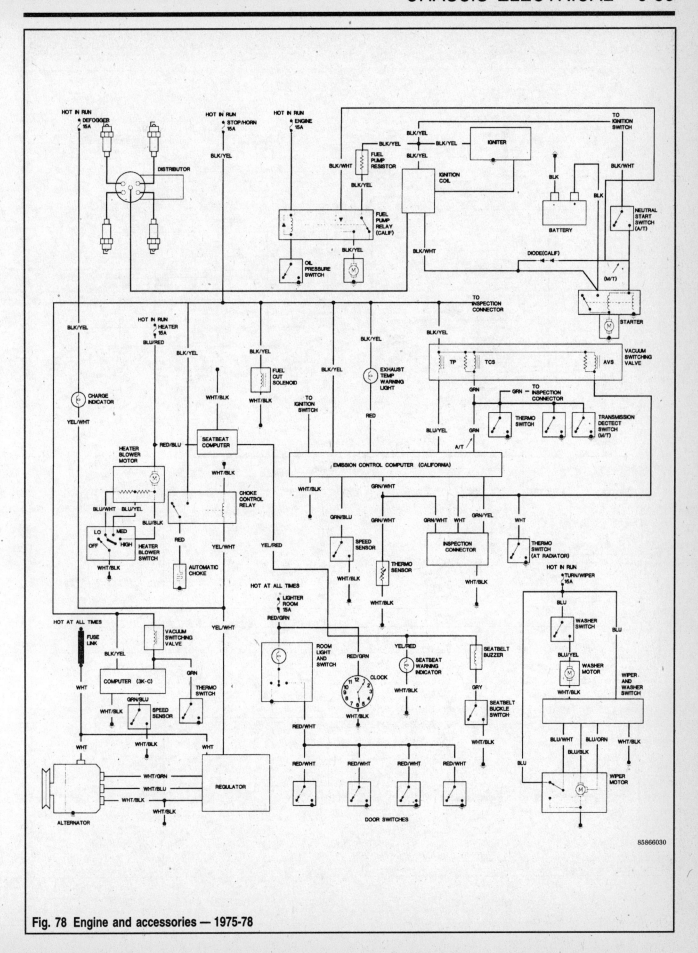

Fig. 78 Engine and accessories — 1975-78

85866030

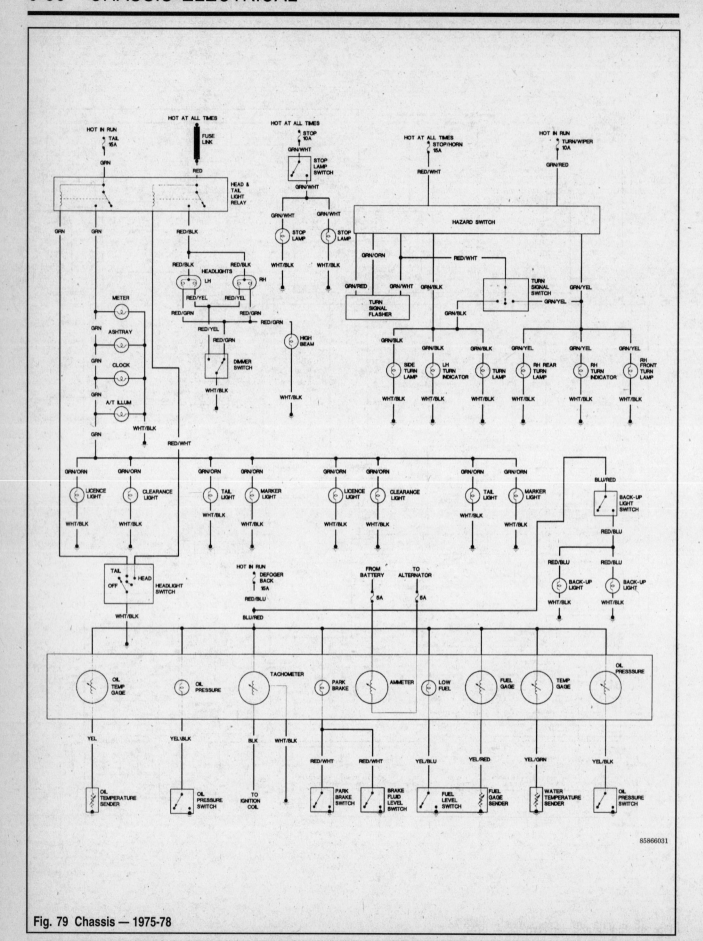

Fig. 79 Chassis — 1975-78

85866031

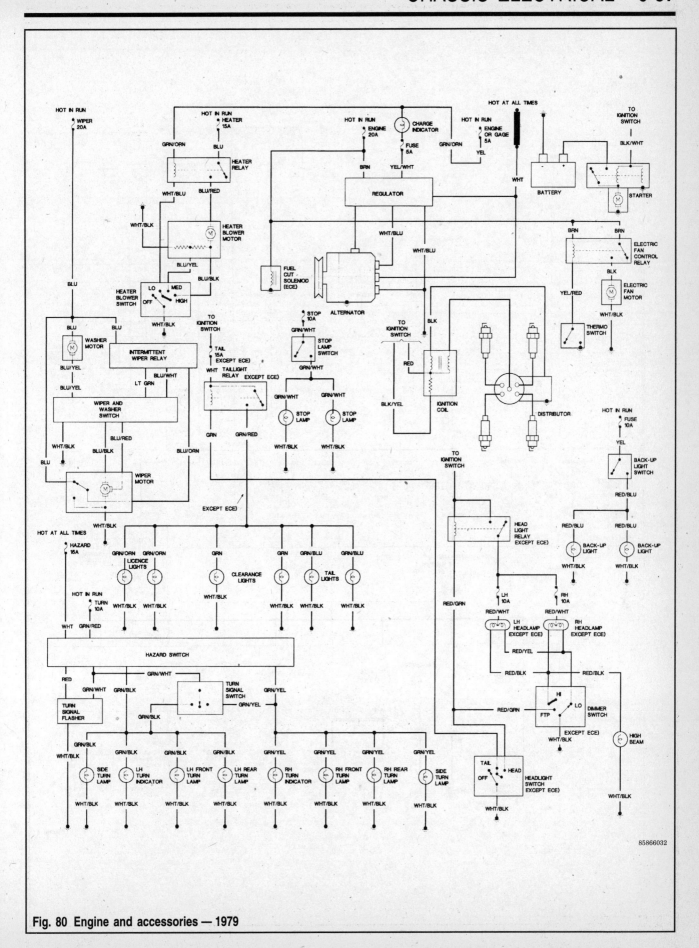

Fig. 80 Engine and accessories — 1979

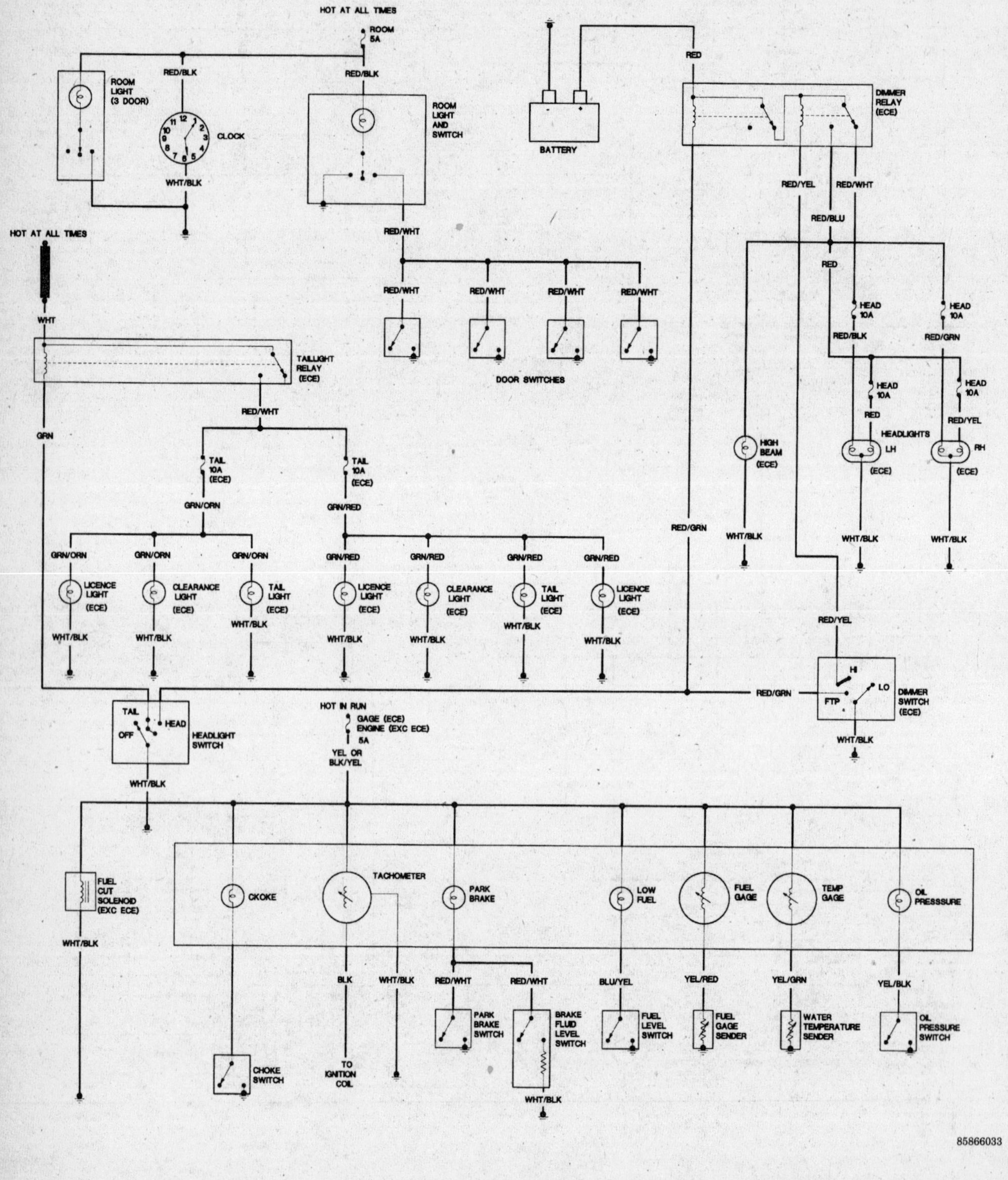

Fig. 81 Chassis — 1979

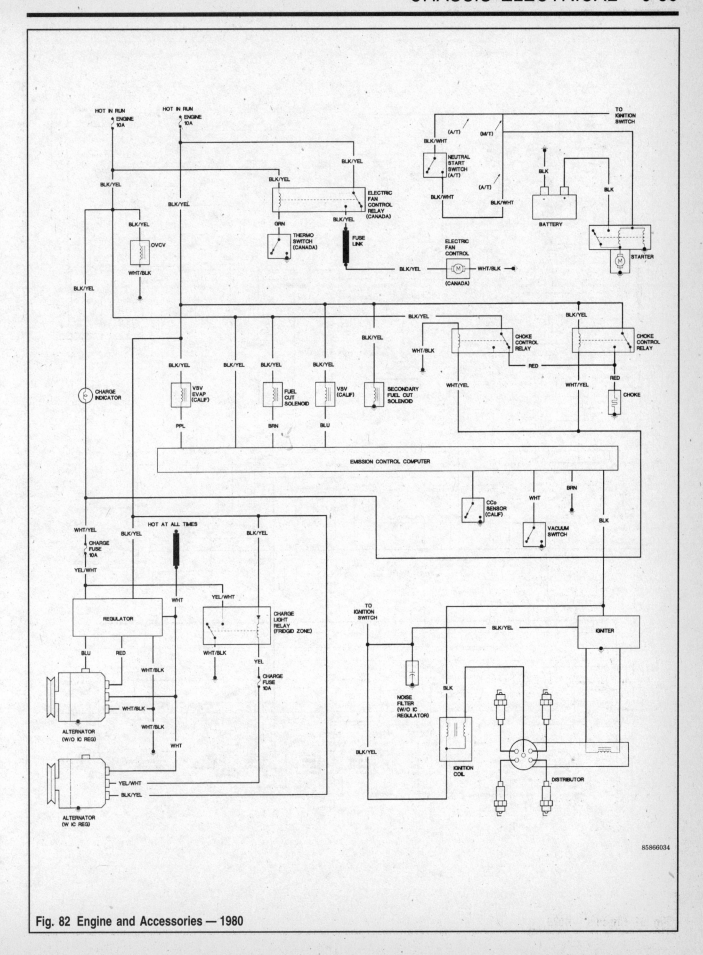

Fig. 82 Engine and Accessories — 1980

85866034

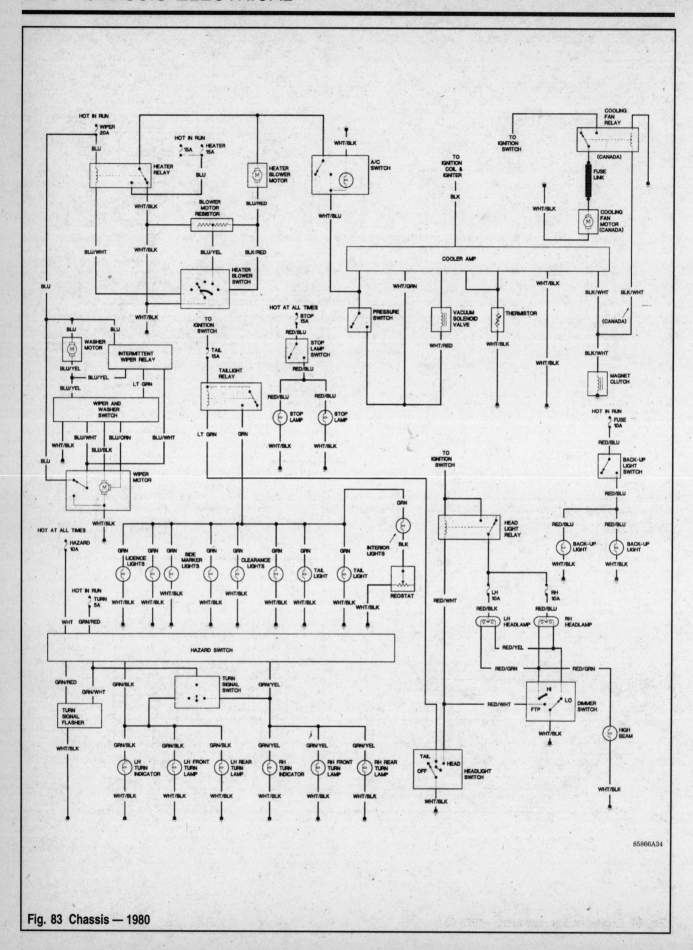

Fig. 83 Chassis — 1980

85866A34

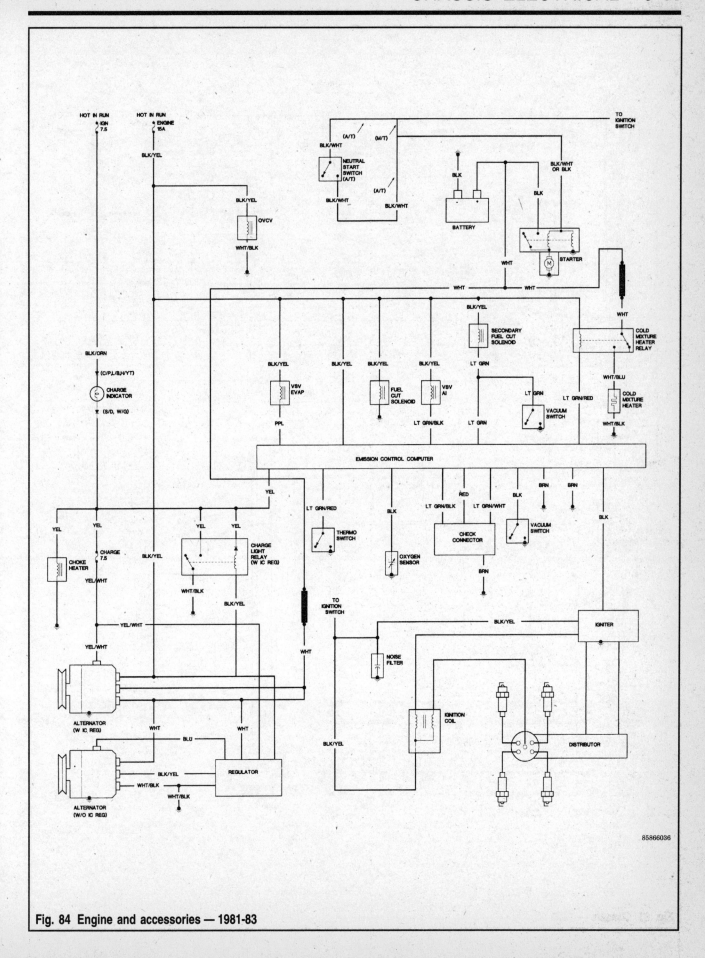

Fig. 84 Engine and accessories — 1981-83

85866036

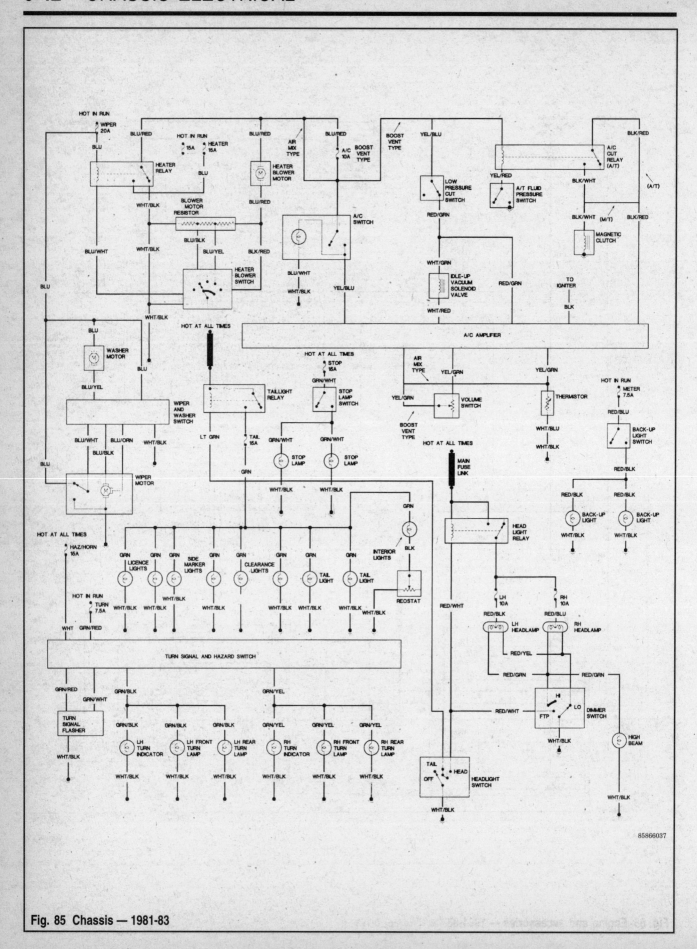

Fig. 85 Chassis — 1981-83

85866037

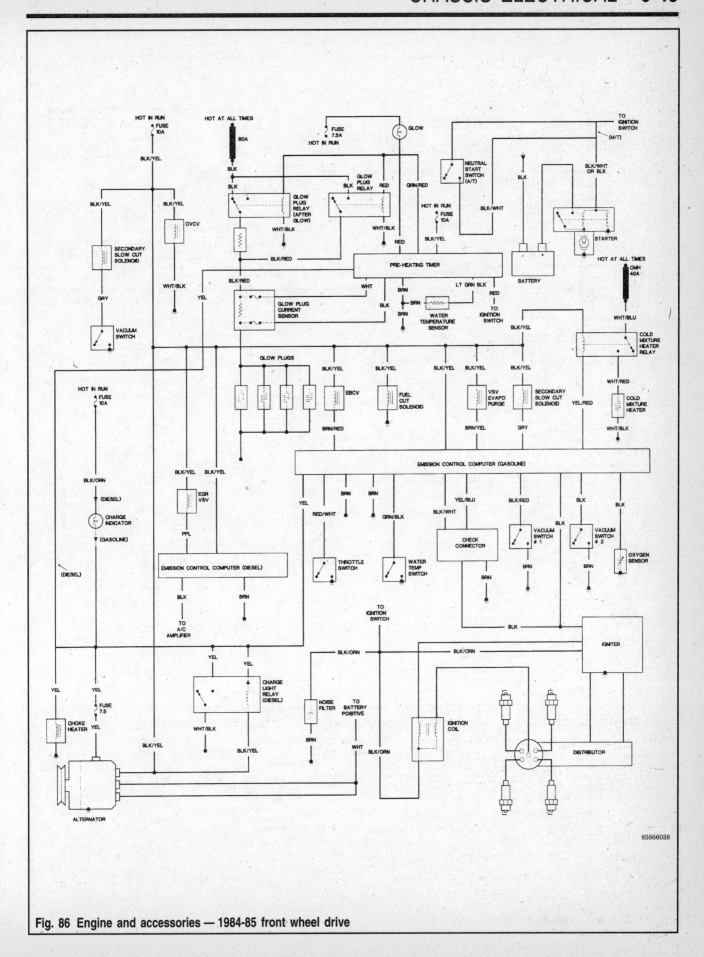

Fig. 86 Engine and accessories — 1984-85 front wheel drive

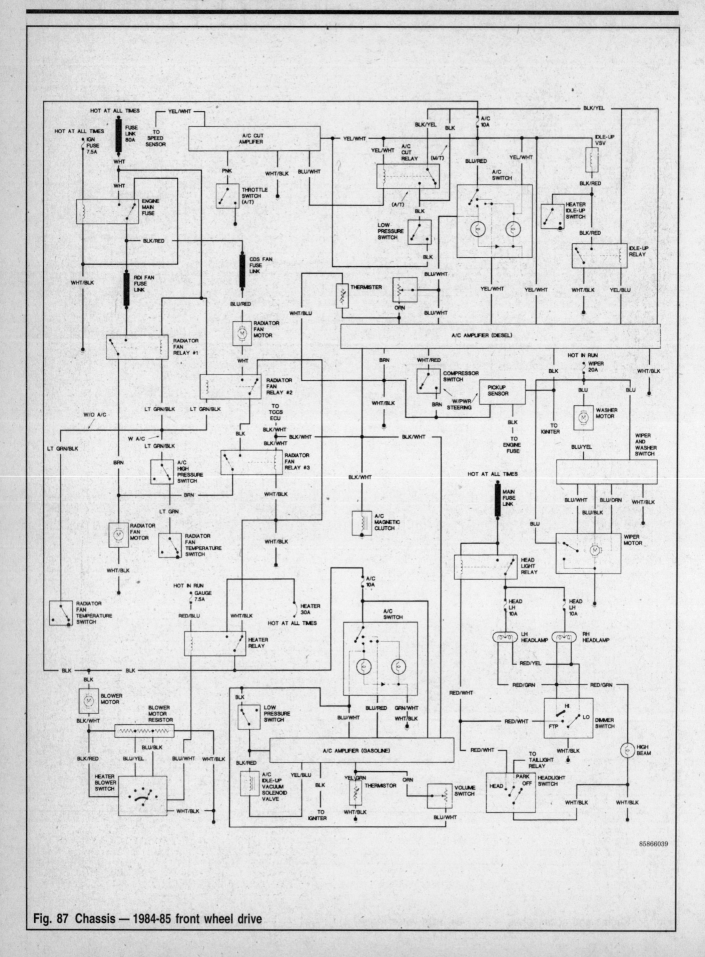

Fig. 87 Chassis — 1984-85 front wheel drive

85866039

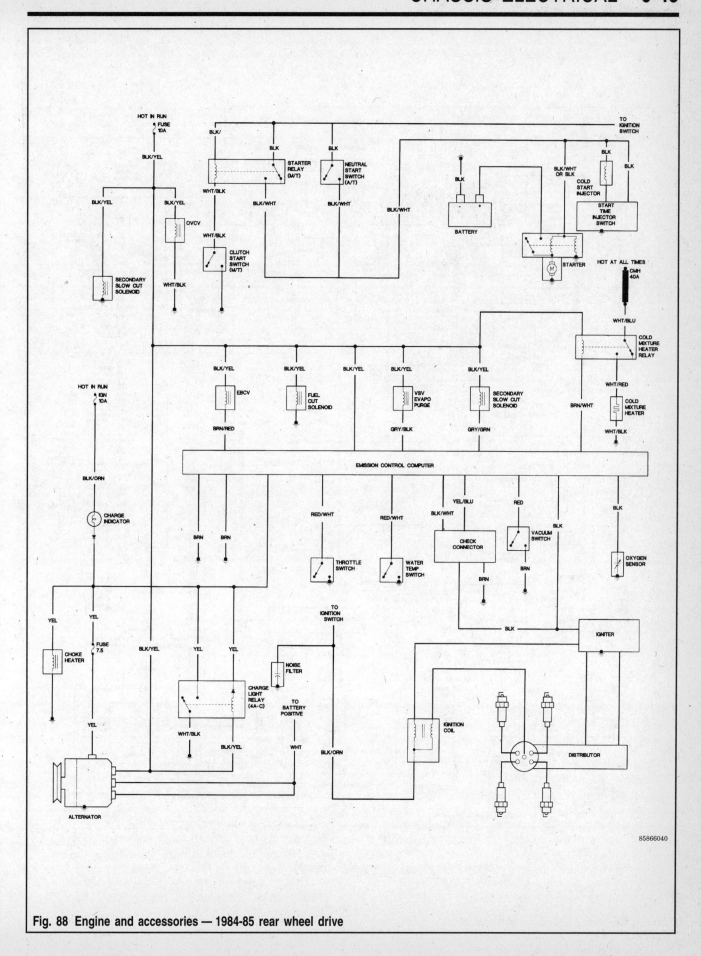

Fig. 88 Engine and accessories — 1984-85 rear wheel drive

85866040

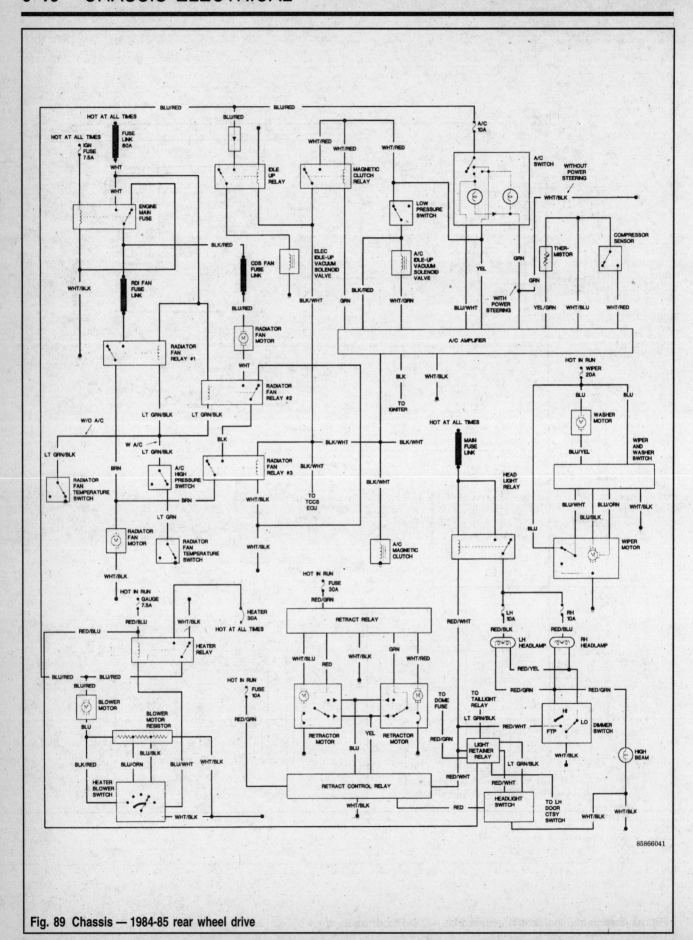

Fig. 89 Chassis — 1984-85 rear wheel drive

85866041

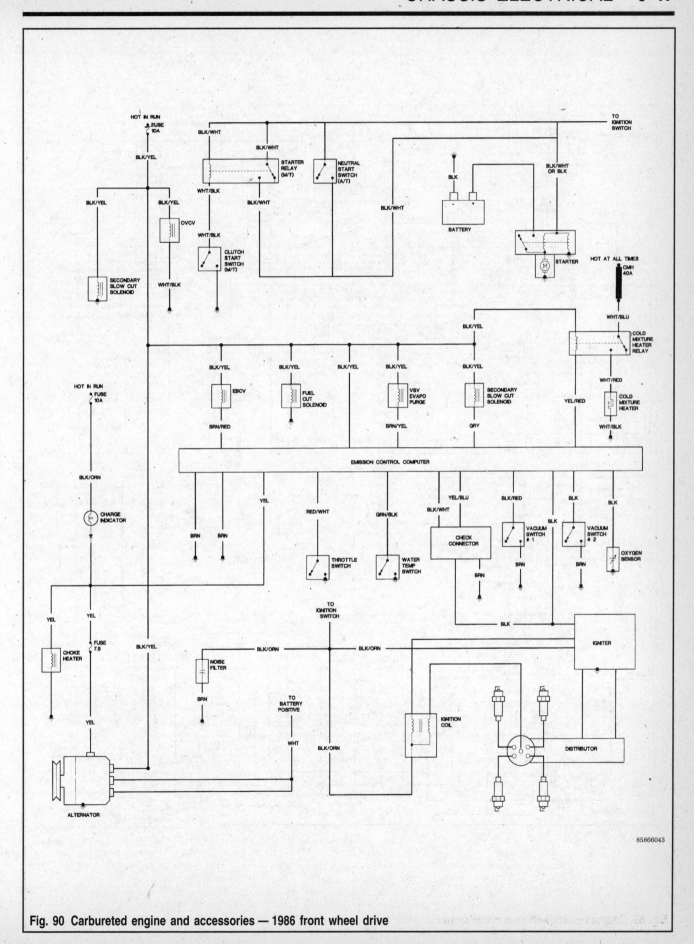

Fig. 90 Carbureted engine and accessories — 1986 front wheel drive

85866043

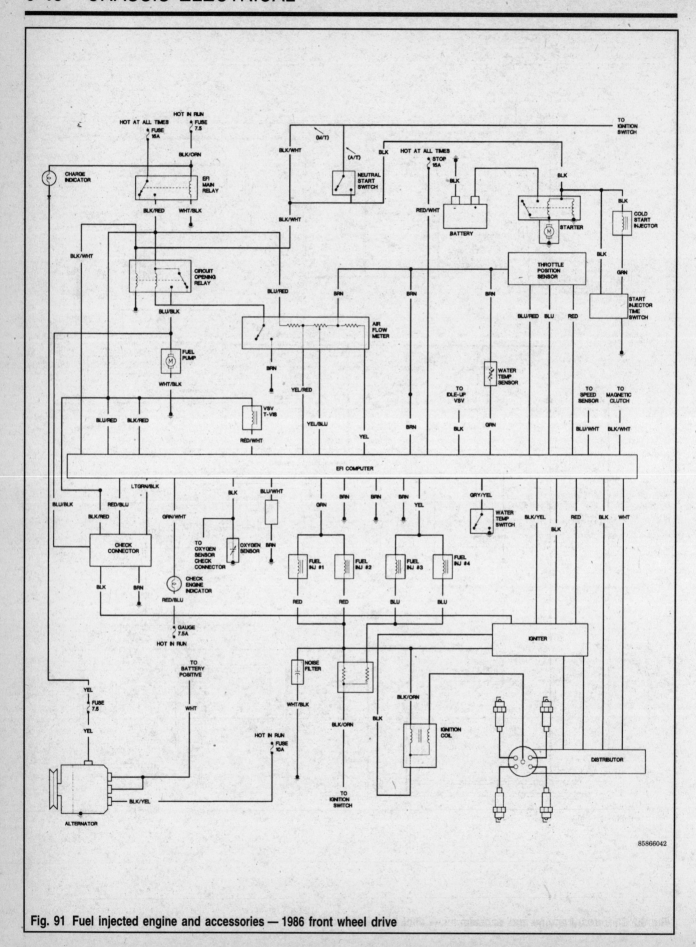

Fig. 91 Fuel injected engine and accessories — 1986 front wheel drive

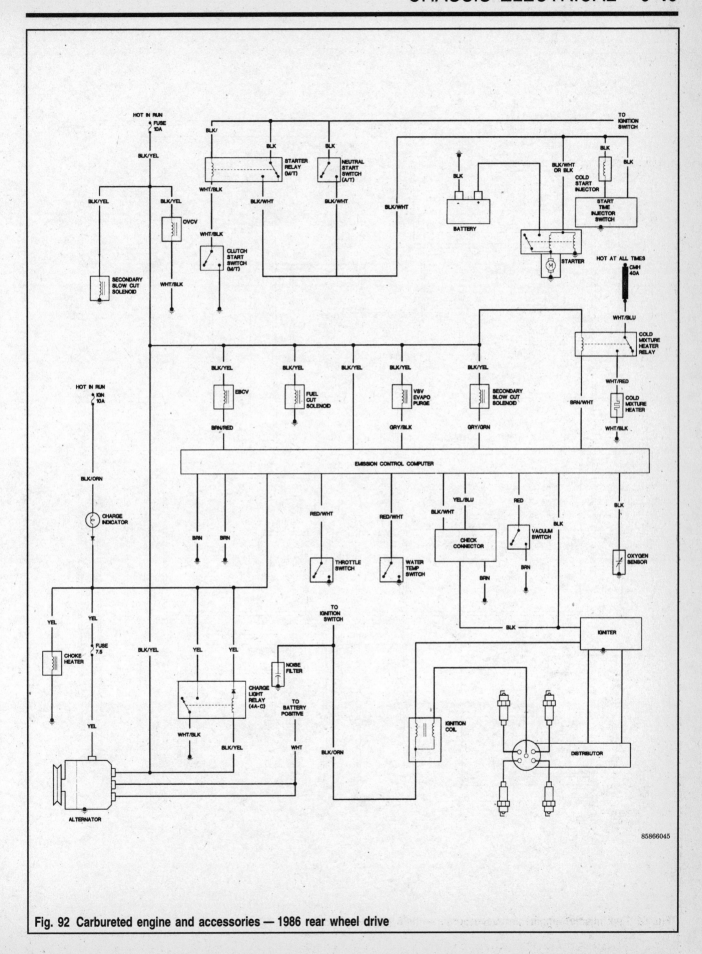

Fig. 92 Carbureted engine and accessories — 1986 rear wheel drive

85866045

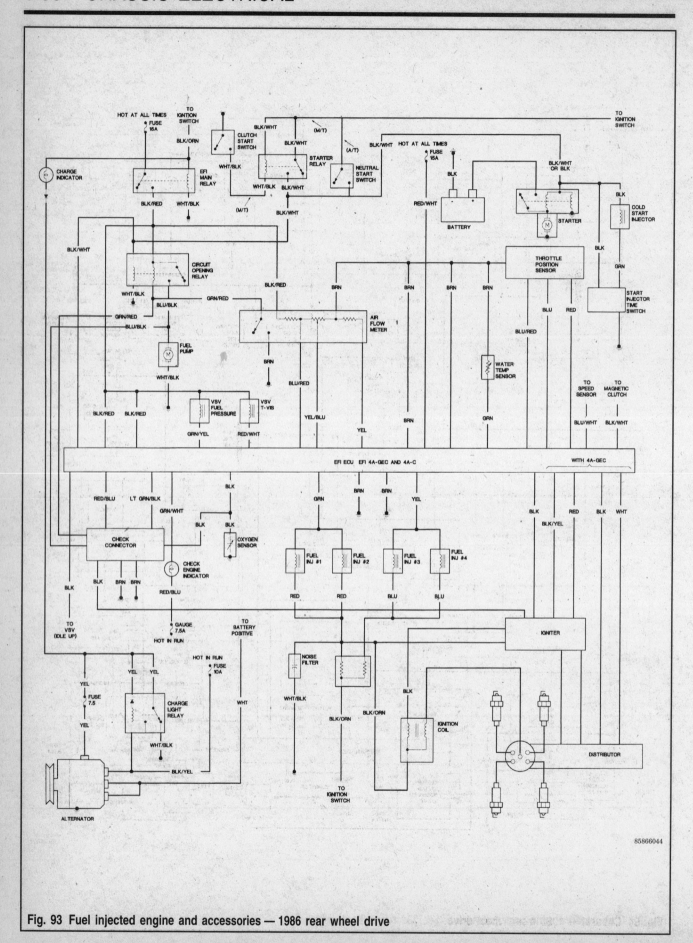

Fig. 93 Fuel injected engine and accessories — 1986 rear wheel drive

85866044

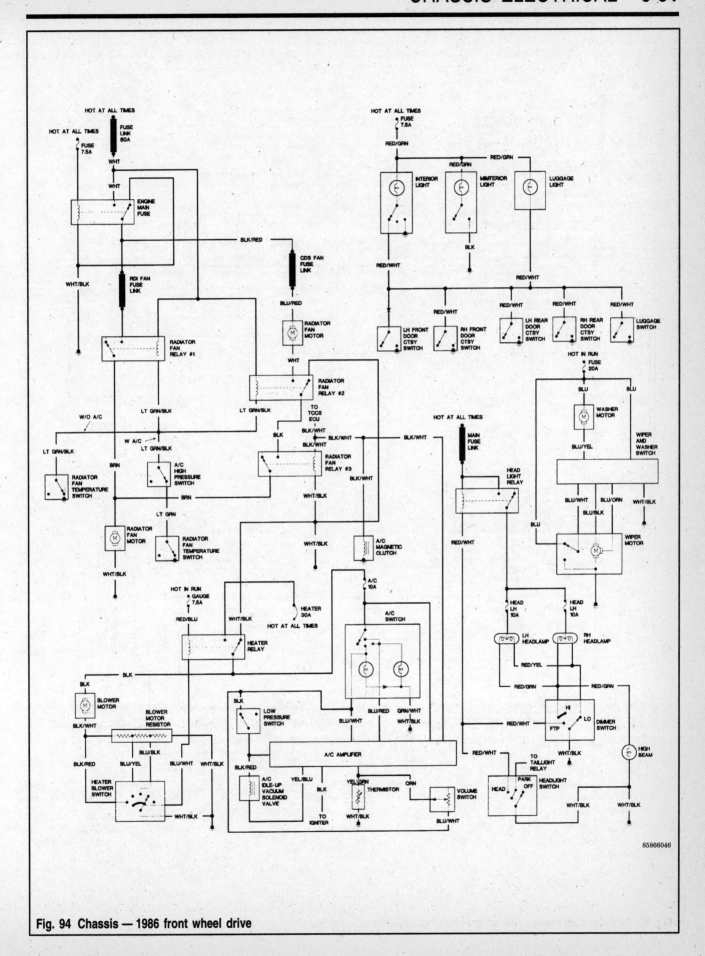

Fig. 94 Chassis — 1986 front wheel drive

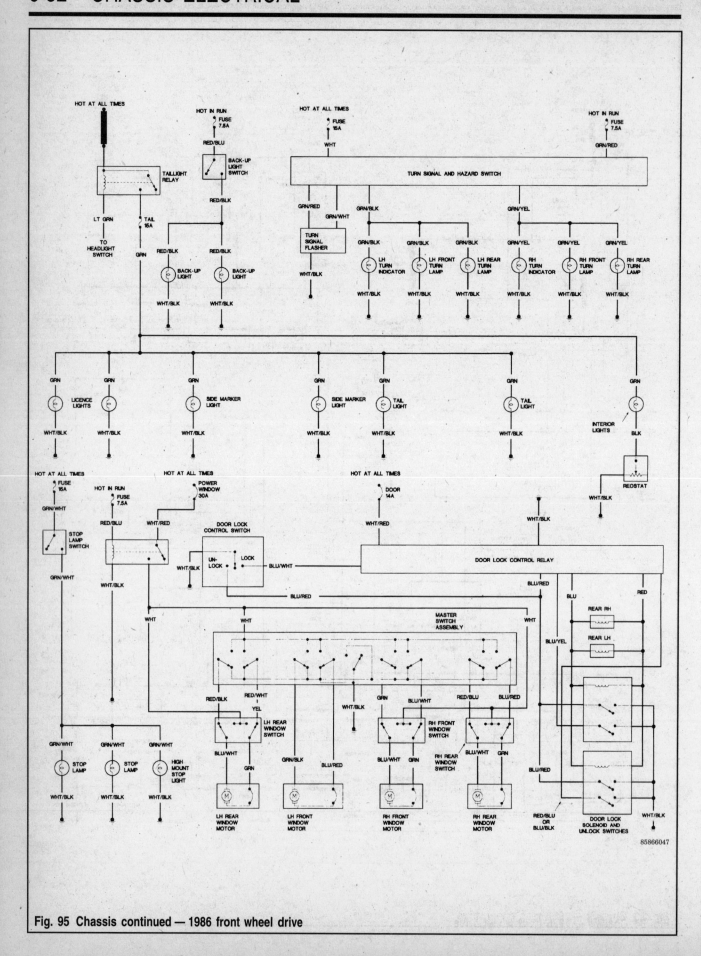

Fig. 95 Chassis continued — 1986 front wheel drive

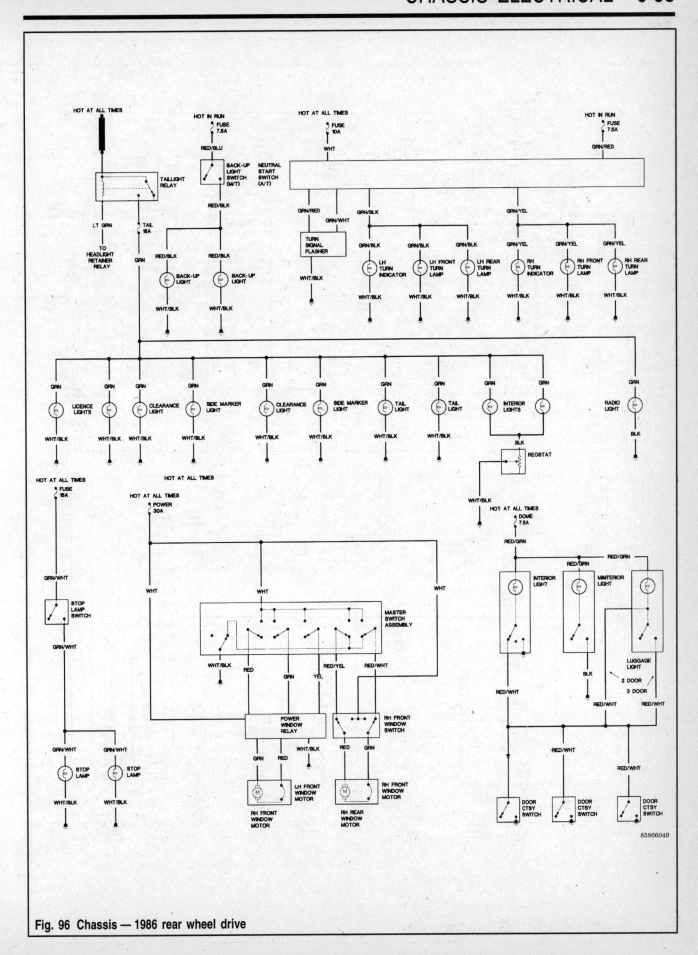

Fig. 96 Chassis — 1986 rear wheel drive

85866049

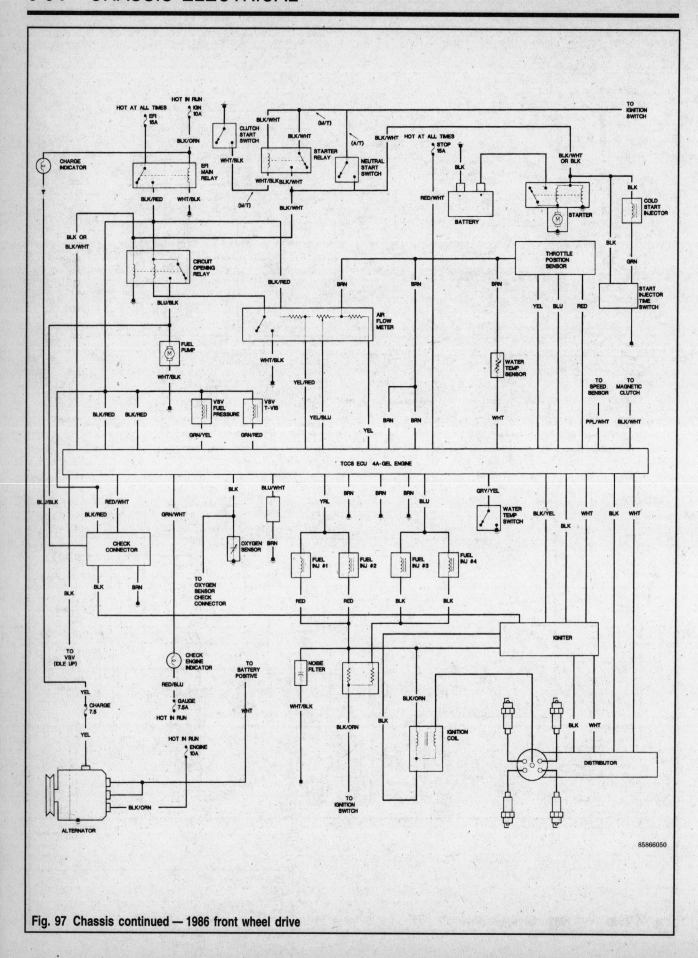

Fig. 97 Chassis continued — 1986 front wheel drive

85866050

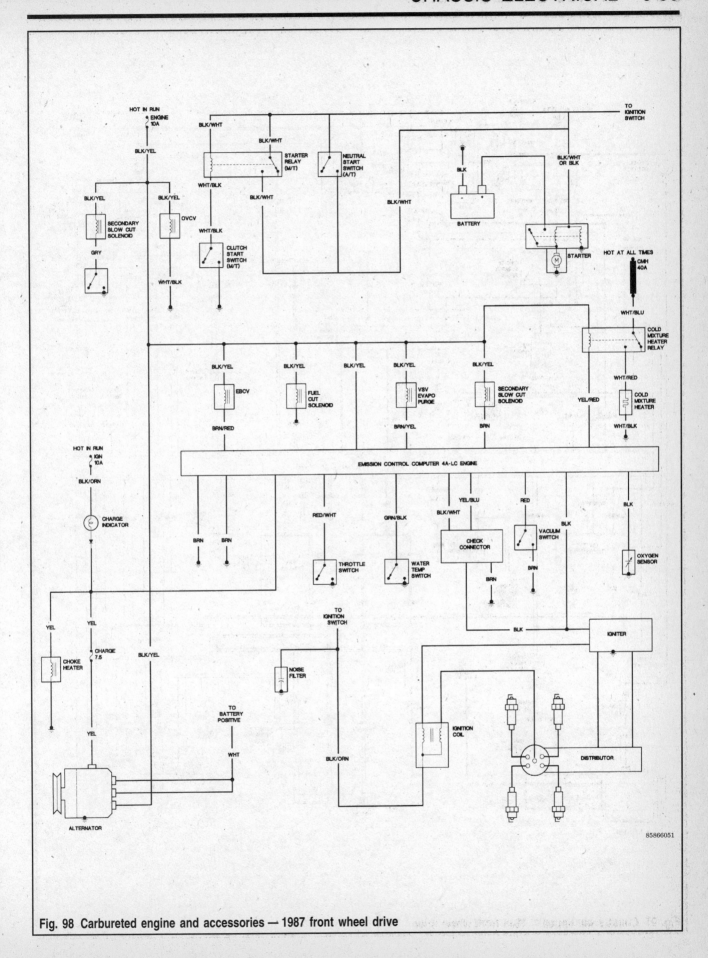

Fig. 98 Carbureted engine and accessories — 1987 front wheel drive

85866051

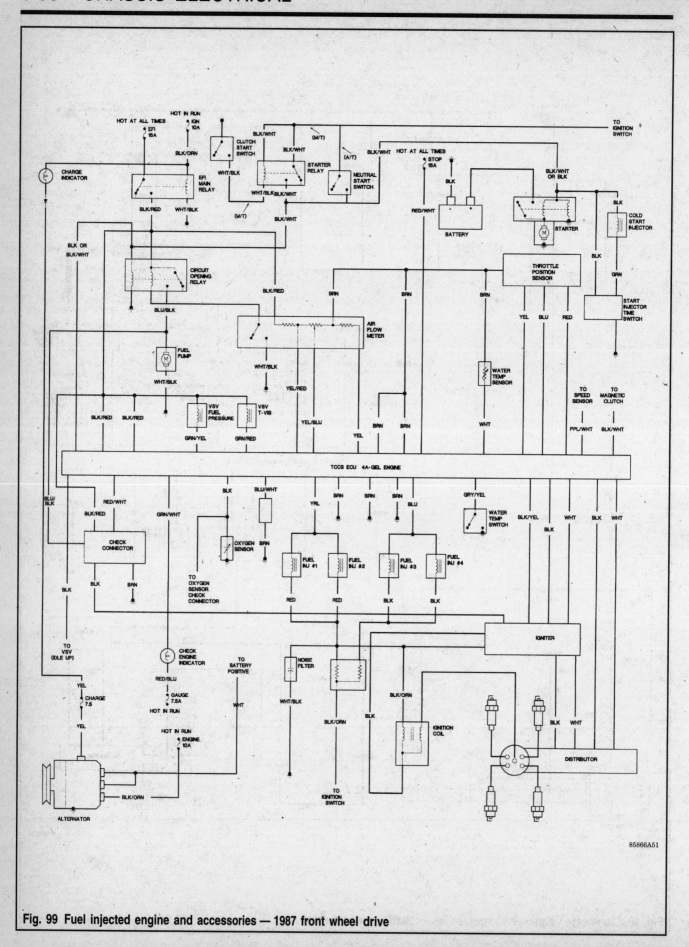

Fig. 99 Fuel injected engine and accessories — 1987 front wheel drive

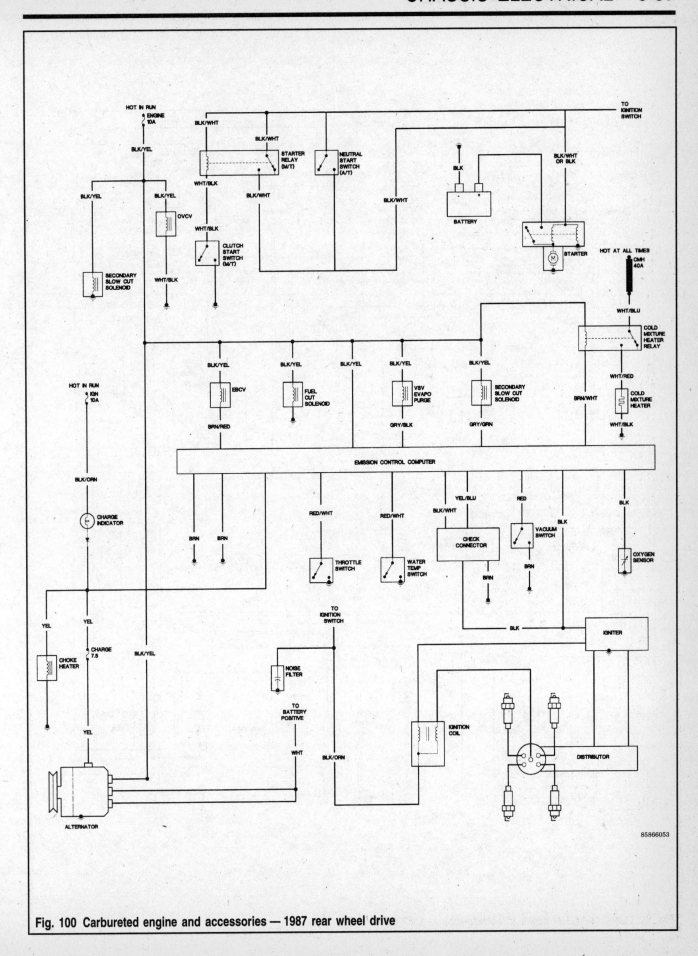

Fig. 100 Carbureted engine and accessories — 1987 rear wheel drive

85866053

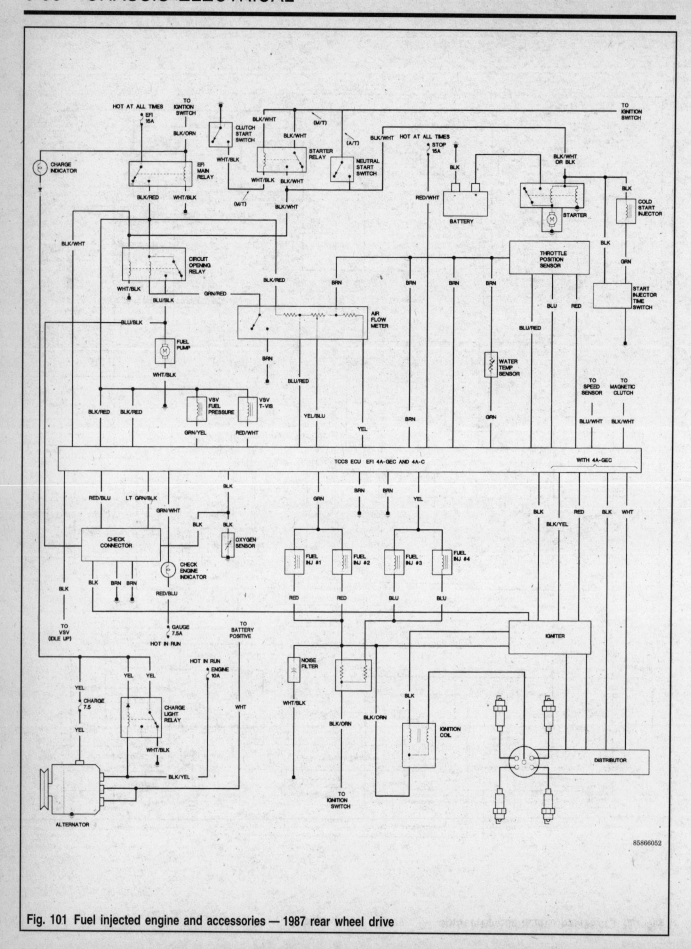

Fig. 101 Fuel injected engine and accessories — 1987 rear wheel drive

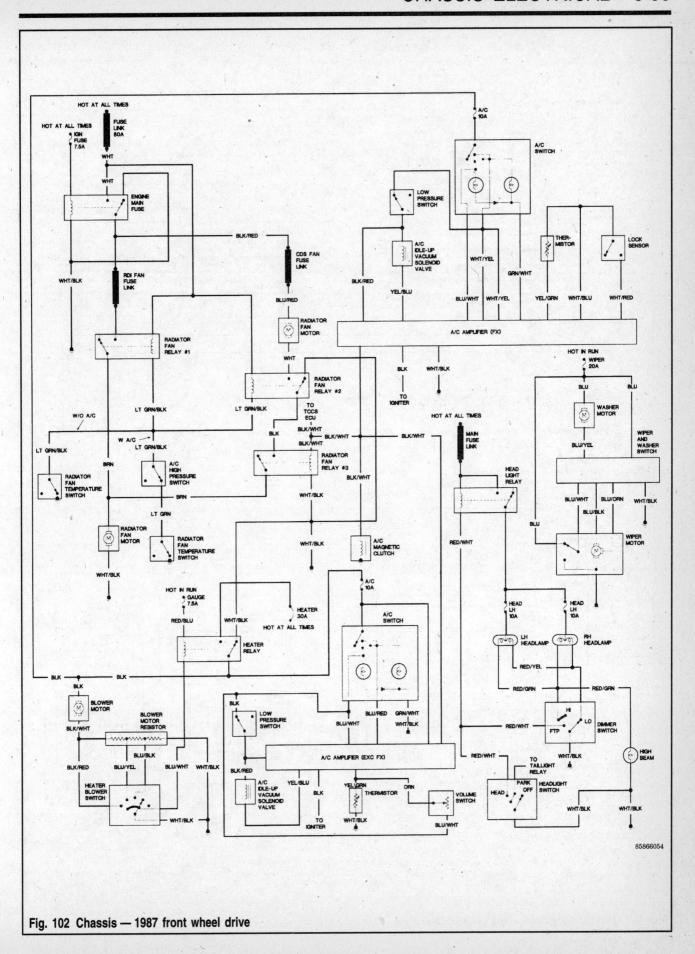

Fig. 102 Chassis — 1987 front wheel drive

85866054

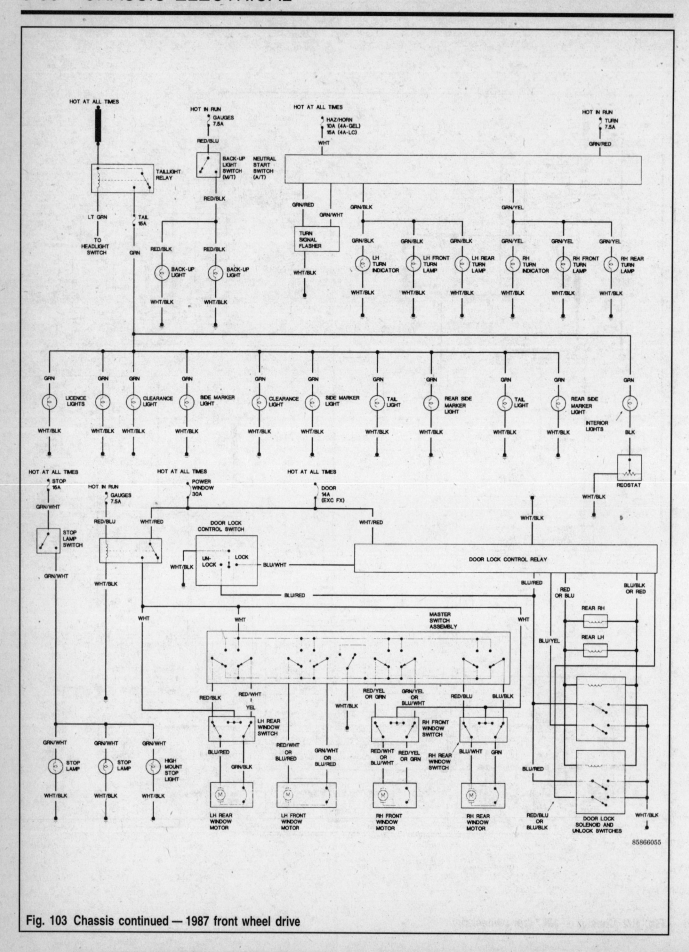

Fig. 103 Chassis continued — 1987 front wheel drive

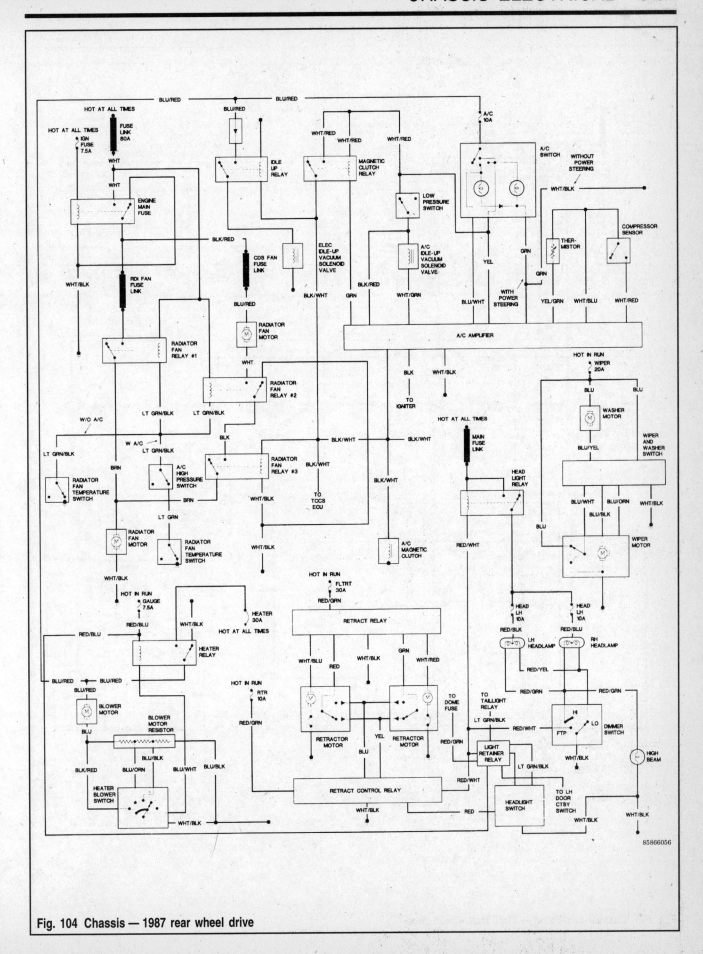

Fig. 104 Chassis — 1987 rear wheel drive

85866056

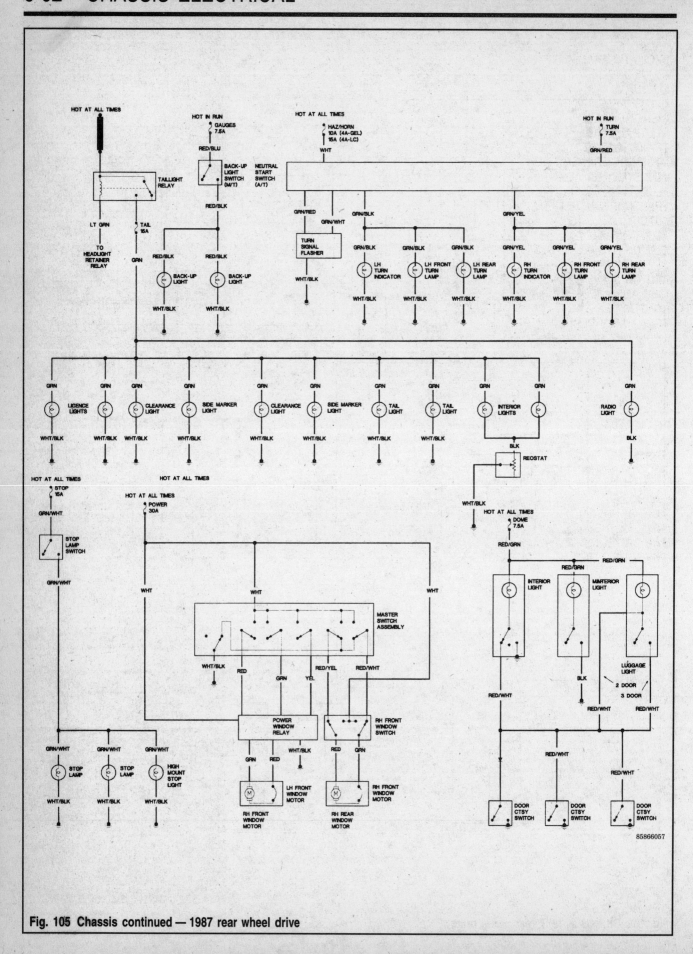

Fig. 105 Chassis continued — 1987 rear wheel drive

85866057

7

DRIVE
TRAIN

MANUAL TRANSMISSION

➡The transmission model identification number is located on the bottom of the Vehicle Identification Number (VIN) plate. For more information refer to Section 1 on transmission identification.

Adjustments

LINKAGE

Most late model passenger cars sold in the US have floor mounted shifters, and internally mounted shift linkages. On some older models, the linkage is contained in the side cover which is bolted on the transmission case. All of the other models have the linkage mounted inside the top of the transmission case itself. No external adjustments are needed or possible on any year or model.

Back-Up Light Switch

REMOVAL & INSTALLATION

The reverse light or back-up light switch is mounted on the side of the transmission housing. Its removal and replacement is easily accomplished by disconnecting the wiring connector from the switch and unscrewing the switch from the case (always replace the mounting gasket below it). A specially sized socket or an equivalent removal tool may be necessary for this service operation. Install the new switch and tighten it 30 ft. lbs. (40 Nm). Reinstall the electrical connector. Turn key to the **ON** position, depress clutch pedal and place shifter in REVERSE position. Check operation of back-up lights.

Transmission

REMOVAL & INSTALLATION

1970-83 RWD

▶ **See Figures 1, 2 and 3**

Working from inside of the car, perform the following:
1. Place the gear selector in **N**. Remove the center console, if so equipped.
2. Remove the trim boot at the base of the shift lever and the boot underneath it on the shift tower.
3. On all Corolla models (except 1600):
   a. Unfasten the snapring from the base of the shift lever.
   b. Withdraw the council spring and the shift lever itself.
4. On Corolla 1600 models only:
   a. Unfasten the four shift lever plate retaining screws.
   b. Withdraw the shift lever assembly.
   c. Remove the gasket.

➡**Cover the hole with a clean cloth to prevent anything from falling into the transmission case.**

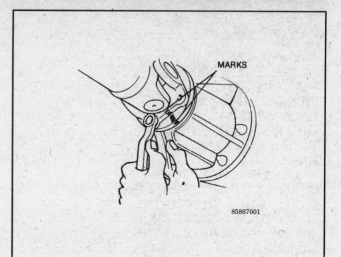

Fig. 1 Matchmark the driveshaft flange to the transmission yoke before removal

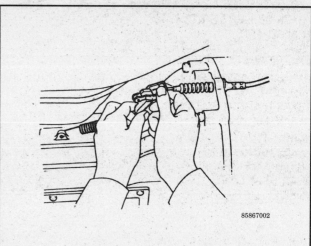

Fig. 2 Disconnecting the clutch cable from the release fork

Working in the engine compartment perform the following:
5. Drain the cooling system and disconnect the cable from the negative side of the battery.
6. Remove the radiator hoses.
7. On Corolla 1200 models, only:
   a. Unfasten the back-up lamp switch connector.
   b. Remove the engine fan.
8. On Corolla 1600 and 1800 models, only:
   a. Remove the air cleaner, complete with hoses.
   b. Unfasten the accelerator torque rod at the carburetor.
   c. Remove the clutch hydraulic line support bracket.
   d. Remove the starter assembly from the left side of the engine.
   e. Remove the upper left hand clutch housing bolt, from the flat at the top of the clutch housing.

➡**Be sure that the car is securely supported with jack-stands. You will be working underneath it.**

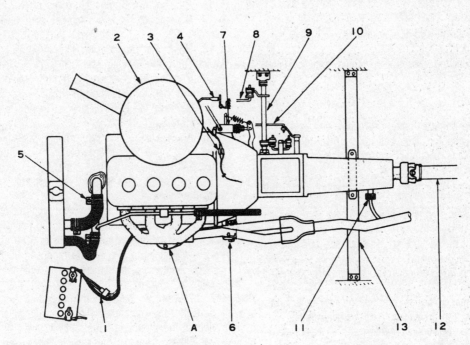

A. Exhaust pipe flange
1. Positive battery cable (+)
2. Air cleaner
3. Back-up lamp connector
4. Torque rod
5. Radiator hose

6. Exhaust pipe clamp
7. Master cylinder w/line support
   bracket
8. Accelerator linkage
9. Pivot—not applicable in USA

10. Bellcrank—not applicable in the
    USA
11. Speedometer cable
12. Driveshaft
13. Rear supporting crossmember

85867003

Fig. 3 Transmission mounting

9. Drain the transmission oil.
10. Detach the exhaust pipe from the manifold and remove the exhaust pipe support bracket.
11. Remove the driveshaft.

➡It will be necessary to plug the opening in the end of the transmission with an old yoke or if none is available, cover it with a plastic bag secured by a rubber band.

12. Unfasten the speedometer cable from the right side of the transmission.
13. On Corolla 1600 and 1800 models, only:
   a. Remove the clutch release cylinder assembly from the transmission and tie it aside, so that it is out of the way.
   b. Unplug the back-up lamp switch connector.
14. Support the front of the transmission with a jack.
15. Unfasten the engine rear mounts. Remove the rear crossmember.
16. Remove the jack from under the transmission.

17. On Corolla 1600 and 1800 models, unbolt the clutch housing from the engine and withdraw the transmission assembly.

➡**Remove the brace, if so equipped.**

18. Perform the following on Corolla 1200 model, before removing the transmission:
   a. Remove the cotter pin from the clutch release linkage.
   b. Remove the clutch release cable.
   c. Separate the clutch housing from the engine by removing the bolts which secure it.

To install:

19. Installation is performed in the reverse order of removal, but remember to perform the following during installation.
20. Apply a light coating of multipurpose grease to the input shaft end, input shaft spline, clutch release bearing, and driveshaft end.

21. On Corolla 1200 model, apply multipurpose grease to the ball on the end of the gearshaft lever assembly and clutch release cable end.

➡ **Install the clutch housing-to-engine bolts in two or three stages.**

22. Fill the transmission and cooling system.
23. Adjust the clutch.
24. Check to ensure that the back-up lamps come on when R is selected.

1984 and Later RWD

1. Disconnect the negative battery terminal.
2. Loosen the distributor pinch bolt and turn the distributor body so it doesn't come in contact with the dash panel.
3. Remove the center console box.
4. Remove the trim boot at the base of the shift lever and the boot underneath it on the shift tower.
5. Unfasten the four shift lever plate retaining screws, withdraw the shift lever and remove the gasket.
6. Raise the front of the vehicle and drain the transmission fluid.
7. Disconnect and remove the front exhaust pipe at the manifold.
8. Matchmark the two flanges, remove the four bolts and nuts, then disconnect the driveshaft from the differential.
9. Remove the center support bearing and its heat shield from the vehicle underbody.
10. Remove the driveshaft.

11. Disconnect the speedometer cable and position it out of the way.
12. Disconnect the back-up light switch connector at the switch.
13. Remove the clutch release cylinder.
14. Disconnect the two electrical leads and remove the starter.
15. Raise the transmission slightly so as to remove the weight from the rear support.
16. Remove the rear engine mount. Remove the stiffener plate and then remove the transmission mounting bolts.
17. Remove the transmission down and toward the rear.
   To install:
18. Apply a light coating of multipurpose grease to the input shaft end, input shaft spline, clutch release bearing, and driveshaft end.
19. Installation is in the reverse order of removal. Please note the following:
   a. Align the input shaft spline with the clutch disc and then push the transmission fully into position. Install the two upper set bolts and tighten them to 53 ft. lbs. (72 Nm).
   b. Tighten the rear engine mount to 38 ft. lbs. (52 Nm).
   c. Tighten the transmission and stiffener plate mounting bolts to 27 ft. lbs. (37 Nm).
   d. When reconnecting the driveshaft to the differential, be sure that the matchmarks made earlier align and then tighten the mounting bolts to 31 ft. lbs. (42 Nm).
20. Fill the transmission and cooling system.
21. Adjust the clutch.
22. Check to ensure that the back-up lamps come on when R is selected.

MANUAL TRANSAXLE

➡ **The transaxle identification number is located at the bottom of the engine compartment identification plate. No linkage adjustment is necessary for these models. For more information on transaxle identification, please refer to Section 1.**

Adjustments

SHIFT LEVER FREE-PLAY

▶ **See Figure 4**

1. Remove the console.
2. Disconnect the shift control cables from the control shift lever assembly.
3. Using a dial indicator, measure the up and down movement of the shift lever; it should be about 0.0059 in. (0.15mm).
4. If necessary to adjust the free-play::
   a. Remove the shift lever cover-to-housing screws and the cover.
   b. Remove the snapring, the shift lever, the shift lever ball seat and the bushing.
   c. Select the correct shift lever bushing and reverse the removal procedures.
5. Recheck the shift lever movement.

CLUTCH SWITCH

▶ **See Figure 5**

1. Check that the engine DOES NOT start when the clutch pedal is released.
2. Check that the engine STARTS when the clutch is depressed.
3. If necessary, adjust or replace the clutch start switch:
   a. Loosen the clutch switch locknut and adjust the switch to the proper clearance 0.08-0.24 in. (2.0-6.0mm) with a feeler gauge set.
   b. Retighten the locknut and check for proper operation.

Shift Cables

REMOVAL & INSTALLATION

▶ **See Figure 6**

The shift control cables are precisely adjusted at the factory during assembly and cannot be accurately adjusted in the field. Should either of the cables become stretched and therefore out of adjustment, the individual cable must be replaced. Any attempt to adjust the shift cables can cause poor shifting and/or transaxle damage.

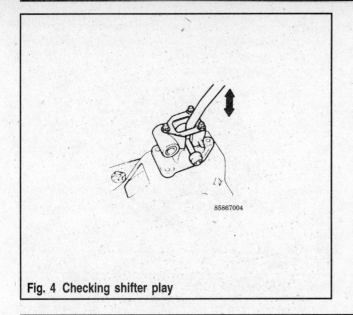

Fig. 4 Checking shifter play

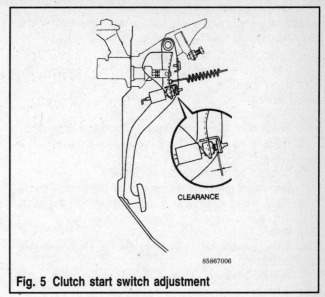

Fig. 5 Clutch start switch adjustment

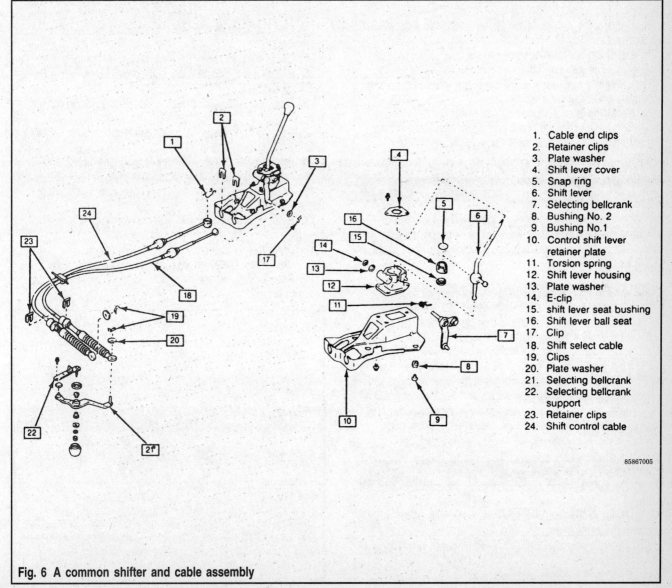

1. Cable end clips
2. Retainer clips
3. Plate washer
4. Shift lever cover
5. Snap ring
6. Shift lever
7. Selecting bellcrank
8. Bushing No. 2
9. Bushing No.1
10. Control shift lever retainer plate
11. Torsion spring
12. Shift lever housing
13. Plate washer
14. E-clip
15. shift lever seat bushing
16. Shift lever ball seat
17. Clip
18. Shift select cable
19. Clips
20. Plate washer
21. Selecting bellcrank
22. Selecting bellcrank support
23. Retainer clips
24. Shift control cable

Fig. 6 A common shifter and cable assembly

1. Disconnect the negative battery cable.
2. Remove the shift lever knob and the shifter boot.
3. Remove the front and rear center console halves.
4. Remove the center air ducts.
5. Remove the Electronic Control Unit (ECU) mounting nuts and remove the ECU (if so equipped) from under the dashboard.
6. Remove the cable hold-down bracket.
7. Remove the four shifter assembly mounting bolts.
8. Remove the shift cable retainer and end clips from the shifter assembly.
9. Remove the shifter control assembly.
10. Disconnect the cable retainers at the transaxle.
11. Remove the shift cables by pulling them from the outside of the firewall.

To install:

12. Install the new cables by going through the firewall from the outside.
13. Position the cables in their brackets at the transaxle and install the retaining clips.
14. Connect the cables to their transaxle mounts and install the clips.
15. Connect the cables to the shifter and install the clips at the shifter assembly.
16. Install the shifter assembly and its four bolts.
17. Install the cable hold-down brackets.
18. Reinstall the Electronic Control Unit ECU (if so equipped) and the center air duct.
19. Install the front and rear halves of the console.
20. Install the shift lever boot and knob. Connect the negative battery cable. roadtest the vehicle for proper shifter operation.

Back-up Light Switch

REMOVAL & INSTALLATION

▶ See Figure 7

The reverse light or back-up light switch is mounted in the top area of the manual transaxle housing. Its removal and replacement is easily accomplished by disengaging the wiring connector from the switch and unscrewing the switch from the case (always replace the mounting gasket below it). A specially sized socket or an equivalent removal tool may be necessary for this service operation. Install the new switch and tighten it 30 ft. lbs. (40 Nm). Reinstall the electrical connector. Turn key to the **ON** position, depress clutch pedal and place shifter in REVERSE position. Check operation of back-up lights.

Transaxle

REMOVAL & INSTALLATION

▶ See Figures 8, 9, 10, 11, 12, 13, 14, 15, 16, 17, 18 and 19

1. Disconnect the negative battery cable.

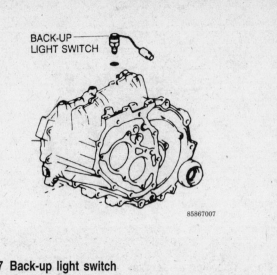

Fig. 7 Back-up light switch

2. Remove the air cleaner case assembly with hose. Remove the coolant reservoir tank.
3. Remove release cylinder tube bracket and cylinder assembly.
4. Disconnect the back-up light switch connector.
5. Remove the ground cable. Disconnect shift cables from the transaxle.
6. Disconnect vehicle speed sensor connector or speedometer cable.
7. Remove the starter set bolt from the transaxle upper side.
8. Remove the 2 transaxle upper mounting bolts.
9. Remove the engine left mounting stay.
10. Install engine support fixture. Raise and safely support the vehicle.
11. Remove the front wheels. Remove the engine under covers.
12. Drain the transaxle oil.
13. Disconnect the lower ball joint from the lower arm.
14. Remove the halfshafts — refer to the necessary service procedures.

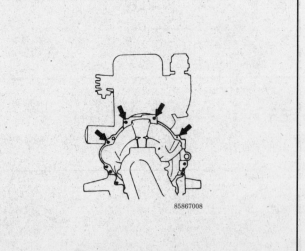

Fig. 8 Remove the upper transaxle set bolts

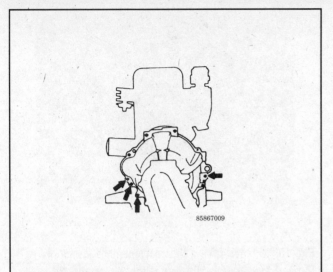

Fig. 9 Remove the lower transaxle set bolts

Fig. 10 If equipped, remove the transaxle shield

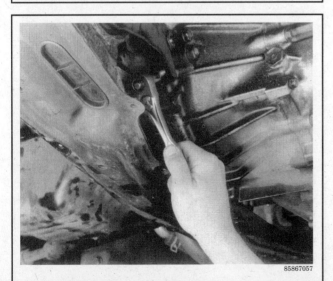

Fig. 11 Unbolt the transaxle bracket

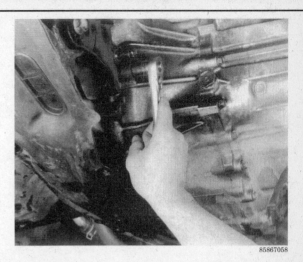

Fig. 12 The transaxle bracket may also have retainers on the rear side of the clutch housing

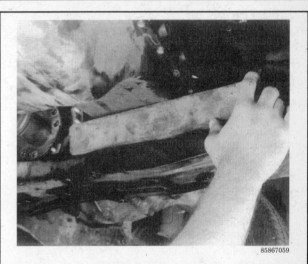

Fig. 13 Support the engine assembly before removing the transaxle

15. Remove the front exhaust pipe.

16. Remove the hole cover, if so equipped. Remove the engine front mounting set bolts.

17. Disconnect engine rear mounting. Remove the engine center support member.

18. Remove the starter. Remove stiffener plate if so equipped.

19. Raise the transaxle and engine slightly with a jack. Remove the engine left mounting set bolts from the front side.

20. Remove the transaxle mounting bolts from the engine front side. Remove the transaxle mounting bolts from the engine rear side. Lower the engine left side and remove the transaxle from the engine.

To install:

21. Align the input shaft with the clutch disc, then install the transaxle to the engine. Torque the engine-to-transaxle bolts to 47 ft. lbs. (64 Nm) for 12mm bolts and 34 ft. lbs. (46 Nm) for 10mm bolts.

Fig. 14 If equipped remove the speedometer cable from the transaxle

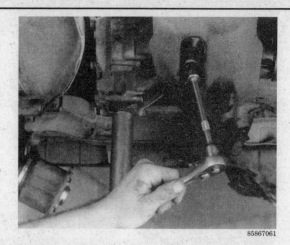

Fig. 15 When removing the crossmember-to-mount bolts, a socket and long extension will usually be helpful.

22. Raise the transaxle and engine slightly, then install the left engine mounting. Install the left engine-to-transaxle mount bolts and torque to 41 ft. lbs. (56 Nm).

23. Install stiffener plate if so equipped. Install starter and connect the electrical wiring to the starter.

24. Install engine center support member. Torque the small bolts to 45 ft. lbs. (61 Nm) and larger bolts to 152 ft. lbs. (206 Nm).

25. Connect the engine rear mounting and torque the bolts to 35 ft. lbs. (48 Nm). Connect the engine front mounting and torque bolts 47 ft. lbs. (64 Nm). Install hole covers.

26. Install front exhaust pipe.

27. Install the halfshafts — refer to the necessary service procedures.

28. Connect the lower ball joint to lower arm.

29. Fill the transaxle with the correct gear oil.

30. Install under covers. Install front wheels and lower the vehicle. Remove the engine support fixture.

31. Install engine left mounting set bolt. Torque the mounting bolt to 41 ft. lbs. (56 Nm).

32. Install engine left mounting stay. Connect vehicle speed sensor connector or speedometer cable.

33. Reconnect the transaxle shift cables. Install ground cable.

34. Connect the back-up light switch connector.

35. Install release cylinder and release cylinder tube bracket.

36. Install coolant reservoir tank.

37. Install air cleaner case assembly.

38. Connect the negative battery cable. Check front wheel alignment.

39. Road test the vehicle and check for abnormal noise and smooth shifting.

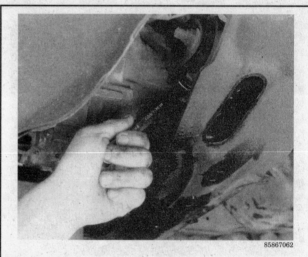

Fig. 16 Some transaxle mount bolts require an open-end or box wrench

Fig. 17 Support the transaxle before removal

Fig. 18 Carefully separate the transaxle from the engine by pulling on the housing

Fig. 19 Removing the transaxle from the engine

Halfshafts

➡ **The axleshafts on front wheel drive vehicles are often referred to as halfshaft assemblies.**

The halfshaft CV-joints are packed with grease for lubrication during assembly. The joints are then covered with rubber CV-boots for protection. If a boot becomes torn or otherwise damaged, it should be replaced immediately to prevent possible damage to the CV-joints from dirt or moisture. The CV-boots should be inspected any time the vehicle is raised to help prevent costly repairs should a CV-joint fail.

REMOVAL & INSTALLATION

▶ **See Figures 20, 21, 22, 23, 24, 25, 26, 27, 28, 29, 30, 31, 32, 33, 34 and 35**

1. Unless air tools are available, remove the cotter pin and hub nut lock before the vehicle is raised. Have an assistant step on the brake pedal and at the same time, loosen and remove the bearing locknut.

2. Raise the front of the vehicle and support it with jackstands. Remove the tires.

3. Remove the cotter pin and lock nut cap.

4. Remove the engine under cover. Have an assistant depress the brake pedal, loosen and remove the six nuts which connect the halfshaft to the differential side gear shaft.

5. Remove the two retaining nuts and then disconnect the lower arm from the steering knuckle.

6. Remove the brake caliper and then position it out of the way. Remove the brake disc.

7. Use a two-armed puller and remove the axle hub from the outer end of the halfshaft.

8. Remove the halfshaft.

➡ **Be sure to cover the halfshaft input hole.**

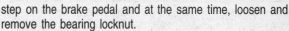

Fig. 20 Use this special tool to remove the halfshaft from the transaxle

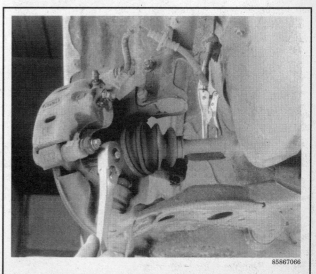

Fig. 21 Remove the caliper mounting plate bolts

Fig. 22 Remove the caliper assembly

Fig. 23 Support the brake caliper out of the way using wire

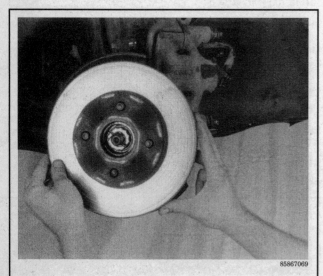

Fig. 24 Remove the brake rotor

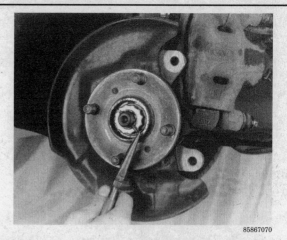

Fig. 25 Unless air tools are available, the cotter pin should be removed with the tire mounted and on the ground

Fig. 26 With the cotter pin out, you are free to remove the hub nut lock

9. Installation is in the reverse order of removal. Please note the following:

a. Install the outboard side of the shaft into the axle hub and then insert the inner end into the differential. Finger tighten the six nuts. Be careful not to damage the boots during installation.

b. Tighten the steering knuckle-to-lower arm bolts to 47 ft. lbs. (64 Nm).

c. With the vehicle on the ground, tighten the bearing locknut to 137 ft. lbs. (186 Nm) and be sure to use a new cotter pin on the locknut cap.

d. Depress the brake pedal and then tighten the six inner retaining nuts to 27 ft. lbs. (36 Nm).

Fig. 27 Loosen and remove the hub locknut

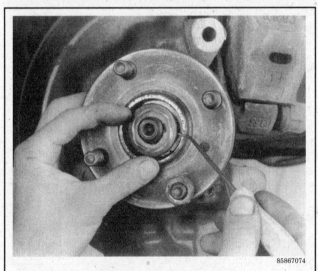

Fig. 28 Remove the hub locknut washer

Fig. 29 Removing the lower strut mounting bolts — the matchmarks are to preserve front end alignment

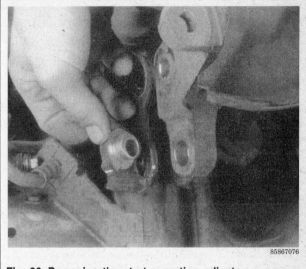

Fig. 30 Removing the strut mounting adjuster

Fig. 31 View of the axle hub assembly mounting holes

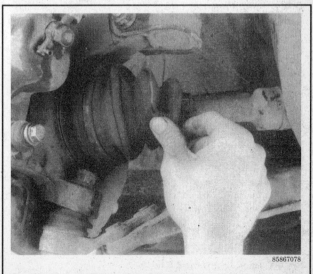

Fig. 32 Inspect the halfshaft boots

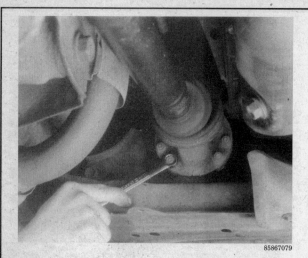

Fig. 33 Removing the halfshaft retaining nuts at the transaxle

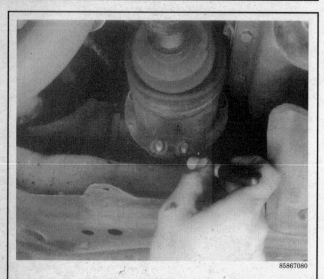

Fig. 34 Mark the halfshaft before separation

Fig. 35 Removing the halfshaft

OVERHAUL

▶ **See Figures 36, 37, 38 and 39**

1. Remove the halfshaft from the vehicle. For details, please refer to the removal and installation procedure found earlier in this section.

2. Before disassembling a halfshaft, check the following to determine it's condition:

   a. Check to see that there is no play in the outboard joint.

   b. Check to see that the inboard joint slides smoothly in the thrust direction.

   c. Check to see that there is no abnormal play in the radial direction of the inboard joint.

3. Remove the CV-joint boot clamps.

4. Place matchmarks on the inboard joint tulip and on the tripod. Remove the tulip from the halfshaft. When matchmarking the tulip to the tripod, never punch the marks.

5. Remove the snapring on the tripod with snapring pliers. Punch matchmarks on the shaft and the tripod and then gently tap the tripod off of the shaft. Never tap on the roller.

6. Remove both boots.

7. Tape the halfshaft splines, then install the boot and a new clamp to the outboard joint.

8. Repeat Step 1 for the inboard joint.

9. Position the beveled side of the tripod axial spline toward the outboard joint. Align the matchmarks made previously, then using a brass drift or hammer, tap the tripod onto the halfshaft.

10. Install a new snapring.

11. Attach the boot to the outboard joint. Pack the boot with grease supplied in the boot kit.

12. Pack the tulip with grease, align the matchmarks and then install the tulip to the halfshaft.

13. Install the boots, making sure that the boot is in the shaft groove. Install new boot clamps and lock them into position as shown in the illustration.

➡**Make sure that the boot is not stretched or contracted when the halfshaft is at its standard length. The halfshaft length for the gasoline engine is right side 27.48 in. (698.5mm) and left side 16.54 in. (420.5mm). The standard length for the diesel engine is right side 27.76 in. (705.5mm) and left side 16.46 in. (418.5mm).**

14. Once the halfshaft is properly assembled, install the shaft back in the vehicle. BE VERY careful not to tear the new boots upon installation or you will have to start all over again.

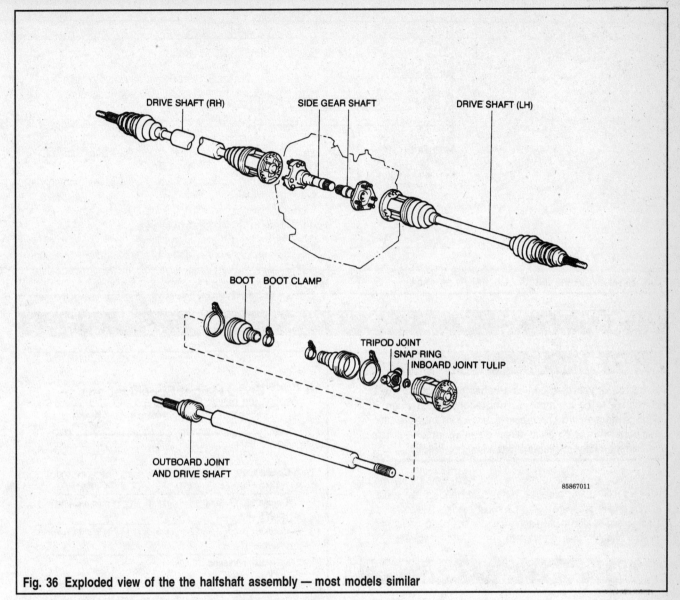

Fig. 36 Exploded view of the the halfshaft assembly — most models similar

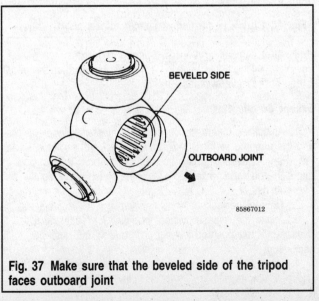

Fig. 37 Make sure that the beveled side of the tripod faces outboard joint

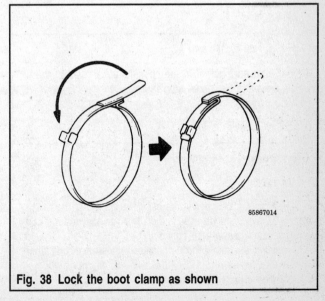

Fig. 38 Lock the boot clamp as shown

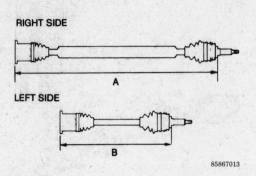

RIGHT SIDE

LEFT SIDE

85867013

Fig. 39 Measure the length of halfshaft as shown

CLUTCH

✳✳CAUTION

The clutch driven disc contains asbestos which has been determined to be a cancer causing agent. Never clean clutch surfaces with compressed air. Avoid inhaling any dust from any clutch area! When cleaning clutch surfaces, use commercially available brake cleaning fluids.

The clutch is a single plate, dry disc type. Some early models use a coil spring pressure plate. Later models use a diaphragm spring pressure plate. On most models, clutch release bearings are sealed ball bearing units which need no lubrication and should never be washed in any kind of solvent.

ADJUSTMENTS

PEDAL HEIGHT

▶ **See Figures 40, 41 and 42**

Adjust the pedal height to the specifications given in the chart, by rotating the pedal stop (nut).

FREE-PLAY

▶ **See Figures 43, 44 and 45**

Corolla 1200

1. Pull on the clutch release cable at the clutch support flange until a resistance is felt when the release bearing contacts the clutch diaphragm spring.
2. Holding the cable in this position measure the distance between the E-ring and the end of the wire support flange. The distance should be 5-6 threads.
3. If adjustment is required, change the position of the E-ring.

Pedal Height Specifications

Model/Year	Height (in.)	Measure Between
Corolla 1200 1975–77	2.2 ①	Pedal pad and floor mat
Corolla 1200 1978–79	6.7	Pedal pad and floor mat
Corolla 1600 & 1800 1975–82	6.5 ②	Pedal pad and floor mat
Corolla 1983–87	6.5 ②	Pedal pad and floor mat

① Pedal depressed
② FWD: 5.85

85867015

Fig. 40 Clutch pedal height specifications chart

4. After completing the adjustment, check the clutch pedal free-play which should be 0.8-1.4 in. (20-36mm) after the pedal is depressed several times.

Except Corolla 1200

1. Adjust the clearance between the master cylinder piston and the pushrod to the specifications given in the Clutch Pedal Free-Play Adjustment chart. Loosen the pushrod locknut and rotate the pushrod while depressing the clutch pedal lightly with your finger.
2. Tighten the locknut when finished with the adjustment.
3. Adjust the release cylinder free-play by loosening the release cylinder pushrod locknut and rotating the pushrod, if necessary.
4. Measure the clutch pedal free-play after performing the above adjustments. If it fails to fall within specifications, repeat Steps 1-3 until it does.

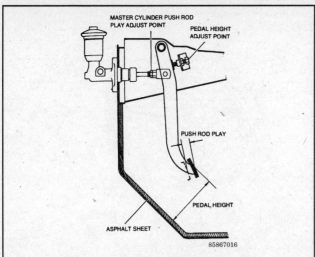

Fig. 41 Clutch pedal adjusting points — all except 1200 model

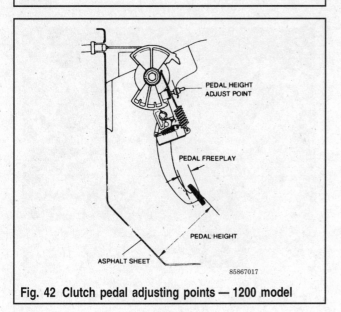

Fig. 42 Clutch pedal adjusting points — 1200 model

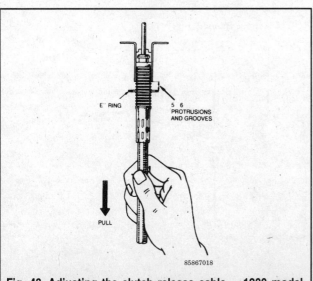

Fig. 43 Adjusting the clutch release cable — 1200 model

Clutch Pedal Free-Play Specifications

Model	Year	Pedal Free-Play (in.)
Corolla 1200	'70–'77	1.00–1.80
	'78–'79	0.80–1.40
Corolla 1600	'71–'79	0.79–1.58
Corolla 1800	'80–'82	0.51–0.91
Corolla	'83–'87	0.51–0.91 ①

① Diesel: 0.20–0.59

85867019

Fig. 44 Specification chart for clutch pedal free-play

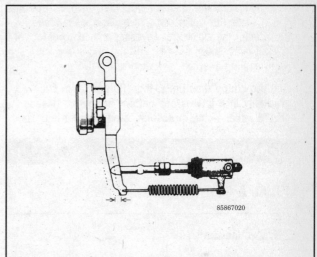

Fig. 45 Release cylinder free-play is the distance between the arrows

Disc And Pressure Plate

REMOVAL & INSTALLATION

▶ See Figures 46, 47, 48, 49, 50, 51 and 52

❋❋CAUTION

The clutch driven disc contains asbestos which has been determined to be a cancer causing agent. Never clean clutch surfaces with compressed air. Avoid inhaling any dust from any clutch area! When cleaning clutch surfaces, use commercially available brake cleaning fluids.

1. Remove the transmission from the vehicle as previously detailed.
2. Remove the clutch cover and disc from the bellhousing.
3. Unfasten the release fork bearing clips. Withdraw the release bearing hub, complete with the release bearing.

4. Remove the tension spring from the clutch linkage, if equipped.

5. Remove the release fork and support.

6. Punch matchmarks on the clutch cover and the pressure plate so that the plate can be returned to its original position during installation.

7. Slowly unfasten the screws which attach the retracting springs, if so equipped.

➡**If the screws are released too fast, the clutch assembly will fly apart, causing possible injury or loss of parts.**

8. Separate the pressure plate (remove the pressure plate retaining bolts evenly in steps) from the clutch cover/spring assembly. Inspect the parts for wear or deterioration. Replace parts as required.

9. Installation is performed in the reverse order of removal. Several points should be noted, however:

• Be sure to align the matchmarks on the clutch cover and pressure plate which were made during disassembly.

• Apply a thin coating of multipurpose grease to the release bearing hub and release fork contact points. Also, pack the groove inside the clutch hub with multipurpose grease.

• Center the clutch disc by using a clutch pilot tool or an old input shaft. Insert the pilot into the end of the input shaft front bearing and bolt the clutch to the flywheel.

➡**Install the clutch disc bolts, then tighten them evenly and gradually in a criss-cross pattern in several passes around the cover — this procedure step is most important.**

Clutch Master Cylinder

REMOVAL & INSTALLATION

1. Remove the clevis pin.

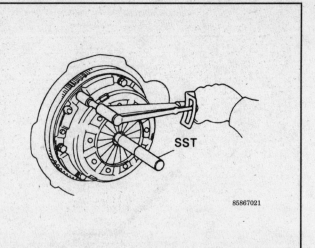

Fig. 47 Use a clutch pilot tool or equivalent to install the clutch assembly

Fig. 48 Inspect the clutch assembly for wear or damage

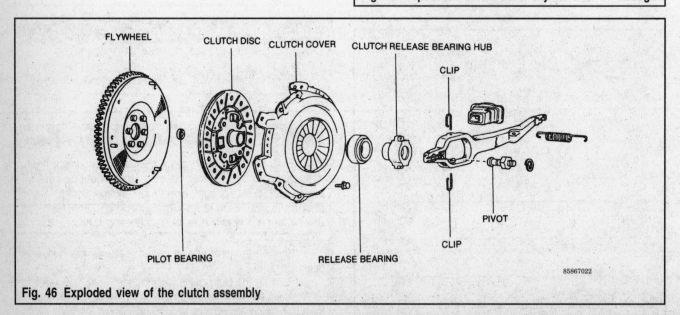

FLYWHEEL   CLUTCH DISC   CLUTCH COVER   CLUTCH RELEASE BEARING HUB

CLIP

PIVOT

CLIP

PILOT BEARING   RELEASE BEARING

Fig. 46 Exploded view of the clutch assembly

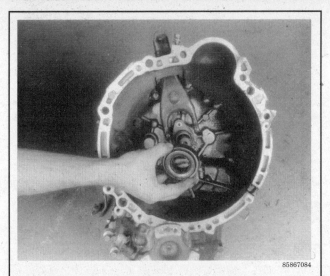

Fig. 49 Removing the clutch release bearing

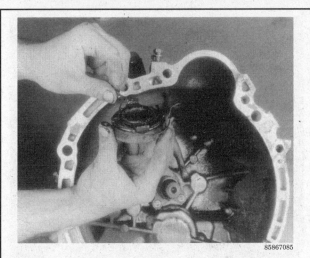

Fig. 50 Removing the clutch release bearing retaining clip

Fig. 51 Installing the clutch assembly — note special tool for assembly installation

Fig. 52 Tighten the clutch disc bolts evenly using a criss-cross pattern

2. Detach the hydraulic line from the tub.

✴✴CAUTION

Do not spill brake fluid on the painted surfaces of the vehicle.

3. Unfasten the bolts which secure the master cylinder to the firewall. Withdraw the assembly.

➡We recommend replacement of the master and clutch slave cylinder as an assembly (one can be replaced without the other) for proper reliability and performance.

4. Service as required. Installation is performed in the reverse order of removal. Bleed and adjust the brake system. Adjust the clutch pedal height and free-play, if necessary.

OVERHAUL

▶ See Figure 53

1. Clamp the master cylinder body in a vise with soft jaws.
2. Separate the reservoir assembly from the master cylinder.
3. Remove the snapring and remove the pushrod/piston assembly.
4. Inspect all of the parts and replace any which are worn or defective.
5. Coat all parts with clean brake fluid, prior to assembly.
6. Install the piston assembly in the cylinder bore.
7. Fit the pushrod over the washer and secure them with the snapring.
8. Install the reservoir.

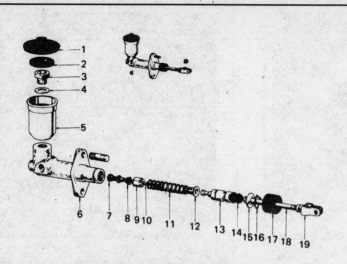

Fig. 53 Exploded view of the clutch master cylinder components

1. Filler cap
2. Float
3. Reservoir setbolt
4. Washer
5. Reservoir
6. Master cylinder body
7. Inlet valve
8. Spring
9. Inlet valve housing
10. Connecting rod
11. Spring
12. Spring retainer
13. Piston
14. Cylinder cup
15. Plate
16. Snap-ring
17. Boot
18. Pushrod
19. Clevis

Clutch Slave Cylinder

REMOVAL & INSTALLATION

▶ See Figures 54, 55, 56, 57, 58, 59 and 60

➡ Do not spill brake fluid on the painted surface of the vehicle!

1. Raise the front of the car and support it with jackstands. Be sure that it is supported securely.
2. If necessary, remove the rear gravel shield to gain access to the release cylinder.
3. Remove the clutch fork return spring.
4. Unfasten the hydraulic line from the release cylinder by removing its retaining nut.
5. Screw in the threaded end of the pushrod.
6. Remove the release cylinder retaining nuts and remove the cylinder.

➡ We recommend replacement of the master and clutch slave cylinder as an assembly (one can be replaced without the other) for proper reliability and performance.

7. Installation is performed in the reverse order of removal. Adjust the pushrod free-play and bleed the hydraulic system.

OVERHAUL

▶ See Figure 61

1. Remove the pushrod assembly and the rubber boot.
2. Withdraw the piston, complete with its cup; don't remove the cup unless it is being replaced.
3. Wash all parts in brake fluid.
4. Replace any worn or damaged parts.
5. Replace the cylinder assembly if the piston-to-bore clearance is greater than 0.006 in. (0.15mm).
6. Assembly is the reverse of disassembly. Coat all parts in clean brake fluid, prior to assembly.

Fig. 54 Clutch slave cylinder installed

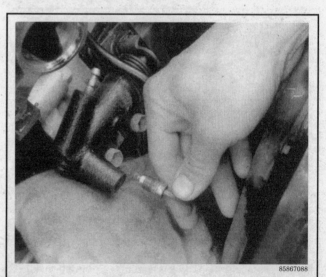

Fig. 55 Remove clutch slave cylinder hydraulic line

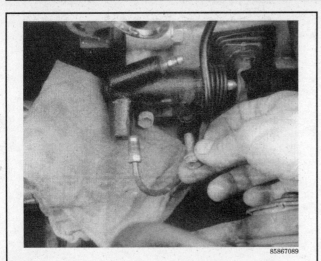

Fig. 56 Remove the clutch slave cylinder mounting bolts

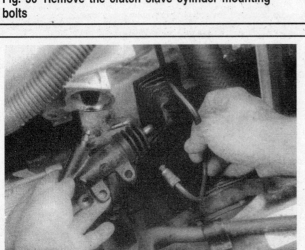

Fig. 57 Remove the clutch slave cylinder assembly

Fig. 58 When installing the clutch slave cylinder assembly place a small amount of grease on the tip of the cylinder

Fig. 59 The clutch slave cylinder assembly must be bled for proper operation

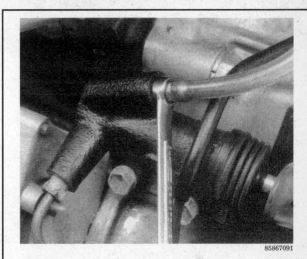

Fig. 60 Place a box wrench and short rubber hose over the bleeder

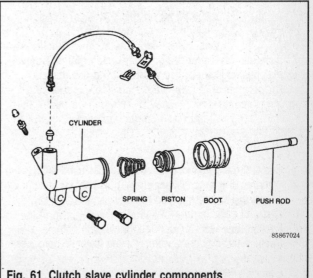

Fig. 61 Clutch slave cylinder components

Clutch Hydraulic System

BLEEDING

1. Fill the master cylinder reservoir with brake fluid.

✳✳CAUTION

Do not spill brake fluid on the painted surfaces of the vehicle. Care must be taken when performing this service operation as fluid will forced out the bleeder hole.

2. Remove the cap and loosen the bleeder plug. Block the outlet hole with your finger.
3. With the help of an assistant pumping the clutch pedal several times, take your finger from the hole while the assistant is depressing the clutch pedal. Allow the air to flow out. Place your finger back over the hole and release the pedal.
4. After fluid pressure can be felt (with your finger), tighten the bleeder plug.
5. Fit a bleeder tube over the plug and place the other end into a clean jar half filled with brake fluid.
6. Depress the clutch pedal, loosen the bleeder plug with a wrench, and allow the fluid to flow into the jar.
7. Tighten the plug and then release the clutch pedal.
8. Repeat Steps 6-7 until no air bubbles are visible in the bleeder tube.
9. When there are no more air bubbles, tighten the plug while keeping the clutch pedal fully depressed. Replace the cap.
10. Fill the master cylinder to the specified level.
11. Check the system for leaks.

AUTOMATIC TRANSMISSION

Fluid Pan And Filter

REMOVAL AND INSTALLATION

1. Remove the transmission drain plug, if so equipped. Drain the fluid from the transmission.
2. Unfasten the pan securing bolts. Carefully lower the pan to the ground.
3. Remove the oil strainer (filter) attaching bolts and carefully remove the strainer. The strainer will also contain some fluid.
4. Discard the strainer or filter. Remove the gasket from the pan and discard it.
5. Drain the remainder of the fluid from the oil pan and wipe the pan clean with a lint-free rag. With a gasket scraper, remove any old gasket material from the flanges of the oil pan and the transmission.

➡**There may be one magnet on the bottom of the pan. This magnet was installed by the manufacturer at the time the transmission was assembled. The magnet functions to collect metal chips and filings from clutch plates, bushings and bearings that accumulate during the normal break-in process that a new transmission experiences. Clean the magnet and reinstall it. This can be useful tool for determining transmission component wear, but more importantly they help to keep the fluid clean.**

To install:
6. Install the new oil strainer or filter. Install and tighten the retaining bolts in their proper locations.
7. Install the new gasket onto the oil pan making sure that the holes in the gasket are aligned evenly with those of the pan. Position the magnets so that they will not interfere with the oil tubes.
8. Raise the pan and gasket into position on the transmission, then install the retaining bolts. Torque the retaining bolts in a criss-cross pattern to 4-6 ft. lbs. (5-8 Nm) on all transmission except A-40. On the A-40 type transmission torque retaining bolts to 17-20 ft. lbs. (23-27 Nm).
9. Install and tighten the drain plug.
10. Fluid is added only through the dipstick tube. Use the proper type of fluid for your automatic transmission. For more information on filling the transmission, please refer to Section 1 of this manual. If you are unsure what type of fluid to use, consult your owner's manual.

➡**Do not overfill the transmission. Do not race the engine when adding fluid.**

11. Replace the dipstick after filling. Start the engine and allow it to idle.
12. After the engine has idled for a few minutes, shift the transmission slowly through the gears and then return it to **P**. With the engine still idling, check the fluid level on the dipstick. If necessary, add more fluid to raise the level to full.

➡**Before recycling the used fluid, check the color of the fluid. It should always be bright in color. It if is discolored (brown or black), or smells burnt, serious transmission troubles, possibly due to overheating, should be suspected. The transmission should be inspected to locate the cause of the burnt fluid.**

ADJUSTMENTS

LOW SERVO AND BANDS

2-Speed

The low and band adjusting bolt is located on the outside of the transmission case so that it is unnecessary to remove the oil pan in order to perform the adjustment.
1. Loosen the locknut on the adjusting bolt.
2. Tighten the bolt until it is bottomed.
3. Back off 3½ turns and hold the adjusting bolts securely while tightening the locknut.

3-Speed Toyoglide

FRONT BAND

1. Remove the oil pan as previously outlined.
2. Pry the band engagement lever toward the band with a small prybar.
3. The gap between the end of the piston rod and the engagement bolts should be 0.138 in. (3.5mm)
4. If the gap does not meet the specification, adjust it by turning the engagement bolt.
5. Install the oil pan and refill the transmission as previously outlined.

REAR BAND

The rear band adjusting bolt is located on the outside of the case so it is not necessary to remove the oil pan in order to adjust the band.

1. Loosen the adjusting bolt locknut and fully screw in the adjusting bolt.
2. Loosen the adjusting bolt one turn.
3. Tighten the locknut while holding the bolt so that it cannot turn.

A-40, A-40D, A-42DL, A130L, A131L, A240L and A240E

No band adjustments are possible. The only external adjustments are throttle and shift linkages.

NEUTRAL SAFETY SWITCH

◆ See Figures 62, 63, 64 and 65

2-Speed

The neutral safety switch used on all 2-speed models is not adjustable. If it malfunctions, it must be replaced. To do so proceed in the following manner:

1. Remove the center console.
2. Unfasten and remove the three screws securing the transmission selector assembly.
3. Disconnect the neutral safety switch multiconnector.
4. Lift transmission selector assembly slightly and unfasten the two neutral safety switch attaching screws.
5. Withdraw the switch.
6. Installation is performed in the reverse order of removal. Position the selector lever in N and install the switch so that installation marks align with each other.

3 Speed (Column Selector)

The neutral safety switch/reverse lamp switch on the Toyoglide transmission with a column mounted selector is located under the hood on the shift linkage. If the switch is not functioning properly, adjust as follows:

1. Loosen the switch securing bolt.
2. Move the switch so that its arm just contacts the control shaft lever when the gear selector is in D position.
3. Tighten the switch securing bolt.
4. Check the operation of the switch; the car should start only in P or N and the back-up lamps should come on only when R is selected.

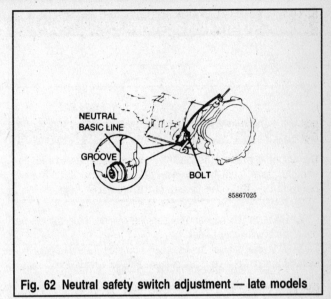

Fig. 62 Neutral safety switch adjustment — late models

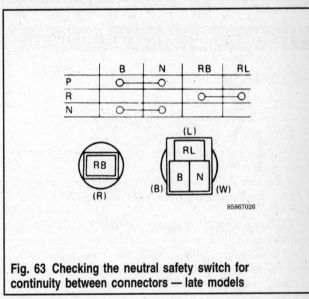

Fig. 63 Checking the neutral safety switch for continuity between connectors — late models

5. If the switch cannot be adjusted so that it functions properly, replace it with a new one. Perform the adjustment as previously outlined.

3-Speed (Console Shift)

Models with a console mounted selector have the neutral safety switch on the linkage located beneath the console. To adjust it, proceed in the following manner:

1. Remove the screws securing the center console.
2. Unfasten the console multiconnector, if so equipped, and completely remove the console.
3. Adjust the switch in the manner outlined in the preceding column selector section.
4. Install the console in the reverse order of removal after completion of the switch adjustment.

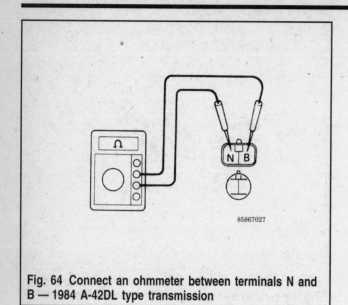

Fig. 64 Connect an ohmmeter between terminals N and B — 1984 A-42DL type transmission

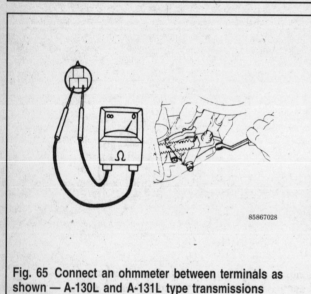

Fig. 65 Connect an ohmmeter between terminals as shown — A-130L and A-131L type transmissions

A-40 and A-40D

If the engine will start in any range except Neutral or Park, the neutral safety switch will require adjustment.

1. Locate the neutral safety switch on the side of the transmission and loosen the switch bolt.
2. Move the gear selector to the Neutral position.
3. Align the groove on the safety switch shaft with the basic line which is scribed on the housing.
4. Tighten the switch bolt.
5. Using an ohmmeter, check the continuity between the switch terminals. If a continuity problem is found (vehicle will start in all or no ranges), replace the switch.

A-42DL, A-130L and A-131L

EXCEPT 1986-87

If the engine will start in any range except Neutral or Park, the neutral safety switch will require adjustment.

1. Locate the neutral safety switch on the side of the transmission and loosen the switch bolt(s).

2. Move the gear selector to the Neutral position.
3. Disconnect the neutral safety switch connector and connect an ohmmeter between terminals N and B on the 1984 A-42DL; and between the correct terminals on the A-130L and A131L. Refer to the necessary illustrations.
4. Adjust the switch to the point where there is continuity between the two terminals.

1986-87

1. Loosen the neutral start switch bolt. Position the gear selector in the N position.
2. As required, disconnect the switch electrical connector. Align the switch shaft groove with the neutral base line which is located on the switch.
3. Tighten the bolt.

SHIFT LINKAGE

▶ **See Figures 66, 67 and 68**

2 and 3 Speed Toyoglide

The transmission should be engaged in the gear selected as indicated on the shift quadrant. If it is not, then adjust the linkage as follows:

1. Check all of the shift linkage bushings for wear. Replace any worn bushings.
2. Loosen the connecting rod swivel locknut.
3. Move the selector lever and check movement of the pointer in the shift quadrant.
4. When the control shaft is set in the neutral position the quadrant pointer should indicate N as well.

➡ **Steps 5-7 apply only to cars equipped with column mounted gear selectors.**

5. If the pointer does not indicate Neutral (N), then check the drive cord adjustment.
6. Remove the steering column shroud.
7. Turn the drive cord adjuster with a Phillips screwdriver until the pointer indicates N.

➡ **Steps 8-10 apply to both column mounted and floor mounted selectors:**

8. Position the manual valve lever on the transmission so that it is in the Neutral position.
9. Lock the connecting rod swivel with the locknut so that the pointer, selector, and manual valve lever are all positioned in Neutral.
10. Check the operation of the gear selector by moving it through all ranges.

A-40 and A-40D

1. Loosen the adjusting nut on the linkage and check the linkage for freedom of movement.
2. Push the manual valve lever toward the front of the car, as far as it will go.
3. Bring the lever back to its third notch (Neutral).
4. Have an assistant hold the shift lever in Neutral, while you tighten the linkage adjusting nut so that it can't slip.

A-42DL, A-130L and A-131L

1. Loosen the adjusting nut on the linkage and check the linkage for freedom of movement.
2. Push the manual lever fully rearward (right side on A-130L, A-131L, A240 L/E), as far as it will go.
3. Return the lever two (2) notches to the Neutral position.
4. Set the gear selector to N, while holding the selector slightly toward the R, have someone tighten the adjusting nut on the manual lever.

THROTTLE LINKAGE

▶ **See Figures 69, 70, 71 and 72**

2-Speed

1. Loosen the locknuts on the throttle linkage connecting rod turnbuckle.
2. Have an assistant depress the accelerator pedal fully.

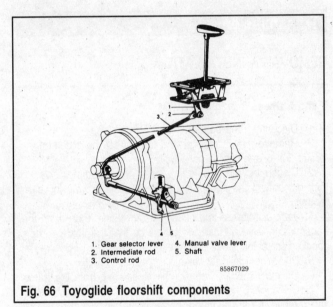

1. Gear selector lever   4. Manual valve lever
2. Intermediate rod   5. Shaft
3. Control rod

Fig. 66 Toyoglide floorshift components

Fig. 67 Adjusting the shift linkage — A-40, A-40D and A42DL

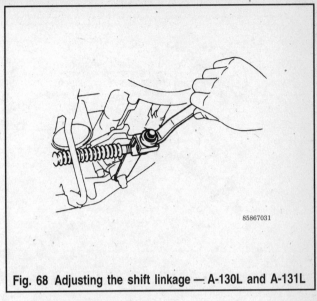

Fig. 68 Adjusting the shift linkage — A-130L and A-131L

3. Hold the throttle butterfly to the fully opened position.
4. Adjust the length of the rod so that the pointer lines up with the mark on the transmission case.
5. Tighten the locknut.

3-Speed Toyoglide

1. Loosen the locknut at each end of the linkage adjusting turnbuckle.
2. Detach the throttle linkage connecting rod from the carburetor.
3. Align the pointer on the throttle valve lever with the mark stamped on the transmission case.
4. Rotate the turnbuckle so that the end of the throttle linkage rod and the carburetor throttle lever are aligned.

➡ **The carburetor throttle valve must be fully opened during this adjustment.**

5. Tighten the turnbuckle locknuts and reconnect the throttle rod to the carburetor.
6. Open the throttle valve and check the pointer alignment with the mark on the transmission case.
7. Road test the car. If the transmission hunts, i.e., keeps shifting rapidly back and forth between gears at certain speeds or if it fails to downshift properly when going up hills, repeat the throttle linkage adjustment.

A-40, A-40D, A-42DL, A-130L and A-131L

1. Remove the air cleaner.
2. Confirm that the accelerator linkage opens the throttle fully. Adjust the link as necessary.
3. Peel the rubber dust boot back from the throttle cable.
4. Loosen the adjustment nuts on the throttle cable bracket (rocker cover) just enough to allow cable housing movement.
5. Have an assistant depress the accelerator pedal fully.
6. Adjust the cable housing so that the distance between its end and the cable stop collar is 2.05 in. (63mm) on vehicles through 1979. On 1980 and later vehicles it should be 0-0.4 in. (0-10mm).
7. Tighten the adjustment nuts. Make sure that the adjustment hasn't changed. Install the dust boot and the air cleaner.

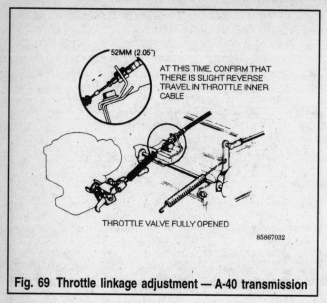

Fig. 69 Throttle linkage adjustment — A-40 transmission

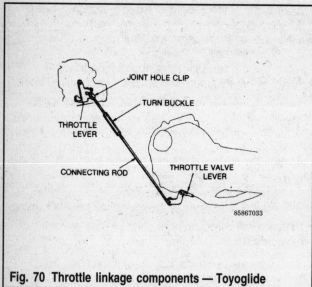

Fig. 70 Throttle linkage components — Toyoglide

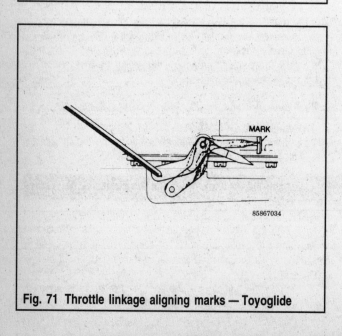

Fig. 71 Throttle linkage aligning marks — Toyoglide

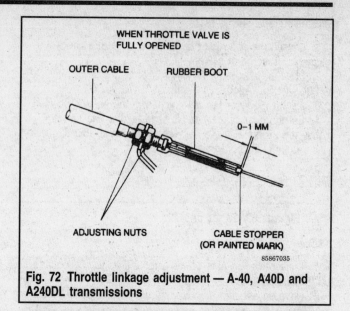

Fig. 72 Throttle linkage adjustment — A-40, A40D and A240DL transmissions

Transmission

REMOVAL & INSTALLATION

2 and 3 Speed Toyoglide (RWD)

1. Disconnect the battery.
2. Remove the air cleaner and disconnect the accelerator torque link or the cable.
3. Disconnect the throttle link rod at the carburetor side, then disconnect the backup light wiring at the firewall (on early models).
4. Jack up the car and support it on stands, then drain the transmission. Use a clean receptacle so that the fluid can be checked for color, smell and foreign matter.
5. Disconnect all shift linkage.
6. On early models, remove the cross-shaft from the frame.
7. Disconnect the throttle link rod at the transmission side and remove the speedometer cable, cooler lines and parking brake equalizer bracket.
8. Loosen the exhaust flange nuts and remove the exhaust pipe clamp and bracket.
9. Remove the driveshaft and the rear mounting bracket, then lower the rear end of the transmission carefully.
10. Unbolt the torque converter from the drive plate. Support the engine with a suitable jackstand and remove the seven bolts that hold the transmission to the engine.
To install:
11. Reverse the order of the removal procedures.
12. Install the drive plate and ring gear, tighten the attaching bolts to 37-43 ft. lbs. (50-58 Nm).
13. After assembling the torque converter to the transmission, check the clearance, it should be about 0.59 in.
14. Before installing the transmission, install the oil pump locator pin on the torque converter to facilitate installation.
15. While rotating the crankshaft, tighten the converter attaching bolts, a little at a time.
16. After installing the throttle connecting second rod, make sure the throttle valve lever indicator aligns with the mark on

the transmission with the carburetor throttle fully opened. If required, adjust the rod.

17. To install the transmission control rod correctly, move the transmission lever to N and the selector lever to Neutral. Fill the transmission with automatic transmission fluid (Type F only), then start the engine. Run the engine at idle speed and apply the brakes while moving the selector lever through all positions, then return in to Neutral.

18. After warming the engine, move the selector lever through all positions, then back to N, and check the fluid level. Fill as necessary.

19. Adjust the engine idle to 550-650 rpm with the selector lever at Drive. Road test the vehicle.

20. With the selector lever at 2 or D, check the point at which the transmission shifts. Check for shock, noise and slipping with the selector lever in all positions. Check for leaks from the transmission.

A-40, A-40D and A-42DL (RWD)

▶ **See Figure 73**

1. Disconnect the battery.
2. Remove the air cleaner and disconnect the accelerator torque link or the cable.
3. Mark and remove the back-up light wiring.
4. Remove the upper starter mounting nuts using a socket wrench with a long extension.
5. Raise the car and support it securely with jackstands. Drain the transmission.
6. Remove the lower starter mounting bolt and lay the starter alongside of the engine. Don't let it hang by the wires.
7. Unbolt the parking brake equalizer support.
8. Matchmark the driveshaft and the companion flange, to ensure correct installation. Remove the bolts securing the driveshaft to the companion flange.
9. Slide the driveshaft straight back and out of the transmission. Use a spare U-joint yoke or tie a plastic bag over the end of the transmission to keep any fluid from dripping out.
10. Remove the bolts from the cross-shaft body bracket, the cotter pin from the manual lever, and the cross-shaft socket from the transmission.
11. Remove the exhaust pipe bracket from the torque converter bell housing.
12. Disconnect the oil cooler lines from the transmission and remove the line bracket from the bell housing.
13. Disconnect the speedometer cable from the transmission.
14. Unbolt both support braces from the bell housing.
15. Use a transmission jack to raise the transmission slightly.
16. Unbolt the rear crossmember and lower the transmission about 3 inches (76mm).

17. Pry the two rubber torque converter access plugs out of their holes at the back of the engine.

18. Remove the six torque converter mounting bolts through the access hole. Rotate the engine with the crankshaft pulley.

19. Cut the head off a spare bolt to make a guide pin for the torque converter. Install the pin on the converter.

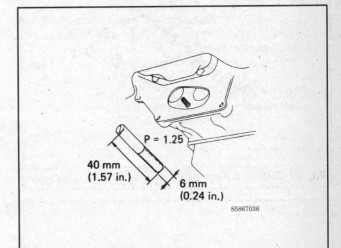

Fig. 73 Cut the head off a spare bolt to fabricate a guide pin — A-40, A-40D and A-42DL type transmissions

20. Remove the converter bell housing-to-engine bolts.

21. Push on the end of the guide pin in order to remove the converter with the transmission. Remove the transmission rearward and then bring it out from under the car. Don't catch the throttle cable during removal.

To install:

22. Reverse of removal for installation.

23. Install the two long bolts on the upper converter housing and tighten them to 36-58 ft. lbs. (48-78 Nm)

24. Tighten the converter-to-flex plate bolts.

25. When installing the speedometer cable, make sure that the felt dust protector and washer are on the cable end.

26. Tighten the cooling line and exhaust pipe bracket mounting bolts evenly. Tighten the cooling lines.

27. Align the matchmarks made on the driveshaft and the companion flange during removal. Tighten the driveshaft mounting bolts.

28. Be sure to install the oil pan drain plug.

29. Adjust the throttle cable.

30. Fill the transmission to the proper capacity. Use only type F (ATF) fluid. Start the engine, run the selector through all gear ranges and place it in P. Check the lever on the dipstick and add type F fluid, as necessary.

31. Road test the car and check for leaks.

AUTOMATIC TRANSAXLE

Identification

The automatic transaxle identification code is stamped on the VIN plate under the hood.

Fluid Pan

REMOVAL, INSTALLATION AND FILTER SERVICE

▶ **See Figures 74 and 75**

1. To avoid contamination of the transaxle, thoroughly clean the exterior of the oil pan and surrounding area to remove any deposits of dirt and grease.

2. Position a suitable drain pan under the oil pan and remove the drain plug. Allow the oil to drain from the pan. Set the drain plug aside.

3. Loosen and remove all but two of the oil pan retaining bolts.

4. Support the pan by hand and slowly remove the remaining two bolts.

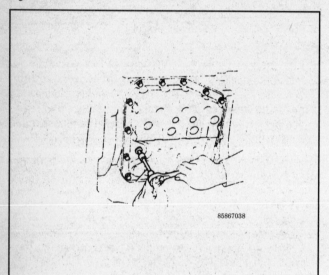

85867038

Fig. 74 Removing the automatic transaxle oil pan

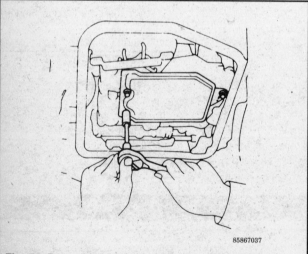

85867037

Fig. 75 Removing the automatic transaxle oil filter (strainer)

5. Carefully lower the pan to the ground.

6. Remove the 3 oil strainer (filter) attaching bolts and carefully remove the strainer. The strainer will also contain some fluid.

➡**One of the 3 oil strainer bolts is slightly longer than the other 2. Make a note of where the longer bolt goes so that it may be reinstalled in the original position.**

7. Discard the strainer. Remove the gasket from the pan and discard it.

8. Drain the remainder of the fluid from the oil pan and wipe the pan clean with a lint-free rag. Using a gasket scraper, remove any old gasket material from the flanges of the pan and the transaxle. Remove the gasket from the drain plug and replace it with a new one.

➡**There may be anywhere from one to three small magnets on the bottom of the pan. These magnets were installed by the manufacturer at the time the transaxle was assembled. The magnets function to collect metal chips and filings from clutch plates, bushings and bearings that accumulate during the normal break-in process that a new transaxle experiences. Clean the magnets and reinstall them. They can be useful tools for determining transaxle component wear, but more importantly they help to keep the fluid clean.**

To install the filter and pan:

9. Install the new oil strainer. Install and tighten the retaining bolts to 7-8 ft. lbs. (10-11 Nm) in their proper locations.

10. Install the new gasket onto the oil pan making sure that the holes in the gasket are aligned evenly with those of the pan. Position the magnets so that they will not interfere with the oil tubes.

11. Raise the pan and gasket into position on the transaxle, then install the retaining bolts. Torque the retaining bolts in a criss-cross pattern to 43 inch lbs. (4.9 Nm).

12. Install and tighten the drain plug.

13. Fluid is added only through the dipstick tube. Use the proper type of fluid for your automatic transaxle. For more information on filling the transaxle, please refer to Section 1 of this manual. If you are unsure what type of fluid to use, consult your owner's manual.

➡**Do not overfill the transaxle. Do not race the engine when adding fluid.**

14. Replace the dipstick after filling. Start the engine and allow it to idle.

15. After the engine has idled for a few minutes, shift the transmission slowly through the gears and then return it to P. With the engine still idling, check the fluid level on the dipstick. If necessary, add more fluid to raise the level to full.

➡**Before recycling the used fluid, check the color of the fluid. It should always be bright in color. It if is discolored (brown or black), or smells burnt, serious transmission troubles, possibly due to overheating, should be suspected. The transmission should be inspected to locate the cause of the burnt fluid.**

Adjustments

THROTTLE CABLE

▶ **See Figure 76**

To inspect the throttle cable operation, remove the air cleaner assembly and depress the accelerator cable all the way. Check that the throttle valve opens fully. If the throttle valve does not open fully, adjust the accelerator link as follows:

1. Remove the air cleaner.
2. Fully depress the accelerator cable.
3. Loosen the adjustment nut.
4. Adjust the cable housing so that the distance between the end of boot and the stopper is 0-0.04 in. (0-1mm).
5. Tighten the adjusting nuts.
6. Recheck the adjustment.

SHIFT CABLE

1. Loosen the control cable lever swivel nut.
2. Push the control lever to the right as far as it will go.
3. Bring the lever back two notches to the Neutral position.
4. Place the shift lever in Neutral.
5. Hold the lever, lightly, toward the R range side and tighten the swivel nut.

Neutral Safety Switch

The neutral safety switch in addition to preventing the vehicle from starting with the transaxle in gear also actuates the back-up warning lights.

REMOVAL & INSTALLATION

1. Disconnect the neutral start switch connector.

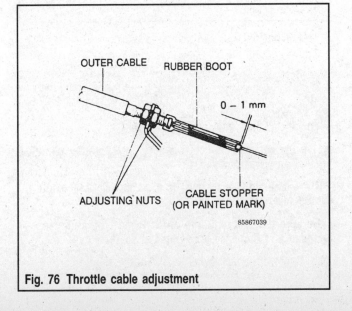

Fig. 76 Throttle cable adjustment

2. With a pair of needlenose pliers, remove the clip that connects the manual control cable to the manual shift lever.
3. Unstake the lock nut and remove the manual shift lever.
4. Remove the neutral start switch with the seal gasket.

To install:

5. Install the neutral start switch making sure that the lip of the seal gasket is facing inward.
6. Install the manual shift lever.
7. Install the locknut and torque to 61 inch lbs. (6.9 Nm). Stake the nut with the locking plate.
8. Engage the switch connector.
9. Adjust the neutral start switch.
10. Connect the transaxle shift cable and install the clip.
11. Adjust the transaxle shift cable.
12. Check the operation of the switch and adjust as necessary.

ADJUSTMENT

▶ **See Figure 77**

If the engine starts with the shift selector in any position except Park or Neutral, adjust the switch as follows:

1. Loosen the two neutral start switch retaining bolts and move the shift selector to the Neutral range.
2. Align the groove and the neutral basic line. Maintain the alignment and torque the bolts to 48 inch lbs. (5.4 Nm).

Transaxle

REMOVAL & INSTALLATION

1. Disconnect the negative battery cable.
2. Remove the air cleaner.
3. Disconnect the neutral start switch.
4. Disconnect the speedometer cable.
5. Remove the shift control cable.
6. Disconnect the oil cooler hose.
7. Remove the water inlet pipe.

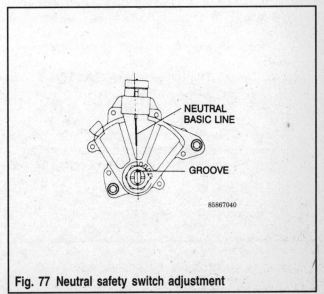

Fig. 77 Neutral safety switch adjustment

8. Raise and support the vehicle on jackstands.
9. Drain the fluid.
10. Remove the engine undercover.
11. Remove the front and rear transaxle mounts.
12. Support the transaxle with a jack.
13. Remove the engine center support member.
14. Remove the halfshafts.
15. Remove the steering knuckles.
16. Remove the starter motor.
17. Remove the flywheel cover plate.
18. Remove the 6 torque converter bolts, through the opening covered by the cover plate.
19. Remove the left engine mount.
20. Remove the transaxle-to-engine bolts, then slowly and carefully back the transaxle away from the engine.
21. Installation is the reverse of removal. Observe the following torques:
   • Transaxle-to-engine bolts: 12mm 47 ft. lbs. (64 Nm): 10mm 25 ft. lbs. (35 Nm)
   • Torque converter bolts: 13 ft. lbs. (20 Nm)

REAR DRIVELINE

Driveshaft and U-Joints

REMOVAL & INSTALLATION

▶ **See Figures 78, 79 and 80**

✳✳CAUTION

Be sure that the car is securely supported. Remember, you will be working underneath it.

1. Raise the rear of the car with jacks and support the rear axle housing with jackstands.

➡**Be sure to matchmark the yoke flange to the mounting flange on the drive pinion.**

2. Unfasten the bolts which attach the driveshaft universal joint yoke flange to the mounting flange on the differential drive pinion.
3. On models equipped with three universal joints, perform the following:
   a. Withdraw the driveshaft subassembly from the U-joint sleeve yoke.
   b. Unfasten the center support bearing from its bracket.
4. Remove the driveshaft end from the transmission.
5. Install an old U-joint yoke in the transmission or, if nothing is available, use a plastic bag secured with a rubber band over the hole to keep the transmission oil from running all over the place.
6. Withdraw the driveshaft from beneath the vehicle.
To install:
7. Installation is performed in the following order. Apply multipurpose grease on the section of the U-joint sleeve which is to be inserted into the transmission.
8. Insert the driveshaft sleeve into the transmission.

➡**Be careful not to damage any of the seals.**

22. Fill the unit with Dexron II ATF.

Halfshafts

REMOVAL & INSTALLATION

Refer to Manual Transaxle Halfshaft Removal and Installation in this section for the necessary service procedures.

OVERHAUL

Refer to Manual Transaxle Halfshaft Overhaul in this section for the necessary service procedures.

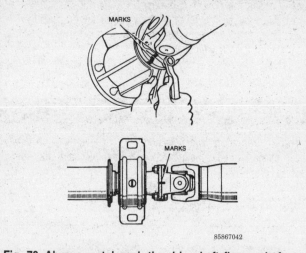

Fig. 78 Always matchmark the driveshaft flanges before separating them

9. For models equipped with three U-joints and center bearings, perform the following:
   a. Adjust the center bearing clearance with no load placed on the driveline components; the top of the rubber center cushion should be 0.04 in. (1mm) behind the center of the elongated bolt hole.
   b. Install the center bearing assembly.

➡**Use the same number of washers on the center bearing bracket as were removed.**

10. Secure the U-joint flange to the differential flange with the mounting bolts.

➡**Be sure that the bolts are of the same type as those removed and that they are tightened securely.**

11. Remove the jackstands and lower the vehicle.

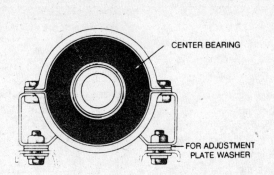

Fig. 79 Center bearing adjustment — most models similar

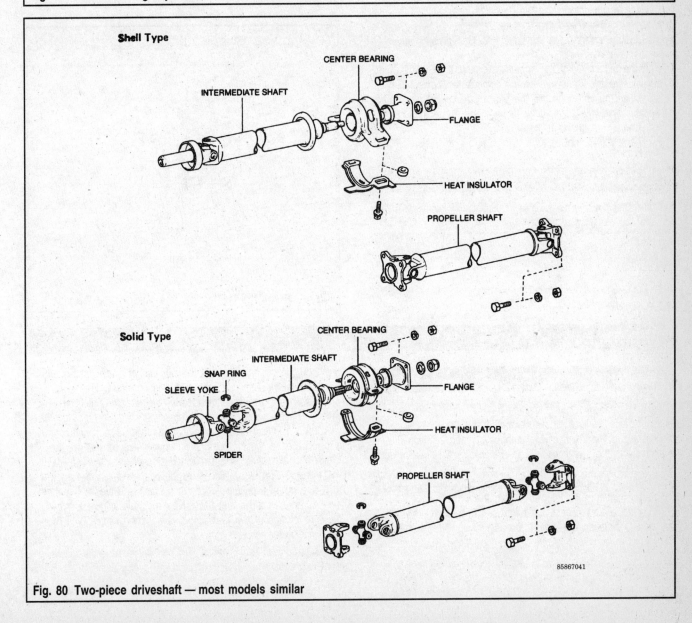

Fig. 80 Two-piece driveshaft — most models similar

U-JOINT OVERHAUL

▶ See Figures 81 and 82

➡The U-joints on some late model vehicles are non-serviceable, the entire driveshaft must be replaced in the event of U-joint problems.

1. Matchmark the yoke and the driveshaft.
2. Remove the lockrings from the bearings.
3. Position the yoke on vise jaws. Using a bearing remover and a hammer, gently tap the remover until the bearing is driven out of the yoke about ½ in. (13mm).
4. Place the tool in the vise and drive the yoke away from the tool until the bearing is removed.
5. Repeat Steps 3 and 4 for the other bearings.
6. Check for worn or damaged parts. Inspect the bearing journal surfaces for wear.

To assemble:

7. Install the bearing cups, seals, and O-rings in the spider.
8. Grease the spider and the bearings.
9. Position the spider in the yoke.
10. Start the bearings in the yoke and then press them into place, using a vise.
11. If the axial play of the spider is greater than 0.002 in. (0.05mm) select lockrings which will provide the correct play. Be sure that the lockrings are the same size on both sides or driveshaft noise will result. If the U-joint is in doubt replace the joint or entire driveshaft, as necessary.
12. Check the U-joint assembly for smooth operation.

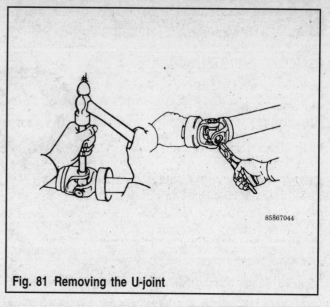

Fig. 81 Removing the U-joint

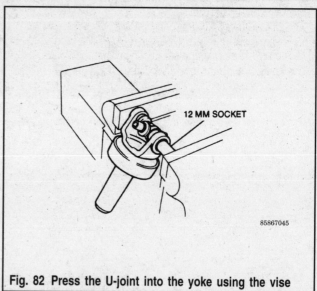

12 MM SOCKET

Fig. 82 Press the U-joint into the yoke using the vise

REAR AXLE

Axle Ratio

The drive axle of a car is said to have a certain axle ratio. This number (usually a whole number and a decimal fraction) is actually a comparison of the number of gear teeth on the ring gear and the pinion gear. For example, a 4.11 rear means that theoretically, there are 4.11 teeth on the ring gear for each tooth on the pinion gear or, put another way, the driveshaft must turn 4.11 times to turn the wheels once. For example, on a 4.11 rear, there might be 37 teeth on the ring gear and 9 teeth on the pinion gear. By dividing the number of

teeth on the pinion gear into the number of teeth on the ring gear, the numerical axle ratio (4.11) is obtained. This also provides a good method of ascertaining exactly which axle ratio your vehicle is equipped with.

Another method of determining gear ratio is to jack up and support the car so that both rear wheels are off the ground. Make a chalk mark on the rear wheel and the driveshaft. Put the transmission in neutral. Turn the rear wheel one complete turn and count the number of turns that the driveshaft makes. The number of turns that the driveshaft makes in one complete revolution of the rear wheel is an approximation of the rear axle ratio.

Rear Axle Shaft

REMOVAL & INSTALLATION

Rear Wheel Drive

▶ **See Figures 83 and 84**

1. Raise the rear of the car and support it securely by using jackstands.

❋❋CAUTION

Be sure that the vehicle is securely supported. Remember, you will be working underneath it.

2. Drain the oil from the axle housing.
3. Remove the wheel cover, unfasten the lug nuts, and remove the wheel.
4. Punch matchmarks on the brake drum and the axle shaft to maintain rotational balance.
5. Remove the brake drum and related components.
6. Remove the rear bearing retaining nut, if so equipped.
7. Remove the backing plate attachment nuts through the access holes in the rear axle shaft flange.
8. Use a slide hammer with a suitable adaptor to withdraw the axle shaft from its housing.

➡**Use care not to damage the oil seal when removing the axle shaft.**

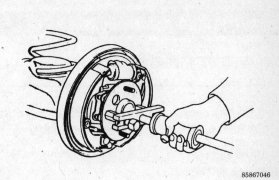

85867046

Fig. 83 Using a slide hammer to remove the axleshaft

9. Repeat the procedure for the axle shaft on the opposite side. Be careful not to mix the components of the two sides.
10. Installation is performed in the reverse order of removal. Coat the lips of the rear housing oil seal with multipurpose grease prior to installation of the rear axle shaft. Torque the bearing retaining nut, if so equipped to (1970-74 models) 15-22 ft. lbs. (20-30 Nm) (1600 models) 26-38 ft. lbs. (35-51 Nm) and (1800 models) 44-53 ft. lbs. (60-72 Nm).

Front Wheel Drive

Refer to Section 8 for repair procedures.

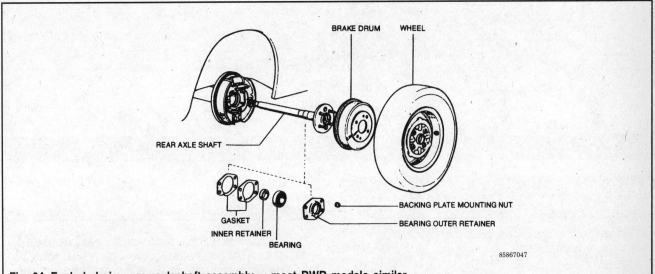

Fig. 84 Exploded view rear axleshaft assembly — most RWD models similar

FRONT AXLE

Front Axle Hub and Bearing

REMOVAL & INSTALLATION

Rear Wheel Drive

Refer to Section 8 for service and repair procedures.

Front Wheel Drive
▶ See Figure 85

1. Remove the cotter pin from the bearing locknut cap and then remove the cap. Have an assistant step on the brake pedal and then loosen the locknut.

2. Raise the front of the vehicle and support it with jackstands. Remove the wheel.

3. Remove the brake caliper mounting nuts and then position the caliper out of the way. Pull off the brake disc.

4. Remove the cotter pin and nut from the tie rod end, then using a tie rod end separator tool, remove the tie rod.

5. Place matchmarks on the shock absorber lower mounting bracket and the camber adjustment cam, then remove the bolts and separate the steering knuckle from the shock.

6. Remove the two ball joint attaching nuts and disconnect the lower arm from the knuckle.

7. Carefully grasp the axle hub and pull it out from the halfshaft.

➡**Be sure to cover the halfshaft boot with a cloth to protect it from any damage.**

8. Clamp the steering knuckle in a vise.
To install:

9. Remove the dust deflector. Remove the nut holding the steering knuckle to the ball joint. Press the ball joint from the steering knuckle.

10. Remove the deflector from the hub. Use a slide hammer to remove the inner oil seal. Remove the snapring retainer with the correct tool.

11. Remove the disc brake dust shield. Use a two armed puller and remove the axle hub from the steering knuckle.

12. Remove the inner bearing races (inside and outside). Remove the oil seal from the knuckle.

13. Position the old bearing inner race (outside) on the bearing. Use a hammer and drift to carefully knock out the bearing.

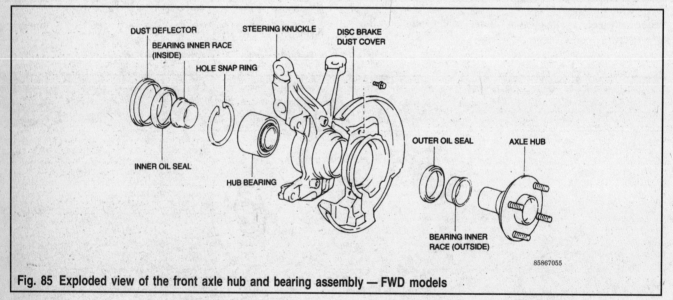

Fig. 85 Exploded view of the front axle hub and bearing assembly — FWD models

14. Press a new bearing into the steering knuckle.

15. Use a seal driver and install a new oil seal into the knuckle.

16. Install the brake dust cover. Apply grease to the oil seal lip and the bearing inner race. Press the hub into the knuckle.

17. Install a new snapring. Press a new seal into position. Install the remaining components and the steering knuckle in the reverse order of removal. Please note the following:

   a. Tighten the ball joint nut to 14 ft. lbs. (19 Nm) then replace the nut with a new one, and tighten to 82 ft. lbs. (111 Nm).

   b. Tighten the steering knuckle-to-shock absorber bolts to 105 ft. lbs. (142 Nm) except for diesel models on which the bolts should be tightened to 152 ft. lbs. (206 Nm).

   c. Make sure the vehicle is on the ground with brakes applied before attempting to tighten the locknut. Tighten the bearing locknut to 137 ft. lbs. (186 Nm) and always use a new cotter pin.

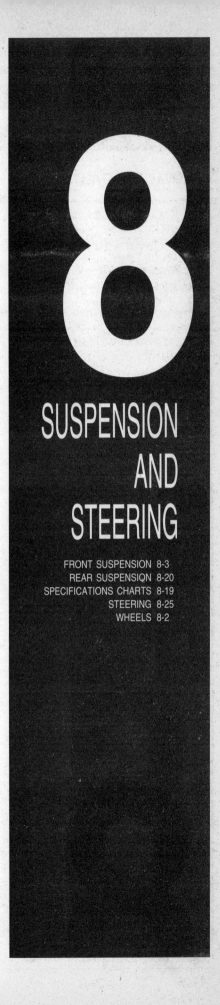

8

SUSPENSION
AND
STEERING

WHEELS

Wheels

REMOVAL & INSTALLATION

▶ **See Figures 1 and 2**

1. If using a lug wrench or breaker bar, loosen the lug nuts before raising the vehicle.
2. Raise the vehicle and support it safely.
3. Remove the lug nuts and wheel from the vehicle.

To install:

4. Install the wheel and hand tighten the lug nuts until they are snug.
5. Lower the vehicle and torque the lug nuts EVENLY in a crisscross pattern.

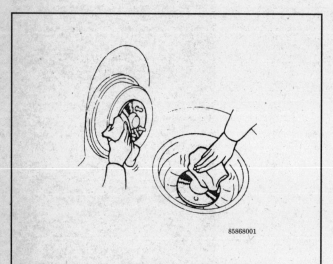

Fig. 1 Wheels should be cleaned and inspected whenever they are removed

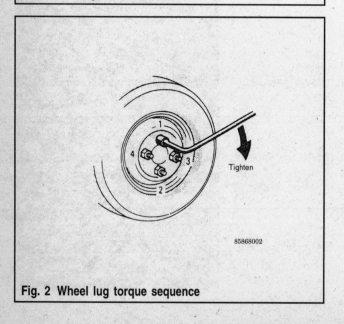

85868002

Fig. 2 Wheel lug torque sequence

INSPECTION

Before installing on wheels, check for any cracks or enlarged mounting holes. Remove any corrosion on the mounting surfaces with a wire brush. Installation of wheels without a good metal-to-metal contact at the mounting surface can cause wheel nuts to loosen. Recheck the wheel nuts after 1,000 (1600 Km) miles of driving.

Wheel Lug Studs

REPLACEMENT

Front Wheel

▶ **See Figure 3**

1. Raise and support the vehicle safely. Remove the front wheel.
2. Remove the front brake caliper and disc rotor.
3. Drive out the hub bolt with suitable punch.

To install:

4. Install the new hub bolt and draw into place using the nut and a stack of washers. The new hub bolt must be fully seated in the hub assembly.
5. Install front brake disc and front brake caliper.
6. Install front wheel and lower the vehicle.

Rear Wheel

DRUM BRAKES

1. Raise the vehicle and support safely.
2. Remove the wheel.
3. Remove the brake drum from the vehicle.
4. Drive the lug bolt out of the axle hub, with a suitable punch.

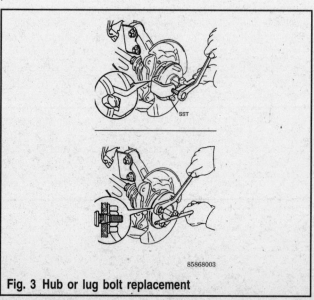

85868003

Fig. 3 Hub or lug bolt replacement

To install:

5. Draw the lug bolt into the axle hub using the nut and a stack of washers.

6. Install the brake drum onto the vehicle.

7. Install the wheel and lower the vehicle.

DISC BRAKES

1. Raise the vehicle and support safely.

2. Remove the rear wheel.

3. Remove the rear caliper and brake rotor.

4. Remove the wheel lug bolt by tapping the bolt through the hub with a hammer.

To install:

5. Draw the new lug bolt into the hub using the nut and a stack of washers.

6. Install the brake rotor. Install rear brake caliper.

7. Install the rear wheel and lower the vehicle.

FRONT SUSPENSION

▶ **See Figures 4 and 5**

The front suspension system is of the MacPherson strut design. The struts used on either side are a combination spring and shock absorber with the outer casing of the shock actually supporting the spring at the bottom and thus forming a major structural component of the suspension.

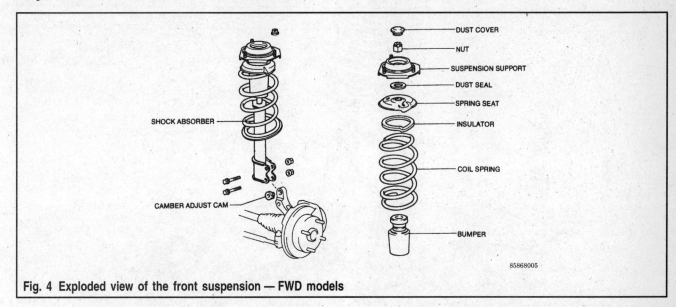

Fig. 4 Exploded view of the front suspension — FWD models

The wheel hub/steering knuckle is attached to the bottom of the strut. A strut mounting bearing at the top and a ball joint at the bottom allow the entire strut to rotate in cornering maneuvers. The strut assembly, steering arm and the steering knuckle are all combined in one assembly; there is no upper control arm. A rubber bushed transverse link (control arm) connects the lower portion of the strut to the front crossmember via the ball joint; the link thus allows for vertical movement.

❋❋CAUTION

Exercise great caution when working with the front suspension. Strut coil springs and other suspension components are under extreme tension and result in severe injury if released improperly. Never remove the nut on the top of the shock absorber piston without using the proper spring compressor tool.

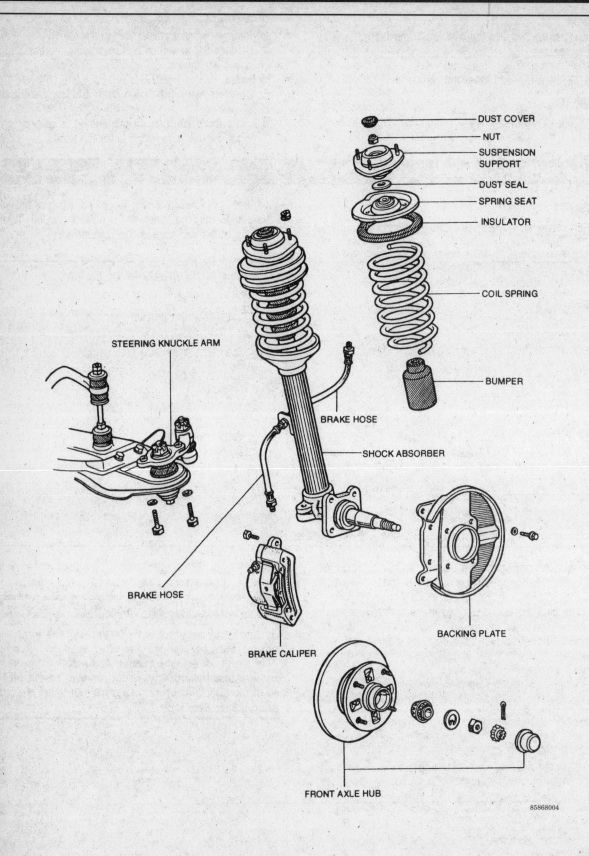

DUST COVER
NUT
SUSPENSION SUPPORT
DUST SEAL
SPRING SEAT
INSULATOR
COIL SPRING
BUMPER
STEERING KNUCKLE ARM
BRAKE HOSE
SHOCK ABSORBER
BRAKE HOSE
BACKING PLATE
BRAKE CALIPER
FRONT AXLE HUB
85868004

Fig. 5 Exploded view of the front suspension — RWD models

MacPherson Struts

The struts are dangerous parts and retain the springs under tremendous pressure even when removed from the car. For this reason, several expensive tools and substantial specialized knowledge are required to safely and effectively work on these components. If spring and shock absorber work is required, it may not be a bad ideal to remove the strut involved yourself and then consider taking it to a repair facility which is fully equipped and familiar with the car.

TESTING

➡On MacPherson strut shock absorbers, if oil is leaking from the cylinder portion of the assembly the shock absorber must be replaced.

The function of the MacPherson strut shock absorber is to dampen harsh spring movement and provide a means of dissipating the motion of the wheels so that the shocks encountered by the wheels are not totally transmitted to the body of the car and, therefore, to you and your passengers. As the wheel moves up and down, the shock absorber retracts and extends, thereby imposing a restraint on excessive movement by its hydraulic action.

A good way to see if your shock absorbers are working properly is to push on one corner of the car until it is moving up and down for almost the full suspension travel, then release it and watch its recovery. If the car bounces slightly about one more time and then comes to a rest, you can be fairly certain that the shock is all right. If the car continues to bounce excessively, the shocks will probably require replacement.

REMOVAL & INSTALLATION

▶ See Figures 6, 7, 8, 9, 10, 11, 12, 13 and 14

➡We recommend replacement of the struts in sets for added safety and reliability

1. Remove the hubcap and loosen the lug nuts.
2. Raise the front of the car and support it on the chassis jacking plates provided with jackstands.

❄❄CAUTION

Do not support the weight of the car on the suspension arm; the arm may deform under its weight.

3. Unfasten the lug nuts and remove the wheel.
4. Detach the front brake line from its clamp.
5. Remove the caliper and wire it out of the way.
6. Unfasten the three nuts which secure the upper shock absorber mounting plate to the top of the wheel arch.
7. Remove the two bolts which attach the shock absorber lower end to the steering knuckle lower arm.

➡Press down on the suspension lower arm, in order to remove the strut assembly. This must be done to clear the collars on the steering knuckle arm bolt holes when re-

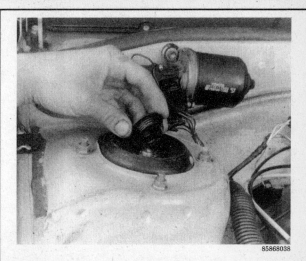

Fig. 6 Remove the dust cover on MacPherson strut assembly

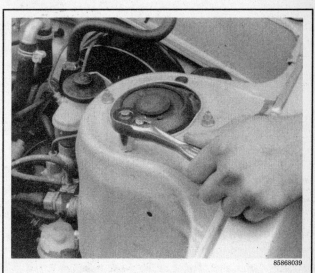

Fig. 7 Remove the suspension support retaining nut

Fig. 8 Cleaning the brake fitting before removal

Fig. 9 Using a back-up wrench, remove the brake line from the brake hose

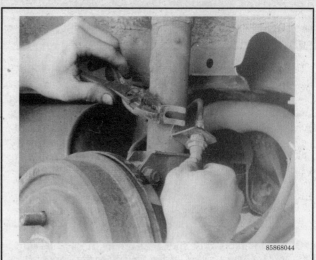

Fig. 11 After retaining clip is removed, unthread the fitting and remove the line

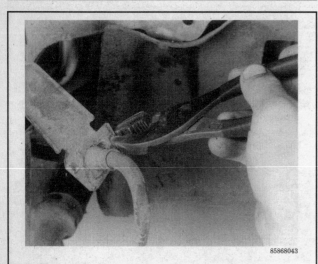

Fig. 10 Using pliers, remove the brake hose/line retaining bracket clip

Fig. 12 Mark the lower MacPherson strut mounting to maintain alignment during installation

moving the shock/spring assembly. The steering knuckle bolt holes have collars that extend about 0.20 inch. (5mm) Be careful to clear them when separating the steering knuckle from the strut assembly.

To install:

8. Align the hole in the upper suspension support with the shock absorber piston rod end, so that they fit properly.

9. Always use a new nut and nylon washer on the shock absorber piston rod end when securing it to the upper suspension support. Torque the nut to 29-40 ft. lbs. (39-54 Nm).

➡**Do not use an impact wrench to tighten the nut.**

10. Coat the suspension support bearing with multipurpose grease prior to installation. Also after installation, pack the space in the upper support with multipurpose grease.

11. Tighten the suspension support-to-wheel arch bolts to the following specification:
- RWD: 11-16 ft. lbs. (15-22 Nm)
- FWD: 23 ft. lbs. (31 Nm)

12. Tighten the shock absorber-to-steering knuckle arm bolts to the following specifications:
- RWD: 50-65 ft. lbs. (68-88 Nm)
- FWD gas: 105 ft. lbs. (142 Nm)
- FWD diesel: 152 ft. lbs. (206 Nm)

13. Adjust the front wheel bearing preload — refer to procedures in this section.

14. Bleed the brake system.

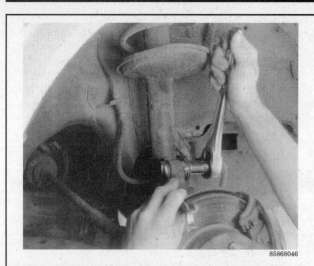

Fig. 13 Using a socket wrench and back-up wrench remove the lower MacPherson strut mounting

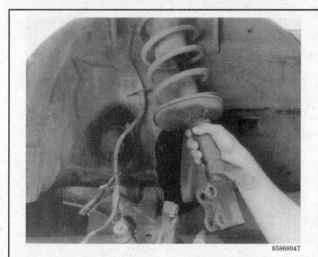

Fig. 14 After removing the lower mounting bolts remove the MacPherson strut assembly from the vehicle

OVERHAUL

Coil Springs

▶ See Figures 15, 16, 17 and 18

✳✳CAUTION

The coil springs are retained under considerable pressure. They can exert enough force to cause serious injury. Exercise extreme caution when disassembling the strut for coil spring removal. This procedure requires the use of a spring compressor. It cannot be performed without one. If you do not have access to this special tool, do not attempt to disassemble the strut.

➡We recommend replacement of the coil springs in sets for added safety and reliability

1. Remove the strut assembly.

2. Fabricate a strut assembly mounting stand. Bolt the assembly to the stand and then mount the stand in a vise.

➡Do not attempt to clamp the strut assembly in a vise without the mounting stand as this will result in damage to the strut tube.

3. Attach a spring compressor tool and compress the spring until the upper spring retainer is free of tension.

4. Use a spring seat holder to secure the support and then remove the nut on the strut bearing plate.

5. Remove the bearing plate, the support, the upper spring retainer, then slowly and cautiously unscrew the spring compressor until all spring tension is relieved. Remove the spring and the dust cover.

➡Do not allow the piston rod to retract into the shock absorber. If it falls, screw a nut onto the rod and pull the rod out by the nut. Do not use pliers or the like to grip the rod as they will damage its surface, resulting in leaks, uneven operation or seal damage. Be extremely careful not to stress or contact the rod.

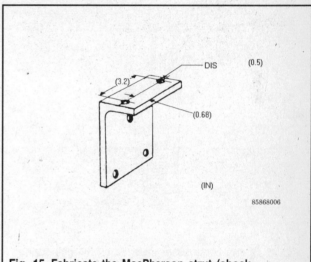

Fig. 15 Fabricate the MacPherson strut (shock absorber) stand and mount it in a vise

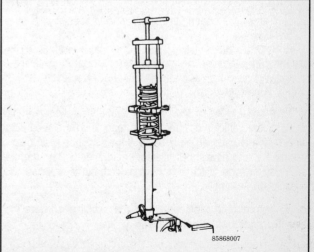

Fig. 16 Spring compressor installed on the coil spring for removal

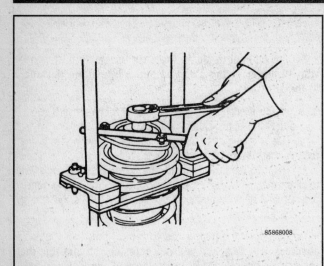

Fig. 17 Hold the upper mount with a rod while loosening the piston rod nut

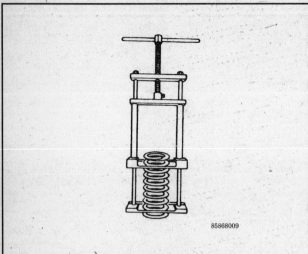

Fig. 18 Spring compressor installed on the coil spring for installation — leave the upper coils free

6. Installation is in the reverse order of removal. Please note the following:
- Pack the bearing in the suspension support with multipurpose grease
- Use a new retaining nut and tighten it to 29-39 ft. lbs. (39-53 Nm)

Shock Absorbers

There are 2 types of MacPherson strut shock absorbers used for the vehicles covered in this manual. The non-cartridge type, which is used on early model vehicles, They must be overhauled and new shock absorber fluid added. Then there is the cartridge type which is not overhauled, but is replaced as a complete assembly.

➡**We recommend replacement of the shock absorbers in sets for added safety and reliability**

NON-CARTRIDGE TYPE (OVERHAUL TYPE)

◗ **See Figures 19, 20, 21, 22, 23, 24, 25, 26, 27 and 28**

➡Disassemble the shock absorber in a clean place. Do not allow dust or dirt to get on the disassembled parts. The piston rod is high precision finished, even a slight scratch can cause fluid leakage so be careful when handling the piston rod.

1. Remove the strut assembly.
2. Remove the coil spring.

❋❋CAUTION

Do not attempt spring removal without the proper tools. Thoroughly read the spring procedure before proceeding.

3. Remove the wheel hub and the brake disc.
4. Attach the assembly to the mounting plate and clamp it in a vise.
5. Use a ring nut wrench and remove the ring nut at the top of the strut tube.
6. Use a needle and pick the gasket out of the strut tube.
7. Remove the guide, the rebound stopper and the piston rod.
8. Pull the cylinder out of the strut tube, then use a long blunt instrument to drive the base valve out of the bottom of the cylinder.
9. Empty all oil out of the tube.

➡Rebuilding kits are available through your local Toyota dealer.

To install:
10. Press the base valve into the bottom of the cylinder.
11. Slide the cylinder into the strut tube.
12. Slide the piston rod and the rebound stopper into the cylinder.
13. Fill the cylinder with NEW shock absorber fluid (about 315cc).
14. Press the rod guide and its gasket into the top of the strut tube.
15. Tape the end of the piston rod to avoid damaging the oil seal inside the ring nut.
16. Coat the oil seal with multipurpose grease and then install the ring nut on the piston rod.
17. Using a ring nut wrench, tighten the ring nut until the top of the piston rod is 3.15-3.54 (80-90mm) inch above the top of the strut tube. Torque the nut to 73-108 ft. lbs. (99-146 Nm).
18. Installation of the remaining components is in the reverse order of removal.

CARTRIDGE TYPE (SEALED UNIT)

◗ **See Figures 29 and 30**

1. Remove the strut from the vehicle.
2. Position a bolt and two nuts between the bracket at the lower portion of the shock absorber shell and clamp shock absorber in a vise. The bolt acts as a spacer to allow for clamping without crushing the bracket.

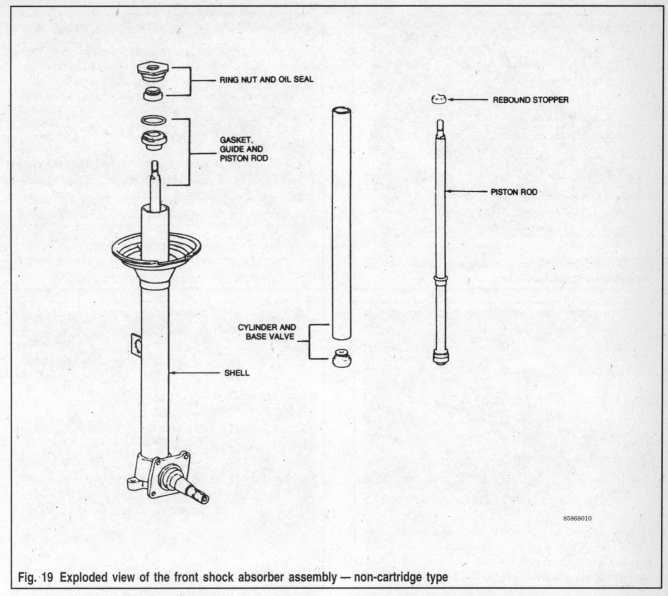

Fig. 19 Exploded view of the front shock absorber assembly — non-cartridge type

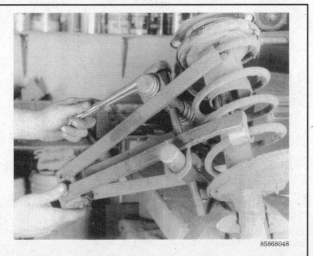

Fig. 20 Install the compressor tool squarely on the strut assembly in order to compress the spring

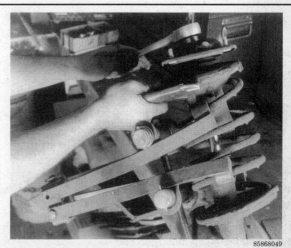

Fig. 21 While using vise-grips to hold the plate, use a socket wrench to loosen the support nut

Fig. 22 After removing the retaining nut, remove the suspension support assembly

Fig. 25 Remove the bumper on the strut assembly

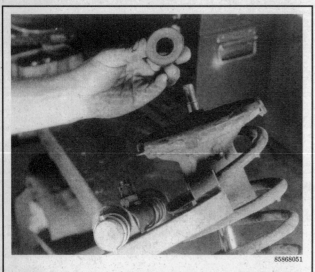

Fig. 23 Remove the dust seal on the strut assembly

Fig. 26 Remove the lower spring seat

Fig. 24 Remove the spring seat on the strut assembly

Fig. 27 Check the threads on the retaining nut for damage before installing the piston rod in the strut

Fig. 28 Check the O-ring for proper installation before installing the piston rod assembly

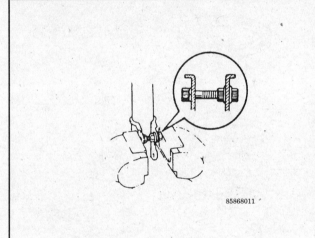

Fig. 29 Install a bolt in the lower bracket to secure shock absorber in a vise

3. Using suitable spring compressor such as SST No. 09727-22032 or equivalent, compress the coil spring.

✳✳CAUTION

Failure to fully compress the spring and hold it securely is extremely hazardous.

4. Using SST No. 09727-22032 or suitable clamping device, hold the spring seat so that it will not turn and remove the center nut. Discard the nut.

5. Slowly release the coil spring tension.

6. Remove the suspension support, dust seal, spring seat, spring insulators, coil spring and bumper.

7. While pushing on the piston rod, make sure that the pull stroke is even and that there is no unusual noise or resistance.

8. Push the piston rod in and then release it. Make sure that the return rate is constant.

9. If the shock absorber does not operate as described, replace it.

➡ If a shock absorber is replaced, the old one should be drilled at the center to vent the internal gas. Wear safety goggles and drill a small hole 0.08-0.12 inch (2-3mm) into the base of the shock absorber (not through bracket). The gas within the strut is colorless, odorless and non-toxic, but should be vented to make the unit safe for disposal.

To install:

10. Install the lower insulator.

11. Install the spring bumper onto the piston rod.

12. Compress the coil spring with the spring compressor tool.

13. Align the coil spring end with the lower seat hollow and install.

14. Install the upper insulator.

15. Face the OUT mark of the spring seat toward the outside of the vehicle.

16. Install the dust seal onto the spring seat.

17. Install the suspension support.

18. Install a new suspension support nut and torque to 34 ft. lbs. (47 Nm).

19. Release the spring compressor.

20. Pack multi-purpose grease into the suspension support and install the dust cover.

Upper Ball Joint

Vehicles covered by this repair manual do not utilize an upper ball joint as part of the front suspension assembly. For more details please refer to the overview of the front suspension earlier in this section.

Lower Ball Joint

INSPECTION

▶ See Figure 31

1. Straighten the front wheels and jack up the front of the vehicle.

2. Place an 7.09-7.87 in. (180-200mm) wooden block under one front tire.

3. Slowly lower the jack until there is about half a load on the front coil spring.

4. Position jackstands near jack for safety.

5. Make sure that the front wheels are still straight and block them.

6. Move the lower suspension arm up and down and check the vertical play in the joint.

7. Repeat the procedure for the other side.

➡ The maximum ball joint vertical play on Corolla RWD models is 0.098 in. (2.5mm). The maximum ball joint vertical play on FWD models is 0.0 in. (0.0mm).

➡ If the ball joint is checked while disconnected from the steering knuckle, it should have minimal or no free-play and should not twist in its socket under finger pressure.

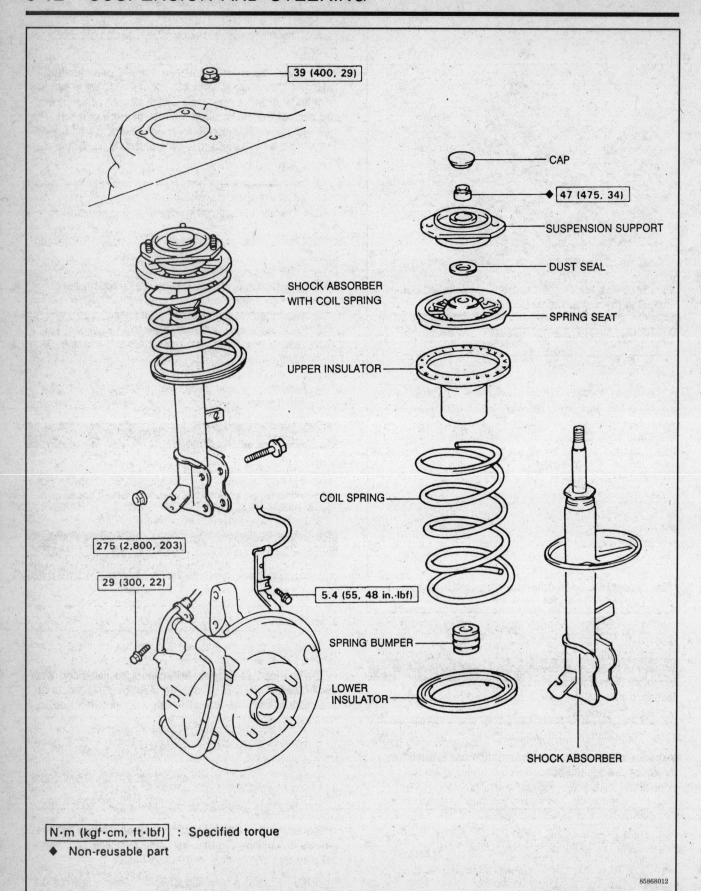

39 (400, 29)

CAP

◆ 47 (475, 34)

SUSPENSION SUPPORT

DUST SEAL

SPRING SEAT

SHOCK ABSORBER
WITH COIL SPRING

UPPER INSULATOR

COIL SPRING

275 (2,800, 203)

29 (300, 22)

5.4 (55, 48 in.·lbf)

SPRING BUMPER

LOWER
INSULATOR

SHOCK ABSORBER

N·m (kgf·cm, ft·lbf) : Specified torque
◆ Non-reusable part

85868012

Fig. 30 Exploded view of the front MacPherson strut/shock absorber assembly — cartridge type

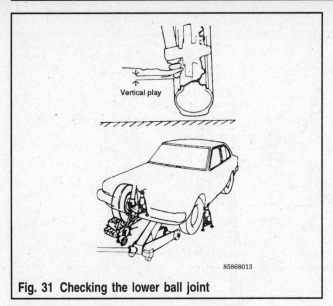

Fig. 31 Checking the lower ball joint

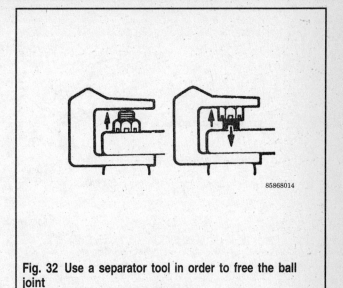

Fig. 32 Use a separator tool in order to free the ball joint

REMOVAL & INSTALLATION

▶ See Figures 32, 33 and 34

➡The use of the correct tools is REQUIRED for this procedure. A ball joint separator is a commonly available tool which prevents damage to the joint and knuckle. Do not attempt to separate the joint with hammers, prybars or similar tools.

RWD Models

To replace the lower ball joint on these models the lower control (suspension arm) assembly must be removed and the unit replaced as an assembly. Refer to the Lower Control Arm removal and installation service procedures.

FWD Models

▶ See Figures 35, 36 and 37

➡This service procedure is for removing the lower ball joint assembly with the lower control arm attached to the vehicle. IF NECESSARY you may remove the Lower Control arm assembly, then remove the lower ball joint from the lower control arm. Refer to the Lower Control Arm Assembly Removal and Installation outlined in this section.

1. Raise and safely support the front of the vehicle. Do not place the stands under the control arms; they must hang free.

➡Do not allow the driveshaft joints to over-extend. The CV-joints can become disconnected under extreme extension.

2. Install a protective cover over the CV-boot.
3. Remove the wheel.
4. Remove the cotter pin from the ball joint nut.
5. Loosen the castle nut but do not remove it. Unscrew it just to the top of the threads and install the ball joint separator. Use the nut to bear on the tool; this protects the threaded shaft from damage during removal.
6. Use the separator to loosen the ball joint from the steering knuckle.

7. Remove the nuts and bolt holding the ball joint to the control arm.
8. Remove the ball joint from the control arm and steering knuckle.

To install:

9. When reinstalling, attach the ball joint to the control arm and tighten the bolts/nuts evenly.
10. Carefully install the ball joint to the steering knuckle. Use a NEW CASTLE NUT and tighten it to 72-76 ft. lbs. (97-103 Nm)
11. Install a NEW COTTER PIN through the castle nut and stud.
12. Remove the protector from the CV-boot.
13. Install the wheel.
14. Lower the vehicle to the ground. Check wheel Alignment.

Lower Control Arm

REMOVAL & INSTALLATION

RWD Models

➡The ball joint and control arm cannot be separated from each other. If one fails, then both must be replaced as an assembly

1. Remove the front MacPherson strut assembly.
2. Remove the stabilizer bar securing bolts.
3. Unfasten the torque strut mounting bolts.
4. Remove the control arm mounting bolt and detach the arm from the front suspension member.
5. Remove the steering knuckle arm from the control arm with a ball joint puller.
6. Inspect the suspension components which were removed for wear or damage. Replace any parts, as required.

To install:

7. Install the control arm on the suspension member, tighten the bolts partially at first.
8. Complete the assembly procedure and lower the car to the ground.

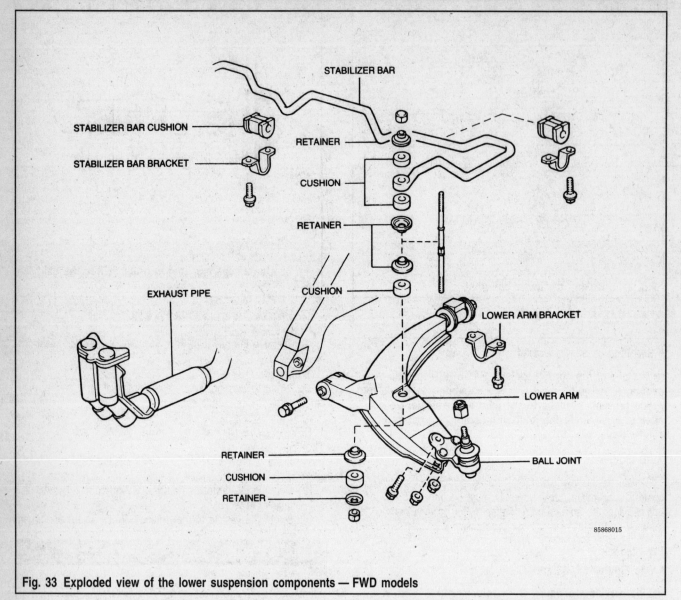

Fig. 33 Exploded view of the lower suspension components — FWD models

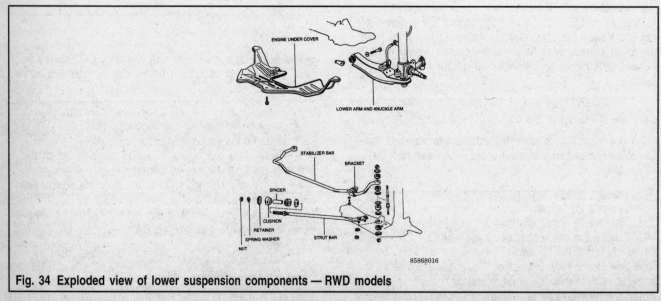

Fig. 34 Exploded view of lower suspension components — RWD models

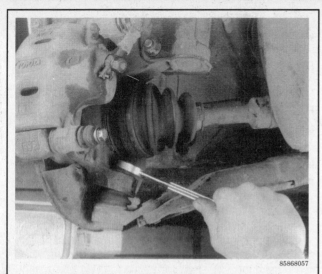

Fig. 35 Removing the lower ball joint retaining nut

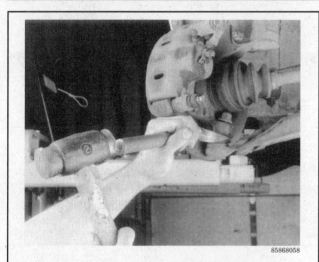

Fig. 36 Using a ball joint removal tool and brass hammer to separate the lower ball joint

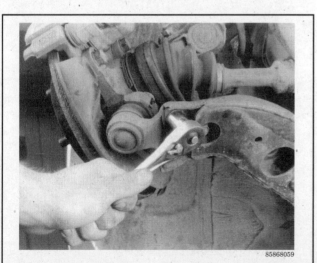

Fig. 37 Removing the lower ball joint-to-lower arm retaining bolts

9. Bounce the front of the car several times. Allow the suspension to settle, then tighten the lower control arm bolts to 51-65 ft. lbs. (69-88 Nm) Tighten knuckle arm bolts to 42-56 ft. lbs. (57-76 Nm), the tie rod end-to-knuckle bolt to 37-50 ft. lbs. (50-68 Nm) and the stabilizer bar nut to 66-90 ft. lbs. (89-122 Nm).

➡️**Use only the bolt which was designed to fit the lower control arm. If a replacement is necessary, see an authorized dealer for the proper part. Use new cotter pins upon installation.**

10. Remember to lubricate the ball joint. Check front end alignment.

FWD Models

➡️**Refer to exploded view of front suspension components as necessary.**

1. Raise and safely support the vehicle. Do not place the stands under the control arms.
2. Remove the nuts and bolts holding lower ball joint-to-lower arm.
3. Remove the nut holding the sway bar link to the control arm, then disconnect the link and bar from the control arm as necessary.
4. Remove the nuts and bolts holding the control arm to the body.
5. Remove the control arm from the car and check it carefully for cracks, bends or crimps in the metal or for corrosion damage. Check the rubber bushing and replace it if any sign of damage or deformation is found.
   To install:
6. Install (replace it if necessary) the bushing and tighten its retaining nut to 76 ft. lbs. (103 Nm).

➡️**Never reuse a self-locking nut and always replace cotter pins. Rock the vehicle up and down to settle the suspension before final torque.**

7. Position the control arm to the body, then install the nuts and bolts. The front nut and bolt should be tightened to 105 ft. lbs. (142 Nm) and the rear to 72 ft. lbs. (97 Nm).
8. Connect the lower arm to the ball joint (steering knuckle). Torque retaining bolts to 47-59 ft. lbs. (64-80 Nm)
9. Reinstall the sway bar and link. Check front wheel alignment.

Stabilizer Bar, Sway Bar and Bushings

REMOVAL & INSTALLATION

▶ **See Figures 38 and 39**

1. Disconnect the sway bar links from the lower control arms. Disconnect stabilizer link from stabilizer bar.
2. Disconnect the sway bar brackets from the body.

➡️**Check the bushings inside the brackets for wear or deformation. A worn bushing can cause a distinct noise as the bar twists during cornering operation.**

3. Disconnect the exhaust system, if necessary.

4. Remove the sway bar from the car. Examine the insulators (bushings) carefully for any sign of wear and replace them if necessary.

To install:

5. Place the bar in position and reconnect the exhaust system using new nuts, if remove to gain clearance to remove the assembly.

6. Install both stabilizer bar brackets and tighten the bolts to 14 ft. lbs. (19 Nm).

7. Connect the sway bar links to the control arms with the bolts, insulators (in the correct order) and new nuts. Tighten the nuts to 13 ft. lbs. (18 Nm). Reconnect stabilizer link (inspect link for wear) to stabilizer bar, torque to 47 ft. lbs. (64 Nm).

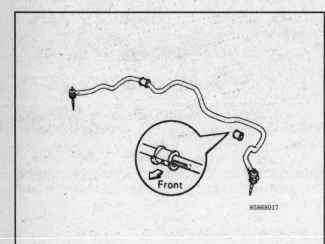

85868017

Fig. 38 The stabilizer bar cushion must be properly positioned during installation

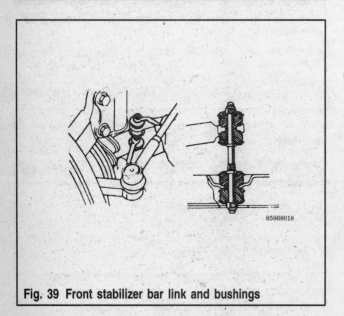

85868018

Fig. 39 Front stabilizer bar link and bushings

Strut Bar

REMOVAL & INSTALLATION

RWD Models

▶ **See Figure 40**

1. Remove the nut, washer, retainer, spacer and cushion from the strut bar where it attaches to the chassis. Do not remove the staked nut.

2. Raise the lower control arm with a floor jack, then disconnect the strut bar assembly.

To install:

3. Check the distance between the staked nut and the center of the bolt hole on the bar. The specification is 14.642 in. (372mm) for RWD. Adjust the staked nut as necessary. Never adjust the staked nut unless required.

4. Raise the lower arm and connect the strut bar.

5. Reconnect the bar and all the hardware to the chassis bracket. Check front end alignment.

Axle Hub, Bearing And Seal

REMOVAL & INSTALLATION

Rear Wheel Drive

▶ **See Figures 41, 42 and 43**

➡ The front wheel bearings on rear wheel drive vehicles are the only wheel bearings which require periodic attention. These wheel bearings are an important maintenance item — refer to Section 1 for correct maintenance intervals.

1. Raise the front of the vehicle and support it with jackstands. Remove the wheel.

2. Remove the front disc brake caliper mounting and position it safely out of the way. Do not let it hang by the brake hose.

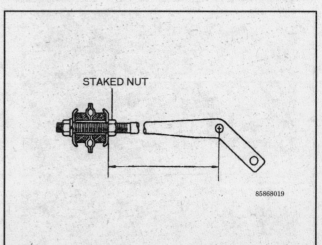

STAKED NUT

85868019

Fig. 40 When installing the strut bar, the distance between the staked nut and the center of the bolt hole must be measured

3. Pry off the bearing cap and then remove the cotter pin, lock cap and the adjusting nut.

4. Remove the axle hub and disc together with the outer bearing and thrust washer.

➡**Be careful not to drop the outer bearing during removal.**

5. Using a small prybar, pry out the oil seal from the back of the hub, then remove the inner bearing.

6. Installation is in the reverse order of removal. Please note the following:

a. Place some axle grease into the palm of your hand and then take the bearing and work the grease into it until it begins to ooze out the other side. Coat the inside of the axle hub and bearing cap with the same grease.

b. Install the bearing adjusting nut and tighten it to 22 ft. lbs. (30 Nm). Snug down the bearing by turning the hub several times. Loosen the nut until it can be turned by hand and then, using spring scale, retighten it until the preload measures 0.8-1.9 lbs.

c. Use a new cotter pin when installing the lock cap.

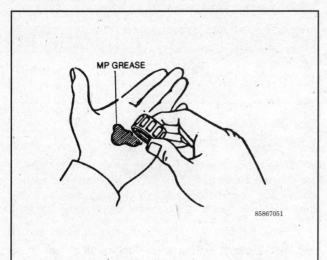

Fig. 42 Pack the wheel bearings with grease — RWD models

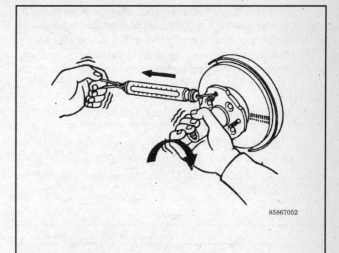

Fig. 43 Use a spring scale to measure the wheel bearing preload — RWD models

Front Wheel Drive

On front wheel drive models, the front axle shafts are part of the drive train. Information on axle shaft and bearing removal or installation can be found in Section 7 of this manual.

Front End Alignment

▶ **See Figures 44, 45 and 46**

Alignment of the front wheels is essential if your car is to go, stop and turn as designed. Alignment can be altered by collision, overloading, poor repair or bent components.

If you are diagnosing bizarre handling and/or poor road manners, the first place to look is the tires. Although the tires may wear as a result of an alignment problem, worn or poorly inflated tires might make you chase alignment problems which don't exist.

Once you have eliminated all other causes (always check and repair front end parts BEFORE wheel alignment), unload everything from the trunk except the spare tire, set the tire pressures to the correct level and take the car to a reputable

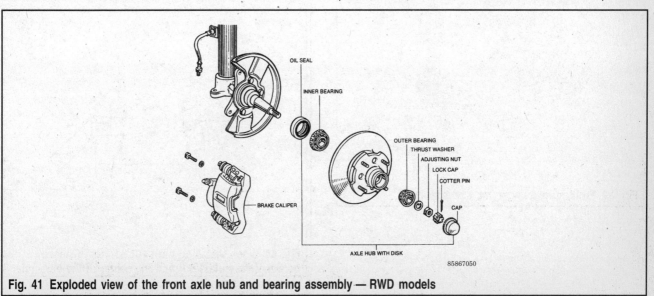

Fig. 41 Exploded view of the front axle hub and bearing assembly — RWD models

alignment facility. Since the alignment settings are measured in very small increments, it is almost impossible for the home mechanic to accurately determine the settings. The explanations that follow will help you understand the three dimensions of alignment: caster, camber and toe.

CASTER

Caster is the tilting of the steering axis either forward or backward from the vertical, when viewed from the side of the vehicle. A backward tilt is said to be positive and a forward tilt is said to be negative.

CAMBER

Camber is the tilting of the wheels from the vertical (leaning in or out) when viewed from the front of the vehicle. When the wheels tilt outward at the top, the camber is said to be positive. When the wheels tilt inward at the top the camber is said to be negative. The amount of tilt is measured in degrees from the vertical. This measurement is called camber angle.

TOE

Toe is the turning in or out (parallelism) of the wheels. The actual amount of toe setting is normally only a fraction of an inch. The purpose of toe-in (or out) specification is to ensure parallel rolling of the wheels. Toe-in also serves to offset the small deflections of the steering support system which occur when the vehicle is rolling forward or under braking.

Changing the toe setting will radically affect the overall feel of the steering, the behavior of the car under braking, tire wear and even fuel economy. Excessive toe (in or out) causes excessive drag or scrubbing on the tires.

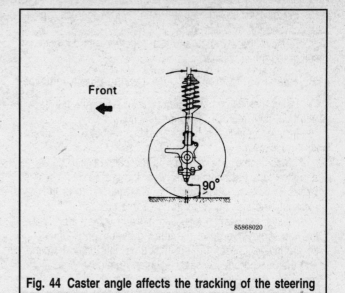

Fig. 44 Caster angle affects the tracking of the steering

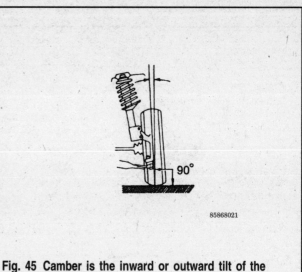

Fig. 45 Camber is the inward or outward tilt of the wheel on the road

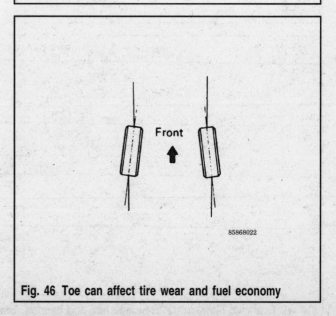

Fig. 46 Toe can affect tire wear and fuel economy

WHEEL ALIGNMENT SPECIFICATIONS: 1970–84

Model		Caster		Camber		Toe-in (in.)	Steering Axis Inclination
		Range (deg.)	Preferred Setting (deg.)	Range (deg.)	Preferred Setting (deg.)		
Corolla	1200	1½P–2⅓	—	½P–1½P	½P	0.04–0.20②	7½P–8½P
	1600 (1970–75)	1½P–2P①	1¾P	½P–1½P	½P	0.04–0.20	7½P–8½P
	(1976–79)	1¼P–1½P	2P	½P–1½P	1P	0.08–0.16③	7¼P–8¼P
	1800 exc. sta. wgn.	1°16′ P–2°16′ P	1°46′ P	33′ P–1°33′ P	1°3′ P	0–.08④	7°55′ P–8°55′ P
	1800 sta. wgn.	1°1/16′ P–2°1/16′ P	1°34P	35′ P–1°35′ P	1°5′ P	0–.08④	7°50′ P–8°50′ P
	1983	1°15′ P–2°15′ P⑤	1°45′ P⑤	35′ P–1°35′ P	1°5′ P	0–.08	8°20′ P–8°30′ P⑥
	1984 RWD	2°15′ P–3°15′ P⑦	2°45′ P⑧	15′ N–45′ P.	15′ P	0–.08P	8°20′ P–9°20′ P
	1984 FWD	25′ P–1°25′ P	55′ P	1°N–0	30′ N	.04N–.04P	12°5′ P–13°5′ P

P—Positive
N—Negative
① 1975 Wagon: ¾P–1½P
② 1978–79 w/bias ply: 0.079″
   w/radial ply: 0.039″
③ 1976–77 (radial): 0–0.08 in.
④ w/bias tires: 0.12 ± 0.04
⑤ 50′ P–2°20′ P; 1°35′ P: Sta. Wag.
⑥ 8°15′ P–8°25′ P: Sta. Wag.
⑦ w/Power Steering: 3°10′ P–4°10′ P
⑧ w/Power Steering: 3°40′ P

85868C01

WHEEL ALIGNMENT SPECIFICATIONS: 1985–87

Year	Model	Caster		Camber		Toe-in (in.)	Steering Axis Inclination (deg.)
		Range (deg.)	Preferred Setting (deg.)	Range (deg.)	Preferred Setting (deg.)		
1985–86	Corolla (RWD)	①	②	½N–1P	¼P	0.04 out–0.12 in	9
	(FWD)	3/16P–1 11/16P	15/16P	1N–½P	¼N	0.04 out–0.12 in	12½
1987	Corolla (RWD)	①	②	½N–1P	¼P	0.04 out–0.12 in	9
	(FWD)	⅛P–1⅝P	⅞P	1N–½P	¼N	0.04 out–0.12 in	12½

① Man. Str.: 2P–3½P
   Pwr. Str.: 3P–3½P
② Man. Str.: 2¾P
   Pwr. Str.: 3¾P

85868C02

REAR SUSPENSION

Shock Absorbers

TESTING

➡On MacPherson strut shock absorbers, if oil is leaking from the cylinder portion of the assembly, the shock absorber must be replaced.

Shock absorbers require replacement if the car fails to recover quickly after hitting a large bump or if it sways excessively following a directional change.

A good way to test the shock absorbers is to intermittently apply downward pressure to the side of the car until it is moving up and down for almost its full suspension travel. Release it and observe its recovery. If the car bounces once or twice after having been released and then comes to a rest, the shocks are all right. If the car continues to bounce, the shocks will probably require replacement.

REMOVAL & INSTALLATION

▶ See Figures 47, 48 and 49

➡We recommend replacement of the shock absorbers in sets for added safety and reliability

Except MacPherson Strut Type

1. Raise the rear of the car and support the rear axle with jackstands.
2. Unfasten the upper shock absorber retaining nuts. Use a tool to keep the shaft from spinning.

➡On some models, upper retaining nut removal may require removing the rear seat. Always remove and install the shock absorbers one at a time. Do not allow the rear axle to hang in place as this may cause undue damage.

3. Remove the lower shock retaining nut where it attaches to the rear axle housing.
4. Remove the shock absorber.
5. Installation is in the reverse order of removal. Tighten the upper retaining nuts to 24 ft. lbs. (32 Nm). Tighten the lower retaining nuts to 32 ft. lbs. (43 Nm).

MacPherson Strut Type

▶ See Figure 50

1. Working inside the car, remove the shock absorber cover and package tray bracket.
2. Raise the rear of the vehicle and support it with jackstands. Remove the wheel.
3. Disconnect the brake line from the wheel cylinder. Disconnect the brake line from the flexible hose at the mounting bracket on the strut tube. Disconnect the flexible hose from the strut.

4. Loosen the nut holding the suspension support to the shock absorber.

✳✳CAUTION

Do not remove the nut.

5. Remove the bolts and nuts mounting the strut on the axle carrier and then disconnect the strut.
6. Remove the three upper strut mounting nuts and carefully remove the strut assembly.
7. Installation is in the reverse order of removal. Please note the following:
   a. Tighten the upper strut retaining nuts to 17 ft. lbs. (23 Nm)
   b. Tighten the lower strut-to-axle carrier bolts to 105 ft. lbs. (142 Nm)
   c. Tighten the nut holding the suspension support to the shock absorber to 36 ft. lbs. (49 Nm). Bleed the brakes.

OVERHAUL

Except MacPherson Strut Type

No overhaul is possible on the regular type shock absorber. If they are defective they must replaced as an assembly. Shock absorbers should be replace in sets.

MacPherson Strut Type

➡Coil spring and shock absorber removal and installation procedures are identical to those already detailed in the previous MacPherson Strut section (Front Suspension). Please refer to these procedures for any work involving the rear struts. If replacement of the MacPherson type shock absorber is required, a small hole must be drilled in the bottom of the strut tube to relieve the gas pressure in the shock before discarding the shock assembly.

Springs

REMOVAL & INSTALLATION

➡We recommend replacement of the springs in sets for added safety and reliability

Leaf Springs

1. Loosen the rear wheel lug nuts.
2. Raise the rear of the vehicle. Support the frame and rear axle housing with stands.

✳✳CAUTION

Be sure that the vehicle is securely supported.

3. Remove the lug nuts and the wheel.
4. Remove the cotter pin (if so equipped), nut, and washer from the lower end of the shock absorber.

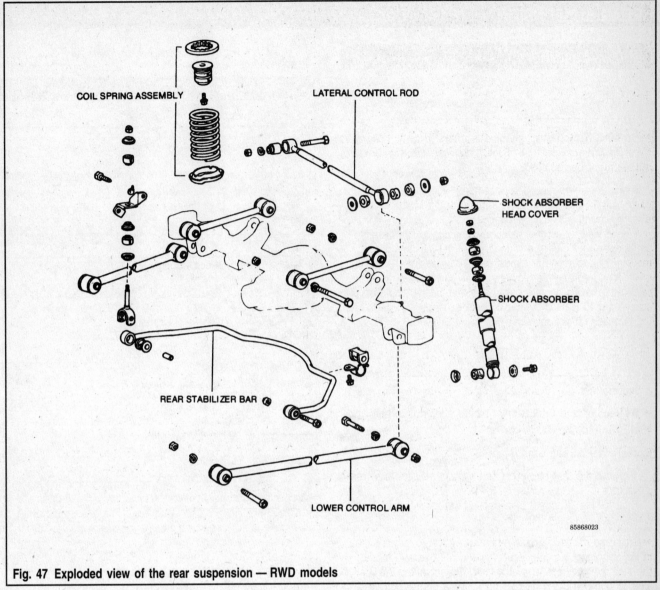

Fig. 47 Exploded view of the rear suspension — RWD models

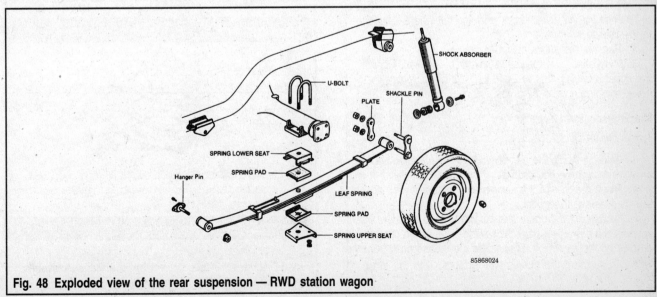

Fig. 48 Exploded view of the rear suspension — RWD station wagon

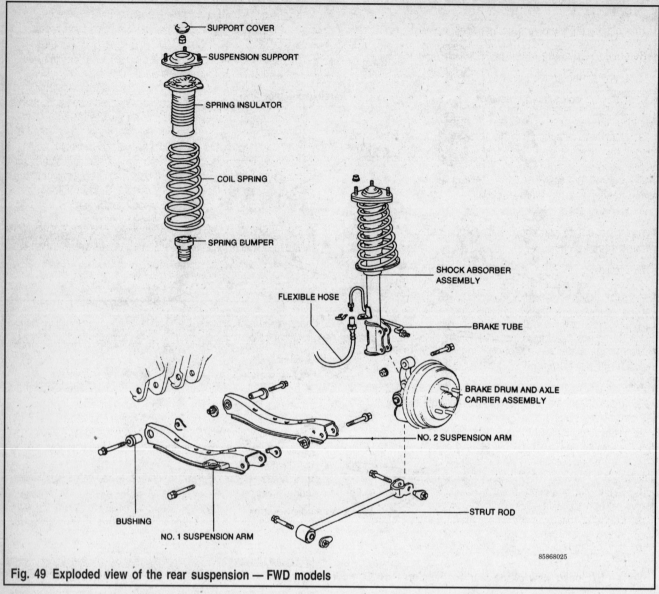

Fig. 49 Exploded view of the rear suspension — FWD models

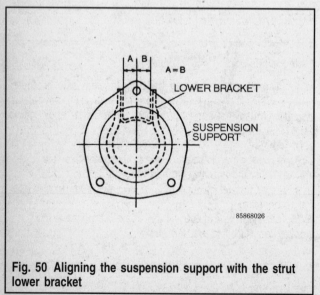

Fig. 50 Aligning the suspension support with the strut lower bracket

Fig. 51 Make sure that the spring is installed correctly in the lower insulator (spring seat)

5. Detach the shock absorber from the spring seat pivot pin.

6. Remove the parking brake cable clamp.

➡**Remove the parking brake equalizer, if necessary.**

7. Unfasten the U-bolt nuts and remove the spring seat assemblies.

8. Adjust the height of the rear axle housing so that the weight of the rear axle is removed from the rear springs.

9. Unfasten the spring shackle retaining nuts. Withdraw the spring shackle inner plate. Carefully pry out the spring shackle with a bar.

10. Remove the spring bracket pin from the front end of the spring hanger and remove the rubber bushings.

11. Remove the spring.

➡**Use care not to damage the hydraulic brake line or the parking brake cable.**

To install:

12. Install the rubber bushings in the eye of the spring.

13. Align the eye of the spring with the spring hanger bracket and drive the pin through the bracket holes and rubber bushings.

➡**Use soapy water as lubricant, if necessary, to aid in pin installation. Never use oil or grease.**

14. Finger-tighten the spring hanger nuts and/or bolts.

15. Install the rubber bushings in the spring eye at the opposite end of the spring.

16. Raise the free end of the spring. Install the spring shackle through the bushings and the bracket.

17. Fit the shackle inner plate and finger-tighten the retaining nuts.

18. Center the bolt head in the hole which is provided in the spring seat on the axle housing.

19. Fit the U-bolts over the axle housing. Install the lower spring seat.

20. Tighten all retaining nuts and bolts.

➡**Some models have two sets of nuts, while others have a nut and lockwasher.**

21. Install the parking brake cable clamp. Install the equalizer, if it was removed.

22. Install the shock absorber end at the spring seat. Tighten the nuts to the specified torque.

23. Install the wheel and lug nuts. Lower the car to the ground.

24. Bounce the car several times. Recheck that all retaining nuts and bolts are tight.

Coil Springs

▶ **See Figure 51**

1. Remove the hubcap and loosen the lug nuts.

2. Jack up the rear axle housing and support the frame with jackstands. Leave the jack in place under the rear axle housing.

✳✳CAUTION

Support the car securely. Remember you will be working underneath it.

3. Remove the lug nuts and wheel.

4. Unfasten the lower shock absorber end.

5. If equipped with a stabilizer bar; remove the bracket bolts.

6. Slowly lower the jack under the rear axle housing until the axle is at the bottom of its travel.

7. Withdraw the coil spring, complete with its insulator.

8. Inspect the coil spring and insulator for wear and cracks, or weakness; replace either or both as necessary.

9. Installation is performed in the reverse order of removal. When reconnecting the stabilizer bar, tighten the bolts finger-tight. When the car is lowered, bounce it a few times to stabilize the rear suspension. Raise the rear axle housing until the body weight rests on the suspension and then re-tighten the nut to 47 ft. lbs. (64 Nm).

Lateral Control Rod

REMOVAL & INSTALLATION

RWD Models

1. Raise the rear of the vehicle and support the axle housing with jackstands.

2. Disconnect the lateral rod from the rear axle housing.

3. Disconnect the lateral rod from the body and remove the rod.

4. Install the arm-to-body nut and finger-tighten it.

5. Position the arm on the axle housing. Then install a washer, bushing, spacer, the arm, bushing, washer and the nut. Finger-tighten the nut.

6. Lower the vehicle and bounce it a few times to stabilize the suspension.

7. Raise the rear of the vehicle again then tighten the control rod-to-body nut to 83 ft. lbs. (112 Nm) and the control rod-to-axle housing nut to 47 ft. lbs. (64 Nm).

Stabilizer Bar

REMOVAL & INSTALLATION

RWD Models

1. Disconnect the stabilizer bar from the rear axle brackets.

2. Remove the stabilizer bar from the vehicle. Examine the insulators (bushings) carefully for any sign of wear and replace them if necessary.

To install:

3. Place the bar in position. Install both stabilizer bar bracket bolts and partial tighten bolts.

4. Lower the vehicle and bounce it a few times to stabilize the suspension.

5. Raise the rear of the vehicle again then tighten the bracket bolts to 14 ft. lbs. (19 Nm).

Upper and Lower Control Arms

REMOVAL & INSTALLATION

RWD Models

➡**On FWD models, refer to the rear suspension exploded views and this procedure as a guide for this service repair.**

1. Raise the rear of the vehicle and support the body with jackstands. Support the rear axle housing with a jack.
2. Remove the bolt holding the upper control arm to the body.
3. Remove the bolt holding the upper control arm to the axle housing and then remove the upper control arm.
4. Remove the bolt holding the lower control arm to the body.
5. Remove the bolt holding the lower control arm to the rear axle housing and then remove the lower control arm.

To install:

6. Position the upper control arm and install the arm-to-body and arm-to-axle housing bolts. Do not tighten the nuts.
7. Position the lower control arm and install the arm-to-body and arm-to-axle housing bolts. Do not tighten the nuts.
8. Lower the vehicle and bounce it a few times to stabilize the suspension.
9. Raise and support the vehicle once again. Raise the rear axle housing until the body is just free from the jackstands.
10. Tighten the upper arm-to-body nut to 87 ft. lbs. (118 Nm). Do the same for the upper arm-to-axle housing nuts.
11. Tighten the lower arm-to-body nuts to 87 ft. lbs. (118 Nm). Do the same for the lower arm-to-axle housing nuts.

Axle Shaft And Bearing

REMOVAL & INSTALLATION

◗ **See Figures 52 and 53**

Front Wheel Drive

➡**No periodic maintenance is required on the rear axle shaft bearing.**

1. Raise and support the rear of the vehicle. On rear disc brake applications remove the brake caliper and suspend it with wire. Remove the rear brake drum or rear brake disc.
2. Check that the bearing play in an axial direction is no more than 0.0020 in. (0.05mm).
3. On rear brake drum models, disconnect and plug the brake tube from the wheel cylinder. Remove the wheel cylinder.
4. Remove the four bolts holding the axle hub to the carrier. Remove the rear axle hub assembly.

5. Using a hammer and chisel, unstake the bearing retaining nut on the axle hub and remove the nut.
6. Using a two armed puller, remove the axle shaft form the axle hub.

To install:

7. Press the axle shaft into the hub and tighten the nut to 90 ft. lbs. (123 Nm). Stake the nut.
8. Position a new O-ring into the axle carrier and then install the axle hub. Tighten the mounting bolts to 59 ft. lbs. (80 Nm).
9. Installation of the remaining components is in the reverse order of removal. Bleed and adjust the brake system.

Rear Wheel Drive

On rear wheel drive models, the rear axle shafts are part of the drive train. Information on axle shaft and bearing removal or installation can be found in Section 7 of this manual.

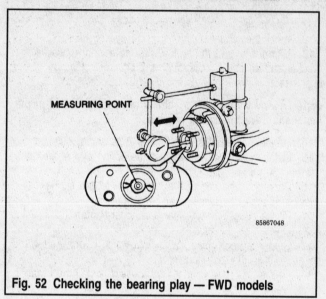

Fig. 52 Checking the bearing play — FWD models

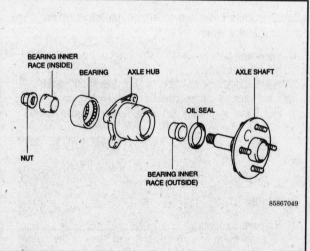

Fig. 53 Exploded view of the rear axle shaft assembly — FWD models

STEERING

Steering Wheel

REMOVAL & INSTALLATION

▶ **See Figures 54, 55, 56, 57, 58, 59, 60, 61 and 62**

Three-Spoke

➡Do not attempt to remove or install the steering wheel by hammering on it. Damage to the energy absorbing steering column could result.

1. Disconnect the negative battery cable. Unfasten the horn and turn signal multi-connector(s) at the base of the steering column shroud.
2. Loosen the trim pad retaining screws from the back side of the steering wheel.
3. Lift the trim pad and horn button assembly or assemblies from the wheel.
4. Remove the steering wheel hub retaining nut.
5. Scratch matchmarks on the hub and shaft to aid in correct installation.
6. Use a steering wheel puller to loosen and remove the steering wheel.
7. Installation is performed in the reverse order of removal. Tighten the wheel retaining nut to 25 ft. lbs. (34 Nm).

Two-Spoke

The two-spoke steering wheel is removed in the same manner as the three-spoke, except that the trim pad should be pried off with a small prybar. Remove the pad by lifting it toward the top of the wheel.

Four-Spoke

➡Do not attempt to remove or install the steering wheel by hammering on it. Damage to the energy absorbing steering column could result.

Fig. 54 Remove the steering wheel horn pad retaining screw

Fig. 55 With the retaining screws removed, lift the horn pad for access to the wiring

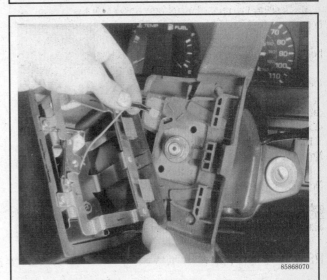

Fig. 56 Disengage the horn pad electrical connection

1. Disconnect the negative battery cable. Unfasten the horn and turn signal multi-connectors at the base of the steering column shroud (underneath the instrument panel).
2. Gently pry the center emblem off the front of the steering wheel.
3. Insert a wrench through the hole and remove the steering wheel retaining nut.
4. Scratch matchmarks on the hub and shaft to aid installation.
5. Use a steering wheel puller to loosen and remove the steering wheel.
6. Installation is the reverse of removal. Tighten the steering wheel retaining nut to 25 ft. lbs. (34 Nm).

Fig. 57 Remove the steering wheel retaining nut

Fig. 58 Matchmark the steering wheel before removing

Fig. 59 Remove the steering wheel with puller tool

Fig. 60 Once the wheel has been loosened by the puller it may be removed from the shaft

Fig. 61 The lower steering wheel cover retaining screws may be deeply recessed in the cover

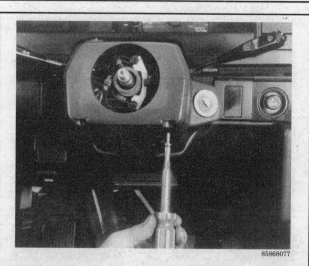

Fig. 62 A magnetic tip screwdriver is especially helpful in removing these screws

Turn Signal/Combination Switch

➡Some earlier models, may utilize a single turn signal switch instead of a combination switch. Removal and installation procedures are essentially the same for either application.

REMOVAL & INSTALLATION

1. Disconnect the negative battery cable.
2. Unscrew the retaining bolts and remove the steering column garnish.
3. Remove the steering wheel (provides easier removal access to steering column covers).
4. Remove the upper and lower steering column covers.
5. Trace the switch wiring harness to the multi-connector. Push in the lock levers and pull apart the connector.
6. Unscrew the mounting screws and remove the switch.
7. Installation is in the reverse order of removal.

Ignition Lock/Switch

REMOVAL & INSTALLATION

▶ See Figures 63 and 64

1. Disconnect the negative battery cable.
2. Unthread the retaining screws and remove the upper and lower steering column covers.
3. Unscrew the retaining screws, then remove the steering column garnish.
4. Turn the ignition key to the **ACC** position.
5. Push the lock cylinder stop in with a small, round object (cotter pin, punch, etc.), then pull out the ignition key and the lock cylinder.

➡You may find that removing the steering wheel and the combination switch will ease removal.

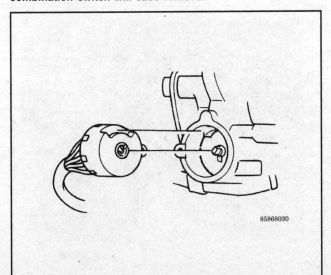

85868030

Fig. 63 Align the switch before installation

6. Loosen the mounting screw and withdraw the ignition switch from the lock housing.
   To install:
7. Install the switch with the switch recess and the bracket tab in the correct position. Install the retaining screw.
8. Make sure that both the lock cylinder and the column lock are in the **ACC** position. Slide the cylinder into the lock housing until the stop tab engages the hole in the lock.
9. Installation of the remaining components is in the reverse order of removal.

Steering Column

REMOVAL & INSTALLATION

1. Disconnect the negative battery cable. Remove the steering wheel.
2. On some models it may be necessary to remove the left side dash trim panel. Unplug the turn signal/combination switch wiring and all electrical connections.
3. Loosen the hole cover clamp screw.
4. Remove the air filter assembly if necessary. Remove the pinch bolt from the yoke.
5. Remove the yoke from the steering gear.
6. Remove the bolts holding the lower column mounting brackets.
7. Remove the bolts holding the upper column to the instrument panel.
8. Remove the column from the vehicle.
   To install:
9. Place the column assembly into position and install the upper and lower bracket nuts and bolts finger-tight.
10. Position the column assembly so the end of the lower support holes touch the mounting bolts.
11. Tighten the upper and lower support nuts and bolts to 19 ft. lbs. (26 Nm).
12. Install the yoke and tighten the pinch bolt to 26 ft. lbs. (35 Nm). Install the air filter, as necessary.
13. Install the hole cover clamp.
14. Install the combination switch and all electrical connections.
15. Install the steering wheel. Install side dash trim panel as necessary.

Tie Rod Ends

REMOVAL & INSTALLATION

▶ See Figures 65, 66, 67, 68, 69, 70, 71, 72, 73 and 74

1970-82 Models

1. Raise and support the vehicle. Measure the exposed thread on the tie rod end for correct installation.
2. Working at the steering knuckle arm, pull out the cotter pin and then remove the castellated nut.
3. Using a tie rod end puller, disconnect the tie rod from the steering knuckle arm.

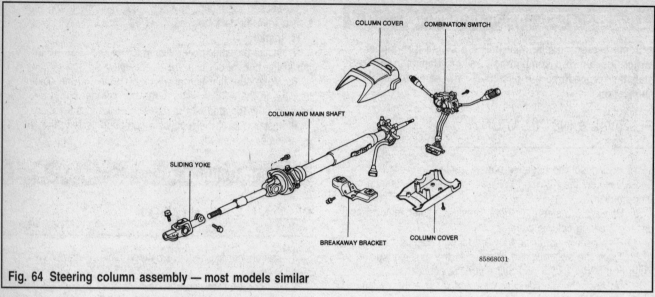

Fig. 64 Steering column assembly — most models similar

4. Repeat the first two steps on the other end of the tie rod (where it attaches to the relay rod).

To install:

5. Turn the tie rods in their adjusting tubes (use exposed thread specification as guide for length) until they are of equal lengths.

6. Turn the tie rod ends so that they cross at 90°. Tighten the adjusting tube clamps so that they lock the ends in position.

7. Connect the tie rods and tighten the nuts to 37-50 ft. lbs. (50-68 Nm)

8. Check the toe. Adjust if necessary.

1983 and Later Models

1. Raise the front of the vehicle and support it with jack-stands. Remove the wheel.

2. Measure the exposed thread on the tie rod end for correct installation.

3. Remove the cotter pin and nut holding the tie rod to the steering knuckle.

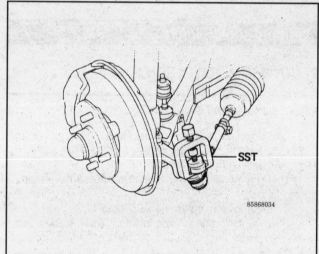

Fig. 66 Remove the tie rod end from the steering rack using a separator tool — FWD models

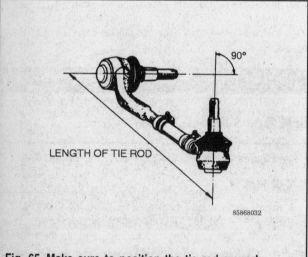

Fig. 65 Make sure to position the tie rod properly before installation — RWD models

Fig. 67 Remove the tie rod end cotter pin

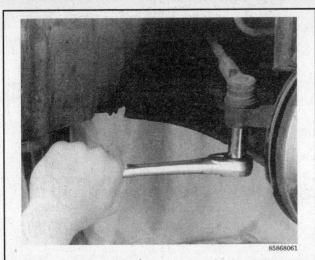

Fig. 68 Using a deep socket wrench remove the tie rod end lower retaining nut

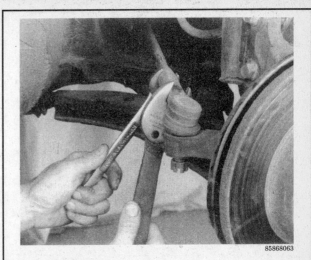

Fig. 70 Loosen the tire rod adjusting tube locknut before removing

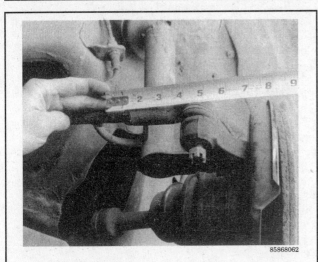

Fig. 69 Measure the exposed thread on the tie rod end for correct installation

Fig. 71 Loosen the tie rod end with a separator tool

4. Using a tie rod removal tool, press the tie rod out of the knuckle.

5. Matchmark the inner end of the tie rod to the end of the steering rack or adjusting tube.

6. Loosen the pinch bolt or locknuts and pull the tie rod off of the steering rack or adjusting tube.

7. Repeat Steps 2-5 on the other side of the vehicle.

To install:

8. Install the tie rod ends onto the rack ends or adjusting tubes (use exposed thread specification as guide for length). On rear wheel drive models tighten the pinch bolts to 14 ft. lbs. (19 Nm). On front wheel drive models tighten the locknuts to 35 ft. lbs. (47 Nm).

9. Installation is in the reverse order of removal. Always use NEW cotter pins.

Fig. 72 After the separator tool is used, the tie rod end may be removed from the steering knuckle

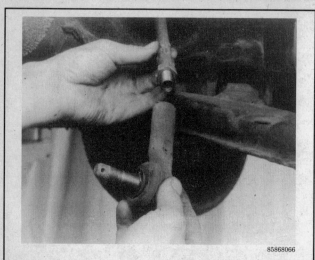

85868066

Fig. 73 After the locknut is loosened, remove the tie rod end from the steering rack assembly

Manual Rack And Pinion Steering Gear

Adjustments

Adjustments to the manual steering gear/rack and pinion are not necessary during normal service. They are preformed only as part of overhaul.

REMOVAL & INSTALLATION

▶ **See Figure 74**

1. Remove the cover from the intermediate shaft.
2. Loosen the upper pinch bolt. Remove the lower pinch bolt at the pinion shaft.
3. Loosen the wheel lug nuts.
4. Elevate and safely support the vehicle.
5. Remove both front wheels.
6. Remove the cotter pins from both tie rod joints and remove the nuts.
7. Using a tie rod separator, remove both tie rod joints from the knuckles.
8. Remove the nuts and bolts attaching the steering rack to the body.
9. If possible slide assembly out the wheel well opening. Remove any necessary component to gain working access to remove the rack and pinion assembly from the vehicle. Remove the rack assembly.
   To install:
10. Install the rack assembly. Secure it with the retaining bolts and nuts and tighten them to 43 ft. lbs. (58 Nm).
11. Install any component which were removed for access.
12. Connect the tie rods to each knuckle. Tighten the nuts and install new cotter pins.
13. Install the front wheels.
14. Lower the car to the ground.

15. Install the lower pinch bolt at the pinion shaft. Tighten the upper and lower bolts.
16. Install the cover on the intermediate shaft. Check front end alignment.

Power Rack And Pinion Steering Gear

Adjustments

Adjustments to the power steering gear/rack and pinion are not necessary during normal service. They are preformed only as part of overhaul.

REMOVAL & INSTALLATION

▶ **See Figure 75**

1. Remove the intermediate shaft cover.
2. Loosen the upper pinch bolt and remove the lower pinch bolt.
3. Place a drain pan below the power steering rack assembly. Clean the area around the line fittings on the rack.
4. Loosen the front wheel lug nuts.
5. Safely elevate and support the vehicle.
6. Remove the front wheels.
7. Remove the cotter pins and nuts from both tie rod joints. Separate the joints from the knuckle using a tie rod joint separator.
8. Support the transaxle with a jack.
9. Remove the rear bolts holding the engine crossmember to the body.
10. Remove the nut and bolt holding the rear engine mount to the mount bracket.
11. Label and disconnect the fluid pressure and return lines at the rack.
12. Remove the bolts and nuts holding the rack brackets to the body. It will be necessary to slightly raise and lower the rear of the transaxle to gain access to the bolts.
13. Remove the rack through the access hole.
    To install:
14. When reinstalling, place the rack in position through the access hole and install the retaining brackets to the body. Tighten the nuts and bolts to 43 ft. lbs. (58 Nm).
15. Connect the fluid lines. Always start the threads by hand before using a tool to the rack.
16. Install the nut and bolt holding the rear engine mount to the mount bracket.
17. Reinstall the engine crossmember bolts and tighten.
18. Remove the jack from the transaxle.
19. Connect the tie rod ends to the knuckles. Tighten the nuts and install new cotter pins.
20. Install the wheels and lower the vehicle to the ground.
21. Connect the intermediate shaft to the steering rack. Tighten all necessary connections. Install the intermediate shaft cover.
22. Add fluid and bleed the system.
23. Have the alignment checked and adjusted at a reliable repair facility.

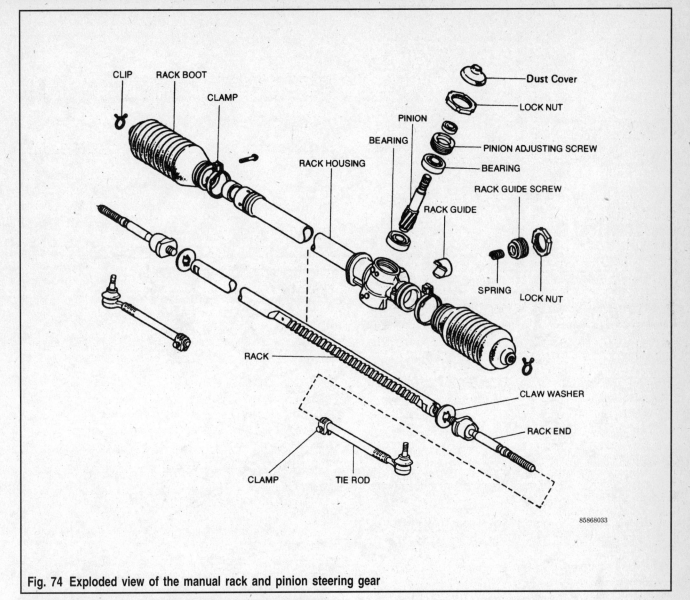

Fig. 74 Exploded view of the manual rack and pinion steering gear

Power Steering Pump

REMOVAL & INSTALLATION

▶ See Figures 76 and 77

➡On some models, an idler pulley assembly type adjustment is used instead of bracket type adjustment.

1. Remove the fan shroud.
2. Unfasten the nut from the center of the pump pulley.

➡Use the drive belt as a brake to keep the pulley from rotating.

3. Withdraw the drive belt.
4. Remove the pulley and the Woodruff key from the pump shaft.

5. Detach the intake and outlet hoses from the pump reservoir.

➡Tie the hose ends up high, so that the fluid cannot flow out of them. Drain or plug the pump to prevent fluid leakage.

6. Remove the bolt from the rear mounting brace.
7. Remove the front bracket bolts and withdraw the pump.
To install:
8. Install the pump and all necessary brackets.
9. Tighten the pump pulley mounting bolt to 25-39 ft. lbs. (34-53 Nm)
10. Adjust the pump drive belt tension. The belt should deflect about 0.4 inches when 22 lbs. pressure is applied midway between the air pump (if so equipped) and the power steering pump.
11. Fill the reservoir with Dexron®II automatic transmission fluid. Bleed the air from the system.

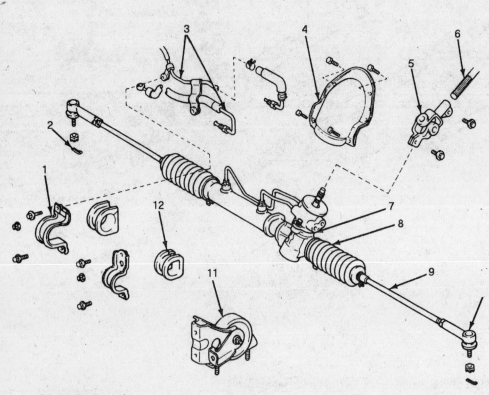

1 Mounting bracket
2 Cotter pin
3 Pressure and return lines
4 Column hole cover
5 Universal joint (yoke)
6 Intermediate shaft
7 Steering gear housing
8 Boot
9 Tie rod
10 Tie rod end
11 Engine mount
12 Grommet

85868035

Fig. 75 Exploded view of a power rack and pinion steering gear assembly

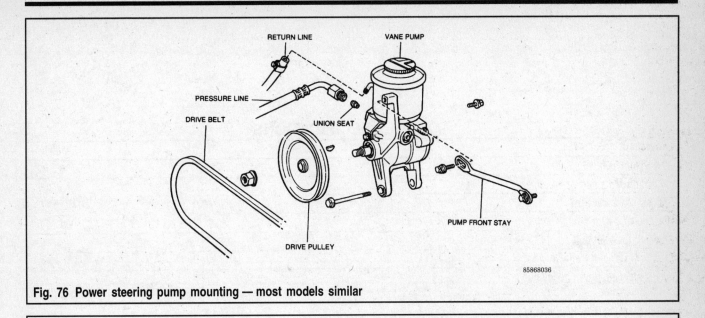

Fig. 76 Power steering pump mounting — most models similar

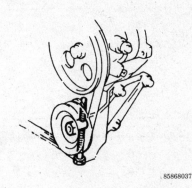

Fig. 77 Power steering pump equipped for idler pulley type adjustment

BLEEDING

1. Raise the front of the vehicle and support it securely with jackstands.

2. Fill the pump reservoir with DEXRON®II automatic transmission fluid.

3. Rotate the steering wheel from lock-to-lock several times. Add fluid as necessary.

4. With the steering wheel turned fully to one lock, crank the starter while watching the fluid level in the reservoir.

➡**Disconnect the high tension lead from the coil; do not start the engine. Operate the starter with a remote starter switch or have an assistant turn the switch from inside of the car. Do not run the starter for more than a few seconds without stopping to allow the motor to cool.**

5. Repeat Step 4 with the steering wheel turned to the opposite lock.

6. Start the engine. With the engine idling, turn the steering wheel from lock-to-lock two or three times.

7. Lower the front of the car and repeat Step 6.

8. Center the wheel at the midpoint of its travel. Stop the engine.

9. The fluid level should not have risen more than 0.2 inch (5mm). If it does, repeat Step 7 again.

10. Check for fluid leakage.

TORQUE SPECIFICATIONS

Component	U.S.	Metric
Tie rod lock nut	41 ft. lbs.	56 Nm
Tie rod end to steering knuckle	36 ft. lbs.	49 Nm
Ball joint to lower arm	72–76 ft. lbs.	97–103 Nm
Hub bearing lock nut	137 ft. lbs.	186 Nm
Steering joint set bolt	26 ft. lbs.	35 Nm
Stabilizer bar to lower arm	13 ft. lbs.	18 Nm
Power steering pump pulley nut		
4A-GE engine	28 ft. lbs.	38 Nm
Power steering gear bracket to body	43 ft. lbs.	59 Nm
Manual steering gear bracket to body	43 ft. lbs.	59 Nm
Front shock upper suspension support nut	29–40 ft. lbs.	39–54 Nm
Front shock absorber-to-knuckle		
RWD models	50–65 ft. lbs.	68–88 Nm
FWD models (gas engine)	105 ft. lbs.	142 Nm
FWD models (diesel engine)	152 ft. lbs.	206 Nm
Rear shock absorber		
Upper mounting nuts	24 ft. lbs.	32 Nm
Lower mounting nuts	32 ft. lbs.	43 Nm
Rear suspension arm-to-body	87 ft. lbs.	118 Nm

85868999

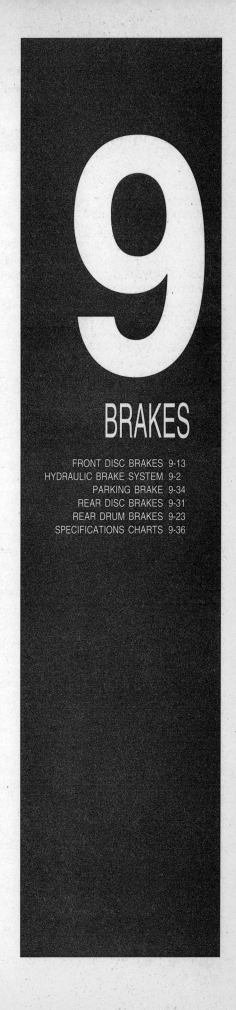

9

BRAKES

HYDRAULIC BRAKE SYSTEM

Basic Operating Principles

Hydraulic systems are used to actuate the brakes of all automobiles. The system transports the power required to force the frictional surfaces of the braking system together from the pedal to the individual brake units at each wheel. A hydraulic system is used for two reasons.

First, fluid under pressure can be carried to all parts of an automobile by small pipes and flexible hoses without taking up a significant amount of room or posing routing problems.

Second, a great mechanical advantage can be given to the brake pedal end of the system, and the foot pressure required to actuate the brakes can be reduced by making the surface area of the master cylinder pistons smaller than that of any of the pistons in the wheel cylinders or calipers.

The master cylinder consists of a fluid reservoir and a double cylinder and piston assembly. Double type master cylinders are designed to separate the front and rear braking systems hydraulically in case of a leak.

Steel lines carry the brake fluid to a point on the vehicle's frame near each of the vehicle's wheels. The fluid is then carried to the calipers and wheel cylinders by flexible tubes in order to allow for suspension and steering movements.

In drum brake systems, each wheel cylinder contains two pistons, one at either end, which push outward in opposite directions.

In disc brake systems, the cylinders are part of the calipers. One cylinder in each caliper is used to force the brake pads against the disc.

All pistons employ some type of seal, usually made of rubber, to minimize fluid leakage. A rubber dust boot seals the outer end of the cylinder against dust and dirt. The boot fits around the outer end of the piston on disc brake calipers, and around the brake actuating rod on wheel cylinders.

The hydraulic system operates as follows: when at rest, the entire system, from the piston(s) in the master cylinder to those in the wheel cylinders or calipers, is full of brake fluid. Upon application of the brake pedal, fluid trapped in front of the master cylinder piston(s) is forced through the lines to the wheel cylinders. Here, it forces the pistons outward, in the case of drum brakes, and inward toward the disc, in the case of disc brakes. The motion of the pistons is opposed by return springs mounted outside the cylinders in drum brakes, and by spring seals, in disc brakes.

Upon release of the brake pedal, a spring located inside the master cylinder immediately returns the master cylinder pistons to the normal position. The pistons contain check valves and the master cylinder has compensating ports drilled in it. These are uncovered as the pistons reach their normal position. The piston check valves allow fluid to flow toward the wheel cylinders or calipers as the pistons withdraw. Then, as the return springs force the brake pads or shoes into the released position, the excess fluid reservoir through the compensating ports. It is during the time the pedal is in the released position that any fluid that has leaked out of the system will be replaced through the compensating ports.

Dual circuit master cylinders employ two pistons, located one behind the other, in the same cylinder. The primary piston is actuated directly by mechanical linkage from the brake pedal through the power booster. The secondary piston is actuated by fluid trapped between the two pistons. If a leak develops in front of the secondary piston, it moves forward until it bottoms against the front of the master cylinder, and the fluid trapped between the pistons will operate the rear brakes. If the rear brakes develop a leak, the primary piston will move forward until direct contact with the secondary piston takes place, and it will force the secondary piston to actuate the front brakes. In either case, the brake pedal moves farther when the brakes are applied, and less braking power is available.

All dual circuit systems use a switch to warn the driver when only half of the brake system is operational. This switch is located in a valve body which is mounted on the firewall or the frame below the master cylinder. A hydraulic piston receives pressure from both circuits, each circuit's pressure being applied to one end of the piston. When the pressures are in balance, the piston remains stationary. When one circuit has a leak, however, the greater pressure in that circuit during application of the brakes will push the piston to one side, closing the switch and activating the brake warning light.

In disc brake systems, this valve body also contains a metering valve and, in some cases, a proportioning valve. The metering valve keeps pressure from traveling to the disc brakes on the front wheels until the brake shoes on the rear wheels have contacted the drums, ensuring that the front brakes will never be used alone. The proportioning valve controls the pressure to the rear brakes to lessen the chance of rear wheel lockup during very hard braking.

Warning lights may be tested by depressing the brake pedal and holding it while opening one of the wheel cylinder bleeder screws. If this does not cause the light to go on, substitute a new lamp, make continuity checks, and, finally, replace the switch as necessary.

The hydraulic system may be checked for leaks by applying pressure to the pedal gradually and steadily. If the pedal sinks very slowly to the floor, the system has a leak. This is not to be confused with a springy or spongy feel due to the compression of air within the lines. If the system leaks, there will be a gradual change in the position of the pedal with a constant pressure.

Check for leaks along all lines and at wheel cylinders. If no external leaks are apparent, the problem is inside the master cylinder.

DISC BRAKES

Instead of the traditional expanding brakes that press outward against a circular drum, disc brake systems utilize a disc (rotor) with brake pads positioned on either side of it. Braking effect is achieved in a manner similar to the way you would squeeze a spinning phonograph record between your fingers. The disc (rotor) is a casting with cooling fins between the two braking surfaces. This enables air to circulate between the braking surfaces making them less sensitive to heat buildup and more resistant to fade. Dirt and water do not affect braking action since contaminants are thrown off by the centrifugal action of the rotor or scraped off the by the pads.

Also, the equal clamping action of the two brake pads tends to ensure uniform, straight line stops. Disc brakes are inherently self-adjusting.

There are three general types of disc brake:
1. A fixed caliper.
2. A floating caliper.
3. A sliding caliper.

The fixed caliper design uses two pistons mounted on either side of the rotor (in each side of the caliper). The caliper is mounted rigidly and does not move.

The sliding and floating designs are quite similar. In fact, these two types are often lumped together. In both designs, the pad on the inside of the rotor is moved into contact with the rotor by hydraulic force. The caliper, which is not held in a fixed position, moves slightly, bringing the outside pad into contact with the rotor. There are various methods of attaching floating calipers. Some pivot at the bottom or top, and some slide on mounting bolts. In any event, the end result is the same.

DRUM BRAKES

Drum brakes employ two brake shoes mounted on a stationary backing plate. These shoes are positioned inside a circular drum which rotates with the wheel assembly. The shoes are held in place by springs. This allows them to slide toward the drums (when they are applied) while keeping the linings and drums in alignment. The shoes are actuated by a wheel cylinder which is mounted at the top of the backing plate. When the brakes are applied, hydraulic pressure forces the wheel cylinder's actuating links outward. Since these links bear directly against the top of the brake shoes, the tops of the shoes are then forced against the inner side of the drum. This action forces the bottoms of the two shoes to contact the brake drum by rotating the entire assembly slightly (known as servo action). When pressure within the wheel cylinder is relaxed, return springs pull the shoes back away from the drum.

Most modern drum brakes are designed to self-adjust themselves during application when the vehicle is moving in reverse. This motion causes both shoes to rotate very slightly with the drum, rocking an adjusting lever, thereby causing rotation of the adjusting screw.

POWER BOOSTERS

Power brakes operate just as non-power brake systems except in the actuation of the master cylinder pistons. A vacuum diaphragm is located on the front of the master cylinder and assists the driver in applying the brakes, reducing both the effort and travel he must put into moving the brake pedal.

The vacuum diaphragm housing is connected to the intake manifold by a vacuum hose. A check valve is placed at the point where the hose enters the diaphragm housing, so that during periods of low manifold vacuum brake assist vacuum will not be lost.

Depressing the brake pedal closes off the vacuum source and allows atmospheric pressure to enter on one side of the diaphragm. This causes the master cylinder pistons to move and apply the brakes. When the brake pedal is released, vacuum is applied to both sides of the diaphragm, and return springs return the diaphragm and master cylinder pistons to the released position. If the vacuum fails, the brake pedal rod will butt against the end of the master cylinder actuating rod, and direct mechanical application will occur as the pedal is depressed.

The hydraulic and mechanical problems that apply to conventional brake systems also apply to power brakes, and should be checked for if the tests below do not reveal the problem.

Test for a system vacuum leak as described below:
1. Operate the engine at idle without touching the brake pedal for at least one minute.
2. Turn off the engine, and wait one minute.
3. Test for the presence of assist vacuum by depressing the brake pedal and releasing it several times. Light application will produce less and less pedal travel, if vacuum was present. If there is no vacuum, air is leaking into the system somewhere.

Test for system operation as follows:
4. Pump the brake pedal (with engine off) until the supply vacuum is entirely gone.
5. Put a light, steady pressure on the pedal.
6. Start the engine, and operate it at idle. If the system is operating, the brake pedal should fall toward the floor if constant pressure is maintained on the pedal.

Power brake systems may be tested for hydraulic leaks just as ordinary systems are tested.

Adjustments

DISC BRAKES

All disc brakes are inherently self-adjusting. No periodic adjustment is either necessary or possible.

DRUM BRAKES

▶ See Figures 1, 2 and 3

Except Corolla 1200

The rear drum brakes used on all models in this manual, except the Corolla 1200, are equipped with automatic adjusters which are actuated by the parking brake mechanism. If this mechanism is working properly no periodic adjustment of the drum brakes is necessary . If the pedal travel is greater than normal, it may be due to a lack of adjustment at the rear. In a safe location, drive the car backwards at low speed. While backing, pump the brake pedal slowly several times. Neither the speed of the car or pedal pumping speed has any effect on the adjustment. The idea is to apply the brakes several times while backing. Drive forward and check the pedal feel by braking from moderate speed. It may take 2 or 3 passes in reverse to bring the pedal to the correct travel; each brake application moves the adjuster very little. It will take several applications to take up excess clearance.

If brake shoe-to-drum clearance is incorrect and applying/releasing the brakes in reverse does not adjust it properly, the parts will have to be disassembled for repair.

An alternate method of adjustment can be used when the brakes have been disassembled or when the reversing method does not work.

1. Elevate and safely support the vehicle. If only the rear wheels are elevated, block the front wheels with chocks. Once the vehicle is firmly on stands, release the parking brake.

2. Remove the rear wheels.

3. Remove the brake drum. It will not come off if the parking brake is applied.

✳✳CAUTION

Brake pads and shoes may contain asbestos, which has been determined to be a cancer causing agent. Never clean the brake surfaces with compressed air! Avoid inhaling any dust from brake surfaces! When cleaning brakes, use commercially available brake cleaning fluids.

4. If the brake drum cannot be removed easily:

a. Insert a screwdriver through the hole in the backing plate and hold the adjusting lever away from the star wheel.

b. Using another screwdriver or a brake adjusting tool, turn the wheel to reduce the tension (increase the clearance) on the brake shoes, then remove the drum.

5. Use a brake drum measuring tool with both inside diameter and outside diameter capability. Measure the inside diameter of the brake drum and record the reading.

6. Measure the diameter of the brake shoe assemble at the friction surface. Use the adjusting wheel to adjust the brake shoes until the diameter of the shoes is either 0.02 inch (0.60mm) on new models or 0.01 inch (0.33mm) on older models less than the diameter of the drum. This small clearance is important; incorrectly adjusted cause drag and premature wear on the shoes or a loss of braking.

7. Install the brake drum(s) and install the rear wheel(s).

8. Apply the parking brake and lower the car to the ground.

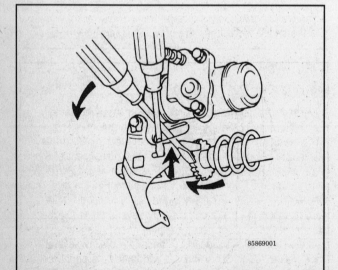

Fig. 1 Backing off the rear drum brake adjuster

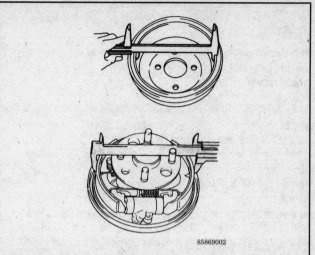

Fig. 2 Measuring the diameters of the drum and shoe assemblies

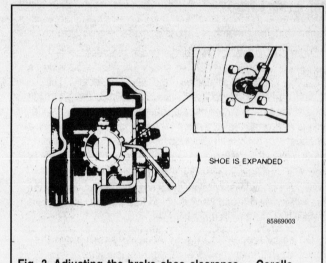

Fig. 3 Adjusting the brake shoe clearance — Corolla 1200

Corolla 1200

Corolla 1200 models are equipped with rear drum brakes which require manual adjustment. Perform the adjustment in the following order:

1. Chock the front wheels and fully release the parking brake.

2. Raise the rear of the car and support it with jackstands.

✳✳CAUTION

Be sure that the car is securely supported. Remember; you will be working underneath it.

3. Remove the adjusting hole plug from the backing plate.

4. Expand the brake shoes by turning the adjusting wheel with a starwheel adjusting tool or appropriate thin-bladed tool.

5. Pump the brake pedal several times, so that the shoes contact the drum evenly.

➡**If the wheel still turns when your foot is removed from the brake pedal, continue expanding the shoes until the wheel locks.**

6. Back off on the adjuster just enough so that the wheel rotates without dragging.

7. After this point is reached, continue backing off for five additional notches.

8. If a problem is encountered getting the wheel to rotate freely the wheel, back off one or two more notches. If after this, it still drags, check for worn or defective parts.

9. Pump the brake pedal again, and check wheel rotation.

10. Reverse Steps 1-3.

BRAKE PEDAL

The correct adjustment of the brake pedal height, free play and reserve distance is critical to the correct operation of the brake system. These three measurements inter-relate and should be performed in sequence.

Pedal Height
▶ **See Figure 4**

1. Measure the pedal height from the top of the pedal pad to the floor. Correct distances are: 6.4-6.8 inches (161-171mm) for RWD, 5.9-6.3 inches (147-157mm) early model FWD, or 5.4-6.0 inches (134-149mm) late model FWD. Always use the above specifications as a guide for this adjustment.

2. If it is necessary to adjust the pedal height, loosen the brake light switch and back it off so that some clearance exists between it and the pedal arm.

➡**On some models, it may be necessary to remove the lower dash trim panel and air duct for access.**

3. Adjust the pedal height by loosening the locknut and turning the pedal pushrod.

4. Return the brake light switch to a position in which it lightly contacts the stopper on the pedal arm.

Pedal Free-play
▶ **See Figure 5**

1. With the engine **OFF**, depress the brake pedal several times until there is no vacuum held in the booster.

2. The free-play distance is between the "at rest" pedal position and the position at which the beginning of pedal resistance is felt. This represents the distance the pedal pushrod moves before actuating the booster air valve. Correct free-play is 0.1-0.2 inch (3-6mm) for all models.

3. If adjustment is necessary, adjust the pedal pushrod to give the correct clearance. After adjusting the pedal free-play, recheck the pedal height.

4. Double check the adjustment of the brake light switch.

Pedal Reserve Distance
▶ **See Figure 6**

1. With the transmission/transaxle in P or N and the parking brake fully released, start the engine and apply normal braking effort to the pedal. Depress the pedal fully, but don't try to put it through the floor.

2. While the pedal is depressed, have a helper measure the distance from the top of the pedal pad to the floor. This distance is the extra travel available to the pushrod if it must work without vacuum assist or if the brakes are worn or severely out of adjustment. If the pedal height and pedal free-play are correctly adjusted, the pedal reserve distance must be at least to specification. The reserve distance can be greater than specified but must not be less. If the reserve distance is less than specification, the brake system must be diagnosed for leaks or component failure.

3. The reserve distance specification is 3 inches (75mm) on RWD models or 2.4 inches (60mm) on FWD. Always use the above specifications as a guide for this adjustment.

Brake Light Switch

▶ **See Figure 7**

The brake light switch is located at the top of the pedal arm. It is the switch which turns the brake lights on when the

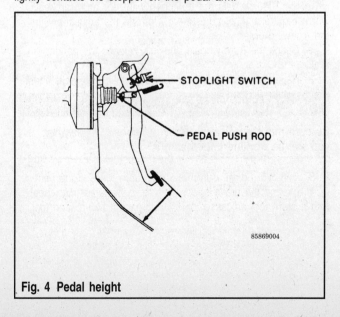

Fig. 4 Pedal height

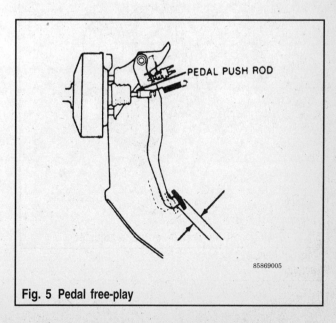

Fig. 5 Pedal free-play

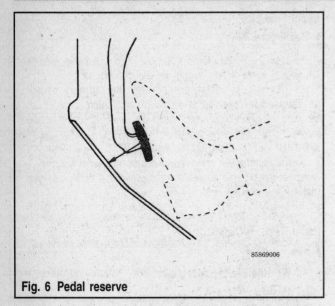

Fig. 6 Pedal reserve

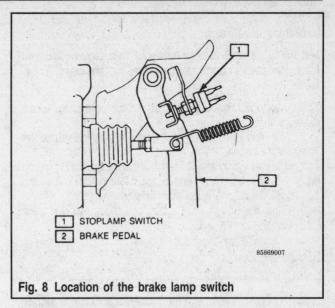

| 1 | STOPLAMP SWITCH |
| 2 | BRAKE PEDAL |

Fig. 8 Location of the brake lamp switch

brakes are applied. The plunger type switch is held in the off position by the normal position of the brake pedal; when the pedal moves during brake application, the switch plunger moves forward and the brake lights are turned on.

The switch is almost always the first place to look for the cause of the brake lights flickering over bumps or staying on without use of the brakes. If the brake lights fail to work with the brakes applied, check the fuse first, then check the switch.

REMOVAL & INSTALLATION

▶ See Figure 8

1. Remove the wiring from the switch terminals. Put a piece of tape over each exposed wiring connector; one wire terminal may be HOT even though the ignition is OFF. If it accidentally touches metal, a fuse will blow.

➡ On some models, it may be necessary to remove the lower dash trim panel and air duct for access.

Fig. 7 View of the brake light switch — most models similar

2. Loosen the locknut closest to the brake pedal arm. Unscrew the switch from the nut and remove it from the bracket.

3. Install the new switch and tighten the retaining nuts finger-tight when the switch plunger is lightly compressed against the stopper on the pedal.

4. Connect an ohmmeter across the terminals of the switch. Move the brake pedal and check the on off behavior of the switch. Adjust the switch so that the switch comes on at the bottom of the pedal free-play. This brings the brake lights on just as the brakes apply but no sooner.

5. Tighten the locknuts to hold the switch in position.

6. Remove the tape and connect the wiring to the switch.

Master Cylinder

REMOVAL & INSTALLATION

▶ See Figures 9, 10, 11 and 12

➡ Be careful not to spill brake fluid on the painted surfaces of the vehicle; it will damage the paint.

1. Unfasten the hydraulic lines from the master cylinder.

2. Detach the hydraulic fluid pressure differential switch wiring connectors. Disconnect the fluid level sensor wiring connectors, if necessary.

3. Loosen the master cylinder reservoir mounting bolt.

4. Then, do one of the following:

    a. On models with manual brakes remove the master cylinder securing bolts and remove the clevis pin from the brake pedal. Remove the master cylinder.

    b. On models with power brakes, unfasten the nuts and remove the master cylinder assembly from the power brake unit (vacuum booster).

To install:

5. Before tightening the master cylinder mounting nuts or bolts, screw the hydraulic line into the cylinder body a few turns by hand-NEVER use a wrench to start threads.

Fig. 9 Removing the brake line from the master cylinder assembly

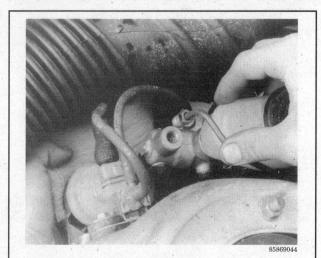

Fig. 10 View of the line removed from the master cylinder

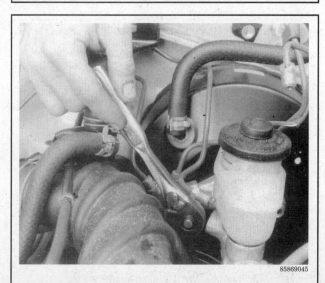

Fig. 11 Removing the master cylinder mounting bolts

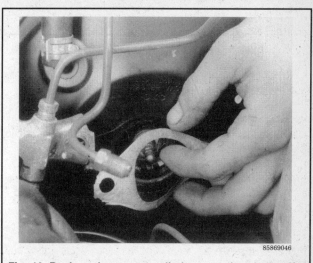

Fig. 12 Replace the master cylinder mounting gasket if necessary

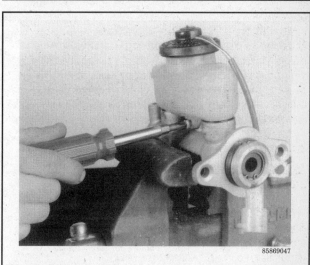

Fig. 13 Remove the master cylinder reservoir assembly retaining screw

6. After installation is completed, bleed the master cylinder and the brake system as outlined later in this section.

➡When replacing the the master cylinder it is best to BENCH BLEED the master cylinder before installing it to the vehicle. Mount the master cylinder into a soft jawed vise or suitable equivalent (do not damage the cylinder). Fill the cylinder to the correct level with new DOT 3 type brake fluid. Block off all the outer brake line holes but one, then position a long wooden dowel in the bore to actuate the brake master cylinder. Pump the brake master cylinder 3 or 4 times (push in and out with the dowel) until brake fluid is released and no air is in the brake fluid. Repeat this procedure until all brake fluid is released from every hole and no air is expelled.

OVERHAUL

▶ **See Figures 13, 14, 15, 16, 17, 18, 19, 20, 21, 22 and 23**

1. Remove the reservoir caps and floats. Unscrew the bolts which secure the reservoirs to the main body.

2. Remove the pressure differential warning switch assembly. Then, working from the rear of the cylinder, remove the boot, snapring, stop washer, piston No. 1, spacer, cylinder cup, spring retainer, and spring, in that order.

3. Remove the end-plug and gasket from the front of the cylinder, then remove the front piston stop bolt from underneath. Pull out the spring, retainer, piston No. 2, spacer, and the cylinder cup.

4. Remove the two outlet fittings, washers, check valves and springs.

5. Only remove the piston cups from their seats if they are to be replaced.

6. After washing all parts in clean brake fluid, dry them with compressed air if available or allow them to air dry. Inspect

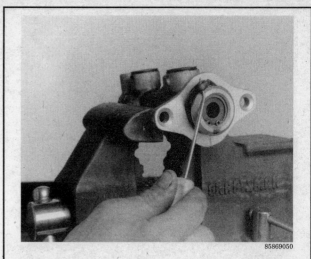

Fig. 16 Remove the master cylinder rubber mounting seal

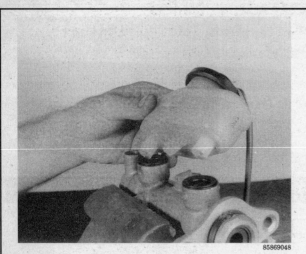

Fig. 14 With the bolt removed separate the reservoir from the master cylinder assembly

Fig. 17 Remove the piston snapring using a suitable pair of snapring pliers

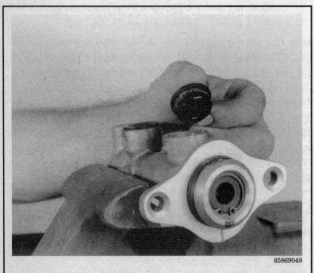

Fig. 15 Remove the master cylinder reservoir grommet

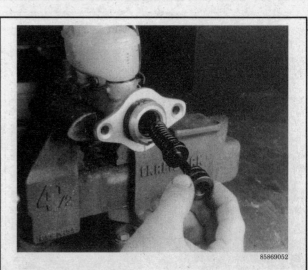

Fig. 18 Withdraw the No. 1 piston assembly from the bore

Fig. 19 Remove piston stopper bolt with a suitable driver

the cylinder bore for wear, scuff marks, or nicks. Cylinders may be hones slightly, but the limit if 0.006 inch (0.15mm) In view of the importance of the master cylinder, it is recommended that it be replaced, rather than overhauled, if worn or damaged.

7. Assembly is performed in the reverse order of disassembly. Absolute cleanliness is imperative. Coat all parts with clean brake fluid prior to assembly.

8. Bleed the hydraulic system and the master cylinder.

Proportioning Valve

A proportioning valve is used on all models to reduce the hydraulic pressure to the rear brakes because of weight transfer during high speed stops. This helps to keep the rear brakes from locking up by improving front-to-rear brake balance. The proportioning valve is located in the engine compartment, near the master cylinder.

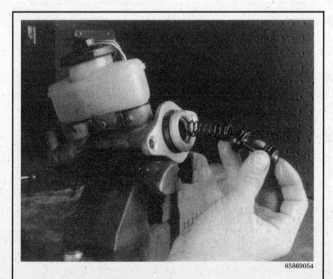

Fig. 20 Withdraw the No. 2 piston assembly

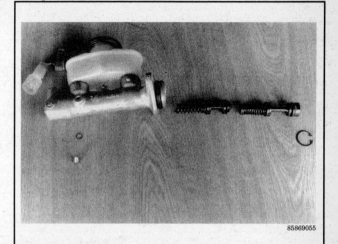

Fig. 21 Exploded view of the master cylinder assembly — most models similar

REMOVAL & INSTALLATION

1. Disconnect the brake lines from the valve unions.
2. Unfasten the valve mounting bolt, if used.
3. Remove the proportioning valve assembly.

➡**If the proportioning valve is defective, it must be replaced as an assembly; it cannot be rebuilt.**

4. Installation is the reverse of removal. Bleed the brake system after it is completed.

Vacuum Booster

➡**Vacuum boosters can be found only on models equipped with power brakes.**

REMOVAL & INSTALLATION

1. Remove the master cylinder as previously detailed.
2. Locate the clevis rod where it attaches to the brake pedal. Pull out the clip and then remove the clevis pin.
3. Disconnect the vacuum hose from the booster.
4. Loosen the four nuts and then pull out the vacuum booster, the bracket and the gasket.
5. Installation is in the reverse order of removal.

OVERHAUL

Asian Type
▶ **See Figure 24**

1. Unscrew the nut at the front of the booster and remove the pushrod.
2. Loosen the retaining nut and then unscrew the clevis.
3. Pull off the rubber boot.
4. Pry out the air filter retainer from around the back of the booster and then remove the three filter elements.

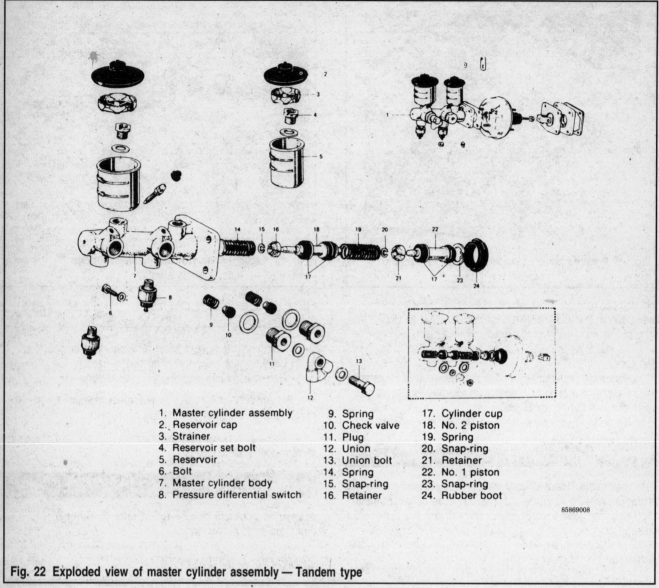

1. Master cylinder assembly
2. Reservoir cap
3. Strainer
4. Reservoir set bolt
5. Reservoir
6. Bolt
7. Master cylinder body
8. Pressure differential switch
9. Spring
10. Check valve
11. Plug
12. Union
13. Union bolt
14. Spring
15. Snap-ring
16. Retainer
17. Cylinder cup
18. No. 2 piston
19. Spring
20. Snap-ring
21. Retainer
22. No. 1 piston
23. Snap-ring
24. Rubber boot

85869008

Fig. 22 Exploded view of master cylinder assembly — Tandem type

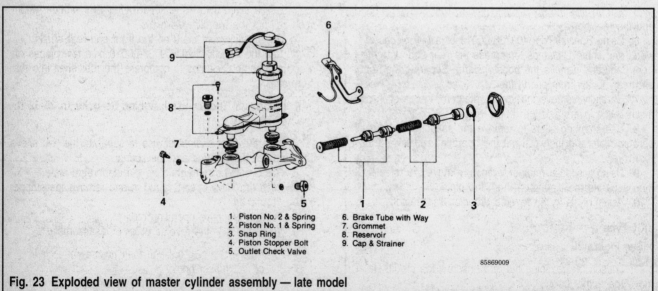

1. Piston No. 2 & Spring
2. Piston No. 1 & Spring
3. Snap Ring
4. Piston Stopper Bolt
5. Outlet Check Valve
6. Brake Tube with Way
7. Grommet
8. Reservoir
9. Cap & Strainer

85869009

Fig. 23 Exploded view of master cylinder assembly — late model

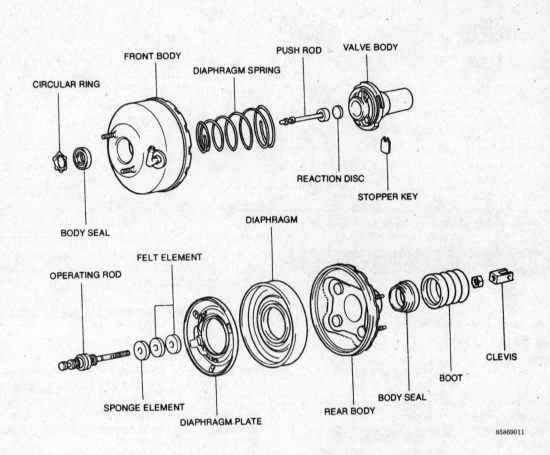

Fig. 24 Exploded view of the vacuum booster assembly — ASIAN type

5. Put an alignment mark across the front body, the band and the rear body.

6. Using Special Tool #09738-00010 or a few pieces of wood and some C-clamps, compress the rear body into the front body and remove the booster band. Separate the front and rear bodies from each other.

7. Carefully, remove the spring retainers, the reaction plate, the reaction levers and the rubber ring.

8. Use snapring pliers to remove the snapring in the diaphragm plate and then pull out the operating rod toward the rear.

9. Using a special retainer wrench, remove the retainer and then separate the diaphragm from the plate.

10. Assembly is in the reverse order of disassembly.

JKK Type

▶ See Figure 25

1. Loosen the retaining nut and unscrew the clevis. Remove the rubber boot.

2. Use a screwdriver to remove the air filter retainer and then pull out the two filter elements.

3. Put an alignment mark on the front and rear shells.

4. Use the Special Tool #09738-00010 or a few pieces of wood and some C-clamps to compress the rear shell into the front shell.

➡**If the Special Tool is used, tighten its bolts to 35-52 ft. lbs. (47-70 Nm).**

5. Turn the front shell clockwise to separate the two shells, then remove the pushrod and the spring.

6. Remove the diaphragm from the diaphragm plate.

7. Push the valve operating rod in and remove the stopper key.

8. Pull out the valve operating rod.

9. Assembly is in the reverse order of disassembly.

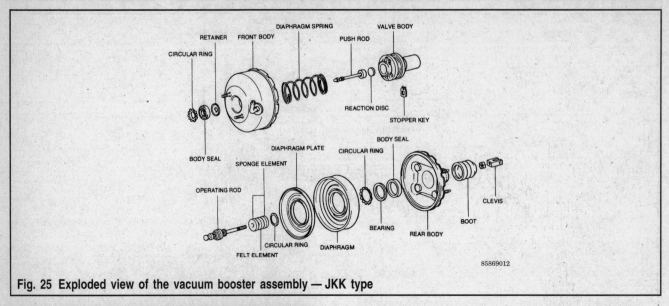

Fig. 25 Exploded view of the vacuum booster assembly — JKK type

Brake Hoses

INSPECTION

1. Inspect the lines and hoses in a well lighted area. Use a small mirror to help see concealed parts of the hose or line. Check the entire length and circumference of each line or hose.

2. Look for any sign of wear, deformation, corrosion, cracking, bends, swelling or thread damage.

3. The slightest sign of leakage requires IMMEDIATE ATTENTION.

4. Check all clamps for tightness and check that all lines and hoses have sufficient clearance from moving parts and heat sources.

5. Check that any lines passing through grommets pass through the center of the grommet and are not forced against the side of the hole. Relieve any excess tension.

6. Some metal lines may contain spring-like coils. These coils absorb vibration and prevent the line from cracking under strain. Do not attempt to straighten the coils or change their diameter.

REMOVAL AND INSTALLATION

1. Elevate and safely support the vehicle.
2. Remove the wheel.
3. Clean all dirt from the hose junctions.
4. Place a catch pan under the hose area.
5. Using 2 wrenches one should be line or flare wrench, disconnect the flexible hose from the steel brake line at the strut assembly.

➡When disconnecting a brake line fitting always use 2 wrenches (one should hold brake line and flare/line wrench used to loosen fitting) to prevent damage to the fitting or brake line.

6. If equipped with disc brakes, disconnect the brake hose union bolt at the brake caliper. If equipped with drum brakes, disconnect the hose from the steel pipe running to the wheel cylinder.

7. Remove the hose retaining clips and remove the hose from the vehicle.

8. If the system is to remain disconnected for more than the time it takes to swap hoses, tape or plug the lines and caliper to prevent dirt and moisture from entering the system.

9. Install the new brake hose into the retaining clips.

10. Connect the hose to the caliper (disc brakes) and tighten the union bolt to 22 ft. lbs. (30 Nm) or connect the hose to the short line running into the wheel cylinder and tighten the fitting to 11 ft. lbs. (15 Nm).

11. Connect the steel brake line to the hose at the strut. Start the threads by hand and make sure the joint is properly threaded before tightening. Tighten the fitting to 11 ft. lbs. (15 Nm).

12. Install the wheel. Bleed the brake system. Refer to the necessary service procedures.

13. Lower the car to the ground.

Bleeding the Brake System

▶ **See Figures 26 and 27**

It is necessary to bleed the hydraulic system any time the system has been opened or air has been trapped within the fluid lines. It may be necessary to bleed the system at all four brakes if air has been introduced through a low fluid level or by disconnecting brake pipes at the master cylinder.

If a line is disconnected at one wheel only, generally only that brake needs bleeding. If lines are disconnected at any fitting between the master cylinder and the brake, the system served by the disconnected pipe must be bled.

➡Do not allow brake fluid to splash or spill onto painted surfaces; the paint will be damaged. If spillage occurs, flush the area immediately with plenty of clean water.

1. Fill the master cylinder reservoir to the "MAX" line with brake fluid and keep it full throughout the bleeding procedure.

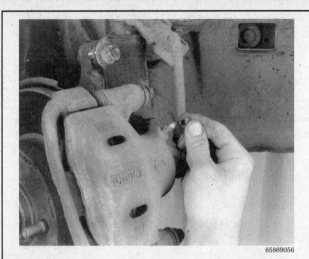

Fig. 26 Remove the bleeder cap on the brake caliper before opening bleeder valve

Fig. 27 Bleeding the front brake caliper

2. If the master cylinder has been removed or disconnected, it must be bled before any brake unit is bled. To bleed the master cylinder:

a. Disconnect the front brake line from the master cylinder and allow fluid to flow from the front connector port.

b. Reconnect the line to the master cylinder and tighten it until it is fluid tight.

c. Have a helper press the brake pedal down one time and hold it down.

d. Loosen the front brake line connection at the master cylinder. This will allow trapped air to escape, along with some fluid.

e. Tighten the line, then release the pedal slowly and repeat the sequence (steps c d e) until only fluid runs from the port. No air bubbles should be present in the fluid.

f. Finally, tighten the line fitting at the master cylinder.

g. After all the air has been bled from the front connection, bleed the master cylinder at the rear connection by repeating all procedure steps.

3. Once the master cylinder has been bleed-the individual wheel cylinders and calipers may be bleed as follows:

a. Place the correct size box-end or line wrench over the bleeder valve and attach a tight-fitting transparent hose over the bleeder. Allow the tube to hang submerged in a transparent container of clean brake fluid. The fluid must remain above the end of the hose at all times, otherwise the system may ingest air instead of fluid.

b. Have an assistant pump the brake pedal several times slowly and hold it down.

c. Slowly unscrew the bleeder valve ($\frac{1}{2}$ turn is usually enough). After the initial rush of air and fluid, have the assistant slowly release the brake pedal. When the pedal is released, tighten the bleeder.

d. Repeat steps until no air bubbles are seen in the hose or container. If air is constantly appearing after repeated bleedings, the system must be examined for the source of the leak or loose fitting.

➡**If the entire system must be bled, begin with the right rear, then the left front, left rear and right front brake in that order. After each brake is bled, check and top off the fluid level in the reservoir. Do not reuse brake fluid which has been bled from the brake system.**

4. After bleeding, check the pedal for sponginess feel. Repeat the bleeding procedure and check brake adjustment, if necessary.

FRONT DISC BRAKES

Disc Brake Pads

✳✳CAUTION

Brake pads and shoes may contain asbestos, which has been determined to be a cancer causing agent. Never clean the brake surfaces with compressed air! Avoid inhaling any dust from brake surfaces! When cleaning brakes, use commercially available brake cleaning fluids.

INSPECTION

▸ See Figure 28

For proper inspection, the disc brake caliper and the brake pads themselves must be removed. Some later models may have an inspection hole in the brake caliper, but this allows only a small portion of the pads to be seen.

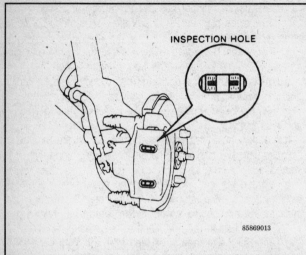

Fig. 28 Front disc brake caliper inspection hole — late models

WEAR INDICATORS

▶ **See Figure 29**

The front disc brake pads are equipped with a metal tab which will come into contact with the disc after the friction surface material has worn near its usable minimum. The wear indicators make a constant, distinct metallic sound that should be easily heard. The sound has been described as similar to fingernails on a blackboard or a field full of crickets. The key to recognizing that it is the wear indicators and not some other brake noise is that the sound is heard when the car is being driven WITHOUT the brakes applied. It may or may not be present under braking but is heard during normal driving.

It should also be noted that any disc brake system, by its design, cannot be made to work silently under all conditions. Each system includes various shims, plates, cushions and brackets to suppress brake noise but no system can completely silence all noises. Some brake noise either high or low

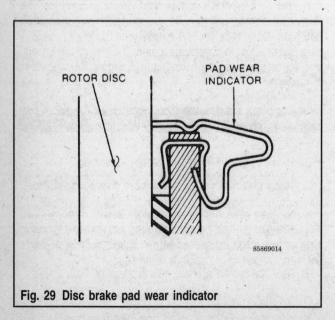

Fig. 29 Disc brake pad wear indicator

frequency can be considered normal under most conditions. Such noises can be controlled and perhaps lessened, but cannot be totally eliminated.

REMOVAL & INSTALLATION

➡ **We recommend replacement of the disc brake pads in axle sets for added safety and reliability.**

Rear Wheel Drive
▶ **See Figure 30**

1970-79 MODELS

1. Raise and support the front of the vehicle on jackstands. Remove the front wheel.
2. Siphon a sufficient quantity of brake fluid from the master cylinder reservoir to prevent the brake fluid from overflowing when removing or installing pads. This is necessary as the piston must be forced into the cylinder bore to provide sufficient clearance to remove the pads.
3. Remove the four clips that hold the caliper guides in position.
4. Lightly tap out the guides (keys). Remember the correct positioning.
5. Lift the caliper off of the mounting bracket. It may be necessary to rock it back and forth a bit in order to seat the piston so it will clear the brake pads. Position the caliper out of the way and support it with wire so it doesn't hang by the brake lines.
6. Remove the brake pads from the mounting bracket. Do not remove the support springs.
7. A support plate is under each pad; they are not interchangeable and must be replaced correctly. Remove the support plates.
8. Inspect the brake disc (rotor) as detailed in the appropriate section.
9. Inspect the caliper and piston assembly for breaks, cracks or other damage. Overhaul or replace the caliper as necessary.

To install:

10. Replace the support plates in their original positions.
11. Place the new pads in the support bracket over the support springs.
12. Push the piston all the way back into its bore (a C-clamp may be necessary for this operation).

➡ **The piston must be turned back into its seated position on certain models. Check piston type before seating.**

13. Position the caliper over the pads and onto the mounting bracket.
14. Install the caliper guides (retaining keys) and then install the guide retaining pins.
15. Refill the master cylinder with fresh brake fluid.
16. Install the tire and wheel assembly. Lower the vehicle, then pump the brake pedal several times to bring the pads into adjustment. Road test the vehicle.

➡ **If a firm pedal cannot be obtained, bleed and adjust the brake system. Do not attempt to move the vehicle until a firm pedal is obtained.**

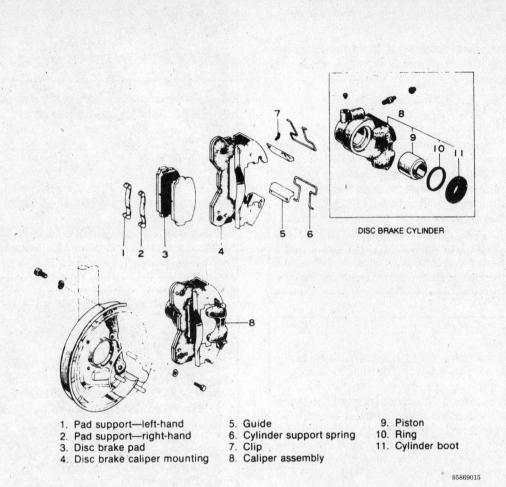

DISC BRAKE CYLINDER

1. Pad support—left-hand
2. Pad support—right-hand
3. Disc brake pad
4. Disc brake caliper mounting
5. Guide
6. Cylinder support spring
7. Clip
8. Caliper assembly
9. Piston
10. Ring
11. Cylinder boot

85869015

Fig. 30 Exploded view of the front disc brake assembly with guide plates — 1970-79 models

1980 AND LATER MODELS

▶ **See Figures 31, 32, 33, 34, 35, 36, 37, 38, 39, 40 and 41**

1. Raise and support the front of the vehicle on jackstands. Remove the wheel.

2. Siphon a sufficient quantity of brake fluid from the master cylinder reservoir to prevent the brake fluid from overflowing when removing or installing the brake pads. This is necessary as the piston must be forced into the cylinder bore to provide sufficient clearance to remove the pads.

3. Compress the piston in the caliper assembly if necessary.

4. Remove the lower guide bolt. Swing the caliper upward and install a bolt into the torque plate to secure the caliper.

5. Lift out the brake pads and anti-squeal shims.

6. Remove the anti-rattle springs, pad guide plate and support plate.

7. Check the brake disc (rotor) as detailed later in section.

8. Examine the dust boot for cracks or damage, then carefully push piston back into the cylinder bore. Use a C-clamp or other suitable tool to bottom the piston. If the piston is frozen, or if the caliper is leaking hydraulic fluid, it must be overhauled or replaced.

To install:

9. Compress the piston in the caliper assembly. Install new pad support plates, guide plates and anti-rattle springs into the torque plate.

➡**Be careful of the proper installation direction.**

10. Install new pad wear indicator clips onto each pad. Install a new anti-squeal shim onto the backing of the piston side pad, then position the pads into the torque plate.

11. Remove the bolt from the torque plate, swing the caliper into position, insert the guide bolt and tighten it to 14 ft. lbs. (19 Nm).

12. Refill the master cylinder with fresh brake fluid.

13. Install the tire and wheel assembly and then pump the brake pedal several times to bring the pads into adjustment. Road test the vehicle.

➡**If a firm pedal cannot be obtained, bleed and adjust the brake the system. Do not attempt to move the vehicle until a firm pedal is obtained.**

FWD Models

▶ **See Figure 42**

1. Raise and support the front of the vehicle on jackstands. Remove the wheel.

2. Siphon a sufficient quantity of brake fluid from the master cylinder reservoir to prevent the brake fluid from overflowing the master cylinder when removing or installing the brake pads. This is necessary as the piston must be forced into the cylinder bore to provide sufficient clearance to remove the pads.

3. Remove the two caliper mounting bolts and then remove the caliper from the torque plate. It may be necessary to rock

Fig. 33 View of the front disc brake system

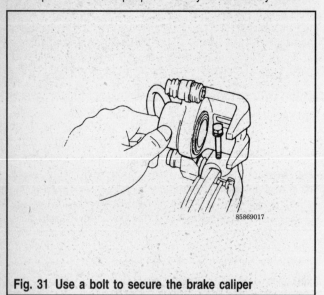

Fig. 31 Use a bolt to secure the brake caliper

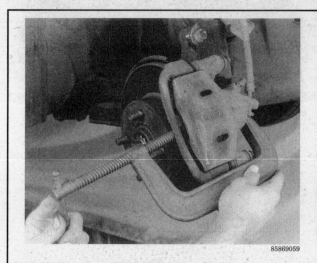

Fig. 34 Compress the front brake caliper using a C-clamp

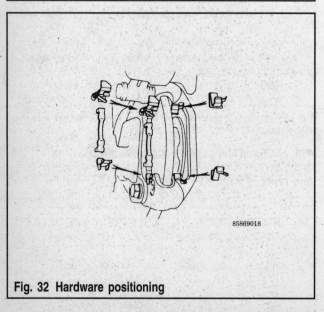

Fig. 32 Hardware positioning

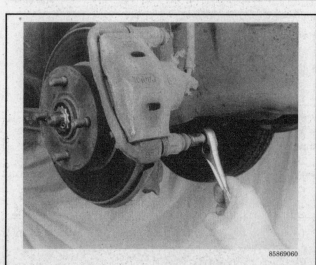

Fig. 35 Remove the lower retaining bolt or pin of the brake caliper

Fig. 36 Swing the brake caliper upward to remove the brake pads

Fig. 37 Remove the outer brake pads

Fig. 38 Remove the inner brake pads

Fig. 39 Remove the brake pad support plate (brake hardware) keep one side together for quick reference upon installation

the caliper back and forth a bit in order to seat the piston so it will clear the brake pads. Position the caliper out of the way and support it with wire so it doesn't hang by the brake line.

4. Remove the two anti-squeal springs, then lift out the brake pads and the anti-squeal shims.

5. Remove the four pad support plates.

6. Check the brake disc (rotor) as detailed in the appropriate section.

7. Examine the dust boot for cracks or damage, then carefully push the piston back into the cylinder bore. Use a C-clamp or other suitable tool to bottom the piston. If the piston is frozen, or if the caliper is leaking hydraulic fluid, the caliper must be overhauled or replaced.

To install:

8. Install four new pad support plates into the torque plate.

9. Install new pad wear indicator clips onto each pad. Install new anti-squeal shims onto the backing of each pad, then position the pads into the torque plate.

➡**Make sure that the arrow on the pad wear indicator clip is pointing in the direction of rotor rotation when the pad is installed into the torque plate.**

10. Install the two anti-squeal springs.

11. Position the caliper on the torque plate, insert the mounting bolts and tighten them to 18 ft. lbs. (24 Nm).

12. Refill the master cylinder with fresh brake fluid.

13. Install the tire and wheel assembly. Lower the vehicle, then pump the brake pedal several times to bring the pads into adjustment. Road test the vehicle.

➡**If a firm pedal cannot be obtained, bleed and adjust the brake system. Do not attempt to move the vehicle until a firm pedal is obtained.**

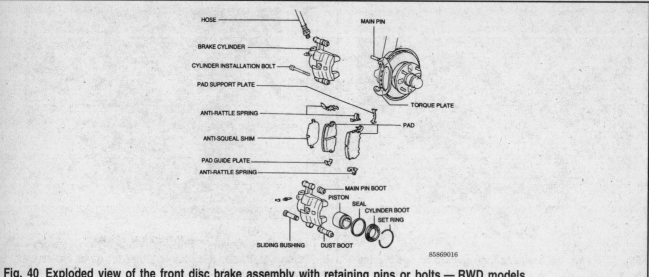

Fig. 40 Exploded view of the front disc brake assembly with retaining pins or bolts — RWD models

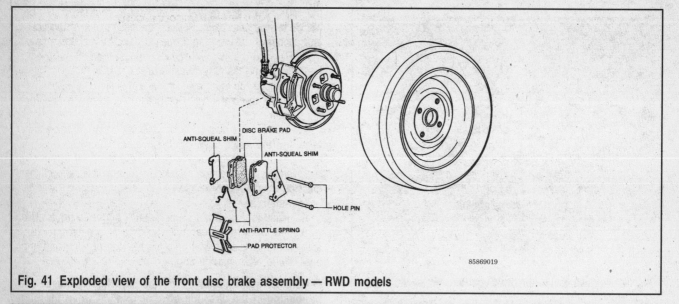

Fig. 41 Exploded view of the front disc brake assembly — RWD models

Disc Brake Caliper

REMOVAL

▶ **See Figures 43, 44, 45 and 46**

➡**We recommend replacement of the disc brake calipers in axle sets for added safety and reliability.**

1. Raise and safely support the front of the vehicle on jackstands. Set the parking brake and block the rear wheels.
2. Siphon a sufficient quantity of brake fluid from the master cylinder reservoir in order the brake fluid from overflowing when removing or installing the calipers. This is necessary as the piston must be forced into the cylinder bore to provide sufficient clearance to install the caliper.

➡**Disassemble brakes one wheel at a time. This will prevent parts confusion and also prevent the opposite caliper piston from popping out during installation.**

3. Disconnect the hose union at the caliper. Use a pan to catch any spilled fluid and immediately plug the disconnected hose.
4. Remove the two caliper mounting bolts or guide plates, then remove the caliper from the mounting bracket.

OVERHAUL

▶ **See Figures 47, 48, 49, 50, 51, 52, 53 and 54**

1. On some early models you must first remove the two bridge bolts in order to split the caliper halves.
2. Carefully remove the dust boot from around the cylinder bore.
3. Apply compressed air to the brake line union to force the piston out of its bore. Place a rag or block of wood to protect the piston. Be careful, the piston may come out forcefully.

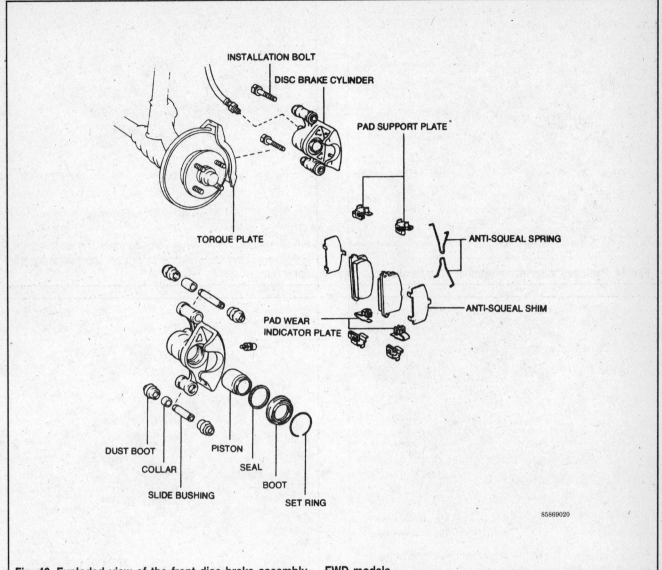

INSTALLATION BOLT

DISC BRAKE CYLINDER

PAD SUPPORT PLATE

TORQUE PLATE

ANTI-SQUEAL SPRING

ANTI-SQUEAL SHIM

PAD WEAR
INDICATOR PLATE

DUST BOOT   PISTON

COLLAR   SEAL

SLIDE BUSHING   BOOT

SET RING

85869020

Fig. 42 Exploded view of the front disc brake assembly — FWD models

85869065

Fig. 43 Clean the brake hose union at the caliper before removal

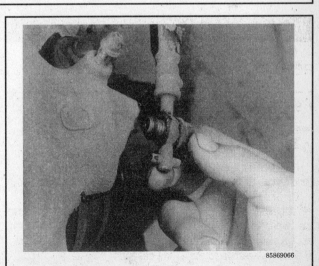

85869066

Fig. 44 Remove the brake hose union at the brake caliper assembly

Fig. 45 Remove the caliper assembly from the vehicle

Fig. 46 After the brake caliper is removed check the torque plate retaining bolts

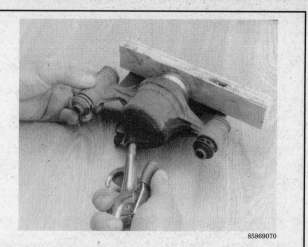

Fig. 47 Compressed air is used to force the piston from the bore — note the wood is to protect the piston from damage

Fig. 48 Remove the piston from brake caliper

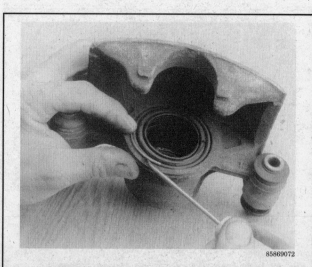

Fig. 49 With a small tool carefully remove the set ring from the brake caliper

4. Remove the seal from the piston. Check the piston and cylinder bore for wear and/or corrosion. Replace components as necessary.

Assembly is performed in the following order:

5. Coat all components with clean brake fluid.

6. Install the seal and piston in the cylinder bore, after coating them with the rubber lubricant supplied in the rebuilding kit. Seat the piston in the bore with your fingers.

7. Fit the boot into the groove in the cylinder bore.

8. Install the caliper cylinder assembly.

INSTALLATION

1. Use a caliper compressor, a C-clamp or large pair of pliers to slowly press the caliper piston back into the caliper.

2. Install the caliper assembly to the mounting plate. Before installing the retaining bolts or guide plates, apply a thin, even coating of anti-seize compound to the threads and slide surfaces. Don't use grease or spray lubricants; they will not hold

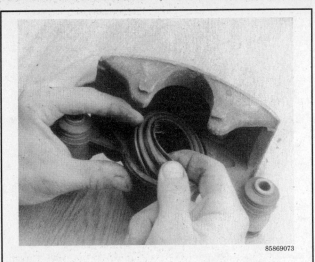

Fig. 50 After removing the set ring remove the dust boot

Fig. 51 With the piston removed check the cylinder bore for wear

Fig. 52 With a small tool remove the seal from the brake caliper

Fig. 53 After piston is removed always replace this seal upon installation

Fig. 54 Exploded view of the brake caliper assembly

up under the extreme temperatures generated by the brakes. Tighten the bolts.

3. Install the brake hose to the caliper. Always use a new gasket and tighten the union to about 17 ft. lbs. (23 Nm).

4. Bleed the brake system.

5. Remove the 2 lugs holding the disc in place and install the wheel.

6. Lower the vehicle to the ground. Check the level of the brake fluid in the master cylinder reservoir; it should be at least to the middle of the reservoir.

➡If a firm pedal cannot be obtained, bleed and adjust the brake system. Do not attempt to move the vehicle until a firm pedal is obtained.

Brake Disc

REMOVAL & INSTALLATION

▶ See Figures 55, 56 and 57

➡ If necessary, check the disc runout. Front wheels bearings must be adjusted properly before runout check is made. Refer to Brake Specifications Chart in this section.

➡ We recommend replacement of the brake disc in axle sets for added safety and reliability.

1. Remove the brake pads and the brake caliper, as detailed earlier in this section.
2. Loosen the bolts which secure the caliper mounting bracket. Remove the torque plate or caliper mounting bracket.
3. On RWD models, remove the grease cap from the hub. Remove the cotter pin and the castellated nut. Remove the wheel hub with the brake disc attached. Remove the disc from the brake hub assembly.
4. On the FWD models, simply remove the disc from the axle hub.
5. Perform the disc inspection procedure, as outlined in the following section.
To install:
6. On RWD models, coat the hub oil seal lip with multipurpose grease and install the disc/hub assembly. Adjust the wheel bearing preload — Refer to Section 8.
7. On FWD models install the brake disc on the axle hub assembly.
8. Install the caliper bracket or torque plate. Install the brake caliper assembly.
9. Bleed the brake system.

➡ If a firm pedal cannot be obtained, bleed and adjust the brake system. Do not attempt to move the vehicle until a firm pedal is obtained.

INSPECTION

▶ See Figures 58 and 59

Examine the disc. If it is worn, warped or scored, it must be replaced. Check the thickness of the disc against specifications — refer to brake Specification Chart in this section. If it is below specifications, replace it. Use a micrometer to measure the thickness.

Fig. 55 Removing the brake rotor — all models similar

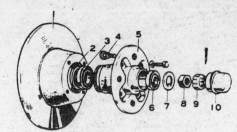

1. Disc
2. Oil seal
3. Tapered roller bearing
4. Hub bolt
5. Hub
6. Tapered roller bearing
7. Washer
8. Nut
9. Adjusting lock cap
10. Grease cap

Fig. 56 Brake disc assembly — 1970-79 models

The disc runout should be measured before the disc is removed and again, after the disc is installed. Use a dial indicator mounted on a stand to determine runout. If runout exceeds 0.006 inch (0.15mm), replace the disc.

➡ Be sure that the wheel bearing nut is properly tightened. If it is not, an inaccurate runout reading may be obtained.

REAR DRUM BRAKES

Brake Drums

✳✳CAUTION

Brake pads and shoes may contain asbestos, which has been determined to be a cancer causing agent. Never clean the brake surfaces with compressed air! Avoid inhaling any dust from brake surfaces! When cleaning brakes, use commercially available brake cleaning fluids.

REMOVAL & INSTALLATION

▶ See Figures 60 and 61

➡ We recommend replacement of the brake drums in axle sets for added safety and reliability.

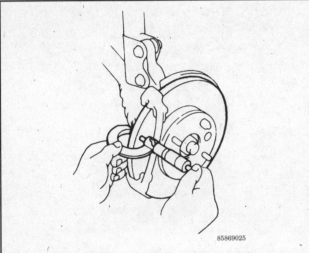

Fig. 58 Never use a rotor which is below minimum thickness

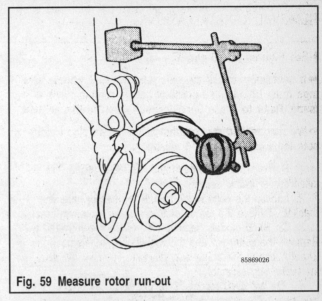

Fig. 59 Measure rotor run-out

1. Remove the hub cap (if used) and loosen the lug nuts. Release the parking brake.
2. Block the front wheels, raise the rear of the car, and support it with jackstands.

✳✳CAUTION

Support the car securely.

3. Remove the lug nuts and the wheel.
4. Remove the brake drum retaining screws, if equipped.
5. Remove the brake drum. Tap the drum lightly with a rubber mallet in order to free it. If the drum cannot be removed easily, insert a tool into the backing plate hole and hold the automatic adjusting lever away from the adjusting bolt. Using another tool relieve the brake shoe tension by turning the adjusting bolt clockwise. If the drum still will not come off,

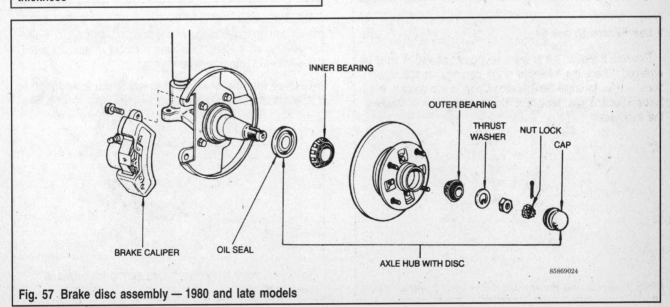

Fig. 57 Brake disc assembly — 1980 and late models

use a puller; but first make sure that the parking brake is released.

➡**Don't depress the brake pedal once the drum has been removed.**

6. Inspect the brake drum.

7. Brake drum installation is performed in the reverse order of removal.

INSPECTION

1. Clean the drum.

2. Inspect the drum for scoring, cracks, grooves and out-of-roundness. Replace or turn the drum, as required.

3. Light scoring may be removed by dressing the drum with fine emery cloth.

4. Heavy scoring will require the use of a brake drum lathe (refer to a local machine shop) to turn the drum.

Brake Shoes

▶ **See Figures 62, 63, 64, 65, 66, 67, 68 and 69**

✳✳CAUTION

Brake pads and shoes may contain asbestos, which has been determined to be a cancer causing agent. Never clean the brake surfaces with compressed air! Avoid inhaling any dust from brake surfaces! When cleaning brakes, use commercially available brake cleaning fluids.

INSPECTION

▶ **See Figure 70**

An inspection hole is provided in the backing plate of each rear wheel which allows the brakes to be checked without removing the drum. Remove the hole plug and check the lining

Fig. 60 Remove the tire to remove the brake drum from the vehicle

85869078

Fig. 62 Clean the drum brake components before removal

85869080

Fig. 61 Removing the brake drum — all models similar

85869079

Fig. 63 Remove the brake return spring with special brake tool

85869081

Fig. 64 Using the special type brake spring hold-down tool remove the hold-down spring washer

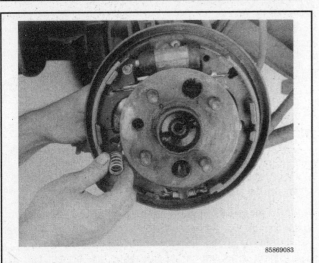

Fig. 65 After removing the hold-down spring washer remove the brake hold-down spring

Fig. 66 Remove the inner brake hold-down spring washer

Fig. 67 Remove the rear brake shoe with brake hardware still attached

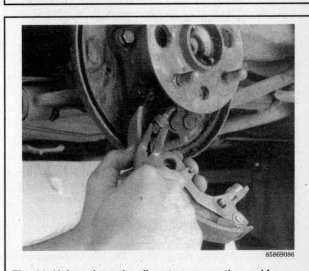

Fig. 68 Using vise grip pliers to remove the parking brake-to-brake shoe spring

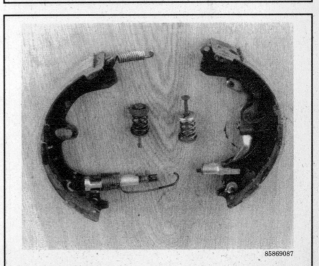

Fig. 69 Exploded view of brake shoes and hardware — most models similar

thickness through the hole. If below minimum, the shoes will need replacement. Always replace the plug after checking, making certain it is properly seated and tight.

It should be obvious that this method doesn't provide a lot of information about how the brakes are wearing since it only shows one part of one shoe, but is a quick and easy first check. The only way to see the friction faces of the shoes is to remove the brake drums. No generalities can be drawn between the left and right side shoes, so both drums must be removed to perform a proper inspection.

With the drums removed:

1. Liberally spray the entire brake assembly with an evaporative brake cleaner. Do not use other solvents, compressed air or a dry brush.

2. Measure the thickness of the friction surface on each shoe at several different locations. If any measurement is below the minimum thickness, replace all the shoes as a set. Refer to Brake Specifications Chart in this section.

3. Check the contact surfaces closely for any signs of scoring, cracking, uneven or tapered wear, discoloration or separation from the backing plate. Anything that looks unusual requires replacement.

4. If the shoes are in otherwise good condition except for glazing (a shiny, hard surface), the glaze may be removed by light sanding with emery cloth. Also lightly sand the inside of the drum to de-glaze its surface. Do not attempt to rub out grooves or ridges; this is best done with a resurfacing lathe. After sanding the components wash them thoroughly with aerosol brake cleaner to remove any grit.

REMOVAL & INSTALLATION

▶ **See Figures 71, 72, 73, 74 and 75**

➡The brake shoes can be removed and replaced using everyday hand tools, but the use of brake spring tools and assorted specialty tools makes the job much easier. These common brake tools are available at low cost and can greatly reduce working time. Record the location of all brake hardware (spring etc.) before starting this service

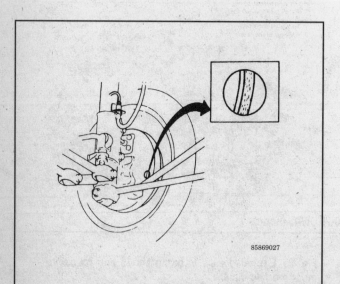

85869027

Fig. 70 Rear brake shoe inspection hole — most models

procedure. Work on one side at a time, so that the other side may be used as guide. Do not apply the brake pedal while the drum is removed.

➡We recommend replacement of the brake shoes in axle sets for added safety and reliability.

1. Perform the Brake Drum Removal procedure as previously detailed.

2. Unhook the shoe tension springs from the shoes with the aid of a brake spring removing tool.

3. Remove the brake shoe securing springs.

4. Disconnect the parking brake cable at the parking brake shoe lever.

5. Withdraw the shoes, complete with the parking brake shoe lever.

6. Unfasten the C-clip and remove the adjuster assembly from the shoes. Inspect the shoes for wear and scoring. Have the linings replaced if their thickness is less than minimum specifications (refer to Brake Specifications chart in this section). Check the tension springs to see if they are weak, distorted or rusted.

7. Inspect the teeth on the automatic adjuster wheel for chipping or other damage.

To install:

➡Grease the point of the shoe which slides against the backing plate. Do not get grease on the linings.

8. Attach the parking brake shoe lever and the automatic adjuster lever to the rear side of the shoe.

9. Fasten the parking brake cable to the lever on the brake shoe.

10. Install the automatic adjuster or strut and fit the tension spring on the adjuster lever.

➡When assembling the rear shoe and the automatic adjuster, check the clearance between the shoe and the lever using a feeler gauge. Clearance should be 0-0.0138 inch (0-0.35mm); if not within specifications, adjustment can be made by replacing the shim on the adjusting lever shaft. Shims are available in 0.04 inch (1mm) increments from 0.008-0.024 inch (0.2-0.6mm). There is also one measuring 0.035 inch (0.8mm). To replace the shim, remove the C-clip, install a shim of the proper thickness and then install a new C-clip.

11. Install the securing spring on the rear shoe and then install the securing the spring on the front shoe.

12. Hold one end of the tension spring over the rear shoe with the tool used during removal; hook the other end over the front shoe. Install all necessary springs

➡Be sure that the wheel cylinder boots are not being pinched in the ends of the shoes.

13. If equipped, test the automatic adjuster by operating the parking brake shoe lever.

14. Install the drum and adjust the brakes as previously detailed.

Wheel Cylinders

If wheel cylinders are leaking or seized, they should be replaced. The units are inexpensive enough to often make

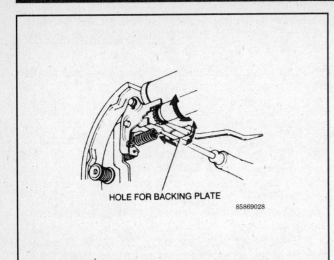

HOLE FOR BACKING PLATE

85869028

Fig. 71 Backing off the brake shoes to remove the brake drum

replacement a better choice than repair. Even if the pistons and seals can be replaced, the internal bore can rarely be restored to perfect condition. A faulty repair can reduce braking effort on the wheel or cause a leak which soaks the brake shoes in fluid.

When inspecting the cylinders on the car, the rubber boots must be lifted carefully and the inner area checked for leaks. A very slight moistness usually coated with dust is normal, but any accumulation of fluid is evidence of a leak and must be dealt with immediately.

REMOVAL & INSTALLATION

➡ **We recommend replacement of the wheel cylinders in axle sets for added safety and reliability.**

1. Remove the brake drums and shoes as detailed earlier in this section.

2. Working from behind the backing plate, disconnect the hydraulic line from the wheel cylinder.

3. Unfasten the screws retaining the wheel cylinder and withdraw the cylinder.

4. Installation is performed in the reverse order of removal.

➡ **However, once the hydraulic line has been disconnected from the wheel cylinder, the union must be replaced on early models. This step is not necessary on newer models.**

5. Replace the seat (only if necessary) in the following manner:

   a. Use a screw extractor with a diameter of 0.1 inch (2.5mm) and having reverse threads, to remove the union seat from the wheel cylinder.

   b. Drive in the new union seat with a $5/16$ inch bar, used as a drift. Remember to bleed the brake system after completing wheel cylinder, brake shoe and drum installation.

OVERHAUL

▶ **See Figures 76, 77, 78, 79 and 80**

➡ **It is not necessary to remove the wheel cylinder from the backing plate if it is only to be inspected or rebuilt.**

1. Remove the brake drum and shoes. Remove the wheel cylinder only if it is going to be replaced.

2. Remove the rubber boots from either end of the wheel cylinder.

3. Withdraw the piston and cup assemblies.

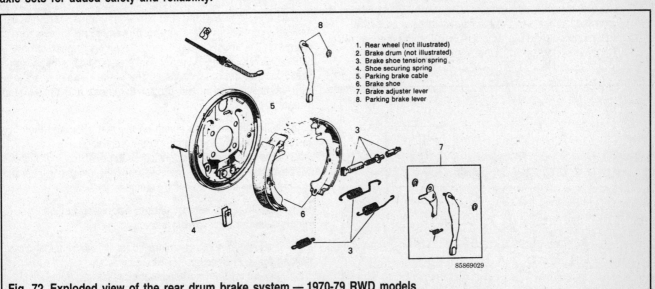

1. Rear wheel (not illustrated)
2. Brake drum (not illustrated)
3. Brake shoe tension spring
4. Shoe securing spring
5. Parking brake cable
6. Brake shoe
7. Brake adjuster lever
8. Parking brake lever

85869029

Fig. 72 Exploded view of the rear drum brake system — 1970-79 RWD models

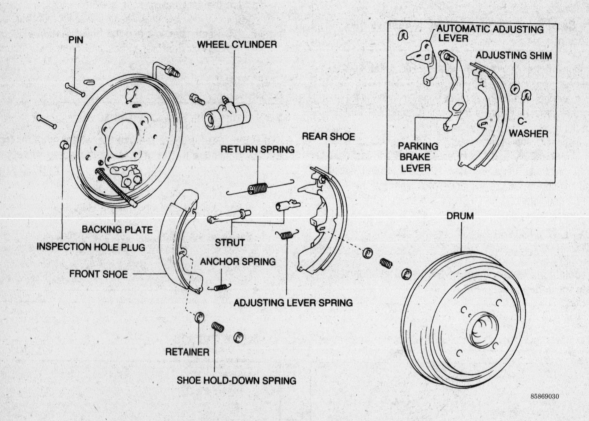

PIN

WHEEL CYLINDER

AUTOMATIC ADJUSTING LEVER

ADJUSTING SHIM

RETURN SPRING

REAR SHOE

C-WASHER

PARKING BRAKE LEVER

BACKING PLATE

DRUM

INSPECTION HOLE PLUG

FRONT SHOE

STRUT

ANCHOR SPRING

ADJUSTING LEVER SPRING

RETAINER

SHOE HOLD-DOWN SPRING

85869030

Fig. 73 Exploded view of the rear drum brake system — FWD models

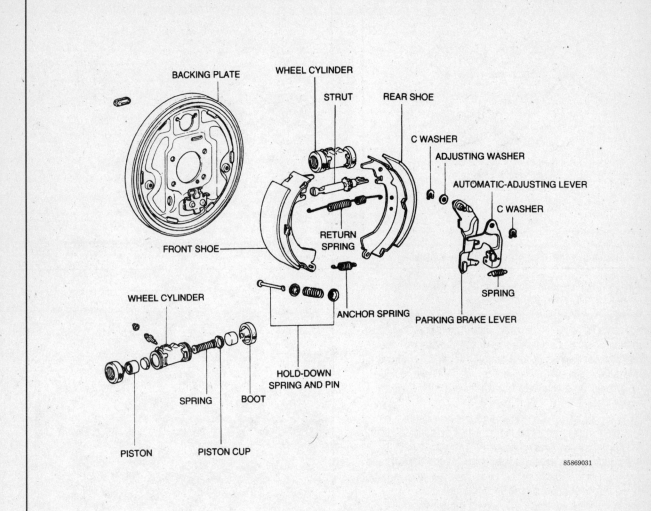

Fig. 74 Exploded view of the rear drum brake system — 1980 and later RWD models

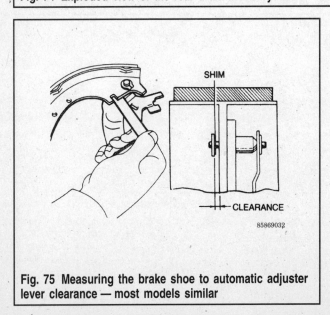

Fig. 75 Measuring the brake shoe to automatic adjuster lever clearance — most models similar

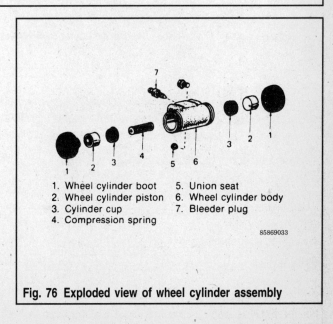

1. Wheel cylinder boot
2. Wheel cylinder piston
3. Cylinder cup
4. Compression spring
5. Union seat
6. Wheel cylinder body
7. Bleeder plug

Fig. 76 Exploded view of wheel cylinder assembly

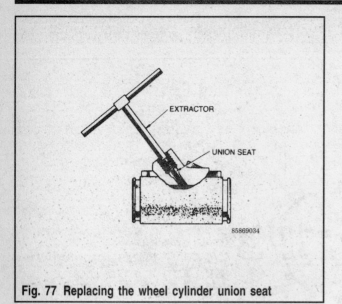

Fig. 77 Replacing the wheel cylinder union seat

4. Take the compression spring out of the wheel cylinder body.

5. Remove the bleeder plug (and ball), if necessary. Check all components for wear or damage. Inspect the bore for signs of wear, scoring and/or scuffing. If in doubt, replace or hone the wheel cylinder (with a special hone). The limit for honing a cylinder is 0.005 inch (0.1mm) oversize. Wash all the residue from the cylinder bore with clean brake fluid and blow dry.

To assemble:

6. Soak all components in clean brake fluid, or coat them with the rubber grease supplied in the wheel cylinder rebuilding kit.

7. Install the spring, cups (recesses toward the center), and pistons in the cylinder body, in that order.

8. Insert the boots over the ends of the cylinder.

9. Install the bleeder plug (and ball), if removed.

10. Assemble the brake shoes and install the drum.

Fig. 78 Remove the rubber dust boot on the wheel cylinder

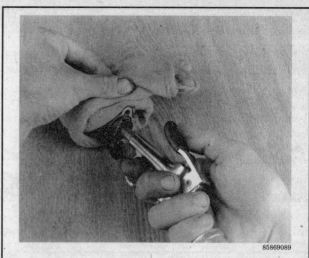

Fig. 79 Use compressed air to gently free the wheel cylinder piston

Fig. 80 Exploded view of the wheel cylinder assembly

REAR DISC BRAKES

✳✳CAUTION

Brake pads and shoes may contain asbestos, which has been determined to be a cancer causing agent. Never clean the brake surfaces with compressed air! Avoid inhaling any dust from brake surfaces! When cleaning brakes, use commercially available brake cleaning fluids.

Brake Pads

INSPECTION

The rear brake pads may be inspected without removal. With the rear end elevated and supported, remove the wheel(s).

View the inner and outer pads through the cut-out in the center of the caliper. Remember to look at the thickness of the pad friction material (the part that actually presses on the disc) rather than the thickness of the backing plate which does not change with wear.

Remember that you are looking at the profile of the pad, not the whole thing. Brake pads can wear on a taper which may not be visible through the window. It is also not possible to check the contact surface for cracking or scoring from this position. This quick check can be helpful only as a reference; detailed inspection requires pad removal.

REMOVAL & INSTALLATION

▶ **See Figures 81, 82, 83, 84 and 85**

➡**We recommend replacement of the disc brake pads in axle sets for added safety and reliability.**

1. Raise and safely support the rear of the vehicle.
2. Remove the wheel and temporarily fasten the rotor in position with the lug nuts.
3. Check the pad thickness by looking through the center hole provided at the top of the caliper. Minimum thickness should be 0.039 inch (1mm).
4. Open the bleeder screw on the caliper and bleed off a small amount of brake fluid.
5. Disconnect the clip that attaches the parking brake cable. Pull the cable from the brake cable bracket at the caliper.
6. Remove the lower (closer to the ground) caliper mounting bolt. Pivot the caliper upward on the upper mounting bolt. Loosen the upper bolt slightly if required.
7. Take note of the position of the brake pads and mounting hardware while removing them. Remove the two brake pads, the two anti-squeal shims, two anti-rattle springs. pad support plate and two pad guide plates. Disassemble and assemble one side at a time so that the other side can be use for reference.

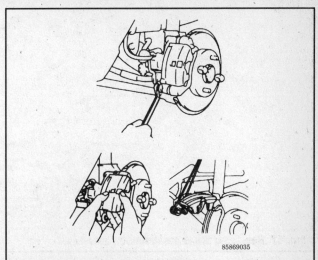

Fig. 81 Correct method of raising the rear caliper for access to the brake pads

To install:

8. Check the rotor thickness and runout. Service as required. Assemble the brake pads in the support bracket in the reverse order of removal.

✳✳WARNING

The caliper piston must be turned clockwise to retract it back into the caliper bore. Special Toyota tool SST 09719-14020 (09719-00020) or the equivalent is required.

➡**Do not attempt to push the caliper into the caliper bore otherwise damage to the parking brake adjuster will occur.**

9. Turn the caliper piston clockwise, back into the caliper bore.
10. Lower the caliper and fit the brake pad protrusion (rear of inner pad) into the stopper groove in the caliper piston. Align as required.
11. Finish lowering the caliper, taking care not to wedge the boot between the metal of the support bracket and caliper. Install the lower mounting bolt, then tighten the mounting bolts to 14 ft. lbs. (19 Nm).
12. Connect the parking brake cable. Adjust the parking brake by pulling and releasing the apply lever.
13. Install the rear wheel. Lower the vehicle. Fill the master cylinder and bleed the brake system.

Caliper

REMOVAL

➡**We recommend replacement of the disc brake caliper in axle sets for added safety and reliability.**

1. Raise and safely support the rear of the vehicle.
2. Remove the wheel.

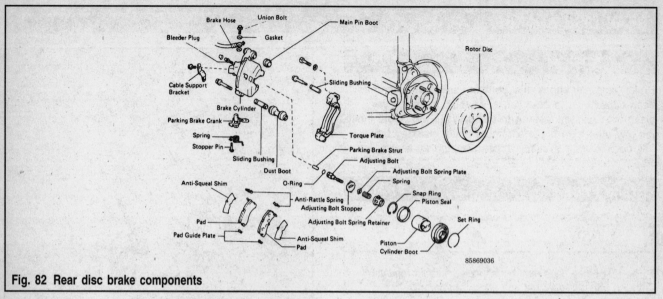

Fig. 82 Rear disc brake components

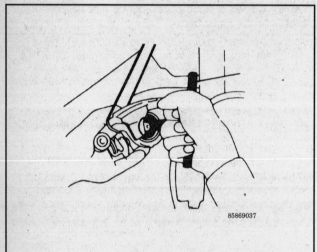

Fig. 83 Using the special tool to retract the rear caliper piston

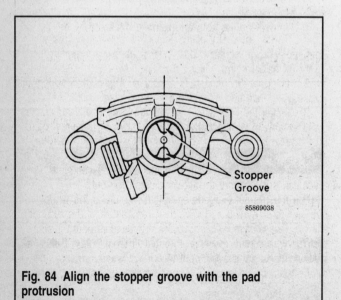

Fig. 84 Align the stopper groove with the pad protrusion

3. Place a suitable container (to catch the brake fluid) under the brake hose to caliper mounting. Disconnect the brake line at the caliper.

4. Remove the brake pads and mounting hardware.

5. Remove the upper mounting bolt and remove the caliper.

OVERHAUL AND INSTALLATION

➡**Modify this service procedure by omitting steps, as necessary**

1. Remove the upper mounting bolt bushing and boot.

2. Remove the piston boot snapring and piston boot.

3. Use the special service tool or equivalent (mentioned in Pad Removal) to turn the caliper COUNTERCLOCKWISE out of the caliper bore.

4. Remove the piston seal from the caliper bore.

➡**Special Service Tool SST 09756-00010, or the equivalent, is required to turn the internal parking brake adjusting nut so that snapring removal is possible.**

5. Position the SST onto the parking brake adjuster nut (bottom of caliper bore) and tighten the nut slightly.

➡**Use the SST or suitable equivalent to ensure that the internally mounted spring will not fly out, causing injury or damage to the caliper bore. DO NOT tighten the adjuster TOO much.**

6. Remove the internal retainer snapring with suitable pliers. Remove the SST.

7. Remove the adjuster spring retainer, spring, spring plate and stopper together with the adjusting bolt.

8. Remove the strut. Remove the torsion spring from the parking brake crank lever.

9. Turn the crank to a position where it will not catch on the stopper pin and remove it from the caliper.

10. Remove the crank boot.

11. Inspect all parts, service as required.

12. Install the parking crank boot into the caliper. Install the parking brake crank and torsion spring.

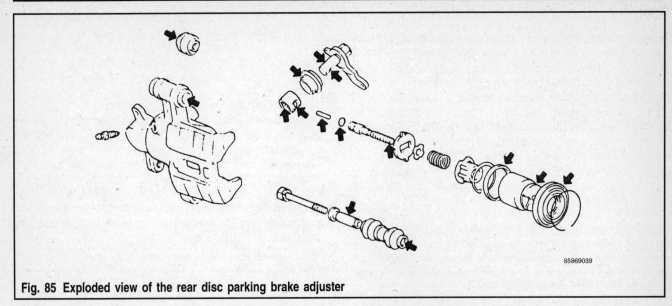

Fig. 85 Exploded view of the rear disc parking brake adjuster

13. Check the clearance of the cable support bracket to caliper. Clearance should be 0.0197-0.0275 inch. (0.5-0.7mm) Adjust the clearance with the cable support mounting bolt.

14. Install the strut into the caliper bore. Adjust the needle bearings so that they will not catch on the hole.

15. Install a new O-ring on the adjuster bolt. Assemble the stopper, washer, spring and spring case to the adjuster bolt. Use the SST and fully tighten down by hand. Position the marked surface of the stopper upward. Align the notches on the spring case with the notches on the stopper.

16. Install the adjuster assembly into the caliper. Install the snapring with the opening in the snapring facing the bleeder hole. Remove the SST. Pull upward on the adjuster assembly and check that it is secured.

17. Move the parking brake lever crank by hand to insure that the adjuster bolt moves smoothly.

18. Install the piston seal in the caliper bore groove.

19. Assemble the piston into the caliper bore by using the SST and slowly screwing in the piston CLOCKWISE. Screw in the piston until it will not descend any further. Align the center of the piston stopper groove with the positioning protrusion on the lower edge of the caliper.

20. Install the piston boot. Install the upper mounting bushing and boot.

21. Install the brake pads and caliper in the reverse order of removal. Tighten the mounting bolts to 14 ft. lbs. (19 Nm). Connect the parking brake cable. Connect the brake hose.

22. Install the wheel and lower the vehicle.

23. Fill the master cylinder reservoir. Adjust the parking brake and bleed the brake system. Check for fluid leakage.

Brake Rotor

REMOVAL

➡️**We recommend replacement of the brake rotor in axle sets for added safety and reliability.**

1. Raise and safely support the rear of the vehicle on jackstands. Block the front wheels.

2. Siphon a sufficient quantity of brake fluid from the master cylinder reservoir to prevent the brake fluid from overflowing when removing or installing the brake pads. This is necessary as the piston must be forced into the cylinder bore to provide sufficient clearance to install the pads.

3. Remove the wheel.

➡️**Disassemble brakes one wheel at a time. This will prevent parts confusion and also prevent the opposite caliper piston from popping out during pad installation.**

4. Remove the brake caliper — refer to the necessary service procedures.

5. If the rotor is to be measured, install all the lug nuts to hold the rotor in place. If the nuts are open at both ends, it is helpful to install them backwards (tapered end out) to secure the disc. Tighten the nuts a bit tighter than finger-tight, but make sure all are at approximately the same torque. Follow the measurement and inspection procedures listed under INSPECTION, in this section.

6. Remove the mounting bolts holding the mounting bracket to the rear axle carrier.

7. Remove the lug nuts and remove the rotor.

INSPECTION

Run-out

1. Mount a dial indicator with a magnetic or universal base on the strut so that the tip of the indicator contacts the rotor about ½ inch (12mm) from the outer edge.

2. Zero the dial indicator. Turn the rotor one complete revolution and observe the total indicated run-out.

3. If the run-out exceeds specifications, clean the wheel hub and rotor mating surfaces, then remeasure. If the run-out still exceeds maximum, remove the rotor and remount it so that the wheel studs now run through different holes. If this re-indexing does not provide correct run-out measurements, the rotor should be considered warped beyond use and either resurfaced or replaced.

Thickness

The thickness of the rotor partially determines its ability to withstand heat and provide adequate stopping force. Every rotor has a minimum thickness established by the manufacturer. This minimum measurement must not be exceeded. A rotor which is too thin may crack under braking; if this occurs the wheel can lock instantly, resulting in sudden loss of control.

If any part of the rotor measures below minimum thickness, the disc must be replaced. Additionally, a rotor which needs to be resurfaced may not allow sufficient cutting before reaching minimum. Since the allowable wear from new to minimum is about 0.04 inch (1mm), it is wise to replace the rotor rather than resurface it.

Thickness and thickness variation can be measured with a micrometer capable of reading to one ten-thousandth of an inch. All measurements must be made at the same distance in from the edge of the rotor. Measure at four equally spaced points around the disc and record the measurements. Compare each measurement to the minimum thickness specifications.

Compare the four measurements to each other and find the difference between each pair. A rotor varying by more than 0.013mm can cause pedal vibration during stops. A rotor which does not meet these specifications should be resurfaced or replaced.

Condition

A new rotor will have a smooth, even surface which rapidly changes during use. It is not uncommon for a rotor to develop very fine concentric scoring (like the grooves on a record) due to dust and grit becoming trapped by the brake pad. This slight irregularity is normal, but as the grooves deepen, wear and noise increase as well as stopping may be affected. As a general rule, any groove deep enough to snag a fingernail during inspection is cause for action or replacement.

Any sign of blue spots, discoloration, heavy rusting or outright gouges require replacement of the rotor. If you are checking the disc on the car (such as during pad replacement or tire rotation) remember to turn the disc and check both the inner and outer faces completely. If anything looks questionable or requires consideration, choose the safer option and replace the rotor. The brakes are a critical system and must be maintained at 100% reliability.

Any time a rotor is replaced, the pads should also be replaced so that the surfaces mate properly. Since brake pads should be replaced in axle sets (both front or both rear wheels), consider replacing both rotors instead of just one. The restored feel and accurate stopping make the extra investment worthwhile.

INSTALLATION

1. Place the rotor in position over the studs and install two lug nuts finger-tight to hold it in place.
2. Install the mounting plate to the rear axle carrier and tighten the mounting bolts.
3. Install the brake caliper assembly.
4. Install the mounting bolt(s) and tighten it to 14 ft. lbs. (19 Nm).
5. Remove the lug nuts holding the disc, install the rear wheel and install all the lug nuts.
6. Depress the brake pedal once or twice to take up the excess piston play.
7. Lower the car to the ground and fill the master cylinder reservoir to the correct level. Final tighten the lug nuts.

PARKING BRAKE

Cables

REMOVAL & INSTALLATION

▶ **See Figure 86**

➡**This procedure should be used as a guide to Parking Cable replacement. You may need to modify or ignore steps, as applicable for your model.**

1. Elevate and safely support the car. If only the rear wheels are elevated, block the front wheels. Release the parking brake after the car is supported.
2. Remove the rear wheel(s).
3. If equipped with drum brakes, remove the brake drum and remove the brake shoes. Then remove the parking brake retaining bolts at the backing plate.
4. If equipped with disc brakes, remove the clip from the parking brake cable and remove the cable from the caliper assembly.
5. Remove any exhaust heat shields which interfere with the removal of the cable.
6. Remove the 2 cable clamps.
7. Disconnect the cable retainer.
8. Remove the cable from the equalizer (yoke).

➡**With the rear cables removed from the equalizer, replacement of the front cable simply requires accessing and releasing the other end of it (on the parking brake lever). Make sure a new cable is routed exactly as the component it is replacing was routed.**

To install:

9. When reinstalling, fit the end of the new cable into the equalizer and make certain it is properly seated.
10. Install the cable retainer, and, working along the length of the cable, install the clamps.

➡**Make certain the cable is properly routed and does not contain any sharp bends or kinks.**

11. Feed the cable through the backing plate and install the retaining bolts.
12. If equipped with disc brakes, connect the cable to the arm and install the clip.
13. If equipped with drum brakes, re-install the shoes. The cable will be connected to the shoes during the installation process.
14. Reinstall the wheel(s) and lower the car to the ground.

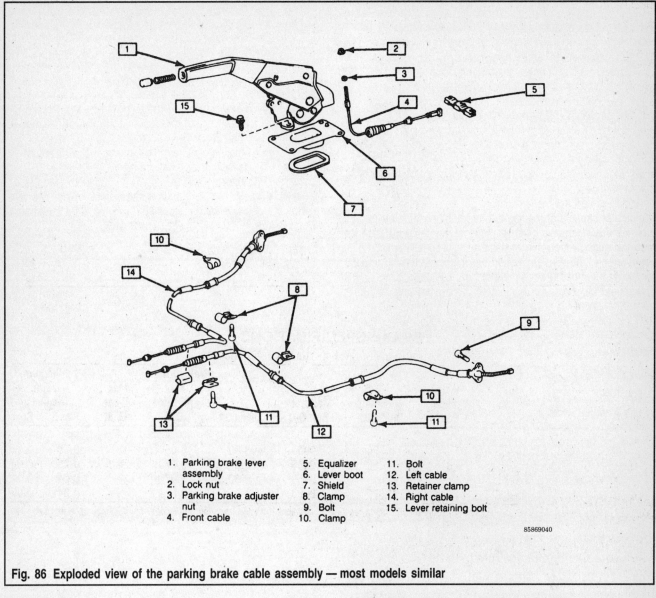

1. Parking brake lever assembly
2. Lock nut
3. Parking brake adjuster nut
4. Front cable
5. Equalizer
6. Lever boot
7. Shield
8. Clamp
9. Bolt
10. Clamp
11. Bolt
12. Left cable
13. Retainer clamp
14. Right cable
15. Lever retaining bolt

85869040

Fig. 86 Exploded view of the parking brake cable assembly — most models similar

ADJUSTMENTS

▶ See Figure 87

➡ On Corolla 1200 models, the rear brake shoes must be adjusted before performing this procedure. See the section on brake adjustments at the beginning of this section for details. On early models use these specifications only as a guide-more adjustment may be necessary.

Pull the parking brake lever all the way up and count the number of clicks. The correct range is 4-7 clicks rear drum brake type and 5-8 clicks rear disc brake type for full applica-tion. A system which is too tight or too loose requires adjustment.

➡ Before adjusting the parking brake cable, make certain that the rear brake shoe or rear brake pad clearance is correct. Refer to the necessary service procedures.

1. Remove the center console box.
2. At the rear of the handbrake lever, loosen the locknut on the brake cable.
3. Turn the adjusting nut until the parking brake travel is correct.
4. Tighten the locknut.
5. Reinstall the console.

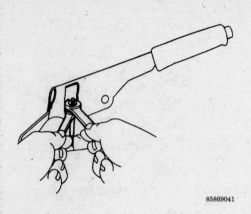

85869041

Fig. 87 Parking brake adjustment

BRAKE SPECIFICATIONS

(All measurements given are inches unless noted.)

Model	Lug Nut Torque (ft. lbs.)	Master Cylinder Bore	Brake Disc		Brake Drum			Minimum Lining Thickness	
			Minimum Thickness	Maximum Run-Out	Diameter	Max. Machine O/S	Max. Wear Limit	Front	Rear
Corolla									
1200	65–86	0.626	0.350	0.0060	8.00	8.050	8.14	0.25	0.04
1600	65–86	0.813	0.350	0.0060	9.08	9.070	9.16	0.25	0.04
1800 ('80–'82),	66–86	—	0.453 ①	0.0059	9.00 ②	9.079 ③	—	0.04	0.04
1600 ('84–'87)	65–86	—	0.827	0.0060	—	9.079 ③	—	0.04	0.04

NOTE: Minimum lining thickness is as recommended by the manufacturer. Due to variations in state inspection regulations, the minimum allowable thickness may be different than recommended by the manufacturer.

① RWD: 0.669
   FWD: 0.492
② FWD: 7.874
③ FWD: 7.913

85869C03

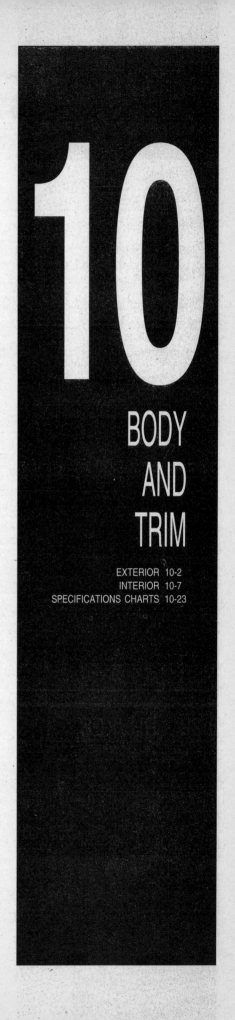

10

BODY

AND

TRIM

EXTERIOR

Doors

REMOVAL & INSTALLATION

▶ **See Figure 1**

1. Pull the door stopper pin upward while pushing in on the claw. Leave the claw raised after removing the pin.
2. Place a wooden block, rubber pad or other soft surface under the door for protection, then support it with a floor jack.
3. Remove the door mounting bolts, then remove the door. Special box wrenches are available to make accessing door hinge bolts easier
4. Installation is the reverse of removal. Adjust the door as necessary to achieve proper fit and prevent body interference.

ADJUSTMENT

▶ **See Figures 2, 3, 4 and 5**

➡**Since the centering bolt is used as the door hinge set bolt, the door cannot be adjusted with it installed. Replace the bolt with one which contains a washer, refer to the necessary illustration.**

1. To adjust the door in the forward/rearward and vertical directions, loosen the body side hinge bolts, then move the door to the desired position.
2. To adjust the door in the left/right and vertical direction, loosen the door side hinge bolts, then move the door to the desired position.
3. Adjust the door lock striker as necessary by slightly loosening the striker mounting screws, and hitting the striker lightly

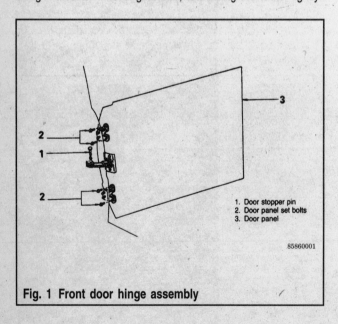

1. Door stopper pin
2. Door panel set bolts
3. Door panel

85860001

Fig. 1 Front door hinge assembly

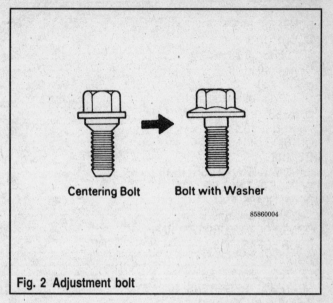

Centering Bolt → Bolt with Washer

85860004

Fig. 2 Adjustment bolt

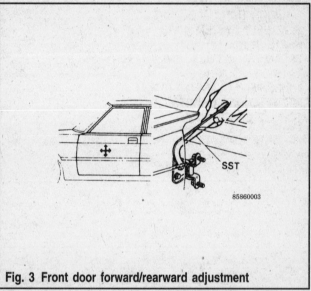

SST

85860003

Fig. 3 Front door forward/rearward adjustment

with a rubber or brass mallet. Tighten the striker mounting screws when proper adjustment has been achieved.

Hood

REMOVAL & INSTALLATION

▶ **See Figures 6, 7 and 8**

➡**An assistant is not only helpful for this procedure, but will help prevent paint damage.**

1. Protect the painted areas such as the fenders with a protective cover or equivalent.

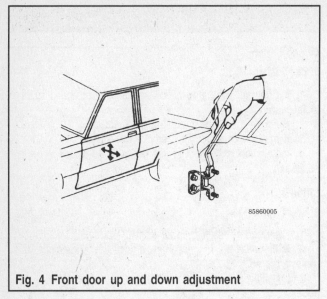

Fig. 4 Front door up and down adjustment

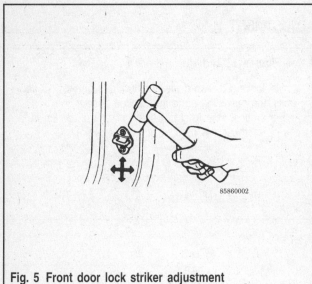

Fig. 5 Front door lock striker adjustment

2. If equipped, disconnect any hood mounted wiring or hoses (such as underhood compartment lights or wiper washer hoses).

➡On most vehicles covered by this manual you have a choice of hood removal procedures, either you can remove the hood from the hinges or the hood and hinges from the body. In either case be sure to matchmark the position of the hinges to the component (hood or fender) from which they are being removed.

3. Matchmark the hood hinges to the vehicle body or to the hood depending on which bolts are being removed.

➡If the hood is being replaced and you are using the old hinges, it probably makes more sense to leave the hinges attached to the body.

4. Loosen the hinge-to-vehicle body or hinge-to-hood retaining bolts, as desired. In both cases, be sure to have an assistant help steady the hood. If the hinge-to-hood retaining bolts

Fig. 6 If equipped, disconnect any hood wiring or hoses

are being removed, be careful that the hood does not slide back on the hinges contacting the cowl or windshield.

5. With the aid of an assistant remove the retaining bolts and lift the hood (or hood and hinge assemblies) away from the car.

6. Installation is the reverse of removal procedure. Be sure to use the hinge alignment marks made during removal to help assure proper installation.

7. Align the hood to the proper position, then tighten the hinge mounting bolts.

8. Don't forget to reconnect any wiring or hoses which were disconnected during removal.

ALIGNMENT

▶ **See Figures 2 and 9**

➡Since the centering bolt is used as the hood hinge set bolt, the hood can not be adjusted with it installed. Replace the bolt with one which contains a washer, refer to the necessary illustration.

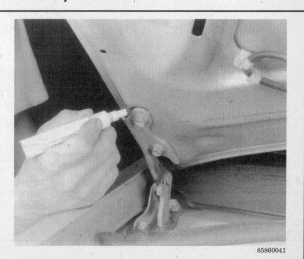

Fig. 7 Matchmark the hood hinges before removal in order to assure correct installation

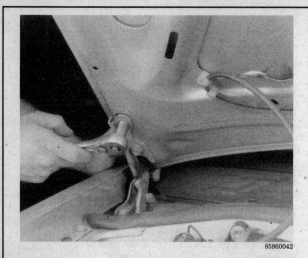

Fig. 8 BE SURE to support the hood while loosening the hinge bolts

1. For forward/rearward and left/right adjustments, loosen the body side hinge bolts, then move the hood the desired position.

2. For vertical adjustment of the hood's front edge, turn the cushion at that edge.

3. For vertical adjustment of the hood's rear edge, increase or decrease the number of washers or shims.

4. Adjust the hood lock by loosening the bolts and repositioning as necessary.

Luggage Compartment Lid (Trunk)

➡An assistant is not only helpful for this procedure, but will help prevent paint damage.

Fig. 9 Adjust hood (vertical direction) and hood lock

REMOVAL & INSTALLATION

Coupe/Sedan
▶ **See Figure 10**

1. Matchmark the hinge-to-lid alignment to assure proper installation.
2. Remove the hinge mounting bolts.
3. It may be necessary to remove the torsion bar.
4. Installation is the reverse of removal. Adjust as necessary.

Liftback
▶ **See Figure 11**

1. Disconnect the lift cylinder from the body.
2. Matchmark the hinges, then remove the hinge bolts and remove the lid.
3. Installation is the reverse of removal. Adjust as necessary.

ADJUSTMENT

▶ **See Figures 12 and 13**

1. For forward/rearward and left/right adjustments, loosen the bolts and move the hood the desired position.
2. For vertical adjustment of the front end of the lid, increase or decrease the number of washers.

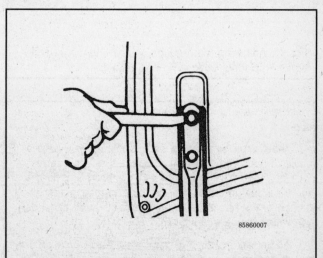

Fig. 10 The luggage compartment lid may be removed once the retaining bolts are withdrawn — Coupe/sedan

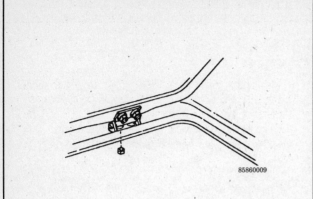

Fig. 11 When removing the liftback, unbolt the lid from the hinge or the hinge from the body, whichever is easier

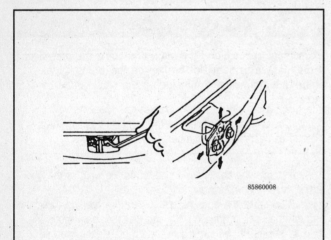

Fig. 12 Adjusting the luggage compartment lock and striker — Coupe/sedan

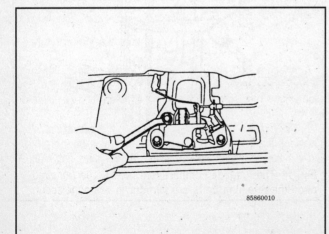

Fig. 13 Adjusting the luggage compartment lock and striker — liftback

Lift Cylinder

REMOVAL & INSTALLATION

▶ **See Figure 14**

➡️Do not disassemble the cylinder because it is filled with pressurized gas. If the damper cylinder is to be replaced, drill a 0.08 in. (2mm) hole in the bottom of the REMOVED damper cylinder to completely release the high pressure gas before disposing of the assembly.

Coupe/Sedan

1. Disconnect the lift cylinder upper end from the lid.
2. Disconnect the lift cylinder lower end from hinge.
   To install:
3. Install lift cylinder lower end to hinge.
4. Install lift cylinder upper end to lid. Adjust the lid as necessary.

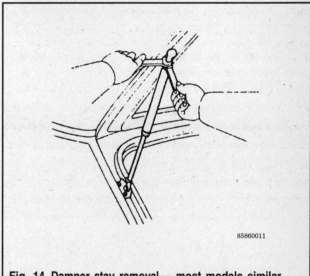

Fig. 14 Damper stay removal — most models similar

Liftback

1. Remove the roof side inner garnish, as necessary.
2. Disconnect the lift cylinder lower end from the body.
3. Remove the lift cylinder upper end from the backdoor.
4. Installation is the reverse of the removal procedures. Adjust the liftback as necessary.

Bumpers

REMOVAL & INSTALLATION

➡️This is a general procedure for front and rear bumpers assemblies — modify the service steps as necessary for your vehicle.

1. If necessary to ease access, raise and safely support the vehicle.

2. Disengage all electrical connections at the bumper assembly.

3. Remove the bumper retainers, then remove the bumper assembly. Be careful as these are often heavy components. Remove the shock absorbers from the bumper as necessary.

➡The shock absorber is filled with a high pressure gas and should not be disassembled.

4. Install shock absorber and bumper assemble in the reverse order of the removal. Align the bumper assemblies for the correct fit as necessary.

Grille

REMOVAL & INSTALLATION

The grille can usually be removed without removing any other parts. The grille is held on by a number of fasteners. Raise the hood and look for screws placed vertically in front of the metalwork. Other screws may be positioned horizontally, in front of or recessed in the grille. Remove the retainer screws and lift the grille from the vehicle.

Upon installation, make sure that all the retainers are installed in their original locations. As grilles are often made of thin materials, do NOT overtighten the fasteners or you may crack the grille mounting tabs.

Outside Mirror

REMOVAL AND INSTALLATION

▸ **See Figure 15**

Manual And Electric

1. On manual mirrors, remove the setting screw and knob. Tape the end of a thin screwdriver or equivalent and pry retainer loose to remove the cover.
2. Remove the 3 retaining screws.
3. On electric mirrors, disengage the electrical wiring from the mirror then remove the mirror assembly.
4. Remove the mirror assembly.
5. Installation is the reverse of the removal procedure. Cycle the mirror several times to make sure that it works properly.

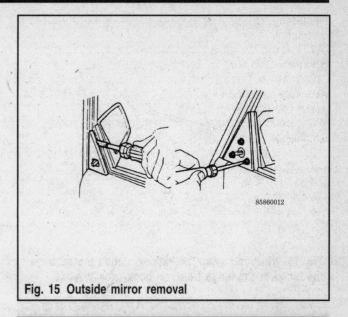

85860012

Fig. 15 Outside mirror removal

Antenna

➡**On most applications the mast and cable are one piece. If the mast is damaged or broken on these units, the entire antenna assembly, including the cable, must be replaced.**

REPLACEMENT

1. Remove the console side panel, to the right of the accelerator pedal as necessary.
2. Disconnect the antenna cable from the radio by reaching through the back of the console and disconnecting the cable from its socket. If you can't quite reach or release the cable, the radio will have to be loosened in the dash and disconnected from the front.
3. Remove the two screws holding the hood release lever and move the lever out of the way.
4. Remove the lower left dashboard trim and disconnect the speaker wiring.
5. Remove the left side kick panel.
6. Remove the retainer(s), then remove the left side cowl trim.
7. Attach a long piece of mechanic's wire or heavy string to the end of the antenna wire. This will track up through the pillar as you remove the old antenna and can then be used to pull the new line into place.
8. Remove the two attaching screws at the antenna mast. Remove the antenna and carefully pull the cable up the pillar. Use a helper to insure the end inside the car does not snag or pull other wires.

To install:

9. Remove the mechanic's wire or twine from the old cable and attach it to the new cable. Make sure it is tied so that the plug will stay straight during installation.
10. With your helper, feed the new cable into the pillar while pulling gently on the guide wire or string. Route the antenna cable properly under the dash, making sure it will not catch on

the steering column or pedal linkages. Use tape or cable ties to secure it.

11. Remove the guide line from the antenna cable. Route the antenna into the radio and install the connector.

12. Install the attaching screws holding the mast to the pillar. Make sure the screws are properly threaded and that both the screws and their holes are free of dirt or corrosion. A poor connection at these screws can affect antenna and radio performance.

13. Install the left side cowl trim and the left side kick panel.

14. Connect the speaker wiring and install the lower left dashboard trim.

15. Install the hood release lever.

16. Install the console side panel.

Fenders

REMOVAL & INSTALLATION

1. Remove or disconnect all electrical items attached to the fender which is being removed.

2. If necessary, remove the front bumper assembly.

3. Remove the inner fender liner.

4. Remove all bolts attaching the fender and the brace to the firewall and the radiator/grille panel.

5. Remove the rear attaching bolts through the pillar opening and remove the fender from the vehicle.

➡**DO NOT attempt to open/close the door on that side of the vehicle unless you verify that there will be no interference with the newly installed fender.**

6. To install, reverse the removal procedure. Align all body parts after installation.

INTERIOR

Door Panels

REMOVAL & INSTALLATION

▶ **See Figures 16, 17, 18 and 19**

1. Remove the door inside handle (pull handle) and arm rest, if so equipped.

2. Remove the regulator handle snapring with a tool or pull off the snapring with a cloth.

3. Remove the door lock lever bezel, inside handle bezel and door courtesy light, if so equipped.

4. Remove the door trim retaining screws.

5. Loosen the door trim by prying between the retainers and the door trim (tape the prytool before use) then disconnect the power window switch, if so equipped.

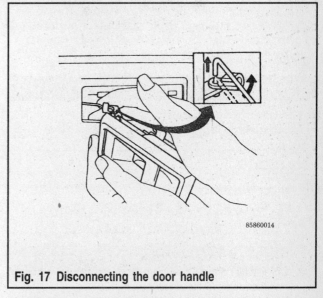

85860014

Fig. 17 Disconnecting the door handle

6. Installation is the reverse of removal procedure. Handle the door trim panel with care after removal.

Interior Trim Panel

REMOVAL & INSTALLATION

The interior trim panels are generally retained by screws. push type fasteners or spring loaded fasteners. To remove the spring type fasteners, apply light hand pressure to separate the trim. To remove the push type fasteners, insert a clip remover tool or the blade of a screwdriver (that has been taped to protect the surfaces) between the trim panel and the fastener to be removed, then carefully pry the retainer upward.

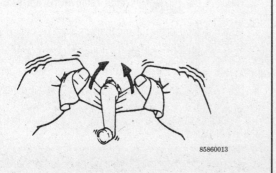

85860013

Fig. 16 A soft cloth may be used to remove the door regulator handle snapring

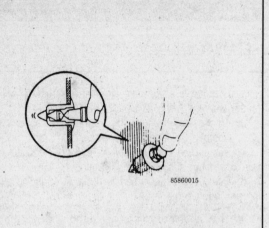

Fig. 18 Locking the door panel with locking clips

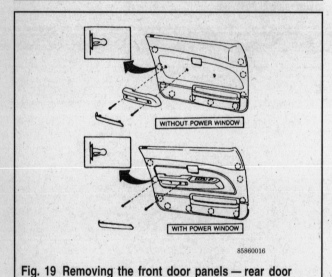

WITHOUT POWER WINDOW

WITH POWER WINDOW

85860016

Fig. 19 Removing the front door panels — rear door panels similar

Heater/AC Registers

REMOVAL & INSTALLATION

1. Disconnect the negative battery cable.
2. If necessary, remove the trim panel.
3. Remove the 2 mounting screws, then remove the register.
4. Installation is the reverse of the removal procedure.

Defroster Nozzle

REMOVAL & INSTALLATION

To remove the nozzle, first remove all retaining screws, then tape the end of a screwdriver and insert it between the de-

froster nozzle and the panel. Gently pry the nozzle out. To install, push into place by hand, then secure using the retainers.

Heater Ducts

REMOVAL & INSTALLATION

To remove the ducts, remove the retaining screws and separate the ductwork. To install, position pieces of duct together (assuring a tight connection between pieces), then install the retaining screws as required.

Door Locks

REMOVAL & INSTALLATION

1. Remove the inside door trim panel and access cover.
2. Disconnect the links from the outside handle and door lock cylinder.
3. On models with power door locks it will be necessary to disengage the connectors from the door lock solenoid and key unlock switch.
4. Remove the door lock retaining bolts or screws, then remove the door lock.
5. Installation is the reverse of removal procedure.

Door Lock Cylinders

REMOVAL & INSTALLATION

1. Remove the door trim panel.
2. Carefully remove the water deflector shield from inside the door. Take your time and don't rip it.
3. Disconnect the link rod running between the lock cylinder and the lock/latch mechanism.
4. The lock is held to the door by a horse-shoe shaped retaining clip. Slide the clip free of the lock and remove the cylinder from the outside of the door.
   To install:
5. Install the new cylinder and install the clip. The retaining clip has a slight bend in it and will install under tension. Do not attempt to straighten the clip.
6. Connect the link rod.
7. Install the water deflector shield, making sure that it is intact and firmly attached all the way around.
8. Reinstall the door trim panel.

Tailgate Lock

REMOVAL & INSTALLATION

1. Disconnect the negative battery cable.
2. Remove the back door inside garnish trim.

3. Remove the trim panel.

4. Disconnect the links from the door control and door lock cylinder.

5. Remove the bolts and the door lock control with the solenoid.

6. To remove the door lock cylinder, remove the retaining screws and then remove the cylinder.

To install:

7. Install the door lock cylinder and secure with the retaining screws.

8. Install the bolts and the door lock control with the solenoid.

9. Connect the links to the door control and door lock cylinder.

10. Install the trim panel.

11. Install the back door inner garnish trim.

12. Connect the negative battery cable.

Sedan Trunk Lock

REMOVAL & INSTALLATION

1. Disconnect the negative battery cable.
2. Remove the inside trunk garnish trim.
3. Remove the bolts and the door lock assembly.
4. The installation is the reverse of the removal procedure.

Door Glass and Regulator

REMOVAL & INSTALLATION

▶ See Figures 20, 21, 22, 23, 24, 25, 26, 27, 28, 29, 30, 31, 32, 33 and 34

Front Door Glass

EARLY MODEL

➡Refer to exploded view of door assembly components as a guide for this repair.

1. Remove the door trim panel.
2. Carefully remove the water deflector shield and lower the window glass fully.
3. Remove the outer weatherstrip.
4. Remove the sash channel mounting bolts.
5. Carefully remove the glass through the top of the door.
6. Remove the window regulator mounting bolts and remove the regulator
7. If the window glass is to be replaced:
   a. Remove the sash channel from the glass.
   b. Apply a solution of soapy water to the sash channel.
   c. Install the channel to the new glass using a plastic or leather mallet to gently tap the sash into place. Be sure to support the glass on a protective surface while installing the sash. Note that the sash channel must be exactly positioned on the glass or the bolt holes will not align at reinstallation.

To install:

8. Install the regulator and tighten the bolts evenly.

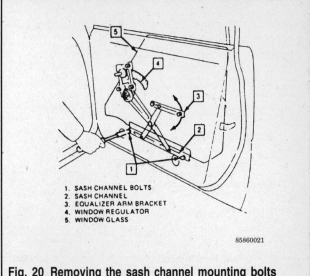

1. SASH CHANNEL BOLTS
2. SASH CHANNEL
3. EQUALIZER ARM BRACKET
4. WINDOW REGULATOR
5. WINDOW GLASS

85860021

Fig. 20 Removing the sash channel mounting bolts

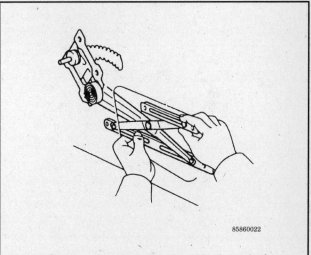

85860022

Fig. 21 Remove the regulator assembly through the access hole in the door

9. Install the window glass and install the sash channel mounting bolts.

10. Wind the window slowly up and down to observe its movement and alignment. The position of the glass can be adjusted by moving the equalizing arm bracket up or down. Make small adjustments and work for a perfectly aligned window.

11. Install the outer weatherstrip.

12. Install the water deflector, making sure it is intact and properly sealed.

13. Install the door trim panel.

LATE MODEL

➡Refer to exploded view of door assembly components as a guide for this repair — modify this service procedure as necessary.

1. Remove the door trim panel.
2. Carefully remove the water deflector shield and lower the window glass fully.
3. Remove the glass channel mounting bolts.

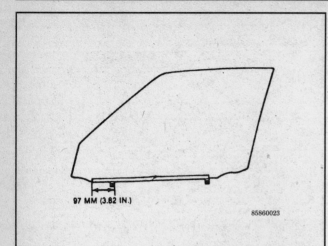

Fig. 22 Correct placement of the regulator sash channel is critical for proper glass alignment

97 MM (3.82 IN.)

85860023

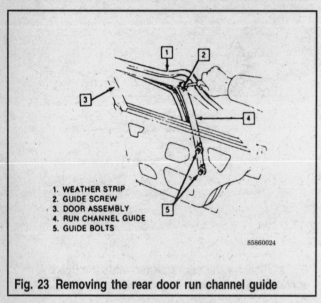

1. WEATHER STRIP
2. GUIDE SCREW
3. DOOR ASSEMBLY
4. RUN CHANNEL GUIDE
5. GUIDE BOLTS

85860024

Fig. 23 Removing the rear door run channel guide

4. Remove the window glass by lifting it through the top of the door.

5. Disconnect the window regulator as follows:

a. For power windows, disengage the electrical connector and remove the 4 mounting bolts. The regulator will be removed with the motor attached.

b. For manual windows, remove the 3 mounting bolts.

6. Remove the two mounting bolts holding the equalizer arm bracket.

7. Remove the window regulator.

➡**If the motor is to be removed from the power window regulator, install a large stopper bolt through the regulator frame before removing the motor. When the motor is removed, the spring loaded gear will be disengaged, causing the gear to rotate until the spring is unwound. Install the stopper bolt to prevent possible injury by the spinning gear.**

To install:

8. Before installing the regulator assembly, apply a light coat of lithium grease to the sliding surfaces and pivot points of the regulator. Do not apply grease to the spring.

9. Install the regulator:

a. With power windows, install the 4 mounting bolts and connect the motor wiring.

b. With manual windows, install the 3 mounting bolts.

10. Install the bolts holding the equalizer arm bracket.

11. Place the glass into the door and install the glass channel retaining bolts.

12. Adjust the door glass by moving the equalizer arm up or down as necessary to get the window level in the frame.

13. Install the water deflector, making sure it is intact and properly sealed.

14. Install the door trim panel.

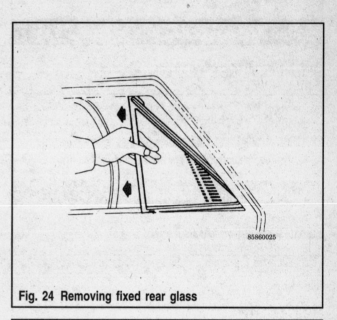

85860025

Fig. 24 Removing fixed rear glass

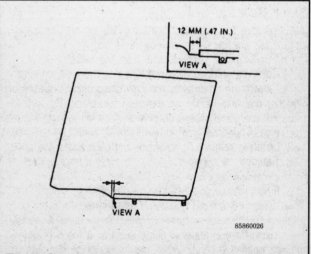

12 MM (.47 IN.)

VIEW A

VIEW A

85860026

Fig. 25 Correct placement of sash channel on rear glass

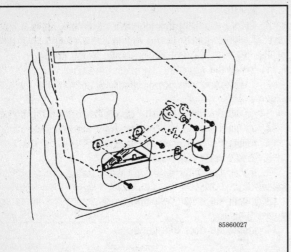

Fig. 26 Front door window regulator — most models similar

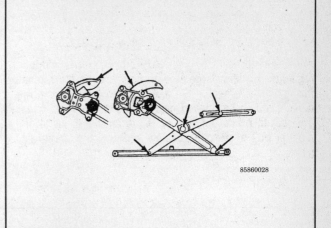

Fig. 27 Points to be lubricated before installing front or rear regulator — do not lubricate the spiral spring

Rear Door Glass

EARLY MODEL

➡The movable window glass cannot be removed without removing the fixed glass. Refer to exploded view of door assembly components as a guide for this repair.

1. Remove the door trim panel.
2. Carefully remove the water deflector shield and lower the window glass fully.
3. Remove the outer weatherstrip.
4. Partially remove the door weatherstrip to remove the run channel guide upper retaining screw.
5. Remove the rubber or felt run channel.
6. Remove the lower run channel guide bolts and the guide.
7. Pull the fixed glass forward and remove it. Place it in a safe and protected location, away from the work area.
8. Remove the sash channel bolts.
9. Carefully remove the glass through the top of the door.
10. Remove the mounting bolts and the window regulator.
11. If the window glass is to be replaced:
   a. Remove the sash channel from the glass.
   b. Apply a solution of soapy water to the sash channel.
   c. Install the channel to the new glass using a plastic or leather mallet to gently tap the sash into place. Be sure to support the glass on a protective surface while installing the sash. Note that the sash channel must be exactly positioned on the glass or the bolt holes will not align at reinstallation.

To install:

12. Install the regulator and tighten the bolts evenly.
13. Install the window glass and sash channel bolts.
14. Reinstall the fixed glass and make certain it is correctly positioned.
15. Install the run channel guide and install the two lower retaining bolts.
16. Install the felt or rubber run channel. Make certain there are no twists or kinks in the channel.
17. Install the channel guide top screw and secure the weatherstrip.
18. Wind the window slowly up/down to observe its movement and alignment. The position of the glass can be adjusted

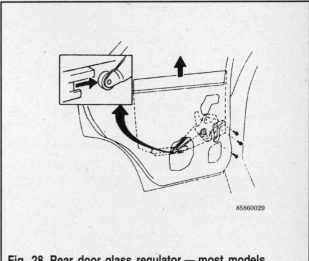

Fig. 28 Rear door glass regulator — most models similar

by moving the equalizing arm bracket up/down. Make small adjustments and aim for a perfectly aligned window.

19. Install the outer weatherstrip.
20. Install the water deflector, making sure it is intact and properly sealed.
21. Install the door trim panel.

LATE MODEL

➡Refer to exploded view of door assembly components as a guide for this repair — modify this service procedure as necessary.

1. Remove the door trim panel.
2. Carefully remove the water deflector shield and lower the window glass fully.
3. Remove the glass from the regulator arm.
4. Loosen the weatherstrip at the glass channel run's rear edge.
5. Remove the rear channel guide top and bottom screws.
6. Lift the door weatherstrip and remove the screws holding the window filler panel.

7. Remove the door glass by pulling it upward.

8. If equipped with power windows, disconnect the motor wiring connector.

9. Remove the bolts and the window regulator.

➡**If the motor is to be removed from the power window regulator, install a large stopper bolt through the regulator frame before removing the motor. When the motor is removed, the spring loaded gear will be disengaged, causing the gear to rotate until the spring is unwound. Install the stopper bolt to prevent possible injury by the spinning gear.**

To install:

10. Before installing the regulator assembly, apply a light coat of lithium grease to the sliding surfaces and pivot points of the regulator. Do not apply grease to the spring.

11. Install the regulator, tightening the bolts evenly.

12. If equipped with power windows, connect the motor wiring.

13. Install the glass into the door and connect the regulator.

14. Install the window filler panel and its 2 screws.

15. Install the rear glass guide channel.

16. Install the window weatherstrip.

17. Install the water deflector, making sure it is properly sealed.

18. Install the door trim panel.

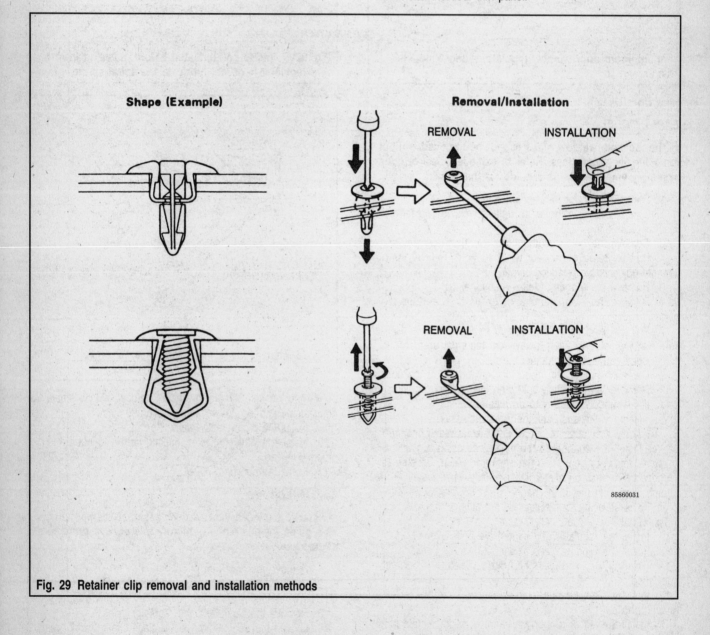

Fig. 29 Retainer clip removal and installation methods

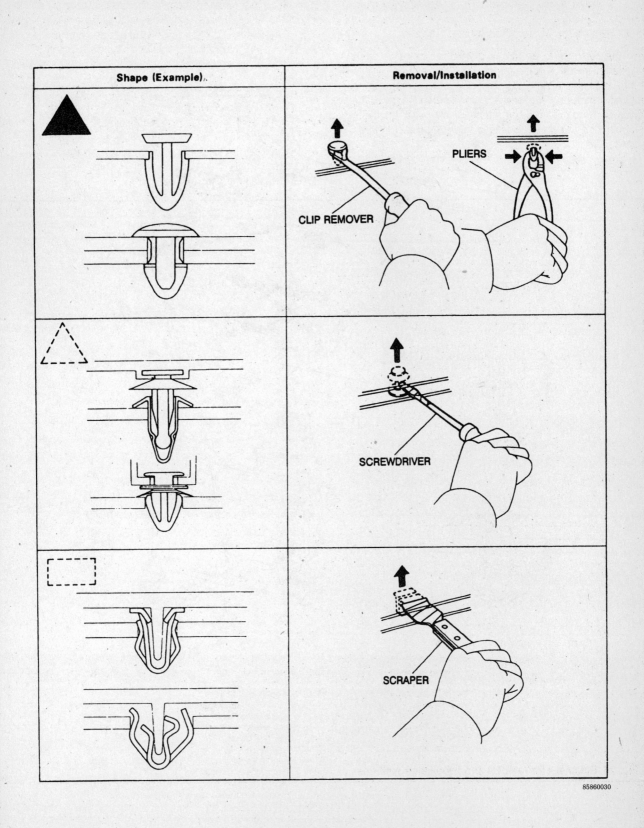

Shape (Example).	Removal/Installation

PLIERS

CLIP REMOVER

SCREWDRIVER

SCRAPER

85860030

Fig. 30 Retainer clip removal and installation methods

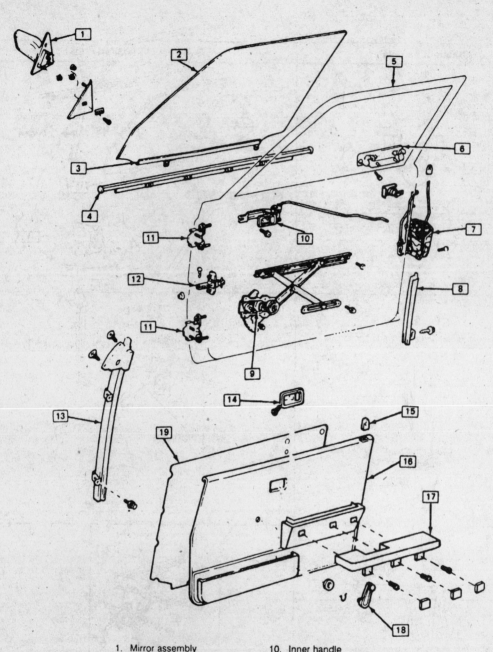

1. Mirror assembly
2. Window glass
3. Sash channel
4. Door belt molding
5. Door assembly
6. Outer handle
7. Door latch/lock
   assembly
8. Rear run channel guide
9. Window regulator
10. Inner handle
11. Hinge
12. Door check
13. Front run channel guide
14. Inner handle bezel
15. Lock knob
16. Door trim panel
17. Armrest
18. Window winder handle
19. Water deflector shield

85860017

Fig. 31 Exploded view of the front door assembly components — early models

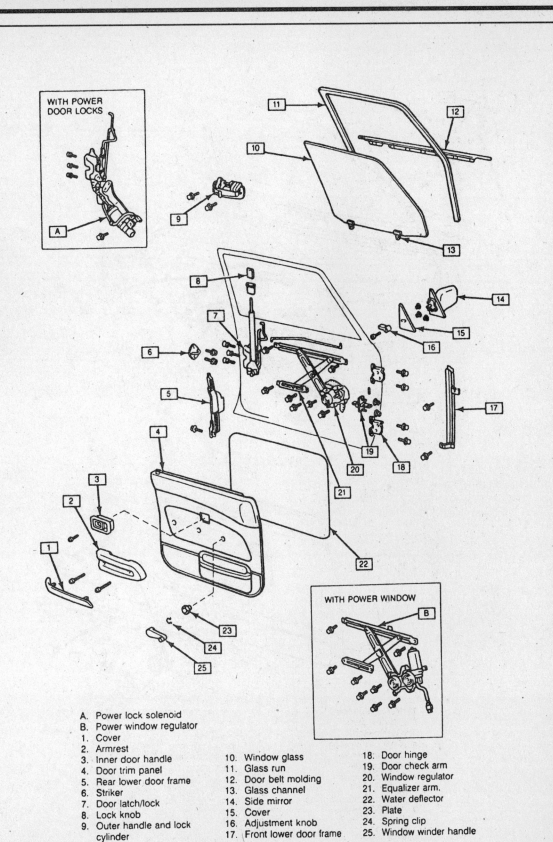

WITH POWER
DOOR LOCKS

WITH POWER WINDOW

Fig. 32 Exploded view of the front door assembly components — late models

A. Power lock solenoid
B. Power window regulator
1. Cover
2. Armrest
3. Inner door handle
4. Door trim panel
5. Rear lower door frame
6. Striker
7. Door latch/lock
8. Lock knob
9. Outer handle and lock
   cylinder
10. Window glass
11. Glass run
12. Door belt molding
13. Glass channel
14. Side mirror
15. Cover
16. Adjustment knob
17. Front lower door frame
18. Door hinge
19. Door check arm
20. Window regulator
21. Equalizer arm.
22. Water deflector
23. Plate
24. Spring clip
25. Window winder handle

85860018

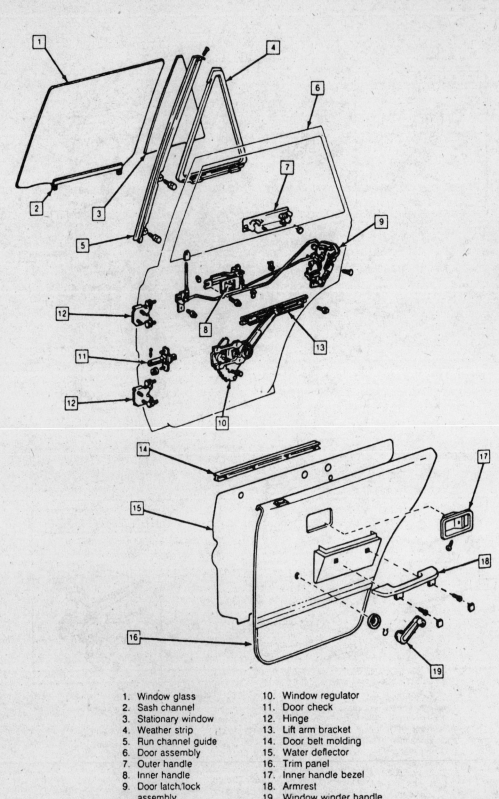

1. Window glass
2. Sash channel
3. Stationary window
4. Weather strip
5. Run channel guide
6. Door assembly
7. Outer handle
8. Inner handle
9. Door latch/lock assembly
10. Window regulator
11. Door check
12. Hinge
13. Lift arm bracket
14. Door belt molding
15. Water deflector
16. Trim panel
17. Inner handle bezel
18. Armrest
19. Window winder handle

85860019

Fig. 33 Exploded view of the rear door assembly components — early models

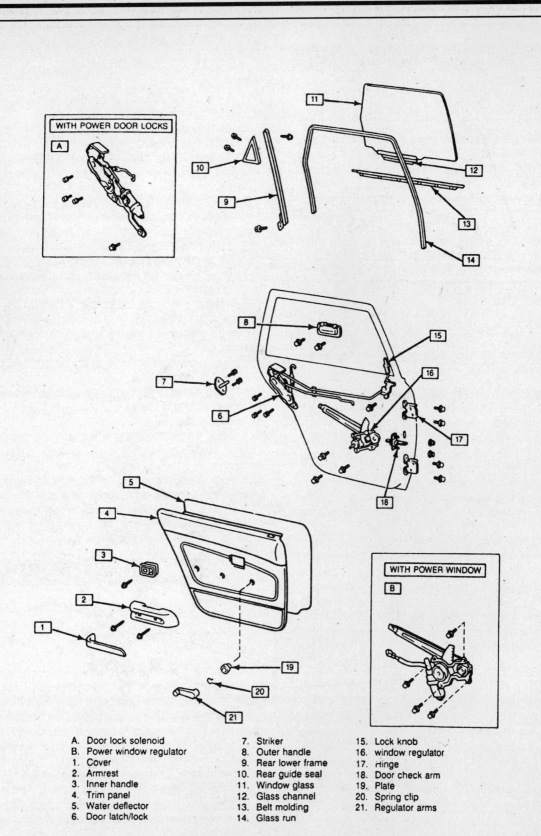

A. Door lock solenoid
B. Power window regulator
1. Cover
2. Armrest
3. Inner handle
4. Trim panel
5. Water deflector
6. Door latch/lock

7. Striker
8. Outer handle
9. Rear lower frame
10. Rear guide seal
11. Window glass
12. Glass channel
13. Belt molding
14. Glass run

15. Lock knob
16. window regulator
17. Hinge
18. Door check arm
19. Plate
20. Spring clip
21. Regulator arms

85860020

Fig. 34 Exploded view of the rear door assembly components — late models

Windshield Glass

REMOVAL & INSTALLATION

➡ Extreme care must be taken when removing, installing or resealing a windshield. The windshield will crack if stress is exerted in the wrong direction, even if the pressure is very slight. Undesirable stress on the windshield could take place during a number of operations. Damage could occur days after the repair has been completed, caused by the body of the vehicle flexing during normal vehicle operation, or during the removal of the outer moldings before any repair work has been done. This should be realized before the job of removing a windshield is undertaken. If you are in doubt, refer all glass work to reputable glass repair shop.

REMOVAL & INSTALLATION

◗ See Figures 35 and 36

1. Disconnect the negative battery cable.
2. Remove the sunvisors, holders and the front assist grip.
3. Remove the inner rear view mirror.
4. Remove the front pillar garnish.
5. Remove the hood, wiper arms and the cowl panel (louver).
6. Remove the hood weather-strip by pulling upward. Take care not to tear the weather-strip during removal.
7. Remove the retainer screws and the outside windshield molding.
8. Tape the end of a scraper and insert between the body and the upper windshield molding. Pry the molding upward and remove from the clips. Remove the molding from the vehicle.
9. Push piano wire from the interior of the vehicle outward and tie to an object (such as a small wooden dowel) to act as a handle to each end of the wire. Apply tape to the outer body

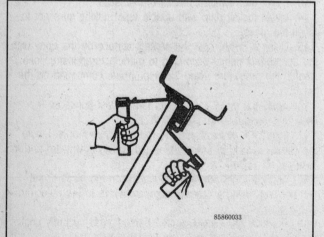

85860033

Fig. 35 Removing glass from the vehicle

surfaces to avoid scratching the finish. With the aid of a helper, cut the adhesive by pulling the piano wire around the windshield.
10. Carefully remove the glass from the vehicle.
To install:
11. Clean all adhesive off of the body of the vehicle. Clean all contact surfaces with an appropriate cleaner.
12. Remove old fasteners and replace with new parts.
13. Clean the removed glass of all adhesive using an appropriate cleaner. Do not touch the contact area after cleaning.
14. Install new retainers to their original location. Install the spacer.
15. Position the glass onto the vehicle making sure all contacting parts of the glass are perfectly even and don't make contact with any fasteners.
16. Mark the position of the glass and remove.
17. Clean the contact surfaces of the glass.
18. Install the air dam with double tape making sure not to touch the glass.
19. Using a brush, coat the contact surface on the body with the appropriate primer according to manufactures instructions. Repeat the procedure using the appropriate compound on the glass.
20. Apply windshield adhesive to the contact points in a bead 0.39 in. (10mm) thick.
21. Install the glass aligning to the reference marks. Insure the correct sealing of the air dam. (lip curling downward and in the bead of sealer)
22. Apply a slight downward pressure on the glass to set into position. Using a spatula, apply adhesive to the outer rim of the glass.
23. Remove any excess sealer. Fasten glass securely until sealer sets. Water test once the sealer is fully dry.
24. If no leaks are present, carefully install the moldings, interior trim components, cowl panel, wiper arms and the hood.
25. Connect the negative battery cable.

Back Window Glass

REMOVAL & INSTALLATION

◗ See Figure 37

➡ Extreme care must be taken when removing, installing or resealing a rear glass. The rear glass will crack if a stress is exerted in the wrong direction, even if the pressure is very slight. Undesirable stress on the rear glass could take place during a number of operations. Damage could occur days after the repair has been completed, caused by the body of the vehicle flexing during normal vehicle operation, or during the removal of the outer moldings before any repair work has been done. This should be realized before the job of removing a rear glass is undertaken. If you are in doubt, refer all glass work to reputable glass repair shop.

1. Remove the rear seat and the rear cushion (on sedan and coupe models only) from the vehicle.
2. Remove the wiper arm, if so equipped. Remove the inner roof garnish and back door trim panel (on station wagon models only).

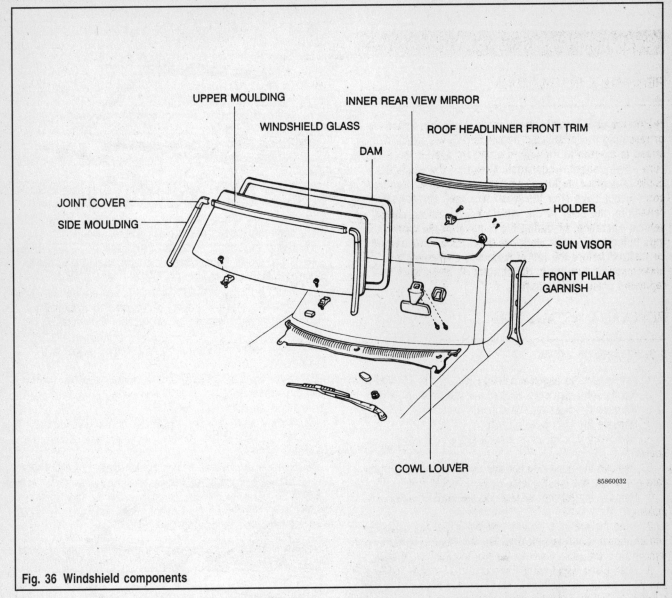

UPPER MOULDING

WINDSHIELD GLASS

DAM

INNER REAR VIEW MIRROR

ROOF HEADLINNER FRONT TRIM

JOINT COVER

SIDE MOULDING

HOLDER

SUN VISOR

FRONT PILLAR GARNISH

COWL LOUVER

85860032

Fig. 36 Windshield components

3. On all models so equipped, disengage the rear window defogger electrical connection.

4. Remove the interior assist grips and the rear portion of the headlining.

5. Using a knife, remove the back window molding by cutting off the lip portion of the molding which is over the glass.

6. Remove the back glass in the same manner as the front windshield (using tool made from piano wire — refer to the procedure earlier in this section for details) and remove the glass retainers.

To install:

7. Clean all adhesive off of the body of the vehicle. Clean all contact surfaces with an appropriate cleaner.

8. Remove all old fasteners and replace with new parts.

9. Clean the removed glass of all adhesive and clean with an appropriate cleaner. Do not touch the contact area after cleaning.

10. Install new retainers to their original location.

11. Position the glass onto the vehicle making sure all contacting parts on the glass are perfectly even and don't make contact with any fasteners.

12. Mark the position of the glass and remove.

13. Clean the contact surfaces of the glass.

14. Install the air dam with double tape making sure not to touch the glass.

15. Using a brush, coat the contact surface on the body with the appropriate primer according to manufactures instructions. Repeat the procedure using the appropriate compound on the glass.

16. Apply the glass adhesive to the contact points on the body in a bead 0.39 in. (10mm) thick.

17. Install the glass aligning to the reference marks. Insure the correct sealing of the air dam. (lip curling downward and in the bead of sealer)

18. Apply a slight downward pressure on the glass to set into position. Using a spatula, apply adhesive to the outer rim of the glass.

19. Remove any excess sealer. Fasten glass securely until sealer sets. Water test once the sealer is fully dry.

20. If no leaks are present, carefully install the moldings, interior components, trim panels and wiper arm if so equipped.

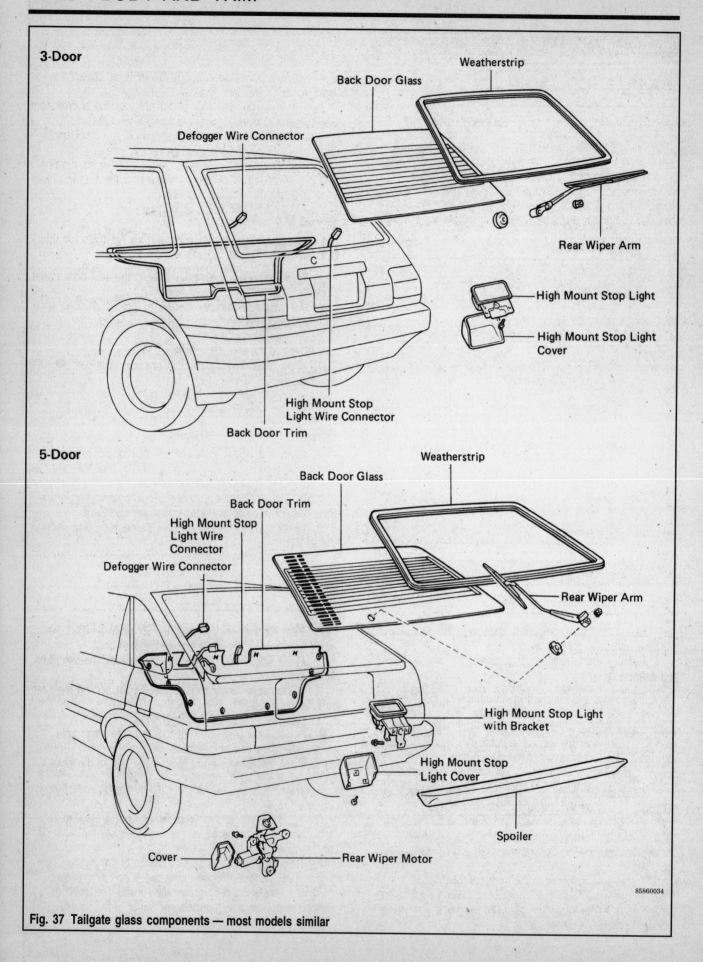

Fig. 37 Tailgate glass components — most models similar

Inside Mirror

REMOVAL & INSTALLATION

▶ **See Figure 38**

The inside mirror is removed by carefully prying off the plastic cover and removing the retaining screw. The inside mirror is designed to break loose from the roof mount if it receives moderate impact. If the mirror has come off due to impact, it can usually be remounted by installing a new mirror base rather than an entire new mirror. If the glass is cracked, the mirror must be replaced.

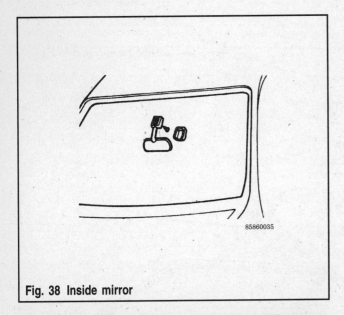

85860035

Fig. 38 Inside mirror

Seats

REMOVAL & INSTALLATION

▶ **See Figures 39, 40 and 41**

Front Seats

The front seats are removed by disconnecting the 4 mounting bolts holding the seat to the floor rails. The bolts may be under plastic covers which can be popped off with a small tool. The seat assembly will come out of the vehicle complete with the tracks and adjuster. When reinstalling the seat, make certain that the bolts are properly threaded and tightened. SEAT MOUNTING AND RETENTION IS A CRITICAL SAFETY ITEM. NEVER ATTEMPT TO ALTER THE MOUNTS OR THE SEAT TRACKS.

Rear Seats

BENCH SEAT CUSHION

1. Pull forward on the seat cushion releases. These are small levers on the lower front of the cushion.
2. Pull upward on the front of the seat cushion and rotate it free. It is not retained or bolted under the seat back.
3. To reinstall, fit the rear of the cushion into place under the seat back.
4. Push inward and downward on the front of the cushion until the releases lock into place. Make sure the seat is locked into place and the releases are secure.

BENCH SEAT BACK

➡**The seat bottom cushion need not be removed for this procedure, but if it is, access will be improved.**

1. Remove the two lower bolts holding the seat back to the body.
2. Pull outward and push upward on the bottom edge of the seat back. This will release the seat back from the L shaped hangers holding it.
3. Remove the seat back from the vehicle.
4. When reinstalling, carefully fit the seat back onto the hangers.
5. Swing the back down and into place.
6. Install the lower retaining bolts.

SPLIT/FOLDING SEAT CUSHION

1. At the front lower edge of the seat cushion, remove the 2 bolts holding the seat cushion to the body. The bolts may be concealed under carpeting or trim pieces.
2. Pull upward on the front of the seat cushion and rotate it free. It is not retained or bolted under the seat back.
3. To reinstall, fit the rear of the cushion into place under the seat back.
4. Push inward and downward on the front of the cushion until it is in place and the bolt holes align.
5. Install the retaining bolts and tighten them.

SPLIT/FOLDING SEAT BACK

1. Push the seat back forward into a folded position. Remove the carpeting from the rear of the seat back.
2. At the side hinge, remove the bolt holding the seat back to the hinge.
3. At the center hinge, remove the 2 bolts holding the seat back to the hinge.
4. Remove the seat back from the car.
5. Reinstall the seat back. Tighten the side hinge bolts, then tighten the center hinge bolts.
6. Install the carpeting and trim on the rear of the seat back.

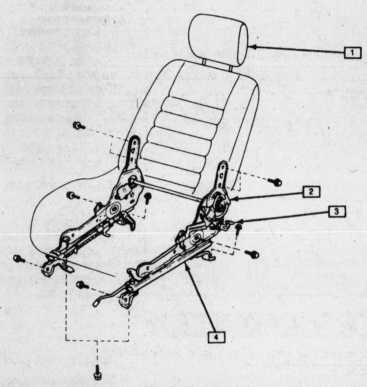

1. Head restraint
2. Recliner mechanism
3. Recliner actuator handle
4. Seat adjuster

85860036

Fig. 39 Front seat components — most models similar

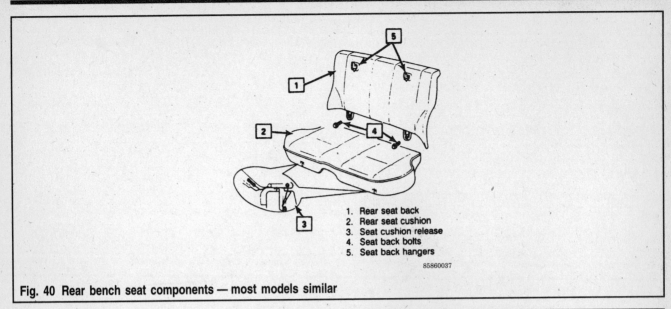

1. Rear seat back
2. Rear seat cushion
3. Seat cushion release
4. Seat back bolts
5. Seat back hangers

85860037

Fig. 40 Rear bench seat components — most models similar

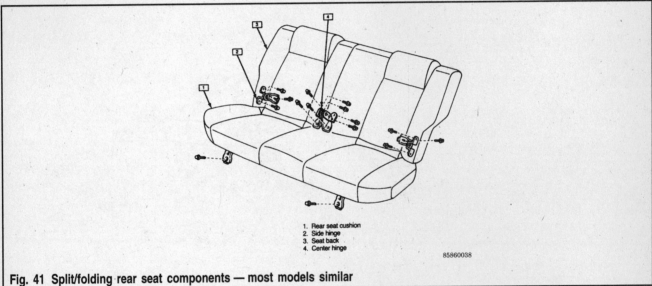

1. Rear seat cushion
2. Side hinge
3. Seat back
4. Center hinge

85860038

Fig. 41 Split/folding rear seat components — most models similar

Seat Belt System

REMOVAL & INSTALLATION

▶ **See Figure 42**

Front Seat

1. Remove trim cover at upper shoulder anchor bolt.
2. Remove the anchor bolts.
3. Remove the lower cover on the outer retractor. Unbolt the retractor from the inner floor panel.
4. Remove the retractor portion of the seat belt.
5. To remove the buckle end of the seat belt, remove the cover on the base of the belt and remove the mounting bolt.
6. Installation of the belts is the reverse of the removal procedure. Torque the upper shoulder mounting bolt to 32 ft.

lbs. (43 Nm), the lower retractor mounting bolt to 9 ft. lbs. (13 Nm), and the buckle retainer bolt to 32 ft. lbs. (43 Nm).

7. Do not remove safety belts from any vehicle. Inspection of the seat belts for proper operation is recommended for the safety and is required in most states by law.

Rear Seat

1. Remove trim cover at upper shoulder anchor bolt.
2. Remove the upper shoulder anchor bolt.
3. Unbolt the outer belt anchor from the body panel. Removal of the rear seat is required. Unbolt the lower end of the belt under the retractor from the side panel.
4. Remove the retractor portion of the seat belt.
5. To remove the center belt buckle, remove the seat cushion and the center belt mounting bolt.
6. Installation is the reverse of removal. Torque all belt mounting bolts to 32 ft. lbs. (43 Nm).

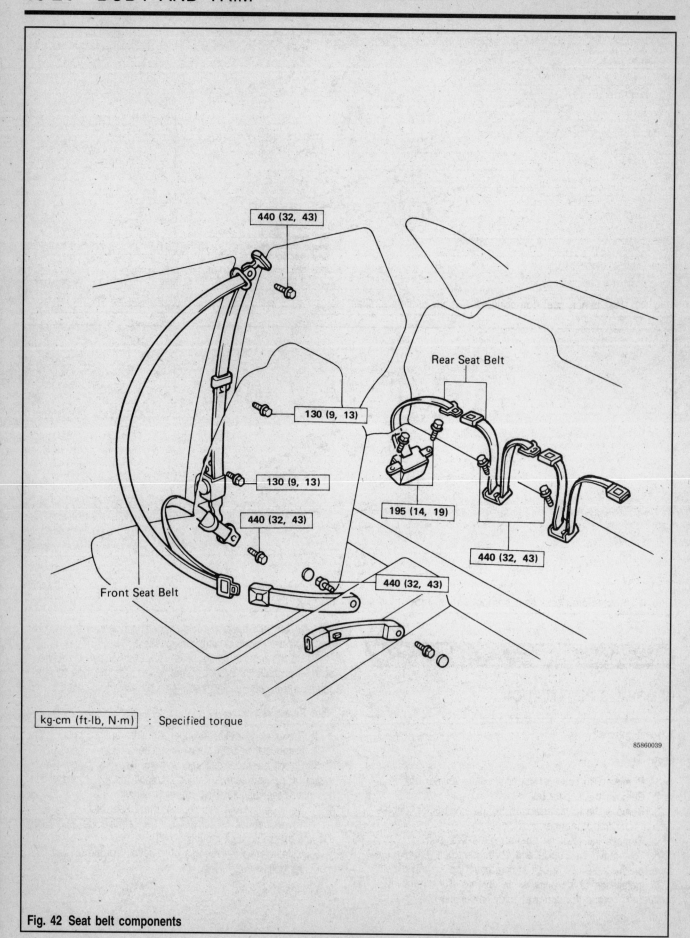

440 (32, 43)

Rear Seat Belt

130 (9, 13)

130 (9, 13)

195 (14, 19)

440 (32, 43)

440 (32, 43)

440 (32, 43)

Front Seat Belt

kg-cm (ft-lb, N·m) : Specified torque

85860039

Fig. 42 Seat belt components

TORQUE SPECIFICATIONS

Component	U.S.	Metric
Hood hinge to hood bolts	10 ft. lbs.	14 Nm
Hood lock to body	74 inch lbs.	8.3 Nm
Front door hinge to body	21 ft. lbs.	28 Nm
Front door window regulator to inside panel frame	48 inch lbs.	5.4 Nm
Front door lock to panel	48 inch lbs.	5.4 Nm
Rear door hinge to body	21 ft. lbs.	28 Nm
Rear door window regulator to inside panel frame	48 inch lbs.	5.4 Nm
Rear door lock to panel	48 inch lbs.	5.4 Nm
Tailgate hinge to body	9 ft. lbs.	13 Nm
Tailgate hinge to tailgate	9 ft. lbs.	13 Nm
Trunk lid hinge to body	48 inch lbs.	5.4 Nm
Trunk lid hinge to trunk lid	74 inch lbs.	8.3 Nm
Front seat track to body	27 ft. lbs.	37 Nm
Rear seat cushion hinge to body	14 ft. lbs.	19 Nm

85860999

GLOSSARY

AIR/FUEL RATIO: The ratio of air to gasoline by weight in the fuel mixture drawn into the engine.

AIR INJECTION: One method of reducing harmful exhaust emissions by injecting air into each of the exhaust ports of an engine. The fresh air entering the hot exhaust manifold causes any remaining fuel to be burned before it can exit the tailpipe.

ALTERNATOR: A device used for converting mechanical energy into electrical energy.

AMMETER: An instrument, calibrated in amperes, used to measure the flow of an electrical current in a circuit. Ammeters are always connected in series with the circuit being tested.

AMPERE: The rate of flow of electrical current present when one volt of electrical pressure is applied against one ohm of electrical resistance.

ANALOG COMPUTER: Any microprocessor that uses similar (analogous) electrical signals to make its calculations.

ARMATURE: A laminated, soft iron core wrapped by a wire that converts electrical energy to mechanical energy as in a motor or relay. When rotated in a magnetic field, it changes mechanical energy into electrical energy as in a generator.

ATMOSPHERIC PRESSURE: The pressure on the Earth's surface caused by the weight of the air in the atmosphere. At sea level, this pressure is 14.7 psi at 32{248}F (101 kPa at 0{248}C).

ATOMIZATION: The breaking down of a liquid into a fine mist that can be suspended in air.

AXIAL PLAY: Movement parallel to a shaft or bearing bore.

BACKFIRE: The sudden combustion of gases in the intake or exhaust system that results in a loud explosion.

BACKLASH: The clearance or play between two parts, such as meshed gears.

BACKPRESSURE: Restrictions in the exhaust system that slow the exit of exhaust gases from the combustion chamber.

BAKELITE: A heat resistant, plastic insulator material commonly used in printed circuit boards and transistorized components.

BALL BEARING: A bearing made up of hardened inner and outer races between which hardened steel balls roll.

BALLAST RESISTOR: A resistor in the primary ignition circuit that lowers voltage after the engine is started to reduce wear on ignition components.

BEARING: A friction reducing, supportive device usually located between a stationary part and a moving part.

BIMETAL TEMPERATURE SENSOR: Any sensor or switch made of two dissimilar types of metal that bend when heated or cooled due to the different expansion rates of the alloys. These types of sensors usually function as an on/off switch.

BLOWBY: Combustion gases, composed of water vapor and unburned fuel, that leak past the piston rings into the crankcase during normal engine operation. These gases are removed by the PCV system to prevent the buildup of harmful acids in the crankcase.

BRAKE PAD: A brake shoe and lining assembly used with disc brakes.

BRAKE SHOE: The backing for the brake lining. The term is, however, usually applied to the assembly of the brake backing and lining.

BUSHING: A liner, usually removable, for a bearing; an anti-friction liner used in place of a bearing.

CALIPER: A hydraulically activated device in a disc brake system, which is mounted straddling the brake rotor (disc). The caliper contains at least one piston and two brake pads. Hydraulic pressure on the piston(s) forces the pads against the rotor.

CAMSHAFT: A shaft in the engine on which are the lobes (cams) which operate the valves. The camshaft is driven by the crankshaft, via a belt, chain or gears, at one half the crankshaft speed.

CAPACITOR: A device which stores an electrical charge.

CARBON MONOXIDE (CO): A colorless, odorless gas given off as a normal byproduct of combustion. It is poisonous and extremely dangerous in confined areas, building up slowly to toxic levels without warning if adequate ventilation is not available.

CARBURETOR: A device, usually mounted on the intake manifold of an engine, which mixes the air and fuel in the proper proportion to allow even combustion.

CATALYTIC CONVERTER: A device installed in the exhaust system, like a muffler, that converts harmful byproducts of combustion into carbon dioxide and water vapor by means of a heat-producing chemical reaction.

CENTRIFUGAL ADVANCE: A mechanical method of advancing the spark timing by using flyweights in the distributor that react to centrifugal force generated by the distributor shaft rotation.

CHECK VALVE: Any one-way valve installed to permit the flow of air, fuel or vacuum in one direction only.

CHOKE: A device, usually a moveable valve, placed in the intake path of a carburetor to restrict the flow of air.

CIRCUIT: Any unbroken path through which an electrical current can flow. Also used to describe fuel flow in some instances.

CIRCUIT BREAKER: A switch which protects an electrical circuit from overload by opening the circuit when the current flow exceeds a predetermined level. Some circuit breakers must be reset manually, while most reset automatically

COIL (IGNITION): A transformer in the ignition circuit which steps up the voltage provided to the spark plugs.

COMBINATION MANIFOLD: An assembly which includes both the intake and exhaust manifolds in one casting.

COMBINATION VALVE: A device used in some fuel systems that routes fuel vapors to a charcoal storage canister instead of venting them into the atmosphere. The valve relieves fuel tank pressure and allows fresh air into the tank as the fuel level drops to prevent a vapor lock situation.

COMPRESSION RATIO: The comparison of the total volume of the cylinder and combustion chamber with the piston at BDC and the piston at TDC.

CONDENSER: 1. An electrical device which acts to store an electrical charge, preventing voltage surges.
2. A radiator-like device in the air conditioning system in which refrigerant gas condenses into a liquid, giving off heat.

CONDUCTOR: Any material through which an electrical current can be transmitted easily.

CONTINUITY: Continuous or complete circuit. Can be checked with an ohmmeter.

COUNTERSHAFT: An intermediate shaft which is rotated by a mainshaft and transmits, in turn, that rotation to a working part.

CRANKCASE: The lower part of an engine in which the crankshaft and related parts operate.

CRANKSHAFT: The main driving shaft of an engine which receives reciprocating motion from the pistons and converts it to rotary motion.

CYLINDER: In an engine, the round hole in the engine block in which the piston(s) ride.

CYLINDER BLOCK: The main structural member of an engine in which is found the cylinders, crankshaft and other principal parts.

CYLINDER HEAD: The detachable portion of the engine, fastened, usually, to the top of the cylinder block, containing all or most of the combustion chambers. On overhead valve engines, it contains the valves and their operating parts. On overhead cam engines, it contains the camshaft as well.

DEAD CENTER: The extreme top or bottom of the piston stroke.

DETONATION: An unwanted explosion of the air/fuel mixture in the combustion chamber caused by excess heat and compression, advanced timing, or an overly lean mixture. Also referred to as "ping".

DIAPHRAGM: A thin, flexible wall separating two cavities, such as in a vacuum advance unit.

DIESELING: A condition in which hot spots in the combustion chamber cause the engine to run on after the key is turned off.

DIFFERENTIAL: A geared assembly which allows the transmission of motion between drive axles, giving one axle the ability to turn faster than the other.

DIODE: An electrical device that will allow current to flow in one direction only.

DISC BRAKE: A hydraulic braking assembly consisting of a brake disc, or rotor, mounted on an axle, and a caliper assembly containing, usually two brake pads which are activated by hydraulic pressure. The pads are forced against the sides of the disc, creating friction which slows the vehicle.

DISTRIBUTOR: A mechanically driven device on an engine which is responsible for electrically firing the spark plug at a predetermined point of the piston stroke.

DOWEL PIN: A pin, inserted in mating holes in two different parts allowing those parts to maintain a fixed relationship.

DRUM BRAKE: A braking system which consists of two brake shoes and one or two wheel cylinders, mounted on a fixed backing plate, and a brake drum, mounted on an axle, which revolves around the assembly.

DWELL: The rate, measured in degrees of shaft rotation, at which an electrical circuit cycles on and off.

ELECTRONIC CONTROL UNIT (ECU): Ignition module, module, amplifier or igniter. See Module for definition.

ELECTRONIC IGNITION: A system in which the timing and firing of the spark plugs is controlled by an electronic control unit, usually called a module. These systems have no points or condenser.

ENDPLAY: The measured amount of axial movement in a shaft.

ENGINE: A device that converts heat into mechanical energy.

EXHAUST MANIFOLD: A set of cast passages or pipes which conduct exhaust gases from the engine.

FEELER GAUGE: A blade, usually metal, of precisely predetermined thickness, used to measure the clearance between two parts.

FIRING ORDER: The order in which combustion occurs in the cylinders of an engine. Also the order in which spark is distributed to the plugs by the distributor.

FLOODING: The presence of too much fuel in the intake manifold and combustion chamber which prevents the air/fuel mixture from firing, thereby causing a no-start situation.

FLYWHEEL: A disc shaped part bolted to the rear end of the crankshaft. Around the outer perimeter is affixed the ring gear. The starter drive engages the ring gear, turning the flywheel, which rotates the crankshaft, imparting the initial starting motion to the engine.

FOOT POUND (ft.lb. or sometimes, ft. lbs.): The amount of energy or work needed to raise an item weighing one pound, a distance of one foot.

FUSE: A protective device in a circuit which prevents circuit overload by breaking the circuit when a specific amperage is present. The device is constructed around a strip or wire of a lower amperage rating than the circuit it is designed to protect. When an amperage higher than that stamped on the fuse is present in the circuit, the strip or wire melts, opening the circuit.

GEAR RATIO: The ratio between the number of teeth on meshing gears.

GENERATOR: A device which converts mechanical energy into electrical energy.

HEAT RANGE: The measure of a spark plug's ability to dissipate heat from its firing end. The higher the heat range, the hotter the plug fires.

HUB: The center part of a wheel or gear.

HYDROCARBON (HC): Any chemical compound made up of hydrogen and carbon. A major pollutant formed by the engine as a byproduct of combustion.

HYDROMETER: An instrument used to measure the specific gravity of a solution.

INCH POUND (in.lb. or sometimes, in. lbs.): One twelfth of a foot pound.

INDUCTION: A means of transferring electrical energy in the form of a magnetic field. Principle used in the ignition coil to increase voltage.

INJECTOR: A device which receives metered fuel under relatively low pressure and is activated to inject the fuel into the engine under relatively high pressure at a predetermined time.

INPUT SHAFT: The shaft to which torque is applied, usually carrying the driving gear or gears.

INTAKE MANIFOLD: A casting of passages or pipes used to conduct air or a fuel/air mixture to the cylinders.

JOURNAL: The bearing surface within which a shaft operates.

KEY: A small block usually fitted in a notch between a shaft and a hub to prevent slippage of the two parts.

MANIFOLD: A casting of passages or set of pipes which connect the cylinders to an inlet or outlet source.

MANIFOLD VACUUM: Low pressure in an engine intake manifold formed just below the throttle plates. Manifold vacuum is highest at idle and drops under acceleration.

MASTER CYLINDER: The primary fluid pressurizing device in a hydraulic system. In automotive use, it is found in brake and hydraulic clutch systems and is pedal activated, either directly or, in a power brake system, through the power booster.

MODULE: Electronic control unit, amplifier or igniter of solid state or integrated design which controls the current flow in the ignition primary circuit based on input from the pick-up coil. When the module opens the primary circuit, the high secondary voltage is induced in the coil.

NEEDLE BEARING: A bearing which consists of a number (usually a large number) of long, thin rollers.

OHM:(Ω) The unit used to measure the resistance of conductor to electrical flow. One ohm is the amount of resistance that limits current flow to one ampere in a circuit with one volt of pressure.

OHMMETER: An instrument used for measuring the resistance, in ohms, in an electrical circuit.

OUTPUT SHAFT: The shaft which transmits torque from a device, such as a transmission.

OVERDRIVE: A gear assembly which produces more shaft revolutions than that transmitted to it.

OVERHEAD CAMSHAFT (OHC): An engine configuration in which the camshaft is mounted on top of the cylinder head and operates the valve either directly or by means of rocker arms.

OVERHEAD VALVE (OHV): An engine configuration in which all of the valves are located in the cylinder head and the camshaft is located in the cylinder block. The camshaft operates the valves via lifters and pushrods.

OXIDES OF NITROGEN (NOx): Chemical compounds of nitrogen produced as a byproduct of combustion. They combine with hydrocarbons to produce smog.

OXYGEN SENSOR: Used with the feedback system to sense the presence of oxygen in the exhaust gas and signal the computer which can reference the voltage signal to an air/fuel ratio.

PINION: The smaller of two meshing gears.

PISTON RING: An open ended ring which fits into a groove on the outer diameter of the piston. Its chief function is to form a seal between the piston and cylinder wall. Most automotive pistons have three rings: two for compression sealing; one for oil sealing.

PRELOAD: A predetermined load placed on a bearing during assembly or by adjustment.

PRIMARY CIRCUIT: Is the low voltage side of the ignition system which consists of the ignition switch, ballast resistor or resistance wire, bypass, coil, electronic control unit and pick-up coil as well as the connecting wires and harnesses.

PRESS FIT: The mating of two parts under pressure, due to the inner diameter of one being smaller than the outer diameter of the other, or vice versa; an interference fit.

RACE: The surface on the inner or outer ring of a bearing on which the balls, needles or rollers move.

REGULATOR: A device which maintains the amperage and/or voltage levels of a circuit at predetermined values.

RELAY: A switch which automatically opens and/or closes a circuit.

RESISTANCE: The opposition to the flow of current through a circuit or electrical device, and is measured in ohms. Resistance is equal to the voltage divided by the amperage.

RESISTOR: A device, usually made of wire, which offers a preset amount of resistance in an electrical circuit.

RING GEAR: The name given to a ring-shaped gear attached to a differential case, or affixed to a flywheel or as part a planetary gear set.

ROLLER BEARING: A bearing made up of hardened inner and outer races between which hardened steel rollers move.

ROTOR: 1. The disc-shaped part of a disc brake assembly, upon which the brake pads bear; also called, brake disc.
2. The device mounted atop the distributor shaft, which passes current to the distributor cap tower contacts.

SECONDARY CIRCUIT: The high voltage side of the ignition system, usually above 20,000 volts. The secondary includes the ignition coil, coil wire, distributor cap and rotor, spark plug wires and spark plugs.

SENDING UNIT: A mechanical, electrical, hydraulic or electromagnetic device which transmits information to a gauge.

SENSOR: Any device designed to measure engine operating conditions or ambient pressures and temperatures. Usually electronic in nature and designed to send a voltage signal to an on-board computer, some sensors may operate as a simple on/off switch or they may provide a variable voltage signal (like a potentiometer) as conditions or measured parameters change.

SHIM: Spacers of precise, predetermined thickness used between parts to establish a proper working relationship.

SLAVE CYLINDER: In automotive use, a device in the hydraulic clutch system which is activated by hydraulic force, disengaging the clutch.

SOLENOID: A coil used to produce a magnetic field, the effect of which is produce work.

SPARK PLUG: A device screwed into the combustion chamber of a spark ignition engine. The basic construction is a conductive core inside of a ceramic insulator, mounted in an outer conductive base. An electrical charge from the spark plug wire travels along the conductive core and jumps a preset air gap to a grounding point or points at the end of the conductive base. The resultant spark ignites the fuel/air mixture in the combustion chamber.

SPLINES: Ridges machined or cast onto the outer diameter of a shaft or inner diameter of a bore to enable parts to mate without rotation.

TACHOMETER: A device used to measure the rotary speed of an engine, shaft, gear, etc., usually in rotations per minute.

THERMOSTAT: A valve, located in the cooling system of an engine, which is closed when cold and opens gradually in response to engine heating, controlling the temperature of the coolant and rate of coolant flow.

TOP DEAD CENTER (TDC): The point at which the piston reaches the top of its travel on the compression stroke.

TORQUE: The twisting force applied to an object.

TORQUE CONVERTER: A turbine used to transmit power from a driving member to a driven member via hydraulic action, providing changes in drive ratio and torque. In automotive use, it links the driveplate at the rear of the engine to the automatic transmission.

TRANSDUCER: A device used to change a force into an electrical signal.

TRANSISTOR: A semi-conductor component which can be actuated by a small voltage to perform an electrical switching function.

TUNE-UP: A regular maintenance function, usually associated with the replacement and adjustment of parts and components in the electrical and fuel systems of a vehicle for the purpose of attaining optimum performance.

TURBOCHARGER: An exhaust driven pump which compresses intake air and forces it into the combustion chambers at higher than atmospheric pressures. The increased air pressure allows more fuel to be burned and results in increased horsepower being produced.

VACUUM ADVANCE: A device which advances the ignition timing in response to increased engine vacuum.

VACUUM GAUGE: An instrument used to measure the presence of vacuum in a chamber.

VALVE: A device which control the pressure, direction of flow or rate of flow of a liquid or gas.

VALVE CLEARANCE: The measured gap between the end of the valve stem and the rocker arm, cam lobe or follower that activates the valve.

VISCOSITY: The rating of a liquid's internal resistance to flow.

VOLTMETER: An instrument used for measuring electrical force in units called volts. Voltmeters are always connected parallel with the circuit being tested.

WHEEL CYLINDER: Found in the automotive drum brake assembly, it is a device, actuated by hydraulic pressure, which, through internal pistons, pushes the brake shoes outward against the drums.

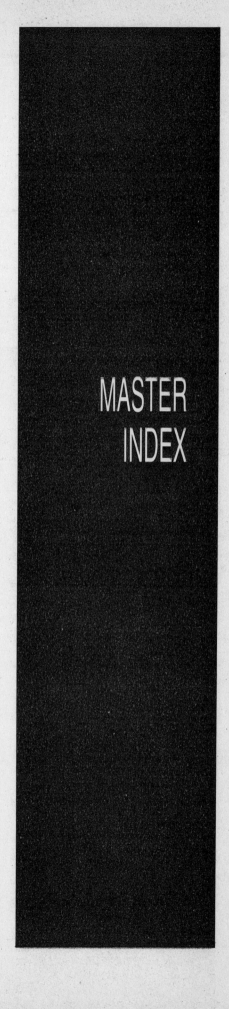

MASTER INDEX